# OFFICE MANAGEMENT AND CONTROL

# OFFICE MANAGEMENT AND CONTROL

## THE ACTIONS OF ADMINISTRATIVE MANAGEMENT

By GEORGE R. TERRY, Ph.D.
School of Business
Northwestern University, and
Management Consultant, Chicago

FIFTH EDITION
1966

RICHARD D. IRWIN, INC.

HOMEWOOD, ILLINOIS

To the
Memory of My Mother

110,16

# PREFACE

THIS is the *Fifth Edition of Office Management and Control.* Since the appearance of the original edition, back in 1949, this important area of management has undergone constant and significant changes. New developments emerge almost daily; fantastic machines are perfected; and conceptual ideas refined for assembling, processing, distributing, and retaining information—the product of the office. Why these numerous efforts? Essentially for one purpose: so that management members can manage effectively. With all these changes has come greater recognition of office management as a vital activity in today's enterprises, be they in business, government, or the military. Both the dynamics and the growing essentiality of the office suggest this new fifth edition. It incorporates not only all major improvements, but also takes into account the suggestions and experience of many users of the previous edition. The result is a completely up-to-date, comprehensive, balanced, and helpful book which it is believed meets the requirements of the office-management teacher, student, and practitioner.

The study of office management is challenging. The need for accurate and timely information is universal because papers and their effective processing are basic in modern administration. How to get *what* information to *which* people poses difficult problems. New office machines, especially the computer, have sharpened our focus upon information handling. Tremendous quantities of records can be turned out in a matter of minutes. Systems and procedures innovation and analysis are supplying effective and needed tools. Old techniques of decision making, corresponding, filing, quality controlling, work measuring, and employee motivating and training, are giving way to new ideas, new approaches, and new achievements. The urge for lower office costs, more helpful information, and greater office efficiency moves forward as a strong and steady force.

The chief stabilizer of office-management study is getting the necessary office work done in the best way. This was stated in the first edition, some years ago, and is still true. Hence, the basic objective of this fifth edition remains the same: namely, to present fundamental principles and successful practices used in getting office work accomplished. Practices change, new ones are developed and found superior. As a result, the interpretations given principles are modified, but their basic concepts offering fundamental guides to thought and action tend to be enduring.

Office management is here viewed as a distinct activity made up of fundamental functions comprising what can be termed a management process. Past experience with this approach in previous editions demonstrates its effectiveness and completeness. The management-process approach gives a logical, readily comprehended, and inclusive arrangement of office-management material and reveals the distinct anatomy of management as well as the vital interrelations of its various activities. Examples of current office operations are sprinkled throughout the book. Charts and illustrations are included where it is believed they will be advantageous to the reader.

Featured in this edition are several brand new chapters, major revisions of a number of chapters, and updating of the entire book. The writing is tightened; the total number of chapters reduced. Forty-five new case problems are added as well as many thought-provoking and review questions to facilitate study of the material. Retained are only the most effective of former case problems and questions, as revealed from usage of the book. In essence, new and ample material is provided for purposeful participation in studying office management so that emphasis can be given to implementing needed action as well as to acquiring helpful knowledge.

Contributing immensely in the preparation of this edition were the exchange of ideas and the discussion of office management problems with practicing managers of office work, teachers, and students. To these people I am indebted for their helpfulness, viewpoints, and suggestions. They made pertinent information available and stimulated my thinking about office management. Their number is too large to enumerate here, but to each of them warm and sincere appreciation is extended.

*April, 1966*                                        GEORGE R. TERRY

# TABLE OF CONTENTS

Methods. Systems and Procedures in Office Management. Advantages of Systems and Procedures. Systems and Data Processing. Basic Observations about Systems. Who Designs Systems and Procedures?

## PART 4. OFFICE MANAGEMENT—PLANNING

tion. Forecast the Environment. Determine Alternatives. Select the Alternative. Gaining Acceptance of Selected Plan. LR and SR Planning. Common Types of Office Plans. Planning Office Forms. Functional Considerations. Physical Considerations.

Top Management Backing. System Design. Define System Boundaries. Secure Data and Facts. Organize and Consolidate Data and Facts. Establish System Premises. Evolve the System Design. Procedure Design. Implementing the System or Procedure. Improving Systems and Procedures. Principles of Office Work Simplification. Planning for Improving Procedures. Select the Office Procedure to Be Improved. Get All the Facts about This Procedure. Analyze and Evaluate These Facts. Devise the Improvement. Process Chart. Movement Diagram. Procedure Flow Chart.

Office Method Study. Approach to Planning Office Methods. Which Method to Improve? Getting All the Facts. Therbligs. Using the Questioning Approach. Developing the Improved Method. Providing a Suitable Workplace. Application of the Improved Method. The Left- and Right-Hand Chart. Production Study Chart. Operator-Machine Activity Chart.

Selection of Office Equipment and Machines. Equipment and Machine Selection Factors. Depreciation and Trade-in. Buy or Lease. Maintenance. Office Chairs. Office Desks. Modular Office Furniture. Posting-Tray Unit. Punched-Card Machines. Arrangement of Data on Card. Basic Punched-Card Machines. Special Punched-Card Machines. Usage of Punched-Card Machines. Marginal Notched-Card Machines. Accounting Machines. Descriptive Accounting Machine. Nondescriptive Accounting Machine. Addressing and Listing Machines. Miscellaneous Equipment and Machines.

Basic Considerations. Space Planning and Office Systems and Procedures. Space Planning and Functional Analysis. Who Goes Where? CRAFT. Basic Layout Guides. Space Standards. Steps in Office Layout. Overall Space Estimates. The Private Office. Movable Partitions. Modular Equipment. Reception Room. Conference Room. Wardrobe Facilities. Planning the Office Move.

Office Lighting. Sources of Light. Basic Designs of Lighting Systems. Arrangement of Fixtures. Office Lighting as an Investment. Color Conditioning in the Office. Selection of Colors. Color and Lighting. Music Conditioning. Air Conditioning. Temperature, Humidity, and Ventilation. Sound Conditioning. Locating the Office. Adaptability of the Space. The

Building Facilities. Proximity of Office Building to Business Factors. The Cost Involved. Natural Lighting and Ventilating Provided. Characteristics of the Building. Freedom from Dirt and Noise. Stability of the Tenants. Own or Rent. Provisions of Lease.

## PART 5. OFFICE MANAGEMENT—CONTROLLING

Controlling of Office Forms. Determine What Is Being Accomplished. Evaluation of Present Forms. Applying Corrective Measures. Gains from Controlling Forms. Controlling Office Supplies. Controlling and Standards. Extent of Standards. Advantages of Standards. Means of Expressing Standards. Change and Standards. American Standards Association, Inc. Office Standardization—Meaning and Implication.

The Problems of Quantity Variation. Quantity Controlling Efforts. Means of Controlling Office Work Fluctuation. Routing. Scheduling. Dispatching. Office Quality Control. Office Quality Control Approaches. Statistical Quality Control. Chance and Assignable Causes. Control Chart. Implementing SQC in an Office.

Office Work Measurement. Measuring Unit. Modified Work Measurement Units. Timing Office Work. Preliminaries of Office Time Standards. Subjective Judgment. Past Performance Records. Work Sampling. Standard Time Data. Stopwatch Study. Standard Data from Stopwatch Study. Examples of Office Time Standards. PERT.

Cost and the Office Manager. Approaches to Cost Reduction. Items Offering Greatest Cost Reduction Opportunities. Cost Consciousness among Employees. Establish Effective Cost Control Program. Determining What Is Being Accomplished Costwise. Evaluating the Cost Expenditure. Applying Corrective Action if Necessary. Why Use a Budget? Kinds of Budgets. All Budgets Concern the Office Manager. Preparation of the Budget. The Budget Period. Revision of Budget. Making Budgeting More Effective.

Evaluation of Manuals. Types of Office Manuals. Manual of Policies. Manual of Operations. Manual of Office Rules and Regulations. Historical Manual. Multiple-Purpose Manual. Sources for Manual Material. Preparation of Manuals. Distribution of Manuals. Manual Maintenance.

## PART 6. OFFICE MANAGEMENT—ORGANIZING

Management and Organizing. Objective and Organizing. Meaning of Organizing. Relation of Office to Organization of Enterprise. Organizational Content and Placement of the Office. The Office Services

## INDEX

# PART 1

# INTRODUCTION

*Let us begin our study of office management with a dis-*
*cussion of what office work is, its reasons for being, and*
*its essential features and characteristics. With such back-*
*ground knowledge we can better understand what we are*
*managing in office management and, further, we can com-*
*prehend how management is applied to this work. Hence,*
*the subjects (1) the concept of office work and (2) manag-*
*ing office work comprise the first two chapters.*

# CHAPTER 1

# THE CONCEPT OF
# OFFICE WORK

The very first step toward success in
any occupation is to become
interested in it.
            —*William Osler*

A DISCUSSION of office management can begin logically by directing attention to the concept of office work, or to that which is being managed. Obtaining a better understanding of the nature and characteristics of, and facts about, office work will assist us in grasping more realistically the problems, challenges, and opportunities which office management offers.

At first inquiry, there is a temptation to state quickly that office work is work performed in an office. But a moment's reflection brings about the recognition that this answer is incomplete. Office work is performed, for example, by retail salespeople in a store, papers are filled out by shop employees in a factory, and bank employees work with papers all day long. Could we define office work as paper work? Certainly paper work is important in modern enterprises. We have more papers in business and government affairs today than ever before. Every activity is preceded, started, accompanied, stopped, and recorded for future reference by a piece of paper. Is paper work the same as office work? To a degree, yes, but some office work—for example, telephoning and processing data electronically—does not involve paper work.

Viewing office work as a means, we can ask, "Why is office work performed?" The answer: to provide *information*. Here is the most comprehensive and meaningful word for office work as the term is popularly used. An office manager deals with the work designed to provide proper and adequate information to the right person at the right time and in the right form. The office is the fountainhead of information. This is what makes office work so important. This is why office work is growing so rapidly. This is the reason so much effort is being directed to how office work should be performed.

## WHAT IS INFORMATION?

Information is meaningful data—words, figures, or symbols—that convey usable knowledge. What is usable depends upon the following:

1. *Objective of the recipient.* If information is to help, it must assist the recipient in what he is trying to do.

2. *Accuracy of the data transmission and processing.* The real essence and significance of the information must be retained regardless of how it is handled and manipulated.

3. *Time.* Is the information current? Does it have maximum value by virtue of being the latest available?

4. *Space or place.* Is the information available at the right place? This implies that the information is supplied to the proper recipients.

5. *Form.* Can the information be used effectively? Does it show needed relationships, trends, and areas requiring managerial attention; and does it emphasize pertinent situations?

6. *Semantics.* Is the relationship between the words and their intended meaning absolutely clear? Is there any likelihood of misunderstanding? The word "duck," for example, may mean a type of cloth, a type of fowl, or to move quickly.

It is well to point out that, as defined above, not all data are information. There are today many useless records and reports being prepared and distributed. In contrast, there are gaps of information that need to be bridged by useful data. Generally, it is the responsibility of the office manager, administrative manager, or whatever his title, to supply needed information in order that the entire enterprise can be managed efficiently.

## INFORMATION DEVELOPMENT

Information is supplied either to a manager or a nonmanager. What information is supplied depends upon the recipient's job, but in any event it should be what the recipient needs, wants, and uses, qualified by what information is available and feasible to obtain. The recipient, together with the information compiler, should decide what information to provide. In these efforts, however, the quantity of information must be carefully controlled. This is an especially important consideration today when, by means of computers and other electronic machines, it is possible to compile information in 15 minutes that takes a man two days to read and two weeks to assimilate.

In addition, there are new requirements placing greater and greater demands upon the supplying of information. A number of factors are responsible. High on the list is the growth and complexity of enterprises. As companies expand, merge, and diversify, there is a greater need for formal information to keep personnel adequately informed. Another contributing cause is the growth in the number of executives. The trend is toward more management members over specialized areas, and this necessitates the distribution of information to a wide range of executives within relatively short periods. Also, the force of competition, both domestic and foreign, can be cited. The managers of a company, for example, may have to decide where to locate a branch factory or warehouse for maximum marketing impact. The information requirements necessary to reach this decision are large and involve digestion of a considerable number of facts. In addition, the increasing expenditures for research and development, and the resulting new processes and new products, accelerate the need for accurate information on financial needs, production activities, and other phases of a business. In turn, these changes increase the complexity of the information and emphasize the need to schedule efforts economically. Lastly, information of various types has been developed because it is required of enterprises by government. In this catgory are data relating to taxes, and compliance with regulations and numerous legal requirements. Without proper information, managers are unable to comply with the law. More will be stated in connection with some of these factors later in this chapter.[1]

In brief, information development has come about because today's mode of operation simply does not permit either the successful manager or the successful nonmanager to carry in his head all the information needed to carry out his work effectively. The manager needs information on cost, sales, production, personnel, plans, accomplishments, inventories, machines, customers, prices, markets, and taxes. The nonmanager requires work instructions, scheduling data, deadline dates, evaluation of efforts, and notices of work changes. These represent masses of data which must be collected and put into easily accessible form in order to have maximum value and benefit. Also, it should be pointed out that machine availability to handle the information quickly and properly is contributing toward the status of information development. For several decades there has been a continuous parade of new office machines designed to accomplish office work more efficiently. And the pace is quickening. Computers are making deep modifications in office work methodology, and they are destined to cause even greater changes in the future.

## SUPPLYING INFORMATION

Supplying needed information requires fundamentally four activities. These include data (1) collecting, (2) processing, (3) retaining, and (4)

---

[1] See page 14.

distributing. Figure 1–1 shows this concept graphically. First of all, the data must be collected; and, as discussed in the following paragraphs, there exist major sources of data in most enterprises. Next, the collected data must be processed. In brief, the descriptive information must be arranged according to a predetermined pattern, numerical values must be calculated, and helpful relationships must be shown. Typically, some information is either retained by the office for additional data, when available, to be added to what has been processed, or is retained simply for future reference purposes. Lastly, the processed data are distributed to those requiring the information and include all types of communication. More will now be discussed for each of these four activities.

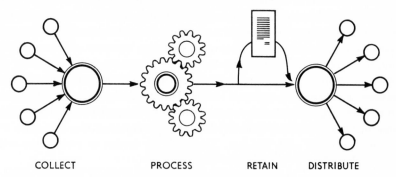

COLLECT        PROCESS        RETAIN    DISTRIBUTE

FIG. 1–1. Data must be collected, processed, retained, and distributed to provide information needed to manage an enterprise effectively.

### THE COLLECTING OF DATA

Practically every operation in a modern enterprise gives rise to data. While the terms may differ from enterprise to enterprise, depending upon the type of enterprise, the following operations or activities can be considered basic sources of data.

| *Operation or Activity* | *Gives Rise to Need for:* |
|---|---|
| Purchasing | Vendors' list, prices, quotations, delivery dates |
| Receiving | Receipt of material, inspection, quantity |
| Stockkeeping | On hand, coming in, location, allocation |
| Production | Process times, orders, waiting times |
| Selling | Customers' orders, sales analysis, price |
| Delivery | Date, carrier information, bills of lading |
| Billing | Customer's name, merchandise, price |
| Collecting | Credit, invoice, discounts |
| Disbursing | Payroll, materials purchased, taxes |

Actually, all this type of information is obtained from data expressed as words, numbers, and symbols. The challenge is to put the proper data together and make them available to the proper party at the proper time. For instance, under purchasing, for a vendors' list to be useful, it should contain (1) names, preferably alphabetically, by type of commodity or by location; (2) terms of sale; (3) past experience with vendor; (4) name of representative with vendor; and (5) telephone number. Likewise, certain data must be put together meaningfully for (say) billing, collecting, and disbursing.

## THE PROCESSING OF DATA

Data processing is a series of planned operations upon information in order to achieve a desired objective or result. Usually, a step-by-step arrangement, a formula, or pattern is followed to arrive at a result that shows the data in some standard and useful form. Bookkeeping, inventory record keeping, payroll, accounting, and the solving of mathematical equations are all included under the heading of processing of data.

The performance of the operations in predetermined sequence and the devices or machines employed to perform these operations constitute a data-processing system. There are many types of devices and hence many types of data-processing systems, that can be employed. For example:

1. The device may be simply pen and paper.
2. The device may be an adding machine and an accounting machine.
3. The device may be a computer.

Likewise, the sequence of operations may differ from one system to another, depending largely upon the goal and the devices to be utilized. However, regardless of the data-processing system, *the plan of processing is always of human origin.* Furthermore, the system is, or should be, performed essentially to serve human beings. Data are processed to put them into a form that has greatest utilization.

## BASIC ELEMENTS OF DATA PROCESSING

Specifically, what are some basic elements of data processing? In answering this question, many will mention "writing" and "calculating," and a few will include "storing." But study of the processing effort reveals that there are not three but eight basic elements of processing. These are shown in Figure 1–2. The reason each element is performed and the result obtained from applying each element to the data are also included in the figure. To illustrate, sorting (No. 4) is performed to classify the data and results in the data being related to one or more bases.

It would be difficult to overstate the importance of these basic elements of data processing. They serve as the nucleus around which all paper work revolves. Various combinations of these elements, in kind as well as in

| Basic Element of Data Processing | Why Performed | Results in: |
|---|---|---|
| 1. Reading | To interpret data by going over characters, words, and symbols | Awareness of data existence |
| 2. Writing, typing, card punching, or paper-tape perforating (frequently called *input*) | To facilitate processing by putting data on or in medium, i.e., alphabetical or numerical marks on paper, holes in paper, magnetic areas on tape, and magnetic ink on paper | Start of data processing |
| 3. Recording or printing (frequently called *output*) | To obtain results of processing, the data—in medium form for processing purposes—are converted to form easily read by a human being, if not already in that form | End of data processing |
| 4. Sorting | To classify the data | Data being related to one or more bases |
| 5. Transmitting | To disseminate the data | Data availability for specific purpose and place |
| 6. Calculating | To manipulate the data mathematically | Numerical data being added, subtracted, multiplied, or divided |
| 7. Comparing | To check data for accuracy and completeness | Quantitative and qualitative inspection of data |
| 8. Storing | To retain or keep the data | Data being available when needed |

*Note:* The meaning of each of the following terms, frequently used in office management, is included in the above listing:

a) "Interpreting" (usually associated with No. 2 or No. 3) is imprinting the meaning of the punched holes in a punched card on that card.

b) "Reproducing" (usually associated with No. 2) is duplicating an exact copy of a punched card.

c) "Collating" (usually associated with No. 4) is merging sets of related data into a single set.

d) "Segregating" (usually associated with No. 4) is separating sets of related data into several sets.

FIG. 1–2.   The basic elements of data processing.

degree, are required to supply the needed information which the office is expected to furnish.

## PROCESSING AND PRODUCTION UNIT EMPLOYED

The development and use of the modern electronic computer has brought emphasis and recognition to the basic elements of data processing. Terminology such as "input," "output," "transmitting," and "recording" is commonplace with computer installations. However, these terms are actually not exclusive with computer usage. These elements of processing are basic and universal. They exist in all data processing, whether noncomputer processing or computer processing.

To highlight this important fact, Figure 1–3 is included. In this figure, the basic elements of data processing are shown across the top, while the common office productive units are listed vertically in the left column.[2] The basic elements of processing performed by each production unit are

| OFFICE PRODUCTION UNIT EMPLOYED | READING | WRITING, TYPING, ETC. | RECORDING, PRINTING | SORTING | TRANSMITTING | CALCULATING | COMPARING | STORING |
|---|---|---|---|---|---|---|---|---|
| | 1 | 2 | 3 | 4 | 5 | 6 | 7 | 8 |
| ACCOUNTING MACHINE | | V | V | V | | V | V | |
| ADDING AND CALCULATING MACHINES | | V | V | | | V | | |
| ADDRESSING MACHINE | | | V | V | | | | |
| COMPUTER WITHOUT SPECIAL ATTACHMENT | | | V | V | V | V | V | V |
| COPYING MACHINE | | | V | | | | | |
| ELECTRONIC READER | V | V | | | | | | |
| HUMAN BEING | V | V | V | V | V | V | V | V |
| MICROFILM UNITS | | | V | | | | | V |
| PNEUMATIC TUBE | | | | | V | | | |
| PUNCHING MACHINE | | V | | | | | | |
| SORTER | | | | V | | | | |
| TABULATOR | | | V | | V | V | V | |
| TELAUTOGRAPH | | V | V | | V | | | |
| TELEGRAPH | | V | V | | V | | | |
| TELETYPEWRITER | | V | V | | V | | | |
| TYPEWRITER | | V | V | | | | | |

*Header note: BASIC ELEMENT OF DATA PROCESSING*

FIG. 1–3.   Each office production unit performs specific basic elements of data processing.

indicated by the check marks. For example, an accounting machine performs the basic elements of writing, recording, sorting, calculating, and comparing. In contrast, a copying machine performs just one basic element of processing—recording. A human being performs all the basic elements of data processing.

This figure helps to identify the makeup of information. It assists in grasping the important overall picture of what is managed by the office

---

[2] Office production units or machines are discussed in detail in Chapter 18.

manager and in understanding better the role and operation of various office production units. It also demonstrates that what has been done with papers for years is still being done, whether essentially by hand, by ordinary office machine, or by computer.

## THE RETAINING OF DATA

The very nature and reason-to-be of much paper work requires that data be retained. The more obvious reason is to keep it for future reference. The decision regarding what to retain, for how long a period, and under what arrangement is a vital part of providing needed information. However, equally important is the retaining of data either mentally, manually, or mechanically so that subsequent data can be appended to the already existing fund and thus keep the information current.

The retaining of data for subsequent processing and bringing them up to date has been emphasized by the use of the computer—the function of its so-called memory unit. But data retention is also basic in paper work performed by hand, in placing papers in a file so that they can be located easily for future reference, or where records are kept solely in the owner's head.

## THE DISTRIBUTING OF DATA

Collecting, processing, and, when necessary, retaining data are insufficient for information to be utilized by employees and customers. The information must also be distributed to those who have need for it. This task includes the proper placing and timing of the information. It includes all the means of communication such as mail, telephone, telegraph, intercommunication systems, and electronic communication devices.

An employee's effectiveness depends upon the accuracy, timeliness, and precision with which his contribution is geared to the overall plan. When this thesis is followed, reports are distributed only to employees who are in a position to take direct action; only information which, directly or indirectly, helps get the job done is provided. Violations of these rules in the distributing of data are common sources of inefficiency in office management.

## CHARACTERISTICS OF OFFICE WORK

Pointing out the important distinguishing features about work performed for informational purposes serves to supply the concept of what is being managed in the area of office management. Accordingly, the major characteristics of this work will now be discussed.

1. *A facilitating function.* Office work is a facilitating function; it is

the essential medium through which the various activities of an enterprise are fused together. In a sense, office work can be called the "catalytic agent" of modern management.[3]

The work of the office assists in efforts to increase output, lower costs, stimulate employees, pay wages, purchase materials, and ship orders. The individual work of practically every department in an enterprise is implemented by office work. For example, a credit department cannot operate successfully without current records of creditors, amounts and dates due, lists of delinquent accounts, credit histories of customers, and a quantity of correspondence.

Of special importance is the facilitating action of office work in decision making. Information is gathered and analyzed in relation to a set of alternative solutions to a problem in order to reach a decision. Likewise, information is the basis for communicating. For example, the exchanging of ideas and suggestions among people to develop the alternatives, the reporting of the decision to others so that implementation can take place, and the reporting back to evaluate what is being accomplished are all predicated upon communicating.

*2. A service work.* Another distinguishing feature of office work is that it is a service work. In and of itself, office work serves little purpose; it is performed to help others do their work more effectively. For example, office work is a service to the top executive officers, to the production department, to the sales department, and to the finance department. It helps supply top executives with data which are necessary in order to manage the enterprise. By means of records, the production department is helped to improve its service and to lower costs, the sales department is aided in its work of selling the product, and the finance department is assisted in maintaining written evidence of the financial status of the enterprise.

Unfortunately this concept is frequently overlooked. In their zeal to improve office efforts, some embrace the thought that information is the end product and that giving it to the proper personnel insures that the desired action will result therefrom immediately. This is tremendously misleading. Most managers and nonmanagers are not concerned primarily with securing, processing, and giving information. They have other important work to do. The information they receive is supposed to help them do their respective jobs. The intent is to keep them effective in their particular area and in doing what they are hired to do, namely, managing, selling, performing production work, or financing, and not in preparing, reading, or discussing reports and records.

---

[3] "Catalytic agent" is a term used in chemistry and means an element the presence of which is necessary to bring about a desired reaction between other elements but which does not itself enter into the reaction. In a similar manner, office work brings about a desired reaction of business elements but does not enter into the reaction itself.

Service is the primary objective of the office. Consideration for office costs, as well as for the utility, quality, and quantity of the office services, is also important; but these should be recognized as secondary objectives. An eagerness to slash all costs or a decision to compile only records which the office believes are useful might result in failure to provide the necessary office services to the other departments. Thus, losses occur in these departments that probably far exceed the savings in operation. However, the service should be evaluated in terms of cost; elaborate and excessive service usually means waste, while, on the other hand, inadequate service represents false economy.

3. *Volume determined by outside.* Unlike many major business activities, the volume of office work is determined by factors outside the office. These factors include the number of shipments, the amount of collections, the number of open accounts, the quantity of sales letters, the number of factory employees, and the number of items manufactured or sold—all factors outside the control of the office.

This unique characteristic makes for problems in office management. For example, provisions for fluctuations in the work load must be provided, even though the timing and extent of the variation are wide and usually cannot be accurately forecast. Also more often than not decisions made by nonoffice management members and about which the office management member has little or nothing to say affect significantly the work managed by the office management members.

4. *An indirect contributor to profit.* No profit is realized directly from office work, since it acts through the operative departments, such as the production, sales, and finance departments.[4] In this sense, office work contributes indirectly, not directly, to the profit-making ability of the enterprise. However, some feel that office work produces profit. This belief stems primarily from considering the office as a complete unit within itself.

However, the fact that the office does not contribute directly to profit making means that it is usually on the defensive insofar as justifying expenditures is concerned. It is, for example, unlike sales, where by spending so much it is hoped to realize a resultant gain in sales and also in profits. In dealing with the management of office work we must constantly seek to justify the work and its cost and to point out wherein it is good management to make the expenditure.

5. *Contents.* The predominant type of work making up office work is typing and calculating. Various studies reveal that these two types account for nearly one-half of all office time. Other important activities include checking or proofing, filing, telephoning, duplicating, and mailing

---

[4] "Profit," as used here, is the residual income accruing to the owner of an enterprise after he has paid all the economic aids of production—that is, rent on all land used, interest on all capital used, and wages to all labor used.

and these, together with typing and calculating, constitute nearly 90 percent of office employees' work time. As office mechanization advances this pattern changes somewhat, but it is interesting to note that typing remains a very essential activity whether manual, semimechanized, or full automation of performing office work is followed. This is due to the fact that currently typing is usually necessary to put the input information into a form acceptable for receiving by the machine. However, as we employ more machines that read and convert ordinary written data into "machine language," the volume of typing probably will decline. The common office activities mentioned above are fully discussed in Part II of this book, and office automation is included in Part III.

6. *Dispersion.* Office work is not performed exclusively in any one department; some of it is performed in every department of an enterprise. The swing to mechanization, and especially to computers, has resulted in much office work being handled within a single location; but there is still considerable paper work in other areas—for example, in the purchasing, engineering, or inspection department. Furthermore, a milling machine operator in a factory usually performs some clerical work in the normal course of his daily duty. Where financial incentives and production control are used, the operator may be responsible for a considerable amount of clerical work, yet he is not classified as an office worker. Likewise, most salesmen are accountable for sizable amounts of paper work; and the same is true of many employees of a personnel department, who are quick to point out the voluminous paper work used in the execution of their tasks.

Figure 1–4 indicates the dispersion of paper work and the basic functions of business. Selling gives rise to the order entry acknowledgment, and the subsequent paper work flow affects many departments, whether the goods are shipped or assembled from stock, or needed raw materials are obtained to take care of the customer's order. What we are saying is that information is required by people throughout an entire organization, as well as by certain others outside the organization, in order for the enterprise to function effectively.

7. *Personnel performing.* One of the interesting developments among office employees is the increasing proportion of women in this category. In the year 1870, for example, only 2 percent of office personnel were women; by 1930, the percentage was nearly 50; by 1950, the number of women office employees reached 60 percent of the total; and in 1965, women held nearly 71 percent of all office jobs.

There is, however, a tendency for certain office jobs to be occupied by men. These include accountant, programmer, analyst, collection clerk, credit clerk, and correspondent. Other office jobs are commonly held by women. In this group are the jobs of file clerk, machine operator, tape librarian, receptionist, typist, stenographer, and telephone operator. Still other jobs are held by either men or women and include those of bookkeeper, cashier, mail clerk, and private secretary.

Also, the proportion of office workers to total workers varies considerably with different industries. For example, nearly one-half of the workers in finance, insurance, and real estate are office workers. In contrast, the proportion is about 11 percent in manufacturing and only 0.3 percent in agriculture, forestry, and fisheries.

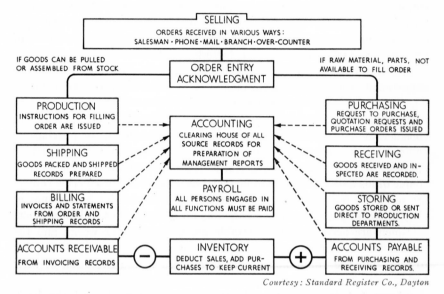

*Courtesy: Standard Register Co., Dayton*

FIG. 1–4. Records permeate an entire enterprise. Information is required by every department.

## GROWTH OF OFFICE WORK

As mentioned in the beginning of this chapter, information development has taken place rapidly. The growth has been especially sharp during the past several decades. Let's look at some specifics. Verification of the growth can be made in a number of ways, but the increase in the number of office employees is probably most conclusive, particularly when one observes the productive capacity of present-day office equipment and machines to enable a large work volume per employee. The rate of growth in the number of office employees has been much greater than that in either our total working force or our total population. For example, in the United States, during the period 1870–1940, the total working force increased less than four times, while the number of clerical workers increased fifteen times. From 1940 to 1965, the total population increased 48 percent, the total working force expanded 56 percent, and the number engaged in clerical occupations increased approximately 138 percent.

The basic information concerning the growth in total population of the United States, in the total working force, and in clerical and kindred workers is set forth in Figure 1–5. The ratio of clerical to total working force has been calculated for each year, and these values are shown in the last column to the right. For example, in 1870, the ratio of clerical to total working force was 2.4 percent; whereas in 1965, this ratio had increased to

| Year | Total Population of the United States | Total Working Force | Clerical Workers | Percentage— Clerical to Total Working Force |
|---|---|---|---|---|
| 1965 | 194,700,000 | 70,169,242 | 10,963,761 | 15.6 |
| 1960 | 181,057,000 | 66,681,537 | 9,783,632 | 14.6 |
| 1950 | 151,230,000 | 55,835,340 | 6,866,374 | 12.3 |
| 1940 | 131,950,000 | 45,166,083 | 4,612,356 | 10.2 |
| 1930 | 123,080,000 | 48,829,920 | 4,025,324 | 8.2 |
| 1920 | 106,970,000 | 41,614,248 | 3,111,836 | 7.5 |
| 1910 | 92,410,000 | 38,167,336 | 1,718,458 | 4.5 |
| 1900 | 76,090,000 | 29,073,233 | 1,068,993 | 3.7 |
| 1890 | 63,056,438 | 22,735,661 | 801,505 | 3.5 |
| 1880 | 50,262,382 | 17,392,099 | 518,439 | 3.0 |
| 1870 | 39,904,593 | 12,505,923 | 305,502 | 2.4 |

Source: U.S. Department of Commerce, Bureau of the Census, "Statistical Abstract, 1965" (Washington, D.C.: U.S. Government Printing Office, 1965), pp. 5, 216, 228.
U.S. Department of Commerce, Bureau of the Census, "1955 Annual Report on the Labor Force" (Washington, D.C., March, 1956), pp. 3–5.
U.S. Department of Commerce, Bureau of the Census, "1950 Census of Population," Vol. I: "Population" (Washington, D.C.: U.S. Government Printing Office, 1953), pp. 110–12.
U.S. Department of Commerce, Bureau of the Census, "Sixteenth Census of the United States, 1940," Vol. III: "Population" (Washington, D.C.: U.S. Government Printing Office, 1943), p. 76.
U.S. Department of Commerce, Bureau of the Census, "Fifteenth Census of the United States, 1930," Vol. V: "Population" (Washington, D.C.: U.S. Government Printing Office, 1933), pp. 10–22.
U.S. Department of Commerce, Bureau of the Census, "Twelfth Census of the United States, 1900," Special Reports: "Occupations" (Washington, D.C.: U.S. Government Printing Office, 1904), pp. 1 and li.

FIG. 1–5. Total population of the United States, total working force, number of clerical workers, and percentage of clerical workers to total working force for the years 1870–1965.

15.6 percent. Each decade since 1870 has shown a greater percentage of the total working force performing clerical work. Stated differently, in 1870, about one worker in forty was an office worker; in 1965, about one in seven was an office worker.

## REASONS FOR GROWTH

We have already stated the major factors contributing to the growth in information development which has brought about the increase in office personnel.[5] For emphasis we might restate that one major consideration is the industrial growth of the United States with its specialization and its

---

[5] See page 4.

need for other activities to keep the industrial growth virile. For example, during the period 1900–1960, the number engaged in manufacturing occupations increased from 6 million to 16.4 million, and the number engaged in "service industries" spurted from 4 million to nearly 14 million. We commonly associate the growth of our economy with manufacturing efficiency—improved methods, better machines, and more effective controls. But this growth has brought with it expenditures sometimes overlooked in that obtaining, processing, and distributing information for attaining these manufacturing gains costs nearly as much as does the direct production labor.

Likewise, growth in government has been mentioned as a cause for the increase in office personnel. To supply the ever expanding requests by government for information necessitates more and more office employees by private enterprises. Also, from the government's side, both the amount of its clerical work and the number of governmental office employees have also increased. There were nearly 5 million office workers in public administration work in 1965.[6]

Finally, some portion of the growth in office personnel and office work is undoubtedly due to inadequate efforts to control it. The preparation of essential paper work only, the extended use of efficient office machines, the adequate motivation of office employees, and the development of proper systems, procedures, and methods are examples of efforts which assist in reducing the amount of paper work.

## WILL GROWTH CONTINUE?

Opinions differ regarding the future growth of office work. Some believe it will continue to grow at a rate exceeding that of all other types of work. They view it as basically a self-perpetuating situation—more people, more paper; more paper, more people. They point out that we have become attuned to the use of the products of the office.

In contrast, many believe that the upward trend in office work cannot continue. They insist we are drowning in a sea of paper and that some office work has become a ritual performance for its own sake. They observe that the past increase in office work has resulted in an overwhelming increase in overhead costs and that this process cannot continue indefinitely.

## THE FUTURE OF THE OFFICE

A number of available studies point out that there exists considerable waste office work. The exact amount is unknown, but the gains to be won

---

[6] U.S. Department of Commerce, Bureau of the Census, *Statistical Abstract, 1965* (Washington, D.C.: U.S. Government Printing Office, 1965), pp. 440–45.

by eliminating just a portion of this unnecessary processed information staggers the imagination. It seems that a simple approach could be followed: (1) Eliminate the unnecessary paper work being done, and (2) perform the necessary paper work more efficiently. The first criterion is to determine what office work serves effectively a definite and essential need, that is, provides essential information. Opinions, of course, will differ in this evaluation. The second criterion stresses such things as simplification of the office processes, training of office employees, and more office mechanization.

But an interesting paradox should be noted. Based on much of our experience to date, our ability to handle a large volume of paper work at a low unit cost, as exemplified by many mechanized processes, is actually a problem, not a solution. Enormous quantities of data are processed and made up into reports of all kinds, copies of papers are run off with little effort, and memoranda are quickly prepared. In each case copies are distributed to many members of the enterprise. Receipt of them signals the reading of them. This takes time as does subsequent thinking about them and answering or expressing opinions about them to others. In addition, the papers are filed, eventually the need for additional filing equipment is generated, and more floor space is needed. The net result is that what was thought and intended to decrease paper work actually has increased it. The answer lies in more rigid control of "what is necessary paper work" and this is essentially a human, not a machine contribution.

Increased emphasis will probably be placed upon analysis and interpretation of information made available by the office. As more facts are needed and can be made available within a reasonable period, the task of determining what data are necessary, and why, will take on new and increasing meaning. But the facilitating and service elements of office work will remain of prime importance. Determining and providing essential information effectively, and thus contributing to the success of the entire enterprise, will continue to be the vital task of office management.

Some feel that the whole concept of information needs drastic revision. In their opinion much of the present information is incomplete, too late, unreliable, and poorly organized to have maximum value. Facts for today's decisions reach managers next week. Reams of detailed data are supplied, but helpful summaries and relationships are lacking. Distinction between the critical and the immaterial is not indicated. The need is for a complete reorientation of information. What we now have is outmoded. In an economy such as ours, where manufacturing techniques, products, and markets change as rapidly as they do, we cannot operate an enterprise on fragmented and historical facts that are basically an extension of the past.

Certainly there are elements of truth in these contentions. The challenge is great and it is reasonable to assert that with the need and importance of information being increasingly recognized, fundamental changes for the better will evolve. Then too, there are some who believe the office of the future will not employ papers. Information will be supplied to a great extent by means of drums, tapes, and wires—media of certain office machines. To illustrate, payroll checks might be replaced with information fed by wire from the employer's machine directly into the bank's machine for credit to the individual employee's account. Collectors will receive payment by drawing on their customers' checking accounts. Whether these things come about is conjectural, but the trend toward greater mechanization is taking place.

As office mechanization increases, it would seem that clerical personnel will become more technically proficient, require more training, become more productive, and receive higher wages. But the many problems stemming from the relationship of the employee to a machine, the degree of work specialization, and the acquisition of work satisfaction by the employee are likely to be multiplied.

## QUESTIONS

1. Discuss several important factors that are responsible for the growth development in the supplying of information.
2. What is the meaning of information from the viewpoint of the modern office manager?
3. Explain the meaning of Figure 1–3 in your own words.
4. What is meant by the statement, "Office work is a service work"? Of what importance is this in office management?
5. Discuss the retaining of data in handling the work of the office.
6. What is a data-processing system, and why is it important in performing office work?
7. Select three common types of paper work found in an office with which you are familiar; and, for each type, name the basic elements of data processing required to prepare the paper work.
8. In the typical business enterprise, enumerate five activities giving rise to data; and, for each activity, give the type of common data which are created.
9. Can office work do a service job without being facilitating? Can it be facilitating without doing a service job? Explain.
10. What is meant by each of the following:
    a) The office is the fountainhead of information.
    b) Output of data.
    c) Types of work making up office work.
    d) Basic elements of data processing.

11. In your opinion has the availability of many mechanized processes for performing office work added to or subtracted from the tasks of office management? Justify your answer.

12. What is your opinion regarding the future growth of office work?

## CASE PROBLEM

### Case 1–1.  The Fairchild Company

Mr. Arnold Scott, president of the Fairchild Company, is concerned about the present operations of his company. He has certain ideas about what he feels is wrong and about what corrective actions are needed. However, after thinking the situation over he decided to appoint Mr. Edward Peterson, an outsider and an executive with an excellent business background, to study the company and make recommendations as to what should be done. Mr. Peterson was named special assistant to Mr. Scott two months ago. Since his appointment, Mr. Peterson has studied various documents of the company and has held several interviews with key personnel. From the former source, he has found out that (1) net profits of the company were $100,000 a month a year ago and for the past month were $52,000, (2) sales have dropped $700,000 during the past year to a current level of $4,200,000 annually, (3) cost of purchased items has remained fairly constant, (4) labor costs are sketchy and incomplete, and (5) credits to customers due to monthly rejects of goods shipped have increased from $32,000 a year ago to $278,000 as of last month.

Interviews by Mr. Peterson have disclosed the following. The sales manager, Mr. Herbert Hawkinson, indicates that deliveries are too slow, production promises mean little, for they are not kept, credit records of the company maintained by the central office do not reflect current data, and faulty material is being shipped—the present checking for quality is inadequate. Mr. Clarence Williard, vice-president in charge of production, points out that rush orders have become the rule, not the exception, and are accepted when production facilities are already taxed to capacity, sales personnel do not allow sufficient time to fulfill orders, and the cancellation of a customer's order takes excessively long to reach the factory—sometimes being received several days after the order has been shipped. Mr. Williard has volunteered the information that an important area of difficulty is Mr. Scott's private secretary, Mrs. Alice Beaulieu, who is not articulate in summarizing and communicating information to the executives of the company. As Mr. Williard expresses it, "She is a nice person but can't shake loose the data other executives are holding. Papers remain on her desk and also on Mr. Scott's desk too long. She doesn't seem to be able to farm out her work to others when necessary. She insists on completing all reports by herself, and she either has Mr. Scott sold on how she operates or he doesn't recognize the shortcomings of these ways of doing business." From the controller, Mr. Peterson has learned that about six months ago an order to economize was given him (the controller) by Mr. Scott. Since then several of his people have left the company claiming they had gotten higher paying jobs for the same work with other companies. No attempt was made to keep them by granting a wage increase. The controller states he has experienced great difficulty in acquiring competent help and he understands this is also true of the factory.

## Problems:

1. From the viewpoint of office work, what is the major problem here?
2. What actions do you recommend the company take? Why?
3. Outline how you would try to gain acceptance for your recommended actions.

# CHAPTER 2

# MANAGING
# OFFICE WORK

He who would arrive at the appointed
end must follow a single road and
not wander through many ways.
*—Seneca*

THE recognized need for proper information, the cost of obtaining such information, and the advent of new tools and techniques for getting this information have placed office management in the limelight. With greater amounts of office work being generated and retained, it became quite evident that the cost of this work was a major expenditure. In the interests of efficiency and economy, adequate management had to be placed over office work. Most of us spend far more time and energy working with papers than we realize. Studies reveal, for example, that spending 15 percent of our work time with paper is common and in the case of some executives the figure skyrockets to 75 percent and more. The need is to provide not just information but the right information in the right form at the right time and place for maximum help to the recipient. This requires that the collecting, processing, retaining, and distributing of information be achieved with appropriate attention given to productivity in performing this information work and to supplying it at the lowest cost consistent with acceptable service.

## CONSIDERATIONS OF MANAGEMENT

Office management is one—and a most important one—of the various specialized areas of management. Among the other areas are manufacturing management, sales management, personnel management, finance management, farm management, city management, traffic management, and credit management. Although the areas of application differ, the concept of management is the same regardless of its area of application. This is important. It means that management is a universal concept. Furthermore, it is made up of definite fundamental functions or activities. Hence, the statement can be made that management is a universal activity. Its definite fundamental functions are applied to different areas; but the application varies with regard to type of function, amount, quality, and timing, depending upon the circumstances as the manager sees them and what he is trying to accomplish.

## OBJECTIVES

To clarify the meaning of office management, it is helpful to begin with consideration of the predetermined objective or objectives. Office management concerns the achievement of certain desired goals or results; and basically, the efforts of the office manager center around ways and means to accomplish these goals. There is a mission to perform, a project to initiate, a service to supply.

Examples of objectives of office management are the following:

1. To furnish all necessary and complete information when, where, and to whom it is required for the efficient operation of the enterprise.

2. To provide adequate records and reports at lowest possible cost.

3. To assist the enterprise in keeping competitive.

4. To supply accurate paper work and assist in rendering service to the customer.

5. To make better and better written records at lower and lower costs.

Such statements may sound purely academic, but they serve a practical purpose in that they point out the sought-for goal. They define the target. Other objectives, subordinate but related to the overall goal, can be used to designate the aims for specific office groups or individuals.

An interesting illustration concerns the U.S. Navy. Reports, forms, files, manuals, and procedures threatened to develop into a gigantic paper peak that could seriously damage naval combat readiness. Accordingly a project called SCRAP (Selective Curtailment of Reports and Paperwork) was started by the Navy in 1964. Its objective: "The prompt and drastic reduction of paperwork in the operating forces to that required by a Need to Know or Need to Act." Initial efforts were directed to three areas: (1) reports and forms, (2) directives, catalogs, and external correspondence, and (3) internal correspondence. To date excellent results have been achieved. Illustrative of "selective curtailment" accomplished is that 30 of 61 field activities have been relieved of preparing lengthy, complicated, and costly monthly reports.

Figure 2–1 shows the means by which a manager's efforts are directed toward accomplishing the objective. By means of information a manager establishes the policies, systems, and procedures to be utilized, which in turn guide the utilization of the basic resources of men, materials, machines, methods, money, and markets. The consolidated force of these resources moves and directs the work flow toward the objective. The effectiveness of this work flow is revealed by information returned to the manager, who can, if necessary, adjust the policies, systems, or procedures.

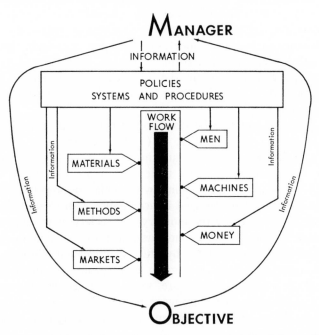

FIG. 2–1. Utilizing information, the manager formulates policies, systems, and procedures which guide the actions of the basic resources—men, materials, machines, methods, money, and markets—toward the objective. In turn, information is reported back to the manager of the accomplishment of the work flow so that adjustments, if necessary, can be made.

The cycle is continuous: information for policies, systems, and procedures; for basic resources; for work flow evaluation; for policies, systems, and procedures.[1]

## TYPES OF OBJECTIVES

Indefinite, overly generalized, and difficult-to-measure objectives accomplish very little. "To improve paper work efforts," while commenda-

---

[1] For discussion of systems and procedures, see Chapter 9; for policies and procedures see Chapter 16.

ble, is of little value in establishing guidelines and channeling efforts. We need specifics, such as which paper work, in which departments, and what reasonable expectancies. We can use the term *result* objective to identify those objectives that set forth the end accomplishment. That is, they emphasize what we want to achieve. Frequently they are expressed in general terms. In contrast, there are *how-to* objectives which stress the means for realizing the end goals. How-to objectives are more complex, more specific, and more difficult to state, but exceedingly helpful and, in fact, necessary for accomplishment of result objectives.

Objectives may be specific or general, written or unwritten, long or short term, temporary or permanent, or applicable to certain segments of the office only. Whatever their form or content, these objectives are set and accepted, for without them the meaning of management becomes nebulous and there is no satisfactory basis for determining the effectiveness of management.

Office objectives can also be classified as pertaining primarily to (1) service, (2) social responsibilities, or (3) profit. Service is of foremost importance in the objectives of managing office work because this work is done to assist others in doing their work more effectively. Also of significance is the objective dealing with social responsibilities which stresses the attainment of the goal in accordance with certain moral and ethical codes as set forth by the industry and society in which the enterprise operates. Lastly objectives emphasizing profit or gain to the owners can be assisted tremendously by office management. Performing the office work more effectively can mean more profit inasmuch as lower expenditures for clerical work are made. Greater emphasis of the importance of the office to management and profit is in order. Acceptance of this obligation by office management members strengthens their status and identifies their role.[2]

## OFFICE MANAGERIAL FUNCTIONS

Objectives can be achieved only through action. The initiating and carrying out of definite and purposeful actions to achieve an objective is the content of management. This content is made up of a process—called the management process—consisting of fundamental functions or activities including:

1. *Planning*—to lay out a means or a course of action, giving consideration to the factors influencing the particular situation.

---

[2] The concept of profit as the objective of any enterprise or segment of an enterprise is actually quite limited. Profit, as such, can be the indirect or the direct aim, depending upon the thinking of the particular company involved. Profit is residual in nature, a by-product resulting from other direct goals.

2. *Controlling*—to determine what is accomplished, evaluate it, determine the "feedback," and apply corrective measures, if needed, to insure results in keeping with the plan.

3. *Organizing*—to distribute the planned work to be done among the members of the work group, establish proper work relationships among them, and supply the proper work environment.

4. *Actuating*—to stimulate and maintain the desire of the members of the work group to execute their respective work enthusiastically in order to achieve the predetermined objective in accordance with the plan.

These four fundamental functions are the distinguishing characteristics of management. They apply universally to management, be it production management, sales management, finance management, or office management. Specifically, they are the means used by an office manager to perform office management. They distinguish the office manager from the nonoffice manager. The student of office management will do well to fix these functions in mind for they provide an all-inclusive viewpoint of office management activities and assist greatly in the understanding of office management.

## OFFICE MANAGEMENT PLANNING

The fundamental function of planning in office management includes the methodic technique of looking ahead and selecting a course from among alternative actions in order to accomplish a predetermined aim. It is a foreseeing action—related facts and assumptions are considered and established for the purpose of determining what must be done, when, by whom, where, and how. Planning requires visualization of future action. It includes determination of proposed actions and knowing what steps will produce the desired results and in what sequence they should be taken.

Effective planning necessitates creative, reflective, and imaginative thinking. Such vision marks the progressive office manager; and in today's office, planning is rapidly becoming ever more important. It is the core of much modern managerial thinking. Perhaps more than ever before, office management planning contains a dynamic element due to the pace at which technology and innovations are being made available to the office and introduced into our economy. In these changes, office managers should contribute, not simply adjust, to the plans, thus adding to the progress and advancing the status of the office management field. Good planning emphasizes prevention rather than correction of delays. It anticipates and defines future possible difficulties and makes provision to care for them.

Consider the illustration of a company which, wishing to mechanize its weekly payroll procedures, purchased, without proper planning, a specialized machine costing $15,000. The machine performed all the payroll work very satisfactorily and required only 1½ days a week to do it. About six months later, the manager decided to mechanize accounts payable and accounts receivable, and hence purchased a general-purpose accounting machine costing $7,500. Within a short period, the capacity of this machine proved too small, so an additional and identical machine was purchased at the same price. The total capacity of the second general-purpose accounting machine was not required, so efforts were undertaken to find work to utilize it full time. It was discovered that the entire weekly payroll work could be done on it. This eliminated the need for the original specialized payroll machine. Its cost, or $15,000, could have been avoided by proper planning. But is having all the work done on two $7,500 general purpose accounting machines the best plan? Could one $10,000 general-purpose accounting machine have accomplished the total work? Adequate planning would have encompassed initially a broader scope of paper-work activities for consideration. Specifically, the needs not only for payroll but for accounts payable and accounts receivable should have been considered. Furthermore, the alternative possibilities would be evaluated and the best course of action developed. In addition, the dispersion of the various necessary records, papers, and information within and outside the typical enterprise help to point out the vital nature of planning in office management work.

## OFFICE MANAGEMENT CONTROLLING

A long-standing function of a manager is to check results in order to see if the work is progressing satisfactorily and in keeping with what is expected, that is, in accordance with the planning. "Follow-up" is an essential part of management and is included under the term "controlling." The best plan may not bring about the desired results. Variances, misunderstandings, and unexpected events may occur. Such contingencies must be quickly ascertained so that corrective action can be taken.

In order to apply controlling to any activity, measurable performance factors must be established. These include such things as quantity, quality, cost, or time bases. The actual performance is compared with the expected or preestablished standard. For example, the number of payroll cards processed per hour is compared to the number expected for acceptable performance, and deviations from the established base are subject to analysis and evaluation.

Much of the office manager's contribution to the entire enterprise is in the area of controlling. Records and information help provide answers to the question: "How well is the work being done?" However, controlling within the office area is a chief consideration of this book, since it is an essential part of office management. Controlling must be exercised by the office manager to carry out his office management activity successfully. In instances where the office manager is in charge of all office work, some of which is done by people other than those in the office, and which people also decide certain matters involving paper work, the function of office management controlling takes on added importance.

## OFFICE MANAGEMENT ORGANIZING

Organizing means literally to make organic—i.e., serviceable or helpful —by means of establishing a structure or a definite operating relationship among various components of the entire entity. An office manager organizes the work for which he is responsible by apportioning it in an orderly fashion among the various structural units for achieving the task. The personnel for each structural unit are selected, delegated appropriate authority, and held responsible for the satisfactory completion of their respective work. If, within the company, no group exists from which personnel can be selected, the manager must recruit and hire the needed personnel from outside the company. In addition, the personnel are provided proper workplaces, that is, the appropriate equipment, machines, lighting, and work area. In brief, organizing deals with the establishing of proper relationships among the components of the work to be done, designating the people who are going to do it, and providing the work environment in which the tasks will be done.

Knowledge and skill in organizing are vital in office management. Organizing makes it possible for the office manager to spread his influence and to get goals accomplished effectively through a group. Organizing is a key to group efficiency. It helps the group serve as a unit with all its efforts blended together toward a specific objective.

## OFFICE MANAGEMENT ACTUATING

The fundamental function of actuating includes the creating and maintaining of the desire by each member of the work group to achieve the objective in accordance with plans. The work of planning, controlling, and organizing does not accomplish the predetermined goal. The plan must be put into effect by people working willingly at prescribed tasks and at given times and places. To accomplish this, people must be properly motivated to work along these guided lines. This activity constitutes managerial actuating.

The type of person, the component activity to be performed, the facilities provided, and the manager's judgment determine the measures utilized to execute this actuating function. Leadership, human-relations practices, training programs, and proper compensation are among the more common means.

Actuating concerns intangible subject areas, but success in these areas brings high rewards. When members of the work group are inspired to use their highest attainable skills and capacities, when they are genuinely interested in their work, when they are enthusiastic about accomplishing their assigned tasks, and when they believe in and understand the plan and how the objective is to be accomplished, the burden of management is lightened, and the accomplishments attained frequently are startling even to the experienced manager proficient in actuating efforts.

Figure 2–2 recapitulates the concept of the basic office management functions in a concise tabular form. It serves to fix in mind the process of management as a distinct activity consisting of planning, controlling, organizing, and actuating.

| Basic Office Management Functions | Performed by People, but Concerned Primarily with. . . . |
|---|---|
| PLANNING AND CONTROLLING<br>Determining the future courses of action and seeing that they are accomplished within reasonable limits. | . . . things and materials.<br>What procedure? Equipment? Machines? Cost? Accuracy? Time limits? |
| ORGANIZING AND ACTUATING<br>Dividing the work, maintaining proper work relationships among members of the group, and getting them to want to accomplish what the manager wants them to do. | . . . employees and their work.<br>Who does what? Who reports to whom? What motivates whom? How acquire dedication to work? |

FIG. 2–2. The basic office management functions.

## INTERDEPENDENCE OF FUNDAMENTAL FUNCTIONS

The four fundamental functions of office management are interdependent—they should never be thought of as being mutually exclusive. Each depends upon the others. Actually, there is no sharp delineation designating the terminating of one function and the starting of another in the process. For instance, planning constitutes a part of determining the work-to-be-done components, an activity included under organizing. And controlling influences the establishing of proper relationships among the organizational units normally included under organizing.

Nor is there a definite sequence of the functions which the office manager must follow. In presenting the fundamental functions, the sequence of planning, controlling, organizing, and actuating was followed. But a manager performs only the function or functions required by the situation and in the order deemed advisable. Thus, actuating efforts may be employed, followed by planning and subsequently by controlling.

## OFFICE MANAGEMENT IS A DISTINCT ACTIVITY

From what has been stated, it follows that office management is a distinct entity; it can be studied, and proficiency in it can be attained. Management is not a person or a group of people. One who performs the activity of management is a manager. Hence, those who perform this activity of management in the office work area are office managers.

The concept of management as an activity, and of those performing this activity as managers, helps to clarify thinking on this subject. Unfortunately, many common expressions used to describe the work of the office manager are not very helpful. For example, identifying an office manager as the one who "runs" an office or the person who "tells" employees what office work to do provides little assistance. Also, the fact that a person has subordinates reporting to him does not make that person a manager in the true meaning of management. Having a group of faithful followers is not a guarantee that management exists.

To reiterate, an office manager, to qualify as an office manager, performs four fundamental functions making up the management process. The use of this management process marks the essential difference between a clerk and an office manager, or between an accountant and the manager of the accounting department. Knowing how to write letters, for example, is not sufficient to manage the correspondence department. Office management is a distinct entity, it is an activity in itself, and it requires the use of certain knowledge, skills, and practices.

## OFFICE MANAGEMENT AND THE BASIC RESOURCES

As has already been pointed out, a manager regulates, starts, or stops a work flow and hence work accomplishment by utilizing the six basic resources of men, materials, machines, methods, money, and markets. These six resources are sometimes referred to as the "six M's." A manager conveys his managerial wishes to his associates and helpers by means of information which is derived from his application of the management functions, i.e., planning, controlling, organizing, and actuating.

Figure 2–3 shows this concept in graphic form. To reiterate, effective management requires knowledge of the objectives, i.e., knowing what is to be accomplished is a prime requisite. In most cases, planning helps to set forth the objectives. With the stated goals as a background, an office manager utilizes the "six M's" which are shown intertwined at the left of the figure. They are subjected to planning, controlling, and organizing. The men, or members of the work group, are actuated to want to achieve the objectives and help insure that the end results will be the stated objectives.

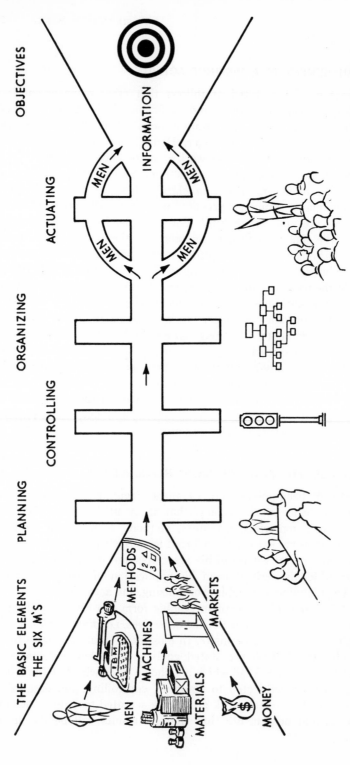

FIG. 2–3. The objectives of the office are obtained by subjecting the "six M's"—Men, Materials, Machines, Methods, Money, and Markets—to the application of the managerial functions of planning, controlling, and organizing, and, in addition, subjecting the basic element of Men to the activity of actuating.

## DEFINITION OF OFFICE MANAGEMENT

Office management can be defined as *the planning, controlling, and organizing of office work, and actuating those performing it so as to achieve the predetermined objectives.* It deals with the life cycle of business information and data from their creation through their maintenance, distribution, and retention, if of permanent value, or destruction if obsolete.

Several observations should be made concerning the definition given above. First, office management is considered in the broad, inclusive sense. It includes managerial efforts over office work anywhere in an enterprise. It is not confined to efforts of the person called "the office manager" or some similar title, nor to the work performed in "the office" only.

Second, office management is not a purely mechanistic activity. The effective application of the fundamental functions of office management is fraught with great difficulties. No fixed formula can be followed in all cases. There is an art of management as well as a science or body of knowledge of management. The art of management deals with skill or the application of knowledge. This is of special importance in management. One may have all the facts and pertinent relationships but fail to use them effectively.[3]

Office management necessitates the ability to make decisions. Each of the fundamental functions of management requires decision making in its execution. Determining the course of actions to follow (planning) or appraising a situation (controlling) involves decision making. Decisions should be based on adequate facts, and these facts are often difficult to obtain. The successful manager carefully distinguishes between facts and opinions and utilizes only those data which are definitely related and pertinent to the problem at hand. Frequently, all the facts cannot be secured, in which case the best decision based on the known facts should be made, with the realization that future adjustments may be necessary. Normally, decisions should be based on a logical or reasoned approach, with due regard given to the intent of the enterprise.

Lastly, office management members must be able to exercise ingenuity. To a considerable extent, all managerial progress is dependent upon the creation and the development of successful ideas. Most improvements start as ideas—for example, a better way of performing an office task, a simplified means of securing applicants, and the rearrangement of data on the paper form to make calculating easier. Such ideas stem from observation and thinking.

---

[3] Science, scientific management, and the art of management are discussed in the immediately following pages.

## COMMON APPROACHES IN APPLYING THE MANAGEMENT PROCESS

In applying the management process, an office manager can follow one of several general approaches. Among these are (1) the scientific approach, (2) the systems and procedures approach, (3) the artistic approach, (4) the conventional approach, and (5) the observational approach. All are utilized, all are valid.

## SCIENTIFIC OFFICE MANAGEMENT

Today we hear a great deal about the scientific approach which employs the "scientific method." When followed faithfully, this approach contributes much fundamental knowledge to office management and, based on past performance, has greatly enriched our current office management practices.

"Science" is a body of knowledge discovered by means of the scientific method, which knowledge has been accumulated and accepted in reference to the discovery or understanding of truth. The facts which make up this body of knowledge are expressed by statements or data generally believed to be representative of the phenomena and supposedly free from bias and prejudice. Science is entirely objective; there is no place in it for personal influence, likes, and dislikes.

The scientific method consists of well-defined steps taken either to confirm or to disprove a stated proposition under consideration. The method tests the proposition under carefully prescribed and controlled conditions. These steps are shown in Figure 2–4. In essence, a tentative solution to a stated problem is tried out under specific and known conditions. In a sense, it can be viewed as controlled experimentation.

Frederick W. Taylor is generally credited with beginning the application of the scientific method to management. He conducted many studies or tests under controlled conditions, i.e., employing the scientific method, and obtained vast new funds of knowledge. Among his important conclusions were that high wages were compatible with low unit costs; that standards were needed to control production; that employees, materials, and procedures should be scientifically selected; and that cooperation between management and nonmanagement members was required for highest productivity.[4]

---

[4] These fundamentals are expounded in F. W. Taylor, *Scientific Management,* which comprises the previously published works *Shop Management, The Principles of Scientific Management,* and *Testimony before the Special House Committee* (New York: Harper & Bros., 1947), pp. 1–47 and 130–31.

| BASIC ACTION | STEPS | |
|---|---|---|
| CREATE | 1. RECOGNIZE THE PROBLEM | |
| | 2. MAKE PRELIMINARY OBSERVATIONS AND ANALYSIS | |
| | 3. DRAW UP A HYPOTHESIS OR TENTATIVE SOLUTION TO THE PROBLEM | |
| PROVE | 4. MAKE A THOROUGH AND DETAILED ANALYSIS | |
| | 5. COLLECT ADEQUATE DATA | |
| | 6. CLASSIFY THE DATA COLLECTED | |
| | 7. MAKE A TENTATIVE ANSWER TO THE PROBLEM | |
| CONCLUDE | 8. TEST THIS SOLUTION OR ANSWER | |
| | 9. ADJUST IN LIGHT OF RESULTS UNDER STEP 8. | |
| | 10. STATE THE ANSWER TO THE PROBLEM | |

FIG. 2–4.  The scientific method consists of well-defined steps.

## SYSTEMS AND PROCEDURES OFFICE MANAGEMENT

The use of systems and procedures in office management is not new, but during recent years the recognition of this viewpoint as an approach to office management has grown tremendously. It is modern, inclusive, and extremely effective. A systematic collection and effective use of data and information can be designed. By such a system each individual in an enterprise is provided with the information he needs to discharge his duties, to delegate tasks to his subordinates, and to facilitate his other and sundry managerial responsibilities.

The utility and practical value of the systems and procedures approach has been enhanced by the electronic computer. It is now feasible to process large volumes of information rapidly and accurately. Hence, our thinking in office management and the boundaries of information handling for a specific project are greatly increased. The former constraints imposed by information applying to an isolated activity or limited number of activities are no longer valid. We can now look upon an enterprise as a unit and consider all information handling efforts within this unit or the entire enterprise. The systems and procedures approach permits us to adopt this broader picture, to coordinate all the efforts dealing with information, facts, and figures and to eliminate needless duplication and voids in paper-work handling.

The systems and procedures developed and adopted automatically encompass the plans, policies, relationships, and controls used by the manager and supply the required written managerial records. Under this approach there may be a tendency to stabilize given ways of achieving office work and to a degree this is highly desirable. But improvements in the existing systems and procedures should be sought as new ideas and new machines become available. The systems and procedures approach is destined to grow in importance. Actually there is some systems and procedures management in every type of management; it is a necessary supplement to each of the other managerial types.

## ARTISTIC OFFICE MANAGEMENT

By artistic office management is meant the approach emphasizing the art of management. Art stresses the skill in bringing about a desired result. The art of management enhances the other approaches of management. For example, it assists in implementing the science of management and the knowledge and concepts derived from the systems and procedures approach. In other words, the art of management emphasizes adroitness in applying the fund of management knowledge. Skill in perceiving where and when to take certain actions or to refrain from any action is essential to managerial success.

Judgment, experience, understanding, and feeling appear to be important in developing an art of management. Management really becomes personalized and a part of the manager when the art of management is developed and employed. By its successful application managerial achievements soar to heights consistent with highest professional levels.

## CONVENTIONAL OFFICE MANAGEMENT

The adherence to custom characterizes conventional office management. It follows the manner and method which have been handed down from the past; emphasis is placed on doing a managerial task in a manner similar to that which one's predecessor used. The fundamental theme is expressed by the statement: "What was good enough for my father is good enough for me." The follower of conventional management seldom asks why or questions the purpose of a particular managerial activity. He is little concerned with efforts to discover new managerial techniques.

## OBSERVATIONAL OFFICE MANAGEMENT

This type is characterized by the use of observations as the basic media for managing an operation. The observational manager observes how other managers achieve their goal and uses this information in determining his own course of action. He copies and attempts to select what he believes to be the best of his fellow managers' techniques and then applies them to his own particular problems. The observational manager's attitude is: "Find out how the other fellow performs a managerial task similar to one which you have—then solve your managerial problem by using the same approach and method."

Observational management helps to distribute managerial ideas and techniques among managers. Furthermore, it requires little effort. Most managers like to discuss their activities, especially those in which they are successful. Also, observational management offers dynamic sources of information for the changing managerial problems, but does not necessarily contribute to the improvement of managerial techniques. An office practice which works well for one office might produce poor results for the firm which copies it, as a result of differences in objectives, in the size of the office, or in the personnel of the two firms. Nevertheless, observational management is used by many managers of small offices where the facilities and time may make other approaches difficult to follow.

## OFFICE MANAGEMENT ACTIVITIES

The activities included in office management are quite numerous; among them are the following:

1. Maintaining adequate office services and communication facilities.
   *a*) See that correspondence work—stenographic and typing—is performed.
   *b*) Handle incoming and outgoing mail.

  *c*) Supply reception and messenger service.

  *d*) File records and reports.

  *e*) Maintain papers of permanent value; destroy those that are obsolete.

2. Deciding the extent of office automation to be used.

  *a*) Select and utilize office electronic machines.

  *b*) Develop the format for information derived from machines.

  *c*) Handle the training and transferring of employees in keeping with mechanization plans.

  *d*) Establish integrated data processing (IDP).

3. Determining the complete course of action to accomplish the office work.

  *a*) Keep informed of latest developments in performing office work.

  *b*) Develop office systems, procedures, and methods.

  *c*) Apply work simplification to office work.

  *d*) Coordinate the work of the office with that of the nonoffice.

  *e*) Specify and purchase office furniture, machines, and supplies.

  *f*) Arrange the office layout—location of office furniture and machines.

  *g*) Determine effective work environment—adequate lighting, elimination of noise, and proper ventilation.

  *h*) Select the office location.

4. Measuring and evaluating quantity and quality of office work.

  *a*) Establish standards for office work.

  *b*) Schedule and dispatch office work.

  *c*) Maintain quality of office work.

  *d*) Time-study office operations.

  *e*) Keep office costs within acceptable limits.

  *f*) Prepare office budget.

  *g*) Write office manuals.

5. Providing an effective office organization.

  *a*) Apportion the work among the organizational units.

  *b*) Maintain proper balance among the various office activities.

  *c*) Establish definite and known relationships among organizational units.

  *d*) Know the individual jobs in the office.

  *e*) Assign proper personnel to organizational units.

  *f*) Delegate authority.

  *g*) Fix responsibility among personnel.

  *h*) Provide for proper work facilities.

6. Inspiring the office personnel to do the best of which they are capable.

  *a*) Motivate office employees.

  *b*) Give adequate supervision.

    *c*) Analyze and evaluate office jobs.
    *d*) Give office training programs.
    *e*) Provide adequate communication among office employees and between office and nonoffice units.
    *f*) Administer office salary plan.
    *g*) Promote office safety.

## THE CHALLENGE OF OFFICE MANAGEMENT

Opportunities are abundant in the field of office management. The rapid growth in the amount of work and in the number doing it have emphasized the need for managers trained in this field. As the importance and contributions of the office are gaining greater recognition, the status of the qualified office manager is increasing.

Challenges are indeed numerous for the executive specializing in the managing of information handling. Among the more significant challenges are (1) increasing the number of office executives with the management viewpoint, (2) applying greater creativity to office management, (3) reducing the amount of unnecessary paper work performed, (4) improving office systems, procedures, and methods, (5) using effectively the "automated office," (6) establishing more and better office standards, (7) developing better means of motivating office employees, and (8) attracting and acquiring the better graduates from schools for office jobs.

There exist in companies almost everywhere vast possibilities for qualified executives. This is especially true for office managers. Indeed, the future is brilliant for the qualified office manager who recognizes the real importance of information handling, can manage it effectively, and can contribute to the successful operation of the entire enterprise.

## THE TITLE "OFFICE MANAGER"

Since office work is present in every phase and level of management, it follows that most executives have something to do with office work, although this is not their primary responsibility. Any department head or other executive can improve the management of the office work under his direct supervision by applying the managerial practices developed in this book. He need not necessarily have a large clerical staff. However, when the scope and extent of activities are limited, the degree of specialization may be somewhat reduced.

The scope of the office manager's job is quite flexible. Strictly speaking, the one in charge of managing office work is the office manager. As already stated, in some enterprises the office manager has charge of the work done by all the departments of the office; in other enterprises, he is the general manager not only of the office work in the office but of all office work, whether it is done in or out of the office.

## THE ADMINISTRATIVE MANAGER

In actual practice, the one in charge of managing office work is not always titled "office manager." He may have the title of "controller," "systems analyst," "manager, office procedures," "auditor," "manager, information," "chief clerk," "manager, office services," "administrative services manager"; or he may have no title at all.

Since about 1960, the title "administrative manager" has gained considerable favor. Many believe that this title is more descriptive of the managing of information and better denotes the company-wide range of activities centered in the office. This can be viewed as another change in the current evolution of the office. As one speaker so aptly described it: "The office has become the nerve center of the enterprise."

With this change, the person in charge of office work, whatever his title, has been given greater authority and responsibility, and more company-wide activities have been transferred to the office area. Recognition of this significant growth and trend is encompassed by the title "administrative manager," which is winning favor, and the trend seems likely to continue. In many cases, the duties and title of the office manager have changed. Demanded are new approaches and patterns of thought. Fresh viewpoints and contributions of information technologists, office administrators, and trained paper-work analysts are reshaping the concept of the office manager's role. He is proving himself to be an indispensable adjunct to the top management of the company and is gaining greater recognition and occupying an increasingly important role in the overall management of the enterprise.

## QUESTIONS

1. Office management is defined by some as the accomplishment of office work by others. Does acceptance of this definition mean that actuating office employees represents and is the same as office management? Discuss.
2. Briefly identify each of the following:
   - *a*) Office management.
   - *b*) Result objectives.
   - *c*) Universal concept of management.
   - *d*) Systems and procedures office management.
3. Visit an office with which you are familiar and find out its major objectives. What do you deduce from the information obtained?
4. Do you agree with the following statement? "To achieve objectives requires action. This being true, planning can be considered nonproductive because nothing is achieved simply by planning." Elaborate on your answer.

5. Describe the meaning of Figure 2–1 in your own words.

6. Relate an example of artistic office management.

7. What steps of the scientific method do you feel are probably most difficult to apply to office management problems? Discuss.

8. What title for the person in charge of office work do you prefer? Justify your answer.

9. Relate an experience in some phase of business, preferably dealing with office work, which illustrates poor controlling.

10. How successful do you believe an office manager can be by following the approach of conventional management in his work? Discuss.

11. Briefly relate your reaction to this statement: "The key to being an expert office manager is to know how to practice effective organizing. It is dividing the office work fairly and properly among personnel that counts and this is exactly what managerial organizing does."

12. Discuss five current major challenges of office management.

## CASE PROBLEMS

### Case 2–1.   National Co-operative

James Wellington is an accountant and has been in the employ of National Co-operative for eight years. During the past two years his work and attitude have declined. His work is filled with errors and poor grammar and misspellings are frequent in the reports he writes. His work requires extra checking. Jim has taken to monopolizing the telephone with long personal conversations and spends considerable office time in extended coffee breaks and long lunch hours. There is evidence, fairly well covered up, of hostility between Jim and his immediate supervisor, Mr. Harold M. Harwich.

Mr. Harwich is best described as a patient, tolerant man. He has tolerated the situation with Jim, but has come very near a showdown point several times during the past several months. Two weeks ago he exploded and dashed into his superior's office, the vice-president in charge of finance, and poured out his troubles. Citing several incidents of Jim's work and attitude, Mr. Harwich concluded that Jim's employment must be terminated.

The vice-president of finance agreed. Within a week, a replacement from out of town was hired and put in Jim's job. At the same time, Jim was given four weeks' notice that his employment with National Co-operative was being terminated. He was assigned routine accounting work of a lower level than the work he had been doing. The new replacement did excellent work. He was accurate, wrote better reports, and did more work than Jim had ever accomplished on the job. Mr. Harwich believed he was a great improvement to his department and considered himself lucky to acquire such a worthy new employee.

Jim was bitter. At the end of the second week on his demoted job he succeeded in getting an appointment with the vice-president of finance. During the interview, Jim admitted that he was no angel, but contended you can't fire an employee with eight years' service without giving him a chance to improve. Mr. Harwich never called him on the carpet, never gave him a warning notice, never told him to change his working habits. Jim contended he deserved another chance, preferably in another part of the office where he wouldn't have to be under Mr. Harwich.

## Problems:

1. What is the problem to solve in this case?
2. As James Wellington, what further action would you take? Why?
3. Evaluate Mr. Harwich's actions.
4. What action do you recommend the vice-president of finance take? Why?

### Case 2–2.   The Sullivan-Culbert Company

Mr. Culbert, in charge of sales, has received many dealer complaints during the past several months. Delays in billing, incorrect invoices, and mistakes in pricing and discounts are mentioned most frequently. He has spoken several times about these complaints to Mr. Buffington who is in charge of the office. Mr. Buffington states that there is a sufficient number of employees in the office to get the work out promptly and correctly. The difficulty is that they just do not work. He has repeatedly cautioned them about the quality of their work, but it does no good. Office help is difficult to find, so he cannot be too severe. Probably the whole condition is a part of growing pains which the company is now experiencing due to adding new products and expanding distribution nationally.

Mr. Culbert also spoke with Mr. Sullivan, president of the Company, about the dealer complaints and the status of the office work. Subsequently, Mr. Sullivan talked with Mr. Buffington. It was decided that Mr. Buffington should proceed to correct the office situation, using all reasonable and necessary means.

Mr. Buffington took the following measures:

1. Hired an additional six male clerks and eight female typists.

2. Wrote a personal note to each office employee stating that the quality of the office work must be improved.

3. Stated that all office supervisors would become working supervisors in order to locate sources of mistakes in papers being prepared. Any employee caught preparing an incorrect billing or invoice would be given five demerits. A total of fifteen demerits means automatic employment termination.

4. Indicated his greater activity in work of credit extensions, collecting accounts, and trying to keep sufficient cash and funds on hand to meet the needs of the expanding business.

5. Made it clear that if the quality of the office work did not improve, changes in personnel would be made.

6. Appointed Mr. Herbert Welsh as his assistant to whom all office supervisors would report. However, carefully stated that decisions involving major issues remain his (Mr. Buffington's) prerogative.

## Problems:

1. What is the main issue in this case?
2. What is your opinion regarding the measures taken by Mr. Buffington?
3. After talking with Mr. Buffington, do you believe Mr. Culbert did the correct thing in seeing Mr. Sullivan? Why?
4. What is your recommendation to Mr. Sullivan? Discuss.

# PART 2

# COMMON OFFICE SERVICES

*An important group of activities dealing with information is commonly called office services. They exist in every office and include corresponding, report writing, mailing, duplicating, calculating, and filing.*

*The following five chapters are concerned respectively with (1) corresponding and report writing, (2) mailing and office communicating, (3) duplicating, calculating, and comparing, (4) filing, and (5) records retention.*

*In each chapter the application of the management process—planning, controlling, organizing, and actuating —is interwoven throughout the discussion. Thus, a practical conceptual pattern of management in these major areas is provided.*

# CHAPTER 3

# CORRESPONDING
# AND REPORT WRITING

Language was given us that we might
say pleasant things to each other.
— *Christian Bouce*

ESSENTIAL to the existence of every enterprise is corresponding and report writing. These are basic activities in supplying necessary information. Paper work even in its most limited concept always includes letters and reports, for these are the common media for keeping interested persons both within and without the enterprise informed on important matters.

## ARE CORRESPONDING AND REPORT WRITING IMPORTANT?

Most executives spend at least two hours a day reading and writing letters and reports. In some cases, they spend twice or three times that amount of time. Many are aware that they probably spend too much time and money in this activity, yet there seems to be a reluctance to let go of the old weighty practices holding them down.

Letters are one of the main carriers of the corporate image. Public relations can be developed tremendously by the use of effective letters. The good will of many companies is due directly or indirectly to their effective correspondence work. Many stories attest to the fact that a friendly, well-written letter paved the way for a million-dollar sale with a previously unknown party. Or what might have been a devastating blow to a company was avoided because the proper letter was sent to a certain party at a particular time. Obviously, such letters are important—worth every ounce of thought and imagination the writer can pour into them. But what about the other letters—the ordinary or supposedly unimportant ones? Individually, they may seem trivial, but their cumulative effect is great. Each one represents an opportunity to make friends and influence others favorably toward your company. This gives them enormous potential.

Likewise, reports are very important because they assist in carrying out the managerial functions of planning, controlling, organizing, and actuating. For example, planning requires information on what must be accomplished, and within what time periods. Reports help to supply this needed information or to suggest possible avenues of approach which might reveal potent information.

A report is a formal presentation of summary information dealing with utilization of resources or status of operations useful in evaluating progress, making decisions, and directing activities. When an enterprise is small, a manager can keep in personal touch with all phases of it, but as growth takes place, various levels of management develop, and the personal means becomes inadequate. To meet these conditions, reports are used to keep executives informed, to develop favorable interdepartmental relationships, and to help get the work accomplished through the work force.

## CLASSIFYING LETTERS AND REPORTS

Efforts to classify letters and reports into major types help to identify them and to designate the main purpose of each communication. Such information can be helpful in managing this area of office services.

Letters can usually be classified into those dealing with complaints, employment, purchasing, sales, or credit. In turn, letters in each of these major groups can be segregated further, as illustrated below.

*Complaints*—the replies are usually of four types:

1. Acknowledgment of complaint and promise to investigate and report later.

2. Adjustment of complaint, giving date and amount, and thanking addressee.

3. Refusal to adjust complaint, with reasons explaining why.

4. Request that the goods be returned for inspection and advise that further consideration will be given.

For *employment*—three types of replies are generally given:

1. Acknowledgment of application, stating that there is no opening at present.

2. Acknowledgment of application and request to report for work.

3. Welcome to newly hired worker of the company and explanation of company policies.

Reports can be classified into many different types, including private, public, company, departmental, restricted, nonrestricted, technical, and nontechnical. However, for purposes of office usage, the three groups of executive, periodic, and special are quite satisfactory. Under each of these classifications are the following:

*Executive reports* stress broad concepts and results rather than details, usually covering a three-, six-, or twelve-month time period. For the most part, they are prepared for members of top and intermediate management levels. They include (1) balance sheet, (2) statement of cost of goods sold, (3) statement of profit and loss, (4) budgetary statement, (5) annual departmental report, and (6) report to stockholders.

*Periodic reports* deal mainly with departmental activities and typically cover weekly, monthly, or quarterly periods. Usually some detailed information pertinent to the operation of the particular department is included. Periodic reports include (1) monthly reports on operation, (2) departmental records of performance, (3) monthly credit reports, (4) purchasing reports, (5) material-handling reports, (6) salesmen's reports, (7) advertising and sales promotion reports, and (8) personnel management reports.

*Special reports* cover activities not covered by other reports. They are published at frequent intervals and include subjects such as product development, marketing research, plant location, company insurance and pension revisions, and various projects of a nonrecurring nature. A portion of a special report dealing with the findings of a market research study is shown in Figure 3–1.

## ARRANGEMENT OF LETTER

A business letter should make a favorable first impression. To do this, it should be well placed on the page, have margins as even as possible, have a uniformity of typing or print, and give a clean and neat appearance.

There is probably no one best form for a business letter. Usually, a general pattern is in common usage; but slight variations are the rule, depending upon the particular needs and wishes of the writer. Most readers are accustomed to the general pattern and look for certain information in certain locations. Figure 3–2 shows the forms of several different types, including (1) indented paragraphs, (2) block paragraphs, and (3) simplified letter. The difference between indented paragraphs and block paragraphs is that in the latter the paragraphs are started at the left margin. In the simplified letter, all material starts at the left margin, the salutation is omitted—in its place the subject of the letter is written—and the complimentary close is omitted. Slight variations from these three forms of letters are employed. One large national distributor, for example, uses the block paragraph form with open punctuation, that is, commas and periods are omitted at end of date, address, and close.

In many instances the situation does not require a letter; a short well-

35–E                    X Research Company                    N 58

## SUMMARY OF FINDINGS

OBJECTIVE:

To obtain a measure of consumer acceptance of Product Y.

RESULTS:

1. Product Y is not as well liked as Product No. 17.
2. The market potential of Product Y is somewhat between 50% and 80% of the market for Product No. 17. These are the limits indicated by consumers' stated preferences and test-package consumption.
3. The preference for Product No. 17 over Product Y prevails in all geographical areas and among all types of consumers. The greatest liking for Product Y was found among women.
4. Product No. 17 is preferred chiefly because it is crisp, easy to eat, and has a sweet, mild flavor.
5. Product Y is preferred by those who like a harder and heavier cereal than Product No. 17. Most cold cereal users, however, thought Product Y too hard to chew.
6. While food value is not a dominant factor in consumers' preferences between cereals, Product Y was the choice of consumers who emphasize this point.

CONCLUSION:

There is a limited market for an expanded cereal that is harder and heavier than Product No. 17. The potential volume of one such cereal—Product Y—is between 50% and 80% of the Product No. 17 market.

FIG. 3–1.   A portion of a special report.

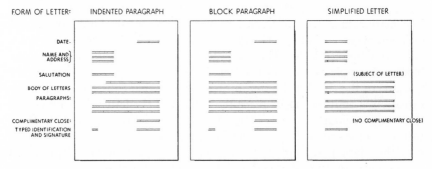

FIG. 3–2.   The respective forms of three different letters used in business.

April 25, 19—
To:                     T. E. Miller
Subject:                Storing purchased parts in our stores.
Objective:              To reduce damage to parts while in transit or in stores.
Scope of Project:       Try to attain:
                            1. Better package design and material.
                            2. Improved physical inventory taking.
                            3. Better utilization of stores space.
                            4. Efficient housekeeping in stores.
Time Required:          Approximately six weeks.
Submitted by:           J. D. Black

FIG. 3–3.   Example of an effective short memorandum.

written memorandum is adequate. Figure 3–3 illustrates an effective memorandum. Terse headings simplify the job of writing because they unify simple sentences into a condensed and informative message.

## SPEED LETTER

In order to simplify the work of correspondence, the so-called "speed letter" is used by many business writers. See Figure 3–4. In this letter, space is provided for a listing of recipients making up a mailing route, and preprinted information is included so that the appropriate information can be indicated by a simple check mark. Additional space is provided for such individual information as may be required.

*A speed letter is a preprinted form designating certain spaces for filling in desired information.* Commonly, three copies are made. The original is retained by the sender; copies No. 2 and 3 are sent to the receiver, who writes in his reply, returns copy No. 2, and retains copy No. 3. Some designs provide spaces for "From" and "To" at the top of the sheet and a line for the "Subject" to be written in, below which is a space for the "Message," and below it, the "Reply."

## FORM LETTERS

As stated above, most letters can be classified into a relatively small number of types. This fact suggests and has led to letter standardization, or the use of form letters. A form letter is *a standardized letter which is used by an enterprise to answer all correspondence on a similar or recurring subject, or which is used to give the same information to many addressees.* A form letter may be sent to accounts past due. Such a letter, keyed

| DEMPSTER CORP.<br>CHICAGO, ILL.<br>SPEED LETTER | | DATE | | |
|---|---|---|---|---|
| TO:<br>1 | LOCATION | | INITIALS | DATE |
| 2 | | | | |
| 3 | | | | |
| 4 | | | | |
| 5 | | | | |

| | |
|---|---|
| APPROVAL | NOTE AND FORWARD |
| AS REQUESTED | NOTE AND RETURN |
| COMMENT | NOTE ENDORST OF ACTION TAKEN |
| FOR YOUR INFORMATION | PER CONVERSATION |
| INITIAL FOR CLEARANCE | PREPARE REPLY |
| NECESSARY ACTION | SIGNATURE |

MESSAGE

| SIGNATURE | TITLE |
|---|---|
| | |

FIG. 3—4.  A well-planned printed form to expedite written communication.

"Delinquent Collection Letter No. 1," is sent to all accounts in arrears, with the appropriate name and address added at the top. After a certain amount of time, a "Delinquent Collection Letter No. 2" may be sent to those accounts which remain unpaid.

The chief advantages in the use of form letters are that they (1) afford a uniform operation, (2) conserve both the dictator's and the typist's time, and (3) help reduce letter costs. On the other hand, there are disadvantages in the use of form letters, including: (1) They are not keyed to the requirements of individual cases, (2) they may be a little stilted, and (3) they are very often discounted by the receiver because of the lack of a personal touch.

Generally speaking, form letters serve a very useful purpose. They are tailored to fit certain conditions and are usually worked over by several correspondents to create the best possible results. They need not be impersonal, and it is not necessary to send the same letter again and again to the same customer. When they are properly handled, there should be no objection to form letters.

## FORM PARAGRAPHS

Form paragraphs are similar in idea to form letters but apply to standardized paragraphs only. Under this practice, letters are composed of form paragraphs plus individual ones. Experts are frequently engaged to develop the form paragraphs.

It is customary for the dictator to use several variants of a form paragraph. This permits some diversity. The approved form paragraphs are listed, keyed, and indexed, and are made available to all correspondents.

## DEVELOPING FORM LETTERS AND PARAGRAPHS

Form letters and form paragraphs can be "armchaired" from handy references, or they can be obtained by actual practice. The latter is recommended. To do this, simply take these steps:

1. For a period of four weeks, make an extra copy of every letter written.

2. At the end of this period, sort the copies by major subject and further by types under each major heading.

3. Determine the types of letters most frequently written and also, under each type, the most frequently used paragraphs.

4. Select the best reply to each frequently asked question and also the best expression of the necessary information.

5. Standardize these forms, and incorporate them as form paragraphs and form letters.

6. Repeat this entire procedure every 12 months; then, adjust and improve form paragraphs and letters as suggested by findings.

For this work, the office manager should enlist the services of all letter-writing people in his office. Participation will not only help win acceptance of the program of improving correspondence but will also utilize the best personnel for this work, raise morale, and increase efficiency.

## FORMAT FOR REPORTS

There is no one best way to arrange the information of a report. In some instances, a standardized format is well established and accepted;

but in many cases, the writer is free to choose the makeup. Material should be presented logically. Aids which will help in the reading should be provided—for example, simple statements, sectional headings, summaries at the beginning, and a table of contents. A reader often glances through a report, noting the various headings and reading a sentence here and there. For this reason, it is advisable to make it possible to obtain a "quickie" on what the report is all about and what it includes. This approach will maintain the reader's interest and lead him to correct conclusions and proper actions.

Every report should follow a carefully developed general outline. The first step in preparing such an outline is to select the information to be included in the report. This is ordinarily dictated by the purpose of the report, what information is available, or what can be uncovered. Next, the items of information should be classified under headings which normally are grouped as major and minor, or as many groups as judgment suggests.

There are a number of general outlines for reports; the following is preferred by many: (1) summary of findings, (2) methodology, (3) detailed results, and (4) appendix. Another outline which is effective and adaptable for many subjects, especially those of a technical nature, includes: (1) summary, (2) objective and scope, (3) equipment used, (4) methodology, (5) data obtained, (6) conclusions, and (7) recommendations. The following has also won favor: (1) introduction and definition of problem, (2) conclusions and recommendations, (3) discussion of procedure and results obtained, and (4) summary. Another is: (1) digest of findings and recommendations, (2) background of study, (3) savings and other benefits to be gained, (4) possible drawbacks, (5) alternatives and why choice of the one recommended, and (6) proposed implementation plan.

It should be observed that in each of these outlines, either the summary, conclusion, or recommendation is included near the beginning of the report. This may seem illogical; but actually it is not. The sequence of items need not be chronologic; however, there should be *some order* in presenting the material. The great majority of report readers want the gist of the findings or the conclusions right away, so it is effective to put this information at the beginning.

The so-called playscript procedure is an effective format for writing. It clearly spells out who does what in a sequential order. Its use is rapidly spreading with wide impact. Figure 3–5 shows this arrangement.

Charts, drawings, pictures, and maps help to convey the meaning to the reader, but they must be carefully selected and employed in "reasonable" amounts for maximum effectiveness. In many cases, the chart or drawing must be explained and significant relations pointed out to the reader, because the exact meaning may not be gained simply by looking at the

PROCEDURE NO. 2

Subject: Retrieving Records from the Center

| Performed By | Action |
|---|---|
| Department Records Clerk | 1. When information is needed from an inactive record, phones Records Center. |
| | 2. Refers to the returned copy of form PSC-418, TRANSMITTAL LIST - INACTIVE RECORDS. Gives the Records Center location carton number, folder, and document wanted. |
| Records Center Clerk | 3. Asks inquirer if this information can be given by telephone. |
| | 3a If phone answer is OK, goes to shelf location, retrieves record, and gives information wanted. |

VARIATIONS

4. If information cannot be given by telephone, and requester wants entire record, asks if a copy will do.

PROCEDURE NO. 3

Subject: Destroying Inactive Records

| Performed By | Action |
|---|---|
| Records Center Clerk | 1. Checks destruction tickler file each month. Pulls out cards indicating the records which are scheduled for destruction. |
| | 2. For each group (same form No. etc.) Fills out form PSC-435, DESTRUCTION NOTICE in 2 copies. |
| | 3. Sends one copy to the department records clerk of the department of "basic interest." |
| Department Manager | 3a. If, upon notice of scheduled destruction, d e c i d e s the group of records should be retained longer, fills out form PSC-445 RETENTION SCHEDULE REVISION. |
| Department Records Clerk | 3b. Sends or takes form PSC-445 to Records Center clerk. |
| Records Center Clerk | 3c. Retains records for an additional 30 to 90 days. |

*Courtesy: "Systemation Letter," Foundation for Administrative Research, Tulsa, Okla.*

**FIG. 3–5.** The effective "Playscript Procedure" is winning wide acceptance.

illustrative material. Pictures are especially helpful in dealing with technical subjects.

## GUIDES FOR EFFECTIVE BUSINESS WRITING

Writing presents a tremendous challenge. One of the most powerful factors in the world is the presentation of helpful ideas and facts in writing that can be clearly understood. Skill in effective writing can be developed. It is not an ability with which some are blessed and which others can never hope to achieve. Writing can be stimulating and it is a powerful tool. It can win men's hearts to a stated cause; it can distribute knowledge; it can implement effective action. A person you have never seen will change his course of action, send an inquiry, or start a new program—as a result of a report or a letter. This should inject a pride of accomplishment in writing really good letters and reports, and inspire one to be satisfied with only the best.

However, too often the challenge of writing is not even recognized, let alone mastered. Much business writing fails to follow Shakespeare's "Speak plain and to the purpose." Consider this exchange of letters between a state highway department and another office.

Will you please forward two more certified copies? We can't send copies to the auditor's office so we must have at least two carbon copies which are certified. We have one carbon now, so we still need two certified copies, one of which must be a carbon. Also, if you send a copy, please send a certified copy rather than a copy of a certified copy. Thank you.

The reply:

I cannot send you two certified copies since it seems the only carbon copy was sent to you previously. Unless I have a carbon copy, I can't obtain a certified carbon copy and without a certified carbon copy, I cannot obtain a copy of a certified carbon copy; therefore, I will have to send two certified copies of carbon copies or have your carbon copy certified and get a copy of your certified carbon copy certified. Please return carbon copy.

This may be an extreme example, but various studies show that much writing is not understood by the recipient. The ideas are jumbled, statements are ambiguous, the sentence structure is poor, and the intended meaning is camouflaged. What can be done to improve our business writing? Following pertinent guides will help considerably. Some rules to remember are:

1. *Make the writing serve a known and definite purpose.* In the case of letters, for example, know exactly what is to be accomplished by the letter. Settle on one main issue and concentrate on it. Letters pertaining to a single subject are easy to understand, and they expedite filing.

Reports are written to help the recipient and should be appropriate to the plan, decision, or directive about which he is concerned. It is essential that the aim of the letter or the report be known to the person preparing it because this knowledge guides the writer and helps him point the communication toward its intended uses.

2. *Keep the recipient in mind.* The aim of a letter or of a report stands a much better chance of accomplishment if its text is understood. To expedite this understanding, the needs, wants, and interests of the recipient should be given prime consideration. What a reader acquires from a written business communication is conditioned by the knowledge he brings to it. That is, a person who has broad training and an extensive background in a particular subject will acquire more from a report in that subject than the individual who does not possess such training and background. For this reason put the reader in the center of what is written. Look at the subject from his viewpoint; visualize the reader while writing, and tailor the material and expressions to him.

In letter writing, for example, the technique of the "you viewpoint" can be followed. To illustrate:

Write:

"You may have quick service if you'll just telephone ORchard 1–7777."

Do not write:

"We wish to call attention to the fact that we are in the dry-cleaning business and have a 15-year record of excellent service. Our telephone number is ORchard 1–7777."

3. *Be factual and unbiased.*   Accuracy is essential to good writing regardless of the scope, subject, medium, or level for which it is intended. The facts should be relevant to the subject; opinions should be identified as such. Irrelevant details should be excluded. What is basic to the stated purpose should be included. Information which is incomplete and not essential to the purpose should be avoided.

The motive and the ideas should be presented without bias. Stress the objective viewpoint. Fundamentally, the writing is being done to inform the reader of the situation or subject as it is. A letter or a report can be colorful, yet not filled with emotional statements. Remember that the content and the words should be tools of straight thinking, not stumbling blocks.

4. *Use short familiar words and simple sentences.*   Word choice is vital; simple words are bold and clear and usually convey the intended meaning. Some writers never use a short, familiar word if they know a big one of similar meaning, and such practice weakens a letter or a report. Employing words in common usage is a good rule to follow. This is well illustrated by a story about Benjamin Franklin. When still a lad, he told his mother: "I have imbibed an acephalous mollusk." His mother, believing young Franklin had swallowed something poisonous, forced him to take a large dosage of medicine to induce vomiting. When he got over the effects of the medicine, he explained to his mother: "I have eaten nothing but an oyster." Whereupon his mother thrashed him for deceiving her. Franklin later advised: "Never use big words when little words will do."

Clear sentences are one of the most helpful ingredients of clear reports. Although variety in sentence length is desirable, short sentences are normally preferred. Some say that no sentence should be longer than 25 words. However, it should be long enough to convey the thought. A practical suggestion is to fit the sentence to the reader's span of attention. Omit involved phrases, and weed out the extra words. Tabulate lists for greater clarity. Unity, coherence, and correct sentence structure are more readily achieved in short than in long, complex sentences. Correct punctuation also helps.

5. *Employ active verbs.*   Present-tense verbs create more interest and convey activity better than past-tense or subjunctive-tense verbs. "He understands" has more vigor than "It is understood by him" or "He should have understood." While some variation is desirable, try to use a good portion of active verbs in your writing.

6. *Use conversational style.*   Letters and reports are communicative devices and are more readily understood when written in a style to which we are accustomed. We are familiar with the conversational style and from it quickly grasp the meaning. Ordinarily we do not use exotic words and long sentences with qualifying phrases in our normal speech. Why insist on using these communication blocks in our written work?

7. *Establish an acceptable mood.* When writing use a tone that wins cooperation or puts the reader in a mood to read the communication and give thought to it. Positive expressions help to accomplish this goal. Greater acceptance and motivation are gained by writing in an optimistic tone. For example, in a letter, write: "We can send you tickets for the November 27 performance," instead of "We cannot send tickets for any performance prior to that of November 27."

Be friendly and let your writing reflect your own natural self. Letters and reports are written to human beings, not merely to names. Write naturally and humanly. Stilted, highly formalized statements are taboo. Avoid "whisker" expressions, examples of which, along with improvements, include

| *Do not use* | *Use* |
|---|---|
| I am not in a position | I cannot |
| My attention has been called | I notice |
| Enclosed please find | We enclose |
| Has come to hand | Referred to me |
| Acquaint me with the facts | Tell me |
| Under separate cover | Separately |
| Contents duly noted | I have read |
| At this time | At present |
| We have reviewed our records | We find |
| It is our opinion | I believe |
| At all times | Always |
| Take pleasure | Are pleased |
| We have yours of the 10th | Your letter of November 10 |
| Your esteemed favor of the 6th and its enclosures | The papers you sent |

8. *Make the writing clear.* This requires knowing what must be included and in what sequence it should be presented. The writer should express each thought so clearly that the reader is certain to understand it. Normally, the transcriber helps in acquiring clarity by straightening out improper sentence structure and switching words. It is well to have a competent person edit a report to insure that the meaning is clear.

Have your writing say exactly what you intend it to say, and mean what the writing says. These eight words form the basis of all great writing: "Write so that you cannot possibly be misunderstood."

9. *Interpret findings adequately.* Care must be exercised to avoid exaggeration or the inclusion of unqualified interpretations which cannot be reasonably derived from the available information. It is usually best to understate rather than to overstate conclusions. Also, recommendations must be practical and sound.

10. *Summarize briefly and make writing conclusive.* Normally, it is best to state the results in a summary statement. Convey the essentials to

the reader easily; under no circumstances should the receiver be required to dig through quantities of words and figures to find out what the writing discloses or is all about.

Be certain to include what action, if any, is desired of the reader, what the writer will do, or what the writer wants done. Be decisive; let the reader know exactly the recommended course or disposition. Avoid double meanings. Long, qualified explanations usually offer little help. Strive to set forth the recommendations so clearly and effectively that they will be followed.

## PROCEDURE FOR HANDLING WRITING WORK

A definite procedure is required to handle the work of writing letters and reports; this cannot be left to chance. Relying upon haphazard methods to accomplish the work promptly is wishful thinking. The following is suggested:

1. *In the case of correspondence, get letters to those who answer them.* Letters on ordinary and routine subjects can be quickly routed to the proper party for reply. In contrast, letters dealing with out-of-the-ordinary subjects frequently offer some difficulty. Frequently, these letters are addressed to the wrong person within the enterprise and must be rerouted. The task of getting letters to the proper persons for answering is usually the responsibility of the head of the mailing department or the office manager.

For reports, the subject area to be covered, time for completion of report, and designation of the writer are basic decisions to be made. In many cases, established policies regarding report writing guide the initial planning steps of report preparation.

2. *Get facts to the correspondent.* To write meaningfully, the writer must have all the facts. To write a sales letter, for example, one must have information on what the product will do, its good points, its price, and the like. Likewise, to compose a report requires access to pertinent information and some knowledge of the facts in the particular subject area.

When filed material is required in order to write a letter, it is obtained in one of several ways. The incoming letter may be (1) routed by the mail room to the filing department, which attaches the filed material to the letter and then forwards both to the writer; or (2) sent directly to the writer, who decides if he needs the file covering previous correspondence and, if so, requests it from the filing department. In some cases, both the writer and the file are located in the same area, so that the writer can himself secure any filed material he needs.

3. *Permit correspondent to analyze facts and to organize the writing.* To a considerable degree, every letter is an effort to have the recipient believe and act toward a subject as the writer does. Hence, the writer

should try to visualize the type of reader to whom he is writing and select an approach that will invoke the reader's response to action. Sometimes, this necessitates guessing or taking a chance. The opening statement, for example, should be designed to get the reader's attention. Following this, the reader's interest should be developed. Then, lead this interest into a desire and finally culminate the entire letter with action—to order the service, to accept the adjustment, to pay the bill, or whatever the case might be. For reports, a simple statement of what the report is about, what it shows, and how the information should be used are of major interest.

4. *Provide correspondent with a stenographer or a dictating machine when ready to dictate.* The assignment of stenographic help to a writer is done by the stenographic supervisor or by the office manager. For corresponding, the stenographer should report to the correspondent at stated times throughout the day; this permits better organization and execution of work on the part of both the stenographer and the correspondent. In actual practice, however, the task of regulating steno-graphic work is not so simple. Most offices have a certain amount of irregular correspondence which is best handled by adapting it to a schedule setting definite hours when emergency dictation can be handled. This helps accomplish all the work with a minimum of confusion. On the other hand, emergency work can be sandwiched in with the regular work. However, when this is done, allowance must be made in the regular schedules.

Many report writers prefer to write out the material in longhand before having it typed. Others put most of their material directly on the machine. The type of material, difficulty of composing, and the amount of statistical tables help determine which procedure to follow.

5. *Get material typed.* The final step is the actual physical work of typing the material, and this is by no means a small job. When completed, the material is sent to the correspondent, who reads, checks, and, in the case of correspondence, signs the letters. Subsequently, the material is prepared for mailing or distributing.

## TYPEWRITERS

Machine selection is a part of planning. In the work of correspondence and report writing, the typewriter is a basic office machine, is widely used, and speeds the handling of all written work. It should be noted, however, that in this day and age many reports are prepared by computers.

A convenient classification of office typewriters is (1) standard and (2) electric. The former is actuated by hand or human energy, i.e., by the depression of a key. While typing, the carriage is moved to the left by

*Courtesy: International Business Machine Corp., New York*

FIG. 3–6.   An IBM "Selectric" typewriter. This is an electric machine adaptable for various "balls of type" supplying various type styles in keeping with different writing demands. The ball of type or selectric element can be quickly interchanged with other elements. A wide variety of elements are offered.

action of a spring. In contrast, the electric typewriter is motivated mainly by electricity. Manual energy is still used to touch the keys, but the energy input is about one-fifth of that required for manual machines. Work done on an electric typewriter is of uniform type impression, and a greater number of copies can be obtained without any increase in manual energy. An electric machine costs more and has fewer moving parts than a standard machine.

Most typewriters on the market today are excellent machines and have many common features which are recognized as standard equipment. Most are equipped with the "set" and "clear" tabulators, either of a single- or decimal-key type. Tabulators are very helpful for the rapid movement and alignment of the carriage which is required in reports and other written work that have frequent indentations. Typewriter platens are available in different degrees of hardness. A soft platen should be used where the number of copies are few and quietness is desired. Conversely, a hard platen is recommended when a large number of copies is required. It causes more noise, however, than does the soft platen.

Figure 3–6 shows a "Selectric" typewriter which is electric and features the innovation of changing selective typing elements, thus making it possible to use the style of type best fitted for the particular writing application. Regular correspondence can be a distinctive type, invoicing of a type that is large, and personal notes of a script style. In general, most typewriters manufactured today are equipped with a standard keyboard. Special keyboards or parts of keyboards, such as engineering, mathematical, chemical, or foreign language signs and marks, are available at an additional cost.

## AUTOMATIC TYPING MACHINES

The automatic typing machine has won wide adoption for the typing of similar letters when they are in (1) large quantities and (2) similar format having slight changes only. It consists of a regular typewriter to which a special mechanism has been attached. The paper is inserted in the

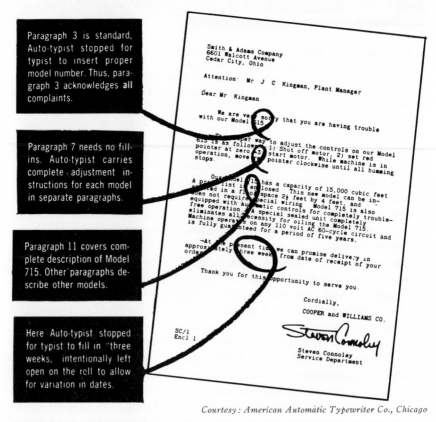

Courtesy: *American Automatic Typewriter Co., Chicago*

FIG. 3–7. A letter typed by an automatic typewriter. Paragraph selection and individual fill-in material are easily handled as described in the illustration.

machine in the same manner as in a regular typewriter; and the date, name, and address are typed in by hand. At the touch of a button, the machine takes over and automatically types the letter, stopping at the first place where a special fill-in is required. This is typed in by hand, and then, after another touch of the button, the machine continues typing the letter to the next stop. Figure 3–7 shows a letter typed in this manner. All paragraphing, spacing, and the like are handled by the machine. If possible, the location of each fill-in should be at the end of a line or paragraph, to provide the required elasticity in space. Words or numbers of varying lengths can be inserted without difficulty. The entire letter has been typed automatically by machine, with the exception of the individualized parts as noted on the illustration.

As many as 200 short letters a day can be typed with this machine. Multiple combinations of machines, requiring one operator, can produce approximately 500 short letters a day. Such a battery is a mass producer, flexible and efficient. For most applications, an operator can employ a battery of four automatic typing machines.

Form letters or paragraphs are originally cut on either (1) a record roll or (2) a tape. This perforating work is done in the individual office or at the local service office. The record roll, resembling that used on a player piano, is mounted in the machine and, when released, passes over a trucker bar in which a vacuum is maintained. Any opening in the roll causes a change in pressure, which actuates the type, thus causing the machine to write. The capacities and details of operation vary with the machine and the manufacturer. About 20 different letters or an equivalent of

*Courtesy: American Automatic Typewriter Co., Chicago*

FIG. 3–8.  An automatic typewriter featuring push-button controls.

form paragraphs can be placed on one record roll. The operator selects the material to be machine-typed by means of simple controls. In one method, a series of push buttons is used to make the operation entirely automatic. See Figure 3–8.

FIG. 3–9.   An automatic writing machine that is actuated by a punched tape.

When a perforated tape is used, the operation of the automatic typewriter is quite similar to that described above. Such a typewriter unit is illustrated in Figure 3–9. The holes in the tape cause the mechanism to operate specific typewriter keys which result in the desired letter. Perforated tape is being used more and more to operate office machines automatically. Its growth has been stimulated by the application of source data automation (SDA) which is described in Chapter 11.

## PRODUCING LETTERS BY DUPLICATION PROCESS

To produce a substantial quantity of written material exactly alike, any one of several duplicating means described in Chapter 5 is satisfactory. Duplicating is fast and economical. It is used for both letters and reports. When used for letters, the name and address are omitted, and simply "Dear Sir" is put on each letterhead, with the name and address on the envelope only. As an alternative, the name and address can be typed carefully on the letter, but it will not match precisely the duplicated part of the letter. However, with typing skill and experience, satisfactory results are possible.

Another possibility for volume mailings is to use a "window letter." A preaddressed card is attached to the back and top of the duplicated letter, so that the name and address appear at the normal location and can be read through a window opening in the letterhead. The card also serves as a business reply card with necessary postage and name and address of the sender on the reverse side. This arrangement is illustrated in Figure 3–10.

For correspondence, a machine is available that will write a complete letter from blank paper in one run—individual name and address, salutation, letterhead in color, date, text, and facsimile ink signature—all with one operator. Since the same basic process is used at the same time, the name and address are perfectly matched with the text of the letter. In addition, the machine will print and personally identify a reply card. Sheets of paper are fed automatically to the machine, which progressively

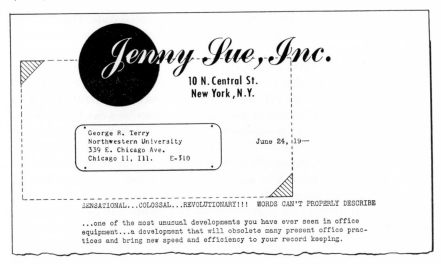

FIG. 3–10. A "window letter" which features the use of a preaddressed card to individualize a form letter. The card, also used as a business reply card, is held in place either by a pocket in the back or by slots into which opposite card corners are inserted (as illustrated). The name and address appear through a window opening in the letter. The mailing can also utilize window envelopes.

prints name, address, salutation, letterhead, date, body of letter, closing, and signature. The machine speed is 100 complete letters per minute.

## WHICH BASIS—PERSONAL OR MACHINE?

Either a personal or a machine basis can be followed in writing letters and reports. Under the personal basis, the dictator talks to a stenographer, who manually takes down the statements in shorthand. Later, these notes are transcribed. When the machine basis is used, the dictation is recorded on a machine and subsequently played back to the transcriber, who types the letter.

Advocates of the personal basis are quick to point out that a feeling of close cooperation, better understanding of the type of letter to be written, and consideration for the important human element are induced when letters are dictated to a stenographer. Second, the personal basis permits the transcriber to work from written notes, which are usually easier to comprehend than audible data. Third, with diligent and reasonable effort, shorthand can be mastered. Fourth, the cost of a machine is avoided, as well as the costs of operation, special supplies, and maintenance. Fifth, dictation is possible anywhere. A special machine need not be available. However, a machine for recording dictation can be used. The notes are printed in letters on a tape in accordance with a special code. The machine looks like a small typewriter and requires special training for proficient operation.

The important advantages of the dictating machine basis include the following: First, dictation is expedited—material can be dictated when it is on the dictator's mind. His thoughts can be recorded as they occur to him. Second, the distribution of work among transcribers can be balanced. Steady and even work throughout the day frequently minimizes the number of transcribers needed. Third, the transcriber's time is saved, since her presence is not required while the dictation is being recorded. Fourth, convenience is provided. The dictator can work independently; he can dictate at his convenience; he need not wait for his stenographer. Fifth, the dictator is alone; thus, concentration and clearer and better thinking are encouraged.

## DICTATING MACHINES

A dictating machine consists of a recorder unit used by the dictator, and a transcriber unit used by the typist to play back the recorded dictation; or a combination unit featuring both recording and transcribing. The latter is practical when the dictator and transcriber can plan their day for separate periods of dictation and transcription.

The recorder is equipped with either (1) hand microphone, recommended for ordinary dictating practices or when the surroundings are somewhat noisy; or (2) desk microphone, for recording over-the-desk conference discussions or important telephone conversations, assuming the consent of both parties has been obtained. Furthermore, when the recorder is equipped with a foot-control device, the desk microphone permits free use of both hands during correspondence dictation. It is possible to start and stop the recorder as desired and to listen to what has been dictated. A signaling device is also provided whereby the amount of dictation and places of correction can be indicated. There is usually a backspacer for repeating dictation and voice-control adjustments to regulate speed, volume, and tone.

Most dictating machines use a recording medium of either (1) plastic belt, (2) plastic disk, or (3) wax cylinder. One plastic belt medium is an endless belt of thin, tough plastic, 3½ inches wide and 12 inches in circumference. It withstands rough handling, accommodates about 15 minutes of dictation, and serves as a permanent, one-time recording medium. As many as five belts, nested one within the other, will fit into a small business envelope and can be mailed for a few cents. Figure 3–11 shows a dictating machine using a plastic belt.

The plastic disk is also a satisfactory medium. The disk can be used once, then thrown away or filed for future reference. One hundred disks are approximately 1 inch in thickness; and three sizes are available—3, 5, and 7 inches in diameter, respectively—for 4, 15, and 30 minutes of recording. The disks are light, tough, and unbreakable, which makes it possible to send them conveniently through the mail. Wax cylinders are also in use, but they are used with older equipment. Cylinders are shaved after usage to remove the engraved surface so that the cylinder can be used again for dictation. A wax cylinder will record about eight one-page letters and can be shaved about 65 times.

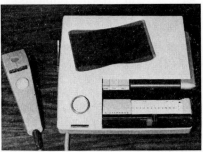

*Courtesy: Dictaphone Corp., New York*

FIG. 3–11.   Taking up less space than a letter and weighing about eight pounds, this fully automatic dictating machine is a recorder-transcriber unit and employs a plastic belt as the medium.

## CONTROLLING LETTER AND REPORT WRITING

Unnecessary letters and reports are a tremendous waste of time, money, and energy. The office manager should see to it that only necessary materials are prepared and that they fulfill a vital need.

In the typical enterprise too many letters are written. A number serve no genuine purpose and others are replies to communications which do not require an answer. The habit of writing reports tends to remain long after the original need for the report has ceased. Periodic revaluation of the necessity for all reports should be followed. In the case of operative reports, all that is needed is the statement that activities are proceeding according to plans or that they are within acceptable limits. This latter can be called a "tolerance report." If plans are not being fulfilled, the recipient wants to know what is out of line and how best to correct it. Such a report can be termed an "exception report." In neither case is it necessary to write a complete report describing in minute detail all the activities in order to determine whether things are all right or to identify the exceptions requiring managerial attention.

To gain some idea of the extensiveness of writing work, the following simple investigation can be made. Determine the payroll for one month for employees engaged in letter and report writing. Add to this the monthly investment in machines, space, and supplies. View this total in relation to the number of letters and reports written. Compare it also to total office expense. In most cases it represents a sizable percentage.

Answers to these questions aid in attaining better controlling:

1. Is this written material really necessary?
2. Does this written material satisfy the purpose for which it is intended?
3. To whom are copies sent? Should they be sent?
4. Can one copy serve several present recipients?
5. Can the readability be improved by illustrations, better English and grammar?
6. Is the best means being used to produce the written material?
7. Is it worth the cost?
8. Should it be automated?

When given sufficient thought and properly applied, the answers to these questions will assist in writing better—not bigger—letters and reports. And office managers will have achieved a noteworthy accomplishment.

Some believe that using the "reply at bottom" type of letter lessens correspondence work and makes controlling efforts easier. In this type of letter, the answer or comment is written in the margin or at the bottom of an incoming letter. A copy is then made and sent to the interested party, the original being retained for the files. This practice may not be suited for all correspondence, but when satisfactory it does save considerable typing and filing space.

The distribution of reports merits special attention. Too often distribution is made to a long list which includes names of persons who neither need nor read the report. Many practices reputed to be truthful are cited in office management circles regarding efforts to screen the distribution of reports. One such practice is to review the distribution list and remove the names of certain individuals believed nonessential as report receivers. No notice is given those whose names are removed. Subsequently, in most instances, the absence of the report is not noticed by the new nonreceiver; seldom is a complaint or an inquiry made about the report.

It may be argued that the additional cost of running off extra copies of a report is relatively small; that is, to make 24 copies costs little more than to make 14 copies. But while the cost of labor, paper, and machine time for the differential 10 copies may be relatively small, the fact still remains that 10 more people receive the report. They take time to look it over, become interested in functions or problems which may not be their concern, waste some of their time on these "foreign" activities, and require additional filing space and help to retain the reports for some doubtful future reference.

Additional specific suggestions include the adoption of better correspondence and report writing standards designed to attain improved quality and quicker service. Also, some measurement of quality and of output should be determined, for only by such means will a manager be able to determine the success of efforts toward improving the work of writing. Consideration for accuracy, clearness, conciseness, completeness, and naturalness can be used to rate the quality of the work. Output might best be determined by sorting letters according to type and counting the number of each type written during the period of a week or two weeks. For reports, number of pages, by type, usually gives satisfactory results.

An accounting of such things as the machine assigned to each correspondent, the amount of work turned out by each machine, the extent of machine idleness, and the amount and frequency of repairs can also be employed. These data, plus proper follow-up, will help to improve the work output. Desirable in certain instances is the drawing of a daily record or chart for each stenographer or typist, showing the amount of work completed, the amount currently being handled, and the amount scheduled to be done. This information can be used to distribute the work evenly among all employees and to check accomplishment with task.

The use of an office manual is another effective means of controlling. Manuals provide the employee with standard practices and instructions in a form that is convenient and easy to use. They help the employee to help himself and assist in eliminating many needless errors.[1]

## COST OF LETTERS AND REPORTS

Cost is among the best approaches for controlling the writing of letters and reports. Few realize what it costs to write a letter or a report. Figure 3–12 shows an estimate of time and cost factors in writing a typical one-page letter. Observe that for the personal basis the cost per letter is $2. Even a form letter costs 28 cents. The cost varies, of course, depending on

| | Personal Basis | Machine Basis | Form Letter |
|---|---|---|---|
| Planning the letter | 13 min. | 13 min. | 0 min. |
| Dictating the letter | 13 " | 8 " | 0 " |
| Transcribing and typing | 7 " | 9 " | 3 " |
| Checking and signing | 3 " | 3 " | 2 " |
| Total Time | 36 min. | 33 min. | 5 min. |
| Labor cost @ $2.50/hr | $1.50 | $1.38 | $0.21 |
| Supplies and office overhead | 0.50 | 0.50 | 0.07 |
| Total Cost | $2.00 | $1.88 | $0.28 |

FIG. 3–12. Estimate of time and cost to write a one-page letter (original and three carbon copies).

[1] See Chapter 25 for discussion of office manuals.

the length, difficulty of material, method of transcription, and nonproductive time.

The cost for large quantities of almost identical letters can be reduced considerably by using the automatic typewriter. One operator with four machines will produce approximately 500 one-page letters a day. For this volume and using a five-year depreciation basis for a battery of four machines, direct labor cost of $20 a day, the cost figures about 6 cents a letter.

Likewise, the cost for identical letters produced by a duplicating process is less than for those individually typed, the exact figure depending mainly upon the process used and the quantity involved. Of course, costs for a letter individually typed and those for a duplicated letter are not strictly comparable, since it is unlikely that quantities of identical letters would be individually typed.

The cost of a report depends upon many factors. Expense of gathering data and the time of the writer are key costs. Studies show that what appears to be a simple 20-page report may cost upward of $1,500 to prepare. Most executives underestimate what a report costs. Computer-prepared reports also usually mean a considerable expenditure.

Some office managers have informed the recipient of a report what it costs to prepare it and have indicated that in the future his unit or department will be charged for this work. If the costs do not justify the use made of the reports, the recipient will request his name to be withdrawn from the distribution list. Discretion and judgment must be exercised in this approach, but it is effective.

## BUSINESS WRITING AND MANAGEMENT ORGANIZING

In the office letter writing is done by different employees located in many different departments. Many top executives prefer to handle their correspondence work in their own unit, i.e., by their secretaries and themselves. However, the bulk of correspondence work is usually performed by correspondents who either have transcribers permanently located in the various departments performing letter writing or have transcribers in a centralized transcribing department or "pool."

Whatever the organizational arrangement, the producing of letters requires coordination among various personnel. For example, the dictator must correct or redictate if the transcriber's work is in error, the dictator cannot be effective if the file clerk supplies the wrong materials, and the transcriber cannot be efficient if the dictator does his work poorly. The organizational relationship should foster the needed cooperation and coordination among those engaged in letter-writing work.

Likewise, many employees have the task of report writing. In some cases, the total job content is report writing; in others, a report is required but once a week or month. Report writing can be found in almost any organizational unit—it is not confined to "the office." For example, the assistant sales manager may have the responsibility of writing the monthly sales report; the technician, a research report; and the personnel manager, a report on the company's industrial relations.

## ACTUATING—CORRESPONDENCE AND REPORTS

A program which acquaints all correspondence personnel with effective letter-writing fundamentals, enumerates specific practices preferred by the enterprise, and supplies the best writing tools will help tremendously in attaining effective letter writing. Many actions can be taken. For example, Mutual of New York undertook a comprehensive correspondence simplification program and, among other things, drafted a series of "guide letters" for its correspondents. Figure 3–13 shows an example. These letters were meticulously prepared to give customers the answers they wanted in understandable terms and in a friendly, helpful manner.

It frequently is helpful to appoint a correspondence counselor. He or she may be selected from among present employees, or the services of a consultant may be used. The duties of the counselor include those of an adviser, a teacher, and a salesman for effective writing within the enterprise. He is the nominal head of the program for correspondence improvement.

Regular meetings at which correspondents will discuss the principles of good letter writing should be established. The counselor acts as the group leader, and letters written by the employees can be criticized. It is also possible to hold conferences with individual employees. Frequently, this method is more effective than the group meetings, for samples of the employee's work can be inspected and personalized help can be given. The belief is widespread that typically a writer has only two or three writing weaknesses, not all of them. Intensive corrective work to remedy these few faults, not discussing over and over again all the defects of writing with him, is the real road to improvement.

Each correspondence employee should be kept busy at the level of skill for which he or she is hired. Stenographers should not be tied down to typists' jobs. Correspondents should not spend a great deal of their time filing. High-salaried executives should not dictate letters in those cases where a correspondent will do an equally effective job. Full utilization of all correspondence facilities is the goal. In addition, the machines must be kept in good repair to insure high volume and quality of work.

The same motivating techniques can be used for writers of reports. But in this area, it is extremely helpful to establish the importance of report writing. This will add prestige to the writer as a doer of work that is needed and is beneficial to all members of the enterprise. More spe-

<u>Example of The "Long" and "Short" of It</u>

<u>DEATH CLAIM - EXPLAINING AGE ADJUSTMENT</u>

<u>Original</u>

We are enclosing a letter addressed to the payee under
the above numbered policy, explaining the adjustment
which we made because of a difference in the Insured's
age.

Will you see that we are furnished with the best
evidence available as to the correct date of birth?  A
copy made by a notary of a family or public record,
made at or near the time of birth, of the date of birth
together with a statement by the notary as to the date
of publication of the book from which the record is
obtained, and by whom the record was made and when, is
the most satisfactory evidence.  Form 3593 covers such
information.  If no such record is obtainable, an
affidavit to that effect should be furnished together
with the best information available with a full
statement as to its source and why it is believed to
be correct.

Please forward the above information to us at your
earliest convenience.

Yours very truly,

<u>Revised</u>
<u>To Manager</u>

DCA-14    We will gladly make adjustments on this claim, if
necessary, when correct birthdate is established.  If
(name) is unable to complete Form 3593, please get an
affidavit stating why the date is believed correct and
return with the best evidence available.

Also, kindly give the enclosed  letter* of explanation.

Thank you.

*  Key No. DCA-15

<u>Original</u> <u>160</u> <u>Words</u>:  <u>Revised</u> <u>53</u> <u>Words</u>:  <u>Saving</u> <u>67</u> <u>Per</u> <u>cent</u>

Note:  The Original is a splendid example of a letter
that goes to great unnecessary length in stating
the obvious.  Notice that the Revised states all
that a manager need be told to know how to proceed.

*Courtesy: Mutual of New York*

FIG. 3–13.   A guide letter furnished company correspondents to assist them in writing more effectively.

cifically, it should be pointed out to the writer how report writing will help him, that reports can be a means to desirable ends—to get certain actions started and others curtailed. The reading of good reports is also helpful. A study of expressions, choice of words, and organization of material can be especially beneficial. Regular meetings to encourage the exchange of ideas helpful to writers are another effective medium. Also, writers should be told to draft their material currently—while it is on their minds. Make a brief written note when you think of an idea which you can use in your writing. Ideas come when least expected and are easily forgotten unless noted.

## BETTER DICTATING AND TYPING PRACTICES

The dictator should follow these simple suggestions: (1) have complete information at hand and organize his thoughts before dictating, (2) refrain from unnecessary interruptions, (3) speak clearly, pronounce each word correctly, and avoid the "ah" and "oh" when thinking about the next sentence, (4) be concise—avoid unnecessary details and repetition, and (5) relate complete working instructions—number of copies, general makeup of material, and whether rough draft or final copy is desired.

Proper instructions, adequate supervision, and regular practice are essential for attaining typing proficiency. The office manager should do everything possible to promote these essentials. In addition, he should provide a good working area, including adequate space, good lighting, a posture chair, a desk or stand which insures a comfortable work arrangement, and supplies within easy reach.

## QUESTIONS

1. Of the several guides offered to improve business writing, select and discuss the three you believe are probably most important.
2. What is an automatic typing machine, and when and how should it be used from the viewpoint of effective office management?
3. Fully justify the belief that letters and reports are important in modern business.
4. In your opinion, what is the best way to get report writers to want to improve their writing?
5. Discuss the cost of letters.
6. Identify clearly each of the following:
    a) "Speed letter."
    b) "Guide letters" for correspondents.
    c) "Whisker" expressions.
    d) A written report.
7. Discuss the form or arrangement of material of a business letter. Of a report.
8. Do you favor the use of the "reply at bottom" type of letter? Why?
9. Under what specific conditions would you recommend the use of the personal basis—stenographer and shorthand—to accomplish correspondence work? Of the machine basis—a recording and transcribing machine?
10. Discuss several effective techniques for controlling business-writing activity in an office.

11. Secure a report written for an executive. Study its contents, and determine the main purpose it is intended to serve. Assuming that the purpose is a valid one, explain in what specific ways you feel this report can be improved.

Sources for reports are friends in business, government reports, and various articles in newspapers and magazines available in the library.

12. Do you agree with the following: "Admittedly, some reports cost a lot of money to prepare, but the cost is usually minor when the report is viewed in the light of its importance. Reducing the funds allocated for report writing is foolish economy. Greater and more tangible savings can usually be acquired elsewhere in an enterprise." Elaborate on your answer.

## CASE PROBLEMS

### Case 3–1.  Haskins-Beckett, Inc.

You have been asked to assist Haskins-Beckett, Inc. in improving the corresponding work of its office. The office manager believes that group instruction in the general practices of good letter writing will aid in overcoming various individual defects of the correspondents, but wishes to supplement these efforts with an analysis of each correspondent's work. These personal analyses will reveal specific faults. Furthermore, suggestions for improvement will be indicated on a Letter Analysis Card given each correspondent.

The office manager hands you a copy of a letter written by employee R. L. Brunn. It reads as follows:

May 16, 196–

Mr. Sidney M. Wyatt
President
Kells Manufacturing Company
13672 N. Oakton Street
Kansas City, Missouri

Dear Mr. Wyatt:

This letter will acknowledge your letter of May 7th in which you requested a copy of our booklet, "Cutting Filing Costs" and also our booklet, "Designs for Destiny," describing our products and services.

It is a distinct pleasure to learn that you are endeavoring to resolve your present difficulties of filing and that we can anticipate hearing from you. We are of the opinion that our extensive experience can be of unusual assistance to you.

A copy of each of the requested booklets is enclosed herewith.

Kindly advise us if we can be of further aid.

Very truly yours,

*R. L. Brunn*

B:s                                    Advertising and Sales Promotion

## Problems:

1. What are your suggestions to the office manager for improving corresponding work in his office?

2. Enumerate the main faults of the letter to Mr. Wyatt.

3. Indicate a format for the Letter Analysis Card and show what might be typical entries for the above letter.

### Case 3–2.   Whitehurst Vending, Inc.

Arnold Pierson, president of this corporation, has jotted down the following notes covering items to be included in his report to shareholders for the year just ended.

1. Sales are down—$40,272,396 this year compared to $49,335,840 last year. But sales of the general products line are up 20 percent. The general products line is the growth area of our business. Included in the general products line are vendors for milk, coffee, candy, cigarettes, and hot and cold foods.

2. Earnings this year—61 cents per share; last year—$1.07 per share.

3. Paid four quarterly dividends of 12½ cents a share; total for year, 50 cents.

4. Federal income tax $1,825,000 this year.

5. Believe new dollar-bill and coin change units will result in substantial sales by the company.

6. Anticipate very minor adjustment problems from new coins of different composition and weight.

7. Inventory may be high, but we are in a position to capitalize on rapidly expanding automatic retailing sales on cards, and toiletries look good. Especially suited semiattended locations are motel lobbies, service stations, and drugstores. Refreshments (carbonated drinks) continue to be our big market.

8. Experimenting with all-automatic grocery. Running tests here. Will permit grocers to expand with displays in places such as apartment houses, parking lots, and service stations. Market is tremendous here.

9. A new hospitalization and group insurance program was started. Higher benefits to employees are provided by the modified plan.

10. Company outlook is favorable. With business adjustments back of us, we can reasonably look forward to a greatly improved sales and profit picture this forthcoming year.

## Problems:

1. Prepare the report to shareholders that you feel appropriate for Mr. Pierson to have distributed.

2. What are the major features of your report? Elaborate.

CHAPTER **4**

# MAIL AND OFFICE

# COMMUNICATING SERVICES

The easiest thing of all is to deceive
one's self; for what a man wishes he
generally believes to be true.
—*Demosthenes*

SUCCESS of any enterprise depends in great measure upon the ability to communicate effectively and this, in turn, is conditioned by proper use of communicative devices. The various communicative services in an enterprise, such as the mail handling, telephone, and messenger services, must be operated in an efficient manner for sustained high office productivity to exist. There are no substitutes for these office services. They must be provided if the office work is to be accomplished effectively.

## SELECTING THE COMMUNICATIVE MEANS

Typically, a business enterprise has a variety of communicative means available to it. These include such means as mail, telephone, teletypewriter, intercommunication systems, messenger service (either personal or mechanical), television, and a host of others which will be discussed in this chapter. Before the proper means can be selected, however, it is necessary to know what the real communicative needs of the company are. Various considerations enter into the picture. Without this knowledge, a hodgepodge, overlapping, and noncoordinated communicative system that is not tailored to serve best the requirements of the company is likely to develop. Among the major considerations are:

1. *The quantity and type of communications that should be provided.* This information, segregated for supervisors, salesmen, customers, vendors, and the general public, will provide helpful, factual, and basic data.

72

2. *The cost of the communication.* An approximate cost range from the minimum to the maximum, and related to the service provided, is helpful.

3. *The importance of speed.* Certain devices transmit messages in a matter of seconds, others require several days. Adequate planning reduces much of the need for speed in communicative devices.

4. *Are written or oral communications needed?* The former tend to be more specific, provide evidence, and help to lessen misunderstandings. In contrast, oral communications are quicker, cost less, and are superior when an exchange of ideas to reach a mutual agreement is desired.

5. *The length of the communication.* Certain devices are ideal for lengthy communications, while others are designed for short, terse messages.

6. *The effect of peak load periods.* Volumes vary and the capacity of the selected communicative means must satisfy the peak load.

To gain a quick comparison of various communicative means, Figure 4–1 has been included. This indicates differences for basic considerations among the several means. Discussion of these characteristics is contained on the following pages.

| | | | | COMMUNICATION MEANS | | | | |
|---|---|---|---|---|---|---|---|---|
| *Is Communication* | *Mail* | *Tele-phone* | *Tele-type-writer* | *Tele-graph* | *Tel-auto-graph* | *TV* | *Inter-com* | *Per-sonal Mes-senger* |
| An oral message? | No | Yes | No | No | No | No | Yes | Yes |
| A written message? | Yes | No | Yes | Yes | Yes | No | No | Yes |
| Operative when nonattended? | Yes | No | No | Yes | No | No | No | Yes |
| Suitable for handling illustrations and drawings? | Yes | No | No | Yes (Wire-fax) | Yes | Yes | No | Yes |

FIG. 4–1. Comparison of common communicative means on basic service factors.

## THE COMMUNICATION OF MAIL

It is doubtful that a modern enterprise could exist without mail; it is imperative that some written means of offering the services of the enterprise and of issuing answers to inquiries, statements, and invoices be available. Promptness and accuracy are the major requisites of satisfactory mail service. From the managerial viewpoint of the individual enterprise, there are five keys to follow faithfully: (1) keep mail routes up to date, (2) use efficient means for sorting, delivering, and picking up mail, (3) minimize the address reading for mail handling, (4) mechanize wherever volume is sufficient, and (5) know and apply proper postage rates.

One of the greatest steps forward in mail addressing is the Zip Code. This is a five-digit code designed to expedite and economize mail handling, by quickly identifying destination area, and to facilitate optical reading equipment to be used by many large U.S. post offices. The first digit designates one of ten national service areas. The second digit identifies the service subdivision, the third digit the post office in that subdivision, the last two digits the post office station from which the mail to that addressee is delivered. Figure 4–2 shows the Zip Code National Areas along with

## ZIP CODE NATIONAL AREAS

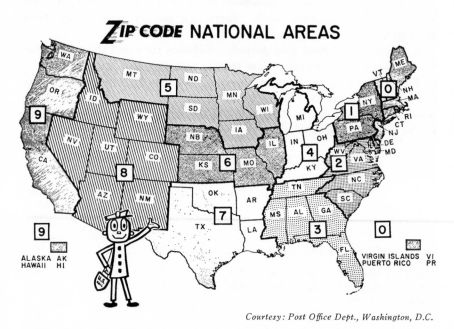

Courtesy: Post Office Dept., Washington, D.C.

FIG. 4–2.   The Zip Code national areas and authorized two-letter abbreviations for the various states.

authorized two-letter state abbreviations. Using these abbreviations will enable city, state, and Zip Code to be written on one line by most addressing machines. Note that Colorado is CO, Connecticut is CT, Illinois is IL, and Texas is TX. National Code Area No. 6 includes Illinois, Missouri, Kansas, and Nebraska. Figure 4–3 shows the Zip Code for Illinois. Chicago, for example, is 606; the second digit—zero—identifies the northeast part of Illinois, the third digit—6—identifies the Chicago Post Office. To these three digits is added the local zone number in Chicago. Hence, a Zip Code for an address in Chicago, Illinois, is 60611.

There are nearly 600 major post offices and sectional centers and about

42,000 different Zip Codes. The program starts with mass users of second- and third-class mail. They are required to update their mailing lists to include the full Zip Codes. Beginning January, 1967, all such mailers must presort their mail to the full five-digit Zip Code before mailing. Eventually all business mailers will be included in the complete Zip Code usage.

*Courtesy: Post Office Dept., Washington, D.C.*

FIG. 4–3.   Zip Code for subdivisions in state of Illinois.

## MANAGEMENT OF MAIL ROOM

The work of the mail room is greatly simplified and performed more quickly by using the proper number of units correctly arranged. Mail handling is an important activity and warrants adequate space and competent personnel. The work of handling *incoming mail* consists of fairly well-defined and uniform steps including:

1. *Receiving and opening the mail.* Mail is delivered to the office either by the postman or a company representative who calls for it at the post office. The latter is preferred by many large enterprises, especially in the case of the first morning mail, because when called for at an early hour, it can be distributed by the time the office formally opens. In this event, employees handling incoming mail should report for work about one-half hour before the regular opening office hour.

Mail is opened either by hand or by machine, depending upon the volume of mail. For manual means a good standard is 15 pieces per minute. Machines will open as many as 500 letters per minute. Mail marked "Personal" or addressed to specific individuals is not company mail and may or may not be opened, whichever is the policy of the company. The common practice is not to open it. In some instances, mail so addressed is forwarded immediately to the employee's home address.

2. *Sorting and time stamping.* The next step is to remove the contents of the envelopes and, at the same time, sort the mail according to who handles the particular type under question; this might be a department, a

*Courtesy: First National Bank in Dallas*

FIG. 4–4.   Handling the incoming mail in a large bank.

division, or an individual. Usually, the name of the person or of the department to whom the letter is addressed determines where it is to be delivered. When this is not given, a quick scanning of the paper is necessary to determine its proper destination. In exceptional cases, the entire contents must be read.

Figure 4–4 shows a portion of a large mail room. The man in the foreground is opening letters by means of a machine. The man in the background is sorting to the proper compartments in the sorting racks. The general pattern of the various compartments in the rack is similar to that of the mail stations in the office, for in this way the sorted mail can be kept in a logical order for ultimate distribution.

In the case of mail containing money or checks, a listing showing the senders' name and address and the amount enclosed is made out by the mailing department. The cash and checks, along with the listing, are later sent to the cashier department. In other instances, the check is attached to the letter; or in the case of cash, the money is placed in a small envelope and attached to the letter, with appropriate notation. The checks and cash are then delivered to the cashier department.

A letter referring to previous correspondence can either be delivered to the department concerned, which, if necessary, requests the file from the filing department; or it can be sent to the filing department, where the needed file is attached and forwarded to the proper correspondent. The method used depends chiefly upon the number of such letters received and the system of filing used.

At the time the mail is read and sorted, it is customary to stamp the hour and date received on each piece of correspondence. This provides a timed receipt that can be used as evidence in controversial matters regarding the correspondence. It can also be used for checking the efficiency of mail distribution in the office. Either a hand stamp or a machine can be used for the stamping.

3. *Distributing the mail.* This is the final step in the handling of incoming mail and is usually done by messengers, although other means, such as conveyor belts and pneumatic tubes, may be utilized.

For *outgoing* mail, the major areas of mail handling are as follows. Normally, the same employees handle both incoming and outgoing mail.

1. *Collecting and grouping by destinations.* To help in collecting, outgoing mail is usually placed in special desk trays specified as mail stations. Upon receipt at the mail room, the mail is first grouped according to geographical area, then by city, and then by name of addressee. Sorting racks are commonly used for this purpose. All mail of a similar class, and addressed to the same wholesaler, branch, or company, is put together so that it can be mailed as a single piece. Frequently, large Manila envelopes with the address printed or stenciled thereon are used for these large firm mailings. In some instances, each of the outgoing sorting racks contains an addressed envelope which is handy for instant use. Replenishments are made either the first thing in the morning or at regular intervals throughout the day.

2. *Inserting, sealing, and stamping.* If necessary, the material is folded and inserted by the mail department. When ordinary envelopes are used, the name and address on the material must be checked with that on the envelope. Sealing and stamping can be done either by hand or by machine; the volume of mail should determine the method used. It is possible to seal and stamp around 350 letters an hour by hand. It is advisable to appoint one mail-room employee as sole custodian of the stamps. He should control their use either by affixing the postage to the

letters or packages personally or by seeing the letters or packages it is going on before issuing postage to someone else.

When manual operations are used, the stamps are usually kept in an "out in the open" manner, and this may result in stamp losses owing to carelessness in handling and borrowing. To minimize these losses, an accounting should be maintained to show the number of letters mailed in comparison with the amount of stamps purchased. Special care must be exercised in the case of packages.

Many companies now use a meter-mail machine that imprints the postage seal either directly on a letter or, in the case of a package, on an adhesive paper tape which is affixed to the package. At the same time the postage seal is imprinted, a "meter ad," postmark, and date are also imprinted. This is illustrated by Figure 4–5. The machines are offered in an array of capacities and designs; many seal as well as stamp the envelope.

*Courtesy: Pitney-Bowes, Inc., Stamford, Conn.*

FIG. 4–5.    Illustrative of metered-mail imprints, showing "meter ad," postmark, date, and amount of postage.

An important part of this machine is the meter, which is a detachable, portable unit containing the printing die for the postage and a recording mechanism. In buying postage, the meter is taken to the post office and set for a lump sum which is paid in advance. The set meter is then returned to the place of business and inserted into the machine, from which metered stamps can be printed as and when needed. In essence, *a postage-meter machine is a government-licensed device for affixing postage.* Figure 4–6 illustrates a postage-meter machine. Meter mail has many advantages, including the following: (1) Time and effort are saved; (2) stamp losses are stopped; (3) accurate accounting of postal expenditures is provided; (4) date of mailing is shown; (5) quicker handling is provided by the originating post office, since no canceling is required; (6) the prestige of the user is increased; and (7) postmark, slogan, and advertising are added.

3. *Mailing the material.*    It is advisable to post mail at regular intervals throughout the day. This practice smooths out the work load,

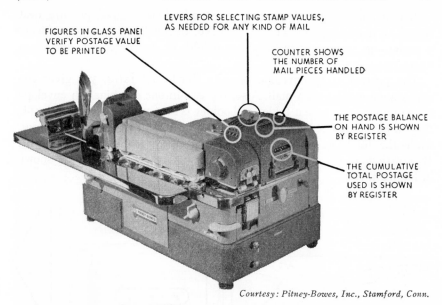

LEVERS FOR SELECTING STAMP VALUES, AS NEEDED FOR ANY KIND OF MAIL

FIGURES IN GLASS PANEl VERIFY POSTAGE VALUE TO BE PRINTED

COUNTER SHOWS THE NUMBER OF MAIL PIECES HANDLED

THE POSTAGE BALANCE ON HAND IS SHOWN BY REGISTER

THE CUMULATIVE TOTAL POSTAGE USED IS SHOWN BY REGISTER

*Courtesy: Pitney-Bowes, Inc., Stamford, Conn.*

FIG. 4–6.  A postage-meter machine, with the important operations of the meter illustrated.

minimizes the usual late afternoon peak, and helps the post office to deliver mail promptly. On distant mail, this practice might save a day. Also, knowledge of train and plane schedules is helpful in expediting mail. It is necessary to deliver certain classes of mail to the post office.

## CONTROLLING MAIL-ROOM OPERATIONS

Most control efforts affecting mail-room operations deal with either cost or conformity with postal standards and requirements. Key mail personnel must know the postal costs and requirements, so that the proper amounts of postage—no more and no less—are affixed. Knowledge of the various classes of mail is basic. In general, first-class mail includes correspondence, securities, and documents; second-class mail, newspapers, magazines, and other periodicals; third-class mail, unsealed printed matter and form letters; fourth-class mail, packages and parcels. Special services, such as registered mail, certified mail, special delivery, and special handling, are available but should be used only under the right circumstances.

The following suggestions should be adopted:

1. *Include Zip Code in the address.* This speeds delivery. The post office offers assistance in providing Zip Codes. Consultation with authorities of the local post office is recommended.

2. *Use standard-sized envelopes.*  Standard-sized envelopes are best suited for most purposes. The No. 9 or No. 10 envelope for correspondence is preferable, since only two horizontal folds in the enclosed material are necessary.

The postage-saver envelope permits third-class rates, yet gives the appearance of first-class mail. Also, the two-in-one combination envelope is recommended where a folder or booklet is sent with a letter. With this type of envelope, the letter or other first-class mail is in one compartment, while the folder or other third-class mail is in another compartment. Illustrations of the postage-saver and the two-in-one envelope are shown in Figure 4–7.

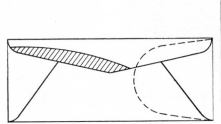 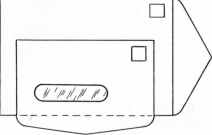

A postage-saver envelope requiring only third-class rate can be top-sealed like a first-class envelope. One end of flap remains unsealed to permit postal inspection.

With the two-in-one combination envelope, first-class mail in one compartment and third-class or fourth-class mail in the other can be mailed as a unit.

FIG. 4–7.   A postage-saver envelope and a two-in-one combination envelope.

3. *Use window envelopes when feasible to do so.*  The risk of getting a letter in the wrong envelope and the necessity of sending individually addressed envelopes to the mail room are eliminated by the use of window envelopes. There is also a saving in cost. With regular envelopes, the labor costs for addressing are about $10 per thousand (assuming a rate of three a minute and wages at $1.80 per hour). Window envelopes cost about $2.50 per thousand more than regular envelopes, so the net saving realized by using window envelopes is $7.50 ($10 less $2.50) per thousand, or 75 percent.

However, some people believe that window envelopes are less attractive and dignified than regular envelopes. Certain types of correspondence are probably best handled by regular envelopes. The final decision in this matter rests with the manager.

4. *Employ enclosed business reply envelopes to increase returns and lower costs.*  A permit, for which no fee is paid, must be obtained to use these envelopes. The postage for such envelopes is of a collect-on-delivery type for which the initial sender pays 7 cents for each reply, based on a 5-

cent regular charge plus 2 cents for the return privilege. If the return is less than 72 percent of the original mailing, the use of business reply envelopes results in savings. When regular stamped envelopes are enclosed, the postage for 100 replies is $5; postage on 72 business reply envelopes is $5.04.

5. *Have posters, books, and guides available to mail personnel so that they can find out and apply the proper mail procedures.* The *United States Postal Guide* (which can be obtained from the Superintendent of Documents, Washington 20402, D.C.) is especially recommended. The office manager should cultivate close cooperation with officials and employees of his local post office. They are always very helpful and can greatly assist in solving mailing problems.

## ACTUATING MAIL-ROOM PERSONNEL

Competent help must be employed if the activities of the mail room are to be performed satisfactorily. Manual dexterity, dependability, and an ability to read rapidly are among the important attributes desirable in mail-room employees. Training designed to inform about postal regulations, company policies affecting mail handling, and the company's organizational units and the specific types of work done by each is strongly suggested and will usually pay big dividends. Some managers hold periodic meetings with the mail-room personnel, briefing them on regulations, postal data, and the importance of accuracy, neatness, and care in handling all mail. After investigating and establishing effective mail-room practices and procedures, the work of handling the mail will normally undergo relatively few changes. They will be more of degree than of kind. Hence, a manual carefully outlining the directions and instructions to be followed will prove highly beneficial.

## TELEPHONE

Good telephone practices aid in building the good will of any enterprise, save time and energy, and help get work accomplished. The telephone has come into wide usage because it provides an inexpensive, convenient, and rapid means of communication. Referring again to Figure 4–1, telephone communication is verbal and is not well suited to convey information concerning drawings, sketches, or dimensions of parts. Conversing over the telephone places the participants in a peculiar relationship. The persons talking can hear but cannot see each other. The impression must rely entirely on the voice—its tone, clearness, and pleasantness; the selection of words; and the manner of speaking. All of these factors, properly blended, constitute the art of telephoning, which can be acquired.

Telephone systems can be classified into three types: (1) the outside

*Courtesy: Illinois Bell Telephone Co., Chicago*

FIG. 4–8. The new Dial PBX provides an easy, part-time job for the attendant.

telephone with extensions handled through a company switchboard (PBX), (2) the private internal telephone (PAX), and (3) Centrex telephone service. The first provides service for external calls coming into or going out of the office and for internal calls between telephones within the office. However, by using the Dial PBX, outbound calls are dialed directly from every desk, so the telephone attendant can handle incoming calls and perform other work. Figure 4–8 shows a Dial PBX. In the second type, private internal telephone (PAX), "inside" calls do not go through the switchboard. Since, in the typical company, more than one-half of the telephoning is internal—between telephones within the company—use of the private internal exchange relieves the regular telephone lines. This clears the way for better service on "outside" calls—those from customers and other important callers. The third type, or Centrex telephone service, features Direct Inward Dialing (DID), that is, all incoming calls, local or long distance, can go directly to the extension, which carries its own number—the usual seven-digit number. Centrex needs no switchboard attendants to handle most calls, insures maximum privacy on every call, saves about one-half minute on each call by dialing directly, and provides itemized telephone billing by individual telephone station. Interoffice calls are handled simply by dialing the last four digits assigned to the extension that is called.

## EFFECTIVE TELEPHONING

Certain characteristics distinguish the seasoned and efficient telephone user. We will comment on a few of these characteristics, first, for the switchboard operator and, second, for the individual using a telephone. For each, there are both technical aspects and speech aspects.

Under switchboard operator, technical aspects include the best way to handle the levers, the manipulation of the cords, the dialing of numbers, and the writing of messages, each of which constitutes an important segment of switchboard telephone efficiency. In addition, correct routing of calls is paramount. The operator must know her setup thoroughly and follow a set procedure for handling unusual requests and other types of time-consuming calls. The best way of performing all these tasks can be found by consulting the telephone company's special representative.

Speech aspects include the proper use of the voice over the telephone, the manner of speaking, and the standardization of certain phrases and words in conversation. Proper practices in these aspects help to obtain faster service, better cooperation, and company good will. It may be well to secure the help of a trained consultant in this field. The following expressions are effective:

1. Identify the company immediately. To illustrate, say:

"Good morning. American Manufacturing Company," or
"American Manufacturing."

2. If the party must be delayed, the operator should say:

"The line is busy right now. Will you wait?"

3. When the caller agrees to wait, the operator should report about every 30 seconds, saying:

"The line is still busy."

When able to complete the call, the operator should say:

"I'll connect you now. Thanks for waiting," or "Here's the line now. Thanks for waiting."

When the caller cannot wait, his name and number should be obtained and the call returned.

The good work of a private switchboard operator must be supplemented by proper telephone techniques on the part of the individual using the telephone. Helpful suggestions of a technical nature include:

1. To be heard clearly, speak directly into the transmitter, with the lips about 1 to 2 inches from the mouthpiece.

2. To hear better in a noisy office, place your hand over the mouthpiece, not over your ear.

3. To attract the operator's attention, move the receiver hook up and down slowly and evenly.

4. Be prepared to take messages or handle inquiries promptly.

5. After finishing a conversation, replace the receiver gently making certain it is all the way down, otherwise the line is either "out of order" or "busy" to anyone calling.

Speech aspects by the individual user emphasize the following:

1. Answer the telephone immediately and identify the department and yourself. For example, say:

"Cost Department, Mr. Allen."

If answering for someone else, give his name and then yours. Say:

"Mr. Brown's office. Miss Kenny speaking."

2. Handle, if possible, but transfer the call when it requires handling by someone else in the company. To do this, advise the calling party he is being transferred to another phone. Say:

"I will transfer you to our accounting division. One moment, please."

Then flash and tell the switchboard operator:

"This call to Mr. Kohl."

3. When using the telephone, do not leave the line unless it is necessary. If this is the case, tell why and for how long. Say:

"Will you excuse me for a moment? I must look at our file on this."

4. On outgoing calls, introduce yourself promptly. Say:

"Hello, Mr. Briggs. This is Spencer of National Sales."

Periodic checkups on the use of the telephone by company personnel are in order. All calls should be handled in the prescribed manner. Data can be obtained on the time required to handle calls and on the manner of speech. Concentrate on the promptness in answering the telephone, helpfulness on all calls, and a pleasing telephone personality. Employees should be informed that periodic checkups are made. When necessary, remedial action should be taken without delay.


## AUXILIARY TELEPHONE SERVICE

It is possible for several executives in different parts of the country to hold a conference by means of a simultaneous telephone hookup known as *conference call service*. The savings in time and trouble from this type of service are obvious. In some instances, the connections are monitored or recorded for possible future reference. When this is done, approval by the parties is necessary. The signal that the call is being recorded is a "beep" tone every 15 seconds.

A perpetual telephone receptionist is afforded by the *automatic answering device*. This unit, about four times the size of a telephone, is linked to the telephone. Incoming calls are answered by a recorded message something like this:

"This is the Avenue Realty Company. Your call is being answered by an automatic answering device. Will you leave your name, telephone number, and message after you hear the 'beep' tone? You may leave a half-minute message for me, and I'll call you when I return. Thank you."

After returning to the office, all messages recorded by the unit are audited and the return calls made. The device is especially convenient not only for small, one-man offices and for medical doctors, but also for large offices during the nonworking hours, thus providing around-the-clock service. The cost is $30 per month after an installation fee of $15.

*Radio-telephone service* provides communication between moving units and any Bell System telephone. It is particularly adaptable for use by trucking, taxicab, and public service companies, and by police and fire departments. For a two-way communication, a mobile unit is called by means of a regular desk telephone. A request is made for the mobile service operator who, by means of radio, signals the driver of the mobile unit. This is done over an approved radio channel. The driver answers the call on his dashboard telephone, and the conversation takes place. In a similar manner, the driver can call his office from his mobile unit. In contrast, the one-way service signals only to the mobile unit. By means of a code, the driver translates the message, such as "Go to Warehouse R immediately."

The *teletypewriter,* or TWX service of the telephone company, provides some 60,000 subscribers with a two-way teleprinter transmission. Speed averages about 75 words a minute. The machine used resembles a large typewriter that transmits messages between stations using telephone lines. Basically the keyboard of the machine is standard and when the keys are depressed, electric impulses reproduce the message in typed form on one machine or on many similar machines, the number being determined by the number of connections desired. To send a message, the TWX subscribers' directory is consulted, the call is placed by number, and the connection is made. Any two teletypewriters can be connected for communication in the same way as two telephones. The communication is two way; a written conversation can be carried out. The service is especially effective over long distances. Charges are made on the basis of time and distance, similar to the long-distance telephone. Rates are approximately two-thirds to one-half those of the telephone. Figure 4–9 shows a teletypewriter.

Additional services include:

*WATS, or wide-area telephone service.* This provides unlimited interstate telephoning within specific areas for a flat monthly rate. It is designed for the customer who makes frequent calls to widely scattered and distant points.

*Leased Private Lines.* These insure availability of the circuit for the customer who is provided exclusive use between two or more locations for a scheduled period each day. This service is preferred when a large volume is sent regularly to a small number of fixed points.

*Courtesy: Illinois Bell Telephone Co., Chicago*

**FIG. 4—9.   A teletypewriter.**

*Dataphone.* Machines are able to talk to each other by means of this service. It is very important in the transmission of data in the language of a computer. Dataphone is fully discussed in Chapter 11, page 252.

## TELEGRAPH

A well-known means of handling communications over relatively long distances is the telegraph. Telegrams secure attention, provide terse businesslike messages, and impel immediate action. They are used for practically all subjects or phrases of business activities.

Telegraphic communications can be sent by any of four main ways: (1) over the counter—giving it to the operator at any branch office; (2) by messenger; (3) by telephone—similar to an ordinary telephone call, charges being made to the telephone account or paid by coins dropped into a public pay telephone; and (4) by mechanical tie lines, such as direct telephone connection which is simply a direct wire between the sender's office and the local telegraph office. There is also a *Telex* service offered by the telegraph company. This includes a teleprinter network so that any Telex subscriber can communicate with any other Telex subscriber. The teleprinter is a machine similar to a typewriter which transmits the typed message electrically to the telegraph office. Transmission is at the rate of 66 words a minute. The message is recorded on paper tape both in the sending office and in the telegraph office. The former serves as the sender's reference copy; the latter is used to transmit the message to a circuit for its destination. Telex subscribers pay special low rates for this service.

The cost of regular telegraphic communications varies with length of message, distance, and speed of delivery. Domestic messages are classified into the following main types: full-rate telegram—most expedient service; base rate applies to 15 words; (2) day letter—deferred slightly in handling; base rate applies to 50 words or less and is roughly 40 percent more than that for a full-rate, 15-word telegram; (3) serial—a deferred message sent in sections to the same addressee during the day; cost is about 20 percent more than for a day letter containing the same number of words; and (4) night letter—an inexpensive overnight service; base rate applies to 50 words or less and is about 75 percent of that of a full-rate, 15-word telegram.

Cablegrams or services to foreign countries are classified as (1) ordinary—the standard full-rate service, (2) urgent—priority over all other messages except government messages, (3) deferred—no priority over other types, and (4) night letter—messages permitting overnight delivery.

Code words are sometimes used for telegraphic communications in order to reduce costs or to insure secrecy. For example, the code word "ROEUZ" might mean: "What action shall I take?" Commercial codes are available, or a special code can be created.

Anything printed or drawn, such as layouts, drawings, or charts, can now be transmitted instantly and accurately by WIREFAX, a special service using telegraph equipment.

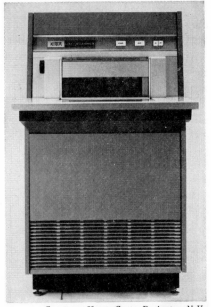

*Courtesy: Xerox Corp., Rochester, N.Y.*

FIG. 4–10. This unit transmits written, typed, or printed documents at high speeds, either within a building or across a continent.

Actually, WIREFAX is a public facsimile system that transmits in units up to 7½ by 9½ inches. Cost depends upon amount and distance. Charges for the initial unit between Chicago and New York are about $5, and each additional unit is about 50 cents.

There are also machines supplying the transmission of printed documents, drawings, and charts. Coaxial cable, private microwave system, or the facilities of common carrier services can be used. The selection depends upon volume, speed, and distance involved. Figure 4–10 shows the unit that converts document images to video transmission signals. Another unit returns these signals to the document images. The quality of the copy is excellent.

## TELAUTOGRAPH

Another well-known means for transmitting messages is the telautograph. As the name suggests, it transmits a handwritten message. The writing is electrically reproduced mainly, but not exclusively, over comparatively short distances. It is popular for communication between main office and receiving room, department and department, and warehouse and main office. In order to send a message, a switch is turned on, and the message is written with a metal stylus on a metal platen. To see what is being written, the sender watches the pen of the instrument writing on a roll of paper. Figure 4–11 illustrates a telautograph. As the message is written, it is reproduced almost simultaneously at one or a number of connected points.

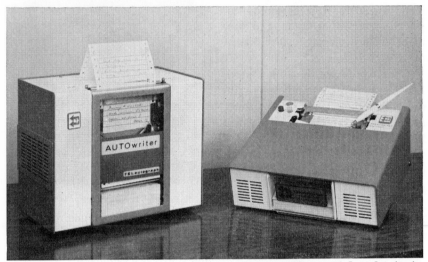

*Courtesy: TELautograph Corp., Los Angeles*

FIG. 4–11. TELautograph receiver and transmitter instruments which handle handwritten messages, including special symbols and sketches.

A telautograph provides economical and high-speed transmitting and receiving of messages. Handwritten records are furnished and can be attached to such things as inquiries, notices, and shipping instructions. It is possible to carry on a written conversation—messages can be sent and received.

## CLOSED-CIRCUIT TELEVISION

One of the newer methods for transmitting messages is television. Although its current application in business is limited, television holds much promise for the future. By means of closed circuits, it is possible to transmit and have instantaneous receipt at many points. Television presents the message visually and in motion—a series of events. However, it does not provide a written message to the recipient.

An interesting application concerns railroad freight car reporting wherein cars move by a TV camera stationed at a strategic point in the freight yard. Pertinent data are viewed on the side of the car and transmitted to a policing and recording center. Floodlights provide proper illumination for both day and night operation.

A television-telephone, enabling the caller to see as well as hear the party at the other end of the line, is available. When the caller lifts the television-telephone, his image appears simultaneously on one-half of his screen and upon one-half of that of the party being called. When the party answers, his image appears on the remaining halves of the two screens. The unit is about the size of a conventional television table model set. Maximum effective distance is several miles. Television-telephone applications include those in large industrial plants to compare drawings and materials, in banks to check signatures, and in penal institutions to serve as an electronic guard.

## INTERCOMMUNICATION SYSTEMS

Quick verbal communication is provided by means of intercommunication systems. Within an enterprise the various individuals or stations are each equipped with a speaking-talking unit. By turning a switch or pushing a button, instant right-of-way is obtained with anyone in the circuit, and conversations can be conducted with great clarity of tone. When privacy is desired, the microphone in the unit can be turned off and a handset substituted.

Many different capacities and features in units are available; usually, it is advisable to consult with the manufacturer or sales representative for specific data regarding individual requirements. The units can be connected in various circuit arrangements, depending upon the needs of the particular enterprise. Figure 4–12 shows models of intercommunication units.

## PAGING SYSTEMS

Important in most companies is the means of locating people through the use of flashing lights, tone bells, and buzzers. These paging devices are usually run by the telephone switchboard operator, or they may be a part of a private internal telephone system or of the intercommunication system. The light or noise outlets are located throughout the office and plant, so that key personnel are free to leave their desks without fear of missing any calls. By means of a code, such as two long and two short rings for the president, one long and one short ring for the controller, and so on, these men are notified of calls. By calling either the switchboard operator or a designated person, the message is obtained. The system is

*Courtesy: Executone, Inc., New York*          *Courtesy: Scan-Am Co., McHenry, Ill.*

FIG. 4–12. Intercommunication units enable the user to converse with any other master station or any staff station in the system. The communication is extremely fast and clear.

quite effective, for it is convenient and is a time-saver to all concerned. The latest paging units feature soft sounds in quiet areas and adequately loud sounds in noisy areas.

### INTERNAL DISTRIBUTION SERVICE

In the normal course of office work, many papers are handled within the enterprise successively by several employees. As already noted, mail is distributed, notices and memorandums must be delivered, and reports must be sent to executives. All these activities necessitate adequate distribution facilities. Either a personal or a mechanical means can be followed. Selection depends upon the specific objectives, but usually the following are of prime concern:

1. The total number of papers and messages.
2. The frequency of the papers and messages.
3. The number of delivery points.
4. The number of papers and messages at each delivery point.
5. The distance between delivery points.
6. The maximum allowable time between delivery points.
7. The expense, including investment and operating costs.
8. The flexibility of the service to meet changing office conditions.

### PERSONAL MEANS FOR CARRYING MESSAGES

The personal method is the oldest and the most common means for distributing papers and messages. To be of greatest benefit, the service must be regular and frequent. Schedules should call for deliveries about every half hour throughout the office. This time interval can be varied, depending upon the needs. In some cases, calls every 15 minutes might be required; in others, calls every hour might suffice. Very often, calls are made with greater frequency in the early morning and late afternoon business hours, in order to take care of the peak loads.

Deliveries can be made either on a desk-to-desk or on a departmental basis. The former is preferable and should be used whenever possible. Desk-to-desk calls insure that the person intended to receive the material actually gets it, that messengers do all the messenger work, and that the distribution and collection are accomplished with a minimum of effort and confusion. In contrast, deliveries by departments require further distribution within each department and often result in costly delays.

The personal method for carrying messages provides excellent training for new, inexperienced employees. They can quickly learn the names of key employees, location of their work stations, layout of the office and plant, and the work of each organizational unit. Some large companies start all young office help as messengers before transferring them to their initially selected jobs.

Adequate control of the messenger service requires close supervision and adherence to these practices:

1. The complete route must be established to include all desks designated as stations. The course to be followed must be defined, and the allowable time for one trip must be known. Adequate rest periods between trips are desirable and usually amount to about 20 percent of the total travel time.

2. All desks designated as stations must be visited on each trip. Even though there is nothing to deliver, there might be something to pick up.

3. Messengers should confine their efforts to the delivery and pickup of written materials along the prescribed routes. The running of miscellaneous errands for members of the office should be forbidden.

4. Each member should be instructed to sort the papers as they are collected, so that on each trip, deliveries can be made to stations not yet called upon. Papers designated for stations already called upon are delivered on the next trip. This eliminates backtracking.

5. A designated area or receptacle for "incoming" and another for "outgoing" messages should be used at each station desk.

6. Each messenger should be provided with an accordion file with one section for each station or some similar arrangement. The file should be equipped with a shoulder strap for carrying, or mounted on wheels for pushing, from station to station.

7. A card-control system provides a check upon the activities of messengers. Several plans are possible.

*a*) The messengers can be required to check in, that is, to sign or punch a card at several well-selected stations along the route. These cards can be collected daily and inspected, and any irregularity of service can be investigated and corrected immediately.

*b*) The messengers can pick up a card and replace it with another at each station on the route. Different cards, identified by number or color, can be used for each trip; and by noting the card in the basket, spot checks can be made to find out if schedules are being maintained.

8. To inform employees politely of the last trip for the day, the messenger can either say, "Good night," or leave a card printed "Last collection has been made" in the basket.

*Courtesy: Merrill Lynch, Pierce, Fenner, and Smith, Inc., New York*

FIG. 4–13.   Effective use of conveyor to transmit papers in an office.

## MECHANICAL MEANS FOR CONVEYING MESSAGES

*Mechanical conveyors* are well suited to convey papers and messages when the work volume is large and fairly constant, and where stations remain fixed. Belt conveyors are probably the most common type used in an office. Brush-off stops can be provided at each station in order to permit the delivery of papers at specific points. Figure 4–13 illustrates a conveyor belt being used to transport orders within a stock brokerage office.

*Pneumatic tubes* are effective, easy to use, and do not require special skill to operate. Material is carried quickly and accurately to its destination. The initial cost of the tubes is rather high, but the maintenance cost is low. The use of pneumatic tubes is most economical where the volume of work is large. Different-sized tubes and tube carriers are offered. For example, a "4-inch tube carrier" is a popular size and has maximum inside length of 14 inches. Rectangular-shaped carriers are also available for handling bulky items. In the case of a large aircraft manufacturer, the installation of pneumatic tubes linking seven buildings into one unit resulted in annual payroll savings of over $100,000. For a medium-sized metal processor, messenger service costs were cut $4,200 a year by use of pneumatic tubes.

## RECEPTION SERVICE

To many visitors, the first impression of a company is frequently gained from the receptionist. Courteous and prompt treatment should be extended visitors in order to build and develop company public relations and good will. The receptionist's basic job is to (1) find out with which person, if any, the visitor should talk; and (2) arrange for the visitor to see the proper person quickly.

A pleasant manner of speech and a winning personality are highly important; but in addition, certain standardized practices have been found most effective. For example, in securing information from callers, the receptionist should ask: "What company do you represent?" or "May I help you?" Should the visitor say he is calling about a personal matter, or words to that effect, it is well for the receptionist to inquire: "Does Mr. —— know you?" If an evasive or a negative reply is given, the receptionist should ask if someone has sent the caller. If no one has, a recommended statement is: "I'll let you talk with Mr. ——'s secretary, who will try to help you."

When the person called on is too busy to see the caller, the receptionist should address the visitor with: "I'm sorry, Mr. —— is busy and will not be able to see you. Can you come back or telephone first for an appointment?" In situations where the person is absolutely not interested in talking with the caller, the receptionist must be tactful and courteous. Refusals to grant short interviews with callers should be held at an absolute minimum; but when necessary, the receptionist might say: "I am sorry, but Mr. —— is not interested in what you have to offer." Under no circumstance should the receptionist suggest that the visitor call later if the person being called upon has no intention of seeing him. Honesty is the best policy.

The receptionist must be fully familiar with what matters are handled by each employee who has callers. Normally, a guide or booklet is available for reference. Customarily, the receptionist keeps a report of callers, including the date, the name of each caller, the name of his company, and the person called on. When individual conditions permit, the receptionist might also perform office work of sorting, stuffing envelopes, typing, or operating the telephone switchboard. However, if there is too much extra work, the regular duties of the receptionist might be neglected. The office manager should watch this carefully.

## TAPE AND WIRE RECORDERS

These devices are being put to a large number of uses, including the recording of inventory counts, personnel interviews, laboratory tests, and sales talks. In the case of inventory counts, the person taking the count is equipped with a microphone attached to the recorder in the office. As the inventory count is obtained, it is spoken and thus recorded. A typist then plays the recording and types the inventory lists. Intermediate paper work, tally sheets, and the like are eliminated. Likewise, interviews with prospective employees or, in the case of lawyers, talks with clients can be recorded and studied for complete information—a more effective practice than the use of handwritten notes, which often inhibit the speaker. However, when conversations are recorded, approval by both parties is necessary. Tape or wire is used in the operation of the machine. The tape is a narrow, thin, flexible, paperlike material coated on one side with magnetic oxide of iron; when wire is used, it is of a special type.

## QUESTIONS

1. Discuss the meaning, use, and advantages of the Zip Code as adopted by the U.S. Post Office Department.

2. What practical suggestions would you give to a newly hired head of the mail room of an office in order to help him succeed on the job?

3. Briefly describe each of the following, pointing out for what type of communication and under what circumstances it is best suited:
   a) Centrex telephone service.
   b) TWX service.
   c) WATS telephone service.
   d) Television.

4. Mr. Burns comes to you for advice concerning the management of the personal messenger service of his company. What specific suggestions would you give him?

5. Discuss a satisfactory approach to the determining of a company's communicative needs.

6. Enumerate key considerations in the effective use of the telephone in a modern office.

7. Under what general circumstances would you suggest that an enterprise use (a) the telegraph, (b) the long-distance telephone, (c) an airmail letter, (d) the teletypewriter, and (e) the telautograph? Give reasons for your answers.

8. Describe fully to what communicative uses you believe television might be applied successfully in the office of the future.

9. State concisely the difference between each of the following:
   a) A window envelope and a business reply envelope.
   b) An automatic answering device for a telephone and TELEX service.

    *c*) Metered mail and nonmetered mail.

    *d*) Postage-saver envelope and regular standard envelope.

10. Do you believe that the management of mail and office communicating services should be under the jurisdiction of the office manager? Justify your viewpoint.

11. Enumerate and discuss briefly the minimum activities you feel necessary to insure adequate control of outgoing mail in a large office.

12. Relate some major considerations in providing a satisfactory reception service?

## CASE PROBLEMS

### Case 4–1.  Reba Products Company

Office manager Albert Stahl firmly believes in employee initiative, self-discipline, and self-imposed responsibility as the marks of a top-notch office employee. "Give them freedom to operate, permit them to see what's to be done, and help them do it the best way," is his manner of expressing it. For office employees to receive personal telephone calls at the office was all right in the views of Mr. Stahl. Generally, the employees did not abuse the privilege. However, Elmer Willis had frequent long personal telephone conversations. Neither Mr. Stahl nor any of his supervisors had talked to Mr. Willis about it. Mr. Stahl hoped that Elmer Willis' own common sense, or that other office employees, would tell Elmer that he was endangering the telephone privilege for all.

One morning the general manager, in showing the office to a good customer, walked past Elmer's desk and observed him talking quite loudly on the telephone. The gist of the conversation marked it as a personal call. Some time later the general manager, in returning to his office, found Elmer still talking on the telephone. Intrigued by the length of the conversation, he waited until it ended, then told Elmer he talked too long on the telephone and that during working hours the telephone was primarily for business calls. Elmer replied, "Yes, I know that. But that call was not more than five minutes and that's certainly reasonable."

The general manager felt Elmer was flippant about the affair and, checking with the switchboard operator, was informed the call was from a suburban area, was paid for by the caller, and lasted 43 minutes. The general manager called Elmer to his office and gave him the information he had received. Elmer insisted the call was not more than five minutes. He added that the switchboard operator must "have it in for me" to report any greater time. When asked, "What do you consider reasonable time for a telephone call?" Elmer replied, "That's too general a question to answer intelligently. Frankly, I figure the telephone is there to help me. As long as I can do my work satisfactorily and the calls are paid for by the caller, I can't see any useful purpose in your playing Sherlock Holmes." At this the general manager informed Elmer that his employment was terminated and told him to get his paycheck from the cashier.

## Problems:

    1. What conditions led to this situation?

    2. Discuss the practices and controls you advocate for use of the telephone for personal calls in an office.

    3. What action do you recommend in this specific case?

### Case 4–2.   Miami Mail Order Company

For years the practice has been followed of having four employees come to work 45 minutes early to open and sort the incoming mail so that all office departments could be in full operation at the regular starting time of 8:45 A.M. Volunteers were used and were permitted to quit at 4:00 P.M. instead of the regular closing time of 4:45 P.M. Over a period of time the company has found it increasingly difficult to obtain the volunteers for the early start work. A week ago one of the early employees served notice that she desired to discontinue the early call. She gave no reason for her action. Requests for a volunteer have brought no response.

### Problems:
1. What alternatives are available to the company?
2. What action do you believe should be taken? Why?

### Case 4–3.   Hoosier Pharmaceuticals, Inc.

This company sells a variety of pharmaceuticals to a large number of customers, including hospitals, drugstores, and physicians' supply stores. Distribution is nationwide, and the company is well known and established. About 75 percent of the company's shipments are in small packages—not over 8 x 8 x 6 inches.

Many of the packages are sent by (1) airmail, (2) special delivery, or (3) special handling, because the customer usually wants the pharmaceuticals as soon as possible. Mailing the packages in this manner incurs additional fees charged by the post office. Special delivery provides immediate delivery at the post office of the addressee; special handling applies to fourth-class mail only and insures prompt and expeditious handling by the post office. Starting at 3:00 P.M., several truckloads of packages are taken to the post office. The last load leaves the company building at 4:30 P.M.

A careful investigation by Mr. Charles Meyers, the office manager, showed that a great majority of the packages could be sent by regular mail, provided the packages were ready to go at stated times throughout the day, and would reach their destinations as quickly as by the use of special mailing services. Mr. Meyers estimated the savings from planned scheduled mailing and the use of regular mailing service at about $65 a day.

He feels that some loss is suffered due to stamp pilferage. Currently, stamps are kept in a desk drawer of the packing room and distributed by Mr. James Lange, the foreman. However, this distribution is loosely handled, in the opinion of Mr. Meyers. The foreman contends that he cannot sit at the desk all day long to issue the proper amount of stamps, nor can he check each package mailed for correct postage. Mr. Meyers has observed that frequently emergency letters or packages must be sent out at times other than regular working hours, that is, at night or on Saturdays and Sundays, during which time an employee not fully familiar with postage rates may be handling the mail. The suggestion has been made that orders to the same customer on the same day could be grouped and packed in the same box, thus reducing handling expense as well as being more convenient for the customer. However, Mr. James Lange disagrees, pointing out that the postage will be about the same and the time spent in grouping orders to the same customer will slow the work of his men.

### Problems:

1. Do you agree with the viewpoints advanced by Mr. James Lange? Why?
2. What action do you recommend be taken? Justify your viewpoint.
3. How should Mr. Meyers proceed in this situation?

CHAPTER **5**

# DUPLICATING, CALCULATING, AND COMPARING

Criticism should not be querulous
and wasting, but guiding, instructive,
and inspiring.
        —*Ralph Waldo Emerson*

OFFICE work involving duplicating, calculating, and comparing is present in every enterprise. Always basic in office operations, these have increased in importance until today they represent essential office services. Copies of papers are needed in the modern office and calculating, along with checking the accuracy of such calculating, are normal in the performance of much work of the office.

## FOCUSING ON DUPLICATING

No office service has undergone more new developments and basic changes during the last several decades than has duplicating. Many new duplicating processes and machines have appeared on the market. This revolutionary expansion of duplicating has brought with it the challenge for adequate management of this office service. Fundamental questions arise. For example, "Are copies really needed?" If so, "What minimum number will suffice?" "Is it better to print computer output on regular forms, or on transparent paper or direct-image master plates for reproduction?" "Should we make or buy most of our office printing needs?"

These are not easy questions to answer; they require sound managerial decisions and actions which are subject to both periodic review and interpretation. Among the basic considerations are:

1. *The quantity, quality, speed, and flexibility of the duplicating service.* What is really required based on reasonable justifications and analysis?

2. *The total investment in duplicating.* This includes not only equipment but personnel and the quantities of paper and supplies held in stock. The cost versus service comparison is also included in this consideration.

3. *The controls utilized.* Duplicating should be scheduled and performed within reasonable time and cost limits. It should insure security of classified information, be adjusted to changing needs, and be properly allocated costwise to units for whom the service is provided.

4. *The logical integration of duplicating with related office work.* Does the duplicating simplify and assist in the essential work being done? Is it in keeping with the major goals sought?

## DUPLICATING PROCESSES

Basic knowledge of various duplicating processes is helpful in selecting the process to utilize. Figure 5–1 shows pertinent information on a comparative basis for a number of different duplicating processes. The contact process, for example, has a relatively high cost per duplicated sheet, enjoys average usage, is usually economical for up to ten copies, is suited for typed or printed material, script, drawings, and pictures, and is produced at the rate of eight copies a minute. Individual requirements should govern the selection and take into account not only the type of

| Process | Relative Cost of Duplicated Sheet | Usage | Usually Economical for Number of Copies Up To: | Main Type of Material for which Suited* | Speed in Sheets per Minute |
|---|---|---|---|---|---|
| Contact | High | Average | 10 | T-S-D-P | 8 |
| Xerography | High | Average | 15 | T-S-D-P | 6 |
| Stencil | Low | Wide | 5,000 | T | 200 |
| Direct | Medium | Average | 300 | T | 150 |
| Offset | Low | Average | 10,000 | T-S-D-P | 150 |
| Indirect | Medium | Limited | 300 | T | 200 |
| Multigraph | Low | Average | 10,000 | T | 150 |
| Whiteprint | Medium | Limited | 500 | T-S-D | 8 |
| Photocopy | High | Limited | 5 | T-S-D-P | 5 |
| Noncarbon | High | Limited | 4 | T | 5 |

* CODE   T = Typed or Printed   S = Script   D = Drawing   P = Picture

FIG. 5–1.   Comparison of various duplicating processes.

data in Figure 5–1, but also such factors as the cost of the equipment and the supplies to run it, the quality of copy desired, time and place considerations, and employees' preferences.

The various descriptions of these duplicating processes are:

1. *Contact.* This means is rapidly growing in popularity and consists basically of placing a sensitized paper in contact with the material to be reproduced and inserting it into the machine, which exposes, develops, and fixes the copy sheet. The process is technically known as thermography and means literally a "burning" process. Dark areas, such as typewritten words, absorb more heat than the blank areas. Exposure to infrared light causes the words of the original to burn an image onto the heat-sensitive

*Courtesy: Minnesota Mining and Manufacturing Co., St. Paul*

*Courtesy: Eastman Kodak Co., Rochester, N.Y.*

FIG. 5–2.   Thermo-Fax Copying Machine featuring speed, economy, and convenience.

FIG. 5–3.   Readyprint Copier for fast, single-copy needs up to 8½ x 14 inches.

copy paper. Representative of the contact process is Thermo-Fax and Readyprint. Figure 5–2 shows a Thermo-Fax copying machine, which makes direct copies in a matter of seconds. Exposure timing is set on the dial on the right of the unit. The original and sensitized papers are placed together and inserted into the machine, which starts automatically and makes the copy. It gives ready-to-use, dry copies and emits no detectable odor. The process is effective wherever carbon is present in the writing, as with pencil or typewriter. Readyprint gives exact copies of letters, including original letterhead and signature, and other papers, is always ready to go, produces top quality copies, and is easy to operate. Figure 5–3 shows a Readyprint Copier.

2. *Xerography* (pronounced zē-rog'-ra-fē). This word stems from the two Greek words meaning "dry printing" and is identified as a dry, fast, electrophotographic copying process. Xerography uses light and static electricity to make copies of anything printed, typed, written, or drawn.

Copies are made on ordinary paper in a matter of seconds. A specially coated plate is charged with positive-charged electricity and is subsequently exposed to the material to be reproduced, *A,* by means of a camera. As a result, the reflection of *A* on the plate is retained and remains charged positively. The remaining area of the plate loses its charge because of light exposure permitted by the camera. Then, a negatively charged powder is adhered to the positively charged *A.* A sheet of paper is placed over the plate and given a positive electric charge. The positively charged paper draws the powder from the plate, forming a direct copy

*Courtesy: Xerox Corp., Rochester, N.Y.*

FIG. 5–4.  The Xerox 914 Office Copier makes perfect copies of all colors as well as rigid three-dimensional objects, in black on white, on ordinary paper or selected paper offset masters.

which is heated in a few seconds to fuse the powder into a permanent print. The copies produced are clear, sharp, and permanent. The same plate can be used hundreds of times. The operation is completely automatic. Figure 5–4 shows the popular Xerox 914 Office Copier. Although not yet commercially available, the xerography principle applied to commercial printing is being studied.

3. *Stencil.*  This is a common means and consists of "typing a stencil," either by typewriter with ribbon removed or nonoperative, by special hand tools (styli), or by a die-impressed operation performed by the manufacturer. The openings thus made in the stencil, i.e., openings caused by the stencil coating being pushed aside and exposing the base fiber, permit ink to pass through so that paper held against the surface receives the image.

Even, sharp, and clear strokes on the stencil give the best results. Corrections can be made on the stencil by using a special fluid to reseal the surface and then retyping. It is also possible to block out and remove an area and replace it by attaching a new portion of stencil. The image or printing is usually in a jet-black color, although several other colors are also available. It is possible to store the stencil for use at a later time; about 5,000 copies can be made from one stencil. A stencil duplicating machine is shown in Figure 5–5.

*Courtesy: A. B. Dick Co., Chicago*        *Courtesy: Ditto, Inc., Chicago*

FIG. 5–5.   A duplicating machine        FIG. 5–6.   A direct or liquid-
using the stencil process.                  process duplicating machine.

4. *Direct or liquid process.*   In this process, the material to be reproduced is put on a master sheet which has behind it a special carbon layer. The carbon places the image in reverse on the back of the master sheet. Different carbons are used for different colors. The master is placed in a machine, and copies are made directly from it in this manner: The copy sheet is slightly moistened with a special fluid before contacting the back side of the master; and as the copy sheet presses against the master, a very small layer of the carbon is removed and impressed on the copy sheet. Four colors can be reproduced in a single machine operation, and about 300 copies can be made from one master. Master sheets can be stored for reruns. Figure 5–6 shows a liquid duplicator.

5. *Offset.*   The offset process is subject to many variations. Basically, the principle involved is that the material to be reproduced is (1) prepared on a plate, which is (2) transferred to an intermediate agent, which is (3) printed on the paper. Frequently, the intermediate agent is made of rubber.

One important offset process is photo-offset. The material to be reproduced is photographed, and the negative is transferred to a sensitized plate. This plate is then used in a photo-offset printing unit. Slight variations in this method are commonly termed "planographing" and "offset lithography." Frequently, a xerography process is used for making offset master paper plates.

A well-known process known as "multilith" is based on this offset principle. Either a metal or a paperlike master can be used. The latter is more widely used, since it can be handled like a piece of paper. That is, a regular typewriter plus pencil, pen, ink, brush, or crayon furnished by the supplier are used in preparing the master. Erasures and corrections are handled as with ordinary paper, and the paperlike masters can be filed in the office like paper sheets. The process is recommended for quantities— over 500 and up to 10,000 copies.

6. *Miscellaneous processes.* There are many more duplicating processes—too many to include all of them here. In addition to the above, however, mention of several others is warranted. The *indirect* process, also known as the gelatin process, consists of putting the material on a master sheet made of special paper; the master sheet is pressed against the gelatin, thus depositing the image on it. Copies are then made by pressing the sheets against the image in the gelatin. *Multigraph* employs either an imprinting or a ribbon process of reproducing. In the former, type, rubber strips, or electrotypes are used. The medium is inked and paper coming in contact with the wet type forms the copy. In the latter, or ribbon process, the duplicating is done through a ribbon similar to that used in standard typing, and the finished work closely resembles original typing. The type used is held in a segment or blanket and consists of up to 70 lines of type. Signature attachments are available, changes or corrections can easily be made in the type, and the process is speedy, as up to 9,000 copies can be run in one hour. *Whiteprint* provides a black on white directly from translucent originals. Additions to the master is a feature. For example, a customer's statement can be typed on a translucent paper and retained as a permanent copy by the company. At the end of each month, a whiteprint is made of the entire statement and is sent to the customer. Advantages include: No copying work is required, errors are held to a minimum, and each month the customer receives the full story on his account. The process is flexible and can handle large sizes of paper. Either the copy is given a light coating of a special solution to develop the copy permanently or it is exposed to controlled aqua ammonia vapors. *Photocopy* is one of the oldest duplicating processes. By photographing a negative, it is possible to make a positive paper print, that is, black lines with white background. Prints can be made in the same size as, or larger or smaller than, the original. *Noncarbon* utilizes carbonless "NCR paper" of the National Cash Register Company. The bottom side of the first sheet is coated with a colorless chemical and the top side of the second sheet with another chemical. Writing on the first sheet reproduces instantly on the second sheet, and similar reaction takes place between the remaining sheets of the pack. Clear copies are obtained, smears and smudges are eliminated, and hands and clothing are not soiled.

## COMPOSITING, COLLATING, AND BINDING

Type compositing, collating, and binding are tasks frequently connected with duplicating work. Type compositing is preparing the type for the master copy. Different styles, sizes, headings, and the like are commonly utilized to make the duplicated material more readable and to highlight important facts. For this work office composing machines are

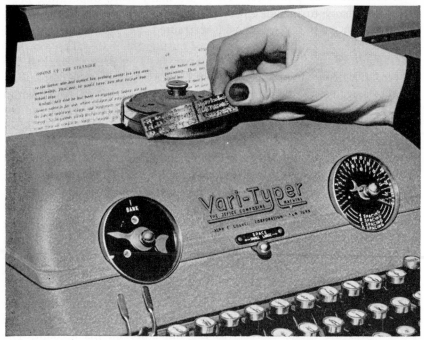

*Courtesy: Addressograph-Multigraph Corp., Cleveland, O.*

FIG. 5–7. Changes from one type to another are accomplished quickly by means of small type fonts weighing less than one-fifth of an ounce. Two such fonts fit into the machine at one time, and changes are made in less time than it takes to refill a mechanical lead pencil.

widely used. They bring the versatility of a well-equipped printing shop into the office and are used to prepare type of all sorts for reports, bulletins, booklets, catalogs, price lists, and house organs, where variety in composition is desired.

Figure 5–7 shows an office composing machine. It resembles a typewriter in both appearance and operation. Each type face is on a removable disk which can be quickly inserted into or removed from the machine. Each disk is complete with capital and lower-case letters, numerals, and symbols. Over 600 different sizes and styles of type, ranging from 5½-

point newspaper style to 14-point Heavy Gothic type, and including boldface headings and italics, are available. Even margins on both the left and the right, similar to those of regular typeset composition, are obtained by typing each line twice. To illustrate: line 1 of the copy is typed in the regular manner on the left half of the piece of paper. Then, it is retyped on the right. The machine spaces the second typing so that both margins are even. The procedure is repeated for each line. When completed, the typed material on the right half of the paper constitutes the finished or master copy.

Collating is the assembling of several different sheets of paper to form a report or booklet. This work can be done manually or by a hand or electrically operated machine. Figure 5–8 shows collating machines.

*Courtesy: Collàmatic, Wayne, N.J.*      *Courtesy: Thomas Collators, Inc., New York*

**FIG. 5–8.** The collating machine on the left is electrically operated. A feed roller at each bin ejects one sheet of paper; the operator grasps the sheets, gathers them, and staples each pack with the electric stapler. The unit on the right is an effective hand-operated collator; as many as 32 sheets can be gathered in one continuous operation.

In many cases, the material is held together by a binding, of which there are many different types. First, there is side wire stitching, i.e., on the side. Also, there is saddle wire stitching, i.e., through the fold at the back of the booklet. Usually, the latter is preferred, since it enables the sheets to remain flat and open once they are placed in that position. Mechanical fasteners are used extensively, including ring or loose-leaf binders, prong fasteners, or screw-post fasteners. Also the use of wire and of plastic bindings has won widespread favor. Wire binding is spun or coiled onto the packet of punched paper; plastic binding is fastened onto the paper via punched holes by means of a clasping action. Plastic binding equipment is available for use in the individual office. Such a binding is advantageous in that (1) a variety of different stock—pages, photographs, samples—can be bound together, (2) various page sizes can be securely bound in one manual, (3) revisions and renewals in the manuals can be made conveniently and quickly right in the office, (4) the cost is reasonable, and (5) the binding is sturdy and durable.

## SYSTEMS AND PROCEDURES AND DUPLICATING

Duplicating is not limited to making copies that provide convenience but is also an essential component in systems and procedures. In some applications, basic information is put on a master and subsequently duplicated as needed onto paper forms designed to direct and control a particular business activity. For example, in purchasing, master sheets for duplicating can be prepared. When an item is to be purchased, its master is withdrawn from the file, and the needed information duplicated on all the purchasing forms. These forms are then processed, and the master is returned to the file for future use. The result is accurate, fast work and much saving in writing time.

An interesting variation of this procedure is used when several of the requisitions to purchase can be assembled for the preparation of one purchase order for one supplier. The requisitions are sent to the

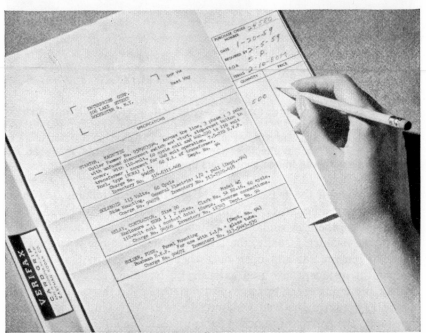

*Courtesy: Eastman Kodak Co., Rochester, N.Y.*

FIG. 5–9. Preparation of purchase orders from component parts is expedited by the use of a duplicating machine.

purchasing department, where the buyer groups them respectively under the names of the vendors whom he selects. The card for each selected vendor is removed from the vendor file and assembled with the requisitions which will make up the purchase order to that vendor. These are placed in a shingled or overlapping position and held in place by a large clip. In addition, a variable information form is added, so that the composition of the purchase order can be completed. Figure 5–9 shows the purchasing requisitions, giving complete specifications, assembled on the left, with the variable information such as purchase order number, date, and quantities being written in on the right. When entries are completed, the entire assembly is placed over a purchasing order master giving heading and shipping instructions—common to all purchase orders—and duplicated. Thus, a complete purchase order is prepared with a minimum of manual writing.

## CALCULATING IN THE OFFICE

In the typical office a considerable amount of adding, subtracting, and multiplying is done in the preparation of different records and reports. This work can be accomplished by working it out longhand with pencil and paper, utilizing charts, slide rule, or a machine. For convenience, the discussion here will be viewed from (1) the mental or personal basis and (2) the machine basis.

## CALCULATING BY MENTAL OR PERSONAL BASIS

The personal basis is commonly used for short and relatively simple calculating work. Different methods can be followed; some represent much less work than others. A few effective short cuts will be included here. *In adding a column of figures, it helps to combine pairs or groups of successive numbers that add up to ten.* The addition can proceed from the top down or from the bottom up. For example, to add:

$$
\begin{array}{r}
5 \\
3 \\
7 \\
6 \\
3 \\
1 \\
4 \\
\hline
\end{array}
$$

say to yourself (working from top down): 5, 15, 25, 29. The 3 and 7, and the 6, 3, and 1, are grouped as units of 10.

*Left-to-right* addition is speedy and accurate. This is accomplished by adding the tens of one number to the tens of the next number, then adding the units, and following this pattern successively to the last number. Thus, in order to add:

$$
\begin{array}{r}
78 \\
81 \\
33 \\
45 \\
\hline
\end{array}
$$

say 78, 158 (78 + 80), 159 (158 + 1), 189 (159 + 30), 192 (189 + 3), 232 (192 + 40), 237 (232 + 5).

*Horizontal addition* is helpful in adding numbers not arrayed in column form. Assume the total is wanted from a number of billings, including $42.50, $1.11, $34.77, $9.81, $7.83, $25.40, and $17.08. It is not necessary to arrange the numbers in the form of columns. Simply add the units, then the tens, then the hundreds, and so forth, and write the sums of the successive additions in the form shown below, then add.

Sum of:

| | | |
|---|---:|---|
| Units................ | 20 | (0 + 1 + 7 + 1 + 3 + 0 + 8) |
| Tens................. | 33 | (5 + 1 + 7 + 8 + 8 + 4 + 0) |
| Hundreds............ | 35 | (2 + 1 + 4 + 9 + 7 + 5 + 7) |
| Thousands........... | 10 | (4 + 3 + 2 + 1) |
| Total.............. | $138.50 | |

*Multiplication by near number* is simple, yet it is not commonly practiced. By this procedure multiplying quickly by numbers near 10, 100, or 1,000 is possible. For example, 368 multiplied by $0.98 consists of

$$
\begin{array}{rr}
368 \text{ times } \$1.00 = & \$368.00 \\
\text{less } 368 \text{ times } \ \ 0.02 = & 7.36 \\
\hline
& \$360.64
\end{array}
$$

In other words, multiplying by 100 is accomplished by simply adding two zeros to the end of the number being multiplied, then adjusting this figure for the amount the multiplier deviates from 100. In like manner, if the multiplier had been $0.12, the multiplier used would be 10 and the calculation would be

$$
\begin{array}{rr}
368 \text{ times } \$0.10 = & \$36.80 \\
\text{plus } 368 \text{ times } \ \ 0.02 = & 7.36 \\
\hline
& \$44.16
\end{array}
$$

*The breakdown method of multiplication* is a time-saver when the personal method of calculating is followed. Actually, this is similar to multiplication by near number and differs in degree, not in type. To multiply by 50, for example, multiply by 100, which is easily done, and take one-half, since 50 is one-half of 100. Likewise, to multiply by 25, take one-fourth of that found by multiplying by 100. To illustrate, $1.95 times

25 equals one-fourth of $195.00, or $48.75. In multiplying $1.95 times 26, an additional amount for one unit, or $1.95, would be added to $48.75, giving $50.70.

*The use of reciprocals* represents another short cut. A reciprocal of a number is one divided by that number, i.e., the reciprocal of four is one-fourth. Calculating work involving percentages and prorating can be expedited by the use of reciprocals because dividing by a number is the same as multiplying by the reciprocal of that number. Assume from the following data that percentage figures are to be calculated:

| Department | Sales | Percentage Total |
|---|---|---|
| A............... | $ 3,905.40 | |
| B............... | 7,041.62 | |
| C............... | 2,052.98 | |
| Total........... | $13,000.00 | 100.00% |

The reciprocal of 13,000.00 is 0.000076923. Multiplying the sales for each department by this reciprocal gives the respective percentages of 30.04, 54.17, and 15.79. Normally a table of reciprocals is used to simplify the work. In many cases, even though machines are employed, the use of reciprocals for this type of calculating is followed. It makes division possible when the machine adds and multiplies only. Also, in some cases it is deemed desirable to have the operator stay with multiplying work only, that is, not mix the work of multiplying with that of dividing.

*Calculating of discounts* is another area where short cuts can be used. Among the important discounts and the reason for granting them are:

| Discount | Reason |
|---|---|
| Quantity: | Less expensive to handle large orders |
| Trade: | Different types of buyers perform different marketing functions |
| Cash: | Inducement for prompt payment |

Customarily, a full or list price is used as the base from which the discount or discounts are applied. When two or more discounts are in effect, each is applied to the net amount remaining after the previous discount has been taken. For example, with a list price of $25.00 and discounts of 30 percent and 10 percent, denoted as 30 and 10, the net price is $15.75, calculated as follows:

| | |
|---|---|
| List price............................ | $25.00 |
| Less 30% (first discount)............... | 7.50 |
| Balance............................. | $17.50 |
| Less 10% (second discount)............. | 1.75 |
| Net price........................... | $15.75 |

This method is too cumbersome. A simpler method follows. A 30 percent discount means 70 percent (100 − 30) remains; hence, the amount can be determined by multiplying the list price by 70 percent. Likewise, a 10 percent discount means 90 percent applies. In the above example, the calculation is therefore

$$\$25.00 \times 0.70 \times 0.90 = \$15.75.$$

Another simple method is to determine the single rate equal to the two discounts. To do this, add the discounts and subtract the sum obtained by multiplying the discounts:

$$0.30 + 0.10 = 0.40$$
$$\text{less } 0.30 \times 0.10 = \underline{0.03}$$
$$\text{Equivalent discount} = \overline{0.37}$$

or $(1.00 - 0.37)$ remains, applying to $25.00 equals:

$$0.63 \times \$25.00, \text{ or } \$15.75.$$

Where the calculating work includes various discounts, it is common practice to make up a table showing the equivalent single discount and the net that is applicable. Such a table is illustrated by Figure 5–10.

| Discount percent | Equivalent | Net |
|---|---|---|
| 10. . . . . . . . . . . . . . . . . . . . . | 0.10 | 0.90 |
| 10 & 5. . . . . . . . . . . . . . . . | 0.145 | 0.855 |
| 10, 5, & 5. . . . . . . . . . . . . | 0.1878 | 0.8122 |
| 20. . . . . . . . . . . . . . . . . . . . . | 0.20 | 0.80 |
| 20 & 10. . . . . . . . . . . . . . . | 0.28 | 0.72 |
| 20, 10, & 5. . . . . . . . . . . . . | 0.316 | 0.684 |
| 40. . . . . . . . . . . . . . . . . . . . . | 0.40 | 0.60 |
| 40 & 5. . . . . . . . . . . . . . . . | 0.43 | 0.57 |
| 40, 5, & 10. . . . . . . . . . . . . | 0.487 | 0.513 |
| 40, 10, & 5. . . . . . . . . . . . . | 0.487 | 0.513 |
| 50. . . . . . . . . . . . . . . . . . . . . | 0.50 | 0.50 |
| 50, 10, & 10. . . . . . . . . . . . | 0.595 | 0.405 |

FIG. 5–10. Discounts, their equivalents, and net amounts.

## CALCULATING BY MACHINE BASIS

Modern office machines have reduced calculating work to very simple tasks. Lengthy columns of figures can be added in a matter of seconds; and if wanted, a written record is available for checking the accuracy or for future reference. Errors due to handwriting figures incorrectly, carelessly, or out of column are eliminated by the machine basis. In this chapter, adding machines and calculating machines will be discussed. Other types of machines, such as a billing or an accounting machine, perform calculating work; these will be discussed in Chapter 18.

*Adding machines* are basically of two types: key-driven and crank-driven. In the former case, the machine mechanism is actuated by depressing a key; in the latter case, the number is "put in the machine" by depressing the key, and the mechanism is actuated by pulling a lever or pressing a motor bar. These two basic types are subject to important variations, including listing or nonlisting, full keyboard or ten-keyboard, and manual or electric.

A listing machine lists or produces a written record of the figures on a tape. This can serve as a machine record, for visual comparison, or as proof of work. Where a long column of numbers, over a hundred, for example, is involved, a listing is usually desired. However, when a nonlisting machine is used and proof of work is required, the work can be checked by going through the addition twice and comparing answers. In some instances, this method is as quick as checking a tape record.

A full-keyboard machine provides a column of keys from 1 to 9 for each digit position. Thus, a five-row machine can handle a number like 628.47. The full keyboard permits high speeds where numbers of four or less digits are involved, because the keys can be depressed simultaneously. A ten-keyboard type has, as the name suggests, ten keys from 0 to 9. Within the machine capacity, all numbers are recorded by means of these ten keys. The number 629.43 would be handled by first presssing the key 6, then 2, and then 9, and so on until the number is completed. The ten-key machine is usually very satisfactory for large numbers. The hand travel is small, since it is confined to ten keys. Numbers with five or more digits are quickly handled on this machine.

The names *manual* and *electric* are self-explanatory, but in both cases the keys are depressed by hand. The manual usually has lower maintenance cost, is lighter, and no electric cords are necessary; the machine can be operated anywhere. In contrast, the electric machine is faster and saves the operator's energy; however, its initial cost is usually greater. Most adding machines can also be used for subtracting, and a number are adaptable for work involving multiplying and dividing. Illustrations of several different types of adding machines are shown by Figure 5–11.

*Calculating machines* are specially built for multiplication and division work, which is really repetitive addition and subtraction, respectively; that is, 3 times 3 is the same as 3 plus 3 plus 3, and 9 divided by 3 is equal to the number of times 3 can be subtracted from 9, i.e., 9 less 3, less 3, less 3. The same considerations apply to calculators as discussed above under adding machines.

Among the latest calculating machines is the Victor 3900 Electronic Calculator which displays its work progress on a built-in 4 x $2\frac{1}{2}$-inch

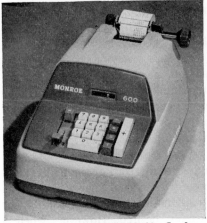

*Courtesy: Monroe Calculating Machine Co., Inc.,*
*Orange, N.J.*

*Courtesy: Burroughs Corp., Detroit*

FIG. 5–11.   Adding machines. *Left:* Listing ten-key model. *Right:* Listing full-keyboard, ten-column-capacity machine.

illuminated display screen. Up to 20 digit figures can be accommodated and multiplying, dividing, adding, and subtracting can be performed in a wink. The machine features very quiet operation—you have to see it to believe it's working—and five display registers, three of which are calculating registers and two are storage registers. The independent memory unit of the machine stores any factor at the touch of a key and brings it back to the processing register at the touch of another key. Figure 5–12 shows this machine.

*Courtesy: Victor Comptometer Corp., Chicago*

FIG. 5–12.   The Victor 3900 Electronic Calculator which is accurate, incredibly fast, and shows its work on an illuminated screen which is a part of the unit.

A fully automatic calculator with simplified listing is shown by Figure 5–13. In multiplying or in dividing, there is no repetition of figures on the tape—just the problem and the answer, as shown in the upper left of the figure. This machine is available with capacity up to $1 trillion. There is also available

a listing calculator featuring a wide range of application, high speed, and interoperation transfers, making it possible to perform sequences of combined operations such as storing data in the machine and recalling for use in subsequent operations. An illustration of this machine and several examples of the calculating work it can perform are shown by Figure 5–14.

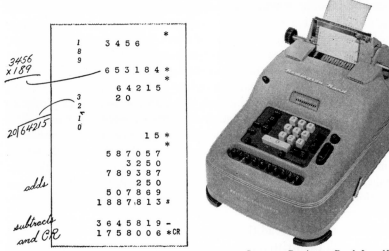

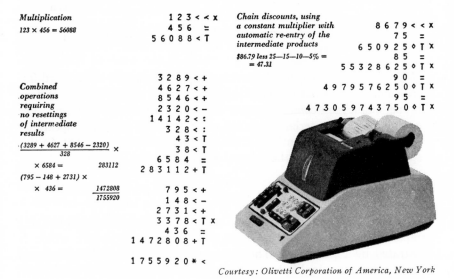

Courtesy: Remington Rand, Inc., New York

FIG. 5–13.   A fully automatic printing calculator, with an example of its work.

## THE OFFICE WORK OF COMPARING

Reading handwritten or typed copy and columns of numbers for accuracy accounts for a sizable portion of office workers' time. Progress in reducing these comparing efforts for checking purposes has been made, as

*Multiplication*

$123 \times 456 = 56088$

```
1 2 3 < < x
  4 5 6   =
5 6 0 8 8 < T
```

*Combined operations requiring no resettings of intermediate results*

$$\frac{(3289 + 4627 + 8546 - 2320)}{328} \times$$

$\times 6584 =$     *283112*

$(795 - 148 + 2731) \times$

$\times \ 436 =$     *1472808*
                    *1755920*

```
3 2 8 9 < +
4 6 2 7 < +
8 5 4 6 < +
2 3 2 0 < -
1 4 1 4 2 < :
    3 2 8 < :
      4 3 < T
      3 8 < T
  6 5 8 4   =
2 8 3 1 1 2 + T

    7 9 5 < +
    1 4 8 < -
  2 7 3 1 < +
  3 3 7 8 < T x
    4 3 6   =
1 4 7 2 8 0 8 + T

1 7 5 5 9 2 0 * <
```

*Chain discounts, using a constant multiplier with automatic re-entry of the intermediate products*

*$86.79 less 25—15—10—5% = = 47.31*

```
8 6 7 9 < < x
    7 5   =
6 5 0 9 2 5 ◊ T x
    8 5   =
5 5 3 2 8 6 2 5 ◊ T x
    9 0   =
4 9 7 9 5 7 6 2 5 0 ◊ T x
    9 5   =
4 7 3 0 5 9 7 4 3 7 5 0 ◊ T x
```

Courtesy: Olivetti Corporation of America, New York

FIG. 5–14.   A listing automatic calculator with a wide range of applications. Illustrations of the printed tape supplied by the machine are shown.

evidenced by proofing masters only of duplicated material, personal basis shortcuts for checking calculations, and proofing devices on office machines. For the most part, material to be checked falls into two categories: (1) material that requires exact comparison with the original and (2) material that necessitates general checking for correctness of intended meaning and satisfactory appearance.

When exact comparison is required, it is common for one employee to read from the original while another employee checks the material. A word-for-word comparison is made. The employee reading indicates headings, quotations, and punctuation marks, and spells difficult words. Care must be exercised by the employee checking to catch omissions, misspelled words, and incorrect syllabifications. Along with this, an examination is made to see that the general format, margins, and appearance are correct.

In checking numbers read the columns vertically. Place the original list side by side with the written list, so that the numbers are matched on the same line. This helps to eliminate possible error. The doubling of figures and using the comma division should also be practiced whenever possible. For numbers that repeat, use the expression "two times," "three times," and so forth. To illustrate:

| When the number is: | Say: | | | | |
|---|---|---|---|---|---|
| 157 | One | fifty-seven | | | |
| 2157 | Twenty-one | fifty-seven | | | |
| 2,157 | Two | one | fifty-seven | | |
| 3,845,157 | Three | eight | forty-five | one | fifty-seven |
| 341 ⎫ 341 ⎬ 341 ⎭ | Three | forty-one | | | —three times |

Material requiring general checking is carefully read, but a word-for-word comparison is not made. Frequently, general checking work is done by one employee—commonly the one who wrote the material. The meaning of the material must be clear and the general appearance satisfactory. Special attention should be given dates and amounts. In this respect, comparison with the original is recommended.

## UNIT ANALYSIS COMPARATIVE REPORTS

The summarizing of much data in a neat and concise form emphasizing comparisons describes the unit analysis comparative report which is illustrated by Figure 5–15. The data are written on specially designed forms held in place by binder rings through holes at the top of each form. At the close of each period, such as a month, the data for the current month are posted in the left-hand column of a strip and the year to date

| PERIOD JANUARY THIS YEAR | PERIOD FEBRUARY THIS YEAR | PERIOD MARCH THIS YEAR | PERIOD APRIL LAST YEAR | PERIOD APRIL THIS YEAR | OPERATING REPORT | % OF SALES | TO DATE APRIL THIS YEAR |
|---|---|---|---|---|---|---|---|
| | | | | | SALES | | |
| 60,125 | 62,411 | 63,147 | 51,675 | 57,355 | PRODUCT A | 55.2 | 243,038 |
| 51,312 | 61,387 | 62,298 | 44,375 | 55,467 | PRODUCT B | 44.8 | 230,464 |
| 111,437 | 123,798 | 125,445 | 96,050 | 112,822 | TOTAL | 100.0 | 473,502 |
| | | | | | COST OF SALES | | |
| 42,066 | 42,439 | 43,571 | 35,643 | 41,295 | PRODUCT A | 69.9 | 169,371 |
| 35,462 | 43,279 | 43,921 | 30,234 | 38,272 | PRODUCT B | 70.0 | 160,934 |
| 77,528 | 85,718 | 87,492 | 65,877 | 79,567 | TOTAL | 70.0 | 330,305 |
| | | | | | GROSS PROFIT | | |
| 18,059 | 19,972 | 19,576 | 16,032 | 16,060 | PRODUCT A | 30.1 | 73,667 |
| 15,850 | 18,108 | 18,377 | 14,141 | 17,195 | PRODUCT B | 30.0 | 69,530 |
| 33,909 | 39,080 | 37,953 | 30,173 | 33,255 | TOTAL | 30.0 | 143,197 |
| | | | | | COST OF SALES ADJUSTMENTS | | |
| 1,211 | 657 | 752 | 418 | 456 | INVENTORY ADJUSTMENTS | | 3,076 |
| 2,075 | 1,947 | 1,846 | 1,157 | 1,411 | OVER OR UNDER ABSORBED BURDEN | | 7,279 |
| 3,286 | 2,604 | 2,598 | 1,575 | 1,867 | TOTAL | 1.9 | 10,355 |
| 30,623 | 35,476 | 35,355 | 28,598 | 31,388 | GROSS PROFIT AFTER ADJ. | 28.1 | 132,842 |
| | | | | | GENERAL EXPENSES | | |
| 6,317 | 7,185 | 7,321 | 5,732 | 6,930 | ADMINISTRATIVE – SCHEDULE A | | 27,763 |
| 8,245 | 9,345 | 8,560 | 7,048 | 6,742 | SELLING – SCHEDULE B | | 32,892 |
| 3,612 | 4,762 | 5,121 | 3,848 | 4,637 | SHIPPING – SCHEDULE C | | 18,132 |
| 2,098 | 2,417 | 2,860 | 2,461 | 2,420 | BRANCH – SCHEDULE D | | 9,795 |
| 20,272 | 23,709 | 23,862 | 19,089 | 20,729 | TOTAL EXPENSES | 18.7 | 88,572 |
| 10,351 | 11,767 | 11,493 | 9,509 | 10,659 | NET PROFIT FROM OPERATIONS | 9.4 | 44,270 |
| | | | | | OTHER INCOME | | |
| 251 | 187 | 252 | 142 | 210 | INTEREST EARNED | | 900 |
| 516 | 518 | 675 | 567 | 572 | DISCOUNT ON PURCHASES | | 2,281 |
| 122 | 158 | 145 | | 112 | DIVIDENDS RECEIVED | | 537 |
| | | 250 | | | PROFIT ON SALE OF ASSETS | | 250 |
| 218 | | | | | PROFIT ON SALE OF INVESTMENTS | | 218 |
| 1,107 | 863 | 1,322 | 709 | 894 | TOTAL OTHER INCOME | .9 | 4,186 |
| | | | | | OTHER DEDUCTIONS | | |
| 376 | 112 | 87 | 123 | 75 | INTEREST PAID | | 650 |
| 678 | 458 | 567 | 482 | 420 | DISCOUNT ON SALES | | 2,123 |
| | 100 | | | | LOSS ON SALE OF ASSETS | | 100 |
| | | | | | LOSS ON SALE OF INVESTMENTS | | |
| 1,054 | 670 | 654 | 605 | 495 | TOTAL OTHER DEDUCTIONS | .6 | 2,873 |
| 53 | 193 | 668 | 104 | 399 | NET | .3 | 1,313 |
| 10,404 | 11,960 | 12,161 | 9,613 | 11,058 | NET PROFIT BEFORE TAXES | 9.7 | 45,583 |
| | | | | | TAXES | | |
| 55 | 55 | 55 | 45 | 55 | CAPITAL STOCK | | 220 |
| 145 | 152 | 159 | 127 | 121 | STATE INCOME | | 577 |
| 3,675 | 3,742 | 3,815 | 2,655 | 3,420 | FEDERAL INCOME | | 14,652 |
| 3,875 | 3,949 | 4,029 | 2,827 | 3,596 | TOTAL TAXES | 3.1 | 15,449 |
| 6,529 | 8,011 | 8,132 | 6,786 | 7, | NET PROFIT FROM ALL SOURCES | 6.6 | 30,134 |

JUST LIFT UP

*Courtesy: Royal-McBee Co., New York*

FIG. 5–15. Comparative and accumulative operating and financial information is presented in an effective arrangement.

figures in the right-hand column; the center of the strip is used for identifying information. By properly positioning the newly completed monthly strip in the binder, comparisons between figures for the current month and those of previous periods are supplied. In the illustration, for example, comparisons are expedited between (1) April this year and previous months of this year and (2) April this year and April last year. If desired, additional data can be included by adding columns to the right. The unit analysis method assists in presenting calculated data in a convenient and usable pattern, in determining trends, measuring the efficiency of the operations, and highlighting the status of different components making up the entire activity.

## PEGBOARD AND PAPER STRIPS

Pegboard accounting, also known as shingle-strip and summary-strip accounting, is another type of strip arrangement for accumulating or summarizing a large number of items with minimum time, maximum accuracy, and convenience. The equipment consists of a special board and ready-made paper strips, about 2 to 3 inches wide and 16 inches long, fastened to the board. Original data are written on the strips. These strips are held in alignment by means of holes across the top which fit into a peg strip at the top of the board. The arrangement of the paper strips is offset so that a vertical margin of each strip is exposed, thus disclosing a column of figures. Quick summaries and "recaps" can be run off. A movable horizontal bar is used to guide the eye to the proper line across the forms.

Pegboard accounting is particularly effective in making distribution analyses of various kinds, including cost, payroll, stock control, and sales, and it can be designed to serve almost every type of business. The boards are made in various sizes, ranging from approximately 20 x 18 inches to 36 x 18 inches. The advantages of the use of peg strips include the following: Copying of the data is eliminated—the original forms are used to obtain final results; accurate information can be provided; flexibility is permitted, since variations in the number and kind of distributions are possible; and the cost is economical—there is a minimum of handling, and the equipment required is simple.

## CONTROLLING OF DUPLICATING, CALCULATING, AND COMPARING

The controlling efforts over duplicating, calculating, and comparing work should be thorough and understood by all affected by them. Scheduling of work in economic lot sizes is especially important, and the necessary follow-ups to insure delivery of work when promised are likewise essential. The quality of duplicating and accuracy in calculating and comparing must be watched, for unless proper attention is directed to it, the work tends to get marginal and below satisfactory standards.

For duplicating, urgency of material is usually important, but normally a first-come, first-serve basis is satisfactory. Grouping the work and establishing its sequence for each duplicating machine gives orderliness to the duplicating efforts. Rigid controls over the issuance of papers are usually in order. The use of a requisition form showing the duplicating process preferred, the number of copies, size of paper, date needed, destination, and general comments is effective.

Likewise an accounting of how much time is spent on each duplicating, calculating, and comparing job is normally needed to exercise really

| DUPLICATING REPORT | | | | | | | |
|---|---|---|---|---|---|---|---|
| Hours and Activity Report | | | Week Ending | | | | |
| Regular jobs:<br>Special jobs:<br>Machine down time: | | | Total paid hours:<br>Time available: | | | | |
| Std. Hrs. Operation | Unit | Activity | Std. Hrs. | | | | |
| | | | Std. | All. | Taken | Diff. | |
| Stencils<br>Run copies<br>Gather and staple<br>Plastic binding | Stencil<br>Copy<br>Copy<br>Fin. unit | | .040<br>.00008<br>.00004<br>.025 | | | | |
| Material<br>20# stock | Ream | | | | | | |

FIG. 5–16. Comparative data are helpful in controlling the work of duplicating.

effective control. In the case of duplicating, a form like that illustrated in Figure 5–16 can be used. Reasonable levels of performance should be established and made known to the employee. The lack of proper work loads per employee for duplicating, calculating, and comparing work is one of the biggest sources of poor management of these services. Also, helping the employees to become cost-conscious about their work supplies a strong, positive force toward achieving adequate control. However, when corrective action is required, it should be taken immediately.

## ORGANIZING IN DUPLICATING, CALCULATING, AND COMPARING

Duplicating lends itself to a centralized organizational unit. Such an arrangement makes for better utilization of the necessary equipment and machines, encourages adequate supervision, fixes responsibility, and expedites the development and the retaining of efficient operators in duplicating work. Depending upon the individual circumstances, however, duplicating is found as a part of the correspondence organizational section, or whatever unit utilizes duplicating most. Also, in recent years, with the availability of low-cost, easy-to-operate machines, such as those using the contact process giving several copies of letters, billings, or notices that are needed in a hurry, the trend is to disperse these machines throughout the office, placing them at locations where they are used frequently and are convenient to the person needing the copies.

Calculating and comparing are normally organized on a decentralized basis because they are common to many office jobs. However, where volume of work warrants, it is satisfactory to have a centralized computing or comparing group, which is usually a part of the organization unit having the largest quantity of these types of work—probably the bookkeeping section.

Calculating requires employees with a *number sense,* that is, an ability to recognize relations that exist between numbers and to think of numbers in their broad relations. Placing this type of person in calculating work will bring the best results. Comparing is detailed, repetitive work and requires reading skill, patience, and a passion for accuracy. Proper personnel selection for comparing work will greatly strengthen the organization utilized.

## ACTUATING IN DUPLICATING, CALCULATING, AND COMPARING

The employee's desire to turn out good quality work within reasonable periods in these office services must be developed and maintained. Basic training is paramount and should include proper use of any equipment that is used. Machine instructions should be given in a step-by-step, easy-to-follow manner, and amply illustrated. Most machine manufacturers will provide training free of charge through their sales representatives. Many people have the capacity for acquiring acceptable competency, but this ability remains dormant until properly developed through training. It is erroneous and wasteful to place an employee in these services and assume that he knows how to do every aspect of the work properly.

All employees need definite work goals, but this is especially so for those in duplicating, calculating, and comparing. The nature of these types of work seems to require that a sense of accomplishment be emphasized by management. Also, the employee's desire to have the manager know what is being achieved must be satisfied. Furthermore, full utilization of employee's time should be stressed. Too little or too much work can result in a dissatisfied employee. Or expecting the work to be accomplished within practically no time at all can dull the employee's enthusiasm. Team effort is especially important because those in duplicating, calculating, and comparing usually perform several different tasks throughout the day. It is therefore desirable to maintain a congenial group.

## QUESTIONS

1. Point out the major differences between the concepts in each pair of the following:
   a) Multigraph and multilith duplicating processes.
   b) Pegboard accounting and contact duplicating process.
   c) Office composing machine and a unit analysis comparative report.
   d) Side wire stitching and saddle wire stitching.

2. As you see it, in the management of duplicating work, which is most important: planning, controlling, organizing, or actuating?

3. What are the major topics of information regarding collating and binding with which an office manager should be familiar?

4. What duplicating equipment would you recommend for each of the following?
   a) Eight copies of a chart 8½ x 11 inches.
   b) Copy of a letter.
   c) A company president's speech of 15 pages, copy to be made for each of 8.000 employees.
   d) Copy of photograph.
   e) One hundred copies of a one-page announcement.
   f) A copy of a map 8½ x 15 inches.

5. Discuss duplicating as an essential component of office systems and procedures.

6. Do you favor having duplicating work on a centralized or on a decentralized organizational arrangement? Why?

7. Discuss the office work of comparing, noting its identity, importance, and probable future as a basic office activity.

8. Explain the following terminology used in connection with adding machines:
   a) Listing and nonlisting.
   b) Key-driven and crank-driven.
   c) Full keyboard and ten-key keyboard.
   d) Manual and electric.

9. By the near-number or breakdown basis, multiply each of the following:
   a) 427 by 13.
   b) 728 by 25.
   c) 956 by 9.
   d) 6,131 by 50.

10. In your opinion, could the work of comparing in the office be considered controlling work? Explain.

11. Give a brief description identifying each of the following:
    a) Shingle-strip accounting.
    b) Horizontal addition.
    c) A number sense that a person should acquire.
    d) The reciprocal of a number.

12. Discuss the subject, "The Controlling of Duplicating, Calculating, and Comparing."

## CASE PROBLEM

### Case 5–1.   Butler Products Company

Stencil-duplicated material has been processed and used in the office of the Butler Products Company for a number of years. Last year, for example, there were duplicated 1,780 memorandums of one page each, 307 reports of six pages each, and 155 reports of eight pages each. For each memorandum, an average of nine copies was made; for the six-page reports, eight copies; and for the eight-page reports, six copies.

Current costs of the company are 25 cents each for a stencil; ink, about $20 a year; labor for typing or operating the duplicator, $2.20 per hour; paper, $1.70 for 500 sheets when purchased in quantity. It requires approximately one minute per line to prepare stencils. The memorandums average 15 lines and the reports are 20 lines to a page. It takes about 12 minutes to put the stencil on the machine, adjust it, and later remove and file it. Speed of the machine is 75 sheets a minute. For hand collating and stapling of reports, a flat rate of 10 cents per report can be used.

Since the present duplicating machine is worn and must be replaced in the near future, the office manager believes that in addition to the stencil method, both the contact and the xerography methods should also be investigated for possible adoption. With this thought in mind, he has compiled cost data as follows. For the contact method, sensitized paper, one of which is needed for each page duplicated, costs 4 cents each, depreciation on the contact machine will be $65 per year, compared to $85 per year for a new stencil machine. Material costs, in addition to sensitized paper sheets, will approximate $30 per year for the contact machine, which it is estimated will produce 200 copies an hour. This includes the work of loading the machine. For xerography, output can be estimated at 350 copies an hour, machine lease cost at $375 a month, and machine supplies at about $0.001 per duplicated sheet. For either the contact or the xerography method, work of adjusting the stencil and removing it from machine are not required.

### Problems:

1. Based on cost, which duplicating process should the office manager select? Substantiate your answer.

2. In addition to cost, what other important factors should be considered by the office manager in arriving at a decision?

3. What should be the decision of the office manager? Why?

### Case 5–2.   The Vitek Company

Upon receipt of a customer's order, it is entered in two ledgers; one is by items, the other by salesman. This is done in order to determine total weekly sales for each item and for each salesman. To illustrate, suppose an order for six hair shampoo size No. 2 and two dozen toothpaste giant size is received from the Baker

Drug Store, located in the territory of John Doe, a Vitek Company salesman. Entered in the hair shampoo size No. 2 ledger are date, saleman's name, quantity, and the amount of sales dollars. In the toothpaste giant-size item ledger are entered date, salesman's name, quantity, and sales dollars. Also in the John Doe salesman ledger are entered date, code number of the Baker Drug Store, quantity, item, and sales dollars.

The Vitek Company manufactures and distributes toilet preparations nationally. Most of the items are offered in several different sizes. The total number of products, including the various sizes of each, is 38. The company has a sales force of 54 salesmen operating out of four branches. The main office is located in Detroit. Weekly reports by each branch are sent to the main office, where they are analyzed and made up into a final company report.

## Problems:

1. Suggest an improved manual means of tabulating the sales data in order to simplify the work and reduce the chances of error.

2. Write a brief description of your proposed means, giving sufficient details to convey complete understanding of your proposed plan.

CHAPTER **6**

# FILING

When a man's knowledge is not in
order, the more of it he has the
greater will be his confusion.
                    —*Herbert Spencer*

To HELP provide information when needed, data are stored according to some arrangement so that they are readily available. In the normal course of business, reference to written information concerning plans, decisions, thoughts, contracts, obligations, drawings, research, and transactions is utilized quite frequently. To supply this needed office service requires filing, which can be defined as follows: *Filing is the placing of papers in acceptable containers according to some predetermined arrangement so that any paper, when required, can be located quickly and conveniently.* Emphasis is upon the "finding," not the "storing" aspect. Placing the information in safekeeping is important; being able to find it promptly, when wanted, is vital. One needed paper lost or mislaid can delay a dozen employees in their work.

## FILING—IMPORTANCE AND ARRANGEMENT

Each year, greater quantities of papers must be filed; and the problem of how best to handle them for quick reference, what arrangement to follow, what policies to adopt, and what equipment to utilize multiplies the need for competent office managerial action. The office is unique in that it stores many of its "products." This is a necessary part of its service. As we create more records, demand more information, and require more controls, filing has grown in importance. Every record and paper created and processed must have proper disposition. If it does not, or if we permit nonessential and excessive papers to be produced and filed, we are adding to the problem of filing. Fundamental are the facts that (1) filing is an integral part of paper work processing and (2) when searching for information, there should be as few places as possible to look, preferably only one.

The type of material handled, the nature and size of the enterprise, and the peculiarities of the particular business influence the selection of the arrangement of papers in the file. Numerous ready-made filing arrangements are offered on the market. Different manufacturers stress different features. The arrangement selected should provide for distinct divisions of the material, allow for possible expansion, and be inclusive of all the material to be handled.

There are four basic filing arrangements: (1) alphabetical, (2) numerical, (3) geographical, (4) chronological. Various modifications and combinations of these are possible and, in fact, are commonly used. For example, subject filing by an alphabetical arrangement is widely used, an alphabetical-numerical plan is often employed; and in many alphabetical files, the material in each subdivision is arranged chronologically, i.e., the latest paper always on top. Likewise, under the geographical plan it is customary to arrange the subdivisions alphabetically.

## ALPHABETICAL FILING

The alphabetical arrangement, or some modification of it, is the most widely used form of filing. It stresses the name or topic as the important item. The filing is by dictionary order. If the first letter is not sufficient for determining the proper place of the material, the second and, if necessary, the third and fourth succeeding letters are used. See Figure 6–1. For any given total of names, the probable number which will occur in each

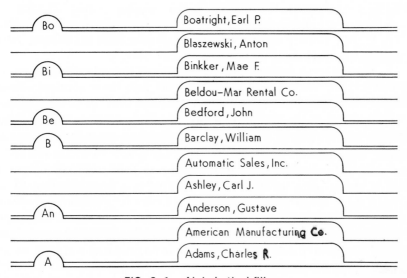

FIG. 6–1. Alphabetical filing.

subdivision of the alphabet is known. For example, names beginning with the letters *S*, *B*, *M*, and *H*, respectively, are most common; those beginning with *X*, *Q*, and *U* occur least frequently. For a given quantity of names, there are usually about three times as many names under *B* as under *A*, twenty times as many under *H* as under *I*, and ten times as many under *T* as under *U*. Information of this sort is utilized scientifically in determining filing guide subdivisions, which can be purchased as standard equipment. Sets ranging from 24 to some 2,600 subdivisions are available.

To provide for expansion, sets are available that permit the inserting of additional subdivisions to the original set. For example, a set of 300 subdivisions is converted into one of 400 subdivisions simply by adding an expansion package of 100 subdivisions. None of the original subdivisions are discarded; there is no waste.

The advantages of alphabetical filing are that direct reference is provided, a quick check is offered on misfiled material, and common names are grouped. It is sometimes considered "the natural way to file." Figure 6–2 illustrates a modern alphabetical filing arrangement for correspondence. From this illustration, the following can be observed:

1. The primary guides, or partitions segregating the material, give the chief breakdowns of the alphabet and are identified by green tabs occupying the first three positions which are shown along the top left portion of the guide.[1] These tabs are marked with letters and numbers, i.e., $A = 1$, $Abr = 2$, $Ad = 3$, $Ag = 4$, etc. The number expedites the filing work. When considering the letter *d*, it is a little difficult to recall that *d* is between *c* and *e*. In contrast, no thought is required to remember that the number 3 is between 2 and 4.

2. Individual folders containing regular correspondence are filed behind their proper primary guide and tabbed in the fifth or extreme right position: "1. Aaron, Carl"; "1. Abbott, A. M."; etc.

3. Miscellaneous folders, used for occasional and miscellaneous correspondence, are marked with red tabs in the first three positions. These folders correspond in identification and number with the primary guides and are placed in the back of each primary-guide spacing. When regular material is moved to the transfer file, the miscellaneous folders are moved also and serve as primary guides in this file.[2]

4. Auxiliary guides, tabbed in the fourth or right-center position, are used to simplify and to speed the filing by dividing primary-guide spacings according to individual needs. Auxiliary guides may include (*a*) common titles and names, such as "American," "Brown," "Smith," and "United States"; (*b*) alphabetical listings which segregate the material under the

---

[1] Tabs are located by position along the width of the guide. At the left is the first position, and moving to the right are the second, third, fourth, and fifth positions; the fifth position is at the extreme right.

[2] The transfer of filed material is discussed in Chapter 7.

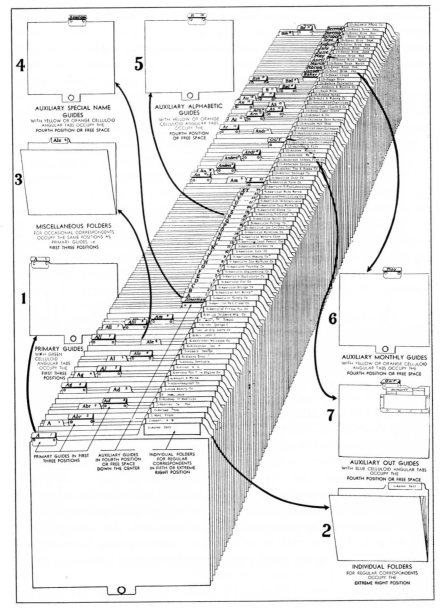

FIG. 6–2. Filing arrangement under a modern alphabetical correspondence-filing plan.

common title or name—"American Art Works" or "American Bridge Co.," for example; and (c) monthly listings which separate the material under the common title or name by months—"Baker Bros.—Jan.," "Baker Bros.—Feb.," and "Baker Bros.—March."

5. Out guides are tabbed with blue in the fourth position and are inserted in the file when any folder is taken out. Each out guide is equipped with a holder device for a charge-out card. Entries on this card show when a folder is removed, by whom, and when returned. Out guides

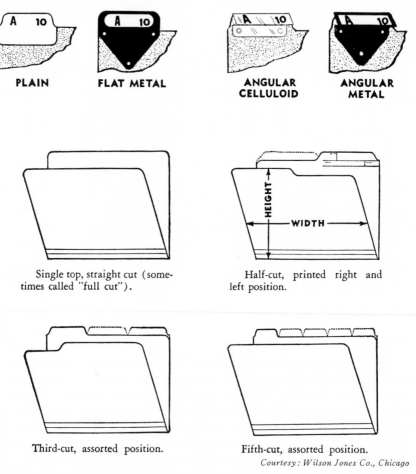

PLAIN        FLAT METAL        ANGULAR            ANGULAR
                              CELLULOID           METAL

Single top, straight cut (some-     Half-cut, printed right and
times called "full cut").           left position.

Third-cut, assorted position.       Fifth-cut, assorted position.

*Courtesy: Wilson Jones Co., Chicago*

FIG. 6–3. *Top:* Styles of tabs for file guides. *Bottom:* Offset cuts at top of file folders.

are also available in folder form, in which case spaces are ruled on the side in order to record data on removals.[3]

It will be of interest to note here that tabs for file guides are available in several types and, to expedite filing, the top of file folders are cut in a choice of various "positions." See Figure 6–3.

---

[3] The subject of charging material out is discussed on page 135.

## SUBJECT FILING

A modification of the alphabetical arrangement is subject filing, in which the arrangement of material is according to subject or descriptive feature instead of name. For example, all material pertaining to insurance is put in one main division and all material on taxes in another division. If necessary, subdivisions of each subject are made. For Insurance, the subdivisions might be Accident, Fire, and Group; and the material is usually filed alphabetically under each classification. The choice of subject heading should be inclusive and descriptive of the contents. Any logical grouping based on usage is permissible. Idiomatic terminology should be used. If employees habitually ask for the file on Employment, it is not helpful to insist upon filing such material under Applications for Employment.

Subject filing helps to indicate the main classifications for separate files in an office. To illustrate, a separate file may be used for each main subject, such as costs, orders, personal, purchases, and taxes. Subheadings are included under each main subject, for example, under Orders are Adjustments, Collections, Complaints, Correspondence, and Shipments. In addition, subject filing places all material of a common descriptive feature together, so that it can be used conveniently. Common examples of subject filing include executive files, files of material going between home office and branches, interdepartmental written material, research data, clippings, and notes.

## PHONETIC FILING

Another interesting modification of the alphabetical arrangement is phonetic filing. In many instances, a name can be spelled in different ways. For example, the name "Barnett" can also be spelled "Barnet," "Bornet," "Bornett," and so forth. Under which spelling is such a name filed or found? Poor handwriting and errors in transcribing might add further to the filing perplexity. To meet this problem, a system of file indexing based on the pronunciation or sound of the name has been developed.

Under this system, all names are coded by use of the "Soundex Code," which is:

| Code Numbers | Key Letter Equivalents |
|---|---|
| 1 | b, f, p, v |
| 2 | c, g, j, k, q, s, x, z |
| 3 | d, t |
| 4 | l |
| 5 | m, n |
| 6 | r |

The letters a, e, i, o, u and w, h, y are not coded. In addition, the following practices apply:

1. The initial letter is not coded but is used as a prefix to code a number which always has three digits.

2. The zero is used where there is no key letter equivalent.

3. Doubled key letters are coded as one, that is, *rr* as *r*.

4. A key letter and its equivalent are likewise coded as one, that is, *ck* as *c*.

To illustrate, the name "Barnett" would be coded B—653; "Barnet," B —653; and "Bornet," B—653. Thus, all names which sound alike, although spelled differently, have an identical filing location and thus can be quickly located. A phonetic filing system is a special type of alphabetic-numeric arrangement. Among the important advantages of phonetic indexing are the following: Ninety percent of all family names are grouped automatically, duplications are detected, unlimited expansion and flexibility are provided, the effect of transcribing errors is minimized, and a uniform and precise indexing method is provided.

## NUMERICAL FILING

In this filing arrangement, each item filed has a number, and location of the material is by numerical sequence. Numerical files are used for such material as bank checks, invoices, engine numbers, and papers pertaining to freight cars. However, the numerical arrangement is not confined to prenumbered material. Items such as letters, memorandums, and notices are also filed according to this plan; and in such cases, an auxiliary alphabetical card file is employed to learn the proper filing number. The system of numbers can be basically one of two types: (1) serial—to provide unlimited expansion, or (2) coded—to indicate specific types of items. An illustration of the latter type is given below:

### Divisions

| 100. *General Sales* | 200. *Production* | 300. *Research* |
|---|---|---|
| 110. Recap of orders booked | 210. Purchasing | 310. Consumer studies |
| 120. Recap of sales shipped | 220. Payroll | 320. Radio ratings |
| 130. Expenditures | 230. Budget | 330. Television surveys |
| 140. Budget | 240. Recap of items completed | 340. Readership records |
| | | 350. Product testing |

The numerical plan offers simple provisions for expansion, some degree of secrecy, ease and speed of operation, and an effective means of identification. Numbers are easy to work with; in fact, most alphabetical filing systems use numbers on the file guides, in addition to the letters, in order to expedite finding. Figure 6–4 shows the arrangement of a numerical file.

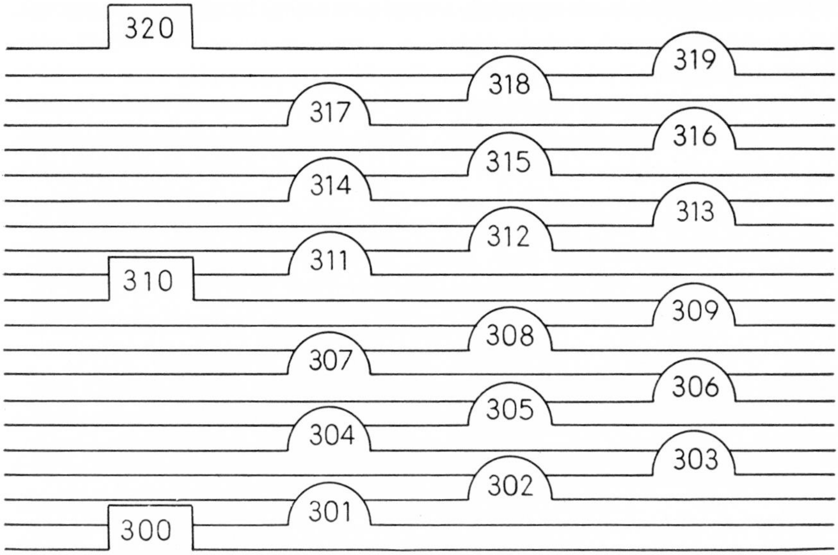

FIG. 6–4. Numerical filing.

In terminal-digit filing, a variation of regular numerical filing, numbers are used, but they are read from right to left instead of the conventional left to right. Hence, records are filed according to the last digit or, more commonly, the last two digits, then the next two or subdivision thereof. To illustrate:

| In Numerical File | In Terminal-Digit File Last-Two Number Breakdown | In Terminal-Digit File Last-Two Number Breakdown with Sub-divisions Thereof |
|---|---|---|
| 160 79 | 3 25 41 | 5 17 41 |
| 174 63 | 5 17 41 | 3 25 41 |
| 325 41 | 1 74 63 | 1 74 63 |
| 517 41 | 1 60 79 | 1 60 79 |

Why file this way? To eliminate misfiles from misreading six or more digits, as happens in regular numerical filing, and to disperse filing activity —the newest records are not placed at one end of the file, causing congested activity in that part of the file.

## GEOGRAPHICAL FILING

The main filing divisions in the geographical arrangement include states, counties, cities, branch-office territories, and salesmen's areas. Usually, the subdivisions are arranged alphabetically; for example, a sales area by cities in alphabetic order, and each city by customers' names in alphabetic order.

The geographical arrangement, sometimes called location arrangement, is easy to understand, simple and direct, and can cover the overall work division, particularly that of sales. The files are generally less unwieldy than is frequently the case with the other basic arrangements. Also, several people can work at the files simultaneously—for instance, one in the Philadelphia file for "Cupper Manufacturing Company" and the other

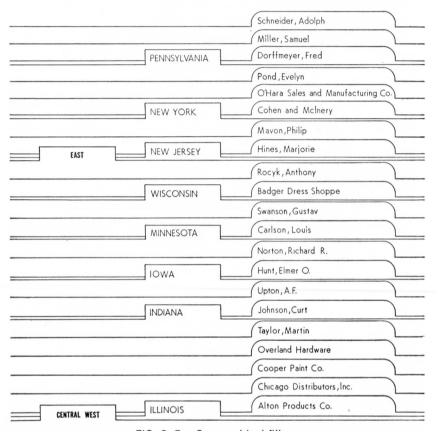

FIG. 6–5.  Geographical filing.

in the Los Angeles file for "Cizzla Sales Corporation." In addition, the geographical arrangement makes it comparatively simple to compile mailing lists by states or cities; and the segregation of material for tax, political, or mailing reasons is readily provided. Figure 6–5 shows a geographical plan of filing.

## CHRONOLOGICAL FILING

The chronological filing arrangement simply arranges material according to its time sequence. The main divisions are either months or weeks, with the subdivisions being days. Some correspondence, bills, and pending accounts payable can be handled on a chronological plan. The advantages of this plan are simplicity, ease of filing, and a convenient signal or reminder of unfinished work, which is shown by the material in the file with reference to a specific date. Figure 6–6 illustrates chronological filing.

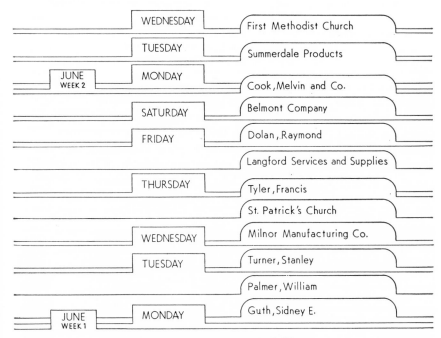

FIG. 6–6.   Chronological filing.

The "tickler file" is an adaptation of chronological filing. Future matters requiring attention are filed under due dates or the time when action should be taken. A glance at the file shows for any given period what matters are to be followed up, what ones are behind schedule, and what ones must be handled in the near future.

## FILE INDEXING

The file index furnishes the key to how the materials are arranged. For any given set of material, a choice is made from several possible indexes. In some cases, the subject is the best index; in others, the name of the customer or the point of destination might be most useful. To illustrate, the following material could be indexed in any one of the several different ways indicated:

| *Material* | *File according to:* |
| --- | --- |
| Catalogs | Date, name of company, or name of product |
| Correspondence | Date, subject, name of company, name of customer, name of seller, point of destination, or point of origin |
| Invoices | Date, name of customer, or number |
| Personnel application forms | Name of applicant, or type of work (subject) |
| Purchase orders | Date, name of vendor, name of product, or number |
| Tax reports | Date, subject, or name of taxing body |

Cross indexing is used when more than one subject is covered by the material or when several indicators are helpful in finding it. A report dealing with the subjects of market expansion and finances could be filed under the subject of markets, sales, future sales, finances, or costs. Cross indexes provide information as to where to place and to find the report; however, numerous cross references should be avoided in order to simplify the work as much as possible. It is best to have these indexes on reference cards which can be maintained in a separate file. To find material on wages, the index card might read:

| | |
| --- | --- |
| Wages | *See also* Compensation |
| | Fringe Benefits |
| | Job Evaluation |
| | Salary |

This means that material on Wages may be found under all five terms. In the opinion of some, when an alphabetical arrangement is used, the cross-reference index should be by number or code. In contrast, when the numerical arrangement is followed, the cross index should be alphabetical.

Essential in most offices is a *basic classification index* which is a categorical grouping of subjects with appropriate detailed subheadings. In addition, *a relative index* is helpful since it shows, in a dictionary type listing, all possible words and combinations by which the material may be requested. All filing indexes should be kept current by making new entries for additional classifications as they occur. Main new sources will be key words, new terminology, or any other means by which material may be requested.

## FILING PROCEDURE

For effective filing, a definite, well-planned filing procedure should be followed. The chief steps in such a procedure include the following:

1. *Checking release for filing.* Before any material is prepared for filing, it must first be checked to be sure it is released for filing. Material which is still being processed or referred to, or which, because of policy, is not retained by the company, should, of course, not be placed in the files.

2. *Reading and marking for filing.* Reading is done to determine the proper filing classification. A marking to indicate this classification can be shown by underscoring or circling a word or two on the paper or by stamping or writing the proper file data in the upper right corner. A colored pencil usually works very satisfactorily, as the contrast aids future reference. If there is a possibility of filing under several headings, it is helpful to consult the cross-reference index to insure use of the best classification for the material.

3. *Sorting.* To expedite filing, the material should be sorted by mark showing the filing classification. Sorting can be performed entirely manually or with the use of a sorting device. In the former, the material is divided into neat piles on a table or desk, each pile being of a different classification. When this method is followed, it is best to sort all material according to major divisions, then each major division by subdivisions, and finally each subdivision as required. Figure 6–7 shows sorting devices

*Courtesy: Erie Railroad, Cleveland*

FIG. 6–7. Sorting waybills in a large office. Approximately three million waybills per year are sorted in this office.

being used in a large office. The device consists of dividers properly indexed and hinged, at intervals of about ¼ inch up to 1 inch, to a common base section. Thus, a series of pockets is formed, and each item of the material to be sorted is dropped into the proper pocket. Different sizes are available, ranging from around 30 up to as many as 2,000 divisions or pockets.

4. *Filing material.* Each piece is filed under the proper classification, with the newest addition always on top or at the front of the contents in its respective folder. This actually amounts to dropping the material into the file at the right place.

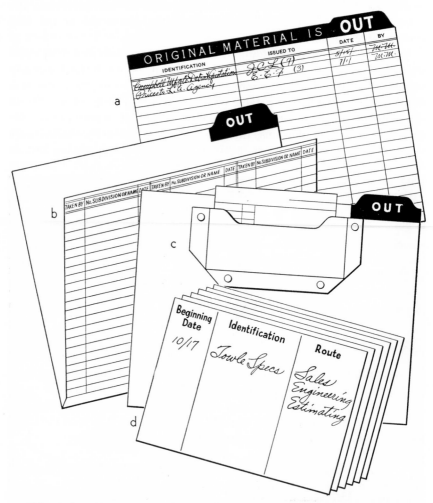

FIG. 6–8.   Media used in controlling charge-outs from filed material: (a) substitution card, (b) out folder, (c) out guide, and (d) multiple charge-out form.

5. *Charging material out.* A definite manner for handling the removal of papers from the file is necessary in order to know where items are, in the event that several people want the papers at the same time, and also to minimize indiscriminate removals from the files. Records of charged-out materials can be handled in any one of four ways as illustrated by Figure 6–8: (*a*) by substitution card, (*b*) by out folder, (*c*) by out guide, or (*d*) by multiple charge-out form.

When the removed material is a single card or piece of paper, its place in the file can be occupied by a substitution card showing the name of the person to whom the material is issued, along with the date and the initials of the file clerk issuing the material. Upon return of the material, the entries on the substitution card are lined out, and the card is reused. Out folders are ordinary file folders with one side printed for the recording of data concerning removals from that folder. The out guide is a pressboard guide with tab printed "Out" and a pocket or device to hold a single charge-out slip. It replaces a folder taken from the file and serves both as a record and as a marker for the borrowed material. When the withdrawn material is to be transferred from one user to another, a multiple charge-out form is used. As shown in Figure 6–8 the date, identification, and route of material are written on the multiple forms. One copy of this form is attached to the substitution card, out folder, or out guide. A second copy is filed in a tickler file for follow-up. Other copies are attached to the material so that, as each individual or department using the material finishes with it, a line is drawn through the name or department on the route list; the top copy is returned to the filing department; and the remaining copies and material are forwarded to the next name on the route list. The returned copy received by the filing department is attached to the tickler file copy; thus, there is a record of who has the material, without clearance of the filed material each time through the filing department.

## FILING PRACTICES

Certain filing practices have been found helpful, and adherence to them will probably bring best results. However, in certain individual cases, slight deviations might work out advantageously, depending upon the circumstances. A complete list of these filing practices is beyond the scope of this book, but the more important ones include the following:

1. Use a sufficient number of guides to help place and find the material quickly. This usually means a guide for each inch of filing.
2. File material *behind* the guides.
3. Use colored tabs and labels to increase identification.
4. Provide, with reference to correspondence files, individual folders

when five or more papers have accumulated. Crowded miscellaneous folders usually show need for more breakdowns of the alphabet.

5. Arrange material in folders so that the latest is at the front.

6. File each name according to (*a*) surname, (*b*) given name or initial, (*c*) middle name or initial, and (*d*) title, if important to retain.

> Alexander, Charles D. (Dr.)

7. File "nothing before something."

> Carter
> Carter, George
> Carter, George L.

8. File alphabetical material in exact sequence of letters, *A* through *Z*, to the last letter of the last word.

> M & A Stores, Inc.
> Maag, Robert C.
> MacArthur, Thomas P.
> Mack, Henry
> MacTavish, Sam W.
> Maleski, Franck C.
> McGuire, William F.
> Mead-Carters Co.

9. Treat compound words as one word.

> Cohen, Julius I.
> Co-operative Sales
> Co-workers Order of Bart
> Cutter, Frederick J.

10. Spell out abbreviated names.

> Safety Tool and Tire Company
> Saint Louis Poultry and Egg Company
> Saint Paul Club
> Salk, Meyer L.
> Street, Theodore P.

11. Spell out numerals and abbreviations.

> First National Bank
> Three Thirty-Three Lake Building
> Young Women's Christian Association

12. When names are identical, file by city; then state; and if necessary, by street address in city.

> Carson, John M.
>   Bangor, Maine
> Carson, John M.
>   Springfield, Mass.

> Carson, John M.
> 3719 Lyndale Road
> Springfield, Ohio
> Carson, John M.
> 5127 Western Street
> Springfield, Ohio

13. To save time with alphabetic material, sort by first segregating into four groups, such as A–F, G–L, M–R, and S–Z; then, sort each group according to the first letter. For numeric material, first sort 0–2, 3–5, and 6–9; then sort each group by the first digit.

14. Transfer material to inactive file regularly and at stated intervals.[4]

## FILING CABINETS

Filing cabinets are available in many different sizes and types, but those for cards—3 x 5 inch or 5 x 8 inch—letter, and legal-size papers are most popular. The equipment is available in sizes from one to six drawers. The one- and two-drawer models are used on a desk or table; the three-drawer is desk height and is usually used beside a desk, providing ready accessibility to papers frequently used. Four-drawer models are used for counter purposes. The five- and six-drawer files provide extra filing capacities for the floor space occupied. A standard file drawer holds about 5,000 sheets of paper, 300 file folders, and 26 file guides.

The mechanical details of files differ with the manufacturers. Most files feature a ball-bearing, full progressive sidearm suspension which provides smooth rolling action of the drawer and permits easy opening and closing. A sliding, adjustable device known as a "follower" holds the papers upright in the drawer. It can be pulled up tight and snapped or locked in position; a slight force releases the device and permits it to be moved to another position. In some models the material is placed in hanging or suspending folders which transfer the weight from the drawer bottom to two top rails on either side, running the length of the drawer. Suspended folders provide fingertip ease of filing and the folders cannot slump. The equipment is available with or without locks, insulated for fire protection, and in several colors and finishes to harmonize with the color scheme of the office.

## SIDE-FILING OR LATERAL CABINETS

Proponents of this type of filing cabinet stress the ease of getting to all filed material, the fast handling of filing work—25 percent more than that with other types, and savings in floor space—about 50 percent compared

---

[4] Transfer of filed material is discussed in the following chapter on records retention.

with a regular four-drawer based on filing inches per square foot of floor area. Lateral filing cabinets can be divided into four groups: (1) drawer, (2) box, (3) shelf type, and (4) suspension. The first is similar to a regular end-opening filing cabinet, but in the side-file the drawer opens from the side. These units can be equipped to handle either regular or suspension folders. All material can be reached easily. The second, or box, consists of top and side open-edged metal boxes or trays hooked onto the rails of a freestanding metal frame, which is assembled without nuts, bolts, or screws. The frame is tailored to fit individual needs and the

*Courtesy: Tab Products Co., San Francisco*

FIG. 6–9.  Detail of the cutaway box permitting working folder corners. The box type is for records not requiring closed storage.

boxes, into which the material is placed, hang at a slight angle, creating a stair-step effect to expedite the filing work. Top- or side-tab folders can be used. Figure 6–9 shows the detail of this type filing. The third, or shelf type, features compartments of filed material exposed for ready accessibility, as shown by Figure 6–10. Folders can be slid out instead of lifted out, separators within compartments can be supplied if desired, and open file doors serve as work surfaces. In the fourth, or suspension, filed material is contained in special folders suspended from a pair of rods. The folders, provided with labels at front edge, are available in many different sizes to accommodate different sizes and weights to be filed. Figure 6–11 shows an efficient filing of computer tabulating sheets and supplies and a detail of the file.

Within this category of side filing, modification of the shelf and the suspension types give rise to the so-called open-shelf type of filing

*Courtesy: Tab Products Co., San Francisco*

FIG. 6–10.   Shelf-type steel filing cabinets with retractable doors.

FIG. 6–11.   (Above) Suspension filing used for computer tab forms. (Right) Detail of file construction.

*Courtesy: Robert P. Gillette Co., Inc., Columbia, S.C.*

equipment. This has won wide approval for many odd-sized items such as magnetic reels, paper tapes, artwork, photographs, and line drawings. The units are adjustable with regard to their own size as well as to the space for filed materials, will therefore handle both large and small sizes of materials, and are priced satisfactorily.

## RECIPROCATING FILES

The employee can either go to the work, or the work can be brought to the employee. This latter situation is stressed in reciprocating file equipment. By its use the employee can remain seated with necessary machines and tools located within easy reach, and the file can be moved forward and backward as required. Use of this type of file (1) reduces employee fatigue, (2) eliminates travel time, (3) minimizes waiting time at files, and (4) allows full supervision, since all equipment is at desk-level height and under full view of the supervisor.

## ROTARY FILES

This name applies to filing cabinets mounted on a platform which revolves or to filing cabinets in which the filed material is held to the periphery of a wheel which revolves, thus affording a ready and quick locating means at writing height. In the former type, the arrangement is designed to expedite work methods. It frequently makes one large set of records quickly available to several employees with work stations around the edge of the common file. It can be thought of as a reciprocating file with a circular pattern. (See top view of Figure 6–12.) In the second type, posting is convenient without removal of the filed material. This wheel-type unit provides speedy handling—large motion savings up to 75 percent have been estimated—and compactness. The range of sizes is from small units about the size of a telephone to large units approximately 36 inches high. The capacity varies, of course, with the size of the wheel; for example, a unit having a 21-inch-diameter wheel, handling 5 x 8-inch cards, has a capacity of 6,000 cards. In most cases the filed cards have punched openings at bottom to provide a gripping effect to a retaining rod, but units are available which hold nonpunched cards, folders, photographs, and drawings. Both single- and multiwheel units are offered, as well as a special mechanism for stabilizing the rotation. A four-unit model is shown by bottom view of Figure 6–12.

## MOTORIZED CARD FILES

When the work requires access to a large number of filed cards, a motorized card file may be useful. It is electrically operated and brings in

*Courtesy: Acme Visible Records, Inc., Crozet, Va.*

FIG. 6–12. (*Top*) Six clerks have immediate access to 60,000 customer account records in this rotary file. (*Bottom*) A multiwheel unit of rotary file equipment.

*Courtesy: Wheeldex and Simpla Products, Inc., White Plains, N.Y.*

a few seconds any desired tray of cards in the unit at convenient writing height to a seated operator. The cards are filed vertically, and the trays are removable. Units are available in various card sizes and capacities. Savings in time and effort result from the use of motorized card files.

*Courtesy: Remington Rand, Inc., New York*

FIG. 6–13.  A motorized card file providing an ideal work station with availability to a large number of cards.

Demanding specifications in respect to space limitations, floor layout, and operational problems can be met. A motorized card file unit is shown in Figure 6–13.

## VISIBLE FILES—CARDS HORIZONTAL

The name "visible file" reveals its outstanding feature, namely, providing for the user, at a glance, visible information in the file. Probably the most common and the one we shall discuss first is the type with the cards filed horizontally; however, it is not the only style as we shall later see. The cards are filed horizontally in a shallow slide or tray in such a manner that the bottom margin of each card is exposed, providing for quick visibility. In this margin are pertinent data concerning the information on the major area of the card. Varying widths of margin exposure may be used; standard equipment provides $\frac{3}{16}$-inch to $\frac{5}{16}$-inch margin visibility. Card capacity per tray depends upon the card size and the margin exposure used, but 80 cards per tray is a good average figure. Units are available with different numbers of trays. Each card is fastened in such a way that it can be raised and flipped by pivoting about the top edge. Thus, the complete information on any card can be viewed in full, or additional data can be written on the card with the tray used as an armrest.

In some equipment, the top edge of the card is fastened directly onto the tray; while in other equipment, "pockets" made of strong kraft paper are fastened directly onto the tray and the card is held in place by inserting the bottom edge into a flap made by a U-shaped plastic strip at the bottom of the pocket. The top of the card is held by inserting the corners into slots precut in the pocket.

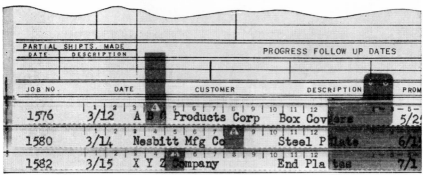

Courtesy: Remington Rand, Inc., New York

FIG. 6–14. An effective follow-up signaling system. On the top card, the signal over the 4 indicates April, the month in which follow-up should be made. The signal at the right of the card at the 3 indicates the day of the month on which the follow-up is due.

Effective signaling to denote certain information on the card is one of the outstanding features of visible filing equipment using cards filed horizontally. By sliding different-colored plastic markers along the visible margins, definite dates or quantities, which are signals for specific actions, are brought out in bold relief. By such signals, a whole tray of cards can be scanned and the items requiring immediate attention quickly spotted. Figure 6–14 illustrates a signaling system for accurate follow-up.

Both manual and electrical visible file units are available. The electric unit eliminates stooping, reaching, pulling out trays, writing at inconvenient levels, and pushing back trays. It excludes many causes of operator fatigue, raises productivity, and saves floor space. One popular unit holds 60 trays, counterbalanced in two equal banks which travel up and down when the unit is actuated. Figure 6–15 shows illustrations of the visible file operated manually and also the unit operated electrically.

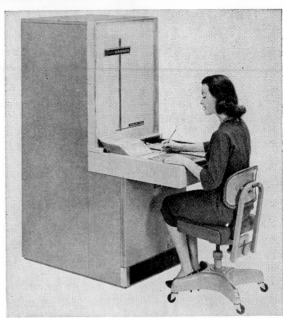

*Courtesy: Remington Rand, Inc., New York*

FIG. 6–15.   Visible file equipment where cards are filed horizontally. On the left is the manually operated unit with tray withdrawn and ready for posting. On the right is the electrically operated unit. The operator presses one of several bars in front of her, causing the desired tray to come out of the unit at writing height in a matter of seconds.

Visible card file equipment is also in book form. Approximately 2,000 cards can be kept in one binder. The book form affords portability and a posting surface always at desk height. Binders are made to lie perfectly flat when open, to lock against any possible accidental shifting of record sequence, and to lift and guide sheets into proper position when the binder is closed.

## VISIBLE FILES—CARDS VERTICALLY

Another type of visible file is that designed for use where cards are filed vertically. With this style, common card sizes are from about 3 to 20 inches in width and 5 to 12 inches in height. They are similar in appearance to the printed forms for machine- and hand-posting work. Two types will be discussed here: (1) the magnetic card and (2) the shingled, clipped-corner card.

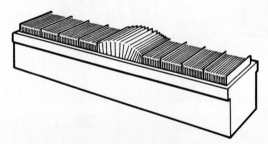

FIG. 6–16.   Side view of magnetic-card visible file. A batch of cards can be fanned out to permit visibility and ease of finding card information.

In the magnetic-card visible file, the records are instantly visible and accessible. They are not fastened in any way to the tray, making rearrangement, removal, or addition of cards to the file a very simple task. Very thin metal strips are included in the cards during manufacture. The unit is powered by magnetic force and operates on the basis of the repellent force of magnets separating one card from the next at any point of reference. A batch of 15 to 20 cards can be fanned out quickly with just a touch of the fingertips, and information on these cards can be read very easily. Figure 6–16 illustrates this type file.

In the shingled clipped-corner card file, one or both of the upper corners of the card are cut away in order to provide diagonal indexing margins; in addition, the horizontal and one of the vertical margins of the card are used for indexing. Cards are placed in the file in an offset arrangement, so that the top, diagonal, and side margins of the card are exposed or visible. The card is held in position by means of a notched arrangement at the bottom of the card which fits into a receiving device at the bottom of the file, and the design is such that cards can easily be inserted or removed. Both sides of the card can be used, and signaling devices similar to those already discussed can be employed. Figure 6–17 shows the arrangement of cards in the file. With this equipment, the finding time is minimized, thumbing through cards is eliminated, and exceedingly quick scanning over large numbers of cards is possible—for example, nearly 7,000 cards, 10 x 5 inches in size, can be accommodated in one file unit.

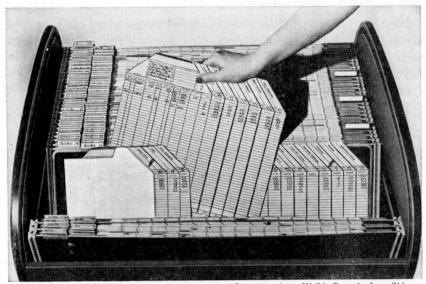

*Courtesy: Acme Visible Records, Inc., Chicago*

FIG. 6–17. The arrangement of cards in a file. Groups of cards can be removed and replaced just as easily as one card. This is commonly called an open tub file.

## FILED STRIPS

Another type of file is the so-called filed strips used when quick reference to records containing a small quantity of data is needed. It is useful for maintaining lists which undergo changes, such as names and addresses of customers, prices, rates, bin locations, directories, reservations, hospital indexes, telephone and switchboard data, and routings.

Either of two methods can be followed. The first consists of (1) typing or otherwise writing the data on scored and special sheet material, which is made of resilient veneer covered on both sides with paper; (2) separating the sections by breaking along the scored line; and (3) placing the strips in a frame by bending them slightly and snapping the ends under the side channels of the frame. The second method consists of writing the data on small die-cut cards which snap or button on a holding frame. This places the cards in an offset arrangement with the upper margin of the card plainly visible. With either method, the frames can be suspended on desk stands, wall brackets, and rotaries. Figure 6–18 shows illustrations of this equipment. To indicate special conditions applying to a particular name, a signaling device of a shape and color code is either slid over, or attached to, a record. Different-colored strips and cards are also available and can be used for signaling purposes, if desired.

*Courtesy: Remington Rand, Inc., New York*

FIG. 6–18. Two types of visible reference record equipment used where the amount of data is small and where fast, frequent reference is required.

## THE CONTROLLING OF FILING

Standards for filing equipment, supplies, handling, and indexing should be developed and followed. With these as a guide, along with periodic follow-ups, the manager can determine whether standards are being followed and whether the level of filing work is satisfactory. Spot checks for accuracy are advisable. For this purpose a committee can be used in order to generate more interest in filing and enhance an awareness of needed improvements. Standards will vary among different companies due to the type of records and the working conditions. However, to give an idea of what can be done, the following expectancies are shown, based on data from a number of companies:

| Task | Units per Hour |
|---|---|
| Sorting letters and filing alphabetically..................180 | |
| Filing 5 x 8-inch cards in an alphabetical vertical file.......315 | |
| Locating and pulling letters from an alphabetical file.......110 | |
| Filing vouchers numerically...........................700 | |
| Marking one-page letters for filing....................220 | |

The existence of duplicate files is a major problem. Adequate controls to minimize the following causes must be enforced: (1) misunderstanding and failure to specify where office files will be located and maintained, (2) lack of determining the number of copies to be filed by particular records or documents, and (3) failure to curb a tendency by management members to create and keep papers for every contingency. It helps to place files in locations convenient to those frequently using them in order to reduce the number of duplicate files.

Cost can be used in file controlling, but its use is not extensive. Some overall cost constraints usually are helpful and should be established. Of the total cost of filing, equipment represents about 12–14 percent, floor space about 10–12 percent, and labor about 70–75 percent. The conclusion is inescapable. Filing labor is vital. Filing requires sizable expenditures. The cost of filing using a four-drawer correspondence file is about $225 per year. Thirty files therefore mean $6,750 annual cost. Substantiating data for one file cabinet per year follow:

| | |
|---|---|
| Rent for 5½ sq.ft. per cabinet and aisle at $2.00 per sq.ft.......| $ 11.00 |
| Depreciation on cabinet................................... | 7.00 |
| Transfer cases........................................... | 8.00 |
| Labor................................................... | 165.00 |
| File guides and folders.................................... | 10.00 |
| Overhead and supervision................................. | 18.00 |
| Miscellaneous........................................... | 4.00 |
| Total............................................... | $223.00 |

Cost data to shed light on the most suitable equipment should be sought. Surplus equipment can be transferred from one area to another, and to control purchases a careful review of all requests for additional equipment should be adopted.

## ORGANIZING AND FILING

From the viewpoint of organizing, filing commonly is on a decentralized basis, which provides accessibility for those needing the files, flexibility in arrangement, and reasonably satisfactory service. However, too frequently there is no one person with fixed responsibility for the overall planning and coordinating of filing activities. One person in charge of all filing helps promote needed study and improvements in filing. Perhaps an arrangement centralized from the viewpoint of managerial operation and decentralized as to the physical location of files is superior. With centralized management authority, the best of filing knowledge and practices from the overall company viewpoint can be put into use. However, the exact organizational plan depends upon individual requirements and understanding them. Filing needs differ. The type of material, the work habits of the employees using the files, the normal filing usage, the flow of work, frequency of records, and information required are several of the more influential considerations.

## FILING AND ACTUATING

Better placement of personnel for filing work is needed. In too many instances, the attitude prevails that the untrained office employee who cannot be fitted in elsewhere because of lack of some office skill should be given filing work. Entirely overlooked is the fundamental truth that filing personnel should possess certain attributes, including a sense of orderliness, accuracy, manual dexterity, quick reading comprehension, and a liking for detail.

Emphasize a realistic approach consisting of these four facets. First, with the assistance of the filing personnel, secure suitable filing equipment and adopt practices to fit the needs of the enterprise. Second, establish what can reasonably be expected from the filing personnel. For example, are all requests clear and complete? Frequently, the file clerk is expected to have an ability to find a piece of paper even though she has never seen it and does not know what it was about, who it was from, or when it was written. Third, make sincere efforts to upgrade filing. All key and office personnel should be made aware of the importance of filing and of the helpful contributions of those performing this work. Fourth, adjust wages of the filing personnel. Of the total cost for filing, most is for labor, and filing can never be more efficient than the people doing the filing.

## QUESTIONS

1. Under what general conditions would you recommend the use of numerical filing? Give reasons for your answer.
2. Name four different types of file equipment; and of this group, discuss the one that interests you the most.
3. Discuss the subject of indexing as an important part of filing.
4. For each of the following filing troubles, suggest a feasible solution:
    *a*) Correspondence papers piled up in miscellaneous folders.
    *b*) Necessity of fingering many folders before finding the right one.
    *c*) Need to search through many papers in a folder to find the one wanted of a certain date.
    *d*) St. Louis correspondence may be found under "St. Louis," "Saint Louis," or "Missouri."

*e*) File drawers jammed tight with material.

*f*) Too many files in which a needed paper might be found.

5. According to the "Soundex Code" determine the code for each of the following names; (*a*) Bohlin, (*b*) Bowling, (*c*) Bowlin, and (*d*) Bowlinn. What conclusion do you draw from your answers?

6. Discuss eight filing practices that you feel are of major significance.

7. Identify each of the following, and explain how it is used:

*a*) Subject filing.

*b*) Out guide for use in charging out filed material.

*c*) Terminal-digit file.

*d*) Primary file guide.

*e*) Tickler file.

8. Discuss the cost of filing. Do you feel that cost is an adequate means of controlling filing work? Why?

9. Identify and discuss application of the suspension type, open-shelf type of side filing.

10. Office manager Arvid Svenson is reasonably certain that present difficulties in his filing department are related to personnel. In general, what actions do you feel Mr. Svenson should take to help remedy the present situation?

11. Explain Figure 6–14 in your own words, using an application of this type filing to illustrate your answer.

12. Discuss the subject, "Controlling Filing Work."

## CASE PROBLEMS

### Case 6–1.  Kedzie Company

The central filing department was operating with a limited number of employees due to vacations. Normally the month of August is a slack period but this August the demands upon filing were greater than expected. Sizing up the situation, Hilda Snell, the supervisor of filing, believed it necessary to switch assignments of two file clerks, Betsy Rice and Jenny Crawford, who were shifted to other filing work than that of their normal jobs. Both Betsy and Jenny disliked the change and complained to their group leader who carried the message to Hilda Snell, who said, "We're in a jam and the company has a perfect right to determine work assignments. The real trouble is they don't want to work. Tell them the switch stands."

The group leader believed it best not to relay this message so did nothing. About an hour later, both Betsy and Jenny said they were ill and left. Two days later each received a registered letter from the company telling them they were suspended for two weeks. The following day each returned to work and presented letters from their medical doctors. The letter of Betsy read: "This is to advise that Betsy Rice has a history of nervous indigestion spells which make her extremely ill and unfit for work during such periods." The other letter stated, "Jenny Crawford periodically suffers sinus discomfort and may find it necessary to stop work during such attacks." The group leader stated she was never aware of their medical problems. Betsy replied, "I became so nervous about the new work I didn't know what

I was doing. And neither Miss Snell nor you would speak with me. I felt miserable and could feel one of my attacks coming on."

## Problems:

1. Do you feel the two weeks suspension is proper? Why?
2. What is the difficulty in this case?
3. What action do you recommend to avoid a reoccurrence of the above difficulty. Elaborate on your answer.

### Case 6–2.  Hennings Construction Company

Custom-built houses in the $27,500–$30,000 price range are constructed by the Hennings Construction Company, which maintains a main office, two construction offices, and an on-the-site sales office. The two construction offices are about 35 miles apart, and the main office is approximately 20 miles from the sales office or either of the construction offices.

The sales office and the construction offices require immediate information on costs, delivery of materials, and dates subcontractors performed work on the houses, and telephone the main office for this type of information. Unfortunately, the desired data are not always available, primarily because the three bookkeepers in the main office are two to four months behind in their work, and each bookkeeper keeps all the pertinent information in her desk drawer until she has posted the cash receipts and the payments to the subtrades, or put the sales through the books.

When a call is received from the sales department or from the construction department, the bookkeepers usually cannot get the information requested until the following day—or in some cases, not for several days. This is because, to find the data requested, it is frequently necessary to search through many papers in the desk drawer and six wooden filing cabinets along the wall of the office. Completed records are placed in these filing cabinets. All information pertaining to purchases, for example, is filed alphabetically, no attention being given to date purchases were made.

Under the present state of affairs, canceled checks and monthly bank statements are not reconciled for periods of two to three months. This work is handled by the chief bookkeeper, Betty Dougherty, who guards the canceled check work and permits no one else to perform this work. Some difficulty is experienced in getting the checks written for accounts payable. None of the bookkeepers want to do this check writing because it takes time from their bookkeeping work.

The situation became so bad that Carl Hennings, president of the company, called in Professor Franklin Swope from a nearby university to review the situation and make recommendations regarding what corrective action to take. Professor Swope studied the entire operations and at the end of two days discovered that:

1. The company managers do not believe in overtime work.
2. Office morale is low.
3. Any change to improve the office operation will be welcomed by Carl Hennings.

4. One key area for improvement is to get the processed papers into the files in accordance with an arrangement that will expedite usage of the filed material.

5. Carl Hennings is thinking of firing the entire office force.

6. Carl Hennings has no objections to the company's having two checking accounts—one for general payables, the other for payroll.

## Problems:

1. What pertinent recommendations do you feel Professor Swope should make to Mr. Hennings? Be specific.

2. What contributions do you believe improved filing management practices and procedures can contribute to this company? Why?

3. What difficulties do you anticipate in implementing the recommendations you feel Professor Swope should make? How would you overcome these difficulties?

CHAPTER 7

# RECORDS RETENTION

The truth is, one's vocation is never some far-off possibility. It is always the simple round of duties which the passing hours bring.
— *John W. Dulles*

THE CREATING and filing of a large volume of records and papers establishes a need for the disposition of all files as soon as they no longer serve any useful purpose. Unless periodic culling of files takes place, there is a staggering amount of file space taken up by routine papers such as outdated correspondence, acknowledgements, inventory records, first drafts of reports, and memoranda. Their presence in the file clutter up the entire contents and make it more difficult to locate important and useful papers as the demand for them arises. You cannot file and forget.

All records go through three different stages: (1) active use—quick access is important, (2) storage—for possible use, and (3) elimination— no longer of use. Recognition of these three basic steps, and of the needless expense incurred by not properly managing this life cycle of all records, suggests actions designed to keep worthless materials out of files, periodically review filed materials to eliminate what is no longer necessary, store certain records in a storage area for possible future use, and preserve only those having permanent value to the enterprise. This is the essential makeup of records retention.

## MEANING OF RECORDS RETENTION

*Records retention deals with the disposition of records and concerns storing those that must be retained and destroying those that are or become worthless.* Records retention is an essential part of records management and must be coordinated with that of other office management activities, so that the necessary paper work is done at lowest cost and yet provides maximum service. The activities of a sound records retention program include provisions to

1. Establish a tight schedule of retention periods for every type of record and all its copies.

2. Remove from active files all materials that should be retained temporarily but are not needed for current operations, employing well-timed and orderly procedures for this work.

3. Destroy obsolete records.

4. Establish and maintain a convenient, safe, and low-cost area for record storage and index the exact location of each type of record.

5. Take charge of all microfilming of records to insure that only necessary copies are made.

6. Show facts on volume and cost of records management and, if necessary, revise activities for greater effectiveness and service.

7. Participate in purchasing decisions for new filing equipment and supplies.

## ADVANTAGES OF RECORDS-RETENTION PROGRAM

Such a program can be quite extensive. It requires good management, foresight, judgment, and especially a steadfastness of purpose. The rewards, however, are high. Better filing efficiency is gained since inactive material is removed, thus reducing finding time. Space savings are also achieved—throwing out records that have become useless means less space is needed. Also, storing useful but inactive records in an inexpensive

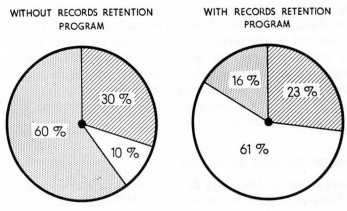

| WITHOUT RECORDS RETENTION PROGRAM | WITH RECORDS RETENTION PROGRAM |
|---|---|
| 30 percent retained in active files | 23 percent retained in active files |
| 60 percent retained in inactive files | 16 percent retained in inactive files |
| 10 percent destroyed | 61 percent destroyed |

FIG. 7–1. Typical disposition of records by companies without and those with records-retention programs.

storage area means dollar savings. And avoidance from accidental or premature destruction of records is assured. Furthermore, the retained records are better protected and safeguarded. Equipment designed especially for storage can be utilized, and the records are not subject to possible mutilation as a result of frequent handling.

Typically about 58 percent of all filed material is eliminated, 16 percent placed in records storage, and the balance, 26 percent, remains in the office area as active material. Think of it. Only one paper in four remains in the office files. The savings in finding time and space are tremendous. The National Records Management Council, Inc., a nonprofit organization, estimates only 5 percent of all records filed are ever referred to after a year and 5 percent of the references made deal with records over five years old. A large public utility reported to be spending nearly $24 million to maintain some 200,000 filing cabinets, adopted a records retention program and trimmed this cost to $17 million and with better service and efficiency. The gains by several other companies are shown by Figure 7–1.

## STEPS IN RECORDS-RETENTION PROGRAM

The objective of a records-retention program is to retain only needed records only as long as they are needed. To this end the program provides a smooth flow of records from the office to storage and eventually to destruction. Such a program requires four steps, made up of these actions: (1) take inventory of records, (2) determine record retention periods, (3) provide effective storage facilities, and (4) transfer the records. These steps are not difficult, but they must be carried out faithfully and carefully to insure success of the program.

## TAKE INVENTORY OF RECORDS

Each company should strive to develop its own records retention based on an analysis of the actual use made of its own records. To copy what another company has decided frequently results in serious shortcomings. The analysis might begin with a cursory review of the entire enterprise to obtain background and understanding of the current work and to spot what records are used and what ones are filed for satisfactory operation. Following this, a survey is in order to determine (1) what is filed; (2) how much is filed—its size and quantity; (3) where it is filed—including the copies, if any; (4) how often it was used during specific preceding periods; (5) when, if ever, it is permanently removed from file; and (6) what is done with permanently removed material. In some instances, this inventory work is expedited by classifying the material by type or by department. Information applicable to several departments can be studied as a group, thus relating the types of information common to the several units. Usually a simple form is used upon which to record the data.

From the survey data, the value of each record is weighed. Questions decided are: Should this record be filed at all? How long should this record remain in the file? Is it advisable to retain this record in storage? Particular attention is paid to records presently having long-term retention. Experience shows that many retention times can be cut measurably below the periods formerly believed necessary.

## DETERMINE RECORD-RETENTION PERIODS

Most offices are confronted with the problem of how long to retain active and inactive file material. The answer lies in knowing what to save and how to store it. This, in turn, depends primarily upon the usefulness of the material to managers, and the legal requirements. The period of retention differs among companies, but there is a tendency toward the development of standard practices.

Group decision making is advisable to determine what papers to retain and for how long a period. Usually, the controller, the legal counsel, the tax counsel, and the manager of records retention should be included in this group; they can decide basic issues essential to the program. For the most part, this group sets forth policy instructions on which operating decisions can be based by the manager of records retention.

Papers that are essential to the company's security should be kept. Proof of assets and liabilities is important. Papers giving proof of ownership, property, inventories, machinery, and buildings are included in this category. Insurance is recovered on proof, not guesswork. Records dealing with transactions should be saved. These include receipt of money, proof of payment, proof of expenses or purchases, and payroll. Also, documents providing proof of usage should be retained, for they are vital in matters dealing with research, engineering, and patents. If the company becomes involved in infringement or other patent-suit claims, certain drawings, properly coded, numbered, and preserved, form the basis for prosecution or defense. Historical data of various types often prove valuable in that they provide trends and statistical analysis helpful in the company's planning efforts. Such data should be retained if there is a reasonable possibility that they will be used in the future or will be referred to for improving decision making by relating the reasons given *why* certain decisions were made in the past with the outcome of such decisions.

Figure 7–2 shows selected retention periods for various records. These values represent the consensus of authorities on record storage and reflect current thinking in this area. However, the statute of limitations, which varies for different documents among states, regulatory activities by

Accounts receivable............... 10
Agreements with employees.......... P*
Annual and monthly reports......... P
Articles of incorporation............ P
Attendance records of employees....... 7
Bids............................ 3
Cash books...................... P
Charge slips..................... 10
Checks canceled.................. 10
Correspondence—
   credit and collection.............. 7
   —purchase..................... 5
Delivery receipts................. 3
Dividend checks.................. 10
Financial statements............... P
General ledger.................... P

Insurance—property............... 8
Labor clock records............... 5
Labor earnings records............. P
Medical histories................. P
Minute book of directors meeting..... P
Paid bills....................... 8
Patent records................... P
Registered mail.................. 5
Requisitions.................... 3
Sales expenses.................. 6
Shipping tickets................. 6
Tax bills and statements........... P
Time and motion studies........... P
Union labor contracts............. P
Wage rates..................... 8

*P = Permanent

FIG. 7–2. Suggested schedule for retention of various records in years.

government agencies, and personal preferences should be considered in the choice. The statute of limitations specifies the length of time a record is alive according to law.

Based on the information obtained from the inventory of records, suggested retention periods, and judgment, records of varying importance can be classified as to their retention. For convenience, they can be divided into four groups:

1. *Nonessential.* Records so classified should never be filed. Since they have value for a short period only—perhaps a few seconds—retaining them is wasteful. Included are pencil notations, routine inquiries, and announcements.

2. *Helpful.* Records in this group can assist, but only for a very limited time, perhaps four to five weeks. After this period, their usefulness is completed. If filed, they should be placed in a separate drawer or cabinet and destroyed as their helpfulness ceases. An example is general correspondence, most of which has a useful life of not over four weeks.

3. *Important.* These include records containing information of value for relatively long periods—up to five or six years. They should first be filed in the office for handy reference; but ultimately, as they lose their current usefulness, they should be transferred to storage. How long they remain in the office depends upon the type of record and the retention period established. Many firms keep records such as invoices, accounts receivable, sales records, quotations, and financial statements in active files for one to two years, then transfer to storage.

4. *Vital.* As the name implies, these records are paramount. They are retained permanently. They may be transferred to the storage area after a given period of time, but they are never destroyed. Vital records include legal papers of incorporation, titles to ownership, deeds, and reports to stockholders.

## PROVIDE A GOOD STORAGE AREA

A clean, dry area should be designated for records retention. Proper conditions of temperature, circulation of air, and humidity should be provided. Traditionally, storage rooms have been the attics of business; they should be regarded as attractive work areas. The floor area must withstand a relatively high weight, as much as 250 pounds per square foot. Location can be either (1) on-site (same as office) or (2) off-site (away from office).

*Courtesy: Bankers Box Co., Franklin Park, Ill.*

FIG. 7–3.   Interlocking fiberboard drawer files form a compact and substantial storage file.

Various types of equipment can be used for storing records. The following are of special interest: (1) specially designed fiberboard drawer files and (2) storage boxes on shelving. A specially designed fiberboard drawer file combines the drawer, shelving, and base, all in one unit. A steel framework carries the entire weight load. The drawer files are interlocking, as illustrated by the right picture of Figure 7–3. The drawers are locked together solidly, each locking to the one below and the one above it. The unit "builds its own steel framework as you stack it." As many as 20 drawers can be stacked in one tier. There is no buckling, sagging, or warping. Different sizes are available for punched cards, letter, and legal-size papers. The total space is devoted to drawer units, which results in a compact, efficient use of storage space giving the high storage ratio of 8 to 1, i.e., the cubic feet of records to square feet of floor space. For bulk storage where reference is infrequent, larger containers with the same interlocking feature can be used. Each container is about 15 inches by 24 inches and holds two boxes, one of which can be used for letter, the other for legal size as shown by Figure 7–4.

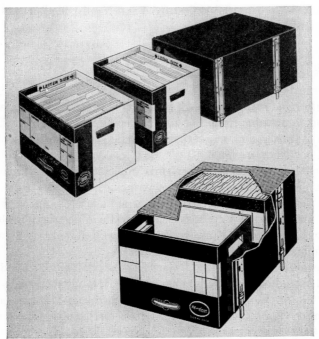

*Courtesy: Bankers Box Co., Franklin Park, Ill.*

FIG. 7–4.　Both storage boxes slide into the stacking shell. This tandem arrangement provides maximum storage in minimum space.

Storage boxes on ordinary shelving are also used. They afford maximum economy in dead records storage. The boxes are built of high-test corrugated fiberboard especially designed to withstand rough usage and to prevent mildew and damage from dirt or moisture. A variety of sizes is supplied so that the stored material fits snugly in the box. The shelving is assembled quickly without tools and can be extended by adding extensional units. The shelving can be dismantled and reassembled in a new location in a matter of minutes.

For records in storage, a system of indexing should be adopted, so that all such material can be located quickly. The information can be kept on small index cards or on sheets in a loose-leaf notebook. It should include subject classification, shelf number, box number or name, and scheduled date for ultimate destruction. If is important that each container be labeled plainly.

At least once a year, a list should be prepared showing what stored original records should be destroyed. It can be compiled readily from data on the index cards. This list is then submitted to the office manager or designated executive for approval and authority to proceed. When this has been granted, the material is destroyed and the list filed permanently for future reference.

## TRANSFER RECORDS

The transfer of records as a part of a records-retention program really starts before the material is filed, in that only material considered to have future worth or value should be filed. Keeping worthless materials out of the files is easier and more realistic than getting worthless materials removed once they are filed.

The systematic transfer of records implements the records-retention program. Several moves are necessary, including transfer from active to inactive files and from inactive files to storage area. In each case the transfer may also lead to a decision for their destruction should the records at that stage be considered worthless. Reference to Figure 7–5 is helpful in discussing the various transfers.

As previously stated, material classified as nonessential should never be filed, but should be destroyed immediately. "Helpful" material is filed in a separate file for the limited period, then destroyed. Material considered important or vital is filed (step No. 1) and subsequently transferred to the inactive file as a normal practice (step No. 2). Material cannot remain in the files indefinitely—the physical space becomes exhausted. As indicated in the figure with a four-drawer filing cabinet, the top drawers can be used for current material and the bottom two for inactive material. This arrangement affords convenient reference to inactive material, necessary from time to time in every office. When the five-drawer file is used, a common arrangement to follow is illustrated by Figure 7–6.

The transferring of material can be done in one of two main ways: (1) the entire unit, or periodically; and (2) the individual, or perpetually. The former requires that all material be transferred at a scheduled time. Usually, an annual basis is used—at the beginning of the calendar year, fiscal year, or busy season. The material remains in the original folders and is moved bodily. New folders are used for the new material in the current file. The individual, or perpetual, means places time limits on individual papers by appropriate marks on the folders. Then, periodically, at intervals of about two or three months—or perpetually, at irregular

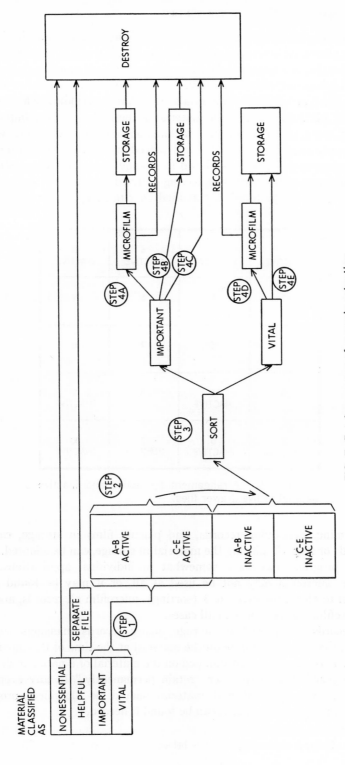

FIG. 7–5. A program of records retention.

intervals—the files are screened, and papers found to have been in the file past the allowable limit are transferred to the inactive file. In cases where the transaction is terminated, i.e., a settlement granted or a sale closed, the material is transferred immediately, regardless of date.

From the inactive files all materials are removed periodically and sorted (step No. 3 of Figure 7–5). The material in these files is either important or vital material. The former is handled in three different ways: microfilmed, records destroyed, films placed in storage, and ultimately destroyed (step 4A); records placed in storage and eventually destroyed (step 4B); or records destroyed, having outlived their span of importance (step 4C).[1] If the material is classified as vital, step 4D, consisting of

| 1 INACTIVE | 3 INACTIVE | 6 INACTIVE | 8 INACTIVE |
|------------|------------|------------|------------|
| 1 | 4 | 6 | 9 |
| 2 | 5 | 7 | 10 |
| 3 | 4 INACTIVE | 8 | 9 INACTIVE |
| 2 INACTIVE | 5 INACTIVE | 7 INACTIVE | 10 INACTIVE |

FIG. 7–6.  Arrangement for active and inactive material in five-drawer files.

microfilming, destroying records, and placing films in storage, can be followed; or step 4E, placing the material in storage, can be adopted.

This program may vary somewhat in individual applications. For example, microfilm may not be used at all, or it may be found more practical to eliminate step No. 3 (sorting), microfilm all records, and use the microfilms for reference in all cases.

If records are placed in storage, many records managers suggest marking the destruction date on the material at the time of its transfer to storage. This may be a date stamped on the material or a notice to destroy in "one year," "two years," or "retain permanently." In any event, as stated above, all transferred material should be classified, properly labeled, and indexed so that it can be found if needed.

---

[1] Microfilming is discussed immediately below.

## MICROFILMING

"Microfilming" is a photographic means of retaining the information given in office papers. The materials are first photographed on film at reduced sizes; then, the film is developed, to serve as the permanent record. Figure 7–7 shows several popular arrangements in microfilming material and a modern microfilming machine.

A

B

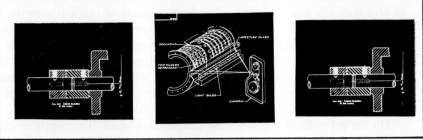

C

*Courtesy: Burroughs Corp., Detroit*

FIG. 7–7. *Top, A:* For standard size letters, 16-mm. film and 17-to-1 reduction are popular. *Top, B:* For infrequent reference, a double line—one for front, the other for back of the document, 23-to-1 reduction, is recommended. *Top, C:* For engineering drawings and ledger sheets, a 17-to-1 reduction and 25-mm. film are used. *Bottom:* One compact machine handles all microfilming needs, including high-fidelity filming to high-clarity reading.

One of the first commercial applications of microfilming was in banks, where it was used in connection with checks. The list of applications grew steadily, and microfilming is now associated with many types of paper materials. It is an accepted part of many records-retention programs. One interesting application is to mount a single microfilm frame into a punched card which carries identifying and classifying data of the microfilmed subject which can be a large engineering drawing, specifications, or photograph. It is an easy matter to store and sort the punched cards, giving quick, accurate handling to what otherwise is a clumsy, time-consuming task.

Microfilming is available to the small as well as to the large enterprise. Outside concerns specializing in microfilming work will microfilm records either in the office of the company or in their own plant. The cost for this service, including film and developing, varies from $4 to $6 for each 1,000 pieces, depending upon the size and quantity of the material, whether hand or automatic feed can be used, and whether one or two sides are to be microfilmed.

The use of microfilming effects a great saving of storage space. About 98–99 percent of storage space can be saved, since one to two file cabinets of film hold the equivalent of a hundred cabinets of original records. In addition, the chances of losing a document are minimized. The photographs on the film are in sequence like links of a chain; once a paper is photographed, there is no danger of the photograph being lost unless the whole roll of microfilm is lost. Furthermore, with microfilm, the retained materials are clean and easily handled; and they reduce the fire hazard, because the film is of the acetate, noncombustible type.

On the other hand, microfilming has its drawbacks. The courts usually prefer original documents, but will accept microfilmed material when failure to produce the original is adequately explained. Usually, microfilming must be established as a regular procedure and one not motivated by any suspicion of fraud. Microfilming may tend to retain temporarily an excess of records because it is easier to microfilm all records and file the films than it is to decide what materials have future use and microfilm them only. Also the use of microfilming requires special equipment; a viewer is the minimum requirement. Furthermore, employees must be trained for the specialized techniques required, and these skills are somewhat different from those required for most office work.

## CONTROLLING AND RECORDS RETENTION

An effective means of control is to limit the quantity of records per employee. The amount permitted will depend upon the type of business operation. In public utilities, for example, an amount of 5 cubic feet of records per employee on payroll is considered satisfactory. For an assembly plant, a comparable figure may be only 1 cubic foot of records; whereas in a purchasing department, the amount may be as great as 12 cubic feet, yet still qualify as an effective records-retention practice.

Cost is used by many companies to keep records-retention work within reasonable limits. Cost for labor and space will vary depending upon the particular location, but cost for equipment is relatively much more uniform. For this latter, an average cost figure is 25 cents per cubic foot of records stored. However, meaningful records-retention cost data should include labor not only for storing but also for finding, and the unit in which the cost is expressed must be meaningful. Cost per cubic foot of records, for example, may not be meaningful for some types of equipment, lineal inches are not appropriate for others, and number of records may be of little value because of the wide variation in type, content, and size of records.

Additional cost information that shows the need to control records retained is that it costs about $1,200 to create the contents for one file drawer of correspondence. Assuming 5,000 papers in one file drawer, one-fifth of them are letters produced at an average cost of $1 each (probably low) and the remaining papers carbon copies at a cost of 4 cents each, the calculations are:

$$1,000 \times \$1.00 = \$1,000$$
$$4,000 \times \ \ 0.04 = \ \ \ \ 160$$
$$\text{Total} = \$1,160$$

Helpful ratios can also be derived. To illustrate, a "usage" ratio reveals the extent to which the materials stored are being used. The formula is:

$$\text{Usage ratio (in \%)} = \frac{\text{Requests} \times 100}{\text{References filed}}$$

For example, if last month, 200 requests were made from 20,000 items stored, the usage ratio in percentage would be $200 \times 100$ divided by 20,000 or 1 percent. This ratio for stored materials will seldom exceed 5 percent. For active materials in the office files, it should run about 15–20 percent. Further analysis of usage ratios can be made, taking into account the rate of reference by type of record versus the age of the record. Such studies assist in better controlling of records-retention efforts.

Another ratio is the "accuracy" ratio, which is calculated by this formula:

$$\text{Accuracy ratio (in \%)} = \frac{\text{Number of items not found} \times 100}{\text{Number of items found}}$$

For 10 items not found and 10,000 found, the ratio is 0.1 percent. For a rating of excellent, the accuracy ratio should not be greater than 0.5

percent. A value of 3 percent or more signifies that remedial action is required. The accuracy ratio can be used for either active only, inactive only, or all stored records.

## HEAD OF RECORDS-RETENTION PROGRAM

In most cases, it is best to have one person in charge of a records-retention program. The person should have adequate authority to direct and maintain the program. To a great extent, the success of the program is determined by the caliber of person heading the unit and the relationship of the records-retention unit to the other office units. Preferably, this head should report to an executive in a high enough organizational level to get top management support and opinions.

Committees should be used to assist the designated head of the records-retention work. As stated earlier in this chapter, a committee to establish policies and decide retention periods for each type of paper is effective, but putting into action and managing the program is better vested in a competent individual. Consultation with department heads is in order because they usually are well qualified to suggest which of their own records probably should be retained and for how long a period.

## ACTUATING AND RECORDS RETENTION

The manager of records retention must instill a feeling of confidence in the records-retention activities and results. All office personnel, as well as key management people, must believe in the accuracy, completeness, and usefulness of the field material. Unless they do, they are quite likely to keep important records in their own desks or special files rather than trust them with records retention.

A manual supplying information on the procedures and practices of the records-retention group is also helpful. Data on the type of material stored, the indexing system, retention schedule, and specific duties of records-retention personnel should be clearly written and made available to anyone whose work is affected by records retention. Such a manual is extremely beneficial for obtaining better understanding and for training new employees in records-retention work.

## QUESTIONS

1. In office management, what is the meaning of records retention, and of what importance is it?
2. Interpret the data given in Figure 7–1.
3. For how long a period do you suggest each item in the following list of filed material be retained:

   *a)* Sales prospect lists?
   *b)* Invoices from suppliers of raw materials?
   *c)* Real estate deeds?
   *d)* Payrolls and pay rates?
   *e)* Application forms from prospective employees?
   *f)* Quotations to customers?

4. Write a two-sentence identifying description of each of the following:
   *a)* "Helpful" material as a classification for records-retention purposes.
   *b)* Fiberboard drawer file.
   *c)* Microfilming.
   *d)* Statute of limitations.

5. Discuss taking an inventory of records as a major part of a records-retention program.

6. Enumerate important considerations in the transferring of records as an essential of a records-retention program.

7. An office which has never had a records-retention program is now interested in establishing one. Suggest an approach which can be followed to meet this purpose.

8. Discuss the physical requirements for a records-retention area.

9. Do you favor the entire-unit or the individual method in the transferring of filed material? Why?

10. Do you agree with the following: "The availability of reliable microfilming machines and supplies solves the retention-of-records problem for most offices. This is substantiated by the fact that accurate copies at a cost of a fraction of a cent each and a saving of over 95 percent storage space are obtained through microfilming."

11. Describe the meaning of Figure 7–5 in your own words.

12. Investigation shows the following facts about the records-retention department of the Newkirk Manufacturing Company. Accuracy ratio 4.5 percent; total employees on payroll, 183; usage ratio = 6.17 percent; current cost of records-retention equipment, $723.45; weekly gross payroll for records retention, $109.70; cubic feet of records in records retention, 714. Evaluate the records-retention work of the Newkirk Manufacturing Company. Substantiate your viewpoint.

## CASE PROBLEMS

### Case 7–1.  Regal Products Company

Company estimates are that 50 file drawers or 75 cubic feet of material annually are placed in records storage. Mr. Mallory Buhl, the office manager, states that the total costs, including space and equipment, currently are 75 cents per cubic foot of records. This is utilizing storage boxes stacked six-high; the boxes cost $5 each, which is amortized over ten years, and each box contains two cubic feet of records.

Recently, Mr. Buhl has been approached by a microfilm service company and requested to change his records storage to a microfilm basis. This service company will microfilm records for a flat fee of $5 per 100-ft. reel, which quotation includes total costs, i.e., machine, material, and labor costs. Mr. Buhl has been informed that approximately 3,500 documents will be photographed on a 100-ft. reel and that there are 3,000 documents per cubic foot.

## Problems:

1. Calculate the company's annual cost for records storage (a) under present operations and (b) under the proposed microfilming arrangement.

2. Other than cost, what important considerations should Mr. Buhl take into account?

3. What decision should be reached? Why?

### Case 7–2.   Martin-Durkee Manufacturing Company

RALPH HESS:   Come in, please. You're Mr. Fred Ford, the management consultant?

FRED FORD:   Yes. Thank you very much.

HESS:   I'll be glad to assist you in every way. I suppose you'd like me to start by discussing what we do here?

FORD:   Yes, if you will.

HESS:   The engineering design division is divided into three sections: design, administration, and design drafting. I am in charge of the latter. We are responsible for all mechanical drafting work in the designing of new products, improvements in the design of existing products, production drawings relative to the building of prototype products, and products to be built under contract to customers.

FORD:   You handle improvements in existing design?

HESS:   Yes, sir.

FORD:   What does the design section handle?

HESS:   They handle the design of new products only. Now, to be able to use the latest commercially offered items as components of design—and this is true for new product design as well, that is, for the design section—it is necessary to have readily available a file of catalogs and design manuals offered by various manufacturers. All these cabinets you see in the room out there are filled with such material. In addition, we have correspondence, blueprints, original drawings, and even samples of various items. Some of these, both papers and samples, are odd sizes and shapes, and are difficult to store; and my guess is that part of what we have out there could be discarded.

FORD:   Do the files out there represent all the stored reference material?

HESS:   No. There are stacks of stuff in a basement room. The material is stacked up in neat little piles on the floor; each stack is tagged, but it's a mess to find anything down there.

FORD:   Do you have need to go to this basement room from time to time?

HESS:   Yes, every once in a while. The men resent being sent there to look for something—all except Harvey Pair, who doesn't seem to mind. In fact, I guess you could say he even enjoys it. Gets lost down there for half a day at a time.

FORD:   About how frequently do you refer to the files out here in this next room?

HESS: That's hard to say. Sometimes, quite often; at other times, maybe just once or twice a day.

FORD: How is the material arranged in these files?

HESS: It's supposed to be alphabetical by manufacturer's name, that is, for the design manuals. General literature from vendors is kept in a separate tier of cabinets, by vendor's name. Several times a week, a young lady from the main office brings current material and files it. But my designers and draftsmen are constantly coming to me and complaining they can't find the material they want, and they insist it was in the files. Sometimes, we find it misfiled; sometimes, the young lady tells us we never did have the material; sometimes, it is lost but turns up later.

FORD: What do you think should be done?

HESS: Well, now. . . . I understand you're the expert, so what I say may not make any sense. But for whatever it is worth, I think there is too much junk in the files—stuff we'll never use. And some way to find what we want would be a big help, too. Why, we've requested new copies of booklets and catalogs from a supplier only to discover before we receive them that we have the same booklets or catalogs in our file. Just could not find them when we wanted them.

## Problems:

1. What further information do you feel Mr. Ford should obtain from Mr. Hess?

2. As Mr. Ford, would you hold any other interviews or make any observations within the company? Why?

3. What recommendations would you make to the company's managers? Discuss.

# PART 3

# THE OFFICE AND AUTOMATION

*Automation has steadily advanced until today it occupies a dominant position in performing office work. The development of this growth, the reasons for adopting office automation, viewpoints vital in this new era of the office, basic concepts of modern processing of data, and the important technical aspects of the automation age are discussed in the following seven chapters.*

*The interesting and challenging subject areas include (1) managing in the new office technology, (2) the systems and procedures approach, (3) the total systems concept, (4) source data automation, (5) electronic computers —technical considerations, (6) electronic computers— managerial considerations, and (7) computerized office applications.*

CHAPTER **8**

# MANAGING IN THE
# NEW OFFICE TECHNOLOGY

The wise man does at once what the fool
does finally.
                                    —*Gracian*

WE ARE moving into a new world much faster than most of us realize.
Spaceships zoom in the vastness of the universe. Supersonic airliners will
soon fly men at speeds of 2,000 miles an hour. Trains are being designed to
go at speeds of 200 miles an hour. And at this moment, scientists are
probing under the ocean nearly ten miles deep for minerals and the
unknown. These developments are all a part of the greatest research
program in the history of mankind.

This pace of progress has stimulated efforts to develop machines and
hasten their application to office work because information is so essential
to all activities and especially to research and development. Significant
office technological advances have been won, yet even greater things to
come are predicted. Routine office jobs are being eliminated, office work is
being accomplished at fantastic speeds, and the makeup of office work is
undergoing significant changes.

## ILLUSTRATIONS OF THE NEW OFFICE TECHNOLOGY

It is no exaggeration to state that nearly every office task can be
automated by the application of electronics, electrostatics, magnetics, or
pneumatics. Scientific breakthroughs are speeding the accomplishments of
the new office technology. For example, now available are electrostatic
printing units capable of printing 72 million characters an hour—or of
printing this entire book in less than two minutes. It is now possible in
digital form to record magnetically on a square inch of tape the words

contained on four pages of this book and, further, to process this amount of information at a rate of 40 pages per second. Machines can multiply two 13-digit figures in 31 millionths of a second, that is, at the rate of 32,000 such multiplications in one second. Work is now being perfected to achieve the amazing reduction of 160,000 to 1 for filming information. This means that the entire contents of three books like the one you are now reading could be recorded on a single film smaller than the size of an ordinary post card. The contents of an entire library could be kept in an ordinary card file.

As indicated above, the new office technology is actually a part of the great technological advances being applied to every branch of industry, and the trend is toward new and better machines. Applications in the factory, in sales, in research, in medicine, in the military, and in transportation are giving greater impetus to the growth in importance of paper work and to its processing in keeping with developments in these other areas. For example, an oil refinery, completely automated, requires only three men to operate the control buttons. And a steel-pipe plant employing automatic machines produces four times as much pipe with one-third the number of employees formerly used. Airplanes are guided in "blind" takeoffs and landings, movements of trains can be controlled, and the course of storms can be charted and weather maps quickly sent to stations across the nation. Managers of retail stores can find which items are selling satisfactorily, which poorly, which items to discontinue, which to promote, which to purchase, and where to display (shelf and location in store), all by means of a point-of-purchase analysis rapidly calculated by an electronic office machine. In another application, voluminous data on the buying habits of soft drink purchasers in a given sales territory are fed into a computer, in addition to data on the composition of newspaper and television audiences in this same territory. Within minutes the most efficient combination of media for a given advertising budget is calculated by the computer.

## SCOPE OF THE NEW OFFICE TECHNOLOGY

The boundaries of the new office technology appear limitless. The advances are neither confined to any one subject area nor to any one type of enterprise. In fact, they defy any arbitrary lines of demarcation. Equipment exists and is operable to take advantage of the new technology. What holds us back or restrains our adoption of the new technology is our limited vision, imagination, and decisiveness. The major issue is basic, not to the type of equipment, but to the managers.

Knowing the kinds of information needed to manage and operate a given enterprise is fundamental. For example, answers to these questions are necessary: What information do you need to know? In what format should it be? How accurate? How frequent? Who should be given all or a part of this information? What do we need to know to plan effectively? How much controlling is needed? Should we emphasize centralization or decentralization in our organizing efforts? To answer these questions requires the ability to determine what information is important, and, once obtaining it, how it will be used. In this connection an understanding of both the nature of the enterprise and its activities is valuable.

To take full advantage of the office technology's offerings, we should also know what specific activities give rise to the information needed to manage the enterprise. Not all activities generate information of equal value. Concentrating our efforts on the really important ones, we can then find out pertinent facts about these key activities, facts such as the channels through which this key information flows, what departments receive it, and what departments use it.

| Purpose of Information | Common Media | For Managerial Activity |
| --- | --- | --- |
| To forecast business conditions | Plans | Planning |
| To allocate resources | Programs | Planning |
| To schedule time use | Reports | Controlling |
| To determine quantity | Reports | Controlling |
| To determine quality | Reports | Controlling |
| To establish standards | Reports and Manuals | Controlling |
| To evaluate performance against standards | Records and Reports | Controlling |
| To inform employees, customers, and stockholders | Letters and Bulletins | Actuating |
| To fulfill commitments to customers and suppliers | Records and Letters | Actuating |
| To meet governmental requirements | Reports | Controlling |

FIG. 8–1. The purpose, media, and for what fundamental managerial activity information is utilized.

Knowing for a given enterprise the information essential for its management and where this information is generated, it is then possible to localize problem areas where there is need for help, and the manner of performing the work in this area can be improved by utilizing more efficient data processing. In other words, an effort is made to match the places where there is a real need for improvement with the places where it is believed help can be supplied.

Figure 8–1 gives a brief summary of selected important information for management purposes. The list is suggestive only. Data for planning purposes are sought and emphasized to achieve better decision making. The possibility of supplying an inclusive background and of analyzing a wide range of alternatives makes planning information valuable. Likewise, control types of information supply a manager with important data, particularly when the information is almost instantaneous with the occurrence of the activity. Production, inventory, and sales are major areas where current control information is essential.

## DEFINITION OF OFFICE AUTOMATION

The word "automation" first appeared in print about 1948. Since that time, this word has stimulated much discussion and controversy; it has been accorded many different meanings. Some consider automation as a synonym for technological change, while others believe it denotes mechanization. Commonly, the word is used solely in connection with the processing of products in a factory; but, while popular, this concept is obviously incomplete, since data processing and the compilation of information have been subjected to technological improvements.

In performing work of any kind, automation means the arrangement whereby one or more machines are operated without human participation except to press the starter button. It is the regulation of processing by which high-speed, self-correcting instruments or machines control the operations of other machines. In a very real sense, automation is the extension of mechanization. If an office machine can be operated and controlled by other machines or devices, office automation can be said to exist. The situation, however, is primarily one of degree and terminology.

Actually, automatic devices are not new. Nineteen hundred years ago, the Romans used a hydraulic float valve to regulate the water level in their reservoirs and tanks. However, today the simultaneous introduction of many electronic devices to control the kind and flow of office work and their outstanding accomplishments are of significant value.

Office automation relieves mankind of menial work. Most office work requires some human cerebration; but when the work is repetitive in nature or subject to exact formulation, it can be effectively handled by machine. By such means, man is free to employ his mind for work which the human brain *alone* can encompass.

## WHY AUTOMATE?

Managers of present-day enterprises need considerable data to help them make effective decisions. As the managerial need for information becomes more and more pressing, the means for supplying this information quickly and completely have been stimulated. This is reason No. 1 why companies automate their data-processing work. In the quick tempo of today, events affecting enterprises seem to occur with increasing rapidity, and many decisions must take into account at least part of these events. Under such conditions, the gathering, processing, and distributing of data must be done as quickly as possible. In certain areas, the tremendous amounts of paper work required can be handled within a reasonable period only by machine. In the case of supplying scientific and research data calculated from mathematical formulas, a machine accomplishes in several hours what would require years of manual calculation.

A second major reason for office automation is to reduce office costs. In some instances, this goal is achieved; but in others, cost reduction is more fancy than fact. One is inclined to believe that in any installation, because of the speed and versatility of office machines used in automation, paperwork costs are reduced. Unfortunately, it is difficult to make accurate comparisons of a "before and after" office automation. Usually, many innovations are effected by automation. The report requirements may change, due mainly to these innovations; and the volume of work may increase, since the processing time is stepped up and "we have the necessary machines." Also, some of the departmental operations may undergo transitions of one type or another. If all factors remained on a status quo basis before and after automation, and there is an adequate volume of work, the costs under automation will be reduced. But a condition that very likely develops is more data processing with approximately the same dollar expenditure.

This does not mean that office automation is not an attractive investment. Quite the contrary, it usually is a good investment; otherwise, managers would not utilize it. A well-planned, -installed, and -managed installation will return a saving of approximately 30–40 percent on the total investment each year. To achieve this return, it is necessary in many cases to operate the equipment five days a week, sixteen hours a day. In each case, individual circumstances govern and must be taken into account for the particular conditions present.

An important reason for office automation frequently overlooked is reduction of errors. Machines seldom commit mistakes; and when they do, it usually is the fault of the person operating them. Office automation tends to integrate data processing and thus minimizes the number of times the data are handled; hence, it reduces the possibilities of committing errors. Higher-quality office work can be viewed as a by-product, even though it is an important contribution of office automation.

As pointed out in Chapter 1, the office work force represents one of the fastest growing groups in our economy. The search for competent office help is continuous. Ways of getting out the necessary work with a limited number of people have been eagerly sought, or an arrangement requiring employment of only the more competent office employees has won favor. Both these conditions are met by automating office work. In many cases, the capacity of the automated system is greater than current needs; and as the clerical work load increases, it will not be necessary to add people, but rather the system can be depended upon to take on most of the additional load. This assures adequate clerical help for perhaps the next decade.

The last reason to be discussed is the desire to have an internal status symbol. Automating office work signifies progress; and in some instances, it appears that equipment was ordered and installed simply because certain executives insisted upon having it. Whether the type and amount of equipment were adequate and proper for their needs was hastily reviewed, and full utilization of the equipment has never been made. Instances of this nature are relatively minor, yet they demonstrate that the basis of some automation is impulsive and personal, not rational and logical.

## THE FEASIBILITY OF AUTOMATION

Automating the paper work of an enterprise can be a detailed and complicated task. For best results, it is imperative that the entire cycle of the work to be automated be taken into account, that the real objectives be carefully defined and used as guides in designing the manner of work performance, and that the proper equipment be selected and employed for the intended use. Actually, two aspects of data processing are involved: (1) the makeup of the paper work itself and (2) the processing of the data as such. Under the former are included the design of the entire cycle, what data are included, in what form, to what form, and how utilized. Under the second point are the actual uses of the equipment typically operating on a continuing basis. These two aspects of data processing are interrelated, and the experts in each area should work together as a team, with each aware of the other's problems.

In some "feasibility" studies, the erroneous assumption is made that office automation is desirable regardless of the current work performance mode. The result is that inefficiencies in paper work are automated or some data are permitted to remain in a form which is incompatible with best automation practices. As a result, both the good and the bad features of the present manner of doing the work are preserved. Experience clearly demonstrates that it is extremely difficult to remove unnecessary data or to change basic procedures once they are incorporated in the office automation arrangement. In fact, a computer when misused is probably the finest device in the world for sealing in existing deficiencies. The proper approach is to conduct a thorough and sound study prior to the decision to use any form of automation. Only in this way is a solid and reliable foundation established for all the subsequent phases of improvement, simplification, and mechanization.

What is included in a thorough and sound study? A number of considerations, including the objectives of the enterprise and the contributions expected of each functional area or organizational unit to the achievement of these objectives. The decision-making activity vested in each management member should be clearly identified so that the information needs of each member can be determined. Familiarity with the organization structure assists in answering who decides what, who is expected to inform whom, and what information is needed. Generally, it is also helpful to know the relative importance of the various basic functions of the enterprise—manufacturing, marketing, financing, engineering, and personnel—in order to obtain some impression of the probable characteristics of the data to be handled. Also, any future increased work loads and contemplated changes should be taken into account, as well as the existing means of performing the work, no matter how primitive, because such facts can have an important bearing upon the recommendations.

Sometimes the term "feasibility of automation" is erroneously interpreted to mean the possible or probable adoption or success of an enterprise in utilizing data-processing equipment. Office automation is a reality. The question to be answered is not the degree of success predicted for certain equipment, but an evaluation of equipment alternatives based on resultant costs, time in process, flexibility of usage, and ability to meet future requirements. A number of different types of office machines can perform the work. For any individual user the question is: Which one will do my paper work best in keeping with my personal needs?

To be sure, equipment manufacturers have developed standardized, practical, and economical ways of processing certain data. We might refer to them as "standardized paper work programs." The processing of payrolls, accounts payable, and purchasing are examples. These can be handled fairly uniformly in company after company, but in many cases they are not, and for any number of reasons. On the other hand, paper work dealing with budgeting, material control, and sales control varies considerably from enterprise to enterprise, presumably because of company size, practices of the business, characteristics of the enterprise, the overall objectives, the product, the service, and personal preference. Consequently they are evaluated individually in many feasibility studies.

Also, too much emphasis may be placed on the practicality or desirability of utilizing particular types of machines and equipment. Attention is focused on speeds, peak loads, scheduling, and other technical considerations. While these are important, it must also be remembered that the data are being processed for utilization, to help somebody do his job better because of the processed data provided to him. Furthermore, concentrating on the processing of the data per se may result in inadequate consideration for such things as acquiring the source data, converting the data into suitable form for machine processing, supplying the processed information in the best format, and getting it to the right personnel at the right time.

## CHANGES IN MANAGEMENT STRUCTURE

One of the most important effects of the new office technology upon the management structure is the increased emphasis given to taking a broader viewpoint or perspective of the entirety, rather than of one single component. The trend of developments appears to be toward the swiftest possible reaction by an *entire* enterprise to any given stimulus. The enterprise is being viewed more and more as a responsive body instead of a cluster of individual and, to some extent, isolated departments. In the future, the work of the office manager will be carried out in more sweeping yet integrated lines. The management of information should be viewed as an activity affecting all parts of an enterprise, and areas outside the enterprise as well. The trend of managerial thinking is definitely toward this broader concept. For example, we are now considering paper work efforts not just within a definite small work center, or within a depart-

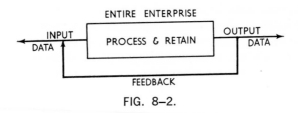

FIG. 8–2.

ment, but within several departments or the entire enterprise. To illustrate, Figure 8–2 has been included. Here, for the study of informational requirements, the entire enterprise is considered a unit. Certain data, termed *input*, are fed into the unit. They include such data as customers' orders, price information from vendors, and information on special technical processes. Within the unit, or the enterprise, the input data are processed, some are retained and some are issued or fed out as *output* data. Price quotations to customers, sales, shipments, and bank checks for payables are illustrative of output data. In addition, the figure includes the concept called *feedback*. This is a selected portion of the *output* used to control for either self-supervision or modification of further processing.[1]

Another effect of the new technology upon the management structure is the emergence of a management information group or department. Such a group will probably become more and more common and will occupy a relatively high organizational level. As office automation increases and experience in obtaining full utilization of office technology is acquired,

[1] There will be much more discussion about the breadth and approach to office work in Chapters 9 and 10.

fuller integration of information will be accomplished. This, in turn, will mean less paper work and reports by personnel of the operating departments. Supervisors, for example, will not be required to spend two to three hours daily on paper work. This shift will enable employees to devote more of their time to their primary function. Also, it is quite likely that a reduction in the size of the clerical staff groups of the operating departments could result. To illustrate, sales analysis of sales and labor costs of production might well be transferred to the information center.

For a given office, automation usually increases relatively the machine cost and decreases the labor cost. In turn, the greater machine expenditure spotlights attention upon questions of depreciation; scheduling and maintaining even work flows, and keeping the mechanized units in top working condition; utilization of records; and format of reports. Automation in the office stresses managerial problems; in the factory, the problems are primarily technical.

Office technology influences the management structure, not only of the large company, but also of the small one. The present and relatively limited routine processing performed by a service bureau for small companies will probably expand to cover more encompassing areas.[2] Equipment considerations alone will not bring this about, but the scarcity of competent and experienced analytical talent will make the service bureau arrangement the logical choice of the small enterprise.

## CONFUSION ABOUT OFFICE TECHNOLOGY

Several factors constitute major obstacles to the complete understanding and utilization of contributions available from office technology developments. These factors include (1) the overemphasis upon technical details, (2) the lack of adequately trained personnel, (3) the adoption of special jargon, and (4) the basically divergent viewpoints or philosophies taken toward computers. Let us examine each of these in some detail.

A tendency to overemphasize technical details is the source of much chaos. To the average layman the need is for what the equipment will do for him rather than how it does it. For some, the "how" is intriguing, but appreciation and use of an automobile, for example, does not necessitate knowing precisely how the thousand separate parts operate. Some people must know all the details, but most people who are involved in the "computer age" are neither technicians nor do they want to be. However, some technical data are essential and should be provided. But too much regard for how the data are processed can result in too little regard for what kinds of data are being provided. The data processing becomes an end in itself rather than a means to an end.

---

[2] Service bureaus are discussed in Chapter 22, p. 506.

Every emerging new field of endeavor suffers from the lack of trained personnel. The office technology is no exception. We have a tendency to minimize the importance of people in office automation. The equipment is in the spotlight, it receives the publicity and glamour. But trained people are needed to design the process and to operate the machines. In certain companies the overflow from other departments has formed the basis for personnel used in the office automation unit, that is, the unit consists chiefly of discarded or reassigned employees. Apparently not much effort has been made to recruit and train new, young, highly intelligent, and proficient people for these vital office jobs. Competent managerial skill is also in short supply. Fantastic office machines are in operation, but in a number of cases management of them leaves much to be desired. All the office equipment in the world falls short of its potential unless we have the manpower to manage it effectively.

Office technology has developed its own jargon. To the newcomer it is comprised of strange terminology unlike anything previously encountered. Words like bit, binary number, access time, real-time, buffer, program, and storage take on special meanings quite different from those previously associated with them. Furthermore, there is confusion about the meaning of certain basic words. Hence, the same word doesn't always have the same meaning. Obviously, this state of affairs makes for difficulties in communication. A sales manager may attempt to learn the intricacies of electronic data processing but become discouraged by the specialized and somewhat stilted language of the technical books recommended to him. Or he may find it a real chore to communicate with the executive in charge of computer activities. In contrast, data-processing personnel encounter difficulty in presenting ideas to sales management personnel. A common complaint of the processor is that he "just can't get through to top and middle managers."

Lastly, confusion about office technology results from widely divergent viewpoints about its identity and contribution. At one extreme is the belief that electronic data processing applies primarily to clerical types of applications, and that this work should be neatly tucked within a well-known major organizational unit such as finance or production where it can be given the proper orientation. In contrast, others contend that electronic data processing includes all types of operations—clerical, production process controls, and engineering problem solving. They look upon computers as highly sophisticated processors of data limited only by man's ingenuity and imagination. Further, they believe that because of its tremendous capacities and possibilities, with information lines cutting across traditional organization lines, the computer should be located in an information center or department reporting to the top executive. These two viewpoints are the extremes of a spectrum which includes many variations between the two limits. Companies have enjoyed benefits by following either of these viewpoints; the approach is not a measure of success. The point here is that divergent viewpoints are present and they condition the use and status of electronic data processing.

## CHALLENGES OF NEW OFFICE TECHNOLOGY

The uses of new techniques and machines to supply needed information multiply daily, and so do the users. The trend is unquestionably upward, whether measured by casual observation, surveys, statements of managers, or the number of office machines in use. Computer manufacturers, for example, now do an annual business of nearly $1½ billion. With this growth, management members are making bigger demands on the office because of the needs for specific information. The effect is to give the manager in charge of information a much larger scope of operations, much more opportunity, and much greater responsibility.

For the most part, basic issues pertaining to data processing are the reflection of basic issues of management. The computer, for example, cannot be viewed as an autonomous "black box" that will solve in some ingenious manner the headaches of managers. The computer is an adjunct to management; its role is to supply information to managers so that they can do their jobs better. But managers have to know their requirements, achieve a clarity of thought, and develop precise plans in order to obtain satisfactory results from a computer. Modern electronic data processing emphasizes the importance of management. Success with automated information efforts depends mainly upon the understanding which managers can and do bring in communicating with processors. Managers must be able to identify corporate objectives and advise of changes when these objectives shift.

One of the outstanding challenges of the new office technology is to improve existent information by streamlining old means of processing essential information into a format that stimulates effective usage of the information. To this end, the office manager should capture the initiative and suggest what types and arrangements of information might be of greatest assistance to the recipient. Too frequently, it is assumed that identical information and reports should continue after automation as existed before automation. The common practice of asking the recipient what information he wants usually results in a continuation of the existent information because the recipient does not know what other types he might have or how what he is receiving might be bettered. In short, he is not an expert in designing the information needs and report structure of his company. Perhaps no one man is—or for that matter, no one group; but certainly, efforts of reasonably skilled people in this area will assist in achieving better information.

An illustration will demonstrate the challenge of information improvement in the typical enterprise, which improvement can usually be won during the time of office automation installation. In a well-known company headquartered in Boston, the vice-president of finance is provided on a monthly basis with information on (1) items having a nonrecurring profit impact, (2) items having a continuing profit impact, and (3) financial managerial subjects requiring policy determination or modification. Such information differs from the rigid and common standardized financial data, yet it provides valuable assistance in vital decision making concerning financial matters.

Various studies among companies regarding their computer installations reveal specific areas for improvement. A rather common occurrence is a lack of determining corporate requirements. Emphasis is placed on data of a certain department rather than on interdepartmental or total operational information. Also, improper or inadequate planning is done resulting in ill-timed crash programs and scheduling difficulties. A complaint of many companies is that the conversion to the computer takes too long. Operations are unduly disrupted, jams occur in the work flow, and the entire mode of work accomplishment is upset.

## OFFICE AUTOMATION AND MANAGERIAL DECISION MAKING

Among the greatest influences of the new office technology is its effect upon managerial decision making. There are three major effects to consider:

1. *It aids in establishing a more sound basis for managerial decision making.* Modern office technology makes it economically feasible to compile data on a current basis. A manager can now know where he is rather than where he has been. To make decisions, reliance need not be placed on facts conditioned by the old traditional lags in information. Furthermore, it is possible to relate different units of measurement regarding company activities. No longer need production reports be expressed as units stamped per day, or shift, and inventory in some other measurement unit. The entire fund of information can be in a measuring unit common and meaningful to all concerned departments. Also, all the interrelated data can be of a comparable time period. For example, the period and frequencies for production reports can be precisely identical to those of inventory, or of sales reports. Thus, valid correlation of the information can be calculated.

2. *It makes feasible the use of new analytical techniques in managerial decision making.* Mathematics has long been applied to engineering and production problems, but it is now being utilized in management decision-making problems. The significant relationships of the important factors are determined and related mathematically. Then, different values for the

variable factors are substituted in the equation and tentative answers calculated. In this way, the best combination of factors for the most desirable answer is determined. In the past, the physical inability of clerical staffs to process all relevant information according to the limits prescribed by the mathematical equation made it impractical to determine many alternative decisions under different sets or conditions or factors. The techniques employed depend upon the problem and conditions under which the factors must operate. Among the more common techniques are linear programming, queuing theory, games theory, and optimization formulas.

3. *It makes possible the pretesting of decisions by means of simulation.* Office automation makes it physically possible to solve tomorrow's problem today, before a real crisis develops. Simulation includes the building of a model of a company that behaves exactly like the real thing; in other words, this model reflects actual operating conditions. Different tentative decisions are followed through to their respective different answers—what would happen as a result of each solution. The best answer can then be selected from various alternatives, and the decision to make for this desired answer is identified.

Simulation provides the answers to "what if" questions. It is made practical through office automation, which can solve problems that are too complex and have too many variables to solve through human effort alone. However, the use of a model to acquire knowledge is nothing new. Engineers have used this technique for years. Models of new designs are constructed and subsequently subjected to varying conditions of operation in order to determine the design providing optimum favorable results. In like manner, the manager using simulation does the same thing.

## HOW MUCH OFFICE AUTOMATION?

Decisions involving office automation are matters of importance to every enterprise. The proper amount or degree of office automation varies somewhat with the circumstance primarily because the meaning of automation is not constant. Automation is not a single entity. It might be the application of a computer to production control or a punched card adopted for handling orders between a factory and several warehouses. It is never accomplished in the sense that further progress in data processing is not possible.

No office is completely automated. Even though technologically possible, at least in the conceptual stage, the fully automated office is not *economically* feasible. And it is the economics of each situation that is a strong determinant of the degree to which automation proceeds. The best current estimates are that some 35–40 percent of the total office work is performed by electronic means in the typical present-day automated office, but it might well be higher. Certainly office automation as we recognize it today is not an office made up of 100 percent robots.

Of particular importance is the achieving of the best correlation between the demands made on the information system and the physical equipment itself. This involves the danger of overmechanization or of undermechanization in the office. From this problem of optimum fit stem many automation difficulties. For example, the equipment may turn out to be too elaborate for the specific company's needs, thus making the equipment investment excessive. Or frequent and expensive breakdowns may occur primarily because too much work or too many different types of work are being attempted with the particular machines. In other cases, the installation cost may greatly exceed estimates—a condition commonly arising from inadequate analysis of necessary informational demands.

Another problem is to determine specifically what work is and what work is not to be done by the machines. Some work is best done by a willing hand and a pencil, especially when the cost of operating the machine is taken into account. Likewise, a policy of charging each department for the machine time of a centralized unit can have the effect of loading too much work on the machine. This comes about quite innocently, in that a department head charged with a machine cost customarily sees to it that he gets something in return. Net result: Some work which should not be handled by the center is sent there for processing. The remedy lies in educating every management member to the economic considerations and limitations of each piece of office equipment and to the idea of total information integration.

In contrast, some offices are not mechanized enough, a state of affairs which commonly arises from indifference, fear, ignorance, or lack of direction or capital. The attitude of "Let us alone; we've been doing it this way since 1930" is one of the chief contributors to this condition. Seldom do office employees demand mechanization or hover around the machine, praising it, after installation. Their normal reaction is not to make any changes. Also, ignorance and the lack of well-defined directions by top managers can lead to undermechanization. Failure to perceive the broad implications of office automation and personal preference for other areas may be cited as the major reasons for this lack of needed direction. In addition, lack of capital may be responsible, but this is a somewhat dubious reason because most installations pay for themselves quickly and easy financing terms are readily available from the equipment seller.

## SOCIAL ASPECTS OF OFFICE AUTOMATION

Social change stimulated by office automation emphasizes employment modifications, which can be viewed as offering either (1) greater opportunities or (2) fewer opportunities, even to the point of mass unemployment. The former is indicative of the attitude under which office automation will come to maturity. It stresses: "What will automation help us do better, or assist us to achieve that has never been achieved?" There is a problem, however, in adapting to this greater opportunity. In this connection, much human effort will shift from manual to mental work and from menial to more challenging tasks. Automation puts at our disposal the means to a materially more abundant life. In the second viewpoint, the dominant force is fear. Employees are quite naturally concerned whether the higher rates of office work performance will result in unemployment or in raising living standards. Past experience seems to indicate that technological advancements have increased the overall level of employment. New demands have developed, the machines themselves creating a large labor force required for their construction and maintenance. However, many people are *displaced,* not *replaced* to other areas of duty. For example, a large installation of electronic office machines in a Chicago office required the shifting of several hundred employees to other jobs. Not a one lost his job; each was trained and placed in new work. This called for real management ability and, of course, necessitated an adjustment on the part of each employee.

To the opponents of office automation the blunt question may be directed: What is the alternative to office automation? The answer appears to be to maintain the status quo and to refrain from utilizing technological progress and faster and better ways of performing office work. Such action would downgrade our offices, our economy, and our society in general. This would be regression on a tragic scale. We would be saying to hundreds of thousands of scientists and engineers striving to advance our office technology that we don't want and will not use this additional knowledge. We must ever be mindful that progress means change and places before us broad challenges and threats which we must meet and conquer; otherwise we shall stagnate.

Many times in the office, the normal rate of attrition will bring about the smaller work force required. But older employees with seniority and relatively little flexibility pose difficulties. In a large insurance company, the personnel whose jobs were eliminated in the advance to more office automation were divided into three classes:

The largest class includes relatively unskilled junior personnel in clerical jobs of a repetitive nature—filing, sorting, recording, and performing other tasks where only a bare minimum of insurance knowledge is required. The second class consisted of personnel with more experience, and many years of seniority, who are in relatively routine jobs which require slightly more knowledge of insurance. Jobs of this class do not require original thinking, nor judgment beyond that necessary to identify an exception to usual routine which must be passed along to higher authority for action. The third class is composed of more highly skilled people engaged in supervisory and senior staff work. Their duties are primarily in the judgment area, and they require a more advanced knowledge of insurance.[3]

The writer of this quotation goes on to say that relocation of the unskilled junior personnel and of the skilled senior people create relatively few problems. It is the experienced employee performing routine jobs not in the judgment area who presents troublesome personnel dislocation difficulties because there are few job openings for a person with these qualifications and usually such an employee is relatively inflexible.

Many are of the opinion that skill requirements will increase for most office jobs as a result of automation. From the overall viewpoint, this might be, but it is well to observe that many jobs of relatively low skill will remain. Certainly training and the need for proficiency in specific skills are emphasized by automation. The person with no skill is hard put to find work.

Undoubtedly, the number of irksome, monotonous tasks is reduced by automation. Much laborious and time-consuming office work is done by the machine. This is desirable from the social point of view and is a benefit to mankind. Many feel that we are at the beginning of what might be described as a second Industrial Revolution, which will substitute machines for human beings in performing mental drudgery, just as the first Industrial Revolution substituted machines for carrying out most back-breaking physical drudgery.

## THINGS TO COME

It is a natural human instinct to anticipate what future progress can be expected in office management and what events of the future might change the office as we know it today. Experience of the present, although limited, suggests possible changes to be expected due to office technology. It appears fairly certain that many of the present ways of performing office work will fall by the wayside. Much of the required writing and calculating will be done automatically by machines which will operate from sound. Communicative devices will probably revolutionize the distribution of information, and it could be that most conferences will be handled on closed TV circuits or some adaptation thereof. Future reproducing processes are almost certain to establish an entirely new concept of filing and storing records. Papers common to our present office will be replaced by some medium such as electronic impulses stored in a computer. Many of these changes may not come about until many years ahead, while others may take place within the present decade.

---

[3] E. W. Martin, Jr., "Practical Problems of Introducing a Computer," *Business Horizons*, Fall, 1960, p. 8 (published by the Indiana University School of Business, Bloomington, Indiana).

It is reasonable to predict that decision making will be improved. The qualification of data, made possible by office improvements, will not only improve the amount and the quality of facts but will reveal pertinent relationships among them. The availability of a wider range of alternatives evaluated factually could reduce decision making based either on intuition or on historical data projection. Also, decision making will be carried out on a broader base. Company goals, not departmental goals, will be stressed; and the interaction of decisions pertaining to departments will be emphasized.

The handling of information will be carefully planned and engineered. The haphazard, "just let it grow as needs develop" attitude will decline to a minor position. Office work will become more closely related to managerial planning and controlling, and will be used to the full. The products of the office will increase in value and importance.

With all these changes, it is logical to state that an office manager's work will take on greater importance. With larger amounts of accurate and timely factual information available, the operational consequences of a decision will be measured more precisely, but the decision cannot be an automatic response to the impact of information. Judgment, consideration for nonmeasurable but influential factors, and responsibility for consequences are not transferred to the office automation equipment. They remain, at least in the foreseeable future, with the manager.

## WHERE ARE WE NOW?

With all these changes, constraints, forces, and innovations in the performance of office work, the total picture presented may be a bit confusing. To summarize, we might ask, "What are the most significant developments of the office technology up to the present time?" It would be easy to list some eight or ten really important changes. However, for purposes of this book, we will compress our list and select only those that are indeed extremely significant. When we do this we have three headings: (1) the systems concept, (2) source data automation (SDA), and (3) the electronics technology. They can be illustrated in the form of a triangle as shown in Figure 8–3.

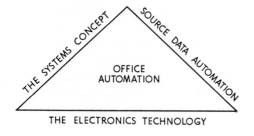

FIG. 8–3. The triangle of office automation.

These constitute the main structural members of office automation as we know it today. These three structural members comprise the nucleus for our discussion of office automation in the chapters immediately following. That is, the next two chapters deal with the systems concept, the third with source data automation, and the following three with the electronics technology.

The systems concept deals with the boundaries within which an analysis of paper work is conducted. It places emphasis upon the entirety, yet stresses the harmonious interrelationships of the parts making up that entirety. Using a systems concept, the analyst tackles the big picture, or the whole, but he is also concerned with how the parts of that picture mesh together into a harmonious unity. The systems concept frees the analyst from the approach of concentrating his efforts upon a single component and successively analyzing each component separately until all the components, or the entirety, are studied. The systems concept is actually not new, but it has gained prominence in the new office technology. The development of the systems concept is a natural outgrowth of having equipment available which can unify office operations among departments, distribute information between widely separated locations, and interrelate data-processing efforts among the traditionally functional divisions of an enterprise. The systems concept supplies the mental medium to conceive and utilize large portions of information projects, which portions are in keeping with the capacities of the physical equipment to be used in processing and handling this information.

Among the initial efforts to improve the processing of data was the idea to put source data into a form so that they could be reused as needed without the necessity of rewriting the source data each time they were to be used. Further, if this form could be made common to all the standard machines of an office, it would be possible to process the data utilizing the type of machine needed without having to rewrite or reenter the information for each machine. Also, the processing of data could be integrated. To illustrate, the punched card into which the data are captured by means of punched holes is a widely known example of a medium which facilitates source data automation. Once the data are captured in the card, they can be processed by a variety of equipment. Without doubt the accomplishment of keeping data in a form reusable between processing steps is one of the outstanding hallmarks in the area of the new office technology.

Third, the electronics technology is so significant that many feel it is synonymous with office technology. The computer is king and the center about which much office automation revolves. What has been accomplished with it staggers the imagination, but even more exciting is to dream what new uses may be made of computers and to strive to discover and ultimately to perfect such disclosures. The computer is without peer as a catalyst for new ideas. It is not just another office tool but a giant marvel awaiting our command. We must, however, know or learn how to direct this force in an effective manner. Computers, while accounting for the biggest share of electronics technology—and in which we are here most interested—are only a portion of the whole story. Automatic control arrangements which unite manufacturing control with data collecting and processing, and communications devices and communications switching devices are also a part of this technological change.

Each of these three major headings or structural members—the systems concept, source data automation, and the electronics technology—has been advanced by tremendous progress in equipment design and availability. Also each has fostered the growth of the other two. These observations are logical because the three developments themselves are outgrowths of a technology—in this case the office technology. And they are interrelated because they come from and have developed within a common major movement—again, the office technology.

## QUESTIONS

1. Discuss the scope of the new office technology.
2. Identify clearly each of the following:
    a) Feasibility of automation.
    b) New office technology.
    c) Feedback.
    d) "Degree of office automation."
3. Do you agree with the following statement: "Although there is much glamour and sophistication about automation in the office, the real reason for its development is the reduction in office costs that it brings about." Why?
4. Briefly describe your concept of "office automation."
5. For any given enterprise, should identical information continue after automation as existed before automation? Why?
6. Discuss the existence of confusion about the possible contributions of the new office technology. What do you recommend to dispel this confusion? Elaborate on your answer.
7. In your opinion, have some companies installed computers in their office in part for reasons of prestige and reputation? Discuss.
8. Discuss several general but important factors to be considered in determining the feasibility of office automation for an enterprise.
9. What is meant by the statement that office automation permits a manager to reach better decisions by means of simulation?
10. As you see it, will office managerial actuating become less important as office automation increases? Justify your viewpoint.

11. Are the social aspects of office automation of major concern to the office manager? Elaborate on your answer.

12. What are the major challenges of the new office technology? Discuss the one you deem vital.

## CASE PROBLEMS

### Case 8–1.   Future Economic Association

In response to an inquiry from Professor Allen Mott, the following letter was received from Mr. John Codley, Secretary of the Future Economic Association:

Dear Professor Mott:

Receiving your recent letter was a genuine pleasure. I am most happy to outline thoughts by members of our association.

Fundamentally, we believe that office machines are making employees obsolete as producers and that action must be taken to insure incomes for all present office employees, whether they work or not. At first, I know this sounds radical, but we are entering an era in the office whereby almost unlimited output, with little human effort, is feasible. Poverty and unemployment are inevitable, as we see it, unless new policies which do away with the current work-reward theory are adopted. Unless positive action is taken, we will be thrown into unprecedented economic and social disorder.

Contrary to statements made by our critics, we do believe that the use of office machines should be encouraged, not repressed. We advocate the use of office machines to perform as much office work as possible. But this technological change must be tuned to the benefit of the individual and utilized humanely as well as rationally. And it is our contention that this necessitates a new concept of "earning income" and divesting income from its traditional partnership to a job.

Under separate cover I am sending you some of our literature that you will find of interest.

Very truly yours,

C:m

John Codley   (signed)
Secretary

## Problems:

1. What are your reactions to Mr. Codley's comments?
2. Write the reply that you feel Professor Mott should make.

### Case 8–2.   Office Machines Research, Inc.

A survey on the subject of office automation has been completed by this corporation. Included in the study were 300 corporations employing a total of 132,740 office employees. Tabulation of the replies shows the following:

1. In your opinion, will office automation in your company continue to increase over the next ten years?

Yes    57.1%    No    36.3%    Don't Know    6.6%

1A. If "Yes," please check the type of office automation anticipated. If "No," go to Question 2.

| | | | |
|---|---|---|---|
| Accounts receivable | 14.1% | Inventory control | 24.6% |
| Accounts payable | 13.7 | Payroll | 6.9 |
| Billing | 10.8 | Production control | 7.4 |
| Information retrieval | 4.8 | Other | 17.7 |
| | | Total | 100.0% |

1B. What are your main reasons for automating?

| | |
|---|---|
| Difficulty in finding needed help | 20.7% |
| Faster processing of data | 21.0 |
| Increased volume of work | 24.1 |
| More accurate processing of data | 14.9 |
| Miscellaneous | 19.3 |
| Total | 100.0% |

2. As of right now, about what percentage of your office work is automated?

| | | | |
|---|---|---|---|
| 100–91% | — | 50–41% | 12.3% |
| 90–81% | — | 40–31% | 38.7 |
| 80–71% | 1.8% | 30–21% | 19.4 |
| 70–61% | 3.6 | 20–11% | 14.8 |
| 60–51% | 5.2 | 10– 0% | 4.2 |

3. In adopting automation in your office, what factors were most difficult to overcome?

| | |
|---|---|
| Belief that cost of automation is too high | 31.9% |
| Converting to the automatic arrangement | 16.5 |
| Finding employees for newly created types of office work | 23.6 |
| Getting employee acceptance | 9.8 |
| Miscellaneous | 11.8 |
| Don't Know | 6.4 |
| Total | 100.0% |

4. During the past ten years has the total office employment of your company increased?

Yes   78.4%   No   15.5%   About same   5.3%   Don't know   0.8%

4A. If answer is "yes," please answer:
In general to what growth factors do you primarily attribute this growth?

| | |
|---|---|
| More office work | 35.7% |
| More services | 20.2 |
| New products | 24.6 |
| Miscellaneous | 10.4 |
| Don't know | 9.1 |
| Total | 100.0% |

4B. If answer is "no," please answer:
In general to what nongrowth factors do you primarily attribute this decline?

| | |
|---|---|
| Automation | 7.0% |
| Business has declined | 13.6 |
| Business has remained same | 55.3 |
| Miscellaneous | 8.4 |
| Don't know | 15.7 |
| Total | 100.0% |

Recap of respondents:

| *Type of business:* | | *No. of Office Employees:* | |
|---|---|---|---|
| Finance | 11.5% | 0–100 | 15.8% |
| Insurance | 8.1 | 101–200 | 44.7 |
| Mfg. | 53.9 | 201–300 | 23.2 |
| Retail | 8.4 | 301–400 | 10.8 |
| Service | 17.0 | 401–500 | 2.4 |
| Other | 1.1 | 501 and over | 3.1 |
| Total | 100.0% | Total | 100.0% |

| *Location:* | | *Title of Respondent:* | |
|---|---|---|---|
| East Coast | 32.3% | Adm. Mgr. | 2.3% |
| SE | 11.2 | Controller | 40.4 |
| Mid-West | 28.1 | Off. Mgr. | 21.7 |
| S Central | 7.0 | Off. Services Mgr. | 5.9 |
| SW | 7.1 | S. & P. Mgr. | 13.3 |
| West Coast | 14.3 | VP Fin. | 8.6 |
| Total | 100.0% | Other | 7.8 |
| | | Total | 100.0% |

## Problems:

1. Discuss major conclusions you derive from this survey.
2. Enumerate additional questions you would have liked asked. Give reasons for desiring answers to these additional questions.

# CHAPTER 9

# THE SYSTEMS
# AND PROCEDURES APPROACH

Doing is the great thing. For if, resolutely,
people do what is right, in time they come to
like doing it.
                              —*John Ruskin*

OFFICE work is being revolutionized by the systems and procedures approach. We are hearing more about "systems," and managers are placing increasing emphasis on systems to meet the need for fast and accurate information and to make effective use of modern technological facilities for processing data. Systems are having a fundamental and broad-based impact upon all functions of an enterprise. Proven techniques, skills, and practices of the systems and procedures approach have been developed to produce meaningful time-saving results. In this and the following chapter we shall discuss the essentials of systems so that a basic comprehension of them is gained and their importance in the current office technology is realized.

## EXISTENCE OF SYSTEMS

There is nothing new about the concept of systems. It is as old as mankind. Early in life we become acquainted with the solar system and later discover that we ourselves have digestive, nervous, and circulatory systems. In business, reference is commonly made to the inventory control system, the marketing system, the financing system, and so forth. Systems have been with us for many years.

For convenience, systems can be classified in any of several ways. The classifications of *physical* systems and *abstract* systems sometimes are helpful. The former includes the human digestive system and the blood circulatory system, for example, while the latter would include the purchasing system and the shipping system of an enterprise. Classifications of similar meaning but with different names are *natural* systems and *man-made* systems. These terms are self-explanatory. Natural systems are those of physical or organic origin; they evolve from sources beyond the control of man, or nearly so. In contrast, man-made systems are designed by man to bring about a desired result by modifying or constraining performance, development, or action of selected basic resources.

## SYSTEM IDENTIFIED

In many instances, an ordinary activity, commonly viewed as a single activity, is in reality made up of many different and relatively less important activities. Upon close examination we recognize the existence of an orderly relationship of some sort among these various lesser activities making up the entirety. And we discover that the interaction among the lesser actions or parts is necessary so that the entirety or end product performed is in keeping with accomplishing a given goal. Systems-minded people have been viewing problems in this light for many years.

Figure 9–1 illustrates graphically an activity common in business and one familiar to most of us. It shows the various activities making up a

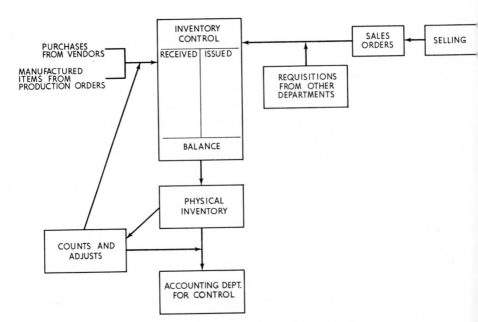

FIG. 9–1.   A system of inventory control.

system of inventory control. In other words to insure adequate amounts of the right types of materials being on hand, we follow a man-made system designed to accomplish our objective. Various activities are coordinated in this effort. As indicated in the upper left of the figure, parts are either purchased from outside suppliers or we make them ourselves. These receipts are balanced with what we need, as revealed by sales orders and requisitions from other departments. Shipment of sales orders are made from storeroom supply. A level of inventory is maintained to permit taking care of the sales orders in this manner. In addition, control of physical counts and the supplying of data to the accounting department are included in the system.

This all appears simple enough, but we must note that a single entry on this chart, such as "purchases from vendors," entails a whole series of actions. From whom is a certain purchase made, when, what papers are used, what information is used to confirm purchase price, and so forth are the types of action involved. We use a term to identify such a sequence of operations for achieving a definite type of informational work. It is office procedure.

We will discuss office procedures more, but for the present we can say that the system shown in Figure 9–1 consists of and ties together three office procedures. Specifically this illustrated system of inventory control is made up of (1) the procedure for purchasing from vendors or from ourselves, (2) the procedure for issuing for sales orders which are shipped from the storeroom supply, and (3) the procedure for determining the physical inventory on hand.

We are now ready to define system. *It is a network of procedures which are integrated and designed to carry out a major activity.* We can think of a system as providing an orderly relationship among the parts and the whole. The large overall picture is included, yet the interrelations of the various parts making up this large picture are each given their proper attention both within the part itself and in its relation to the entirety. That is, the efficiency of each part, as well as the concern for the overall performance of the whole, is retained. In effect, the systems approach brings integration of related activities into the picture. Information which used to be considered and handled as separate entities is brought together. Fragmentation of information is minimized. Highlighted is the composite end result of many different informational activities working in many different ways. We consider the components as a dynamic totality or interaction of parts which is more important than the components themselves.

## THE SYSTEMS VIEWPOINT

From the office management viewpoint, a system can be looked upon as a vehicle of thought and analysis. It is an attitude or way of viewing projects and problems in office management. A system has been called a "think process tool." This identity stresses system as providing the medium of thought and it implies utilization of an encompassing approach, yet retention of and regard for the components making up the entirety employed.

The use of systems in office management stresses conceptual skills of the manager. He must be able to visualize and understand the relationships between the information management job and all functions of the enterprise. For example, he must be able to gain a vivid mental picture of the effect of a change in materials control activity in a plant or in the sales order handling activity. Likewise, the ability to determine the effect of a new production control plan on the current cost control activity must be present.

## EXTENSIVENESS AND INTEGRATION OF INFORMATION FLOW

From what has been stated it follows that the system concept can be applied to many facets of office management. As already indicated (Chapter 8) we can view an entire business enterprise as a system. In this case there are various component activities—producing, selling, financing, and so forth—which, in operation together, make up the entirety. In the same manner, production control, marketing research, handling accounts receivable, and so forth, can be viewed as systems, although in these cases the entirety, or scope of work, included is more limited than that where the entire business enterprise is considered as the system.

The extensiveness and the integration of the information flow arising from various activities are important. Firmly realizing these basic characteristics assists in grasping the fundamental concept of what makes up a system and employing it advantageously in office management work. To demonstrate further the relationships that exist, Figure 9–2 is included. This illustrates vividly the multitude of different, yet integrated, activities involved in receiving, manufacturing, and shipping customers' orders. Production requirements, for example, necessitate parts, labor, a manufacturing program, and facilities planning. Parts are either purchased from vendors or manufactured. If purchased, as shown in the figure, a number of activities are performed, including selecting the vendors, negotiating terms of purchase, following up purchase orders, receiving parts, having them inspected, sending either to raw materials inventory or to assembly, and reporting receipts so that accounts payable can be made. The figure is indicative, but not conclusive. The task of systems integration is never simple. The overall framework is first conceived and then each informational segment, required by certain people to perform their specific work, is fitted into this entirety. Relating each segment to the overall pattern, or system, is vital.

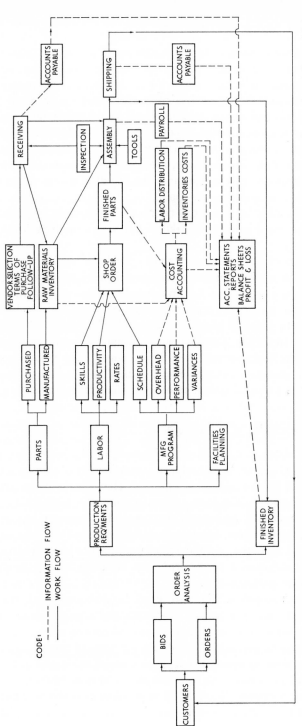

FIG. 9–2. The receiving, manufacturing, and shipping of customers' orders give rise to an extensive informational flow which is integrated by means of office systems.

## SYSTEMS AND OFFICE TECHNOLOGY

Despite the complexity of business, the use of systems was limited until the availability of automated ways of processing data. As the source data automation technique became more widely known and computers became available, managers began to recognize the merit of using the systems concept. A number of the initial automated installations dealt with single isolated activities. Soon it was discovered that either needless duplication existed or certain voids in information were present, especially in relation to isolated activities. Furthermore, the scope of the automated processes and the quantity of data which could be handled within a short period suggested that a broader viewpoint or a larger scope of work be undertaken. In other words, man's concept of what could be accomplished had to be broadened in order to take advantage of the technical advances in data processing.

The systems concept is part of man's need and desire to sharpen his conceptual tools for solving his informational problems. Computers alone, with their capacity, versatility, and speed, cannot supply the answers. What they do is enable man to solve informational problems that heretofore were beyond his scope. Now he has the technical means available, but to utilize them, he must upgrade his conceptual horizons, identify critical informational problems, conceive the solutions to these problems, and evaluate their potential gain. This is a human prerogative and constitutes a vital challenge to modern office managers.

## SYSTEMS, PROCEDURES, METHODS

We stated above that included in the makeup of a system is a network of procedures. Or stated differently, the coordination of related procedures can be thought of as making up a system. Hence, procedures are always included in a system. The term "systems and procedures" is in common usage. It gives recognition to both systems and procedures, but frequently the terminology of either "systems" or "procedures" may be employed. Systems would normally include systems and procedures, whereas procedures may be inclusive of procedures only, although in some instances the concept of systems is also implied.

The term "subsystem" is also used in discussions of systems. A subsystem is an integral part of a system and consists of two or more related procedures. The term, subsystem, is always subordinate to and used in reference to a system. For certain purposes of analysis, the concept of a system and its subsystems is helpful. Considered in and of themselves several related procedures are not referred to as making up a subsystem; they make up a system. To qualify as a subsystem the viewpoint must encompass or imply that the subsystem is subordinate to the system.

Procedures are of special interest in the management of office work. An "office procedure" can be defined as *a series of related clerical steps, usually performed by more than one person, which constitute an established and accepted way of carrying on an entire major phase of office activity*. Procedures are obtained by preplanning the various steps believed necessary to accomplish the work. Procedures are applied to the handling of such things as incoming orders, accounts payable, purchase orders, making up payrolls, sending out statements, and handling mail. An office procedure is broad in scope, frequently extending throughout a large portion of the entire office.

For clarity we will also define methods at this point, but discussion of them will be deferred. The term "method" designates *the manner of work performance of a task consisting of one or more clerical acts by an individual employee*. To a degree, methods become quite routine under an automated arrangement. Methods planning is more important when manual means are followed. A series of methods which are cumulative and integrated make up a procedure. And, to repeat, several procedures which are related and integrated make up a system.

In other words, as we successively narrow our scope of thinking about the manner of work performance, we utilize the concepts of systems, procedures, and methods. It is logical to determine first the system, then the procedures making up this system, and finally the methods making up each procedure. In this way the broad activities are established, coordination is enhanced, the feasibility of automation effectively determined, and the end result of the total effort is clearly visualized. In practice, however, the office planner or analyst gives some consideration to procedures and methods while designing the system and to methods while designing the procedure. This is taking the bottom-to-top viewpoint and this is usually helpful in connection with the top-down viewpoint. The latter viewpoint, however, is dominant. To reverse this approach by starting with methods, tying them together for the procedure, and tying procedures together for the system, is possible, but usually results in coordination difficulties and in excessive work scopes covered by the procedures and the systems.

## SYSTEMS AND PROCEDURES IN OFFICE MANAGEMENT

For many years managers utilized the "look-see" practice in managing their enterprises. By this means the manager had his group working close at hand, gave orders directly to them, and exercised his managerial influences mainly by watching what the members of the group were doing. This overseeing characteristic of management was universal.

In modern business, the "look-see" management is rapidly diminishing. Mainly because of human complexity, size, and number of work specialties, today's manager can no longer look, see, and know the work results.

He must use information as an indirect substitute for the "look-see" technique. Simply strolling by the desks and files to see how things are going, or talking with a few supervisors or group leaders, really doesn't provide much information of any value. The sample is insignificant and certain important criteria are not visible. The modern manager needs (1) a system which provides him accurate information as a substitute for the "look-see" approach and (2) an ability to interpret and understand the real significance of this information. The information is the type needed to help him perform his fundamental managerial functions, namely, his planning, controlling, organizing, and actuating efforts.

Much of today's office work—much in fact of *all* work—is accomplished through systems and procedures rather than by means of direct orders guided by what is obtained from the "look-see" approach. "Management by information" is a term that can be used to describe this new look. The trend in this direction is noticeable. For example, a manager doesn't have to be on the site of his operations. Information centers where decision making takes place are becoming common. All indications point to the increasing importance of management by information and the decreasing use of "look-see" management.

In this change, the emphasis upon systems and procedures in office management is apparent. They are fundamental in obtaining, processing, and distributing information to those who use it and in a form and at a time and place that they need it. Systems and procedures are, indeed, the basis for a completely harmonious and orderly operation of office work. More than this, the success or failure of most enterprises today depend in great measure on how carefully the office systems and procedures are developed and how well they are controlled in expediting the flow of information into and out of the enterprise.

Systems and procedures handle cycles of business activity, that is, they identify and establish sequences of specific activities for achieving definite types of office work. Referring to Figure 9–1 again, this system includes three specific procedures. If well planned this system will establish these procedures as essential to achieve the goal desired, coordinate them, prescribe the precise methods making up each procedure, and synchronize the methods within each procedure. Thus, an effective unity is derived from the various components, and this unity moves efficiently toward accomplishing the stated objective.

A challenge of office planning is to determine what systems and combinations of office procedures and methods is best for a given enterprise. The complexity of modern information handling negates the approach of considering each information requirement as a separate, isolated, and independent entity. The office manager cannot plan piecemeal and add parts together, taking a paper here, a machine there, a tape from still another area, and hope they all will fit together, work right, and give agreeable results. Today, he must start with the objective and work backward, by asking how best this goal can be reached by the use of those facilities available to him or those that can be made available to him. The systems and procedures approach helps tremendously in these efforts.

## ADVANTAGES OF SYSTEMS AND PROCEDURES

The importance of systems and procedures to improved office management are brought out in clear relief by listing their outstanding advantages. Such a list:

1. *Supplies a realistic look at an enterprise.*  There is little question that in the final analysis an enterprise is an entirety. It exists to fulfill definite overall objectives. Each of its parts, departments, or units, no matter how compartmentized, contributes, as a result of the total, to the overall objectives. By adopting the systems and procedures approach it is possible to comprehend the entirety yet appreciate the operation of the various parts, separately and as a group, in achieving a particular goal.

2. *Increases appreciation for the total problem.*  The broad and sweeping scope of systems and procedures enables a manager to see the total problem with its ramifications of various degrees of intensity in different areas of the enterprise. His thinking is focused on concern for the entirety with due regard for each part making up that entirety. What is under study is clearly delineated. In the very real meaning of the word, the relative importance of problems can be ascertained. Systems and procedures cut a swath through limited, departmentized, outmoded, and cobwebbed notions.

3. *Identifies the ingredients and the output.*  It is always helpful to know what is required and what is obtained from any given activity. With the input and output highlighted, an evaluation of the type of data required in order to get certain other derived data can prove helpful in that the feasibility of the work and whether it appears worthwhile can be readily determined.

4. *Brings order and a desirable mode of operation to office work.*  Systems and procedures reduce everyday work to a routine, simplifying the execution of the work and minimizing the task of decision making in the handling of that work. Thus, management members are relieved of many details of execution, making it possible for them to devote most of their time to other work. The carrying out of the usual and frequent tasks is taken care of by the systems and procedures. Thus, only the out-of-the-ordinary or exceptional matters are referred to the executive, who decides what is to be done in these cases. This practice is referred to as the "exception principle" in management literature.

5. *Gives uniformity of actions and formalizes the work.*  Common clerical tasks are handled in an identical manner each time they occur.

Work can be easily located and quick checks on progress can be made. Well-designed paper forms, work habits, and controls can be utilized. In effect, systems formalize the related procedures, and procedures formalize the successive clerical steps so that an omission of any one of them is unusual. Thus, the chances of error are reduced. Furthermore, the possibility of any inaccuracy in the work at any one point is minimized, since an employee becomes particularly efficient and adept at his operation because of specialization and repetition.

6. *Emphasizes accurate and reliable controls.* Systems and procedures show the existence or not of checks and mechanisms whose purpose is to maintain accuracy, reliability, or other types of controls over the data. The overall picture utilized makes it possible to employ only those controls necessary for the whole system, thus lowering costs while retaining needed control over the work. Also, it can be arranged that the development of nonacceptable output triggers corrective action so that the work is kept within the provisions planned for it.

7. *Isolates and identifies problem areas.* The inclusive nature of systems and procedures makes it possible to spot problem areas quickly and accurately. Viewing the entire "work package" as a unit reveals the weak or trouble spots in their true relationship. Whereas an analysis of segment after segment may show no cause for alarm, an examination of the totality will reveal the difficulty. Some errors are magnified, others compensated for or neutralized by the total action and it is this type of helpful information which the systems and procedures approach supplies.

8. *Encourages application of management to broad concepts.* All the fundamental functions of management are promoted by the systems and procedures approach. Planning and controlling are especially stimulated. Uniform management practices are encouraged, thus contributing to an orderly and effective manner of performing the work. Reliance upon rule-of-thumb measures and traditional modes of operation are minimized. Desirable results include greater efficiency, better coordination, a minimum of duplicated efforts and papers, and a more tightly knit and uniform work group.

9. *Facilitates automation of data processing.* Integrated data processing and the computer provide the practical means for handling large volumes of complicated data which apply to and cut across either small or large portions of an enterprise, the entire enterprise, or even the entire enterprise and outside influences. With the physical means available to process such data it is mandatory to have a medium facilitating the conceptualization of how the data might be processed to satisfy definite needs. Systems and procedures supply such a medium.

10. *Simplifies office personnel training.* The duties and operations of each job are clearly defined. Information is determined regarding what the employee must be capable of doing to perform the work satisfactorily.

Selective training programs can be focused on the particular requirements needed by the employee.

11. *Improves the services of the office.* It is by means of procedures that the modern office is able to meet the large demands placed upon it. Getting the work out on time and in an acceptable form is possible through the help of office procedures. They make it possible to render the type of office service desired.

12. *Brings savings in the supplying of necessary information.* The work is kept moving, delay is minimized, employees are guided in their respective tasks, and unnecessary steps are eliminated.

## SYSTEMS AND DATA PROCESSING

The requirements of the system, expressed in written and chart form, are transferred into specific processing activities in order for implementation to take place. In the case of manually or nonautomated processing, this transfer poses no new techniques. It is simply a matter of studying the map or guides and instructions precisely. The identity, sequence, and relationship of the operations are the base requirements. To a degree the same situation exists when source data automation is used. The means and locations for the source data are carefully determined and implemented. The various machines required are secured or made adaptable for the system requirements. The new manner of performing the work is then initiated and periodic follow-ups are made to insure that the processing is satisfactory.

However, when the processing is by computer we encounter a different situation. The system requirements must be transferred into a form which the computer can handle. Specifically, the relationship is between the system design and the computer programming function. What is computer programming? This is answered fully in Chapter 12, but for the present it will suffice to state that computer programming is a detail of the work in the form of a package of instructions for a computer to follow in order to process the work electronically.

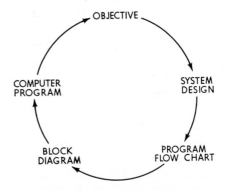

FIG. 9–3. Steps between objective statements are attainments when computer processing is employed.

To get from the system design to the computer program, a program flow chart and a block diagram are used. Figure 9–3 shows the arrangement. An objective is to be accomplished. To this end, a system is designed. The system is expressed in a program flow chart which, in turn, is expressed in the block diagram and computer program.

The program flow chart and block diagram show a detailed breakdown of the step-by-step activity requirements of the system. The extent to which the detail is carried depends upon the complexity and purpose of the work being processed. In some instances extreme details are in order while in other cases "reasonable" details suffice. When necessary details are missing, uncertainty, controversy, and needless discussions result. To illustrate the degree of detail, let us assume the system deals with payroll processing and we have progressed through steps (1) gross pay from straight salary, (2) gross pay from hourly rate, and (3) gross pay from incentive. The next steps are (4) develop deductions, and (5) get new up-to-date balance. Is step No. 4 in sufficient detail? To process it, we must (4.1) determine withholding tax, (4.2) determine F.I.C.A. and (4.3) calculate other approved deductions, i.e., for group insurance, union dues, and purchase of U.S. bonds. Unless these details are inserted in the computer program, the processing will fail. Carried further, we can ask, "Is step No. 4.1, 'determine withholding tax,' in sufficient detail?" Again the answer may be, "No," in which event either the block diagram should include the details or they must be added to the computer program. For step No. 4.1, additional details such as (4.11) exemption amount, (4.12) tax class, (4.13) existence of taxable income, and (4.14) tax amount might be needed.

Symbols are used in the preparation of program flow charts. Widely adopted and recommended symbols and their description are shown in Figure 9–4.

In actual practice the systems man can stop at the system design and let the computer programmer develop from the system the block diagram and the computer program. In contrast, the systems man may extend his efforts all the way through computer programming, and turn over the complete package to the computer operator. Neither of these extremes is recommended. The best arrangement is an overlap in efforts in the area of reasonable details of the block diagram. In this way the systems man gains an understanding of programming and the programmer gains an understanding of the system design work. By developing jointly the graphic documents between system design and computer program, interfunctional cooperation increases, ambiguity of data is minimized, training is facilitated, and interdepartmental flexibility is encouraged.

Figure 9–5 shows the program flow chart for the application of calculating thermal differential means and variances. Beginning in the upper left, the first step is to test if switch B is on. If "Yes," indicated by letter "Y," the next step is to the right; if "No," indicated by letter "N," the next step is downward to Test C, to see if switch C is on. The successive steps progress downward in the left column of the figure to the

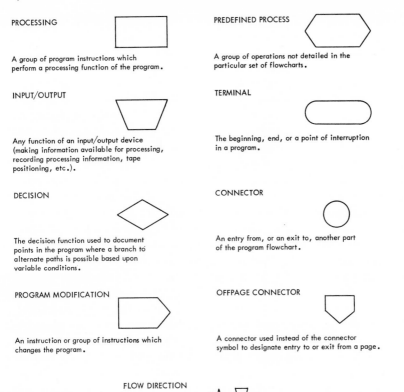

FIG. 9–4.   Program flow chart symbols and their descriptions.

bottom where point A is reached and continue in the column to the right.

From this program flow chart, the block diagram is developed. The start of this is shown by Figure 9–6. Block A is the start and consists of "Test if switch B is on." Moving to the right, block B is the next step, consisting of Test C, which is composed of "Test if switch C is on." Progressing to the right, the next step is indicated in Block C. To the right of each block are two columns for insertion of data needed for conversion to the computer. In block A, for example, in the first column are Y and N standing for "Yes" and "No." In the second column and opposite Y is 2L, meaning if the answer is "Yes," the successive step is 2L; in the same column opposite N is B, meaning if the answer is "No," the successive step is B, or block B, shown to the right of block A. The meaning of 2L is a code for a program modification which in this case is "set time switch to transfer setting" as indicated in Figure 9–5, upper left, as the step

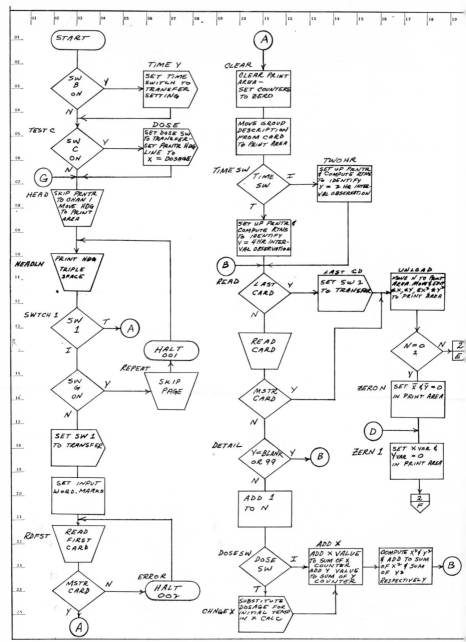

FIG. 9–5.   A program flow chart.

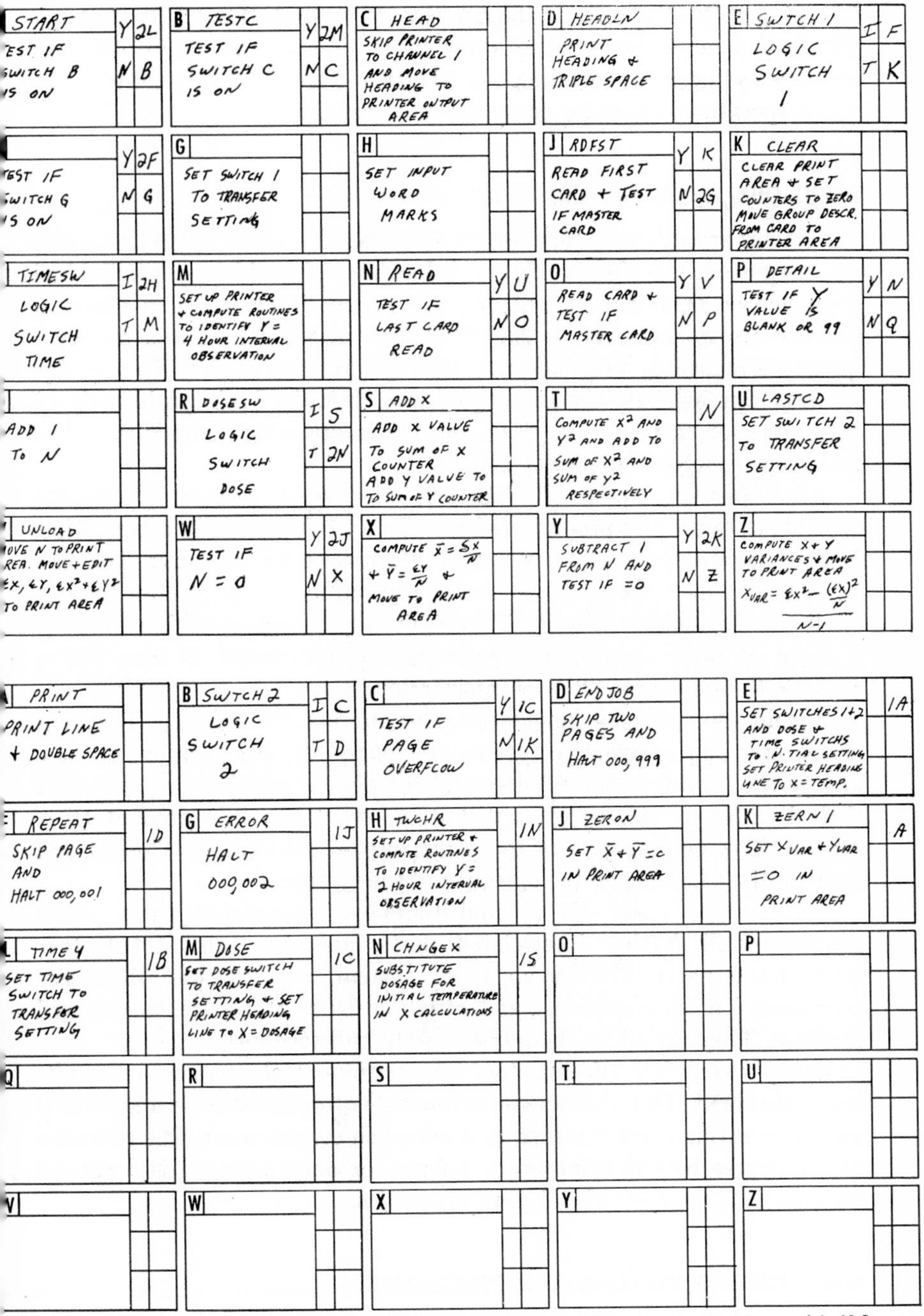

**START** — TEST IF SWITCH B IS ON [Y 2L] [N B]

**B TESTC** — TEST IF SWITCH C IS ON [Y 2M] [M C]

**C HEAD** — SKIP PRINTER TO CHANNEL 1 AND MOVE HEADING TO PRINTER OUTPUT AREA

**D HEADLN** — PRINT HEADING + TRIPLE SPACE

**E SWITCH 1** — LOGIC SWITCH 1 [I F] [T K]

---

TEST IF SWITCH G IS ON [Y 2F] [N G]

**G** SET SWITCH 1 TO TRANSFER SETTING

**H** SET INPUT WORD MARKS

**J RDFST** — READ FIRST CARD + TEST IF MASTER CARD [Y K] [N 2G]

**K CLEAR** — CLEAR PRINT AREA + SET COUNTERS TO ZERO MOVE GROUP DESCR. FROM CARD TO PRINTER AREA

---

**TIMESW** — LOGIC SWITCH TIME [I 2H] [T M]

**M** SET UP PRINTER + COMPUTE ROUTINES TO IDENTIFY Y = 4 HOUR INTERVAL OBSERVATION

**N READ** — TEST IF LAST CARD READ [Y U] [N O]

**O** READ CARD + TEST IF MASTER CARD [Y V] [N P]

**P DETAIL** — TEST IF Y VALUE IS BLANK OR 99 [Y N] [N Q]

---

ADD 1 TO N

**R DOSESW** — LOGIC SWITCH DOSE [I S] [T 2N]

**S ADD X** — ADD X VALUE TO SUM OF X COUNTER ADD Y VALUE TO SUM OF Y COUNTER

**T** COMPUTE $X^2$ AND $Y^2$ AND ADD TO SUM OF $X^2$ AND SUM OF $y2$ RESPECTIVELY [N]

**U LASTCD** — SET SWITCH 2 TO TRANSFER SETTING

---

**UNLOAD** — MOVE N TO PRINT REA. MOVE +EDIT EX, EY, $EX^2$ $EY^2$ TO PRINT AREA

**W** TEST IF N = 0 [Y 2J] [N X]

**X** COMPUTE $\bar{x} = \dfrac{Sx}{N} + \bar{Y} = \dfrac{EY}{N} +$ MOVE TO PRINT AREA

**Y** SUBTRACT 1 FROM N AND TEST IF = 0 [Y 2K] [N Z]

**Z** COMPUTE X+Y VARIANCES + MOVE TO PRINT AREA $X_{VAR} = \dfrac{Ex^2 - \dfrac{(Ex)^2}{N}}{N-1}$

---

**PRINT** — PRINT LINE + DOUBLE SPACE

**B SWTCH2** — LOGIC SWITCH 2 [I C] [T D]

**C** TEST IF PAGE OVERFLOW [Y 1C] [N 1K]

**D END JOB** — SKIP TWO PAGES AND HALT 000, 999

**E** SET SWITCHES 1+2 AND DOSE + TIME SWITCHS TO N. TRIAL SETTING SET PRINTER HEADING LINE TO X = TEMP. [1A]

---

**REPEAT** — SKIP PAGE AND HALT 000,001 [1D]

**G ERROR** — HALT 000,002 [1J]

**H TWCHR** — SET UP PRINTER + COMPUTE ROUTINES TO IDENTIFY Y = 2 HOUR INTERVAL OBSERVATION [1N]

**J ZERON** — SET $\bar{X} + \bar{Y} = 0$ IN PRINT AREA

**K ZERN1** — SET $X_{VAR} + Y_{VAR} = 0$ IN PRINT AREA [A]

---

**TIME 4** — SET TIME SWITCH TO TRANSFER SETTING [1B]

**M DOSE** — SET DOSE SWITCH TO TRANSFER SETTING + SET PRINTER HEADING LINE TO X = DOSAGE [1C]

**N CHNGEX** — SUBSTITUTE DOSAGE FOR INITIAL TEMPERATURE IN X CALCULATIONS [1S]

**O**

**P**

---

**Q**    **R**    **S**    **T**    **U**

**V**    **W**    **X**    **Y**    **Z**

Courtesy: Johnson and Johnson Co., New Brunswick, N.J.

FIG. 9–6.   A block diagram for conversion work to computer.

following a "Yes" answer to the question, "Is switch B on?" By studying Figure 9–5 in conjunction with the block diagram of Figure 9–6, the identity and need for each block of Figure 9–6 is revealed, along with the coded operations which the computer must perform.

## BASIC OBSERVATIONS ABOUT SYSTEMS

Systems are valuable, for they are the means by which related activities are integrated. The effective flow of information, by which each individual employee or organization unit receives proper information in order to perform its work better, is expedited by systems. There are, however, questions regarding what information is proper and needed. To a degree systems can help answer these questions, but the basic problem is to determine for each unit, its goals and the information it needs to utilize management in reaching these goals.

It is important to point out that each unit not only receives information to guide it, but it also produces information of importance to others. That is, there is a receiving and a giving of information by each unit. This can be identified as "input-output" and applies either to one or to a totality made up of a number of units. This input-output characteristic makes for a chain of information which expedites system design. It also makes realistic the expression "flow of information."

Within their defined boundaries, systems are all-inclusive. They cut across common compartmentations recognized by organization, custom, and personal preferences. All essential component activities, regardless of their location or degree of contribution, are taken into account by a system. The guiding rule is to encompass all informational needs and contributions bearing on the objective of the system.

Systems are made up of multitudinous interrelated parts which comprise still further interrelated parts, and, in turn, still further interrelated parts. Within an office system, for example, there are coordinated office procedures, and within an office procedure, coordinated methods. They are all, or should be, closely knit together.

Every system has a feedback of information which gives actual results being obtained. This characteristic follows naturally because a system is an entity within itself designed to accomplish certain work. The revealing of the degree to which this work is over- or underachieved is a natural outgrowth of the system's inherent properties.

## WHO DESIGNS SYSTEMS AND PROCEDURES?

From what has been stated in this chapter, it follows that many, many tasks must be performed by a systems and procedures man and this requires considerable competency. With the increasing emphasis in this area, specialists in systems work have developed. They are termed systems and procedures men or sometimes the names "systems men," "systems engineers," or "systems analysts" are used. How they design a system is discussed in Chapter 16. Illustrative of what can be considered typically the basic functions and duties of a systems designer is shown by Figure 9–7.

---

Title:  Analyst—Systems and Procedures                    Div:  Allen Plant
Dept.:  Staff                                             Job No.:  33

Basic Functions:

Plans, develops, recommends, implements, and coordinates the systems and procedures activities within the Allen Plant. Advises vice-president in charge of this plant on matters of systems and procedures to promote administrative efficiency and reduce clerical costs.

Duties:

Within the authority limits authorized by divisional policies, he has the following duties:

1. Advise and assist the vice-president in regard to proposed systems and procedures.
2. Develop, recommend, and establish an effective cost and inventory system. This includes development of an effective manner for handling receipts and disbursements, handling vendors' and customers' claims, and taking and reporting physical inventories.
3. Review existing systems and procedures periodically in order to introduce improvements and controls to provide better service and lower cost.
4. Develop and maintain a Systems and Procedures Manual for the division to assure conformity to the pattern and format established by the corporation.
5. Coordinate the office mechanization program with all interested staff and operating personnel.

\*     \*     \*     \*     \*

10. Keep informed on current developments in the area of systems and procedures, appraise their value for the division, and recommend adoption when advisable.

Approved _James E. Elgin_
Authorized _Henry Puterbaugh_
Date _July 2, 196—_

FIG. 9–7.  A systems and procedures job description.

---

High on the list of desirable qualifications is conceptual ability, along with imagination and objectivity. He must be able to see future possibilities in untried systems and procedures and anticipate possible trouble areas. Also, the ability to initiate and "dream practical dreams" are genuine assets. In addition, it is helpful to possess a general yet fundamental grasp of the background activities within which the system is designed and operated. The systems designer must constantly update his knowledge of techniques, tools, and equipment. New and better ways are constantly appearing in this special area. Definitely advantageous to the systems and procedures man are mental alertness and curiosity and an understanding of human nature. He must have the ability to work in harmony with top managers, to sympathize with them, and understand their problems, and to push forward in his efforts despite complaints and disappointments. Finally, the art and skill of communication must be developed, for the systems and procedures man must be able to share his ideas, findings, and suggestions clearly and concisely.

## QUESTIONS

1. Discuss why the use of systems and procedures brings orderliness to the accomplishment of office work.

2. Define system and explain in some detail a system with which you are familiar.

3. Relate how the use of systems and procedures has negated the need for the old and familiar "look-see" practice in management.

4. What is your understanding of the statement: "Systems in office management serve as a vehicle of thought and in their design emphasize conceptual skills."

5. Distinguish between the two concepts in each of the following:
    a) Program flow chart and block diagram.
    b) System and procedure.
    c) System and subsystem.
    d) Management by information and a method.

6. What are your reactions to the following statement: "Electronic computers, with all their technical proficiency, versatility, and fantastic speed, cannot alone supply the answers to man's informational problems." Justify your views.

7. Discuss how systems and procedures enable a manager to see the total problem with its ramifications of various degrees in various areas of his enterprise.

8. What interpretation do you give the statement that a system is all-inclusive within its defined boundaries? What significance does this have in office management?

9. Discuss the assistance provided by the use of systems and procedures in spotting problem areas quickly and accurately?

10. Explain the purpose and the methodology followed by Figures 9–5 and 9–6.

11. Is there any significant relationship between systems and electronic computers? Elaborate on your answer.

12. What are some desirable basic qualifications for employment in systems and procedures work?

## CASE PROBLEMS

### Case 9–1.    Alexander and Ramsey, Inc.

A manufacturer of standard and custom-made picture frame mouldings in wood, plastic, and metal, Alexander and Ramsey, Inc., has enjoyed phenomenal growth since its inception some six years ago. Mr. Alexander, one of the owners, has charge of internal operations and has asked your suggestions for improving the customer order handling and purchasing procedures now being followed.

The following describes the present manner of handling the work:

1. Orders are received by mail; a clerk in mail room sorts them by type of material—wood, plastic, or metal.

2. The orders are sent to the billing department for pricing. A listing is made of orders under standard and nonstandard, or custom, headings and under subheadings of (1) sales territory and (2) dollar amount. There is also major segregation by type of material as received from the mail room. Orders for standard items are priced and marked in green pencil, data being taken from a standard price list. Orders for custom items are sent to the factory manager for pricing, which is entered in red pencil.

3. Standard item orders and copy of listings are sent to the sales department. The orders are checked and marked for credit. Custom item orders from the factory manager are checked against listings for receipt of all custom orders, then checked and marked for credit. Listings are used for sales analysis. The orders are sent open account, "2% 10, net 30" where credit standing is satisfactory; otherwise the terms are COD.

4. All orders are then sent to billing where a five-part order form is typed. Copies No. 2 and No. 3 are sent to the factory and used to fill the order. When shipped, copies are so marked, and Copy No. 2 is returned to billing where it is filed chronologically by date of receipt from the factory. Copy No. 3 is filed by the factory.

5. Upon receipt of Copy No. 2 from the factory, billing mails Copy No. 1 to the customer and retains Copies 4 and 5 for its records, one filed alphabetically by customer's name, and one filed numerically by order number.

6. The factory manager places purchase orders with vendors as indicated by his inventory control records or as required for special materials called for by custom orders. The purchase order is typed in duplicate in the factory office, with the original sent to the vendor and the copy for factory files. When the receiving and shipping unit gives notification that the material has arrived, the receiving report is compared to the factory copy of the purchase order, verified, and both papers are sent to accounting for payment.

## Problems:

1. Enumerate several areas in the above paper-work processing that can give rise to difficulties. Why?

2. What specific recommendations would you offer to Mr. Alexander? Why?

### Case 9–2.   Schwab Stores

When Clarence Schwab started his first retail store he paid his two employees in cash. This seemed the simple, direct way and the employees liked it. Now, however, he has five retail stores and a total of 27 people on his payroll. He thinks it might be better to pay by check but believes he should consider what alternatives exist. Sales representatives of several companies have talked with him and all recommend payment by check, using their particular systems. One representative has stated that one of his customers, with approximately the same size payroll as Mr. Schwab, makes a bulk deposit at the bank which credits individual salaries to checking accounts of each individual employee. However, Mr. Schwab wants to give consideration to the overall factors, or what might be termed a broad review of the area, before deciding which is the best system to select to accomplish his goal.

He reasons that the method of payment is but one major factor. There are probably several and, certainly for each of them, the cost of preparation is an important consideration. Currently, he pays weekly but does not feel this will necessarily have to be maintained. He wonders just how important savings would be, since the preparation of only 27 payroll checks is involved. Perhaps considerations other than savings to him are of major significance. He thinks it just might be a good idea to pay an estimated or fixed amount for several periods to each employee and then, for the next period, calculate the exact amount to balance the amount in each account.

## Problems:

1. What are the major alternatives open to Mr. Schwab?

2. Enumerate the advantages of payment by check instead of by cash. The disadvantages?

3. What specific factors should Mr. Schwab take into account?

4. What action should Mr. Schwab take? Why?

# CHAPTER 10

# THE TOTAL SYSTEMS
# CONCEPT

Don't be afraid to take a big step if one is indicated. You can't cross a chasm in two small jumps.

*—David Lloyd George*

THE USE of the systems and procedures approach has proven to be highly effective in defining an informational problem and in evolving the required solution. Further, the potential benefits of office automation are greatest when the systems and procedures approach provides the vehicle of analysis and design regarding what pattern of processing should be followed. In other words, we have progressed in utilizing technological improvements at least to some satisfactory degree by considering elements as a dynamic totality, by viewing this totality as being more important than its components, and by recognizing the interaction of the components as being highly significant.

## THE LOGICAL DEVELOPMENT

Better definition of the problem in its true setting and the extensiveness of systems and procedures led logically to the idea of extending the systems concept to include other related systems as a totality. Why stop with one system? Is not one system related to other systems so that an overall inclusive viewpoint of several systems is not only desirable but entirely practical?

Figure 10–1 shows a system for inventory control and sales. This was derived by adding to the system for inventory control (left portion of figure) the system for sales (right portion of figure). The former, or

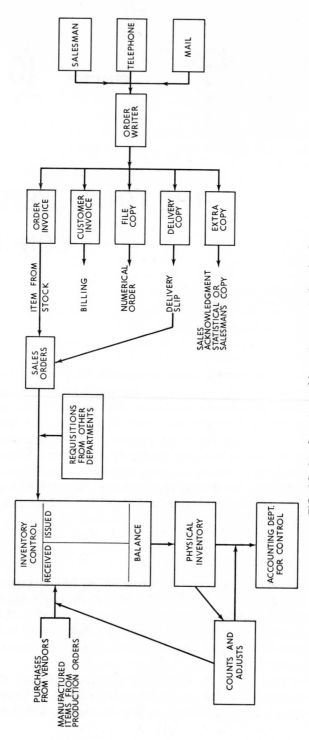

FIG. 10—1. A system of inventory control and sales.

system for inventory control, was discussed in Chapter 9 and illustrated by Figure 9–1. Compared to that shown in Figure 9–1, the system shown in Figure 10–1 is more comprehensive, more meaningful, and more expeditious for utilizing modern office automation equipment. It shows a "bigger picture," the interaction of activities and a greater volume of related work which can be considered in deciding the processing means.

Thus, moving from a single system idea to that of several systems as the vehicle of thought in informational efforts, was a logical development. From the historical viewpoint this was a natural outgrowth. During the early periods of work study, attention was focused on the task of an individual and how it was performed. Expanding this concept the related tasks of several individuals were considered, resulting in the development of a procedure. Later, related procedures were considered and the concept of a system became accepted. Continuing, from considering several related systems evolved the idea of a project, and from many related systems, the idea of an entire enterprise.

Furthermore, during the past few decades there has been a trend to integrated control in which the entire production process from raw materials to finished products, along with all sales efforts, are consolidated. This same trend has led to mergers among enterprises of considerable size. These changes have given emphasis to the need for reliable information of what has gone on and what is proposed should go on, throughout the entire enterprise. In many cases information was far from integrated, and the natural tendency was to try to develop a consolidated information system that would effectively provide the facts that were needed.

Slowly but surely, it became recognized that information is crucially interdependent. What happens in one organizational unit influences what happens in other organizational units. No one bit of information is an island unto itself. It is related to and affects other bits of information. With this fundamental in mind, the natural development was toward a more inclusive and all-encompassing concept about data gathering and processing.

## THE TOTAL SYSTEMS CONCEPT

What is meant by the total systems concept? The answer: The integration of necessary systems within an enterprise to provide timely information derived from rigorously determined relationships and needs of the enterprise. With the total systems concept, a reservoir of information would be available to any management member in the enterprise any time it is needed. The probable impact of any contemplated action in any one segment upon the entire enterprise could be easily and quickly ascertained. Purchasing, marketing, and engineering data could be readily combined with material control, inventory, quality, and production flow information. Research and development progress could be tied in with forecasting; thus where and when to make engineering changes in a product line could be accurately calculated. In brief, complete legal, historical, fiscal, and operational data would be included and interrelated.

A graphic representation indicating the general idea of a total systems concept is shown by Figure 10–2. This is suggestive only and is not intended to be conclusive. Beginning at the top of the figure, top management members, either as individual department heads or as a group, perform basic operations which establish objectives and supply the necessary parameters within which these objectives will be sought. These resulting decisions are forwarded to an Information Service Center which cuts across all organization lines, is centralized, reports to top management members, receives feedback information on actions taken, and regulates information flow. As depicted, the Information Service Center is able to provide top managers with the broad scope of analytical and control data available and in use, plus the information flow related to forecasts, actual performances, feedback, evaluation, and coordination. Thus, effective implementation of information is enhanced and adequate control over it is provided. More specifically, and as shown in the figure, the Information Service Center designs and installs systems, processes data, and supervises information flow. This is done to establish fundamental practices shown on the figure, practices such as stock review, raw materials control, work in process control, product cost reports, and payroll accounting and variance. Feedback is obtained on all these practices by determining for each case the exception to what is wanted (management by exception) and taking the needed corrective action. The automatic feedback is indicated at the bottom of the illustration.

As illustrated, and in most cases, the total systems concept is based on forecasts of requirements over reasonable periods, together with establishment of the optimum manufacturing and selling plans based on the forecast. What is optimum can be from a cost, service, time, or capability viewpoint. Furthermore, implied in the total systems concept are determinations for control limits within which the forecast will remain unchanged, feedbacks of actual requirements compared to the forecasts, and corrective actions either in the form of forecast adjustments or in operations. This is to say that manufacturing and selling efforts are based on the forecasts, not on actual requirements. The latter may vary sufficiently to suggest an adjustment in the forecast, and this is done when the forecast is obviously out of line. But fluctuations within established limits can occur without affecting the forecast.

The total systems concept is so logical that one wonders why we did not get to it sooner or why it is not universally adopted. Actually the reasons are many. During the initial adoption of office automation there was some

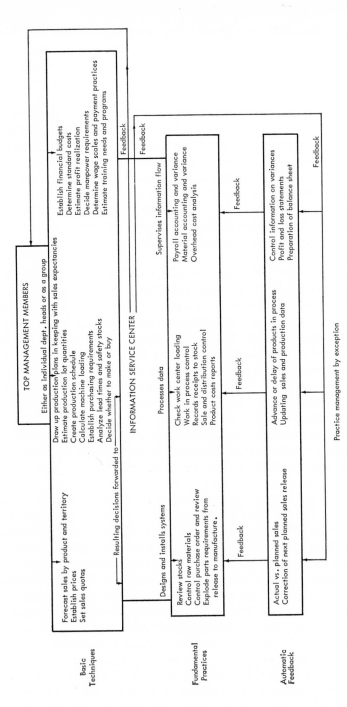

FIG. 10–2. A concept of total systems for an enterprise.

tendency to automate the work that had always been done. The existent systems or procedures were given a sacred, do-not-alter status. Any new information needs were patched onto the old systems or procedures. Reports, records, data of all kinds were seldom culled, and if so, rarely in their entirety. Customarily any inspection was confined to a portion of the entirety. The result was that useless information was permitted to exist, even ignored, without purpose and without controls. In some instances the difficulty probably was in the location and status of the data-processing group. When they alone decide what information they will produce, when they will produce it, and for whom, the total systems concept may suffer. Even when department heads' requests for data are answered, the approach may be strictly departmental, rather than on an enterprise basis, for the department head is most likely to request data of interest to his department only. As a result, other uses for the data processed are not considered.

To facilitate the total systems concept requires three essential factors. First, information handling—including the acquiring, processing, and distributing—must be granted top status and top management attention and backing. The management members must have, or be developed to have, an appreciation for the total systems concept. Changes must be made for the total systems concept to be utilized. They must see information handling as an enterprise activity, not a departmentized or particular specialty for their own isolated use. Second, modifications and improvements of present systems are in order to reflect the completely integrated enterprise-wide total systems concept. Third, new, overall systems should be evolved, installed, and kept up to date. This constitutes a tremendous challenge and a lot of hard work, but it will bring many benefits to everyone in the entire enterprise.

## IDENTIFYING CHARACTERISTICS

In order for the total systems concept to serve as a fundamental approach for guidance in all systems work, we must comprehend its identifying characteristics. To assist in this purpose, Figure 10–3 has been included. Starting at the top and moving clockwise, the circle represents the logical cycle, starting with objectives and eventually ending with objectives accomplished. Efforts to achieve the objectives are constrained by the enterprise's parameters such as contractual obligations, work force, and type of machines. In addition, boundaries are set by outside influences, i.e., those outside the enterprise's control, such as government regulations and trade practices. The efforts taken are guided and integrated by the provisions of the total systems, which can be said to govern the actions to be taken. The sequential work specified by the systems can be either manually or machine operated, subject to the cost and time evaluation involved in any specific circumstance. The work accomplishment brings about results indicated at the bottom of the illustration. The actions taken also supply the feedback essential for internal control. The provisions for the feedback are incorporated in the systems implemented in order to insure validity of the results. What is obtained, or the end of the performance, is subjected to evaluation in terms of its accomplishing the objectives as initially stated.

With this as a background, let us point out the essential characteristics of utilizing the total systems concept. First, and of great significance, is that objectives must be taken into consideration. They are the basis for determining both the formulation and the extent of the total systems

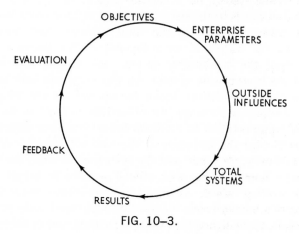

FIG. 10–3.

utilized. Every individual system that is included in the total systems must be justified in terms of its contribution to the objectives. Second, related systems governing performance are integrated into logical total systems. Third, systems can and must be designed within the defined parameters of the enterprise and operative influences outside the enterprise. Lastly, the best means—usually mechanical or automatic—should be considered in the design and application of the systems followed in order that the work is performed most economically in keeping with the objectives and to the end that the right information is delivered to the right people, or where it has maximum value.

## OBJECTIVES AND THE TOTAL SYSTEMS CONCEPT

Objectives are always important in management, but in discussing the total systems concept, objectives warrant special emphasis. What constitutes a system, or a total systems, is determined by the objectives sought. Thus the extent and number of systems we include in a total systems are dependent upon the objectives. An illustration commonly used to bring out this fact will be included here. Although the illustration deals with an automobile, it applies equally to information systems.

With reference to an automobile, the question can be asked, "What is an ignition system?" We would answer in terms something like the following. It is a system actually made up of a combination of several systems designed to make certain activities take place which result in sparks or electric flashes igniting combustible fuel. Note that identification of the several lesser systems is couched in terms of what the total systems are intended to achieve, or in terms of the objectives. We could go into the details of the lesser systems making up the total ignition system, such as the timing system, the condenser system, the spark plug system, and so forth, but this is irrelevant for the point at hand. Next, suppose the question is asked, "What are the total systems that deliver brake horsepower on the wheels of an automobile?" We would answer, the ignition system, the combustion system, the cooling and ventilating system, and the transmission system. All these systems work together to achieve the objective—deliver brake horsepower on the wheels of an automobile. Suppose we change our objectives to include the potential supplying of transportation to a human being. Since our objectives have changed, we change the inclusion of the systems making up the total systems. Specifically, we would add the system of steering, the system of braking, and a human being, with all the systems he brings with him, behind the steering wheel. Again, if our objectives were to include transporting this human being, we get into additional systems such as a system of roads, traffic lights, highway instructions, and so forth.

To reiterate, objectives establish the limits and utilization of the systems making up the total systems concept in any given case. In fact, the total systems concept is meaningful to the degree that the objectives are identified. Furthermore, this means that a total systems is not a grandiose composite of all systems to do all things. Rather, it is an integration of systems designed for the purpose of achieving stated objectives.

Too frequently the total systems idea is applied to objectives that are much too narrow. Existent data should be carefully scrutinized for its essentiality. New data can and should be generated to supply helpful data formerly unavailable or to reveal relationships that are helpful to know. In addition, objectives can include a magnitude that advances managerial effectiveness in that the total systems promote more penetrating thinking by management members, signal the appearance of sudden hazards or opportunities, along with the available alternatives of action to take about them, and highlight the key factors in common occurrences in enterprise.

## ADVANTAGES OF TOTAL SYSTEMS CONCEPT

There are a number of advantages in the total systems concept. Some of these are fairly obvious, others not so evident. It will be helpful to point out these advantages. Foremost is the expediting of planning by means of systems. Planning dealing solely with a major segment of an enterprise may not fill the needs for a broad plan. In some instances, if a narrow scope is followed, it may even work counter to the interests of the enterprise as an entirety. However, when a particular system is planned as a part of a total systems for an enterprise, the system occupies a place compatible in the overall scheme of things and is properly related to the entirety. Also, an important advantage of the total systems concept is the feasibility of considering the impact of important decisions on all parts of an enterprise. It is therefore possible to reach decisions that will maximize profits of an enterprise as a whole, minimize costs of the enterprise as a whole, or to arrive at decisions which provide the most benefits to the enterprise, all parts of the enterprise being taken into account and given recognition in keeping with their respective contributions and value. In addition, the total systems concept makes feasible the utilization of present-day data-processing equipment, especially the highly efficient modern computer. One can reason that the computer served as a catalyst which stimulated thinking toward the total systems concept. Certainly the development of the total systems and the computer are intimately related. Being able to determine what data we want from the entire enterprise viewpoint, and being able to process and transmit these integrated data as needed, has made for a combination significantly important in office management. Improvements and new techniques in developing the total systems are continually being devised and along with them, new capacities and speeds of electronic equipment are being perfected.

Likewise, information is maintained in a single data stream by utilization of the total systems idea. This single vehicle for information serves all phases of the enterprise and normally insures greater accuracy and better format of the information, since decisions in all areas are based on this single uniformity of information flow. Confusion is minimized, standardization increased, and understanding expedited. Furthermore, day-to-day analyses or special studies can be provided. Total systems produce current information related to individual needs. The information is not confined to historical data or traditional reports and records. Neither is it delayed excessively by decision making at many levels and by noncoordinated and time-consuming clerical calculations. Another advantage, commonly overlooked, is that special analyses can be performed as a by-product of the total systems. Usually such analyses can be supplied with very little additional effort. Without total systems special analyses may be too costly or pose so many difficulties as to be considered impractical. Thus additional information helpful in arriving at better and more inclusive decisions is unavailable. Finally, mention of the type of problems solved, and at what cost, should be included. Complex, intricate problems that extend into every facet of the enterprise can be handled satisfactorily by the total systems approach. For by this approach, consideration is given to both the effect upon and contributions to possible solutions to problems of each segment of the enterprise as well as of the totality of the enterprise. The problems can be clearly identified and then related to the activities which they affect. And all this can be accomplished at a relatively low cost.

## SHORTCOMINGS OF TOTAL SYSTEMS CONCEPT

We have already stated that top management attention and backing is one of the essential factors for success in the total systems concept. Actually this backing is not always present and, from a practical viewpoint, its absence constitutes one of the really serious shortcomings in utilizing total systems. How can one account for this situation? Part of the explanation may lie in the fact that most top executives reach the top by way of sales, production, or engineering. Relatively few come up through the accounting, personnel, or information areas. Hence, many have neither a full appreciation of the nature of information problems nor the means to cope with them. Also the area of information and all that goes with it—data, systems, procedures, processing, reports, and so forth —are not exciting subjects to top managers. They look upon a concept such as total systems as being helpful but not essential, useful but not exciting. The general attitude is that their efforts directed to other areas will pay bigger dividends.

The mere scope of total systems encourages numerous areas for specialization. It takes a very competent and informed man to be a good total systems designer and implementer. The tendency is to advocate the overall perspective but to emphasize and practice that about which one knows or thinks he knows the most, either by training or experience. As a result, specialization creeps in and the broad, balanced viewpoint falls by the wayside. A carefully evolved part—or parts—of the total systems is offered as the well-designed total systems, whereas it is only partially so. Furthermore, communication difficulties arise among the specialists. They have trouble conveying their exact needs and suggestions to each other. The total systems concept is evolved on what the meanings are believed to be rather than what they really are.

One of the most serious barriers to total systems, and in fact to all systems, is the temptation to cling to narrow approaches. The complete and full benefits of total systems can never be won by adhering to limited areas. Illustrative of this fact is forms control system. Forms control is a highly important area in office management.[1] It can be viewed and analyzed as a system. But forms are also important in related systems. They are, for example, a data transmission media and can help or hinder the data processing, be it manual or automated. Another example of the need for a broad approach relates to the accounting system approach. The accounting system is certainly essential in enterprises today, yet it is not the sole occupant of a modern systems approach. Related to it and also of great significance are the production control system, the factory machine replacement system, and the credit and collections system. In addition, there is what is termed the mechanization, or automation, system which assumes that the only, or at least the best, means of improving office work performance is via a particular mechanized or automated route. For a given operation, time, and place, this may be true. As equipment is offered on the market, specialists to operate it develop. Usually their interest is mainly in processing the data. When further changes both in the enterprise's informational needs and in the equipment offered on the market take place, these mechanization people may actually represent an inflexibility element in updating the work to meet these current informational needs of the enterprise.

Another drawback to total systems progress and acceptance is the apparently persisting tendency to orientate systems efforts to specific problems as they arise. New systems are designed, or existing systems are revised, to bring about a solution to an immediate difficulty. The initial thinking is focused on patching up or repairing systems already in existence. If this can't be done, a new system is added to the existing old systems. True, service is stressed and this is commendable. But the long term effect of changes in present systems, and the occasional addition of a new one, is to emphasize isolated systems. Their interrelatedness is weakened. It should also be observed that the solving of one problem after another really does nothing to prevent other problems from arising and does not tackle the basic causes of their arising. Seldom followed is a fresh, new overall approach to determine what better systems in their totality might be used to improve the operations and the results.

Finally, there is the hidden characteristic of systems improvements. Changes are not easily discerned and the benefits are intangible. The improvement in service or the reduction in cost is frequently neither as meaningful nor as evident as an increase in sales orders or a new production level attained by a factory force. Closely associated with this hidden characteristic is the desire for protection against possible blame should some part of the systems improvement not work out satisfactorily.

---

[1] Forms control is discussed in Chapter 21.

This takes the form of extra copies, time stamps, initiating of memos, various checks, and logs. But these protective measures can far exceed in cost the delays or errors which they protect against, and they provide little help in determining the source of such delays or errors.

## TOTAL SYSTEMS AND COST

The reduction of cost is commonly one of the reasons for utilizing total systems. Consideration for cost may be altered somewhat where other factors such as capability, time, service, or flexibility are accorded major significance. But cost is always in the picture. Capability, for example, may be traded down slightly in order to keep expenditures within a given amount. The objectives, established or expressed by what the users of the systems want or can be convinced to accept, have a strong influence on the ability to demonstrate savings or other advantages.

|  | *System No. 1* | *System No. 2* |
|---|---|---|
| *One-Time Costs* | | |
| System studies........................ | $ 10,000 | $ 15,500 |
| Conversion to new system.............. | 5,500 | 5,000 |
| Test period........................... | 8,000 | 8,000 |
| Miscellaneous expenses................. | 2,500 | 1,500 |
| Totals | $ 26,000 | $ 30,000 |
| *Recurring Costs* | | |
| Processing equipment (rental) .......... | $108,000 | $137,000 |
| Personnel | | |
| System analysts .................... | 26,000 | 26,000 |
| Operations ........................ | 38,750 | 17,800 |
| Supplies............................. | 22,500 | 14,000 |
| Totals | $195,250 | $194,800 |

FIG. 10–4.   Cost estimates for alternative systems.

In the case of a new system, the cost analysis should take into account *one-time costs,* or those incurred due to design and installation of a new system, and *recurring costs,* or those sustained to operate the new system installed. These concepts are brought out in Figure 10–4, which illustrates a cost comparison between two systems being considered. For system No. 1, the one-time costs consist of system studies, conversion to the new system, a test period to insure satisfactory operation of system, and miscellaneous expenses. These total $26,000 as indicated in the figure. Comparable costs for system No. 2 are $30,000, shown on the right of the illustration. Recurring costs for system No. 1 include processing equipment rental, personnel, and supplies, and total $195,250. Comparable costs for system No. 2 are $194,800.

It is reasonable to prorate the one-time costs over five years. When this is done, we get $5,200 $\left(\dfrac{\$26,000}{5}\right)$ for system No. 1 and 6,000 $\left(\dfrac{\$30,000}{5}\right)$ for system No. 2. Adding the respective recurring costs for each system we get:

|  | System No. 1 | System No. 2 |
|---|---|---|
| Prorated one-time costs | $ 5,200 | $ 6,000 |
| Recurring costs | 195,250 | 194,800 |
| Totals | $200,450 | $200,800 |

These respective totals are for each of the first five years. After that, the costs for each system would be the recurring costs only. This means that based on costs for the first five years, system No. 1 is more advantageous, while after five years, system No. 2 is. Specifically, by selecting system No. 2, costs would be $1,750 greater (5 × $350) but each year thereafter we would save some $450 ($195,250 − $194,800) by using system No. 2 in preference to system No. 1. At the end of nearly nine years from the beginning, we would have recouped the $1,750 disadvantage and go on to benefit by the $450 each year.

|  | System No. 1 | System No. 2 |
|---|---|---|
| Up to Five Years | | |
| One-time costs | $ 5,200 | $ 6,000 |
| Recurring costs | 195,250 | 194,800 |
| Nondisplaceable costs | 122,500 | 122,500 |
| Cost per year | $322,950 | $323,300 |
| Old system costs per year | 323,000 | 323,000 |
| New system savings per year | $ +50 | $ −300 |
| After Five Years | | |
| Recurring costs | $195,250 | $194,800 |
| Nondisplaceable costs | 122,500 | 122,500 |
| Cost per year | $317,750 | $317,300 |
| Old system costs per year | 323,000 | 323,000 |
| New system savings per year | $+5,250 | $+5,700 |

FIG. 10–5.

But is this the whole story? No. We should consider displaceable and nondisplaceable costs. The former are those that are removed with full implementation of the new system, the latter those that are not. Figure 10–5 shows the data taking into account these types of cost. The data are self-explanatory. With nondisplaceable costs of $122,500 and the old system cost of $323,000, for the first five years the cost advantage is in using system No. 1. However, after five years the advantage is with system No. 2. Again, we would select system No. 2 as the better system costwise over the long period.

However, the cost differential between these two systems is small and not very convincing. This would normally lead to giving intangibles considerable weight. Among these would be the relative evaluation of the two systems concerning flexibility, expansion possibilities, safety factor to meet load fluctuations, and preferences of knowledgeable employees. We might also investigate other costs, such as indirect costs of personnel, which in the illustration would probably be higher for system No. 1 since it requires more people as shown by the operations costs of $38,750 annually.

## TOTAL INTEGRATED PERSONNEL SYSTEM

As is well known there is much record keeping in personnel. The work of recruiting, placing, transferring, promoting, counseling, training, and maintaining the traditional information about personnel involves considerable data handling. We should know, for example, each employee's work history, scores on tests, performance ratings, and general qualifications quickly so that the best job possible can be made of maintaining an effective and satisfied work force. What is needed is a way not only to handle personnel information more easily but also to free personnel staff people to do more constructive and creative work. How best can questions such as the following be answered. "What does it cost to recruit, train, and place a man?" "How many present employees have training and experience in operating a vertical boring machine? In conducting marketing research surveys? In public relations work?" "If the retirement age is reduced three years and base wages are raised five percent across the board, what will be the effect on wages and salaries and on the makeup of the work force?"

A Total Integrated Personnel System (TIPS) which is an automated personnel system, has been designed and installed in the Data Systems Division Laboratory of the International Business Machines Corporation in Poughkeepsie, N.Y.[2] By means of this system a complete résumé for each employee is developed and kept updated. An IBM 1410 computer is used. The data for each employee are printed under selected headings with the number of pages varying directly with the amount of data each individual has. Basically the (1) personal data and (2) skills data are brought together in an automated central source from which information for each employee can be generated, including histories, skill searches, résumés, and the like.

Figure 10–6 shows the general arrangement followed from collecting data, centralizing them, and processing to provide information desired.

---

[2] The source of material for this discussion is: T. P. Byrnes and J. Correnti, "TIPS: A Total Integrated Personnel System," (Poughkeepsie, N.Y.: International Business Machines Corporation, May 20, 1964).

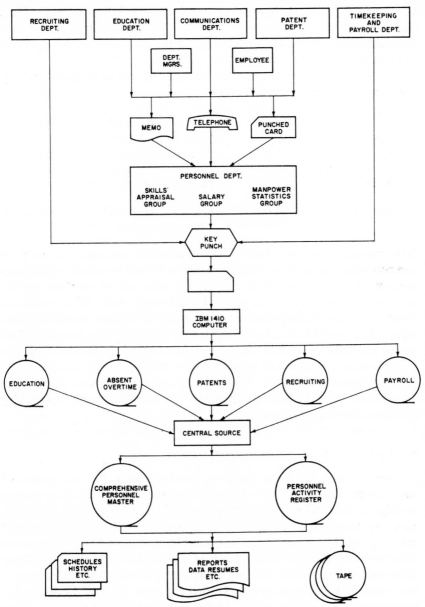

*Courtesy: International Business Machines Corp., Poughkeepsie, N.Y.*

FIG. 10–6.  A comprehensive personnel system.

Referring to the figure, data from the recruiting department are key punched and put into the computer, those from the education department are relayed to the personnel department from whence they are automated, likewise for information from the communications department and from the patent department. It required sound systems designing to provide a means for collecting all these data, preparing them for electronic processing, and providing the means for keeping the data updated by reporting changes and significant events as they occurred.

The end result is that complete information can be obtained quickly from one source. The data include:

| *Classification* | *Typical Inclusions* |
|---|---|
| Personal | Name, address, birth date |
| Education | Course name, degree, scholastic honor |
| Past experience | Work, military service, patents |
| Activities | Professional groups, fraternal associations |
| Skills (several classified types) | Skill description, products worked on, foreign languages, preferences |

The availability of this information, however, does not negate the need for competent personnel management members. It does eliminate much time-consuming routine searching and it identifies those meeting certain standards or criteria to fill a particular manpower need. Who is selected from an approved group remains the manager's decision. In other words, what TIPS provides is (1) a central source for all existing personnel data which are kept up to date, (2) a complete skills inventory to facilitate skills searches, selection of employees for retraining, and transferring of any employee available for reassignment, and (3) a source of classified information helpful in recruiting, manpower scheduling, and determining personnel development needs.

## TOTAL SYSTEMS—A PRESENT EVALUATION

Observe that TIPS is really a total systems for the personnel department. It deals solely with personnel data. As such it is a limited version of the total systems concept but a highly successful accomplishment in that direction. But a short time ago the term "total systems," meaning totally integrated systems, was the rage. This was the utopia for information handling. Today much of the initial enthusiasm has been dispelled. However, this does not mean that the total systems concept is not valid. It would seem to suggest that the work involved in developing total systems for a given enterprise poses greater hurdles and is far more difficult and elusive than first suspected. Also, the complexity of the enterprise's operations, the competitive environment under which it operates, the urgency for a total systems, the caliber of systems men available, the attitude of top managers, and a host of additional factors are contributory. In the case of several large corporations manufacturing in many different locations and distributing nationally and internationally, encompassing relationships with a multitude of vendors, customers, employees, communities, shareowners, and governments, the thought has been advanced that the total systems concept is too broad and too large to use effectively. It is claimed that satisfactory results, at least for the present, are possible with something less than total systems.

The present status is one of degree more than of kind. If total systems cannot be used, some degree of it can. There is unanimity of opinion that within an enterprise a partial total systems is superior to several large but noncoordinated systems. As pointed out above, we specify the extensiveness of the coordination by the statement of the objectives. Literally we say that to accomplish these objectives we will use these integrated systems. Hence, what is a partial total systems may provide the needed results. Our problem may resolve into that of determining precisely and completely the total objectives of the enterprise. This sets the stage for the total systems concept. The day of total systems may not have arrived as yet, but it surely is on its way. As experience, greater skill, and better techniques are developed for systems, along with continued progress in processing equipment, the present hurdles to far-reaching and inclusive integrated systems will be surmounted.

## TOTAL MANAGEMENT INFORMATION SYSTEM

The ultimate of the total systems concept has been referred to by some as the Total Management Information System. This would include the entire enterprise and by means of systematic collecting, processing, and distributing of data would provide all necessary information to each individual in order to give maximum assistance in attaining specific goals. This is to say that each individual is given the information he needs to discharge effectively his responsibilities, to delegate to others his right to make decisions, and to facilitate the fundamental functions of office management—planning, controlling, organizing, and actuating—at all organizational levels.

Because interpretation of "what information is necessary" poses one of the biggest obstacles to a Total Management Information System, let us discuss further this requirement. To identify what information is necessary requires a rigidly monitored approach which stimulates employees to give serious thought to the problem. Simply asking for a statement of their informational needs usually results in incomplete answers, raises questions in the respondents' minds about costs, systems capabilities, means of processing, priorities, and attitudes of superiors. A satisfactory approach is to request each individual to provide answers to the following questions and in this sequence:

1. Specifically, what are your main work objectives?
2. For these work objectives, what are your principal responsibilities?
3. In keeping with these responsibilities, what types of decisions are you called upon to make?
4. What information do you feel you need to reach these decisions from the short-range viewpoint? From the long-range viewpoint? From within the enterprise? From outside the enterprise? From an idealistic viewpoint? From a practical viewpoint?
5. What are the key factors that throttle the work that you are supposed to do?
6. Classify the identified information given in answer to question No. 4 above into the following groups:

   *a*) Absolutely essential.
   *b*) Essential.
   *c*) Desirable.
   *d*) Helpful but really not needed.

Restrictions as to length of answers are in order as this promotes clarity and conciseness and facilitates review. Answers to question No. 4 are vital. The sequence provided builds up to this key question. Answers to questions No. 5 and No. 6 are related. Knowing the key factors (question No. 5) helps to classify the information (question No. 6).

Excellent examples of what can be considered total management information systems are found in the U.S. Air Force. They are the Management Control System (MCS) and the Strategic Air Command (SAC). These are total systems encompassing total operations although they are operated by a subagency. If not truly all-encompassing in their scope, they come very close to it. They are inclusive in keeping with their stated objectives. Also worthy of mention is the total logistics system of the U.S. Air Force. It is worldwide, totally integrated, and covers supply and maintenance. By its operation, service has been upgraded, yet enormous dollar savings have been realized.

The other military services have also been active in developing total management information systems. Both the U.S. Army and the U.S. Navy have active offices of management information. The Department of the Navy's office of management information consists of three top directorships, or organization units, as shown in Figure 10–7. The activities of each unit are clearly indicated in the figure. The reporting of naval program planning and execution by the operating agencies is in essence the makeup of the management information. The office of management information develops systems to generate pertinent information and to help identify problems for top executives of the department.

Available in current literature is an example of what a machinery manufacturer, Farrel Corporation, is doing about a total management information system for improving its profit possibilities and controls.[3] The informational needs of planning, engineering, manufacturing, selling, and financing are integrated and designed to (1) give adequate and consistent planning and engineering documentation for each product line, (2) provide needed manufacturing information including purchasing data, schedules, and labor costs, (3) expedite sales forecasting, market penetration, and sales analyses, and (4) facilitate all fundamental finance information including accounts receivable, accounts payable, expenses,

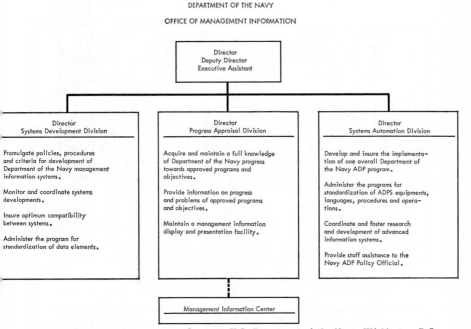

*Courtesy: U.S. Department of the Navy, Washington, D.C.*

**FIG. 10–7.   Makeup of the Office of Management Information of the U.S. Navy.**

payroll checks, and standard cost data and control. With this unified arrangement, the managers of Farrel Corporation believe advantages well worthwhile will be realized including a reduction of materials cost, better manpower utilization, improved flexibility in scheduling, shorter manufacturing cycles, shorter sales delivery periods, improved customer services, and better collection of accounts receivable. With all these gains, the ability to handle a greater volume of business with existent facilities seems likely. Also the new system should supply a broader and deeper knowledge

---

[3] "What Farrel Corporation Is Doing To Maintain and Improve Its Competitive Position," pamphlet published following annual stockholders meeting (Rochester, N.Y.: The Farrel Corporation, March 19, 1964).

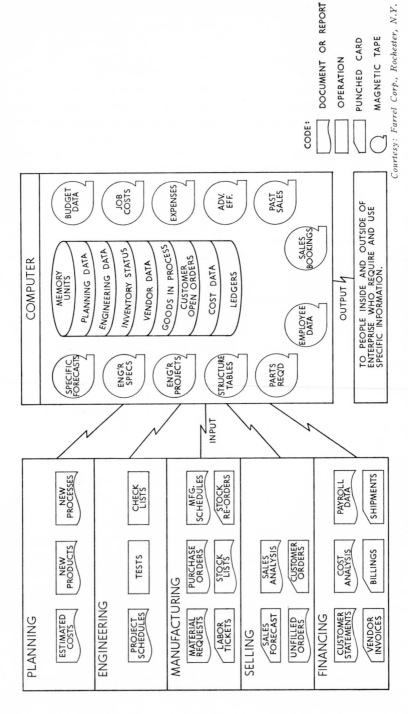

FIG. 10–8. One concept of a total management information system.

*Courtesy: Farrel Corp., Rochester, N.Y.*

of the enterprise and its behavior as a unit. Figure 10–8 is a graphic representation of the system.

## TOTAL SYSTEMS IMPACT UPON MANAGER'S RESPONSIBILITIES

From what has been stated it can be concluded that the use of total systems has an important impact upon a manager's responsibilities. By its adoption the area of decision making formerly given over to middle managers is greatly reduced. For example, decisions dealing with man-hour requirements, work scheduling, the timing and amount of reordering, and machine loading are highly circumscribed. In some instances they are removed from human beings and performed automatically by machines as prescribed by the system. The result is not an adjustment, but an elimination of the middle manager, for these areas are no longer subjected to his judgment and choice.

The need for thorough and adequate planning is emphasized by total systems. In this approach, we are dealing with too large an area to follow a "muddling through" practice. We must know where we are going and how we are going to get there. Not only is breadth of area alone important, but also the changing of relationships among the components, the elimination of some components, and the addition of others to the total picture are equally crucial. The disruptive influences can be large. The risk is high. Hence, to keep the risk and bad influences within known and reasonable limits, planning is resorted to and the determination of future activities is set forth.

Total systems usage tends to promote effective personnel relations. Responsibilities are better identified and known; cooperation is enhanced. The sense of being a part of a worthwhile total effort, of being expected to perform a specific and essential part of the entire work, and of doing it satisfactorily, help to provide an enthusiastic work group and a harmony of interest among the personnel.

## QUESTIONS

1. Enumerate the advantages in using the total system concept in office management.
2. Why is the total systems concept a logical development of the systems and procedures approach?
3. Explain Figure 10–2 in your own words.
4. Why has the total systems concept taken so long to be recognized?
5. Generally speaking is it a good idea to encourage specialization within the total systems idea? Justify your viewpoint.
6. Identify each of the following:
    a) Recurring costs of a system.

*b*) TIPS.

*c*) Total Management Information System.

*d*) Totally integrated systems.

7. As you see it, is the total systems idea a theoretical concept or a practical reality? Why?

8. With respect to the activities within an enterprise, is information crucially independent or vitally interdependent? Give an example to illustrate your answer.

9. Other than those included in this chapter, relate an example showing the importance of objectives in the total systems concept.

10. Of what significance is Figure 10–3? Discuss.

11. Discuss the importance of total systems upon the responsibilities of a manager.

12. Discuss the subject of cost and total systems.

## CASE PROBLEM

### Case 10–1.   Troast Wholesale Plumbers

The assistant sales manager tells Frank Reinhart, a systems analyst, that, upon receipt, a customer's order is time-stamped and checked for credit. If it is found satisfactory, a "Credit OK" stamp is placed on the order; if not, the customer is written a letter requesting payment on his past account or cash for the pending order. Orders with credit approval are posted on customers' order cards, which are used for sales analysis work. Orders are then sent to the storeroom for filling and shipping. Subsequently, when merchandise is shipped and billed, the date and amount of shipment are posted on the customer's card. In response to his question on how the sales department knew the order was shipped, Mr. Reinhart learned that this was by means of a "storeroom packing slip."

He then interviewed Hazel Mead, billing supervisor, who explained that her department receives a "packing slip form 07" which tells them the order is shipped. When they are so informed, this "form 07" is checked with the customer's original purchase order and, if accurate, three billing copies are prepared. The first copy is sent to the customer, the second and third copies are filed respectively alphabetically and numerically in the files of the billing department. The original order is returned to sales, where it is filed, and the packing slip is filed chronologically by date billed.

The purchasing department buys upon requisition from the stockroom. The vendors are selected by looking in the vendor card file. Here the cards are arranged by part numbers and names showing the recommended supplier or suppliers. The purchasing agent can either write or telephone for quotations and base his selection of vendor on the answers received or he can simply select one of the approved vendors. Usually, on orders amounting to less than $100, he selects the vendor based on judgment only. Four copies of a purchase order are made out. Copy No. 1 goes to the vendor, Copy No. 2 goes to inventory control, Copy No. 3 goes to billing for payment, upon receipt of merchandise indicated by a receiving copy slip from the receiving and shipping department, and Copy No. 4 is the copy of purchasing filed by purchase order number.

George Walker, the assistant manager of the stockroom, was interviewed next by Mr. Reinhart. An inventory card record is maintained for each item. When the amount of stock on hand reaches the replenishing point, an amount calculated for each item, a requisition is sent to purchasing to order a specific amount. Stockroom orders are stamped "PI" when they have been recorded in the daily tally sheet of orders for processing and also in inventory card records to reveal inventory depletion due to forthcoming shipping. PI orders are then picked, checked, packed, and shipped. Receiving and shipping, which is subordinate to the storeroom, makes out four copies of a packing slip 07, one of which is sent to billing; the second is a file copy of receiving and shipping; the third is sent to sales, and the fourth is the packing slip enclosed with the merchandise. Further questioning by Mr. Reinhart revealed that the storeroom receives the original customer's order from sales and that from this original a shop or storeroom order is made out. This latter order form highlights storeroom data, such as best sequence for picking items, location of stock in storeroom, and approximate unit weights. After carefully checking the stockroom order, the storeroom sends the original customer's order to the billing department, as indicated above.

## Problems:

1. Currently the processing of a customer's order is viewed as four separate procedures. Do you agree with this viewpoint? Why?

2. Draw a diagram indicating the processing as described above to substantiate your answer to question No. 1.

3. Point out and discuss some areas for improvement in the current processing practices being followed.

# CHAPTER 11

# SOURCE DATA

# AUTOMATION

Nature gave men two ends—one to sit on and
one to think with. Ever since then man's
success or failure has been dependent on the
one he used most.
                              —*George R. Kirkpatrick*

As POINTED out,[1] source data automation (SDA) is a major part of the
current office technology. The identification of SDA is given to data
processing that primarily, but not exclusively, ties together various types
of office machines by common media and integrates their respective
operations so as to form a whole from the various machines utilized.
Computers can be included but they are not a mandatory part of SDA
data-processing equipment.

## IDENTIFICATION AND EVOLUTION OF SDA

In the processing of business data, it is customary to find certain data
copied and repeated over and over again, rearranged according to many
different formats, and originated in or sent to different locations. In
addition, business data are interrelated. For example, data showing price
figures alone mean little. Required, in addition to price, are vendor's name,
address, and terms of sale. Likewise, a single figure showing the quantity
of an item on hand is insufficient. The units of measurement, location,
cost, and source may also be necessary.

Consider the paper work required to handle a customer's order. Raw
materials must be purchased or, if stocked, the inventory records
consulted, release orders to manufacture issued, production-scheduled

---

[1] See Chapter 8.

shipping tickets and bills of lading prepared, and invoices made out to the customer. Much of the information used in preparing these various documents is similar, and the data are written many times. Distribution of the information may be made to a considerable number of locations, some of which are miles apart, as, for example, a branch factory and the central office building.

It is logical to attempt to simplify and integrate the writing of these various office forms. The elimination of duplicate writings can be accomplished by using carbon copies; an accounting machine extends and totals; and information punched in code on cards can be used repeatedly to reproduce all documents required. But in general, these deal with a single process and are not interchangeable among various processes. However, in some instances, as in duplicating copies containing essential information for specific purposes, such as purchasing or production control, the copies serve in several processes, and all the writing is integrated by use of the one master.

The name, source data automation, is self-explanatory. It is the automation of source data—where information begins. Full benefits of automation are thus acquired because the automation applies to the entire range of the data-processing system, not to just the end-product areas. Data recorded are in effect self-perpetuating and can be used over and over for as many times as is necessary to satisfy the varied requirements. To illustrate, the writing for an office operation is put into such a form that subsequent operations requiring this writing can be processed automatically. SDA therefore tends to tie office work together, to integrate it, or to form a whole from the various parts. Mechanization is used. In fact, SDA can be viewed as integrating common machines which are basically dissimilar into a purposeful, coordinated mechanized group.

SDA was introduced in 1954 by executives of the U.S Steel Corporation. They used it for various portions of their paper work operations. Employing the medium of punched cards and perforated tapes, the original data were transferred to one of these media and subsequently processed on any of several common machines. Those work portions which were different for each processing were performed manually, but a large percentage of the total work was automated.

The idea was quickly exploited by many other companies. Some viewed it as a means for utilizing common office machines more effectively, others as an economical way to integrate data, and still others as a way to employ their computers economically and to extend their field of application. Within a short period, "common language" machines or attachments to common machines became readily available. The vast array of equipment, including card-reading machines, paper-tape reading machines, and optical-character recognition machines, made it feasible to keep alive data without the need for direct manual rehandling.

## THE COMMON LANGUAGE LINK

To implement SDA, conventional office machines must be adapted to speak the same language; that is, a basic and direct compatibility, so to speak, between different types of machines, and between machines of different manufacturers, must be achieved. In this manner, data originating on one type of machine can be used later on other types, without human reading, interpreting, and writing.

The common language medium joining all machines utilized is the key to the mechanization aspect of source data automation. The medium is

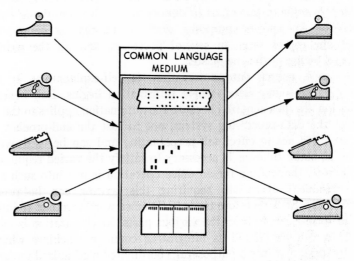

FIG. 11–1. The key to SDA is the common language medium integrating the common office machines.

acceptable to all the machines, permits each to perform its particular task, passes the result on to the next machine, which utilizes this information and passes on the accumulated data. In essence, the group of conventional machines is connected into a harmonious entirety. When the machines are widely dispersed geographically, appropriate media are available for the necessary communication. The idea of the common language link in SDA is shown graphically by Figure 11–1.

There are three common language media in use today: (1) perforated tape, (2) punched card, and (3) edge-punched card. Whatever the medium, it is prepared simultaneously with the initial writing of the data. To reiterate, when a sales order is initially typed, a mechanism attached to the typewriter automatically prepares the medium. As stated above, this medium is then used to operate all subsequent machines required.

Normally, each machine is equipped either to prepare the medium or to "read" it, or both. Figure 11–2 illustrates a nondescriptive accounting machine connected to a tape perforator. In this application, the following is performed in one operation: A voucher is posted, the voucher check is computed and printed, and a voucher register is prepared. Integrated with this operation, a perforated tape is made for subsequent preparation of punched cards used in the processing and the analyzing of the data.

One widely used perforated tape has five rows or channels of perforations. Various combinations of holes in these five channels give a total of 32 symbols, including the 26-letter alphabet, letters, figures, space, carriage

*Courtesy: Burroughs Corp., Detroit*

FIG. 11–2.  Installation of an accounting machine connected to tape perforator providing perforated tape for subsequent integrated data processing.

return, line feed, and blank. A shift symbol provides for numerals. Figure 11–3 shows the five-channel code for perforated tape.

It must not be concluded that perforated tape is limited to five channels. Actually, up to eight channels can be used; this permits more characters and check and control symbols. A seven-channel tape, for example, would require all equipment using this tape to be so equipped for it. As long as the operations are within an enterprise, no particular difficulty would be present; but in dealing with outside firms, difficulty would be encountered if they use tape of a different number of channels.

Punched cards are also a medium for conveying data in an SDA arrangement. The data are put into punched cards which serve to operate all subsequent machines in the process. Historically, this was the first medium used.

The edge-punched card is, as the name suggests, punched along the edge

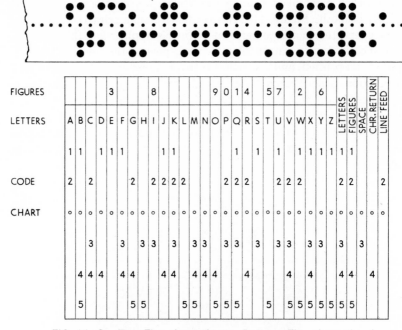

FIG. 11–3. *Top:* Five-channel tape. *Bottom:* Five-channel code.

of the card. The code used is that of the five-channel perforated tape. Cards are easy to handle and file; however, the information on one card is limited by its length, generally about seven inches. This is sufficient, however, for many purposes. Figure 11–4 shows an office machine equipped to utilize edge-punched cards.

## DISTINGUISHING FEATURES OF SDA

All SDA studies should first be systems-oriented and then machine-oriented. SDA demonstrates the need for using the systems approach in order to acquire the overall picture of what work is to be done where and how the total effort is coordinated toward achieving a given goal. This precedes the decisions pertaining to the mechanization of the data processing.

The preservation of source data, determined by thorough systems analysis to be necessary, in a mechanical and reusable form at the time of origination, is another distinguishing feature of SDA. All subsequent processing of the data is performed and preserved in this reusable form. The original data are (1) recorded at the point of origin in a mechanized form, (2) processed exclusively in a mechanized form, and (3) utilized in all subsequent operations, where needed, resulting in the integration of the processing work.

*Courtesy: Commercial Controls Corp., Rochester, N.Y.*

FIG. 11–4. The Flexowriter Programatic prepares documents from unit edge-punched cards automatically. The machine reads, reproduces, or punches card or tape.

SDA is flexible. Machines can be added or subtracted, and the sequence of operations can be changed as requirements of data processing change. With its building block approach, SDA can be engineered to fit a variety of individual needs. Furthermore, nonrepetitive and special entries can be made manually without disrupting the normal progress of the work.

A detailed analysis of the work requirements and how they will be accomplished must be made. Every step of the system followed requires study to insure that the language prepared at one point is exactly as required at another point of use. The selection of the machines and the media also warrant careful analysis.

Although economic considerations are not always governing, quite frequently SDA must be justified on that basis. Usually some equipment is added to make the installation, redesign of office forms may be needed, and retraining of office personnel is required. A detailed cost and time analysis comparing the present to the proposed means of performing the work is essential.

### ACHIEVING SDA

The applications of SDA are practically limitless. Every major system either by itself or along with other systems, offers possibilities. The gains to be realized are usually substantial. For best results, a definite program should be followed, patterned along these steps:

1. *Review areas and departments for study.* This can be started by preparing check lists revealing pertinent facts about present paper-work

activities in the manufacturing, procuring, and distributing departments. Information on the present methods of preparing papers, and their route or travel in the normal operation of the business, is the type to be obtained. By studying and evaluating this information, specific goals will emerge, such as improving production control communication, reducing processing time for purchase orders, providing quick shipping information, sending out invoices promptly, and eliminating copying errors.

2. *Secure top management approval.* Being integrated, SDA will cross departmental lines, involve many employees from different organizational units, and affect what they do. Hence, authorization of and support for the SDA effort must be given by top management; otherwise, the program will be seriously hampered, and little, if anything, will come of it.

3. *Appoint director to head all SDA activity.* With its blessing, top management should appoint an individual to manage the activity, giving him the necessary authority and help to direct the study to a successful installation. Designated groups, carefully selected, should be appointed to assist the director in finding and evaluating all the necessary facts. These groups will include members from the departments affected by proposed changes, systems and procedures personnel, and possibly specialists from a management consultant firm.

4. *Establish target dates.* SDA programs have a tendency to bog down or to extend over long periods unless they are controlled and adherence to a definite schedule is maintained. Target dates for completion of work should be established for each major element in the program. Activities such as finding the facts, charting and analyzing present systems and procedures, and determining recommendations seem to go on and on unless specific dates for their completion are established and enforced.

5. *Gather and analyze pertinent information.* Many details are required, and suitable forms should be used for securing them in order to expedite identification, comparison, and evaluation.[2] All participating members must be supplied proper instruction, so that they observe and understand what information to obtain and how to record it. The analysis should seek to disclose the major advantags and the disadvantages of the present manner of performing the work.

6. *Make recommendation and install.* As study and analysis proceed, possibilities for improvement are disclosed and verified. Substantiation of all gains should be made. Decisions must be made regarding what office machines are to be used and what arrangement of the information on the paper forms will be followed. Finally, the proposal of what to do and why is presented to all interested management members, followed by a discussion to modify the proposal if necessary, but primarily to secure full

---

[2] Discussion of such forms is included under Chapters 15 and 16.

agreement and approval. As soon as practical thereafter, the installation of the program should commence.

In applying the above steps, certain guides are helpful. These include the following: (1) Permit no restricted areas; instead, make the program comprehensive and truly integrated; (2) code first-hand material as much as possible in order to reduce future looking-up time; (3) use an adequate number of control totals between transmissions of data to insure accuracy; and (4) relate data from various sources and for various purposes to the greatest possible extent.

## ILLUSTRATIONS OF SDA

Many applications of recording and accounting are handled simply and effectively by the use of a multientry, flexible-unit combination called Cardatype. The basic machine units include a typewriter, an auxiliary keyboard unit, and a card-feeding and -reading control console. These are illustrated in Figure 11–5.

*Courtesy: International Business Machines Corp., New York*

FIG. 11–5.   Basic machine units for a Cardatype installation.

Consider a manufacturer with a large number of customers. A punched card is prepared in advance for each customer, showing name and address. Also, a separate card is prepared for each item sold, providing information such as the item's description, weight, and price. These are kept in a reservoir file convenient to the operator. Upon receipt of a purchase order, the customer's name card and the cards for each of the items ordered are pulled from the file and fed into the feeding and reading control console, which actuates the typewriter, causing information on the cards to be typed on the paper forms. Semipermanent information, such as preliminary digits of a serial number or the date, is handled by means of the auxiliary keyboard unit, while variable or individualized information is manually typed on the paper forms by means of the typewriter. If it is desired, simultaneously with the writing of the forms, a punched card or a perforated tape can be produced for subsequent processing of the information in a different format for different purposes. Figure 11–6 shows examples of billing performed by this system. Note that the invoice, invoice register, stock selection tickets, and shipping tags are produced. Only the information encircled was inserted by manual key strokes; the rest, or over 95 percent of the work, is automatic—obtained by automating the source data. Several typewriters can be used, if necessary. The console unit performs all computations, such as tax, discount, and net amount. While the unit is handling one invoice, the operator refiles the cards from the previous invoice, so that they are ready for reuse as needed.

Figure 11–7 illustrates an interesting application of SDA for a national manufacturer having four widely separated plants. All production scheduling, stock control, receiving and billing of customers' orders, releases to manufacture, and routing of shipments are made from the centralized office located in a large city, different from that of any of the plants. All customers' orders sent direct to one of the plants by customers are immediately forwarded to the central office. Referring to Figure 11–7, and beginning at the left, the sequence is as follows. Customers' orders are received; edge-punched cards are pulled for customer name and for products ordered, and are sent to the Flexowriter with auxiliary tape perforator. Insertion of the edge-punched cards into the Flexowriter reader causes a six-part invoice and two perforated tapes of the transaction to be typed automatically. Tape No. 1 is sent to a Teletype machine, which, using the tape, transmits the order by means of electrical energy to the proper plant. The tape made at the receiving unit of the plant is used to write a five-part bill of lading and packing slip. Tape No. 2 from the Flexowriter is used in a tape-to-punched card converter. Two sets of punched cards are prepared, one set being used by general accounting accounts receivable, the other set being used for statistical analysis purposes and tabulated open orders file. Plant shipments are teletyped daily to the central office. Upon notice of shipment, the invoice copies are distributed, the accounts receivable copy being sent to general accounting, upon receipt of which the punched card of the transaction in their possession is pulled and sent to tabulating, where costs and other reports are prepared.

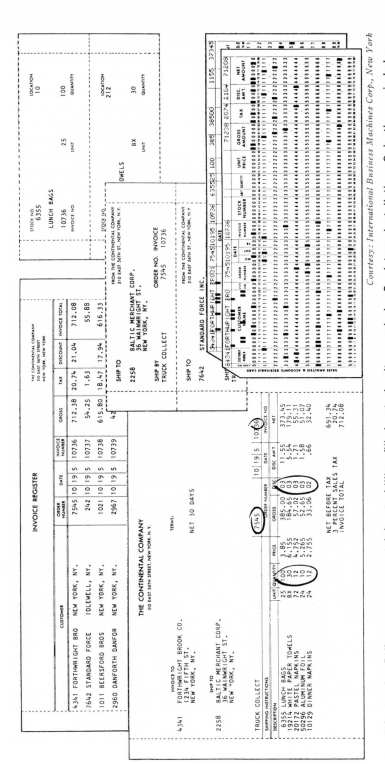

FIG. 11-6. Different papers pertaining to billing filled out simultaneously by Cardatype installation. Only the encircled portions were written by manually operating the typewriter.

*Courtesy: International Business Machines Corp., New York*

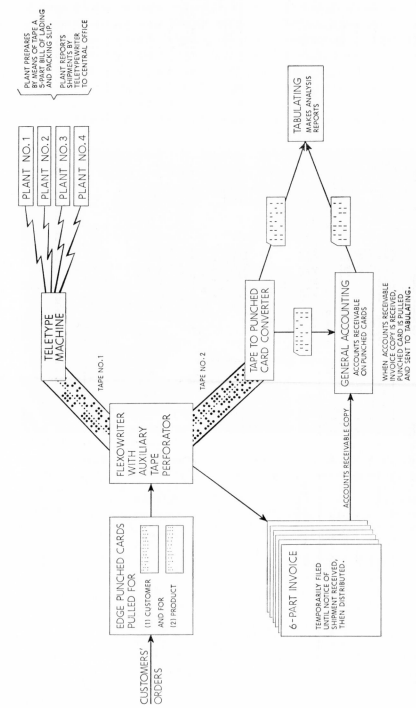

FIG. 11—7. Integrated data processing of order entry, shipping, and billing by a national manufacturer with a centralized office and four widely separated plants.

As indicated in this example, a Teletype machine can be used to transmit the taped information to the various plants. Improvements in communication equipment have been so rapid, however, that it is now possible to send economically and conveniently huge quantities of data over the telephone wires. This is discussed later in this chapter under Data-Phone.[3] Further, machines are available that expedite and combine data collection, handling, and transmission. Specifically, fixed and semi-fixed data (customer's name, address, terms, etc.) are obtained from a

*Courtesy: Teletype Corporation, Skokie, Ill.*

FIG. 11–8. An automated communications set receives, integrates, transmits, and disseminates messages and data of all kinds. The unit illustrated features dual readers that automatically interoperate, a tape punch that simultaneously prints and perforates, and a four-row alphanumeric typewriter keyboard. Its operating speed is 10 characters per second or the equivalent of 100 words per minute.

perforated tape, variable data (date, quantity, etc.) from the machine's keyboard, thus supplying a finished paper product with carbons for processing and filing. In addition, a perforated composite tape of the complete document is made and can be transmitted simultaneously by the machine to several destinations at the same time (cross-country or cross-office), or to a computer, or placed in storage. Figure 11–8 shows the machine offering these advantages.

Mention should also be made of "turn-around documents." Public

---

[3] See page 252.

utility bills on punched cards, magnetic ink bank checks, and bank loan payment forms are representative of turn-around documents now in use.[4] These papers are machine-produced, sent to customers, and returned for further processing—typical of SDA. The initial data do not have to be rewritten in order to perform the additional processing. Also, it is possible for the customer to tabulate or process the data in a number of ways for his own purposes prior to returning the document. This practice is common when the customer is a company or a bank. The use of turn-around documents normally results in faster response in returning documents because they can be processed immediately upon receipt and without costly preparation for processing.

A rapidly expanding application is Numerical Control (NC). Some prefer to call it symbolic control. Logically, it can be considered a part of the general area of SDA. NC is an automatic means of operating a factory machine by feeding a previously prepared punched tape or card with all instructions in numerical form into a mechanism that directs the machine. A computer can also be used, but it is not essential in many NC applications. Computers are more likely to be employed for controlling complete processes such as metal-rolling mills and chemical production than for discrete parts manufacturing.[5] NC instructions are detailed and include every step required to operate the machine in order to obtain a machined part exactly according to blueprint specifications. The old concept of the operator's "running" the machine is eliminated. Basically there are two fundamental types of numerical controlling: (1) positioning and (2) contouring. The former deals with getting the tool and the material in the desired relationship, after which the tool is advanced either automatically or manually to perform the required work. The second type, or contouring, requires that the path of the tool be controlled continuously. In fact, this type is commonly referred to as the "continuous-path" method. There is constant synchronization of the movement of the tool in several axes. Among the advantages of NC are (1) more machine utilization time, less machine setup time, and lower lead times; (2) elimination of fixtures and templates used as guides in manual means; (3) less inspection and fewer rejects; and (4) feasibility of machining otherwise "impossible" parts.

NC has wide application in metalworking, including use with machines for drilling, milling, planning, routing, welding, riveting, tube bending, and coil winding. Figure 11–9 shows a vertical-spindle machine equipped with a Giddings and Lewis Numeridrill (numerical control), made up as shown in the figure of the pedestal-mounted control unit which is immediately back of the operator, and the cabinet housing the electrical control circuits

---

[4] See also Chapter 12, pp. 278–79.

[5] See Chapter 14, pp. 321–23.

*Courtesy: Giddings & Lewis Machine Tool Co., Fond du Lac, Wis.*

FIG. 11–9.  A vertical-spindle machine equiped with Giddings and Lewis Numeridrill featuring five-second automatic tool changer and program combinations of spindle motions for drilling, tapping, boring, milling, and jump feeds. A three-axis control is standard equipment but special controls can be furnished.

which is located to the operator's right and to the rear of the illustration. This vertical-spindle machine with Numeridrill features an automatic tool changer, removing one tool from the spindle and replacing it with another within a time of five seconds.

Large department stores have the problem of inventory control so that the proper quantity and quality of each item are on hand in order to maximize sales and gross margins. To help solve this problem economically, SDA is being used. At the time a customer transaction is originally entered into a National Cash Register, a perforated tape recording is made. The recording shows cash or credit sale; salesperson's number;

customer's number; description of merchandise, including material, size, style, and retail price; and the vendor's number. A prepunched price ticket—actually a small card about 2½ inches wide and 1 inch long— inserted in a unit called a Media Reader automatically starts the tape recorder and produces a detailed record of the item sold. Complete information on inventory control, by units, is thus accurately and economically provided. Figure 11–10 illustrates the machine, tape, and price ticket used for this purpose.

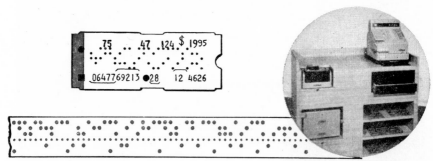

Courtesy: National Cash Register Co., Dayton

FIG. 11–10.  Machine, perforated tape, and price ticket used for effective unit inventory control by large retail outlets.

### SDA AND THE COMPUTER

SDA sometimes includes the use of a computer. This is the case when widely dispersed common office machines are connected with a computer in a central location. When any of the dispersed machines mechanizes the source data which are utilized by the computer serving as the central processing unit, or vice versa, the element of joining machines together for integrating the data processing can be viewed as SDA and a computer. To illustrate, consider a centralized accounting operation that requires that information be consolidated from source data received from widespread locations. This arrangement is shown by Figure 11–11. Data can be sent to the computer headquarters by mail, messenger service, telegraph, or telephone. For any of these communication means, the data can be sent in computer language, but telegraph or telephone provides much faster service. Telegraph has been used extensively, but developments now tie the ordinary telephone to a computer and provide multiple and direct access to it. The development making this possible is called Data-Phone; the machine utilized is illustrated by Figure 11–12.

Regular telephone lines comprising a nationwide network are used, and there are no intermediate steps. To utilize the Data-Phone, a customer picks up the telephone and dials the service number. A dial tone signals connection, after which he inserts an identification card into the device

FIG. 11-11.   Centralized accounting arrangement requiring data from widespread locations.

attached to the telephone, which identification is required by the computer and confirms the customer's right to order. Then, the data, in the language of the computer—punched cards, perforated tape, or magnetic tape—are fed into the device; and these data are transmitted at

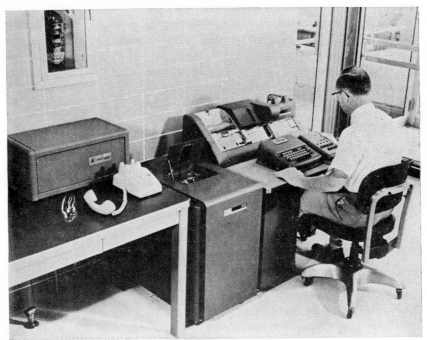

*Courtesy: Illinois Bell Telephone Co., Chicago*

FIG. 11-12.   The units to the left constitute Data-Phone. To the right, punched cards are being prepared.

speeds of up to 1,600 words a minute directly into the computer.[6] Machines talk to one another, cross-town or cross-country. Payment for each Data-Phone call is made just like an ordinary telephone call. Its potential is believed to be so great that in the not too distant future, conversations between machines over regular telephone lines may exceed the volume of voice communications.

## ADVANTAGES OF SDA

Why the widespread adoption of SDA? Some of the more obvious reasons are implied in the above discussion, but several additional comments are warranted. By employing machines adapted to use common language media, much repetitive data processing can be accomplished with a minimum of manual effort. SDA is especially effective where a large part of the data is constant and is continually reproduced from day to day and from paper to paper. There are many such applications in the typical enterprise. In addition, SDA provides practically error-proof processing. Once the data are correctly put into the medium subsequent errors in processing are normally nonexistent. In contrast, with ordinary manual recording and processing of the same data, errors are committed at various points and seem to defy efforts to eliminate them. SDA also lends itself to handling large volumes of data. The machine operations are fast and constant, and machine downtime is held to a minimum. A volume almost impossible to handle within a given period by manual means can be processed efficiently by SDA. Furthermore, deadlines can be met. The processed data are kept current and can be used while they are fresh and in keeping with present requirements.

## QUESTIONS

1. Why should SDA studies first be systems-oriented and then machine-oriented?
2. What is your definition of Source Data Automation; and in general, what purpose does Source Data Automation serve in office management?
3. What is your understanding of the building block approach with reference to SDA?
4. Name and discuss each of the common language media used in SDA.
5. Identify clearly each of the following:
   a) Cardatype.
   b) Numerical Control.
   c) Contouring numerical controlling.
   d) Common language link.
6. Enumerate the main advantages in the use of Numerical Control.

---

[6] Magnetic tape for computers is discussed in Chapter 12, p. 275.

7. Discuss "turn-around documents," pointing out their importance and usage in present-day business activities.

8. Discuss the possibilities and a manner of using SDA for any series of office tasks with which you are familiar, such as (a) processing the purchase orders by a bookstore and its sales to students; (b) maintaining students' records in a large university; (c) handling the requisitions, purchases, and inventory records of a manufacturer; or (d) any selection of office work you care to make. Indicate the means now followed and also the suggested SDA way, and why you feel SDA would prove beneficial in the particular application.

9. Discuss the subject area of "The Computer and SDA," from the viewpoint of office management.

10. How do you justify Numerical Control's being considered a part of SDA? Discuss.

11. In your own words, describe the meaning of Figure 11–7.

12. What is Data-Phone, and how is it used in connection with SDA?

## CASE PROBLEMS

### Case 11–1.   Reeger Manufacturing Company

The main office and factory of Reeger Manufacturing Company in Minneapolis, Minn., employs 677 people. Branch plants are maintained at Wichita, Kans., with 252 employees; Dallas, Tex., with 110 employees; Piqua, O., with 61 employees; and Richmond, Ind., with 88 employees. Most of the office and accounting work of the company is done in the main office in Minneapolis. The outstanding exceptions are the payroll and the direct labor distribution, which are currently prepared manually at the respective plant offices for each plant. It had been assumed that local preparation would be expedient and convenient, but the vice-president of finance states that necessary control is lacking, poor methods are being used by the branch offices, and the cost of performing the work is excessive. The Minneapolis office uses a modern accounting machine which is a part of a modern processing center featuring punched card, tape, and equipment for SDA. At the present time, employees are paid every two weeks, with one week waiting time. That is, on Friday, October 21, an employee is paid for the two weeks ending Friday, October 14. Preliminary inquiry shows that the two-week pay period should be retained, but each plant need not necessarily pay on Friday.

### Problems:

1. Devise a suitable SDA arrangement utilizing the Minneapolis office for preparing all payroll checks and direct labor distribution data. Describe the procedure followed and type of equipment and office forms to be used.

2. What do you envision as the outstanding advantages of your recommended SDA arrangement? Disadvantages? Discuss.

### Case 11–2.   Public Utility Suppliers, Inc.

This corporation, in business for over 50 years, manufactures and handles many different types of equipment and maintenance parts used primarily by public utility companies. About 40 percent of the business is from products manufactured by the company; the remaining 60 percent is jobbed and warehoused by the company for some 18 small manufacturers. General offices are in New York City, but all shipments to customers are made from the corporation's seven warehouses dispersed throughout the United States. Quite a few of the products have a high dollar value and are expensive to handle and ship. Service is important, since usually the ordered items represent materials needed for emergency work.

The records of all sales transactions must be quite detailed. This requirement is brought about not only because the corporation wants to have complete information on its business but also because vendors to the corporation wish complete information concerning sales of their products. Also, the customers need complete data on their purchases to comply with government regulations concerning public utilities.

Currently, when an order is received, it is typed on a five-page multiple copy form. Copy No. 1 is retained by the general office; copies No. 2, 3, and 4 are airmailed to the warehouse nearest the customer's designated place of delivery; and copy No. 5 is mailed to the customer to acknowledge the order. The warehouse, upon shipment of the order, encloses copy No. 4 with the merchandise. Copy No. 2 is returned to the general office, and copy No. 3 is retained by the warehouse for its records. Upon receipt of copy No. 2, the general office matches it with its copy No. 1, which is then completed regarding date of shipment, pricing, etc., and mailed to the customer. Copy No. 2 is retained by the general office for its records.

There is considerable writing required to designate the name of the customer to be billed and the items of each order. The work, as now performed, requires a skilled and experienced order writer who receives a weekly pay of $104. Present rate is seven orders written an hour. The average quantity is 382 orders a day. Study shows it takes about four days, on the average, from the time the order is received until it is shipped. There have been cases where copies No. 2, 3, and 4 were delayed in transit to the warehouse or were not sent to the nearest and proper warehouse.

The president of the company wants to mechanize the entire order-handling paper work and asks you for recommendations.

## Problems:

1. What are your recommendations for this corporation?
2. Enumerate the important assumptions made in answering question No. 1.

# CHAPTER 12

# COMPUTERS—

# TECHNICAL CONSIDERATIONS

How can great minds be produced in a country
where the test of great minds is agreeing
with the opinions of small minds.
　　　　　—*John Stuart Mill*

THE LAST of the three major considerations of the office technology is computers. We will first discuss the main technical considerations of this area, thus gaining a background for a better understanding of the managerial considerations and interesting applications of computers which are set forth in the following two chapters.

A computer is actually a group of mechanical and electronic devices connected into a unit or system to process data. Accurately designated, a computer is an electronic data-processing system. Here is a unit that can take a bundle of facts, process the necessary string of operations, including any or all eight of the basic elements of data processing discussed in Chapter 1, turn out the answers with fabulous rapidity and without error, and proceed automatically to the next bundle of data and process them.

## BASIC TYPES OF COMPUTERS

The basic types of computers are (1) digital, (2) analog, and (3) hybrid digital-analog. Digital computers, or arithmetic machines as they are sometimes described, deal with actual numbers and their answer is a set of numbers or letters, which can be made as accurate as desired. These computers perform according to a set of instructions, or a program, and if required, will perform hundreds and hundreds of repetitive calculations. A digital computer performs the work immediately after it is given a problem. It is a common type of machine for processing business data and represents by far the greatest number of computers in operation today.

An analog computer operates on the basis of using a formula or system to represent that which is being investigated or by duplicating mathematical behavior. It can instantaneously solve a mathematical equation with ten variables. It is actually based on approximations, and both input and output of an analog computer are approximate positions on a continuous scale rather than absolute numbers. Results from the analog computer are never precisely accurate, but they are commonly within 1/20 of 1 percent, which is entirely satisfactory for most applications. Calculating flows and pressures in pipelines and the position of a moving target are accomplished by an analog computer in only a split second, whereas for the same application the digital computer would calculate enormous quantities of data for an hour or so. Many analog computers are used for research and scientific investigation.

A hybrid digital-analog computer is a combination of the first two, digital and analog, utilized to obtain a computer capable of more work than the two can accomplish working separately. This hybrid type is a more recent development. It has been used advantageously for outer space projects and satellite programs. To date there are relatively few hybrid digital-analog computers in use.

## THREE TECHNICAL CONSIDERATIONS

To simplify this duscussion of technical considerations, we can organize our thoughts around three fundamental subject areas. These are: (1) the anatomy of a computer, (2) programming work for computer processing, and (3) coding work for computer processing. The first deals with the essential makeup of a computer. The term, *hardware,* is used to identify the computer itself and its various accessories. The second includes preparing the work for computer handling. The third, or coding, deals with putting the work in a form or language that the computer can handle *Software* is commonly used to identify all programming and coding required to utilize the computer, i.e., to utilize the *hardware* effectively.

## THE ANATOMY OF A COMPUTER

The top portion of Figure 12–1 diagrams the essential makeup of an electronic computer; the bottom portion, the general appearance of actual units. Different models will vary somewhat in detail and specific purposes, but the fundamentals outlined here are common to all computers.

Data in a suitable form such as punched cards, perforated paper tape, or magnetic tape are fed into the input units, where the data are converted into so-called computer language or, more accurately, electric pulses.

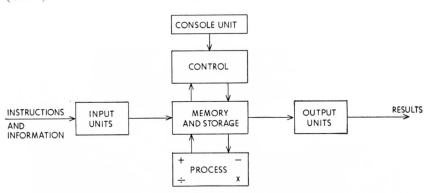

*Courtesy: International Business Machines Corp., New York*

FIG. 12–1. Basic components of an electronic computer.

These data are stored or retained in a memory unit of the computer. The memory units hold standard or current facts and sometimes instructions. When needed, the data are released to the process or computer section.

Directing the entire operation is the control section, which issues a program, or chain of instructions, to the process unit for each new group of data. It can send stored data required by the program, examine any step to select the following one, and start the processing of the next group of data. Frequently, a console unit, illustrated by Figure 12–2, permits a human operator to enter data if necessary, determine the status of the operations, and exercise complete supervision of the processing work. By means of the output units, completed processed data are printed and made available for use.

*Courtesy: Honeywell Inc. Electronic Data Processing Div., Wellesley Hills, Mass.*

FIG. 12–2.   Computer system console unit.

## BASIC OPERATIONAL UNITS

From what has been stated it follows that a series of planned operations are applied to data for processing. These data are entered into the computer by means of an input unit and processed according to programmed instructions by utilizing this input or data already stored within the computer. The end result of the processing is obtained from the computer by means of the output unit. This means that a computer has (1) input-output units, (2) memory and storage units, (3) processing units, and (4) a console controlling unit.

## INPUT-OUTPUT UNITS

Input units supply data to the computer. They "read" data from punched cards, perforated tape, magnetic tape, or magnetic ink characters and make them available to memory and storage units of the computer. Output units convert the processed data from the computer by transferring the "computer language" to a suitable form, such as printed records, punched cards, perforated paper tape, or magnetic tape. In the processing of business data very large quantities of input and of output must be handled. Some output units have a speed equivalent to printing the amount of print on one page of this book in about two seconds. Expressed differently, this is the equivalent of 7,500 paychecks printed in less than one hour.

However, the operating speeds of input-output units are commonly lower than those of the computer processing unit and hence limit the total operation. To alleviate this condition, the computer is used to perform other internal operations on available data while the input data are being fed in, or other devices are employed to perform relatively simple handling and transcribing work. A buffer type of device is also utilized to minimize interruption to the computer processing unit. A buffer is actually an auxiliary storage device which receives data at high speed from the processor, returns control to the processor, and then either feeds the data at high speeds to the processor, or accepts data at high speeds from the processor. This is shown in Figure 12–3.

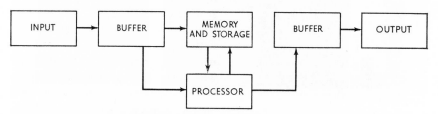

FIG. 12–3.   Illustrating the use of buffering in computer operation.

The term *throughput* and its efficiency are used to explain this same idea of acquiring a maximum of data flow, not in, or not out of the computer, but through the computer. In most data processing it is throughput that governs the performance. That is, the quantity of data taken in, processed, and put out as completed results should be maximized for best computer operation.

## MEMORY AND STORAGE DEVICES

These devices make up the components of the computer capable of storing information which is subject to recall or reference. Varying in type, size, and capacity, the memory and storage devices also serve to store programmed instructions and to provide work area for editing. All data to be processed must pass through what is commonly referred to as "main storage." This storage is supplemented by secondary storage units, which are not directly accessible to the processing unit but instead are connected to the processing unit through the main storage.

Each register, or location, in a memory unit holds one *word*. This may consist of up to 20 digits or letters. A "word" is the basic measurement of storage capacity. Typically, a computer will have 10,000–15,000 registers, but some large scale machines contain up to 300,000 registers. Since references are made to memory and storage units during the processing, the accessibility and capacity of these units and their operation in the computer are paramount. Specifically, we are concerned about the time required to refer to a specific register (location) and obtain the information from it. This is known as *access time*. In addition, the storage capacity of the memory and storage unit is important for we must have enough registers to handle all the information to be processed.

Memory and storage devices in use today are:

FIG. 12–4.   Magnetic core plane as used in a computer.

1. *Magnetic core.* This is illustrated in Figure 12–4. It consists of a series of very tiny cores, or rings of magnetizable material, with wire passed through the opening in two directions. When an electric current is sent through the wires in one direction the core becomes magnetized with a positive charge; in contrast, when the current is sent through the wire in the opposite direction the core becomes magnetized with a negative charge. Thus, the core stores either a positive or negative value, an on or off condition, which represents a portion of a binary configuration.[1]

Magnetic core offers compact size and relatively low access time. The number of cores in a plane and the number of planes determine the storage capacity. Advances in computer design seem to indicate that, for the magnetic core, future reduction in the cost per storage location is a distinct possibility. Access time now is in excess of 4,000 registers per second, which is well above that for any other storage medium.

2. *Magnetic drum.*   A magnetically coated surface of a cylindrically shaped object is the data-bearing medium of a magnetic drum. The data are coded in the form of the location of magnetic spots or dots on this surface.[2] Figure 12–5 illustrates the magnetic drum means. A magnetic drum is mounted on its axis and is rotated to bring the desired information to a magnetic head that reads the information. More than 1,000 characters can be stored within a square inch of surface and are available at a rate of about 25,000 characters per second.

3. *Magnetic disk.* This medium is similar to a phonograph record. The disks are about two feet in diameter, coated on both sides with ferrous oxide recording material, and mounted on a vertical shaft. Data are coded and stored as magnetized spots located in concentric tracks. Reading heads mounted on access arms read or write as directed by the computer

---

[1] See pp. 271–72 for discussion of binary configuration.

[2] See also coding of information under magnetic tape, pp. 275–76.

controlling unit. Storage efficiency is satisfactory, access time is acceptable and if need be can be reduced by using several access arms and "read-
write" heads.

4. *Magnetic tape.* This medium can be described as a metallic or
plastic ribbon of tape with a magnetic surface. Data for storage is coded
and recorded on the tape as spots similar to that of the magnetic drum or

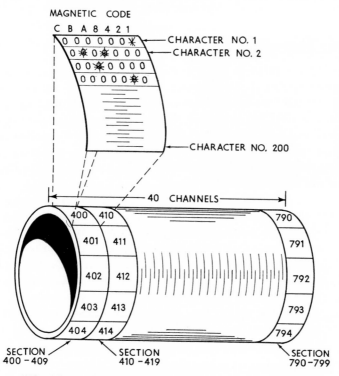

FIG. 12–5.   Magnetic drum storage. In this illustration
there are 200 characters per section, 10 sections per channel,
and 40 channels per drum. This makes 80,000 characters per
drum.

disk. Magnetic tape is a common medium for secondary storage. It has too
great an access time for wide usage as the medium for main storage.
Magnetic tape is widely used for handling input and output data, as
discussed later in this chapter.

## PROCESSING UNITS

There is always a central processing unit made up of a control and
arithmetic-logical section. The former integrates automatically the operation of the entire computer system in keeping with the program of
instructions. This includes controlling the data within the computer such

as regulating the input devices, moving data into or out of memory and storage units, and between memory and storage units and the arithmetic-logical section, and controlling data entering the output units.

As its name implies, the arithmetic-logical section performs arithmetic and logical operations. These include performing according to algebraic equations and calculus as well as basic processing operations such as reading, sorting, transmitting, comparing, and storing.

## CONSOLE CONTROLLING UNIT

By means of this unit the operator can gain a continual picture of the internal operations of the computer. One can view the console controlling unit as actually an integral part of the central processing unit. The operator can start and stop the computer, interrogate for data in memory units, and load data into the computer by means of the console controlling unit. With reference to programming, it is possible to use sense switches to stop processing or to select predetermined program paths. Hence, the flexibility of the program is increased.

There are also cases where not all the program is stored in and accessible to the computer. In such cases, by means of the console controlling unit, programs can be entered directly into the computer step by step as the processing work progresses. Also, the console controlling unit permits tracing a system or a procedure one step at a time and affords high human operator or external control. In some instances, limited data can be entered directly by control buttons on the console. In addition, limited output information may be obtained, thus enabling the console operator to supervise the computer operation.

## GLOSSARY OF COMPUTER TERMS

At this point it will be helpful to insert Figure 12–6. This glossary of selected terms used with computers serves as a convenient review and reference for computer terminology. Familiarity with these terms will assist in grasping the technical significance of computer operation. Some of the terms included in this list concern programming and coding, which will now be discussed.

## PROGRAMMING

The designing of a computer program was discussed in Chapter 9. However, for purposes of emphasis as well as convenience to the immediate discussion, certain basic facts will be reiterated. A data-processing system is designed to handle a specific number and type of operations. When included in the system, a computer is directed to

*Accumulator*—a storage register where results are accumulated.

*Alphameric Characters*—letters of the alphabet, numerical digits, or symbols used for communicative purposes.

*Analog Computer*—one representing variables by physical analogies in continuous form. An analog computer is said to measure, not count.

*Batch Processing*—the means by which a number of similar input items are grouped for processing during the same machine run.

*Buffer Storage*—the temporary storing of information during a transfer of that information. Buffer storage is used to permit simultaneous computation and input or output.

*Checkout*—the determination of the correctness of the computer routine, locating errors in it, and correcting them.

*Compile*—to produce a machine-language routine by translating from ordinary or non-machine program. Concerns programming.

*Digital Computer*—a computer in which information is processed and represented in discrete form. A digital computer counts; it does not measure.

*Hardware*—the mechanical and electrical devices making up a computer.

*Library*—an organized collection of proven and standard routines which can be incorporated into larger routines.

*Location*—a place in a storage unit where a unit of data or an instruction may be stored.

*Loop*—a technique of coding in programming whereby a group of instructions is repeated with alterations of some of the instructions and usually with modification of the data being processed.

*Off-Line*—the operation of input or output devices are not under direct control of the central processing unit.

*On-Line*—the operation of input or output devices are under direct control of the central processing unit.

*Parameter*—a quantity to which arbitrary values may be assigned for such things as decimal point location, record format, and size.

*Parity Check*—a checking means based on making a total number of "on" or "off" in some grouping of binary digits.

*Random Access*—the finding and getting of data in storage is relatively independent of the location of the information most recently obtained.

*Real Time Computation*—data processing by which the computer supplies information to a business activity whenever the information is demanded.

*Register*—a device that holds information while or until it is used.

*Software*—the programming and coding work required for effective computer data processing.

FIG. 12–6.　Glossary of common terms used in computer technology.

perform each basic element of processing by specific instructions, which normally include the identification of the data, the basic elements to be performed, the sequence, and what to do with the results. This complete package of instructions is commonly known as a program. It is developed by "programming," which can be considered as the breaking-down in most complete detail of the work to be electronically processed.

For example, assume that the processing requires multiplication. In this case, the computer must be informed or directed to perform multiplication as well as (1) the operation that precedes the multiplying, (2) the operation that follows the multiplying, (3) the identity and location of the multiplicand, and (4) likewise that of the multiplier. In addition, after the multiplication is completed, the result must be transferred to storage at a specific location in the storage device, from whence it can be discharged, if desired, by the output device or retained in storage for future processing, as the individual case might be. There are certain exceptions to this, however, as for example when magnetic tape ledger records are used as the input medium, in which case part of the stored data are on the tape or strips of the ledgers. Also, in the case of magnetic ink characters being used as the input medium, little of the data is stored in a storage unit of the computer.[3]

In other words, an operation usually involves a chain of operations such as reading, locating information in storage, transferring to the processing device, processing, returning the result to storage, perhaps also returning the initial information to storage, sending out the result from storage to the output device, and finally discharging the result in the prescribed medium from the output device. Thus, the simplest portion of a procedure requires a number of carefully planned steps that must be designated in extreme detail to the computer.

Hence, by means of computer programming, the machine progresses by moving from one minute element of work to the next in a prescribed sequence. In some instances, the sequential element can be either of two possibilities but no more, represented by yes or no, go or no go, on or off, and so forth. If the answer is "Yes," for example, the computer follows the element of this designation. In contrast, if the answer is "No," the alternate element is followed. This means that minute, detailed, sequential steps in the work to be done must be set forth, and where choices arise, the decision must be one of the two alternatives. The computer having the information of the precise element can determine if "yes" or "no" is to be followed. This is illustrated humorously but helpfully by Figure 12–7.

Since a computer program is usually designed and evolved in the form of a flow chart listing the precise step-by-step action to be taken, it is extremely helpful in performing programming work to have an intimate knowledge of existing systems, procedures, and methods. The broad, overall picture should be taken, for one large programming job may encompass many small jobs, thus eliminating duplication and needless waste. In addition, a complete understanding of the purpose for which the finished data are used appears paramount in this work. To illustrate the breadth and detail of this work, it is common for the preparation of customers' invoices to require 1,500 or more steps.

When instructions in the form of programs are placed in the storage device of a computer, they are commonly termed *stored programs*. One computer can be supplied with a number of different programs for different work by simply putting in, or loading, the programs into storage. The stored programs are accessible to the computer, providing it with the

---

[3] Magnetic tape ledger records and magnetic ink characters are discussed later in this chapter, pp. 277–79.

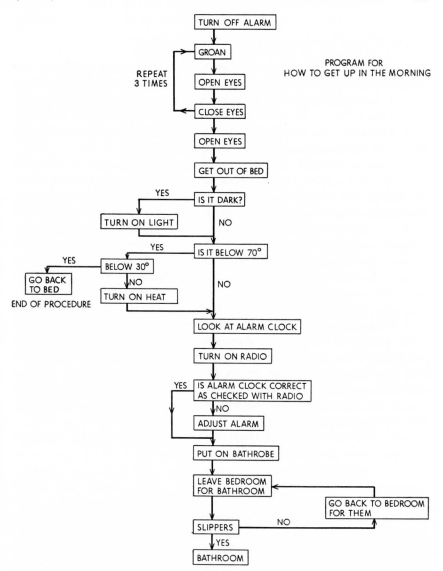

FIG. 12–7. This diagram illustrates how programmers have to instruct the electronic system to work.

ability to alter its own program in response to conditions revealed as the processing takes place. Hence, it can be said that the computer exercises some judgment within the limits established by the programmed operations to be performed. In this sense, it can be stated that computers are capable of making simple decisions.

## BUSINESS AND DATA-PROCESSING PROGRAMMING

Progress in programming has been significant to those wishing to use computers for the processing of normal business data. Typically, this type of work requires many programs providing for relatively small amounts of processing to large quantities of data. Comparatively simple additions, multiplications, and recordings are required. Programming is especially important in adopting computers for business purposes.

In contrast, the use of the computer for research and much scientific work entails a small amount of data being processed many, many times. Frequently, the task of processing is to substitute various values in mathematical formulas and determine whether a critical value, such as the stress in a structure or the amount of chemical produced, is within a safe, allowable technical limit. Processing data for scientific work frequently involves complex mathematics such as extracting square roots, raising numbers to decimal powers as exponents, and handling repetitive processing using different numerical values. Programming for the computer, especially the analog type, to handle this type of work is fairly simple.

It is interesting to note that computers were first used for scientific work, insofar as large-scale commercial usage is concerned. This was probably due to the restricting influence of programming in connection with the computer use. We simply had not figured out how to tell the computer economically the manner of handling much data with little processing. However, during the past decade or so, the rapid strides in the advancement of programming and the knowledge being built up about it are probably the most outstanding factors contributing to computer progress for the processing of ordinary business data.

## COMMON BUSINESS ORIENTED LANGUAGE (COBOL)

To operate a computer, it is necessary to have a network of preprogrammed packages which range from simple service routines to highly complex compilers. A compiler accepts a special code or a natural language, interprets it for the computer, selects the proper routine from a library retained by the computer, supervises the coding, allocates data, assembles a complete program, and gives a report on this program. The first compilers were all algebraic or mathematical, because the language of mathematics is concise and definite. With time, however, attempts were made to orientate the input language of a compiler to the natural language of the user. Subsequently "Math-Matic," "Fortran," and "Unicode" were developed.

With the great interest developing in computers for processing business data, efforts were directed and stimulated toward developing new system languages more suitable for this type of processing. As a result, "Flow-Matic" was pioneered, followed shortly by "AIMACO" and "FACT." The situation seemed to be that each computer manufacturer was developing his own language, a condition not only costly and unnecessary, but extremely difficult for users of several different types of computers. Accordingly, in January, 1960, the Conference on Data Systems Languages, or CODASYL, accepted and approved a plan for perfecting and advancing a common and simplified English language for business system programming. This simplified language is called COBOL and stands for Common Business Oriented Language. Figure 12–8 illustrates COBOL.

---

This language is COBOL:

SUBTRACT   QUANTITY-SOLD   FROM   BALANCE-ON-HAND.   IF BALANCE-ON-HAND IS NOT LESS THAN REORDER-LEVEL THEN GO TO BALANCE-OK ELSE COMPUTE QUANTITY-TO-BUY. . . .

COBOL eliminates the use of detailed and difficult computer language instructions such as:

| 06011 | ' | 12040 | 12047 |
| 06028 | C | 12048 | |
| 06074 | ? | 12046 | 12014 |
| 06145 | S | 12012 | 12010 |

---

FIG. 12–8.  COBOL permits instructions to computers with simple English words of everyday business language.

This advance toward a common computer language suitable for all computers, regardless of their manufacture, is the most significant advance in programming. Once a program is written in COBOL, it need not be rewritten if switching from one data-processing system to another takes place. Exchange of business programs is therefore expedited. Costly and time-consuming rewriting from one machine language to another is eliminated, and the burden of programming is eased by the use of COBOL. As an indirect result of the COBOL influence, many business-oriented "canned" or subroutine programs have been created for each type of computer. Also, automatic compilers and translators have appeared on the market. Thus, another hurdle has been removed, so that the progress of computer processing of business data can continue upward to even greater heights.

## CODING THE WORK FOR COMPUTER PROCESSING

The third and last fundamental subject area in technical considerations of computers is coding the work for computer processing. All information

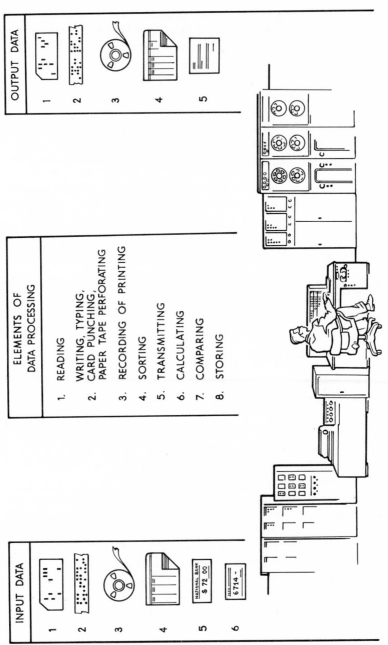

INPUT DATA

1
2
3
4
5
6

ELEMENTS OF DATA PROCESSING

1. READING
2. WRITING, TYPING, CARD PUNCHING, PAPER TAPE PERFORATING
3. RECORDING OF PRINTING
4. SORTING
5. TRANSMITTING
6. CALCULATING
7. COMPARING
8. STORING

OUTPUT DATA

1
2
3
4
5

FIG. 12–9.  Media of input data, processing, and media of output data of an electronic data-processing system.

is conveyed by symbols. In the English language, there are familiar letters of the alphabet, numbers, and punctuation marks. For everyday correspondence, these symbols are recorded on paper according to a prescribed sequence and grouping. When transported to another person reading and writing English, these symbols convey a particular message.

In the same manner, to communicate with a computer system necessitates that the information be expressed in symbols and in a form that can be read and interpreted by data-processing devices. In the case of the computer, this language has been called "computerese." It is language the machine can understand and act upon, in keeping with the desired processing. Man invented "computerese" to utilize the machines. It represents symbols making up a mutual language to provide communication between people and machines. In other words, every detail which the machine is to follow must be put into language that the machine can handle. This includes the use of special codes and numbers which, put on or into the data-transmitting medium, will cause the machine to perform the operation desired.

There are a number of different media that can be used. For input data, the following are included: (1) punched card, (2) perforated paper tape, (3) magnetic tape, (4) magnetic tape ledger record, (5) magnetic ink characters, and (6) imprints of specially formed characters or fonts that are read by machine. The processing of output data, being basically the reverse of that for input data, means that the same media can be used for output data as for input data. However, since output data are either for human use or for subsequent machine use of a relatively limited sort, not all the communication input media are used for output. For the latter purpose, the communication media include (1) punched card (2) perforated paper tape, (3) magnetic tape, (4) magnetic tape ledger record, and (5) ordinary print on paper. The concept of input data, output data, and data processing by a computer is shown by Figure 12–9.

## BINARY MODE

Before discussing each of the data-transmitting media, some fundamentals in their representation of the data should be pointed out. The processing and storage of data within the computer are made possible by coding the data. The more common mode of coding is known as a binary mode, which involves the use of only two possible conditions. For example, holes in a paper tape are either present or absent. Likewise, magnetic spots are either present or absent, electric current is in one direction or in an opposite direction, switches are closed or open, and electric current is on or off. In other words, the base is two, just as decimals refer to a base of ten. Tubes, or transistors, or cores, can exist in only two states—"off" or "on," emitting or not, magnetized in one or the other charge.

One binary digit is called a *bit*. The common arrangement is the binary coded decimal whereby four bit positions represent from left to right the decimal digits, 8, 4, 2, 1. That is, different values are placed on the four positions and the sum of these positions for recording information. There is a combination of these four bit positions to represent any digit from 0 to 9. Figure 12–10 illustrates these combinations.

The handling of zero in a computer is usually noted as ten, i.e., an eight and a two. In the binary position this avoids registering all blanks for zero, for if we did this it would be difficult to determine whether the register is supposed to be zero or the machine has failed to transfer data.

BINARY CODE

|   | 8 | 4 | 2 | 1 | |
|---|---|---|---|---|---|
| DECIMAL | \|<br>↓ IS | \|<br>↓ REPRESENTED | \|<br>↓ | \|<br>↓ BY | TOTAL VALUE<br>(READ ACROSS) |
| 0 | 0 | 0 | 0 | 0 | 0 |
| 1 | 0 | 0 | 0 | ✳ | 1 |
| 2 | 0 | 0 | ✳ | 0 | 2 |
| 3 | 0 | 0 | ✳ | ✳ | 3 |
| 4 | 0 | ✳ | 0 | 0 | 4 |
| 5 | 0 | ✳ | 0 | ✳ | 5 |
| 6 | 0 | ✳ | ✳ | 0 | 6 |
| 7 | 0 | ✳ | ✳ | ✳ | 7 |
| 8 | ✳ | 0 | 0 | 0 | 8 |
| 9 | ✳ | 0 | 0 | ✳ | 9 |

FIG. 12–10.  Illustrating the four bit position and values to represent decimal numbers. For decimal 5, the "bits" of "4" and "1" are "on," "8" and "2" are "off."

Other codes than binary are used by some computers including a numerical coding to the base eight, known as octal notation, a seven-bit alphameric, a six-bit numerical, and a biquinary system indicating numbers to the base five. The number system followed is a technical consideration, and assistance in its understanding is offered by the computer manufacturer both before and after machine installation.

## PUNCHED CARD

The typical punched card is about 7⅜ inches long by 3¼ inches high. In the IBM type, the card is divided into 80 vertical columns, each one containing 12 units which, read from the top down, are: 12, 11, 0, 1, 2, 3, 4, 5, 6, 7, 8, 9. The 12 and the 11 zones are frequently called $R$ and $X$, respectively. Data from original records are put on the cards by means of punched holes; that is, when certain holes are punched in the card, these holes represent definite information. High-speed machines are used for this purpose. The letters of the alphabet number 26, and there are 10 digits (0–9), making a total of 36 characters, each of which must be assigned to coded representation by a positioned hole in the card. Since there are 12 units in a vertical column on the card, it requires three different vertical arrangements totaling 36 (3 × 12) characters to represent all possibilities. This is clearly illustrated by Figure 12–11.

Information represented or coded by means of the presence or absence of holes in specific and exact locations is read as the card travels through a card-reading mechanism. The reading is automatically converted to an electronic language utilized by the computer in its data processing.

It is also possible to record binary information by the use of row binary, in which the data are arranged serially across each row beginning at the lower left, moving across from left to right for each horizontal row, and progressively upward on the card. A punched hole in the card represents "yes," no punch indicates "no." It is also possible to arrange the binary information in parallel columns, with each column of the card containing 12 information bits. For certain computers, where the basic unit of information is a word consisting of a maximum of 36 consecutive bits, a total of three adjacent card columns is used.

## PERFORATED PAPER TAPE

Another common medium for the transmission of data into a computer system is perforated paper tape. It is a continuous recording medium and can be used to record long runs of data, being limited only by the capacity of the storage medium into which the data are being placed.

Most perforated paper tape is either of an eight-channel code or of a five-channel code. A channel runs the length of the tape. In any column across the width of the tape, the number of possible punching positions is equivalent to the number of channels of the tape. That is, in the eight-channel tape, there are eight possible punching positions; and in the five-channel tape, there are five positions.

Figure 12–12 shows the code of an eight-channel paper tape. Observe that the lower five channels, identified as channels 1, 2, 4, and 8, and "check," are used to record numerical characters. As already stated, the sum of the position values indicates the value of the character. For example, 3 is expressed by holes in positions 1, 2, and "check," while 7 consists of holes in 1, 2, and 4. For alphabetic characters, two additional channels at the top, $X$ and $O$, are used with the 1, 2, 4, 8, and "check" channels. The arrangement is similar to that of the 12, 11, or $R$ and X zones of the punched card being used in conjunction with the 0–9 or digit punches of the punched card. To illustrate, the letter $A$ is represented by

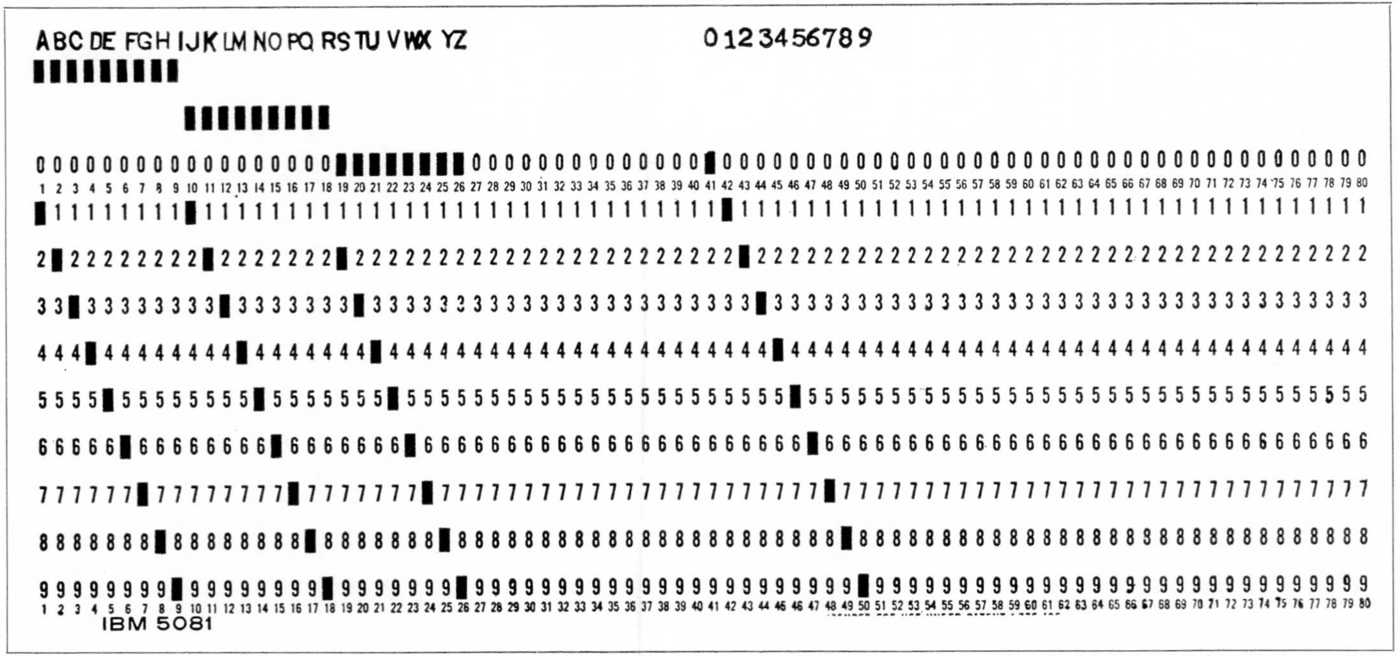

Courtesy : *International Business Machines Corp., New York*

FIG. 12–11.  A code used for punched holes which represent letter and figure data.

holes in the following channels: $X$, $O$, and 1; $K$ by holes in channels $X$, "check," and 2.

The channel identified as "check" is used for verification purposes. Each column is punched with an odd number of holes. If the sum of the holes punched in channels $X$, $O$, 8, 4, 2, and 1 is an even number, a hole in the "check" channel must be present. This explains why the column for the letter $Y$ shows holes in channels $O$, "check," and 8. The "end of line" or "El" channel at the top of the tape is used to indicate the end of a record or the tape.

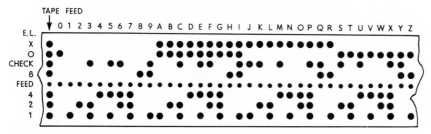

FIG. 12–12.   Code for eight-channel perforated paper tape.

## MAGNETIC TAPE

The principal input medium for computer systems is magnetic tape. It is one-half inch wide, made of plastic, and coated on one side with a metallic oxide. Information recorded on magnetic tape is permanent, but previous recordings are destroyed as new information is put on the tape. It

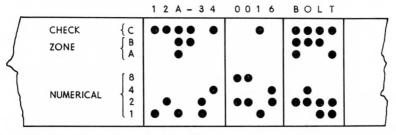

FIG. 12–13.   Coding of magnetic spots on tape to transmit information. This is the seven-bit alphameric code. Translation of the spots is shown at top of sketch.

is possible to utilize the same tape many times, thus saving in recording costs. Magnetic tape is supplied on plastic reels containing approximately 2,400 feet of tape.

The data are recorded on the tape in the form of magnetic dots or spots. The code employed is illustrated by Figure 12–3. Starting at the top, the first channel is $C$, for checking, followed in order by $B$ and $A$, commonly called zone tracks, and 8, 4, 2, and 1, the numerical tracks or channels. In similar manner to that described under binary mode and perforated tape, numbers are coded, using the numerical channels. The number 5 is coded as 4 and 1; and 7 is 4, 2, and 1. The zone tracks are used in combination with the numerical tracks to indicate letters. In this code, for every column, the total spots add to an even number. If for a column the total of the spots in the zone and numerical tracks is an odd number, a spot is added at track $C$.

It is appropriate to state at this point that an electronic system is not infallible. Therefore, it checks itself to find any error. The impulses on channel $C$, or "check," of the tape are used for this purpose. For example, every transfer of information from the memory units might be tested on an odd-even basis. If the sum of the group of digits is an odd number when it is supposed to be even, the machine indicates the error and stops. This is all done automatically by the machine.

The use of magnetic tape as an input medium is further demonstrated by the availability of a hand-operated, portable, magnetic tape digital recorder. Use of this recording machine eliminates the need for punched cards and paper tape for data acquisition and processing. In the case of inventory taking, for example, the bin number, quantity, and material or reference number are recorded on the magnetic tape. Subsequently this tape is fed into the computer, the data processed, and inventory reports printed. The unit has found favor with public utility companies for meter reading. The account or meter number and the reading are recorded by the door to door meter reader. When the tape is filled, it is sent to the computer center where statements to customers, account lists, and reports are prepared. The recording unit is battery powered and handles different sizes of tape cartridges. The maximum cartridge holds about 400 feet of tape. The unit records serially 15-decimal digits per block, a feature which is helpful in attaining error free data collecting.

### INFORMATION INTERCHANGE

These are strong efforts being made to adopt a permutation code whereby all coded information could be interchanged between business machines and computers. To this end the American Standards Association has assisted in developing a standard code which is all-inclusive and provides room for future standardization programs. Figure 12–14 shows this standard code. Its adoption is voluntary by business machine manufacturers, but no doubt it will gradually and surely be utilized. At the same time, the older codes will continue, due to their existence in present machines and to preferences by certain customers for no change.

| $b_4$ | $b_3$ | $b_2$ | $b_1$ | $b_7$=0 $b_6$=0 $b_5$=0 | 0 0 1 | 0 1 0 | 0 1 1 | 1 0 0 | 1 0 1 | 1 1 0 | 1 1 1 |
|---|---|---|---|---|---|---|---|---|---|---|---|
| 0 | 0 | 0 | 0 | NULL | DC$_0$ | b̶ | 0 | @ | P | | |
| 0 | 0 | 0 | 1 | SOM | DC$_1$ | ! | 1 | A | Q | | |
| 0 | 0 | 1 | 0 | EOA | DC$_2$ | " | 2 | B | R | | |
| 0 | 0 | 1 | 1 | EOM | DC$_3$ | # | 3 | C | S | | |
| 0 | 1 | 0 | 0 | EOT | DC$_4$ (STOP) | $ | 4 | D | T | | |
| 0 | 1 | 0 | 1 | WRU | ERR | % | 5 | E | U | UNASSIGNED | |
| 0 | 1 | 1 | 0 | RU | SYNC | & | 6 | F | V | | |
| 0 | 1 | 1 | 1 | BELL | LEM | (APOS) | 7 | G | W | | |
| 1 | 0 | 0 | 0 | FE$_0$ | S$_0$ | ( | 8 | H | X | | |
| 1 | 0 | 0 | 1 | HT / SK | S$_1$ | ) | 9 | I | Y | | |
| 1 | 0 | 1 | 0 | LF | S$_2$ | * | : | J | Z | | |
| 1 | 0 | 1 | 1 | V$_{TAB}$ | S$_3$ | + | ; | K | [ | | |
| 1 | 1 | 0 | 0 | FF | S$_4$ | (COMMA) | < | L | \ | | ACK |
| 1 | 1 | 0 | 1 | CR | S$_5$ | − | = | M | ] | | (1) |
| 1 | 1 | 1 | 0 | SO | S$_6$ | . | > | N | ↑ | | ESC |
| 1 | 1 | 1 | 1 | SI | S$_7$ | / | ? | O | ← | | DEL |

*Courtesy: American Standards Association, Inc., New York*
This material is reproduced from the American Standard Code for Information Interchange, X3.4–1963, copyright 1963 by ASA, copies of which may be purchased from the American Standards Association at 10 East 40th Street, New York, N.Y., 10016.

FIG. 12–14. The standard code for information interchange among information-processing and communications systems. It consists of eight columns of sixteen characters each. Control characters occupy the first two columns, punctuation the third, numbers the fourth, alphabet the fifth and sixth. The last two columns are unassigned, being reserved for future standardization.

## MAGNETIC TAPE LEDGER RECORD

This medium consists of magnetic strips imbedded on the back side of a ledger record. It serves as a dual-purpose record that is readable by machine and by people. Ordinary typing of information on the front side is translated into computer language on the magnetic strips of the same ledger record. The strips are capable of storing a large variety of information. Normally, one of the strips is for positioning purposes prior to an entry being made on the ledger record; the remaining strips contain data, some in what is called a positive coding, some in just the opposite, or negative, code. The positive and negative codes are used for verification purposes and to insure accuracy. An illustration of the magnetic tape ledger record is shown in Figure 12–15.

*Courtesy: Burroughs Corp., Detroit*

FIG. 12–15.   A magnetic tape ledger record.

The advantages of this medium are unique. They include unlimited access to external memory and to familiar, hard-copy accounting data. Also, simultaneous access to both electronic and human language is provided, thus eliminating separate searching operations. Instructions to the machine can be stored on the magnetic tape ledger records along with human language instructions on the front side, thus expediting the handling and processing work. Changes in instructions are easy to make. In addition, the stored information on the magnetic tape is introduced into the machine as needed, or on a random access basis, thus permitting greater processing flexibility and more utility of the internal memory of the computer for processing.

## MAGNETIC INK CHARACTERS

Information can be printed with magnetic ink on ordinary paper. This serves as a medium that can be read by either man or machine. As of the mid-1960's, this medium has been popular for bank checks and deposit slips but has not as yet been extensively adopted for other types of paper work. Study is being given to the extension of magnetic ink to business documents other than checks and deposit slips.

Many are of the opinion that in the near future magnetic ink characters will provide the best means yet devised for automating single documents. The plan is to install an Encoder, which imprints the proper digits, at each point where a charge form, internal debit or credit, and the like are created. Thus, the documents themselves are made the input data, and the need for punching cards or perforating tape is eliminated. The imprinting is such that transit, routing, account number, and amount can be included. Studies indicate the cost would be only about 25 percent that of other appropriate means.

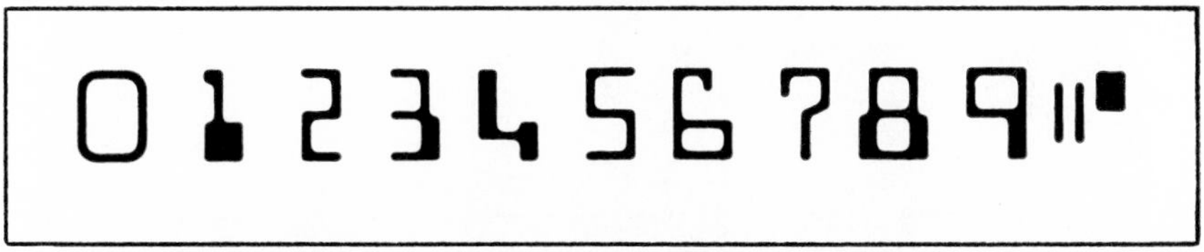

*Courtesy: Moore Business Forms, Inc., Niagara, N.Y.*

FIG. 12–16.   Type font selected for magnetic ink characters. It can be read visually and also provides optimum machine readability.

With reference to bank checks the magnetic ink character numerals and characters are the same style and size for all checks. The information conveyed by these imprints is utilized in processing the check in its journey back to its maker, with the proper bank and individual account being debited or credited. The printing is done with an ink containing iron oxides which are electronically charged and read by magnetic ink character-reading equipment. A special type of design is used in order that the characters can be read visually and maximum machine readability is provided. The printing type employed is of a style called "Font E–13B" and is illustrated by Figure 12–16. The characters are located on the bank documents in specific areas, such as definite distances from the bottom and right edge, in order that the machines may perform automatically and not have to search for the data.

## SPECIAL IMPRINTS FOR MACHINE READERS

There are machines that can do what you are doing right now—reading. A machine reader can read letters and numbers without the use of special ink. Research has demonstrated that to the machine, ordinary printing may be difficult to read because of the variations in normal printing quality. Hence, certain printing type faces resembling conventional type

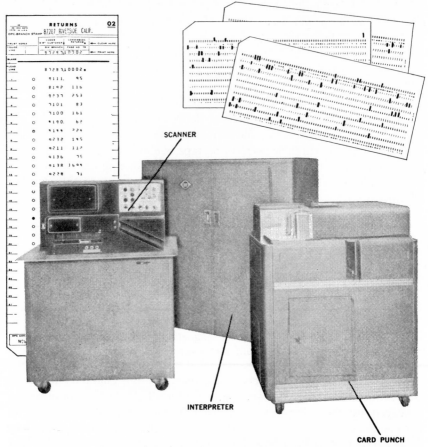

*Courtesy: Farrington Electronics, Inc., Needham Heights, Mass.*

FIG. 12–17. A machine that reads. The unit on the left is the scanner or reader; the center unit, an interpreter; the unit on the right, a card punch machine.

facings have been developed to counter typical printing shortcomings and to meet better the needs of the machine reader. However, the machine can read most printed type, but special imprints are preferred because they give better results. At their present stage of development, most commercially feasible machines are required to read within a relatively small area of the document. It may be an account number, an amount to be paid, or a name and address or a Zip Code number. In the near future, machines to read a page of typed material probably will be available and, beyond that, perhaps a machine to read handwritten material.

Figure 12–17 shows a machine reader. This particular machine reads a varying number of lines from a printed listing and translates these data into punched cards which are fed into a computer. The machine reader of this type actually does two operations: (1) reads and (2) translates what it reads into computer language. In short, the machine performs human reading and eliminates the laborious manual punching required to prepare punched cards or perforated tapes when used as the input medium. Manufacturers of the reader state that when three or more operators are continuously employed in reading and punching, the machine reader is to be preferred.

Being very versatile, the machine reader can be used for the input of data in many different applications. Credit invoices, checks, order cards, and bill stubs of public utility companies are among the more common uses. Its main areas of application can be classified under two groups: (1) where the input information consists of a long number of separate units recorded in a great number of places and must be processed quickly and economically, and (2) where the output data of today becomes the input data of tomorrow. To illustrate, if a statement with a stub consisting of printed material only is sent to a customer who subsequently returns payment and the stub, it is feasible to put critical portions of the printed matter of the stub in a form that the machine reader can easily handle when the stub is returned and becomes input data.

## QUESTIONS

1. Set forth the main differences between a digital computer and an analog computer.

2. Discuss three different memory devices that are used in computers.

3. For a computer, name the basic components and the function of each component.

4. As you see it, is there any substantial difference between the use of magnetic ink characters and the standard magnetic tape as media for data communication? Discuss.

5. Identify clearly each of the following:
   a) Magnetic tape ledger record.
   b) Magnetic drum.
   c) Console controlling unit.
   d) Throughput.

6. What are the important differences between programming for processing business data and programming for processing scientific data? Elaborate on your answer.

7. What is the meaning of binary mode, and how is it used by a computer?

8. Explain the meaning of Figure 12–14 in your own words.

9. Are you of the opinion that magnetic ink for many types of business documents will be common in the not too distant future? Substantiate your answer.

10. Relate briefly the history, present use, and significance of the common business-oriented language as employed for computer operation.

11. What are the present major considerations in the application of the machine that reads.

12. Enumerate and give the chief characteristics of three common media for communicating input data for computer processing.

## CASE PROBLEMS

### Case 12–1.    Grimes Manufacturing Company

A physical inventory of the stock on hand is wanted. The inventory information will be punched into cards showing (1) the item number, (2) the inventory count in units, and (3) the unit price. A separate card will be used for each item number. Cards will be sorted into item number order, or sequence, before being fed into the computer. The dollar amount of each inventory item is wanted along with a listing showing the item number, units on hand, unit price and total value of each item, and a grand total of the dollar amount of inventory.

Currently there are 22,000 inventory items, and it is believed this number might increase in the future to a maximum of 30,000 items. The number of characters required for each inventory item is 20. The computer to be used has magnetic drum storage units. Each of these units has 32 channels with 8 sections per channel. A total of 200 characters is the maximum capacity of each section. In the future the computer will be used for inventory control purposes, hence the inventory information will be retained in the computer.

The manager of the computer unit states that a heading line is to be printed by the computer at the start of each page of output data. Also, he advises that the total value of each inventory item be adjusted to the nearest cent.

### Problems:

1. Draw the diagram for the computer operations, of a block diagram type, showing the sequence of steps required by the computer to process the data.

2. Calculate the amount of storage space required, and draw a sketch showing the arrangement of data on a typical drum storage unit, for this inventory application.

### Case 12–2.    Madison Manufacturing Company

A check and stub unit is to be written by a high-speed printer which is a component of the data-processing center at Madison Manufacturing Company. The printer is made up of a cylinder of print wheels, arranged side by side, which rotate. Raised characters for imprint are located in bands around the rim of the cylinder. Usually, there are some 50 characters in each band. Each character provides one printing position. Opposite each band is a little hammer that presses the paper against the desired character at the proper time while the paper is stopped at each print line. The printer of this company has a printing speed of 700 lines per minute. The maximum number of characters on any one line is 20, and there are six lines to an inch. The printer can skip one or two lines at printing speed; but for three or more lines, it has a speed of 2,000 lines per minute. For estimating purposes, the time required to print a line of less than 20 characters with a distance or length of six inches is the same as that for 20 characters.

The check and stub unit to be printed is 3½ inches by 5¾ inches, the latter being the horizontal distance. Flow of units through the printer is vertical. The check position is to the left, and on it will be printed three lines of ten characters each on the top three lines, plus five lines of six characters each on the bottom five lines. On the stub, the following will be printed:

From top of stub:
Line 1................8 characters
Line 2................6 characters
Line 3................6 characters

From bottom of stub:
Line 1................12 characters
Line 2................12 characters
Line 3................10 characters

For mechanical reasons, a top and bottom border of one-quarter of an inch each must be maintained. No printing can be placed in these borders. In other words, the bottom of Line 1 is five-twelfths of an inch (one quarter plus one sixth) from the top edge. In addition, one-quarter of an inch must be allowed between successive units to compensate for the slight differences in sizes of the units and for a spacing interval for feeding the paper stock through the printer.

## Problems:

1. Draw a layout of the check and stub unit.
2. Compute the printing time for 1,000 check and stub units.

### Case 12–3.   Gibbons Sales Service

A specific problem for a stored-program of a computer deals with the calculation of sales commissions. Currently, salesmen are paid 5 percent of their sales on the first $100 of sales each day and 10 percent on sales in excess of $100 for the same day. To encourage salesmen to sell the higher-priced units, the plan is being revised so that the higher commission will apply before the $100 daily sales level is attained. To this end, the amount by which the average price of units sold by the salesman exceeds $10 will be subtracted from the $100 sales level to determine the amount on which the 5 percent commission will apply. Commissions on sales in excess of this new level will be 10 percent.

To illustrate, salesman James Hendrick sells $150 worth of merchandise, the average price of which is $15. As the plan now is, salesman Hendrick will receive $10, calculated as follows:

5 percent of $100................$ 5.00
10 percent of $ 50................ 5.00
Total...................... $10.00

Under the contemplated revised plan, salesman Hendrick will receive $10.25, calculated as follows:

5 percent of ($100 − [$15 − $10]). . . . . . . . . . . . . . . . . . . . . . . . . . . . . . . . .$  4.75
10 percent of [$150 − ($100 − [$15 − $10])]. . . . . . . . . . . . . . . . . . . . . . .  5.50
Total. . . . . . . . . . . . . . . . . . . . . . . . . . . . . . . . . . . . . . . . . . . . . . . . . . . . . .$10.25

The various detailed operations in proper sequence must be determined so that the work can be processed by the computer.

## Problems:

1. Draw the diagram of computer operations for salesmen's commissions, using the present plan of compensation. Refer to Figure 12–7 and use it as a guide.

2. Draw the diagram for salesmen's commissions, using the contemplated plan of compensation.

3. Briefly discuss the observations you have made in preparing these diagrams, especially from the viewpoint of programming.

CHAPTER **13**

# COMPUTERS—
# MANAGERIAL CONSIDERATIONS

A man's work is in danger of deteriorating when
he thinks he has found the best formula
for doing it.
—*Eugene O'Neill*

THE REAL potential and future of computers for business data processing
is up to the members of management. Computers enhance the functions of
management; they do not replace it. Computers call for better utilization
of the managerial mind, better managerial actions, and better managerial
accomplishments. Significant improvements in management are possible
by use of the computer, but managers must be truly objective and honest
with themselves if they are to gain the benefits which the computer can
bring about. It is erroneous to think that depositing a modern computer in
the midst of inept management policies, outmoded practices, and an
archaic organization will somehow or other cause corrective miracles to
take place.

The awe-inspiring electronic computers, with their fantastic accomplishments, have led some to refer to them as machines that think. This is
not true. The machines do not think. They operate only as instructed and
must be told what to do in the minutest detail. Decision making is not
their prerogative, except that decision making given to them, which
usually includes modifying their own instructions as dictated by progressive stages of their data processing. Managers, not computers, use their
own judgment and their sense of discrimination. Human beings alone have
intelligence, in that they make free decisions based on a personal value
system. The computer has no value system because it does not have a

mind of its own. This means that managers must still think; they cannot turn this vital requirement over to the computer. The simplification and improvement in computer operation have given rise to some erroneously calling a computer a thinking mechanical human being. It is mechanical, all right; but it is not thinking, and it is not a human being.

## MANAGEMENT AND THE COMPUTER

What computers actually do is increase the power and the influence of the human mind, not minimize its importance. They provide help never before believed possible or even conceived. Instead of being overburdened with the processing of data, the human mind can be relieved of such mental drudgery and concentrate its efforts and attention to create, to plan, to ponder and reflect about information, to decide what should be done and whom to inspire. Guesses, hunches, and risks in decision making can be minimized; and decision making on facts and adequate, usable information can be maximized.

Computers increase the responsibility of managers. With the assistance given by computers, the human mind can soar to new heights of accomplishment and acquire knowledge and judgment not yet imagined. The computer can show the way to greater progress, but the accomplishment of hoped-for outputs and gains are regulated by the person issuing the instructions to the computer or figuring out how the computer can be utilized to do what he wants it to do. The potential lies with the manager, not with the moronic metal monster. In essence, computers are tools to be exploited by managers. The challenge is not to be satisfied with the processing of data as such, but to initiate new and revolutionary applications and concepts which are made possible by the use of computers. This necessitates management thinking of the highest order.

## THE COMPUTER AND THE OFFICE MANAGEMENT PROCESS

The computer's effect upon management can probably best be seen by considering its effect upon each of the four fundamental functions of management, namely, upon planning, controlling, organizing, and actuating. The office management process affects and, in turn, is affected by the computer. How the manager can best profit by the opportunities made available by the computer and, in turn, how he can best meet the challenges provided by the computer may be approached most effectively from the viewpoint of the office management process. Under planning, for example, we can ask, "What changes in planning are in order due to the availability of the computer?" "Is the technique and scope of planning being modified by computer utilization?"

## THE COMPUTER AND MANAGEMENT PLANNING

The scope of planning is usually broadened when the possible use of the computer is considered. More activities can be included, the parameters can be pushed back, and a far more inclusive picture of what makes up the totality of the office work can be included. Actually there should be no restricted areas in the initial development stages of computer usage. Compromises can always be made later, but beginning with circumscribed areas inevitably means ending with restricted areas. The usual pattern in the application of a computer is to a smaller range of activities than was initially considered. Seldom can the best results be achieved by confining it to predetermined limits of activities or to certain organizational limits. Computer work commonly cuts across conventional lines originally established for nonautomated purposes.

In planning for computer utilization, an important and initial consideration is to improve existent systems, procedures, and methods, combining reports, records, and office forms wherever possible, and to point the entire effort toward handling only information that is truly essential. It is folly to put into the computer work that you know is unnecessary. Much of this improvement effort can be made by company personnel; but in many cases, the services of a consultant experienced in this area can save much time and direct the work to a satisfactory conclusion. However, excessive reliance upon outside assistance, particularly from manufacturers of computers, may prove unwise. In the first place this is really not the manufacturer's representative's responsibility. Frequently he is neither familiar with the specific and detailed needs of the company nor aware of the human problems confronting company personnel should the decision to use a computer be made. He can and does render valuable assistance in helping the prospect become more aware of what the equipment can do and the possible aids it can provide.

Adequate planning will avoid the establishment of unrealistic deadlines for the changeover. Frequently, it requires more time to get the computer in operation than is at first realized. The usual pattern is pressure for early installation after long delay in trying to decide whether to install it. Planning helps establish practical schedules and ties together the various required activities into a coordinated program.

## THE COMPUTER AND MANAGEMENT CONTROLLING

Periodic follow-up of a computer installation to smooth out operating difficulties is a must. There usually are a number of such difficulties. The follow-up should also include the comparison of "before and after" achievements. By this means areas requiring managerial attention are identified and remedial action is applied to them.

Computer utilization is commonly of a multiproject nature, and this fact emphasizes the importance of establishing effective progress-reporting techniques and carefully monitoring them in order to maintain proper control over each project. Effective reporting techniques are simple, comprehensive, and easy for either the technical or the nontechnical employee to understand. To maintain the support of top management members, it is a good practice to provide them with clear, concise, and up-to-date reports which reveal how each project is progressing and to what extent established goals are being attained.

Job completion dates must be realistic and adhered to; otherwise, control efforts become dissipated. Failure to provide sufficient lead time and allowances for unexpected contingencies is a common cause of establishing completion dates that cannot be fulfilled. The delay of one project aggravates the entire program because work scheduling for a computer closely interrelates all projects within the system. As a result, certain projects may be subjected to completion on a "crash basis," which usually means higher costs and extra follow-up efforts.

## THE COMPUTER AND MANAGEMENT ORGANIZING

For genuine success, the various accomplishments of a computer must be integrated with the operational activities of the company. The computer should not be regarded as a new, mysterious entity separated from the main body of the company or as an interesting, captive consulting facility. To achieve the needed integration between information and action functions, it is essential that those working directly with the computer have a clear understanding of their relationships with members in other units of the company and that the authority of the computer personnel be clearly defined. This brings up questions of organization.

Initially, a common practice was to place the computer in the controller's office. Reasons for this varied, but it was thought that this provided a logical organizational location and was an ideal spot for the computer to prove itself a valuable asset. If not in the controller's office, the computer was quite likely to be located somewhere in the finance department. Recent surveys reveal that currently three out of four computers are the responsibility of the financial executive. In some instances data processing has been moved up in the organization; in others it has been relocated. Quite a number feel that the computer should occupy a separate organizational unit and that the manager in charge should report to the president. This arrangement not only accords great importance to office automation, but it also permits a broad scope of operation and a cutting across traditional organizational boundaries, considerations which probably are necessary for a truly integrated information-processing system to exist.[1]

Organization and office automation give rise to the question: "Should centralization or decentralization be followed?" The situation is primarily whether to have (1) a single large installation to serve the office needs of the various operating units of a big enterprise or (2) a number of smaller facilities, each designed and located to serve the needs of one or several of the company's various operating units. The decision depends upon many factors, including the physical size of the enterprise, the total volume of work, the uniformity of work, and the investment required for the equipment.

From the organizational viewpoint, there is also the task of determining clearly the authority and responsibility assigned to those in charge of the computer. Likewise, each subgroup of the computer unit needs to know how it is to work with other groups and the particular duties that it is expected to carry out. In too many companies this organizational relationship has been permitted to become established mainly on an empirical basis, without proper definition of the authority and responsibility of those in charge of this specialized work.

## THE COMPUTER AND MANAGEMENT ACTUATING

With all the glamour now being associated with the new office technology, it is easy to forget that people are still vital to office management and will continue to be so. It requires people to operate and maintain computers, and it requires people to interpret and utilize the information made available to them. Successful computer usage requires effective managerial actuating.

The adoption of a computer poses the problem of manpower displacement. This, in turn, frequently necessitates the establishment of certain policies to cope with the human considerations involved. Such policies may include (1) telling the office automation story as it is developed, so that all employees will know what is going on, (2) terminating the employment of no employee because of the new machine—normal attrition will take care of any excess, (3) reducing the salary of no employee because of the computer, and (4) changing job content with reassignment, retraining being provided.

Employees to be affected by the change should be encouraged to participate in designing the change. Normally, this practice brings favorable results. Not only are excellent suggestions offered, but by this practice a needed sense of belonging and importance are enjoyed by the employee. High employee participation usually means high employee

[1] The location of the computer in an organization is discussed in detail in Chapter 26, "The Office Organization." See especially pp. 580–85.

cooperation. However, it is a mistake to bypass employees in the planning stages and initially invite them to be a part of the program at the time of installation.

It must be remembered that with the passage of time people tend to become more ready to accept change. The attitude toward office changes almost always becomes more favorable several months after completion of the planning and installation periods than it had been during these periods. People tend to adjust to their surroundings. Experience with new work methods usually demonstrates that many of the fears and unpleasantnesses believed associated with the change actually do not exist or are of much less importance than originally conceived.

Properly handled, the computer system becomes a means of office work that is easier and more practical than any former way. Generally, employees will like the computer way; success or failure depends in large measure upon the quality of actuating efforts performed. The installation should be employee-oriented, not computer-oriented. In the final analysis, the new method is dependent upon the good will, understanding, and cooperation of the employees. To ignore the personnel considerations is certain to invite disaster.

## MAJOR COMPUTER USES

Computers provide better information with respect to both quality and quantity. The various uses of computers are many, but for purposes here can be segregated into five major categories: (1) decision making, (2) controlling, (3) simulating, (4) designing, and (5) specific processing of data. The great majority of computer applications can be classified under one or more of these categories.

In the usual sense of the word, decision making can be considered to mean the selecting from possible problem solutions or courses of action, giving due consideration to the objectives and available information. This concept is quite broad and includes both strategic and operating information and whether actions taken should be on a continuous, periodic, or occasional basis. When computers are utilized, the decision making can be either (1) a programmed and routine type, usually featuring measurable quantities; or (2) a programmed but nonroutine type, where the information is restricting and interpretation is emphasized. For the former, typical decision-making examples are those dealing with such things as the quantity of a product to produce next month or an operating budget for a forthcoming fiscal period. For the latter, representative are decisions concerning the products to be included in a product line, and those relating to level of customer service to be provided to compete successfully. To decide these latter types of questions, information is needed and the computer will supply it. But the information must be studied and interpreted in order to arrive at the decision.

As pointed out in Chapter 2, controlling means "to determine what is accomplished, evaluate it, and apply corrective measures, if needed." When a computer is used for controlling purposes, the facts about what has taken place are put into the machine, in order to obtain specific performance measurements; these values are compared to information showing what is desired; and the respective differences reveal the areas in which corrective action is to be taken. Information on cost, inventory, production runs, and quality of raw materials is illustrative of control material.

Simulating, as pointed out in Chapter 8, is the testing of numerous operating plans to determine the most productive plan. Frequently, but not always, the plans are expressed in mathematical form. However, in all instances, the data must be of a measurable type. In aircraft research, for example, computers are used to simulate different flights for jets. Such factors as allowable pay load, fuel consumption, and speed can be determined accurately without even putting the plane in the air. Likewise by means of a computer, advertising agencies can determine the best combination of media for a particular advertising campaign. The computer is used to try out hundreds of different media combinations and thus reveal the one which maximizes the particular qualities that are being sought. To duplicate manually the information of many combinations would be extremely costly and time consuming. In one such experiment, it required a four-man crew three months to duplicate what the computer provided in six minutes.

A fourth category of computer application is designing. By this is meant the confirmation or rejection of an intelligent guess or hypothesis by the results obtained from carefully directed experimentation. The characteristics of each guess are calculated and checked against specifications. The computer performs these calculations very rapidly. A wide range of possibilities can be considered by the designer; and as a result, the best possible design is identified and used.

Computers are also employed for what may best be termed specific processing of data. This includes the preparation of bank checks, bills, inventory records, and reports of various types. To justify a computer for this work, there usually must be a relatively large volume of work requiring considerable calculating, sorting, or comparing. Otherwise, available machines designed especially to perform the particular work will provide entirely satisfactory results at lower costs.

## ADEQUACY OF PRESENT INFORMATION SYSTEM

A fundamental consideration in determining whether to use a computer is the adequacy of the present information system. Many office executives feel that the first move is a thorough analysis of the present means of work performance in order to spot any weaknesses and to determine any foreseeable inability of the present information system to cope with probable future needs. In addition, the possibilities for improving the present information system should be investigated. In many cases, study brings to light hidden potentials within the existing setup. Taking advantage of these opportunities and improving the present system may adequately fulfill the requirements. A chemical manufacturer found that certain revisions and additions in his current conventional way of processing papers would result in substantial savings, and that the use of a computer was possible but would necessitate a high overhead burden and relatively expensive operating payments.

Adequacy is relative and depends upon what is to be accomplished. When considering the use of a computer most companies want to achieve a savings in clerical cost; a capacity to handle increasing work volume; greater accuracy and uniformity in data processing; the securing of better information in less time; better information upon which to base decisions, including the means to enable the technique of either simulation or design to be employed; and improved service to customers. These objectives are not mutually exclusive, but the selection and weight given to each helps formulate the concept of the ideal computer installation from the viewpoint of the particular company.

The volume of transactions is commonly a deciding factor. Computers handle tremendous work volumes within extremely short periods. When a company is faced with an increasing volume of accounts to be processed, the signal for computer utilization may be at hand. This is especially true when the current noncomputer equipment has limited capacity and prohibits procedural refinement and expansion to more mechanization.

Speed of processing is another important consideration. Reference is commonly made to speed as an outstanding gain in the use of computers. It may be vital, but more often than is the case, speed of processing should be considered in relation to service required. To know that with a computer, information for a report can be completed in two hours, in contrast to four days under the present setup, is convincing, provided the report will be used in two hours and will not be ignored or filed away for four days before any use is made of it. The challenge here is to get management members to improve their usage of the material made available. Perhaps this starts with more rapid processing to make information available more quickly and hence more up to the minute.

In addition, speed of processing may directly influence the company's standard of service in comparison with that of its competitors. When an advantage in service is keenly sought, the computer should be evaluated to determine how much its contribution in speed and service will mean in sales and in customer relations.

Some have reasoned, and admittedly with justification, that the computer industry is in its infancy. The future holds improvements and opportunities for computer applications far above any present usage envisioned. The potential is vast. Companies have ordered and installed computers even though studies indicated an operating loss from them for a number of years. But these decisions were reached because it was recognized that some pioneering with a tool as powerful as a computer is probably necessary, that usage begets further usage with the discovery of new applications, and that firsthand experience gained in the use of computers helps to reap the benefits of computerization. However, it is possible to "go overboard" in deciding such issues and wind up in a precarious managerial position.

## BATCH OR REAL-TIME?

An important managerial decision regarding computer application is whether batch or real-time process scheduling will be used. Under the former means, all incoming computer data are batched or allowed to accumulate and then processed on a scheduled basis, perhaps once a week. In contrast, for the real-time means data are entered into the computer as soon as available and processed immediately. When real-time is used and the computer is "on-line" with the activity being performed, the expression "on-line real-time" is used.

There is no uniformity of opinion as to when a computer arrangement is precisely real-time. Some contend only control applications are real-time because in these applications processing takes place while the related physical manufacturing operations take place. Others give the term broader meaning and include many types of application where the stored information can be removed at random—called "random access"—in contrast to "serial" types of stored data, which must be removed from the computer in the order of their input. The decision on this issue rests with the individual company. How quickly are the processed data wanted? Letting a customer know within five days of order placement when shipment will be made may be entirely satisfactory, and a batch arrangement would be used. On the other hand, information for a seat reservation on an airplane usually requires a real-time arrangement. At the present stage of progress, most payroll, accounts payable and receivable, cost, and sales analyses are on a batch arrangement, but with the development of systems and the movement toward integrating them, the real-time arrangement could well increase significantly in adoption.

## MANAGER-COMPUTER TECHNICIAN RELATIONSHIP

The computer can be a source of controversy between the technician, who knows precisely what the computer can do, and the manager, who can put what it can do to work. It frequently happens that the technician isn't familiar with the manager's needs and, in turn, the manager doesn't understand the technician and is suspicious of the computer because of its far-reaching and revolutionary potential. These divergent viewpoints can be brought together or at least minimized to an appreciable degree. To this end several suggestions are in order.

First, basic policies should be settled before details of the computer utilization are worked out and applied. Computers can open the door to great savings and service opportunities, but to gain them it is necessary and desirable to adjust, delete, and add policies so that the advantages of these opportunities can be won. Almost always needed are statements specifying who is responsible for what decisions, who exercises the prescribed controls, and what the "ground rules" are.

Second, the type of decisions for which the computer will be used should be spelled out. A common practice is to have computer participation in all decisions. This is not only unnecessary but it is also unwise. Too many technicians and specialists get into the act. A simple decision is expanded all out of proportion to its importance. The manager becomes more confused and frustrated. Computers are to assist managers in making better *big* decisions. And our approaches and practices to computer usage should allow the manager and the computer to work together closely.

Also, as pointed out above, computers influence organization and the jobs within it. In some instances the influence results in major modifications; sooner or later there is always some change. Setting forth what these changes probably will be, who will be affected by them and why, tends to smooth the path of application and helps promote good manager-computer technician relationships.

Furthermore, adjustments in long-standing practices assist in acquiring harmonious relationships. Included in the types of popular changes made are (1) elimination of many special files; (2) greater degree of centralized filing; (3) use of "centless accounting"; (4) uniform "days in period" for comparable reports; (5) more data retained on previous functions, such as sales, costs, and collections, to provide helpful trends or comparisons with current data; and (6) greater availability of pertinent data to lower levels of management. In addition, periodic reviews of current computer applications help to uncover other uses and take advantage of available computer time. This state of affairs seems to exist no matter how carefully and thoroughly the initial feasibility study was conducted.

Lastly, the manager should be given basic facts concerning computers and their operation and, likewise, the technician should acquire knowledge of the enterprise and its management. In a sense this is a plea for empathy and, once accomplished, will assist amazingly in acquiring better manager-technician relationships. Mastery of the other's specialty is neither needed nor recommended, but an appreciation and understanding by each of what the other is trying to do, and how he is trying to do it, is mandatory.

## PHYSICAL REQUIREMENTS AND TASKS OF CONVERSION

For computer usage, it is usually necessary to provide nonvarying, disturbance-free electrical power and office space that is regulated as to temperature, dust, and humidity. The layout of the office may have to be changed to place the heavy machine where ample structural support is provided and the flow of office work can most efficiently be handled. Channels under the floor in which to run electrical cables connecting the various units sometimes pose a technical problem, especially when a controlling factor is the maximum lengths of cable specified by the computer manufacturer.

Converting large amounts of written material into language required by the computer can represent a herculean task and too often is brushed off as a minor consideration in a computer installation. Conversion difficulties include inaccuracy and lack of uniformity in existing records, missing papers, unexpected deviations of records from a supposed format, errors in reading or in putting information on tape, the maintenance of an adequate work force to accomplish the conversion work, and the accomplishment of the work within reasonable budget limitations.

The conversion process must also take into account what is known as "application in parallel." This means the practice of continuing the processing of information in the normal way and also through the computer, then comparing the results in order to check the accuracy of the computer program. Normally, the work is run in parallel for several complete cycles, or until the new process is completely "debugged." This can be a very frustrating period. Consistent results are obtained; and then, without warning, inconsistencies occur. Finding and correcting the sources of errors frequently pose major tasks. In some installations, conversion problems are minimized by beginning with areas that are already using punched cards or have been subjected to a certain amount of office mechanization, but there is no guarantee that this approach will eliminate conversion difficulties.

## COMPUTER ECONOMICS

Excluding scientific and military applications, computers are normally used for the direct savings they effect. Savings in clerical payroll of 15–25 percent and in inventory cost of 15 percent are not unusual. In addition to cost savings, other advantages are sought or effected. These include improved customer service, better control over the operation of the enterprise, and increased speed and accuracy in processing data.

As is true for most machines, the larger and more expensive a computer, the lower the unit cost per processing operation. The greater capacity, speed, and versatility of the big computer make its unit cost relatively low. To illustrate, the huge IBM STRETCH computer, with a high usage rate, will perform 100,000 calculations for only 2½ cents. Or this computer will do for less than $1 what it would cost $10 to do on a small computer or perhaps $8,000 with an ordinary desk calculator. Volume and type of work are the key factors.

Three choices are available to the user of a computer: he can (1) buy the computer, (2) rent the computer, or (3) hire a computer service. The cost differs for each of these conditions. With purchase there is a large capital expenditure plus an annual expenditure for operation and maintenance. Rental entails a much smaller expenditure, with standard expenses for operation. Commonly the rental represents about one-third of the total annual operating costs. To hire a computer service requires no capital, operation, or maintenance costs, but a fee for the work performed.

Currently, the rental or lease arrangement represents approximately 80 percent of computer installations. Usually rental agreements contain an option to buy, but few of these options are exercised. Rental or computer service may be favored if there is uncertainty of forecast in computer usage. Also, the small computer user may not be able to justify hiring and training a maintenance crew, which he can avoid by rental or hiring a computer service. Expensive programming for specialty work usually can be minimized by using the computer service. On the other hand, lower net cost in the long run may point to the purchase of the computer as the best decision. The federal government uses a *cost advantage point* in determining whether to buy or lease. This is the point when purchase price plus accrued maintenance equals cumulative rentals for a particular computer. When this point is reached in six years or less, purchase is warranted providing it appears that the computer will meet the job requirements without major modifications. Limited research indicates that it usually takes around six years for computer investment to be recovered. Low point in recovery is the end of two or three years, due primarily to the effect of start-up costs, changeover, and adjustments.

Computer service is offered by over 150 U.S. companies who are specialists familiar with all computers. Some are independent companies, others are service bureaus owned or operated by computer manufacturers. Their charges vary according to factors such as type of computer and the amount of work, but generally charges are considered nominal and in line with the services rendered. The services offered by these companies are ideal for excess work loads and where computer usage is occasional.

It can be seen that many considerations can enter into the decision on which of the three alternatives should be chosen. The total cost can vary widely. Cost is probably most important, but it is not the sole consideration. The company's individual requirements and the manager's judgment are equally influential factors. A helpful comparison of the three basic choices is obtained by forecasting the annual total expenses for the most favorable and suitable arrangement for each choice. This can be projected over a reasonable number of years. Such data, along with attention to nontangible considerations, assist in arriving at a decision.

## WILL IT PAY TO WAIT?

With a field as dynamic and fast-growing as computers, the question arises: "Will it pay to wait in order to obtain a better buy to fulfill our data-processing needs?" Computers, like any other machine, wear out; but experience to date shows that most electronic equipment functions perfectly even after 10 years of use, and engineering estimates are that a usable life of 20–25 years is reasonable. The usefulness of a computer can be reduced by failure of the unit to meet changed requirements. However, proper planning, taking into account probable future needs for 5 to ten years, can minimize most of this loss so that it should not become serious. Furthermore, the utilization of computers employing modular-type design that "grow with the user" helps to meet the problem.

Delay in acquiring data-processing equipment might be thought the best decision when consideration is given to the amazing advances made possible by engineering improvements. In the relatively brief history of computers, improvements have been more in the nature of speed, convenience, and capacity rather than in a radically different basic design. Likewise, computers to serve the special needs of a particular industry or type of application have been developed and employed. In many respects, efforts have concentrated on perfecting components which are made available, but certainly not mandatory, to existing systems. Seldom do these components make the rest of the system obsolete. In the case of rental units, the newest components, as they become available, are commonly incorporated into the system.

The subject of costs and the payout period raise some interesting considerations in deciding the question of whether to wait or to proceed with a computer installation now. The total period in a projected installation must be considered. It is unrealistic and incomplete analysis to begin with some future date and ignore the interim period from the present to the start of that future period. Savings, if any, should be considered from using what is available today. Displacements of this system by future changes can be taken into account.

The data of Figure 13–1, while hypothetical, serve to illustrate a common situation regarding timing and payout period for data-processing systems. Under process system No. 1, a net saving appears in the fifth year, with total savings at the end of ten years being $540,000. Process system No. 2 illustrates waiting until a new machine is on the market and installing it in the third year. Under this arrangement, total savings at the end of the tenth year are $375,000, not as favorable as under process system No. 1, but toward the end of the period increasing yearly at a faster rate than those of system No. 1. However, if system No. 1 is started in the first year and converted to the improved machine, and system No. 2 in the third year, the cumulative savings amount to $690,000, a sizable increase over either those of system No. 1 or those of No. 2 used singly.

In addition, it should be pointed out that the initial conversion to a computer system involves a great deal of work and time. But it is highly probable that the second conversion necessitated by adopting process systems No. 1 and No. 2 will be relatively far less difficult due to previous experience and that the second conversion will stress "debugging" the new system rather than the physical work involved in converting to the new system.

| Year | Process System No. 1 | | Process System No. 2 | | Process System No. 1 and No. 2 | |
|---|---|---|---|---|---|---|
| | Yearly | Cumulative | Yearly | Cumulative | Yearly | Cumulative |
| 1 | − 50 | − 50 | | | − 50 | − 50 |
| 2 | − 65 | −115 | | | − 65 | −115 |
| 3 | − 70 | −185 | − 50 | − 50 | −120 | −235 |
| 4 | +105 | − 80 | − 70 | −120 | + 15 | −220 |
| 5 | + 90 | + 10 | − 75 | −195 | + 75 | −145 |
| 6 | +100 | +110 | +100 | − 95 | +150 | + 5 |
| 7 | +100 | +210 | +100 | + 5 | +160 | +165 |
| 8 | +110 | +320 | +110 | +115 | +175 | +340 |
| 9 | +110 | +430 | +120 | +235 | +175 | +515 |
| 10 | +110 | +540 | +140 | +375 | +175 | +690 |

FIG. 13–1.  Loss or savings for each of three different installations of data-processing systems for a ten-year period (in $000,000).

## THE COMPUTER SELECTION

It has been customary to appoint a committee to select the computer. Normally this gives very satisfactory results. The ideal committee consists of experienced managers, preferably from the upper organizational levels. This group can be supplemented by another group representative of the major areas to be affected by the installation of the computer. In some instances, a committee has been used to carry out the work of studying the status of the present information system; and when this practice is followed, the same committee continues to serve in the selection of the type of computer.

Knowledge about various computers must be acquired by the committee members; and this is best done by attending schools offered by the computer manufacturers, reading available literature on the subject, and conferring with executives of companies having computers in operation. After a period of several months, an effort is made to determine what types of work should be done by a computer and what type of computer appears best for the company's present and reasonable future needs.

Competent consultants can be employed to give assistance in drawing up recommendations pertaining to the company's work to be done on a computer, the type of machine, steps in application, and pitfalls to be avoided in these efforts. The consultant's wide and varied experience can save much time and spark the action to move ahead. But participation by the company personnel is essential, for it provides them with practical insight as to what is going on and why. Furthermore, familiarity with the proposed processing is gained, and the background needed for successful installation and operation is obtained.

The use of a committee can assist in attaining a unified program of preparation and installation. Important groups such as the systems and procedures department, the personnel department, and the departments in which changes will occur can be represented on such a committee. Planning pertaining to the feasibility of automation—the how, when, and where of the changes to be made; and the means for handling these changes, especially with reference to personnel—can be handled quite successfully by a committee.

A number of criteria can be used in the task of selecting a particular computer. Among the more common are (1) completion of operations within a fixed time, (2) cost, (3) the most versatile computer within a given maximum expenditure, (4) specific computer features, (5) proven performance, and (6) the manufacturer. Under this latter consideration, such bases as experience in computer manufacturing, installation and training service, and caliber of maintenance service usually rank high.

## COMPUTER CENSUS

Since 1951, when the U.S. Bureau of the Census installed the first large electronic data-processing system for business data, nearly 20,000 systems have been put into operation. This estimate is for general-purpose systems; it does not reflect specialized installations, as in banks, except in the case of the larger banks where large general-purpose systems are in use. Included in this estimate are the small or desk-size computers, which have opened up a number of users with relatively limited amounts of data processing to be handled. Governmental sources reveal that the number of computers in federal government use as of June, 1965, was nearly 750.

Arbitrary classifications by size of computer system are sometimes followed, including (1) large, (2) medium, and (3) small. Such classifications are actually very broad and rough. The classification "large" includes computer systems renting for over $30,000 monthly. These represent the sophisticated systems with top speeds and special features. "Program interrupt," for example, will usually be included in the abilities of this group. This is the ability of the computer to accept instructions simultaneously by selecting an input or output device ready to join the processing and start this processing at the same time other input and output devices are completing their functions. This raises the "throughput" and assists in conserving valuable processing time. The second group, "medium," constitutes those with rental costs averaging between $5,000–$10,000 monthly. They make up the popular computer systems, widely used and perhaps best known of all computers. Most in this group have mass memory hardware and effective input and output devices. The last group, "small," represents machines renting for around $1,000–$2,000 per month. These have relatively limited capacity but perform satisfactorily within their limits. Punched cards or tape are commonly the input media, tape and printed matter the output media. Many have very limited mass memory, if any, and this condition poses problems in processing, requiring, for example, the referencing of indicative data. Usually the practice is to rely on punched cards or tape for these data as well as the variable data. This results in slower processing, but lower cost.

Figure 13–2 shows a comparison of computers and highlights certain differences among them. For this list the computers were selected arbitrarily, but they do represent many, even though not all, of those in common use. The illustration is intended to be indicative only, not conclusive.

## THE COMPUTER AND RETURN ON INVESTMENT

Some managers believe that their computer investments are not giving adequate return on investment. The computers are providing advantages and improvements, but not in the amount and kind that it is believed they should. This condition stems from various causes including limited competency of computer personnel, lack of sufficient top management interest in computer application, and insufficient managerial effort to determine the economic facts of the computer operations. For example, no study is made of the relative importance of the work being processed, computer time is crowded with menial data "just to keep it busy," no formal method is followed for choosing applications, and no estimates or charges are made of what various computer applications are costing. Many managers, in fact, do not know how much their computer is saving or earning; their operation being based to a great degree on faith.

What is needed is the same type of operational analysis applied to computers as is applied to extensive research projects and expensive marketing projects. Specifically, this involves several important steps. First, carefully estimate the potential gains from a proposed computer application. This is not easy. All work performed in the before and after arrangement must be identified, the effect upon corporate resources and

| Name | Price (Thousands of Dollars) | Average Monthly Rental | Storage Capacity | Media | |
|---|---|---|---|---|---|
| | | | | Input | Output |
| **LARGE:** | | | | | |
| Control Data 1604-A | $1,200 | $37,000 | 6 million words (D)<br>32,000 words (C) | K-MT-PC-PT | K-MT-PC-PT-PR |
| Honeywell 1800 | 1,650 | 30,000 | 1,080 million characters (D)<br>8-32,000 words (C) | K-MT-PC-PT | K-MT-PC-PT-PR |
| IBM 7090 | 3,000 | 65,000 | 280 million characters (D)<br>32,000 words (C)<br>1 million characters (Dr) | K-MT-PC-PT | K-MT-PC-PR |
| RCA 601 | 2,000 | 35,000 | 8-32,000 words (C) | K-MT-PT | MT-PR |
| Univac 1107 | 2,250 | 45,000 | 16-65,000 words (C) | K-MT-PC-PT | MT-PC-PT-PR |
| **MEDIUM:** | | | | | |
| Burroughs 200 | 225 | 6,000 | 480 million characters (D) | K-MT-PC-PT | MT-PC-PT-PR |
| Gen. Elec. 210 | 750 | 14,000 | 4-8,000 words (C) | K-MT-PC-PT | K-MT-PC-PT-PR |
| IBM 1401 | 175 | 4,000 | 20 million characters (D) | MT-PC-PT | PC-PR |
| NCR 315 | 250 | 6,500 | 1-16,000 words (C)<br>10-80,000 words (C) | K-MT-PC-PT | K-MT-PC-PT-PR |
| **SMALL:** | | | | | |
| Gen. Prec. LGP-30 | 50 | 1,200 | 4,000 words (C) | K | PR |
| Monroe Monrobot XI | 25 | 700 | 1-2,000 words (Dr) | K-PC-PT | PC-PT-PR |

CODE:  D = Disk   K = Keyboard   PT = Perforated Tape
      C = Core   MT = Magnetic Tape   PR = Printer
      Dr = Drum   PC = Punched Card

FIG. 13-2. A comparison of computers.

cost estimated, and key adjustments required for the changeover evaluated. To ignore these basic requirements may prove tragic. Assuming the popular, "How can we miss?" attitude can lead to serious difficulties. Second, devise a means for measuring the potential benefits. This necessitates not only identifying what they are, but also evaluating their worth. If the benefit is dollars saved, how does this amount compare with the cost of obtaining them? If less time is to be taken, can and will it be used for accomplishing other work? Third, exercise the required control to see that the expected benefits are obtained. No computer controls itself. Managerial control must be applied to its operation in order to insure successful completion of plans designed to bring about the benefits being sought. Fourth, establish a cost system for charging company departments or accounts for computer operations. This helps to fix responsibility and places computer operations on a sound business-like basis. Here again to establish this practice requires much hard work, but the effort is well worth while. A suggested approach is to (1) determine the present (noncomputer) and proposed (computer) cost of processing the work, (2) charge the original department with the present processing cost, (3) charge the computer department for developing the computer application, and (4) credit the computer department with the savings achieved from the computer application.

## SUGGESTIONS FOR COMPUTER USERS

Many of the problems of computers must be solved in managers' offices rather than in the laboratories of the designing engineers. Experts in the area of computer installation quickly point out that each installation has its unique difficulties, but certain general practices usually aid in achieving complete satisfaction within a minimum of time. Among the suggestions covering these practices are the following:

1. View the computer as a data-processing system, not as a single machine. See it as a means for supplying information to an enterprise, not as a replacement for a single or particular office machine.

2. Learn as much as possible about the various uses of computers. This knowledge will broaden your viewpoint and assist in maximizing utilization of the computer.

3. Have top managers or a top group decide what work should be done with a computer. Do not permit one involved department head to make this decision.

4. Never consider a computer the cure-all for all current paper work ills. A computer assists in attaining improvements, but employees must improve the system. The computer does what it is told to do.

5. In planning a data-processing system, take into consideration the probable needs for the future five to ten years.

6. Always relate computer capability to the specific requirements of the

installation being considered. Capacities and special types of work performed which are not needed by the system at hand are superfluous.

7. With sufficient training, use present personnel for computer operation, as they usually can operate a data-processing system very satisfactorily.

8. Work closely with the computer manufacturer, who is anxious to assist in attaining a completely satisfactory installation.

## QUESTIONS

1. Justify the viewpoint that computers increase the responsibility of managers.
2. Discuss the impact and effect upon management actuating when adoption of a computer is decided.
3. Should an office manager look to a computer as the cure-all for all his current paper work ills? Substantiate your answer.
4. Enumerate three major applications for the computer and discuss one of them fully.
5. Upon what basis and by whom should the selection of the type of computer be made? Elaborate on your answer.
6. As an office manager, would you install a computer even though careful study indicated an operating loss would probably result from it for at least several years? Defend your stand.
7. Does experience tend to show that for a given enterprise it is usually possible, by means of competent managerial planning, to prescribe accurately the uses for a computer prior to its installation? Discuss.
8. Discuss possible major considerations in managerial decision making to determine batch or real-time process scheduling in connection with computer usage.
9. Does not the fact that computers are being improved month after month suggest that the astute manager should wait, if he possibly can, until computers are more perfected, desirable features are available as standard equipment, and the entire unit is less likely to become obsolete? Why?
10. Discuss the various important aspects in the task of converting to computer operation in a typical business enterprise.
11. As an office manager, three choices for acquiring the use of a computer are available—to buy, to rent, or to engage a computer service company. Which choice do you prefer? Justify your selection.
12. Point out several factors essential to good relationships between the manager and the computer technician within a given enterprise.

## CASE PROBLEMS

### Case 13–1.   Beattie, Edgil, and Thurman, Inc.

The majority of the executive committee members of Beattie, Edgil, and Thurman, Inc., an advertising agency commonly referred to as BET, believe strongly that the agency should acquire a computer. Much better service could be provided, they claim, more accurate records would be provided, and it would add to the prestige of the agency. BET is a large agency with headquarters in New York City and branch offices in Detroit and Chicago. Total employment is now 607 people, and clients number over 75. The agency has several well-known national accounts and, while responsible for four leading TV shows, also places much magazine and newspaper advertising.

Mr. Karl Beck, general manager and chairman of the executive committtee, reasons that with the amount of paper work they now have, a computer would certainly be advantageous. In his opinion, the number of accounts payable to different TV stations, publishers, and suppliers, as well as the accounts receivable, payroll, cost reports, and research studies presently conducted, make a computer economically feasible. However, several members of the executive committee dissent, pointing out that processing paper work is really not a major problem of the agency and a continuation of "farming out" much of their specialized processing demands, such as research studies, would appear to be the better decision. They contend the pressing need of the agency is to acquire better creative people, strengthen relationships with leading clients, improve its public image, and reduce operating costs.

After reviewing the various operations in the agency's main office, Herman Noble, representative of a large computer manufacturer, has told Mr. Beck that much of the paper work now being done manually should be automated and that improved systems and procedures should be installed. He estimated that some $2,500 a month could be saved in payroll alone. He added that some of the research work could be put on a computer, but most of this work was special and did not lend itself to a repetitive or standardized processing. He offered to make a survey of the agency's work and submit it to Mr. Beck for his consideration. However, it would be several weeks until such a survey could be started. To Mr. Beck's direct question, "Do you believe a computer is feasible, advantageous, and practical for us?" Mr. Noble replied, "Yes, sir. I certainly do. And I have never been surer of anything in my life." Mr. Beck then indicated that any survey would show the same general conclusion and since the majority of the executive committee agreed, the agency should proceed with the computer acquisition. He told Mr. Noble that agency business demanded his being out of his office a great deal, so he was turning the entire project over to Mr. Levinson, the agency's controller.

After several weeks, Mr. Noble was introduced by Mr. Levinson to the accounts receivable and the accounts payable supervisors, the payroll supervisor, and the assistant director of research. Mr. Levinson requested that they give Mr. Noble complete cooperation, because he was developing computer processing that would be followed in the future. At the same time, to each employee of these four units—accounts payable, accounts receivable, payroll, and research (office only)—a brief letter was given:

> This is to advise you that as soon as possible manual handling of work in your unit will be discontinued and a computer will be installed. This move will necessitate some transferring of employees, but rest assured that this will be worked out to the mutual advantage of all concerned.
>
> Signed   Harry Levinson<br>Controller

The accounts receivable supervisor was unfavorable toward the change. She believed it would necessitate many adjustments, would make the work monotonous, and reduce her importance within the company. She spoke with the payroll supervisor, who also was negative about the contemplated change. Both favored use of late-model accounting machines which, in their opinion, were ideally suited for the accounts receivable and payroll work.

Everything went along as usual for the next five months. Then, one morning, various units of a computer arrived and were located within the accounts receivable area. At the same time, the controller held a meeting in his office with two representatives of the computer company and the accounts receivable supervisor. During this meeting, the representatives carefully explained each step of the new process to be followed. Many questions were asked, and the representatives answered each one of them. The meeting took all morning. After lunch, the controller introduced the representatives to the employees of the accounts receivable department, informed them of the meeting held during the morning, and requested that any questions they might have should be directed to their immediate supervisor, who would either answer the question directly or find out the answer and give it to them. The changeover date was set for three weeks hence; and the names of six employees, with the respective departments to which they were being transferred, were announced.

Two weeks after the changeover date, Mr. Beck, along with Mr. Levinson, visited the accounts receivable department. To Mr. Beck, the employees of the unit appeared confused. He spoke with the supervisor, who said: "Well, it is a mess right now. My desk is piled high with work. We're working overtime but not making much headway. Getting the information on the tape is the big task right now. That will take time. We have a manual that appears to give all the details about the operation. It reads OK, and I must admit that the representatives are very willing to help in every way possible.

Speaking with several employees of the department, Mr. Beck received these reactions: "There are plenty of headaches. I'll stay with it for another week or so; but as of right now, I certainly don't like it." Another employee stated: "We have no precedent to go by. I don't know how to operate this thing. They told me to read the manual, but I don't understand what I'm reading." Another said: "I don't mind the overtime—in fact, I can use the extra money. Other companies use computers—it's the coming thing. This might give me a chance to get ahead."

## Problems:

1. Evaluate the actions of Mr. Beck.

2. Do you feel that, given a reasonable amount of time, the present difficulties in the accounts receivable department will take care of themselves? Why?

3. Would you expect the same conditions to exist in the other units where the computer will first be used as now exist in accounts receivable? Why?

4. What action, if any, do you suggest Mr. Beck take? The controller? Substantiate your viewpoint.

### Case 13–2.  Gordon-Grunow Company

Chairman of the Board Benjamin Coleman commented: "It's about time we took action. Our chief competitor has a solid-state Datiac 999. Our rising labor costs, especially in the white-collar class, are hurting us. In billing, sales analysis, and research and development, we employ 47 clerks and 4 supervisors. Think of it —53 people for this type of work. We must move ahead, men."

Immediately after this board meeting, President Ronald Hall instructed his secretary: "Call the local Datiac office and set up an appointment with its representative." Ronald Hall felt uneasy and insecure in his job. He had come up through the ranks in the sales department; but since his appointment to the presidency three years ago, profits had dwindled, important mergers of competitors had been consummated to the disadvantage of Gordon-Grunow, and the board members were beginning to question Hall's leadership. He was within 20 months of retirement and had a strong desire to end his presidency in a blaze of glory with a significant contribution to the company. He believed the acquisition and use of a computer by the company might be a step in this direction, but interviews with key people during the past six weeks had left him undecided. Now, with the board "breathing down his neck," he believed the computer should be ordered. Problems which were certain to arise could be worked out after they had the computer. And, he reasoned, it would certainly provide faster and more complete information than was now available to company officials.

Generally known throughout the company's office management members, numbering 38, was the fact that Donald Fromberg, the controller, believed he was passed over when Ronald Hall was made president. Approximately the same age as Hall, Donald Fromberg had known him for some 30 years and believed he always had been, was now, and probably always would be a plugging, well-liked, not too intelligent salesman. Mr. Fromberg still nurtured some thought of being president of the company someday; but as the months rolled on, he realized in his more practical moments that such a possibility was getting more and more remote.

Mr. Fromberg repeatedly expressed the opinion in conversations with Mr. Hall that the installation of a computer would open the door to opportunities for savings, but current operations in the office would have to be reviewed thoroughly to take full advantage of the computer system. Comparing the company's paper work with that of other companies, Gordon-Grunow was, in Mr. Fromberg's opinion, in a favorable position. Actually, to take full advantage of a computer, the entire accounting system would have to be revamped and rebuilt from the ground up, and this would cause confusion and involve more cost during a period when cost reduction was a prime need of the company. In reply to Mr. Hall's observation that other companies having computers must have faced the same problems of adapting their accounting system to the computer, Mr. Fromberg agreed that they probably did; but he pointed out that their needs were different from the viewpoint of volume of work, the initial system of record keeping followed, and the cost needs of the company.

Allan Wright, aggressive chief of the company's research and development section, was all for the company's getting a computer. As head of 26 engineers and researchers, Mr. Wright figured the computer would accelerate the work of his unit and would make possible a reduction of 5 engineers from the payroll, leaving his section still able to perform the same amount of research work as was currently being done. These savings in salary alone, contended Mr. Wright, would enable the company to get the computer for practically no new outlay of funds. He strongly urged that the computer be obtained and placed in his unit under his jurisdiction. "We'll make it hum—day and night," he added. "We could start right here in my unit and gradually spread out into the other units of the company. Improved sales analysis, for example, is an area where we could certainly use some help. If the company needs anything, it is sales—a lot more sales."

## Problems:

1. What is the problem as you see it?
2. What is your general impression of Mr. Fromberg? Of Mr. Wright?
3. What do you believe Mr. Ronald Hall should do? Why?

# CHAPTER 14

# COMPUTERIZED

# OFFICE APPLICATIONS

Do not fear to repeat what has already been
said. Men need these things dinned into
their ears many times and from all sides.
The first version makes them prick up their
ears, and the second registers and the third
enters.

—*Lenac*

NEW applications of computers are one of the really basic and dynamic areas of our economy. The list seems almost endless and touches almost every facet of human activity. In this chapter, some idea of the various and interesting types of applications will be briefly discussed. Our purpose is to provide an indication of the part the computer is playing and is destined to play in the future. Let us start with several concise and pertinent at random computer applications and follow these with more detailed discussions of six outstanding applications of computers.

## AT RANDOM COMPUTER APPLICATIONS

Can you envision the work involved in preparing the data and writing nearly 5 million paychecks a month—that's more than 200,000 per day. An agency of the federal government is calculating, writing, and proofing that quantity successfully by means of a computer. In addition, the computer keeps up to date revised addresses, amounts due, and changes occurring from time to time, so that the information and check writing are current and correct for each month. Any corrections or changes can be recomputed by day, month, or year. The computer is practically error-proof.

In operation in 1967 is a super-computer capable of internal processing speeds up to 12 times faster than the ordinary large and powerful computer. This super-computer can perform 8 million additions or 5 million multiplications in one second. It is designed for problems in space exploration, subatomic physics, theoretical astronomy and global weather forecasting. Its cost is $6 million with peripheral equipment.

By means of computerized typesetting systems, type for book matter and newspaper reading matter and classified advertising from unjustified tape made by electric typewriters is now being produced. The computer justifies the line—makes the right margin even, divides hyphenated words correctly, controls line width, selects type sizes and faces. For newspapers, the handling of wire service copy, including programming of corrections and new leads due to later news, are all handled automatically. In one hour about 12,000 lines of 8-point type in 11-pica column width can be produced. In addition, devices handle the output tape to the completion of the finished galleys of completed type are delivered by the linecasting machines. About 600 lines an hour in this width is the speed of the linecasting machine. Thus, about 20 linecasting machines are required for the automated arrangement.

Computers can now talk. An audio response unit makes information within a computer available over the telephone. Words and sounds are recorded by human voice and stored within the computer. Upon inquiry, the words are assembled to form a verbal answer which is transmitted to the caller. Currently about 30 to 125 words are stored, depending upon the flexibility needed and the specific needs of the business. To illustrate, an employee in a branch insurance office in Seattle can obtain policy information from a company computer on the East Coast by dialing several numbers on the telephone. Seconds later he hears a verbal reply to his inquiry. A large department store in Chicago now utilizes a computer-directed credit authorization system that gives a verbal reply to a salesperson's inquiry in less than 30 seconds. All sales-floor telephones in 12 different stores are hooked to the central computer which can handle 10,000 credit approvals daily. However, the computer's capacity is so large that credit applications use less than 5 percent of its time. Hence, the computer is used to prepare over 6 million customer statements a year, write reminder notices to customers, print sales promotion material, and identify probable bad debt accounts.

Computers can also "televise" information. An installation in a well known insurance company retains 400 million characters of customer information and displays, almost instantly, a customer's policy records on a television-type screen. To obtain information on any policy, its number is typed on a machine unit attached to the display screen. In less than a second, the required data are obtained from the computer, converted to visual characters, and displayed on the screen. All transactions such as premium payments and changes of address are checked and posted daily against the master file of information. Within a normal working day, 600,000 policyholders' records can be reviewed and updated.

Equally striking is "Sketchpad," the robot draftsman. The face of a television-type display tube is used like a sheet of paper on which sketches are drawn using an electronic stylus. With Sketchpad, the designer can find out how his new mechanical arrangement will perform without building a model. The computer will animate the drawing, calculate stresses at specified locations, duplicate electric circuit diagrams to determine behavior of current flows, and a variety of other information. Thus, the computer is helpful in creative design. Advantages include increased analysis capability which is more complete in both scope and detail than previously attainable. Heretofore the accepted approach was essentially an art in that designs were formulated largely on the basis of experience and trial and error methods. With the computer, however, most of the possible design parameters can be analytically determined, designs formulated, tested, and detailed drawings provided. The results are improved product quality, elimination of prototype developments, enormous savings of design time, and a revolution of an old established technology.

Beginning in 1968, one of the large airlines will use three big integrated computers with a total of nearly 1 billion characters of random access storage. This capacity will permit 100 percent expansion in keeping with projected passenger growth. A total of 700 printer units will provide agents with copy information and operational messages in addition to the visual readout. The computer installation will enable the agent to issue a ticket with confirmed reservations in several seconds. Cost of the total computer installation: $56 million.

No-check banking and no-cash shopping are also realistic. How is this possible? By debits and credits to bank accounts electronically via the telephone. To pay a bill, a consumer simply inserts a card into a special slot at the back of his telephone and dials his bank's computer number. Then he dials the amount of his bill and within seconds is informed by an electronic voice, described in the above paragraph, that the given amount has been transferred from his account into the account of the company he is paying. Separate cards could be used, each for one company that regularly bills the consumer. Or an individual credit card for use anywhere over a wide communication data network could be followed. The "pay by phone" arrangement can also be used for retail transactions by those subscribing to the system. At the supermarket, for example, a customer at the checkout counter produces his credit card instead of cash. The attendant inserts the card into the supermarket-to-bank telephone. What the customer owes is transferred at once from his bank account to the supermarket's account. Are these dreams of computer-minded men? Not at all. These systems are in existence in several experiments, are proving successful, and signal fantastic changes ahead in bank services and credit.

Claims for improving football are also listed among the computer's accomplishments. By viewing a slow-motion film of all plays during a game, each player is rated on a one-to-seven scale. A score of seven is given for a fumble or for being the cause of a penalty. In contrast, intercepting a pass or successfully blocking two opponents rates a top mark of one. Each player's game record is put into the computer where a play-by-play, game-by-game, or season-by-season analysis and blueprint for victory can be developed. The history of a particular formation or pass pattern is revealed; what is successful and what is not, and the best sequence of plays both for offense and for defense are identified and mastered.

## COMPUTER GRAPHICS

Our first selected application for more detailed discussion is computer graphics. High-speed two-axis plotting of digital computer output for either on-line or off-line operations is now an accomplished fact. Significant applications include engineering drawings, medical research, stress-strain diagrams, calibration curves, meteorological studies, learning curves, water profiles, harmonic analysis, ray tracing, and PERT. The list of applications is constantly expanding. No longer is it necessary to spend long and tedious hours plotting data into graphic form. The computer will do this for us.

The CALCOMP digital incremental plotter is driven by the computer. Direct coupling frequently can be used, but for the larger computer the signal instructions are received by a medium for subsequent use by the plotter off-line. A special adapter converts the computer output to a form suitable for driving the plotter. Figure 14–1 shows the versatile, completely automatic high-speed plotting system. The insert in upper left of this illustration shows a close-up of the plotting unit. Values for preparation of a learning curve are being plotted. The completed chart is removed in a manner similar to that of taking a piece of paper from a roll of wrapping paper. Figure 14–2 illustrates a geologic chart produced automatically by CALCOMP plotter from data in a computer. Figure 14–3 (p. 314) shows a computer-plotter producing a contour map. This unit is applicable to most horizontal geometrical designs including bridge structures, highway designs, and computations for right-of-way projects.

The plotting is produced by movement of a pen relative to the surface of the paper. Each input impulse causes a very minute step, of either .01 inches or .005 inches, on either the $X$-axis or the $Y$-axis. A deflection on the $X$-axis is produced by motion of the drum, on the $Y$-axis by motion of the pen carriage. Signals raise and lower the pen as required. Each step can be in any one of 24 basic step combinations or directions made up of

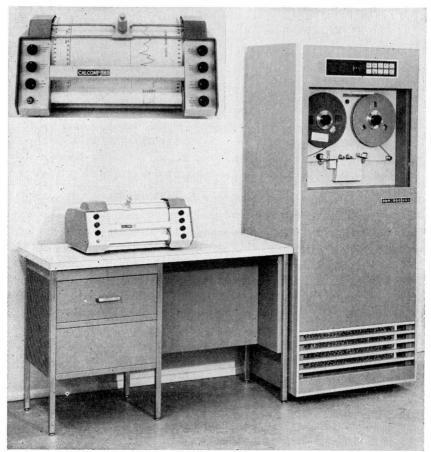

*Courtesy: California Computer Products, Inc., Anaheim, Calif.*

FIG. 14–1.   A magnetic tape plotting system. Featuring a high-speed automatic search, plotting of continuous curve or points, this unit produces graphs up to 29½ inches wide by 120 feet long.

its $X$ and $Y$ values, i.e., the basic step direction for a plotted point can be any of 24 directions within the 360-degree quadrant made up of $X$ and $Y$ values of .01 or .005 inches.

## INFORMATION RETRIEVAL—AUTOMATICALLY

Much of the money spent for research and development will be spent more effectively or not at all when available literature on the subject can be searched thoroughly beforehand. There are thousands of technical journals carrying literally millions of articles on a vast array of scientific subjects. Screening and retrieving what is pertinent to a particular study represents a herculean task for the searcher. In many cases, research is

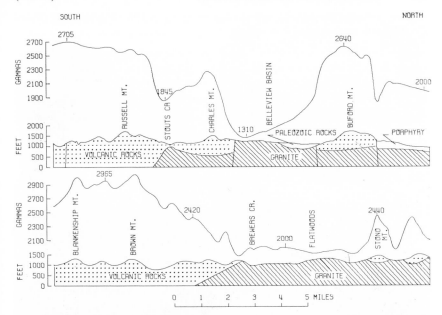

STRUCTURE AND LITHOLOGY FROM AEROMAGNETIC PROFILES OVER THE ST. FRANCOIS MOUNTAINS
*Courtesy: California Computer Products, Inc., Anaheim, Calif.*

FIG. 14–2. Example of chart drawn automatically from data in a computer.

started on a project already completed or in process elsewhere, or not all the available knowledge has been reviewed before launching the new study.

This gives rise to another facet of office technology, called automatic information retrieval. Succinctly stated, this can be called mechanization of the intellectual effort of information input to provide quick screening of voluminous available information on any of a multitude of subjects. It is a terrific time consumer, if indeed physically possible, to follow through all the reports and journals to keep pace with developments in a given field of study. The need is for a fast way to have access to information on specific subjects. This, in turn, requires some means by which masses of data are assimilated, classified, and compressed into complete and understandable indexes; and if desired, the complete information itself can be retrieved quickly.

It is estimated that some $1.5 billion are spent each year for research and development, and a goodly portion of this amount goes for "information services" or searching the literature. Much of this can be handled by the use of computers, but it should be pointed out that other mechanical means are possible and in use. For example, a large pharmaceutical house maintains a punched-card index file on 15,000 drug journal articles that goes back five years. Cost for this arrangement is only $550 a month.

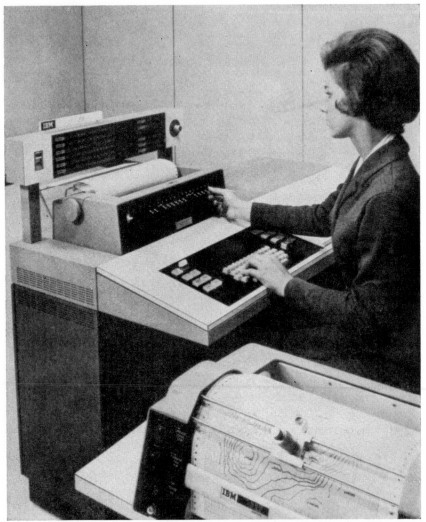

*Courtesy: International Business Machines Corp., New York;
and California Computer Products, Inc., Anaheim, Calif.*

FIG. 14–3. Computer and CALCOMP plotter enables engineers to state problems to the computer and receive immediate answers in printed or graphic form.

Other systems use a combination punched card and microfilm, with the latter located within the center portion of the card. The card is used to locate the title and subject, the microfilm for showing a portion or all of a copy of the original article. The microfilm can be projected on a special screen for reading convenience.[1]

---

[1] See also Chapter 7, p. 163 for reference to this type of application.

Different but closely associated with information retrieval is the belief by many that the computer will help bring about the common world language so long sought. The belief is that as man learns to communicate with machines, this communication will spread to man-to-man communication. Thus, "computerese" may end language barriers. On the other hand, it seems that to eradicate any language of long standing will certainly not be an overnight accomplishment. But communication between men of different languages is an accomplished fact of the computer. It can translate information from one language into another. Such units are feasible, but this application to date has been relatively minor compared to the host of other uses to which computers have been applied.

## VISIBLE RECORD—MICR AUTOMATION SYSTEM

Banks can now enjoy the fastest check handling at the lowest cost per item and highest accuracy in banking history. This is made possible by a visible record computer using MICR (magnetic ink character recognition) source documents. This office automation system is specifically designed

*Courtesy: Burroughs, Inc., Detroit*

FIG. 14–4. The essential units of the visible record–MICR automation system.

for financial accounting. Flexible MICR and punched-card inputs are utilized; electronic processing and retention of accounting records in ordinary visual form (printing on paper) are features of this process. The accounting records are maintained on magnetic tape ledger cards which, as pointed out in Chapter 12, are regular-appearing ledger cards with magnetic tape imbedded on the back side of the card. Information typed on the front side is translated into computer language on the magnetic strips of the same card.

The system is made up of four essential units. These are illustrated in Figure 14–4 and include, viewing from left to right, (1) the sorter-reader,

(2) the record processor and console, (3) the card reader, and (4) the data processor. The latter is the nerve center of the entire system. It performs all calculations, gives instructions, and directs the operations of the other three units.

Encoded MICR items—for example, bank checks in the case of our bank illustration—are read and sorted automatically by the sorter-reader unit to provide on-line and buffered data input for the record processor unit. In other words, the check is read regarding such information as the account number, process control number, and amount from the magnetic ink markings on the check and sorted to a batch of checks, which expedites the posting of the transactions to the check writer's account or statement. The sorter-reader processes mixed items of varying sizes and thicknesses at rates of over 1,500 per minute.

The information read by the sorter-reader is transmitted to the record processor and console, which automatically selects from its file of records the desired record by account number, reads the data stored in the magnetic tapes or strips on the back of the account ledger record, updates both the printed side and the magnetic storage area of each currently active record amount, and returns the ledger record to the file. The recording of data is accomplished by means of a printer capable of over 200 lines per minute, each line consisting of 156 characters. The accounting records are filed by batches in the processor, and the record needed for posting is brought to the front part of the unit for posting operations. Those records requiring special attention are segregated by means of an auxiliary unit called a stacker. Three input stations for forms provide operating versatility. The console supplies the means of communicating between the supervisor and the system.

One of the important functions of the card reader is to supply on-line data input to the system from punched cards. It does this at a rate of 200 cards per minute. In addition, this unit puts programs into the core memory of the data processor, input data for selected data-processing applications, and the processing of exceptional items.

The entire system supplies up-to-the-minute information of current status and previous activity for each account. Simultaneous daily printing of the ledger, statement, and journal avoids the end-of-period statement-printing peaks. In addition, vital analysis of the records can be conducted quickly, the records are balanced step by step to insure complete accuracy, and lower operating costs provide better operational control.

## PROCESSING PUBLIC UTILITY CUSTOMER ACCOUNTS

The preparation of bills for more than 500,000 electric and gas meters is another interesting application of an electronic data-processing system. Readings from the meter readers' reports are typed on a special report using a machine which simultaneously makes a perforated tape of the information. This tape is fed into the computer, which reads the information at high speed. Being given the customer's number and present meter reading, the computer locates the information it has on the particular customer number; subtracts the previous from the present meter reading; computes the cost and discount, if any; and, along with the customer's name and address, sends the processed information to the output unit, where the customer's bill is printed. Subsequently, the bills are sorted automatically by cities and mail zone numbers for putting in the mail.

The monthly bill has the customer's account number preprinted in magnetic ink. This number identifies the account. When bill stubs are returned for crediting customer payments, they are sorted by customer number and read by a sorter-reader unit similar to that described above. From this unit, the information is fed into the computer, which posts the payment to customer ledger cards in the form of magnetic tape ledger cards. Approximately 12,000 customer bills are prepared in one hour. It required about one year to complete the switchover to the new system, but this conversion was accomplished without any inconvenience to the customers of the public utility.

New meter installations and changes of address and number of meter are handled in the same manner as the input of monthly billing data. The new meter is assigned a customer's number; or if the case requires, the new address is added, and the old address is removed from the data in the computer's memory units. These additions and changes create extra work. However, initial estimates placed this work at not more than 2,200 per month, whereas the actual requirements have never exceeded 1,720 in any one month. The system does provide needed flexibility as well as great accuracy and speed.

In addition to processing customer accounts, the company intends to use the computer for the handling of engineering computations and studies. This will facilitate design and planning work so essential to the improvement of new electric and gas facilities necessary to meet future requirements. Other areas for future exploration include payroll, accounts payable, property and plant records, and inventory.

## INVENTORY CONTROL DATA PROCESSING

Like many applications, the work of inventory control, as it is normally thought of, must be modified so that it is in a form that meets the physical operational requirements of computer handling. In this respect, a common arrangement for inventory control by computer is the cumulative or "cum" system, in which all activity is directed toward the new cum or total quantity. Information can be thought of as being gathered by degrees, and quantities increase in number until the entire records are started again from a new base. In essence, if cum is available, inventory is available at the proper time and in the proper quantity. There is no need for balance-of-stores records common in noncomputer inventory control systems.

An understanding of the basic operations performed is essential for comprehending the working of the inventory control data processing. Hence, before discussing what the computer does, a brief description of the basic operations will be given. The initial step is the sales forecast, which is reviewed monthly and adjusted in light of market conditions. A "release for production" is made against the sales forecast, which release authorizes procurement of materials, production schedules, and final assembly. Comparison is made between the cumulative requirements and the amount available. If the latter exceeds the former, no order for parts is entered. On the other hand, if the amount available is less than the cumulative requirements, the deficit is filled by ordering the parts.

*The Data Utilized.* In Figure 14–5, the top illustration shows that for Model 124, the amount released is 5,000; shipped, 2,400; February scheduled shipment, 1,000; March scheduled shipment, 1,500. Thus, the cum for February is 3,400 and for March, 4,900. The data are converted to weekly amounts, as indicated by the middle illustration of Figure 14–5. So far, our data are by model, and each model may require a number of components. Quite probably, some of these components will be common to several models. Our need is to determine the total number of each component that will be required for the scheduled product mix represented by the various models. Assume the monthly data illustrated by the bottom illustration of Figure 14–5 represent these values. The amounts required will be determined primarily on the sales forecasts of each model, with important modifications for in-plant lead time. This is to say that some components are required for subassemblies, others for the final assembly; those for subassemblies must be available in the plant for consumption before the components intended for final assembly. In many instances, the same type of component will be used for the subassembly and again in the final assembly.

For each component, comparisons are now made between the cum and the availability. Based on this comparison, the decision to "order schedule" is determined. Referring to Figure 14–6, the cum requirements for component 1 are 13,400 for the "used to date." As indicated in Figure 14–5, the requirements for the first week of February are 1,500, making the cum 14,900; for the second week, 1,500, making the cum 16,400; and so forth. The availability of component 1 is 22,000, which, compared to the cum of February week A, shows ample supply; hence, no order schedule would be made, and the value of 0 is entered under week A. In like manner, it can be seen that no order schedule for component 1 would

**To Date / February / March**

| Model | To Date Release | To Date Cum Shipped | February Release | February Cum Shipped | March Release | March Cum Shipped |
|---|---|---|---|---|---|---|
| 124 | 5,000 | 2,400 | 1,000 | 3,400 | 1,500 | 4,900 |

**February**

| | Week A | | Week B | | Week C | | Week D | |
|---|---|---|---|---|---|---|---|---|
| | R* | CS* | R | CS | R | CS | R | CS |
| | 250 | 2,650 | 250 | 2,900 | 250 | 3,150 | 250 | 3,400 |

**March**

| | Week A | | Week B | | Week C | | Week D | |
|---|---|---|---|---|---|---|---|---|
| | R | CS | R | CS | R | CS | R | CS |
| | 375 | 3,775 | 375 | 4,150 | 375 | 4,525 | 375 | 4,900 |

## COMPONENT NO. 1 FOR ALL MODELS

**February**

| | Week A | | Week B | | Week C | | Week D | |
|---|---|---|---|---|---|---|---|---|
| | R | CS | R | CS | R | CS | R | CS |
| | 1,500 | | 1,500 | | 1,500 | | 1,500 | |

**March**

| | Week A | | Week B | | Week C | | Week D | |
|---|---|---|---|---|---|---|---|---|
| | R | CS | R | CS | R | CS | R | CS |
| | 1,625 | | 1,625 | | 1,625 | | 1,625 | |

* R = Release; CS = Cum Shipped.

FIG. 14–5. Data utilized in "cum" method of inventory control.

be issued during any of the weeks of February. Even the last week shows the cum will be 19,400, with 22,000 available. Production planning is quite unlikely to match exactly sales forecasts because of the varying need for finished goods inventory, variations in estimated lead times, rates of production, and capacity to produce exactly to requirements. But the system provides reasonable checks between weekly needs and availability, so that deviations are kept within practical limits; thus, satisfactory inventory control is achieved.

COMPONENT NO. 1 FOR ALL MODELS

|  | USED TO DATE | FEBRUARY | | | |
| --- | --- | --- | --- | --- | --- |
|  |  | Week A | Week B | Week C | Week D |
| Cum requirements.......... | 13,400 | 14,900 | 16,400 | 17,900 | 19,400 |
| Available................. | 22,000 | 22,000 | 22,000 | 22,000 | 22,000 |
| Order schedule............ |  | 0 | 0 | 0 | 0 |

FIG. 14–6.

*Automating the Process.* This system is suited to automation. It utilizes a computer designed to approach in-line accounting on a mechanized basis. Such a computer is equipped with a random access storage device which permits the storage of and rapid access to any of many millions of characters comprising the records. The various accounts may be posted in random order. For example, interrelated transactions might involve (1) securing raw materials, for which the transaction is posting receipts to raw material record; (2) making up subassemblies, for which the transactions are posting production of subassemblies to subassembly account and deducting components used in subassemblies from components accounts; or (3) shipping finished goods, which requires for the record a deduction from the finished goods account by the amount of finished goods shipped.

In this application, the equivalent of 62,500 eighty-column punched cards, or 5,000,000 characters, is stored in the storage device of the computer. A total of 50,000 different records of 100 characters each constitutes the master information and previous balances. These 50,000 are prorated among the types of basic information and constitute addresses or identities by which specific records can be located by the computer. This is shown graphically by Figure 14–7.

*The Processing by Computer.* For programming the cum system, each part contained in the bill of materials for each model has a parts record stored in a separate section in the computer. For example, the parts record for a purchased part contains the part number; the percentage allowance for loss, waste, or spoilage; the origin; the cum receipts; and the balance due on open purchase orders.

For the given period of 13 weeks, a master schedule or sales forecast by week by models is punched on a tape which is fed into the computer. This schedule is first processed by the bill-of-material section, or portion showing the materials needed. The computer calculates requirements by periods, namely, by multiplying usage by schedule by shrinkage factor. Next, the schedule period is adjusted for lead time on each piece part. These data are carried forward to the parts record, where they are stored awaiting information from other models. As this information from other models becomes available, it is combined with other like information so that the cum requirements by periods are accumulated on the parts record

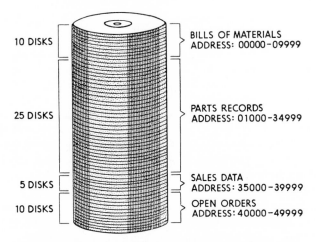

10 DISKS — BILLS OF MATERIALS ADDRESS: 00000–09999

25 DISKS — PARTS RECORDS ADDRESS: 01000–34999

5 DISKS — SALES DATA ADDRESS: 35000–39999

10 DISKS — OPEN ORDERS ADDRESS: 40000–49999

FIG. 14–7.   Each of the 50,000 records has an address or specific location on a disk of the storage unit of the computer.

for each component. When and how much to purchase or make is determined by comparison of the accounts scheduled with the amounts available for each component, as discussed above.

What was previously long, tedious labor required for inventory control is now accomplished in several hours by means of the computer. In addition, it is now a simple matter radically to revise the production program. Information can be quickly obtained regarding the position materialwise if a new production plan is attempted. Shortages and excesses of materials are pointed out, and the status of all components is revealed.

## COMPUTER PROCESS CONTROL (CPC)

One more category of computer applications will be discussed. This application is computer process control (CPC), whereby the computer starts actions and acts upon the results of such actions, thus, in essence, allowing complete automation of the production line. Under this arrangement, the computer makes a running analysis of the process and compensates for changes as they occur. The general arrangement followed is graphically represented by Figure 14–8.

The computer is connected to many and various instruments which provide pertinent readings on variables critical to the process. These readings are analyzed, related, and processed at fantastic speeds, thus recording if the process is progressing satisfactorily or what, if any, part of the production process needs remedial action. If the latter is the case, the computer dispatches back through the communicative network a series of actions that cause individual controls on various pieces of production equipment to make necessary adjustments.

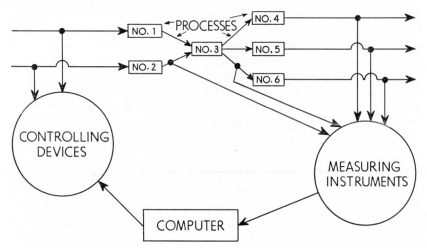

FIG. 14–8.  The general arrangement for computer process control (CPC).

Different processes put different demands upon CPC. Chemical industries typically require a large number of calculations; other industries may necessitate relatively few checks, but they must be made with great rapidity. Complete CPC may cost upward of $1 million, depending upon the complexity of the process. But CPC can be achieved by stages, starting with the computer being used, not as an integral part of the process, but to assist human operators who have complete control of the manufacturing process. Gradually more and more control is given the computer.

Illustrative of CPC is the adaption of blast furnace operations in steel mills to computer control. This arrangement is an off-line application and enables the blast furnace operators to know the ideal and exact conditions for the most efficient operations for producing the best-quality finished product. Indications of difficulties and mechanical failures are detected in advance. A typical blast furnace consumes daily 4,800 tons of raw materials, mainly iron ore, limestone, and coke, and turns out 1,700 tons of iron. The grade of ore, quality of limestone, amount of heat, iron composition and purity desired, and a host of other variables are representative of the type of information which must be properly coordinated to operate the furnace in keeping with predetermined goals.

## CONCLUSIONS ON COMPUTERS

Whatever the use of the computer, it is essential to keep in mind what is to be accomplished—what the real need of the enterprise or the office is. This is fundamental. The better approach might be to analyze and know the needs thoroughly, then get the machines that will best do the required work. On the other hand, knowing the machines and what can be done with them can prove a satisfactory approach. With machine knowledge as a background, it might be possible to adjust the procedures, and the form and type of records determined as essential, to fit what the machine can perform most economically. However, in either event, the real need of the enterprise in terms of its paper-work requirements should receive top priority.

To reiterate, office automation stimulates thinking of office work as a whole, not just of a component of it. All the papers and records should be considered—not simply the payroll records, or the inventory statistics, or the order-handling procedure, or research and development requirements. Automation is geared to volume. There must be a sufficient quantity of work; frequently, this means grouping the components and performing the work for all. The benefits of office automation are numerous; yet problems are entailed that require comprehension, much thought, and study. Difficult decisions must be made. Deeply entrenched habits and beliefs may have to be dispelled. The design of office papers may require revision, the retraining of office personnel may be needed, and an extensive educational job with nonoffice personnel and customers may have to be conducted. Office automation is an area in which a manager *must* manage.

Finally, remember that change is always taking place; the direction and degree of this change in the way paper work is accomplished is, and will inevitably be, modified by the computer. Everywhere, the tempo of technological advance has quickened. The need for more and more information is being accelerated. Discoveries not yet imagined will be made. In such an era, the computer will occupy a role of increasing importance in the hopeful advances of human progress. Properly understood and applied, the computer will assist man in employing his talent, his time, and his ideas most effectively in the pursuit of values which make man so distinctive and his accomplishments so significant.

## QUESTIONS

1. Describe how computers are changing the work of typesetting in the newspaper and printing industries.
2. Do you feel that the major areas of computer applications can be considered fairly well explored as of the present? Substantiate your answer.
3. Identify each of the following:
   a) Computer graphics.
   b) Cum system of inventory control.
   c) Computer process control (CPC).
   d) Sketchpad.
4. In your opinion will "no-cash" shopping be popular by the year 1975? Substantiate your answer.
5. With reference to the six detailed discussions in this chapter, what common attributes do you observe in each? What major differences? Discuss briefly.
6. Could the cum method of inventory control be used for noncomputer data processing in this managerial area? Why?
7. Explain Figure 14–7 in your own words.
8. With reference to the processing of customer accounts by the public utility, determine:
   a) The time required to process the accounts each month.
   b) The percentage of accounts changed each month due to additions and corrections.
   c) Several alternatives to the system currently used for getting the imput and for putting it into the computer.
9. Discuss the meaning, operation, and potential of automatic information retrieval.
10. Consult several business periodicals and read a report on a CPC installation. Relate the interesting aspects of this installation and what would seem to be the limiting factors of additional installations of this particular type.
11. Outside of bank checks and bill stubs, what other types of documents do you feel might be processed advantageously by the use of MICR? Discuss.
12. What are your reactions to this statement: "Computers perform all the calculations required in the designing of a machine or building structure and this ability, plus information retrieval by the computer, leads to these two major conclusions: First, our design engineering work of the future will be performed by robot engineers. Second, the shortage of human engineers will have become a distinct myth." Discuss.

## CASE PROBLEMS

### Case 14–1. The Burton Company

One of the largest department stores in the entire United States, the Burton Company, operates six stores located within a large city and suburban shopping areas adjacent to the city. Studies conducted by the controller, Mr. Lief Huff, show that the paper work performed by the company in connection with the conduct of its business with its customers has been growing, with the costs for this work exceeding the rate of the volume growth. Both the processing and the cost of papers dealing with company purchases and inventory are considered satisfactory by Mr. Huff.

At a top executive meeting yesterday, the controller was authorized to proceed with the necessary work relative to reducing costs and improving the handling of papers created by store customer relations, including such work as the preparing of billings or statements for customers and the processing of customer accounts receivable. Currently, for this work the company uses accounting machines purchased some seven years ago.

A customer extended open credit by the company produces her "charge plate" at the time of making a purchase. This plate is inserted into a small unit on the counter by the store clerk. The plate imprints the customer's number, name, and address upon the purchase order made out by the clerk in longhand. At the same time, the customer's number is relayed to the central credit department, where a check is made to determine if the credit is in good standing. If so, approval is relayed to the originating small unit used by the store clerk who, being thus informed, proceeds with consummation of the sale. On the other hand, if credit is refused, the customer is politely informed of the condition by the clerk, who terminates the sale unless cash payment is made on the account or for the current merchandise being purchased. In some instances, it requires five to ten minutes to get the check on credit. Copies of the orders written by the clerks are sent to the accounting department where reports and records, including monthly statements to customers, are compiled.

Mr. Huff feels the present arrangement can be improved. He is thinking of a computer but feels that all feasible ways of improving the work should be studied. The company has approximately 300,000 customers sold on open account. Of the total number of sales transacted, some 22 percent are cash sales. Peak loads occur during the Easter period, late summer before school starts, and the Christmas period. Accounts are divided by stores, with the statements sent out for each store on approximately the same day of each month. For example, billings for store No. 1 are put in the mail on the second day of each month, and those for store No. 2 on the ninth day of each month. It is estimated that during the past five years, the number of accounts has increased an average of 3 percent per year. It is believed that this growth will continue and may even rise to 5 percent per year.

## Problems:

1. What approach do you recommend that Mr. Huff follow? Why?

2. In your opinion, what are some major considerations that will help determine the feasibility of the use of a computer by the company? Discuss.

3. For computer application, give some important general specifications of the computer recommended and discuss the step-by-step procedure of the computer processing that might be followed.

## Case 14–2.  Twenty-First Century Office

Professor Dean Sager is extremely interested in the development of office automation. He conducted several personal interviews with practicing office managers, and the following are the highlights of the responses he received.

"What will the office be like in a hundred years? I feel almost all the work will be done by machine. It will be a push-button age. Information will be kept right in the machine and will be delivered to you automatically upon request. In many respects, the information won't be on paper at all, but will be on some mechanical medium, like wire or tape, and will be available to us when we want it."

"The term 'office' will be seldom used. Within the next hundred years, 'administrative information center' or something like this will be the common term designating what we currently refer to as the office. But we'll never have a fully satisfactory name for the office because it means so many different things to so many different people in so many different activities."

"The entire concept of office work as we know it today will be different. We will have learned to satisfy our economic wants with a shorter work week and with far less information. We will have found that a manager can have too much information to the point that it confuses instead of helps him. The middle manager will have disappeared from the scene. Office employees will have much higher training and the mode of inquiring and of operating will take place in an entirely different set of conditions."

"In the office of the future, we'll find the executive sitting at a small table; his mail will consist of a tiny packet of plastic transparencies similar to microfilm. These transparencies will be enlarged on a visual screen. If he wishes, he can dictate directly into a machine that will simultaneously either type the letter or paper, or put it on an electronic medium by which it can be quickly transmitted to its recipient. Direct wires connecting the two offices will be unnecessary. The transmission will be wireless, similar to present-day TV."

"The importance of human relations as we know it today will be a thing of the past. Automation will have taken over, and this means a minimum number of people will be required. Minimum people mean minimum trouble. If you have no people, you have no human relations. It's as simple as that."

"Office conferences will be virtually eliminated. Low-cost closed TV circuits connecting executives located in widely separated cities will be commonplace. And this same screen will serve to view wanted materials from a file. In the future, filed material will be housed in narrow wall compartments. By means of a push button, material from a designated file will be brought to view on the executive's screen within a few seconds."

### Problems:

1. What is your reaction to the comments secured by Professor Sager?
2. In your opinion, what might the office be like a hundred years from now?

# PART 4

# OFFICE MANAGEMENT—PLANNING

*Up to this point we have identified the work of the office as being done primarily to supply needed information. We discussed the performance of common office services existent in every enterprise, and we have just finished pointing out in some detail the current status of the office technology, the usefulness of the systems and procedures approach, and the accelerating trend toward more and more office automation.*

*In all these various facets of office management the vital nature of the management process—planning, controlling, organizing, and actuating—are clearly set forth. In fact, office management effectiveness hinges around the astute application of the management process to office activities. This is the essence of desirable office management. Hence, a more thorough study of planning, controlling, organizing, and actuating as they apply to office work is in order.*

*We start with planning. First, we present the general concept of office managerial planning and its application to office forms. Following this, a chapter is devoted to each major area of office managerial planning, including office systems and procedures, office methods, equipment and machines, layout, and office environment and location. In total, six chapters are given to office management planning.*

# CHAPTER 15

# PLANNING AND ITS

# APPLICATION TO OFFICE FORMS

There is no great achievement that is not the
result of patient working and waiting.
—*Josiah Holland*

OFFICE management planning helps establish orderliness and efficiency in getting office work accomplished. It keeps the office moving along smoothly, stressing simplicity, maintaining a work balance, and eliminating nonessentials. Planning assists in producing superior office work in record time with a minimum of effort. Deadlines are met, office equipment and machines are well selected, and the office space is both adequate and efficiently used.

As pointed out in Chapter 2, planning is the basic ingredient of the management process—planning, controlling, organizing and actuating. From planning result plans, and it is in order to make actions conform with these plans that controlling, organizing, and actuating are undertaken. If an office manager's plans are weak or incomplete, his controlling can never attain extraordinary accomplishments, simply because the controlling is being applied to plans that are mediocre. And the same applies to organizing and actuating being applied in conjunction with weak plans.

## THE MEANING OF PLANNING

In Chapter 2 we stated that planning includes the methodic technique of looking ahead and selecting a course from among alternative actions. It is work of a foreseeing nature and requires visualization of future activities. Stated formally, *planning is the visualization and formulation of proposed activities designed to achieve certain results.*

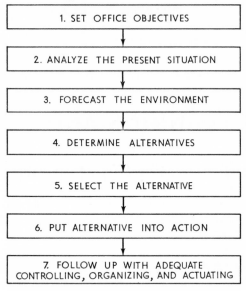

1. SET OFFICE OBJECTIVES

2. ANALYZE THE PRESENT SITUATION

3. FORECAST THE ENVIRONMENT

4. DETERMINE ALTERNATIVES

5. SELECT THE ALTERNATIVE

6. PUT ALTERNATIVE INTO ACTION

7. FOLLOW UP WITH ADEQUATE CONTROLLING, ORGANIZING, AND ACTUATING

FIG. 15–1.   Flow model of office managerial planning.

Planning is made up of definite steps presented as a flow model in Figure 15–1. The first five steps will be discussed in detail. The last two steps, "put alternative into action and follow up with adequate controlling, organizing, and actuating," are included in the figure to indicate the position of planning in the total management process.

SET OFFICE OBJECTIVES

Objectives result from planning; and in turn, planning is affected by objectives. This sounds paradoxical, but it simply signifies the importance of planning as both a determinant of goals and a medium for showing how these goals can be achieved.

For the office manager, the basic objectives are generally set forth by others—members of the board of directors, or top managers. Through planning, these men have determined what goals the enterprise should strive to attain. However, with the basic objectives known, the office manager frequently has to determine certain objectives for his organizational unit and its respective subordinate units. This necessitates planning. The immediate objective of each organizational unit must fit into and be part of the basic objective of the entire enterprise so that integrated objectives from top to bottom are actually stated and known.[1]

Most of the everyday planning of the office manager is determining the type and timing of work in order to achieve given goals. In other words, it involves what sequence of what office work operations should take place in order to accomplish the stated objectives. In this planning, the goals affect the course of action to be followed.

Objectives are vital, not only to planning, but to all management work.

---

[1] For specific examples of office management objectives, see Chapter 2, page 22.

The whole justification for management's existence is that it achieves desired objectives. These objectives set the targets for the entire management process because, as previously stated, the fundamental functions of management—controlling, organizing, and actuating—are essentially activities to implement the plan, which in turn is designed to achieve certain objectives. The obvious is frequently soon forgotten, and this is far too often the story with objectives. No one disagrees with the statement that a common goal must be established in order that a group may work together effectively and management may operate efficiently. But in quite a number of cases, the objectives are not known, are forgotten, or are ignored. This hampers effective management. Periodically, an office manager should state his objectives and then check his activities to see if he is managing toward the achievement of those objectives.

It should be noted that most offices have several objectives. They must of course be compatible, integrated, and to some extent interrelated. Seldom is it wise to try to state the real purpose of an office in one single, inclusive objective. Usually, such a statement is inadequate for managerial purposes. Objectives must be meaningful to every office employee, in terms he can understand, and of a type for which he can strive enthusiastically.

As time and conditions change, objectives are shifted, adjusted, added, or eliminated. There is, however, a stability about many objectives—they do not change perceivably over long periods. Many changes, if made, are slowly evolved, although some take place relatively quickly as a result of emergencies or major events such as legislative acts, world developments, or economic emergencies. But even in these instances, there are frequently forewarnings or indications that a change is likely to occur.

## ANALYZE THE PRESENT SITUATION

With office objectives well developed, the next step of the planner is to create ways of attaining them. To this end he obtains facts and relationships pertinent to his immediate task. He seeks specific knowledge and forms some ideas about what actions of the office resulted in its present position and condition.

Facts are a basic ingredient of practical planning. They should be obtained, carefully evaluated, and possible relationships among them uncovered before attempting to formulate a plan. Sometimes, when the facts are difficult to ascertain or are unpleasant, there is a tendency to discount them or to ignore them in the planning. Such action should be avoided. A planner must face the facts and take into account the actions that the facts dictate. Planning founded upon hopes or opinions may represent wishful thinking and prove impractical in efforts to apply it. Most successful planners stick to the facts. However, this certainly does not imply that visualization of hoped-for achievements cannot be made. Actually achievements are visualized, but the planning to achieve them should be based on facts—on the realities of known information.

Too many rather than too few facts should be sought. Customarily the facts are sorted into common or related groups so that, not only can their meaning and importance be comprehended more easily, but also dependable associations existing between certain types of events or actions can be discovered. This all adds up to the question of which facts are vital, which are important, and which are of little consequence in analyzing the present situation. Further, some ideas about what actions resulted in what outcomes enable the planner to formulate tentative courses of action.

## FORECAST THE ENVIRONMENT

Facts and their relationships, however, provide an insufficient foundation of planning. Why is this? Because planning deals with the future, and facts about the future are unknown. Hence, the planner must assume probable events of the future and include these in his planning; otherwise he cannot plan. Such events are termed premises or assumptions. In other words, premises form the background against which the planner believes future events affecting his plan will take place.

As future events unfold, planning premises change, in turn causing changes in plans. To illustrate, on the premise that sales would increase 20 percent during the coming year, an office manager planned his operations to take care of the additional office work resulting from this anticipated increase in sales. The increase in sales materialized and soon exceeded the 20 percent gain forecast. Concurrently, the office manager had to adjust his plans in keeping with the facts and the new premise established—in this case, an additional 10 percent sales increase.

Actually in forecasting the environment, two problems are involved: (1) determining what conditions should be forecast and (2) determining how to forecast them. Under the former are business forecasts, governmental actions, price structures, population projections, business cycles, quantity of work, quality of work, process used, and market demand studies. In the latter are included past experiences, quantitative measurements, and statistical analysis. All of these are really assumptions about the future upon which the planning efforts are based. In essence, the planner attempts to find out which facts affect office activities and then strives to forecast these factors.

Planning premises within any given enterprise should be harmonious; otherwise, integration of the various planning efforts throughout the enterprise will not be achieved. Specifically the office manager should use premises in keeping with those already established for the entire enterprise. However, alternate premises can and should be considered by an enterprise. This leads, along with a different interpretation of the facts, to alternative plans, discussed in the following paragraphs.

## DETERMINE ALTERNATIVES

Embracing all managerial planning are alternate goals and courses of action. If there is only one goal, attempts to evolve a possible array of related goals from planning are superfluous. Likewise, if there is only one means of achieving a goal, planning becomes a rigid, mechanical activity. The concept of planning in management implies determining a choice from several possibilities. There are a number of worthy goals. Which ones should a manager select? There are a number of means to accomplish a given goal. What means should be given preference by the manager? These questions are answered by planning.

Planning is highly individualized and is greatly influenced by such things as the subject area, the type of plan being created, the people who will carry out the plan, the person or persons doing the planning, the wishes of top managers, and the type of work included. A well-thought-out plan answers each of these questions:

1. *What work has to be done?* This includes the nature of the work, the amount, the time allowed to accomplish it, and when it should start and when it should be finished.

2. *What manner or process will be followed?* For example, will the work be done manually or by machine? If the latter, what kind, etc?

3. *What is the sequence of the work?* How does the work progress from beginning to end? What is the work flow? What organizational unit or units are concerned with the work?

4. *What skill or type of employee is included?* This answers the question: "Who is going to do the work?" The plan spells out this information in detail. For the operative level, instructions to the individual employees should be provided.

It is easy to see that answers to these questions can vary considerably and therefore widely different plans, or alternatives, can be evolved. In addition, it must not be assumed that alternatives are confined to a cause-and-effect relationship as may be derived from step No. 2, or the analysis of the present situation. There is always room for innovation, or the creating of brand-new courses of office actions. Furthermore, conditions are dynamic and the future is uncertain, so planning should provide alternatives making it feasible to change plans when needed. For example, a plan based on premises $A$, $B$ and $C$ may be dissolved when events show premises $B$, $D$, and $E$ are in effect, and another plan substituted, based on these premises $B$, $D$, and $E$. Planning for a range of plans, not just a plan, provides a needed practical aspect and flexibility to plans, so that a manager can perform his work better.

A plan is only as effective as the best of the alternatives developed. It pays to spend time developing alternatives. Unfortunately there is a tendency to discontinue the search for alternatives when a satisfactory course of action is discovered. Good planning minimizes this tendency.

## SELECT THE ALTERNATIVE

This step consists of projecting the probable outcomes from each alternative and then selecting the alternative which will provide the most favorable results. What is favorable is evaluated in terms of the relative importance of the gain to the office and to the enterprise, immediate or long-term accomplishments, and whether tangible or not. Usually the outcome is projected in every case on service, cost, freedom from error, and compatibility with known future requirements. In some instances a ranking of the alternatives is made on the basis of the degree to which they achieve stated objectives. This is a very sound basis. When it is used, care should be taken that the objectives are truly a reasonable totality in scope and not fragmented or in keeping with the goals of one office function only. Of course, if the sought objective is to be fulfilled entirely within one function, the plan will also be functional.

As indicated above, step No. 6 of Figure 15–1 logically follows the selecting of the alternative. A plan must be implemented to bring results. And to insure satisfactory results the remainder of the management process is used, i.e., controlling, organizing, and actuating.

## GAINING ACCEPTANCE OF SELECTED PLAN

In connection with the implementation of a selected plan, there is the consideration of gaining enthusiastic acceptance for it. Logically this is an important part of the plan itself and breaks down into two components: (1) participative planning and (2) strategy determination.

Although planning is a fundamental function of management and all managers require planning in their work, it is common for a manager to follow participative planning by performing planning efforts with others. The practice of consultation with others to gain suggestions, facts, basic information, and advice is democratic, helps to gain hearty acceptance and cooperation of those affected by the plan, and probably gives a better plan than if it were conceived by one person. Joint participation gives recognition to the fact that no matter what is planned, it must be carried out by people and the success of any plan depends in some degree upon people's knowledge, comprehension, and desire to make the plan work. In some cases participative planning is conducted on a highly informal basis; in other cases, it is quite formalized. Committees are used in many offices for planning. Customarily, they are advisory, with the final approval of their recommended plans residing with the manager in charge. Committees provide an excellent means for making employees more aware of the importance of planning and of the difficulties in its formulation.

The approach followed in implementing a plan should be well-thought-out, with the timing and details given special attention. The term "strategy" has been used in this connection, meaning the manner in which the plan is introduced or applied in order to help insure its success. There are many strategies employed by planners. Among the more common are the following:

1. *Strike while the iron is hot.* This stresses proper timing. When a situation appears favorable for adoption of a plan, it should be proposed without delay. Thus, unexpected opposition or difficulties possibly arising in the future are avoided.

2. *Time is a great healer.* This strategy points out that through patience and enforced delay, time is spent; and with it, acceptance of the proposed plan can be won. In other words, with time, events will happen which will make the plan acceptable and, in some instances, requested.

3. *Camel's head in the tent.* The infiltration approach is followed by offering a small portion of the plan and winning acceptance for it; subsequently, successive portions are offered, and accepted, until the entire original plan is in operation.

4. *Mass-concentrated offensive.* Here, the aim is to perform a major surgical operation—cut out the old, install the new—and handle the entire change in the shortest practical time. The rapidity and the "get it over with" aspects feature this strategy.

5. *Sowing seed on fertile ground.* The best place to gain acceptance for a plan is from those who favor it. Under this strategy, favorable members of a group are indoctrinated with the merits of the proposed action. In turn, they explain the plan to other group members, thus enlarging the number favorable to the plan. When sufficient members have been "won to the cause," the plan is formally offered and usually accepted.

These strategies are illustrative. The list is not all-inclusive; there are many, many different strategies. It should also be observed that some strategies are the direct opposite of others. This follows because the situations to which they apply, especially the human element makeup of the group, may be directly opposite. Considerable skill is required to apply strategy successfully in office planning.

## LR AND SR PLANNING

Long range (LR) and short range (SR) are two basic types of planning. LR plans usually are for periods of five years or more. Among the objectives of such plans are utilization of improved office machines and equipment, better utilization of office space, and improved physical working conditions such as better light, ventilation, and sound control. The plan for achieving these goals is carefully devised, with the various necessary activities scheduled and integrated to take place according to a predetermined blueprint of action. LR planning provides perspective to office management; it helps achieve a needed balance of activities. Also, significant savings are made possible by LR planning. In the office of one manufacturer, for example, a 22 percent reduction in space per office employee was achieved and, at the same time, a 36 percent increase in output.

SR planning commonly identifies planning for the immediate future, that is, for the next several months, or possibly a year ahead. It is especially effective in the office for establishing timetables for billing, duplicating work, and other similar activities. Many office training programs are of a short-run type. Likewise, efforts to institute an office machine maintenance program, to improve correspondence, and to raise the efficiency of filing and records retention are suited to SR planning.

## COMMON TYPES OF OFFICE PLANS

Generally speaking, repetitive work is best suited for planning. However, much nonrepetitive work has in its makeup portions of repetitive work; and by analysis, it will be found that more repetitiveness and hence more planning are possible than might at first have been believed. Also, work that is nonrepetitive but is performed frequently can usually be planned successfully.

In office work, most concern is usually given these types of plans: (1) objectives, (2) policies, (3) systems, (4) procedures, and (5) methods. Objectives and planning were discussed several pages back. Policies are formulated by planning and assist in deciding what work must be performed. *A policy is a basic guide to action.* It sets forth overall boundaries within which activities are to take place. Policies result from managerial planning; and they, in turn, affect planning. They tell the intentions of the managers in respect to various activities. For example, a company may have a policy of purchasing each year a quantity of office machines based on an amount determined by a percentage of net sales. This establishes that certain activities are to take place and puts limits upon them. However, it does not set forth what machines are to be purchased. That is, a policy permits planning and decision making within the prescribed limits of the policy.

In Chapter 9, we defined system, procedure, and method.[2] For conven-

---

[2] Pages 197 and 201.

ience we repeat the definitions here. System is a network of procedures which are integrated and designed to carry out a major activity. Procedure is a series of related clerical steps, usually performed by more than one person, which constitute an established and accepted way of carrying on an entire major phase of office activity. The planning of office systems and procedures is the subject of the next chapter. A method is the manner of work performance of a task consisting of one or more clerical acts by an individual employee. The planning of office methods is discussed in Chapter 17.

## PLANNING OFFICE FORMS

The first area to be discussed from the viewpoint of office managerial planning is office forms. This area is discussed first because by means of office forms, essential information in the best format is gotten to people who need it. This is basic in office management. After deciding these fundamentals, we can plan who adds what information where, when, and how. Furthermore, the subject of office forms is an excellent one to illustrate the practical meaning of planning. Office forms are tangible and most of us are familiar with them.

Office forms are sometimes called the raw materials of the office. They are the backbone of nearly every office system and procedure, for the economic processing of paper work requires effective management of office forms. Some choose to use the term *forms management* to characterize this analyzing and improving the role of office forms.

*An office form is a printed piece of paper which provides space for entering records, information, or instructions which are to be conveyed to other individuals, departments, or enterprises.* Common examples include cost tickets, expense accounts, factory orders, requisitions, sales data, purchase orders, invoices, and credit memorandums. Office forms are used because they reduce copying, insure uniformity, serve as work guides, give official sanction to the written work, and implement office mechanization.

In the planning of an office form, it is wise to enlist the help of forms-design engineers for they are trained and experienced in this type of work. They usually are able to suggest improvements. Most manufacturers of office forms offer the services of design engineers. In addition, the users of the form can frequently offer helpful suggestions as well as evaluate a proposed form. The check list shown by Figure 15–2 gives 26 pertinent questions, the answers to which reveal information which is basic in forms planning. A separate sheet is recommended for each form analysis.

By means of forms planning, it is possible to reduce the form size and make the form far more effective. An excellent illustration, revealed by

HAMMERMILL FORM ORDER SHEET • PART 1

# a 5 minute FORM CHECK LIST

[A quick and easy method of checking the efficiency and economy of any form—new or old—before placing your printing order. Read the text at the bottom of this sheet.]

## Necessity

| | OK | ? |
|---|---|---|
| 1 Has the entire system been checked and would a written procedure for the use of this form help put it into more efficient operation? | | |
| 2 Are all copies of the form or report necessary? | | |
| 3 Have the actual users of this form been consulted for suggested improvements, additional requirements and possible eliminations? | | |
| 4 Can the data furnished by this form be combined with some other form or can some other form be eliminated or consolidated with it? | | |
| 5 Has everyone responsible for the form or the form system approved it? | | |

## Purpose

| | OK | ? |
|---|---|---|
| 6 If form is to be sent from one person to another, are proper spaces for "to" and "from" provided? | | |
| 7 Will routing or handling instructions printed on each copy be helpful? | | |
| 8 Should this form be consecutively numbered, or have a place for inserting a number? | | |
| 9 If this is an Outside Contact Form, should it be designed to mail in a window envelope? | | |
| 10 If this form is to take information from, or pass information to, another form, do both have the same sequence of items? | | |
| 11 Have we taken into consideration the number of forms which will be used in a given time (4 to 12 months)—the possibility of changes, and how long the form will remain in use? | | |

## Size and Arrangement

| | OK | ? |
|---|---|---|
| 12 Is the size right for filing, attention value, ample room for information and to cut without waste? | | |
| 13 Is all recurring information being printed, so that only variable items need be filled in? | | |
| 14 Has space been provided for a signature? | | |
| 15 Is spacing correct for handwriting or typewriting? (The Hammermill Form Layout Sheet will help check this.) | | |
| 16 Are the most important items, which should be seen first, prominently placed? (Near the top, if practicable.) | | |

## Wording

| | OK | ? |
|---|---|---|
| 17 Does the form, by title and arrangement, clearly indicate its purpose? | | |
| 18 Is there a proper space for the date? | | |
| 19 Is the form identified by company name and firm name or code number to aid reordering? | | |
| 20 If this is a revised form, can it be distinguished from the previous form? | | |

## Paper and Printing

(SPECIFICATIONS)

| | OK | ? |
|---|---|---|
| 21 Should the form be on colored paper to speed up writing, distribution, sorting and filing; to designate departments or branch offices; to indicate days, months or years; to distinguish manifold copies; to identify rush orders? | | |
| 22 Have we specified paper which will be thoroughly satisfactory, economical enough for form use, consistent in performance and surely available for later reorders? | | |
| 23 Is proper weight of paper used for original and each carbon copy? (Bond Substances 9, 13, 16 and 20. Ledger Substances 24, 28 and 32. Mimeo-Bond Substances 16 and 20. Spirit and Gelatin Duplicator Substances 16 and 20.) | | |
| 24 Are detailed specifications complete? (Paper, type, ink, rules, punch, perforate, score, fold, gather, pad, carbon sheet, stitch, etc.) | | |
| 25 Can other forms, printed on the same paper as this one, be ordered now to reduce production costs? | | |
| 26 Have requirements been estimated correctly and is the quantity to be ordered most economical? (Consider probability of revision and rate of use.) | | |

| Pt. # | Remarks ON POINTS QUESTIONED (?) |
|---|---|
| | |

DATE ____________ 19____ SIGNED ____________

**HOW TO USE THIS FORM** Run through this list and appraise a new or revamped form point by point with an initial (rather than a check mark) either in the column headed "OK" or "?." This will help in working out the most efficient form size and specifications and the best working arrangement of items and copy. Points marked (?) for further study can then be appraised systematically and discussed with those who will regularly use the form. Findings and further details can be elaborated upon in the column for "Remarks" at bottom of the second column.

To pin down responsibility, the person or persons giving the final OK should place their initials opposite the remarks. The whole Check List should be filed with a copy of the form for future reference.

*Courtesy: Hammermill Paper Co., Erie, Pa.*

FIG. 15–2. A form check list which aids in improving office forms.

the "before and after" comparison, is shown by Figures 15–3 and 15–4 on pages 340–41. Note the stated opportunities for better design and also the improvements accomplished.

The planning of office forms can be conveniently considered in terms of functional considerations and physical considerations. The former deal with factors such as the way the form is used, its purpose, the information supplied on it, and the number of copies required. Physical considerations include the ink, print type, paper, and size.

## FUNCTIONAL CONSIDERATIONS

There are seven factors that merit discussion here, including:

1. *Purpose of the form.* The foremost consideration is the job for which the form is to be used. An office form is actually a road map of a job: It shows the flow and sequence of the work. A form should start where the job starts, stop where the job stops, and include the necessary intermediary steps according to the most efficient logical sequence of operations. The form directs employees from the beginning to the end of the job.

2. *Information to include.* Knowing the purpose of the form, the next step is to decide what information the form should include. Help along this line can be secured by answering such questions as:

*a*) What information is needed to accomplish the stated purpose?
*b*) Is the information really vital?
*c*) How is it to be used?
*d*) Who uses it, and in what manner?

A complete list of the items to be included is prepared. Then, a careful review of this list should be made in order to eliminate duplications and information not absolutely necessary.

3. *Sequence of items.* The order should be mainly that of the normal flow of the work, and related items should be grouped. When items are transcribed from one form to another, the items should be arranged in the same sequence on both forms. If instructions are necessary, they should be located just above the portion of the form to which they have reference. This helps to insure that they will be read at the proper time, which is just before filling in the form. All instructions should be brief and to the point.

4. *General pattern of the form.* The method of completion is important. If the work is to be done manually, ample writing space is necessary, and horizontal lines on the form are desirable. Spacing should be three or four lines to the inch.

If the work is to be done by machine, the form should be spaced in accordance with the demands of the machine. The data should be arranged to utilize a tabular alignment, and horizontal lines on the form should be omitted. The following illustrates correct and incorrect arrangement when a machine is used:

|               *Correct*               |        *Incorrect*         |
| :-----------------------------------: | :------------------------- |
| Name:                                 | Name _____  |
| Address:                              | Address _____ |
| S.S. Number:                          | S.S. Number _____ |
| Age:                                  | Age _____ |

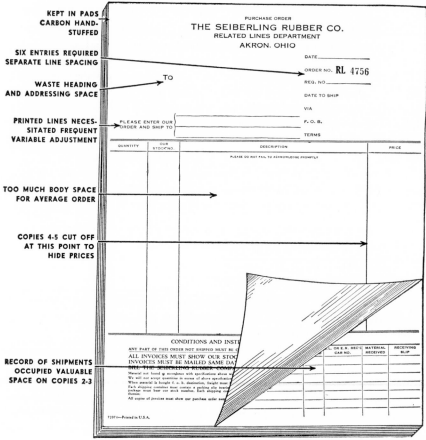

*Courtesy: Standard Register Co., Dayton*

FIG. 15–3.   Original form before redesign.

The use of "boxed" style should be employed whenever appropriate. This style saves filling-in time, conserves space, and improves legibility. It is helpful to provide a reference number for each space to be filled in. By this means, tabulation, comparison, and interpretation of data are expedited. Where long sentences are necessary, it is desirable to have them printed in columnar form instead of across the full width of the sheet, as this expedites reading and makes for better appearance. However, when the information to be filled in is lengthy, the boxed style is usually inappropriate; the regular or "open" style is better. An illustration of a form featuring the boxed style for answers and numbers to expedite machine tabulation is shown in Figure 15–5.

5. *Adequate identification.*   The form name should suggest its purpose. For example, the title "Sales Records" is not complete; "Weekly Sales

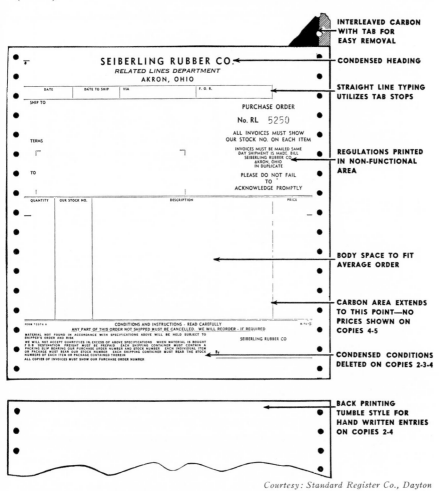

INTERLEAVED CARBON
WITH TAB FOR
EASY REMOVAL

CONDENSED HEADING

STRAIGHT LINE TYPING
UTILIZES TAB STOPS

REGULATIONS PRINTED
IN NON-FUNCTIONAL
AREA

BODY SPACE TO FIT
AVERAGE ORDER

CARBON AREA EXTENDS
TO THIS POINT—NO
PRICES SHOWN ON
COPIES 4-5

CONDENSED CONDITIONS
DELETED ON COPIES 2-3-4

BACK PRINTING
TUMBLE STYLE FOR
HAND WRITTEN ENTRIES
ON COPIES 2-4

*Courtesy: Standard Register Co., Dayton*

FIG. 15–4.  Form after redesign.

Records by Territories" is more descriptive. Usually, the center or the upper left corner is preferable for the location of the name of the company and the upper right area for reference data in filing. Numbering all forms helps identify them and serves as a quick reference. The identification number should be in a convenient location, preferably near the title. In the case of multiple forms, it is usually advisable to number each copy for handy reference. Quick identification can also be gained by using different colors of papers.

6. *Number of copies.* Whether a single or multiple copy form should be used depends mainly upon two considerations: (1) who requires a copy and (2) when the copy is needed. Multiple forms afford a quick means of

**INVESTIGATOR START HERE:**

Is this a personal interview with_____?

IF NOT: Be sure to obtain answers for questions 1, 2, 3
and 4 for this person from an adult member of the family.

|  | 5 | Key No. |
|---|---|---|
| Yes | 1 | |
| No | 2 | |

1. Have you, yourself, tried both of the tubes of tooth
   paste we left you?      6

| If "No," skip rest of ques-<br>tionnaire and interview<br>other family members. | Yes | 1 |
|---|---|---|
| | No | 2 |
| | Don't Know | 3 |
| | | 4 |

AGE GROUPINGS:

| | 10 | | 10 | | 10 |
|---|---|---|---|---|---|
| 0-4 | 1 | 20-24 | 5 | 40-49 | 9 |
| 5-9 | 2 | 25-29 | 6 | 50-59 | 0 |
| 10-14 | 3 | 30-34 | 7 | 60-69 | X |
| 15-19 | 4 | 35-39 | 8 | 70 | R |

2. Which sample tooth paste do you like best?   7

| No. 53 | 1 |
|---|---|
| No. 59 | 2 |
| No Difference | 3 |
| Don't like either | 4 |
| | 5 |

PASTE BRAND:

| 11 | | 11 | | 11 |
|---|---|---|---|---|
| 1 | | 5 | | 9 |
| 2 | | 6 | | 0 |
| 3 | | 7 | | X |
| 4 | | 8 | | R |

3. What is there about the one you prefer that makes you like it?

EDITOR
ONLY
8     8

| 1 | 7 |
|---|---|
| 2 | 8 |
| 3 | 9 |
| 4 | 0 |
| 5 | X |
| 6 | R |

SEX:          12

| Male | 1 |
|---|---|
| Female | 2 |

PRINCIPAL FAMILY      13
PURCHASER:

| Yes | 1 |
|---|---|
| No | 2 |

FIG. 15–5.  A printed form using the boxed style for recording answers, numbers to expedite machine tabulation, and columnar arrangement of material. This form saves time in writing, conserves space, and
expedites reading.

supplying many copies. However, it is best to keep the number of copies
at a minimum. Only the required number of copies should be made; and
extreme prudence and care in this respect is recommended, as excess
papers tend to clutter up an office and contribute to inefficiency.

7. *Type of form.*   There are in general five different types or
arrangements of office forms: single, stub type unit, continuous stub type
unit, fan or **Z** arrangement, and continuous semistrip arrangement. The
single type is used where the original copy only is required, as, for
example, in the case of an employment application form. When necessary,
copies can be obtained simply by using carbon sheets and as many form
sheets as required. Many single-unit forms are used in an office.

The other four arrangements mentioned above are multiple forms.
Illustrations and features of each are given in Figure 15–6.

Multiple forms require only one writing, minimize mistakes, help attain
uniformity, improve departmental coordination, and save time. The
equipment used for multiple forms is either ordinary office equipment or
the same type of equipment with simple attachements, for example, a
special roller on the typewriter platen, or a holder. Figure 15–7 illustrates
units of this sort.

STUB TYPE UNIT

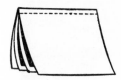

Can be made with stub at top, bottom, either side, or top and bottom. The latter is used when set must be separated into two sections after initial writing for subsequent fill-ins. Carbon is fastened to stub, is used once, and can be of same or different widths and lengths to permit selective coyping.

FAN OR Z

These are provided in continuous strips with perforated accordion folds at left and right edges. The arrangement is available in either packs or rolls. Being joined at alternate sides, the forms can be separated from the strip but still retained in sets. The fan arrangement is available with or without interleaved carbon.

CONTINUOUS
STUB TYPE UNIT

This is the same as the stub-type unit arrangement except that the bottom sheet of each set is attached to the following set by perforations.

CONTINUOUS
SEMISTRIP

This arrangement is similar to the continuous stub type except for the absence of stubs. The forms are perforated at fold. Depending upon method and equipment used, these may be utilized either with or without carbon interleaving.

FIG. 15–6. The main types or arrangements of multiple office forms.

## PHYSICAL CONSIDERATIONS

The following considerations, although technical in nature, are involved in forms planning:

1. *Ink.* The ink selected should provide proper contrast to the paper and should give a clear, uniform, and smooth imprint. Certain printing processes require a certain type of ink. Use of more than one color of ink adds to the cost of the form. As discussed in Chapters 12 and 14, one of the latest "inks" is a magnetic type containing iron oxides. Typing or printing with this type of ink makes impressions on the paper which can be read by electronic means used to put various counting and sorting mechanisms into action.

This attachment, called a "dual feed," makes it possible to produce two records in one operation. Common information is typed on two forms of different size, with independent spacing as the work requires.

*Courtesy: Standard Register Co., Dayton*

FIG. 15–7. A pack holding refold tray used for continuous multiple form.

2. *Print type.* Readability and distinctiveness should govern the selection of print type. For any one form, it is best to keep the type sizes and type styles to a minimum. Items of equal importance should be printed in the same type throughout the entire form. Normally, italic and boldface type should be used for emphasis but confined to words where special stress is required.

3. *Paper.* The five important physical properties of paper are weight, grade, grain, color, and size.

*a)* Weight. Paper is usually sold by weight. Normally, the mill supplies paper in standard sizes according to the different grades and the intended purposes for which the paper is to be used. To illustrate, the purposes and corresponding sizes are shown in this table:

| Use of Paper | Size |
|---|---|
| Bonds, ledgers, general writing | 17″ x 22″ |
| Book papers and offset pages | 25″ x 38″ |
| Cover stock | 20″ x 26″ |
| Newsprint | 24″ x 36″ |
| Bristol board | 22½″ x 28½″ |

A ream is the common measurement for quantity of paper and is approximately 500 sheets. For example, bond paper listed as 17″ x 22″— 20 means that 20 pounds of this grade and size of paper includes approximately 500 sheets. Likewise, bond paper 17″ x 22″—13 means that 13 pounds of this grade and size of paper contain approximately 500 sheets. Comparing these two, the latter sheets would be thinner, since, based on the same size and approximate quantity, their weight is less (13 pounds) compared to the former (20 pounds).

The lightest paper which will give satisfactory results should be used. Among the factors which determine the proper weight of paper are number of copies, amount of handling, purpose of the form, how filed—on edge or side, length of time retained, and whether printed on one or two sides. The following weights are usually recommended:

| Application | Weight of Paper Recommended |
|---|---|
| Legal documents | 28 pound |
| Ledgers | 24 pound |
| Letterheads | 20 pound |
| When 1–4 copies are made | 16 pound |
| When 5–8 copies are made | 13 pound |
| When over 9 copies are made | Tissue |

*b*) Grade. The grade of paper means the quality and is chiefly based on the kinds of materials used in the manufacturing process. Paper is made from rags, mechanical wood pulp, sulfite wood pulp, soda wood pulp, and sulfate wood pulp, which are used in varying amounts, depending upon the kind of paper. The grade selected for a form depends upon such things as the life of the form, the amount of handling, and the appearance. The following table is helpful.

| Life of Form | Grade of Paper |
|---|---|
| 1–5 years | 100 percent sulfite |
| 6–12 years | 50 percent sulfite and 50 percent rag |
| Over 12 years | 100 percent rag |

*c*) Grain. Like wood, paper has a grain characteristic. The direction of the grain is determined by the alignment of the fibers making up the paper. The expression "with the grain" signifies the longitudinal direction of most fibers. Grain direction is the result of the manufacturing process. The grain of paper determines its rigidity. Some processes require that the grain of the paper run with the length of the printing roll. The grain should be parallel to the typewriter platen, because the paper then rolls around the platen better and there is less tendency for the sheets to slip. Paper folds more easily and quickly when it is parallel with the grain. Furthermore, when the graining runs vertically on forms posted by machine or filed on edge, there is less tendency for the forms to buckle and curl.

*d*) Color.   Colored paper for office forms frequently affords an effective medium for securing a strong appeal, a unique identification, and a simple means of facilitating the handling of forms. However, colored paper usually costs more than white.

*e*) Size.   The size of the form is determined by the amount of information, the economical paper size, the size and types of office equipment and machines, and the mechanical requirements. The limitations of the printing process must, of course, be considered in determining the dimensions of a form. Wherever possible forms should be cut from stock sizes of paper. It is advisable to discuss the subject of economical stock sizes with the prospective supplier.

4. *Means of carbonizing copies.*   The providing of carbon paper for use with the forms can be achieved in several ways: (*a*) inserting carbon by hand, (*b*) one-use carbon interleaved into the form, (*c*) carbon in the machine—using a simple "floating carbon" device, and (*d*) spots of wax carbon applied to the back of the form during the manufacturing process.

As indicated in Figure 15–6, some multiple forms provide one-use carbon paper interleaved into position. When the fan and continuous semistrip arrangements are used without carbon interleaving, the "floating carbon" device can be used. In this case, the forms slip over the carbon sheets which remain in the machine, and these sheets are used many times over until the impressions indicate the need for a carbon change. The fourth method, application of spots of wax carbon, makes it possible to apply the carbon to certain parts of a form, thus permitting only certain portions of the original writing to appear on the copies. Frequently, price information or specification data do not appear on all copies, since this information has little value for the purpose of some copies. A similar result can be achieved in the other carbon methods by cutting off certain carbon sheets or blacking out, with a solid mass of dots or other marks, that portion of the form which is not to receive an impression. The carbon mark is not visible on the blackened area.

In Chapter 5 it was stated that carbonless "NCR paper," manufactured by the National Cash Register Company, can be used for making copies simultaneously with the original writing. All that is required is to use NCR paper for the sheets of the form.

## QUESTIONS

1. Does office managerial planning include more than determining what manner or process will be followed? Discuss.
2. Give a complete and concise definition for each of the following:
    *a*) Forms management.
    *b*) Office form.
    *c*) Short range planning.
    *d*) Planning premise.
3. Elaborate on this statement: "Seldom is it wise to try to state the real purpose of an office in one single, inclusive objective."
4. What is the meaning of "strategy determination" in planning, how is it used, and what is sought by its use? Give an illustration to demonstrate your answer.
5. Discuss the performance of the planning step "select the alternative," as adopted in modern office management.
6. Relate four reasons why office forms are utilized.
7. Give an acceptable definition of office management policy, and relate several examples of policies with which you have had experience.
8. Discuss the various means of carbonizing copies of office forms.
9. Explain how the information secured from a check list, as shown in Figure 15–2, can be used to improve office forms.
10. What is meant by each of the following:
    *a*) "Floating carbon" device.
    *b*) Grain of paper.
    *c*) Continuous stub-type unit arrangement.
    *d*) Boxed style for printed office forms.
11. Referring to Figures 15–3 and 15–4, point out and discuss four improvements that you deem of special importance in designing a more effective office form.
12. Discuss the property of weight in the identification and utilization of paper for office forms.

## CASE PROBLEMS

### Case 15–1.  Overton Trust Company

The transfer agent of stock of the Frey Manufacturing Corporation, an Illinois corporation, is the recently appointed Overton Trust Company. Included among the duties of a transfer agent are maintaining an up-to-date list of the corporation's shareholders' names and addresses, disbursing dividends to these owners, and transferring title of any stock certificate of the corporation presented for recording of ownership change.

Upon being presented with a certificate for transfer of ownership, it is the practice of the agent to cancel the old certificate, properly endorsed and assigned, and issue a new certificate for a like number of shares in the name of the assignee, or new owner. The recording of the transfer details, including the adjusting of the transfer records to reflect the change of ownership, requires at least 24 hours. In addition, under Illinois law, it is necessary for the new certificates created by the transfer to be forwarded for countersignature by a registrar, who acts as a check against the overissuance of authorized shares. This registrar must by law be separate from and independent of the transfer agent.

The managers of the Overton Trust Company desire to keep adequate records of transactions, handle the receipt of certificates, cancel them, issue new certificates, forward them to the registrar for countersignature, and subsequently deliver new certificates as quickly as possible to the new owners. The source of certificates presented for transfer can be classified into two types: (1) over-the-counter items, that is, those presented in person to the transfer agent by a broker or an individual; and (2) mail items, that is, those sent to the transfer agent through the mail.

With this in mind, Clark Gates, a member of the office staff at the Overton Trust Company, suggested that a three-section receipt form be used. This form would provide appropriate space for pertinent information, including the name of the stock seller, the number of shares to be transferred, and the old and the new certificate number. The following is a sketch of the proposed three-section receipt.

| Receipt No. .................... Received for transfer of .................... shares of Frey Manufacturing Co. | Receipt No. .................... Received for transfer of .................... shares of Frey Manufacturing Co. | Receipt No. .................... Received for transfer of .................... shares of Frey Manufacturing Co. |
|---|---|---|
| Old Certificate No. .................... | Old Certificate No. .................... | Old Certificate No. .................... |
| New Certificate No. .................... | New Certificate No. .................... | New Certificate No. .................... |
| Section 1 | Section 2 | Section 3 |

For over-the-counter items, the receipt is filled out; and section 3 is given the customer, with the information that the new certificate will be available the following day from the office of the registrar. Transfer of the old certificate will be completed, a new certificate issued, and both, accompanied by section 2 of the receipt form, forwarded by messenger to the registrar. Section 1 will be retained by the Overton Trust Company as a record of the transaction. After the registrar has noted his records and added signature, he delivers the new certificate to the party presenting section 3 of the receipt form. At this time, the recipient is asked to acknowledge delivery of the new certificate by signing a "statement of receipt" appearing on the reverse side of the receipt.

In the case of mail items, the work is handled in similar manner. The three-section receipt form is filled out; the mechanics of transferring are carried out; and the new certificates, together with section 2 of the receipt, are delivered to the registrar. The following day, the messenger of the Overton Trust Company, using section 1, picks up the new certificate from the registrar and returns it to the transfer agent. Meanwhile, section 3 has been retained with the correspondence for identification. As soon as the new certificate is returned to the transfer agent, it is mailed to the transferee with a letter of transmittal, in duplicate, describing the enclosure and asking for acknowledgment of the contents on the duplicate copy. Upon its return, the receipted duplicate copy is filed in the central filing section.

## Problems:

1. Draw a graphic representation of how the three sections of the receipt form will be used for (a) over-the-counter items and (b) mail items. Use any form of graphic representation that you feel helps visualize the paper work followed.

2. Evaluate the plan suggested by Clark Gates.

3. Suggest other practical means for handling the transfer agent's work as described in this case. Which alternative do you prefer? Why?

### Case 15–2.  Pryor Company

Currently, requests for salary increases are typed in duplicate on Form 2297 by each department and the original is sent to the personnel department. This form shows in tabular form the following: (a) employee name, (b) employee number, (c) job, (d) current salary, and (e) recommended increase. On the right margin is space for comments. Ordinarily these papers are made out every two weeks, if needed. The personnel department compiles a tabular master list every two weeks from the Form 2297's received. In addition, the department adds for each emlpoyee listed (a) the salary range for the present job and (b) date of last increase. These entries are on the right portion of the master list. There are also four blank columns headed (a) increase granted, (b) increase refused, (c) effective date, and (d) comments. Copies of these master sheets are distributed to members of the salary committee. Subsequently, at their meeting salary decisions on each listed employee are made and recorded in the proper blank columns of the master list. From this completed list, the personnel department fills out a Form 3229, "Advice of Salary Increase," for each listed employee and Form 3710, which is a tabular listing of the data of personnel department's master list *for employees granted increases only*. Copies of Form 3710 are sent to the payroll department and to the Group Insurance Agency. Form 3229 is sent to the proper department manager, who gives it to the employee.

## Problems:

1. Devise an improved procedure and form which will combine all the necessary information and eliminate duplicate typing and unnecessary work.

2. Briefly describe your recommended procedure and sketch the improved form or forms you recommend.

### Case 15–3.  Hughes, Thomas, and Weaver, Inc.

The assistant officer manager has designed a new customer order and invoice form. He asks you what you think of it. You observe that the size is 7 x 10½ inches; an original and five copies will make up one unit; different colors of paper will be used for each copy; five type styles are used in the composition of the form; and all printing is in black ink except the company's name, which is in light blue. The shipping route is in red, so that it will stand out. The spacing of lines on the form is five to the inch. In answer to your specific questions, the assistant office manager tells you that he intends to get reactions to the form from the company's various sales executives, both in the home office and in district sales offices; a good price from the printer can be secured in quantities of 60,000, which is about a two-year supply; a standard typewriter billing machine, pica type, is used for writing invoices; and in about 40 percent of the invoices written, two extra copies are needed (seven copies total), and these will be inserted in the five-copy pack as required.

### Problems:

1. Outline your reply to the assistant office manager.
2. Discuss the specific recommendations you would make to the assistant office manager.
3. Explain the probable reasons for the weaknesses of the proposed form.

# CHAPTER 16

# PLANNING
# OFFICE SYSTEMS AND PROCEDURES

Life must be lived forwards, but can only be
understood backwards.
*—Sören Kierkegaard*

FEW assignments in office management are as important as planning office
systems and procedures. Sound planning in these areas sets the proper
stage for subsequent effective management, for it is by means of thorough
and carefully derived office systems and procedures that many issues of
office management are settled and the office work accomplished efficiently.
Systems and procedures are comprehensive. They encompass consideration for the process, space, papers, cost, quality, time-use, organization,
and people utilized. They are the common ingredient affecting most office
work.

## TOP MANAGEMENT BACKING

The initial efforts of the system and procedure designer in carrying out
an assignment is to secure top management backing. Unless he has the
blessing and support of top managers he is almost certain to encounter
some difficult obstacles in decisions regarding the proposed system and
procedure and their implementation. Top management support is always a
pleasant possession, but it is especially so in system and procedure
planning. What is acceptable invariably reflects the general philosophy of
the top managers, be they dedicated to the *status quo*, rapid growth,
cautious development, or conservative ways of performing work.

351

In addition, the planner should start his work with a mind free from preconceived ideas of what work modes and machines should be utilized. The facts and demands to be discovered and utilized by him will dictate the plan recommended. During the early stages it is not only interesting but also useful to find out what is motivating the study. Is it really a sincere desire to improve office work? If so, the planner has an ideal assignment. Or is it an organization battle between the leaders of two large departments? Or a struggle between factions vying for corporate power? The planner will do well not to get himself involved in squabbles nurtured by political ambitions.

## SYSTEM DESIGN

System designers differ somewhat in their approach to their work. The essential pattern, however, is similar to that of the five planning steps

| *Five Planning Steps* | *System Design* | *Procedure Improvement* |
|---|---|---|
| 1. Set objectives | 1. Define system boundaries | 1. Select procedure to be improved |
| 2. Analyze present situation | 2. Secure data and facts | 2. Get all the facts about this procedure |
|  | 3. Organize and consolidate facts | 3. Analyze and evaluate these facts |
| 3. Forecast environment | 4. Establish system premises |  |
| 4. Determine alternatives |  |  |
| 5. Select alternative | 5. Evolve the system design | 4. Devise the improvement |

FIG. 16–1. Comparison of major steps in planning, system designing, and procedure improving.

discussed in the preceding chapter. For purposes here we will follow a four-step program for system design. A comparison of the five planning steps to that of the system design program is shown by the first two columns of Figure 16–1. This comparison must not be viewed in a rigid sense. For example, the system designer may well be concerned with setting objectives, but he is more likely to get involved in objectives in order to define the system boundaries which, from the practical view, is his first major step. Likewise, the planning step "analyze present situation" is extremely important and, as shown for the system designer, is made up of: (1) secure data and facts and (2) organize and consolidate facts. Finally, the steps of determining alternatives and selecting an alternative are included in the single system step of "evolve the system design."

## DEFINE SYSTEM BOUNDARIES

Even though tentative, boundaries must be established to define the scope of the study and possible limits of the system. The boundaries serve to establish the framework within which the system evolved will operate. Any statement of system boundaries depends upon objectives sought and these, in turn, are dependent upon the definition of the proposed system and its content. This definition becomes the initial goal of the system designer. Such requirements can be classified as those which are (1) legal —required by law; (2) operational—required for profitable or serviceable operations; and (3) contractual—required by the customer or outsider to the enterprise. These requirements constrain the system design. In this respect, knowledge of the following is required: what activities are to be

| ORGANIZATION UNIT | | | OBJECTIVES | PROCEDURES | CONTROLS | ORGANIZATION | INPUT | OUTPUT | PROCESSING MEANS |
|---|---|---|---|---|---|---|---|---|---|
| NO. | NAME | NO. OF EMPLOYEES | | | | | | | |
| 67 | SALES | 26 | | ✓ | ✓ | | | | |
| 63 | MARKET RESEARCH | 8 | ✓ | ✓ | | | | | |
| 55 | BILLING | 17 | | | | ✓ | ✓ | | ✓ |
| | | | | | | | | | |
| | | | | | | | | | |
| | | | | | | | | | |
| | | | | | | | | | |
| | | | | | | | | | |
| | | | | | | | | | |

FIG. 16–2.   Chart for assisting in determining the scope of a system.

included in the proposed system, what constitutes the input and the output, what processing is to take place, and what manner is followed in handling deviations, exceptions, and malfunctions.

Figure 16–2 illustrates a simple chart helpful in determining the scope of a proposed system. Organization units are listed in the left column, along with the respective number of employees. To the right, heading up the several columns are items which might warrant investigation and study. For example, the check mark opposite "sales department" under "procedures" means that the procedures used merit careful study, or in the case of an existent system being studied, the procedures are believed to be inadequate and changes in them are probably in order for improvement to take place. Opposite "market research," the check mark under "objectives" indicates some question about the clarity or feasibility of the objectives of this department. The check mark under "organization" opposite "billing department" means that the organization form or the relation of the billing department to the total organization of the enterprise should be analyzed. Filling out a chart like this is difficult because it necessitates an ability to conceptualize the system along with understanding and knowledge of the problem area. The latter is quite likely to be meager at the initial stage of the system design. Nevertheless, such a chart can be extremely helpful and its use is beneficial in most studies.

## SECURE DATA AND FACTS

Unless some orderly methodology is followed, the securing of data will be chaotic and wasteful. Data are where you can find them, but care must be exercised in selecting the data and the sources that are utilized. Experience helps the planner to be knowledgeable in data selection, but lacking experience he can proceed to gather data which will be helpful. The following fruitful sources are suggestive only and may supply adequate data in some cases, but merely a starting point in other cases.

1. *Organization charts and manuals.* Organization charts give only sketchy details. However, with organization manuals, they indicate what activities are grouped together, probable authority of the respective members, and the tasks performed. Compiling a list of the tasks performed is especially recommended. From such a list, the identity of the work being done, where it is done, and possible duplications can be ascertained.

2. *Systems, procedures, and methods information.* Any available files of these subjects can be a source of pertinent information. They reveal the manner of work performance currently and in the past. More important, they indicate the managers' probable preferences. In addition, their general quality regarding accuracy, timeliness, and completeness gives clues as to the status of information handling in the particular enterprise. Usually systems, procedures, and methods provide valuable information on the paper forms being used, hence, helpful details are supplied.

3. *Observation of work.* This source is always used and is reliable. Data collected by this means may be compared with data obtained from other sources for purposes of verification. Effective observation requires the knack of purposive watching and a concentration on meaningful actions. This takes some practice, as most laymen are not skilled in observing effectively.

4. *Study of accounting data.* Valuable material applying to existing cost and other financial controls is obtained from this source. Leads as to

what information is considered important, how compiled, and how used are obtained. Sometimes partial, incomplete, or rejected accounting systems are found and for certain types of problems such information proves helpful.

5. *Talks with supervisors and operative employees.* People who are involved currently in processing the data can be helpful. Conversations with personnel normally should be withheld until last because the system designer will then be more certain what questions to ask, better

| Do's | Don't's |
|---|---|
| 1. Do make preparation for the interview; be familiar with and have with you organization charts, manuals, position descriptions, flow charts, and the like. | 1. Don't interrupt the respondent while he is answering your question or giving you information. |
| 2. Do radiate a friendly and genuinely helpful interest in the respondent and an appreciation of his helping you to obtain needed information. | 2. Don't let statements not understood go by; terminate the interview only after you have a clear understanding of the issue. |
| 3. Do keep the interview focused on securing data and facts pertinent to the system design. | 3. Don't ask questions that can be answered "yes" or "no" unless you want an opinion. |
| 4. Do take notes and be a good listener. | 4. Don't play the role of a consultant and suggest solutions to problems posed; this is not the purpose of your interview. |
| 5. Do ask questions designed to verify answers secured from this and other sources. | 5. Don't argue; if violent differences arise, change the subject area and avoid returning to the controversial area for awhile. |
| 6. Do leave the interview feeling you were the interviewer, not the interviewee. | 6. Don't ignore time; be ready to interview at the appointed time and terminate it promptly when the information is obtained or the allotted time expires. Arrange a second interview, if necessary. |

FIG. 16–3. Do's and don't's of interviewing to obtain information for system design.

prepared for the interview—particularly important for noncooperative people—and can thus reduce the time required for the interview. Not all interviews proceed according to plan, however, and the designer may be forced to change his line of questioning or its sequence. Figure 16–3 gives some do's and don't's that apply to talking with supervisors and operative employees.

Attention is called to the fact that the use of questionnaires is not included in the above list. Why not use questionnaires? Primarily because they are very difficult to design and are probably never inclusive of all the information which it is found subsequently must be obtained. Also, the questionnaire method is slow, the total cost high, due mainly to the need for editing and interpreting the information, and many employees object to filling out questionnaires. However, questionnaires are acceptable when a relatively small amount of information is wanted from a large, dispersed group.

## ORGANIZE AND CONSOLIDATE DATA AND FACTS

The data secured from the above step will be, for the most part, a mass of pieces of information, forms, papers, reports, and ideas. They must be related or classified in order to be used effectively. Precisely how the accumulated information should be organized depends upon the makeup of the particular study. It should be emphasized, however, that at this point we are not trying to design the system; we are simply trying to get the information we have in an orderly and easily understood arrangement.

Graphic representation of data is usually easier to comprehend than that in written form. If the data and facts were not collected in graphic form, it is helpful to convert into this type of format. By this means the interrelationships of data will be revealed, duplicated data can be identified and discarded, and a composite picture of fairly large portions of information is gained. When detailed information is needed, the use of symbols on a graphic chart is advantageous. This has already been indicated in Chapter 9.[1] There will be more about the use of charts and symbols later in this chapter.

Among the more common ways of organizing data and facts are by:

1. *The objectives to which they relate.* Generally this supplies broad classifications. The chief drawback is in identifying the objectives. They are not always easy to define clearly and furthermore are commonly compounded so that the classification by objectives does not always give clear and distinct divisions to the data.

2. *Organization.* This is a favorite means for classifying data. It segregates data by who decides what and upon what information a decision is reached. This means associating information—be it in the form of reports, records, or memos—as well as its distribution, to the organization units and their respective personnel. The purpose and use by whom, for each informational segment, serve as the classification. These relations, tied with organization units, reveal the flow of data, at which level, who decides what issues, and the adequacy of the information structure. Consolidating these types of data into a single picture for the entire enterprise provides a blueprint for designing an inclusive and effective system.

3. *Input and output.* This approach is relatively simple and provides meaningful classifications when there are existent systems to be improved.

---

[1] See page 207.

However, to use this basis when there is no precedent from former or present systems, it is necessary to conceive vividly the proposed system and segregate data based on these conceptual notions.

4. *Processing means.* This is advantageous to reveal the current status of the data processing being followed. It is especially helpful in revealing the makeup of the nonautomated processes being utilized and the type of information being obtained.

5. *Major problems or complaints discovered during the collecting stage.* These criteria will separate the information into large classes which in some studies are very helpful. Care must be exercised to include only genuine problems and complaints which appear to be of major significance.

In these efforts to organize the data and facts, attention should also be directed to evaluating them quantitatively, i.e., measurably by cost, accuracy, and employee productivity. This uncovers possible areas for improvement by suggesting the proper integration of activities to obtain desired optimization. Sampling techniques to determine the accuracy of source documents and the reliability of reports and records can be followed. Also, some indexes of employee productivity should be developed. When these are compared to levels of attainment in similar work elsewhere or to what level appears reasonable, the planner has tangible evidence of how efficient the present information work is.

## ESTABLISH SYSTEM PREMISES

Actually the three previous steps in system design provide excellent clues as to what premises should be established. For example, the system boundaries and the organized facts supply information on the quality standards and volume of work that have prevailed. It is a simple matter to project these and establish them as the levels upon which the system design will be made. But events of the future may prove far different than the projections so that the system must be modified. It is best, therefore, to keep the system flexible with built-in means for expanding or contracting as the future shows is necessary.

The process used is perhaps the major premise of any system. The assumption of the use of existing office machines of a company can condition the system design considerably. And the same effect results from the premise to acquire new machines or even a computer. Their means of doing the work shape the system's makeup, yet these means are subject to radical change, as demonstrated by the introduction of new machines and attachments almost daily on the market. Again, system flexibility is the answer.

No part of a system will remain absolutely the same over a period. Some change is inevitable. But for practical purposes, we need to assume some static concept in order to design the system. As conditions change sufficiently, we can adjust our system accordingly.

## EVOLVE THE SYSTEM DESIGN

This step necessitates considerable creativity. New combinations of, and new formats for, information must be considered. The design is motivated by challenge and the opportunity to try out tentatively system patterns that have not been tried heretofore. Nevertheless, the creative requirement can be overstated. To a great extent evolving a system design consists of a lot of hard work, abiding by the "ground rules" or constraints set up, and keeping everlastingly at the planning until a suitable solution is reached. System planning takes time; the work cannot be hurried. Fact-finding and fact-organizing are time-consuming work. Various ideas are tried out, some are retained, many are discarded. The process is one of working back and forth—from the desirable goal backward to what is required at the beginning, and from the beginning through various steps to a logical outcome.

At every part of the system, stress must be given the necessity of the information supplied, to whom it is given, and for what purpose. This is fundamental and must not be ignored. Satisfaction of closing and of due dates for information, peak periods, and volume of work must be given ample consideration so that the needs are met. Any limitations of current equipment should be disclosed, along with specific recommendations as to how to process the required data most advantageously. In this regard, "bench-mark problems" may arise, usually where a computer is used. Relatively speaking, bench-mark problems are not common but when present can seriously curtail design work. A bench-mark problem is the condition of a company having processing equipment dominated by several applications which require some two-thirds of the company's data-processing capacity. When this condition restricts the choice of any additional equipment to that of a complement of the existing equipment, with respect to any new system, a bench-mark problem exists. Usually the term is confined to the situation where an alternate or different type of equipment might be better suited to the needs of a proposed system.

Figure 16–4 lists pertinent questions to aid in system planning. Answers to these questions serve as a stimulus to devising the best possible system and to evaluating designing efforts.

## PROCEDURE DESIGN

In many respects procedure design is similar to system design. The work scope of a procedure is established by the system of which the procedure is a part. Most of the data and facts collected for the system

1. Are the stated objectives and requirements satisfied completely by the system?
2. Does the system perform more efficiently, more accurately, and more quickly than the previous manner of work performance?
3. If organizational changes are required, are these acceptable, and if some are not, will modification seriously restrict the proposed benefits?
4. At what points are employees' judgments, interpretations, and decision making a part of the system? Are there adequate control mechanisms over employees at these points?
5. Are proposed savings to be gained by reducing manpower? If so, will requisitions for manpower be cancelled, present employees transferred, and normal attrition permitted to take care of the labor surplus?
6. Have the information integration requirements been stated clearly, preferably by means of flow charts?
7. Are the inputs of data identified as to source, form, content, and method of transmission?
8. Are the outputs of data identified as to form, content, method of transmission, time requirements, volume, and peak loads?
9. Does the system incorporate adequate feedback and controls?
10. Is the data processing specified regarding type, speed, volume, and other pertinent characteristics?
11. Is the recommended means of data processing completely justified on the basis of clearly stated premises?
12. Are any special purpose requirements included and if so, are they clearly stated and their probable impact upon the system set forth in terms of delivery, delay, maintenance, and cost?

FIG. 16–4.   Questions to assist in designing the best possible system.

can be utilized for designing the procedure. Supplemental data may be needed, however, and these are usually obtained by the same means as those for a system described above.

Although certain limits are in effect for a procedure, due to the constraints of its system, there usually exists a choice of alternative procedures. A certain type and amount of office work can normally be performed in several different ways. In the work of planning procedures the following guidelines are pertinent:

1. *Identify the work to be handled.*   Take a complete picture of the paper work intended to be accomplished by the procedure. With this as a background, identify the type of paper work to be handled. Determine its volume, any characteristic peaks and valleys in its normal flow, and the importance of the time limit for getting the paper work finished. Consider also the present office layout and how the current arrangement will tie in with the procedural requirements. Keep in mind that procedures are far-reaching—they frequently cut across several departments.

2. *Establish the best sequence of the necessary steps.*   Use the minimum number of steps required to do the work adequately. Each step

should make a definite contribution toward the completion of the office work, i.e., each step should be entirely justifiable. There should be no delay, no duplication, and no backtracking.

3. *Hold the writing to a minimum.* As far as possible, the work of copying should be eliminated. Original source data should be used to eliminate posting to or recopying of records. The operations of checking and comparing should be the smallest feasible amounts. Likewise, the number of copies should be limited to a quantity necessary only for carefully selected persons or departments—those really concerned in the operation. There is no merit in making copies and in distributing them simply for the sake of doing so or because they are available.

4. *Wherever possible, put the source data in a form suitable for reuse in subsequent operations.* Actually, this is the basic idea of SDP (source data automation) discussed in Chapter 11. Commonly, the processing of data requires the repeating of identical information on different documents; hence, having such data in a form that expedites duplicating in whole or in part saves time and energy.

5. *Adopt a procedure best suited to the individual need.* The best procedure is tailored to accomplish a specific and particular goal—no more and no less. Frequently, this necessitates modification of a procedure used by another enterprise under similar conditions. Its use by others is no valid justification for adopting a certain procedure, unless it can be shown, by thorough study, that the procedure will accomplish the objective better than any other procedure that could be devised within reasonable time and cost limitations.

6. *Wherever possible, perform multiple operations by machine.* Research studies are now ample to show that multiple office operations are more efficiently performed by machine than by hand. Automatic features of many modern machines, the time required for loading and unloading the machine, and the complexity of much data processing have made mechanization of multiple operations the preferred means.

7. *Give consideration to the personal preference of the employees who will do the work.* Consulting with the employees, getting their ideas as to what the makeup of the procedure should be, and incorporating these ideas whenever possible usually results in obtaining better work. The practice of employee consultation helps to raise morale, gives consideration to the small but important details of the work, and provides due regard for custom and tradition in establishing the procedure.

8. *Perform one type of office work with one procedure.* Attempts to secure a general overall procedure for various yet related types of work result in ineffectiveness. For example, special work processed through a regular work procedure usually results in delaying the former and slowing down the latter. As indicated above, coordinating related procedures

within a given enterprise is accomplished by means of the system design.

A helpful summary check list is shown by Figure 16–5. Answers to these questions provide a penetrating review of the procedure to be followed and help achieve a superior means of getting the office work performed.

---

1. Is it a definite fact that the information produced is not available more simply or economically from another source?
2. Is every part of the information on the record really necessary?
3. Is it possible to eliminate or shorten any proposed step of the procedure, or combine them with other steps?
4. Is any step in the procedure being accepted on the basis that "it has always been done this way"?
5. Can the sequence of the necessary steps of the procedure be changed to expedite the work or make the work less fatiguing?
6. Are the employees designated to do the work specially trained and qualified to do their individual tasks?
7. Are the batches of work large enough to promote efficiency and, on the other hand, small enough for ease in balancing and handling?
8. Are codes being used, and are they simple and short?
9. Are all the workplaces well arranged for performing the work?
10. Are files that are used extensively readily accessible?
11. Does the office layout assist in getting the work to flow smoothly?
12. Are physical conditions such as light, noise abatement, and office temperature the best for proper office work execution?

---

FIG. 16–5.  Helpful questions to ask in efforts to design the best possible procedure.

## IMPLEMENTING THE SYSTEM OR PROCEDURE

Before installing a newly designed or revised system or procedure it is always desirable to test its overall operation. This usually poses some difficulties, due to the unstructured nature of the planned work. A number of runs should be made to insure satisfactory operation as indicated by statistical validity. Pilot or test runs make it possible to detect and correct any shortcomings before large-scale commitments are made. Frequently the approach is to test portions of the system or procedure. Each portion is checked thoroughly. To the degree that successively they are independent they can be tested independently, but, in contrast, if they are dependent serially they must be tested serially. Testing portions helps to simplify the job and expedite understanding and handling the test. But compatibility of the portions is important. As the system or procedure begins to operate, what happens first must satisfy the requirements of those portions that follow.

Modifications may occur as greater insight is obtained from the testing. Redesign of the system or procedure may be in order. However, this is usually confined to certain areas only. Generally a period is scheduled to permit operating personnel to become acquainted with the new plan of work and to gain the necessary proficiency in performing their assigned tasks. Although not planned, usually there are some adjustments to be made to satisfy personnel opinions or complaints.

Eventually, after all sources of difficulty have been removed or corrected, the proposed system or procedure is put into full operation. Now there is a policing period to insure that what is planned is being utilized properly and is functioning satisfactorily. Usually personnel problems dominate the policing period. Characteristic of the initial days during this period are efforts concerning the adaptation of the employees to their new work, adjustments to the working environment, and explanations regarding the equipment.

## IMPROVING SYSTEMS AND PROCEDURES

Much planning of systems and procedures is done to improve what is already being followed. The present way of doing the work may have come about in any of a number of ways, such as by previous planning, observing how others perform similar work, past experience, trial and error, or suggestions by others. It is being done according to some plan, but the belief persists that the work can be done in a simpler and better manner. Greater efficiency is sought and the elimination of waste is paramount. Waste exists when (1) unnecessary office work is done and (2) necessary office work is done inefficiently.

These efforts to improve existing office systems and procedures are commonly accorded unanimity of approval. Much study has been given this subject. There exist, for example, principles to follow and a precise program of action to apply. Some have termed these efforts "office work simplification," which is formally defined as common sense organized to eliminate waste of material, equipment, time, energy, and space in the performance of office work. The possibilities for improvement are limited only by the ability, imagination, and aggressiveness of the analyst. There is no secret formula. Office work simplification is not confined to systems and procedures but is employed to improve a method, a form, an arrangement, a layout, or equipment and machines. In this book, we will discuss it first in relation to office procedures (the same approach would apply in relation to office systems) and second, to office methods, or the individual's job, in the following chapter. This is the correct order; i.e., simplify the procedure, then the method, or elements making up the procedure. To reverse this order would mean that individual jobs would be improved before determining whether they are necessary.

## PRINCIPLES OF OFFICE WORK SIMPLIFICATION

Over a period, many lists of principles or guides to office work simplification have been compiled. Some are quite lengthy; but for our purposes here, six principles will be discussed.

1. *Promote "participation with know-how" by every office employee by means of training in and encouragement of the use of work simplification.* Enthusiastic employees with initiative and imagination in formulating the means and in cooperating in planning efforts to eliminate waste are of fundamental importance. A strong desire that an improved procedure work satisfactorily and an understanding of the reasons for developing procedural improvement to eliminate waste are cardinal considerations. For the most part, these are not won by having an expert simplify the work and then telling the employees how the work should be done. In contrast, these considerations are won by encouraging employee participation in planning the improvement; for in this way, employee interest, self-expression, acceptance, and cooperation are motivated and utilized.

But participation alone is insufficient. Nothing is more frustrating to the employee than to be asked to take part in an activity about which he knows little or nothing. This means the know-how must be supplied. Short, effective training programs are in order. Information and examples must be made available to the office employee. Thus, the "participation with know-how" is supplied.

The best improvements in the manner of office work performance may produce discouraging results because of employee attitudes and reactions. This has been summarized in four words, "employee resistance to change," but such a phrase appears incomplete and actually misleading.

Most office employees dislike being "pushed around," being criticized, and not being informed of developments of changes which affect them. Factors such as these cause the employee to desire the *status quo* and to view with disdain a new means of work performance suggested by outsiders. In addition, fear of the unknown effect of improvements contributes to the employee's noncooperative attitude. At the bottom of this is the employee's natural suspicion of what might happen to him as a result of the change. Typical of these fears are the questions: Will my job be eliminated? Will lower prestige and loss of esteem by fellow employees result? Will my favorite desk location be lost? Is a loss in pay involved? These fears must be eliminated in order to gain the full benefits of procedural improvements.

What is the best way to do this? The answer is primarily employee "participation with know-how" in the work simplification program. A person will usually accept what he himself proposes. Give the employee the technique and the means for improving office work; the resultant improvement will usually have acceptance and the strong will to make it work satisfactorily. Even though the improvement does not represent the zenith of what probably can be done, it is well to remember that an average improvement with employee acceptance and enthusiasm will commonly outproduce a superior improvement with employee passive resistance.

In addition, frank information pointing out the need for improvements to keep the enterprise competitive or to give greater security to the employee should be provided. It is not necessary that an office employee lose his job as a result of work simplification. A policy of retraining and transferring to other jobs can be followed. In many cases, the normal labor turnover will take care of the number of employees needed; those leaving the company are not replaced. But these facts should be explained in simple language to the employees, so that they know what is going on and where they fit into the picture. Also, the ideas of acquiring a real sense of accomplishment and of getting things done the simple way are strong appeals to many office employees. If a manager cannot win the employees' enthusiastic cooperation for the cause of eliminating office waste, it is almost a certainty that no really significant gains are going to be made. And under such a condition, the total potential of office employee productivity will never be reached.

2. *Make the series of activities productive and simple.* As a group, the series of work activities that are adopted should represent the best possible combination for achieving the finished work, taking into account the facilities and conditions under which the work must be accomplished. Simply stated, justify each activity for its essentiality, and eliminate all the unnecessary ones. As far as possible, those contributing directly to the goal, or so-called productive elements of a procedure, should be maximized; and conversely, the nonproductive elements should be reduced to an absolute minimum. Normally, this provides for the greatest productivity.

The more effective series of activities are usually simple in their makeup. Involved ways of performing work should be avoided because they invariably include waste, especially of time and of quality. The specific goals for performing most office work are relatively simple, and the process can be simple. But there is some tendency to get imbued with details or excessively concerned with the frills. These must be guarded against and eliminated for improved work efficiency.

3. *Combine work activities wherever possible to avoid recopying.* It is common to find needless copying of data over and over again in an office procedure. This practice is so prevalent that in some offices it is the accepted manner of getting information processed. There is nothing

uncommon, for example, in having the salesman write an order, his branch office recopy it, the factory recopy certain portions of the order, the billing department recopy on an invoice, and accounts receivable recopy on the proper ledger card. As previously pointed out, most of these writing activities can be combined into a single operation. Source data automation or multiple forms can be used.

4. *Reduce distances traveled to the shortest amounts feasible.* Movement of papers or of people are costly and wasteful; most of them do not represent purposive effort. Therefore, movements should be closely scrutinized; if not essential, they should be eliminated. For office procedures, distances must be traveled, but these should be minimized.

It is usually better to move the paper than the person. Sometimes, the machine can be brought to the work; or mechanical handling devices, such as conveyors, pneumatic tubes, and gravity feeds to deliver or to take away the papers, can be used. When messengers are employed, perhaps more items per trip are in order. Different arrangements of the office layout might also offer worthwhile improvements.

5. *Arrange activities to provide a smooth flow from one clerical step to another or a rhythmic pattern for an employee at a workplace.* Excessive amounts or spurts of unduly heavy work loads tend to discourage the office employee. As a result, the feeling of never "getting on top of the work" or having a sense of accomplishment plagues the employee. In contrast, the situation of carefully throttling the work in order to keep busy is equally annoying. A steady, constant flow of work which is adequate and reasonable is especially significant in determining the most satisfactory office procedure.

Once the paper work starts "through the mill," it should continue to progress until the completion of the procedure. Delays and hesitations should not be permitted. Much time and energy are dissipated by tolerating the jumping around from one batch of work to another, then returning to the initial batch. This applies whether automated or manual means are used. It takes time to adjust to the different batches of work, not to mention the lost time in stopping one and starting another, and in interrupting the smooth work flow. For each employee, a rhythmic pattern of work actions should be encouraged. Planning a certain swing to selected parts of the work helps to lessen fatigue and monotony. Plan for motions to follow curved, not straight lines.

## PLANNING FOR IMPROVING PROCEDURES

The approach used for improving procedures is similar to that followed in all planning. Referring again to Figure 16–1, last column, the steps are: (1) select the procedure to be improved; (2) get all the facts about this procedure; (3) analyze and evaluate these facts; and (4) devise the improvement. Forecasting the environment and establishing premises are omitted, for presumably these remain the same for the improved procedure. Although similar in sequence, the discussion following dramatically points out new material, mainly (1) the use of charts in depicting the facts and (2) the effectiveness of questioning, both in analyzing the facts and in devising the improvement.

## SELECT THE OFFICE PROCEDURE TO BE IMPROVED

Generally speaking, this is a trouble-giving situation, i.e., the number of work activities is too large, the time taken to do the work is excessive, costs are unduly high, or the end result seems unjustifiable. It may be a procedure that limits other office work or one in which labor requirements appear completely out of proportion.

Whatever the procedure selected, it must be defined. This helps to classify the objective and avoids the mistake of attempting to simplify office work without first gaining a clear concept of the work objective. Defining the procedure assists in its simplification because all efforts can be concentrated and directed toward this goal. Questions to help in formulating the definition include: What is the end result of this work? Is it essential? Is this end result achieved now in part or in total by another procedure? How is the information from this office procedure used? Who takes action as a result of this work completion?

## GET ALL THE FACTS ABOUT THIS PROCEDURE

The next step is to find out how the work is currently being handled. Details of the present procedure are obtained from available record sources, i.e., job descriptions, charts, lists, outlines, and sample forms. Supplemental information can be obtained from talks with members of management. This is followed by an inspection of the actual procedure in action, so that the type of work and the equipment used can be observed.

All the facts are needed to perform a competent analysis. To aid in this work and to gain a clear comprehension of them, graphic representations or charts have been developed. Charts serve the following purposes: (1) assist in securing, organizing, and visualizing the facts, (2) aid in analyzing and evaluating these facts, (3) help formulate an improved procedure, and (4) assist in convincing others of the value of the improved procedure. Unless the chart serves one or more of these purposes, it should not be drawn.

There are many different types of charts that can be used. Each chart has a particular purpose and value, and it is neither necessary nor practical to use every type of chart in a particular study. Frequently, more than one chart is used, and the right combination of several charts usually reveals information and clues for work simplification. The major charts for procedure improvements will be discussed in detail later in this chapter.

## ANALYZE AND EVALUATE THESE FACTS

Using the factual information about the entire procedure as a guide, the next step is to analyze and evaluate these facts. This phase might be described as one of challenging each detail of the work. For this purpose, questions pertaining to Why, What, Where, When, Who, and How are extremely helpful. The facts about the selected procedure show what is done, where, when, by whom, and how. To this, the big Why must be added. In other words, the questioning now is: What is being done and Why? Where should it be done and Why? When should it be done and Why? Who should do it and Why? How should it be done and Why? The use of these questions has been referred to as a questioning attitude. The answers help to relate essentials, reveal unnecessary work, and provide clues for improving the procedure.

Every activity of the procedure is subjected to this questioning, and the answers are evaluated in terms of the office work simplification principles discussed above. For example, the answers to the double question: "Where should it be done and why?" should comply with the principle: "Reduce distances traveled to the shortest amounts feasible."

Additional questions of a more specific nature can also be asked. The exact content will depend upon the individual case and to a very great extent upon the initiative and imagination of the questioner. Examples of specific questions include the following:[2]

1. Purpose of operation:
   a) What is the intended use of the form?
   b) Is the form used as intended?
   c) What purpose is served by the report?
   d) Could the information given on the form or the report be obtained from another source?
   e) Do numbers, ratios, or variations best answer and serve the needs of the procedure?
   f) Is the cost of preparing the form or report justified by the results it accomplishes?
2. Design:
   a) Is the design of the form such that all portions are used?

---

[2] Adapted from H. B. Maynard and G. J. Stegemerten, *Guide to Methods Improvement* (New York: McGraw-Hill Book Co., Inc., 1944), pp. 25, 28, 31, 35, 39, 40, 45, and 46.

*b*) Is the size of the form best suited to its use?

*c*) Would a change in color of the form facilitate its use?

*d*) Is the information by which the form will be filed located in the most convenient place from a filing standpoint?

*e*) Can a special type of form, such as Activisible, Kardex, or Key-sort, be used to advantage?

*f*) Can large forms be designed so that, when folded, they will fit in standard files?

3. Process analysis:

*a*) Is the operation duplicated at any point in the procedure?

*b*) Should the form be filed permanently or temporarily, or be destroyed?

*c*) Can two or more records be produced at one writing by combining forms?

*d*) Can the copying of information be eliminated by using original records?

*e*) Is information compiled in the manner best suited for subsequent sorting, filing, or use?

*f*) Should permanent records be made on 35-mm. film to conserve filing space?

4. Inspection:

*a*) Is the form or work legible?

*b*) Is the form or report easy to interpret?

*c*) How is work checked for errors?

*d*) Is it important that all parts of the work be letter-perfect?

*e*) Would the use of mechanical devices improve the accuracy of the work to a desirable extent?

5. Material:

*a*) Is the paper stock used for the form the best for its purpose?

*b*) Is the size of the form most economical from a material standpoint?

*c*) How can waste of forms and office supplies be reduced?

*d*) Are office materials analyzed for suitability and ordered in most economical quantities?

6. Material handling:

*a*) Can the flow of a form through the procedure be expedited by improved office layout?

*b*) Can the amount of time the form is delayed while awaiting action be reduced?

*c*) Is messenger service adequate?

*d*) Can pneumatic tubes or other forms-conveying systems be used to advantage?

*e*) Should special arrangements be made for keeping forms clean during handling in the shop?

## DEVISE THE IMPROVEMENT

Improvement is obtained by seeking to eliminate, combine, change, or simplify the steps of the procedure. Here again the questioning approach is used, along with the principles of work simplification. Figure 16–6 shows the relationships between the key questions asked, the major principles of work simplification utilized, and the resultant actions. For example, answers to the question "What is being done and Why?" following the principles of "promote participation with know-how" and "make activities productive and simple," point out many unnecessary activities that can be eliminated. If so, eliminate them, for this is the

| Key Questions | Major Principles* | Resultant Action | |
|---|---|---|---|
| What and Why? | 1. Promote "participation with know-how." <br> 2. Make activities productive and simple. | Eliminate | |
| Where and Why? <br> When and Why? <br> Who and Why? | 1. Promote "participation with know-how." <br> 3. Combine work activities—avoid recopying. <br> 4. Reduce distances traveled. <br> 5. Provide a smooth flow from one step to another. | Combine <br> or <br> change | the Place <br> the Time <br> the Person |
| How and Why? | 1. Promote "participation with know-how." <br> 2. Make activities productive and simple. <br> 6. Provide pleasant employee surroundings. | Simplify | |

\* Refer to pages 363–65.

FIG. 16–6. Key questions, major principles, and resultant actions used in devising the improvement of an office procedure.

zenith of work simplification. Questions of Where and Why, When and Why, and Who and Why will suggest combining or changing procedural elements as to place, time, and person, respectively. An improved procedure will result. The question "How and Why?" emphasizes simplifying the activity.

The sequence of the questioning and subsequent improvement action is logical and practical. If the activity can be eliminated, there is no need to study it further for possible combination or change. Likewise, the "Who and Why" question precedes the "How and Why" question because the former might lead to improved labor utilization, and this should be determined before the manner of doing the work is improved.

## PROCESS CHART

We will now discuss in detail the major charts used in procedure improvement. The first is the process chart, which shows the successive detailed steps in a process. It is probably one of the most helpful tools in work simplification. The steps are indicated by brief statements and symbols arranged vertically in chronological order, with the first step at the top of the sheet. There are four commonly used symbols: (1) a large circle, ◯, for an operation such as writing, posting, sorting, and filing; it is used whenever anything is being changed or created or added to; (2) a small circle, ○, for transportation such as movement of paper from place to place or the walking of an individual; (3) an inverted triangle, ▽, for storage or delay, such as an office form remaining in place awaiting further action; and (4) a square, ☐, for inspection, which includes checking or verifying, but not changing, the paper. To illustrate, signing a letter constitutes an operation and would be represented by a large circle. Sending the letter to another office unit is transportation and is shown by a small circle. Filing the letter is represented by a storage triangle. Checking the letter for errors constitutes inspection and is represented by a square.

OPERATION – ORIGIN OF RECORD

OPERATION – ADDING TO RECORD

TRAVEL OR MOVE

DELAY – AVOIDABLE

FILE

COPY DISCARDED OR DESTROYED

INSPECTION

FIG. 16–7.   Symbols for process charts preferred by some analysts.

Some recommend the use of symbols modified from those given above.[3] One such set is shown by Figure 16–7. It can be observed that the "operation" has been refined into two types: (1) those that represent origin of the record and (2) those adding information to the record. Likewise, an arrow, symbolic of travel, and a large *D*, standing for avoidable delay, are utilized. A separate symbol for "copy discarded" is also used. Many analysts have found that color is helpful in charting work. For example, the "do" operations, constituting direct processing work and adding value to the product, are distinguished by the use of a special color. In contrast, for the "do" operations used but not adding value, no special color is used. Included in such "do" operations are those for "make ready" and "put away," or those done for preparatory or cleaning-up purposes.

The intended purpose of the process chart and the symbols is to give a clear picture of the office procedure and assist in analyzing and improving

---

[3] Refer again to Figure 9–4 giving the different symbols used with program flow charts when the data processing is by computer.

it. Any reasonable set of symbols can be used; the best is the set that assists the analyst most in his determination to eliminate paper work waste. In addition, it is customary to include on a process chart the time required, the distance covered if movement is involved, and a summary by type of action. This chart can either be drawn for an entire procedure covering many departments, or it may be confined to a part of a procedure.

Figure 16–8 illustrates a process chart. It shows the process of stopping an incorrect charge credit in a large department store. It is drawn for the credit form papers. This work is brought about by the following situation.

An article of merchandise is purchased by a customer, Mrs. John T. Smith, with a charge account. The merchandise is returned, but the clerk incorrectly writes Mrs. John F. Smith on the credit memorandum. Later, the customer telephones and informs the adjusting department of the store that the name is not Mrs. John F. Smith, but Mrs. John T. Smith. Meanwhile, the credit memorandum is in process in either the sales auditing department or the accounts receivable department, both located several floors away from the adjusting department. Hence, a "stop notice" is prepared and a duplicate copy sent to sales auditing or accounts receivable, telling them not to bill the credit memorandum made out to John F. Smith. This stop notice, along with the credit memorandum to John F. Smith, is returned to the adjuster who handled the telephone call.

The placing of the credit memorandum and stop notice on the desk constitutes step No. 1 of the chart illustrated in Figure 16–8. Therefore, on line No. 1, this action is briefly described in the column to the left. This action is an operation, in that something happens to the papers; hence, it is represented by a large-circle symbol and is indicated on the chart by filling in the large circle under "operation" on line No. 1. Appropriate notes are made in the column to the right.

Next, the forms are picked up. Hence, on line No. 2, this action is expressed and represented by a large circle. In a similar manner, the entire process is described and charted. The totals of each action and of the distances traveled are then determined and recorded in the summary table at the top of the sheet. In this illustration, the figures are:

> Operations........................17
> Transportations................... 7
> Storage........................... 5
> Distance traveled.................92 feet

A study of the chart shows that this procedure can be simplified. To do this, the work simplification principles and the questioning attitude, as already discussed, were applied. For example, when step No. 3—placing

PAGE............

## MARSHALL FIELD & COMPANY
### FLOW PROCESS CHART

JOB _Stopping an incorrect charge credit_

SUBJECT CHARTED _Credit form_

CHARTED BY _Ethel Marable_

DATE _November 19—_

DEPT _Customer's Service_ SEC _Adjusting_

| SUMMARY | | | |
|---|---|---|---|
| METHOD | PRES. | PROPD. | SAVG. |
| NO. OF OPERATIONS | 17 | | |
| NO. OF TRANSPORTATIONS | 7 | | |
| NO. OF STORAGES | 5 | | |
| NO. OF INSPECTIONS | | | |
| MAN HOURS OR MINUTES | | | |
| DISTANCE TRAVELED | 92½. | | |

| | DETAILS (PRESENT / PROPOSED) METHOD | OPER. | TRANS. | STORAGE | INSPECT. | DIST. IN FEET | TIME IN MINUTES | WHAT? | WHERE? | WHEN? | WHO? | HOW? | NOTES |
|---|---|---|---|---|---|---|---|---|---|---|---|---|---|
| 1 | Placed on desk | | | | | | | | | | | | Credit and duplicate stop attached—sent from Sales auditing or accounts receivable |
| 2 | Picked up | | | | | | | | | | | | |
| 3 | Placed in drawer | | | | | 2 | | | | | | | |
| 4 | Waits | | | | | | | | | | | | Time indefinite—may have other work of priority nature |
| 5 | Taken out of drawer | | | | | 2 | | | | | | | |
| 6 | Placed on desk | | | | | | | | | | | | |
| 7 | Waits | | | | | | | | | | | | makes out request for claim which acts as "out of file" notice |
| 8 | Attached to request | | | | | | | | | | | | |
| 9 | Carried to central files | | | | | 15 | | | | | | | |
| 10 | Placed in basket | | | | | | | | | | | | |
| 11 | Waits | | | | | | | | | | | | for central file clerk |
| 12 | Picked up | | | | | | | | | | | | |
| 13 | Carried to file cabinet | | | | | 25 | | | | | | | |
| 14 | Waits | | | | | | | | | | | | Looking for claim under correct name |
| 15 | Attached to claim | | | | | | | | | | | | |
| 16 | Carried to out basket | | | | | 25 | | | | | | | |
| 17 | Placed in basket | | | | | | | | | | | | |
| 18 | Waits | | | | | | | | | | | | for pick up |
| 19 | Picked up | | | | | | | | | | | | |
| 20 | Carried to desk | | | | | 15 | | | | | | | |
| 21 | Placed on desk | | | | | | | | | | | | |
| 22 | Stop taken from claim | | | | | | | | | | | | Original stop now placed on claim |
| 23 | Credit voided | | | | | | | | | | | | write "void", claim number and initials |
| 24 | Picked up | | | | | | | | | | | | |
| 25 | Placed in house envelope | | | | | | | | | | | | |
| 26 | Picked up | | | | | | | | | | | | |
| 27 | Carried to house mailbox | | | | | 8 | | | | | | | |
| 28 | Placed in house mailbox | | | | | | | | | | | | |
| 29 | Wait for pickup | | | | | | | | | | | | |

24-01-01 Form 187

FIG. 16–8. A fill-in type of process chart covering the work of stopping an incorrect charge credit.

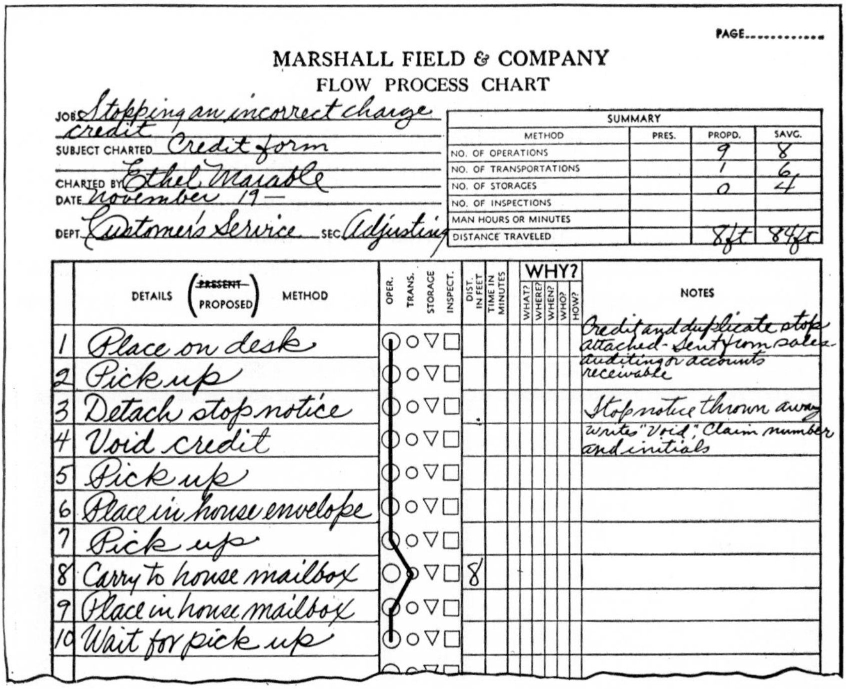

Courtesy: Marshall Field & Co., Chicago

FIG. 16–9. An improved procedure over that shown in Fig. 16–8.

paper in drawer—is subjected to the question "What is done and Why?" it is found to be unproductive and hence can be eliminated. In similar manner, every operation, transportation, storage, and inspection not proved necessary is eliminated; and actions found necessary are combined wherever feasible, or changed to provide better accomplishment of the work. Finally, each necessary step is simplified as much as possible.

Figure 16–9 shows an improved procedure over the one shown in Figure 16–8. In the light of what has been written, it is suggested that a careful comparison of these two charts be made in order to gain an insight as to how a procedure can be improved. Under the new procedure, credits are voided with a claim number on them and sent to sales auditing or accounts receivable. The stop notice can be discarded, since its duplicate is already on the claim. The elimination of requests to pull claims out of the central file accounts for getting rid of steps No. 7 through No. 21 of the original procedure. Also, steps No. 3 through No. 6 have been eliminated; they were simply delaying actions brought about by the makeup of the original procedure. The improved procedure requires eight less operations, six less transportations, four less storages, and less than 10 percent of the former distance traveled.

## MOVEMENT DIAGRAM

A movement diagram portrays motion through space. It is drawn on a scaled layout of the office floor plan so that the movement can be measured and viewed in proper relationship with the physical factors. These charts are helpful in spotting backtracking, visualizing the physical motion involved, and locating congestion and bottlenecks.

Movement diagrams are of two types: those showing paper movement and those showing employee movement. The entire chart should be of one

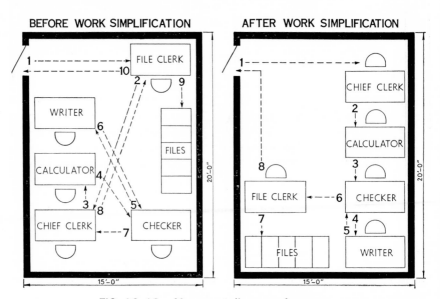

FIG. 16–10.    Movement diagrams for paper.

type or the other. Attempting to follow first one and then the other on the same chart leads to confusion. Figure 16–10 illustrates movement diagrams for paper, showing the movements before and after work simplification. This improvement was gained by changing the office layout.

In many instances, however, the paper is not moved by simply handing it to the person at the adjacent desk or by messenger service; it is carried by the person last working on it to the next successive station. This is part of the procedure. It is therefore apparent that an analysis of employee movement is equally as important as an analysis of paper movement. Charts showing employee movement are especially helpful where the work is nonrepetitive and where the employees operate over a large area. The employee movement chart is similar in appearance to the paper movement chart.

## PROCEDURE FLOW CHART

This type of chart is very effective where multiple-copy forms are used. It depicts graphically the distribution and subsequent steps for each form from physical inception to permanent storage or destruction. Generally, this type of chart is not difficult to construct.

Figure 16–11 shows a procedure flow chart of work performed for handling uniform express receipt-collect shipments. Four separate writings are required for each package. These include separate typings for each of two labels, a packing slip and duplicate, and the copies of the uniform express receipt-collect. As indicated in the chart, the labels are put on the package. One copy of the packing slip is sent to the billing department for filing, the other copy placed in the package. Other operations can be determined from the chart.

A procedure to accomplish the same objective, but with much waste eliminated, is shown in Figure 16–12. As illustrated, a seven-part form is written at one time from the sales order. The writing is checked, and then the copies are sent to the shipping department, where they are distributed and used as indicated on the chart. The total number of operations has been reduced from 30 to 17, a saving of nearly 45 percent. Waste elimination, achieved by planning, has resulted in making activities productive, combining operations, eliminating others, and increasing the accuracy.

## QUESTIONS

1. Relate some of the more common ways to organize data and facts collected for system designing.
2. Do systems and procedures help or hinder the importance of managerial planning? Justify your answer.
3. Identify each of the following by a simple statement:
   *a*) A premise of a system.
   *b*) Questioning attitude.
   *c*) "Bench-mark problem."
   *d*) A "make ready" operation.
4. Name and discuss four common sources of data and information that are used in system designing.
5. Discuss the subject of designing office procedures.
6. What are some important considerations to keep in mind while interviewing to obtain information for use in systems designing? Elaborate on one consideration that you give.
7. Is there a uniform code for symbols used in process charting? Should there be? Why?

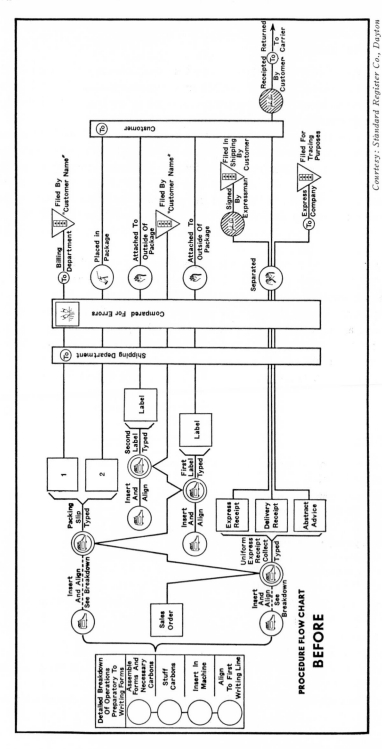

FIG. 16–11.   A procedure flow chart before work simplification.

*Courtesy: Standard Register Co., Dayton*

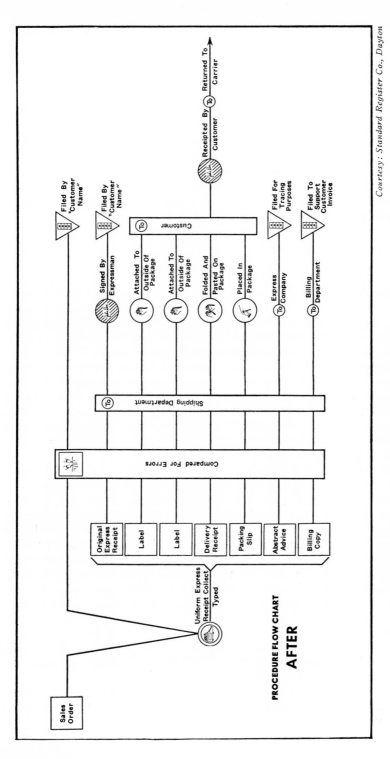

FIG. 16–12. The improved procedure over that shown in Figure 16–11, after work simplification.

*Courtesy: Standard Register Co., Dayton*

8. Discuss some important considerations to be recognized in implementing a system or procedure.

9. Explain Figure 16–6 in your own words.

10. List the six principles of office work simplification, and briefly discuss the one you feel is most important.

11. What are the four major purposes of charts as used in work simplification for office procedures?

12. Do you agree with the following statement: "Whenever a change is made in an office procedure, certain employees will complain, others will not care, and still others will enthusiastically welcome it. It is usually impossible to please all employees all the time. The most expeditious course is to make all the changes for improvement in a procedure at one time and thus gain the benefits as quickly as possible."

## CASE PROBLEMS

### Case 16–1.  Booth Company

About 60 percent of the Booth Company's sales are received from mail orders. Party supplies such as table decorations, inexpensive prizes, flags, novelties, and hobby items including model trains, puzzles, do-it-yourself paintings and ceramic art works are feature items. Because of the tremendous variety offered, it is not always possible to fill a mail order immediately upon its receipt. In these cases, a letter is written stating the reason for nondelivery. A sales correspondent dictates the letters and normally two typists are required to handle the typing of the letters. A copy of the letter is stapled to the customer's order and filed in the "pending sales" file by product type. Before mailing, the correspondent proofs each letter, corrects minor errors, and signs the letter. If mistakes are too serious, the letter is returned to the typist for retyping. Almost all the letters, however, are of satisfactory quality in the first typing.

It is the opinion of William Weston, the office manager, that valuable time is lost in notifying customers of delay in shipping their orders. This results in cancellations, complaints by customers, and poor business relations. He asked his assistant, Roy Samwell, to look into the situation and see what can be done. Accordingly, Mr. Samwell talked with the correspondent and typists, reviewed available company records, and made several investigative studies. From all this, he found that (1) each typist completes about 45 letters a day, but about 10 percent of these are for purposes other than nonshipment of orders; (2) the typists do not like their jobs because the letters are too repetitive and the work is not challenging; (3) salary of the correspondent is $92.50 a week, of one typist $67.50 a week, of the second typist $62.50 a week; (4) most frequent reasons for nondelivery of merchandise given in letters can be classified as (a) obsolete item—no longer available, (b) merchandise on order, will ship in x days; (c) partial shipment being made, remainder will follow shortly; (d) payment not included with order; and (e) insufficient payment sent with order.

With this information from devoting a day to the assignment, Roy Samwell believed he had an acceptable improvement to offer. He proceeded to write his recommendations to Mr. Weston.

Problems:

1. What alternatives of recommendations are available to Mr. Samwell?
2. What action do you recommend to Mr. Weston? Substantiate your views.
3. Outline the chief advantages of your recommended action.

## Case 16–2.  Jefferson Dairy Company

The current procedure for handling collections is as follows: A file card is made out for each customer, showing name, address, monthly due date, and the amounts of credit, debit, and balance. These cards are filed alphabetically according to the customer's surname.

Each collection day, which is monthly, the office clerk goes through the file and makes out a list stipulating the name, address, and amount of accounts due. The collection sheets are given the drivers, who do the collecting. Upon payment, the customer is given a receipt, and the amount paid is written by the driver opposite the proper name on the collection list. From these sheets, the office clerk posts the collection date and amount on the proper file cards.

Office manager Russel Sayer feels that the present procedure requires too much office work and does not permit sufficient flexibility, for example, when only partial payments or advance payments are made. He believes the present procedure can be improved. Mr. Sayer realizes that the common practice is for a dairy to sell the products to the driver, who collects on his own from his customers. However, top managers of Jefferson Dairy Company feel that the present credit arrangement to customers by the dairy gives better control and relieves the driver of much paper work. Market studies indicate that consumers like Jefferson Dairy's way of handling collections. Mr. Sayer states that the company has approximately 12,000 accounts, which is a large number, and that the average amount for each account is $7.18 monthly. Few owe for more than the amount of a month's bill. He believes that any proposed change must of necessity require little or no new office equipment.

Problems:

1. Do you agree with Mr. Sayer, the office manager? Why?
2. Indicate the procedure you recommend for Jefferson Dairy Company. Substantiate your recommendation.

## Case 16–3.  Tostomero Music Publishers

In an effort to reduce waste and cut costs, Mr. Benito Grassi, the president, decided to institute a paper work simplification program in this company. An expert in work simplification was hired for a period of six months. It was believed that within this time the program could be well established, and further use of the expert's services would be unnecessary. During the first day at work, the expert observed the entire office and finally selected the job of opening mail and sorting the contents as the first job for analysis and simplification. The job was improved considerably, and the new method was demonstrated by the expert to the supervisor of the mail department, who agreed that the new method was a big improvement. Together, they went to one of the four employees performing this work and showed her the new method. She was requested to perform the job in the new manner. Within the next day or so, all four employees on this work had been instructed in the new method and were using it.

For the following two weeks, production records kept by the supervisor of the mail department showed that the productivity of the four employees increased approximately 30 percent. It was found that the mail work for the day was nearly finished by midafternoon. Three of the girls were sent to the shipping department, where they were given work of verifying the sheet music gathered for an order against the items called for on that order.

The expert, quite pleased with the achievements to date, reviewed other jobs for analysis. He wrote a short note to Mr. Grassi informing him of the success of the program. The following day, he received a telephone request from the mail department supervisor to come to that department at once. The expert complied, and the supervisor related that the four girls had come to him in a group asking for more money. He told them the plan was to give them an increase but they had beat him to it. Beginning a week from next Monday, their pay would be raised from $60 to $70 a week. The supervisor inquired of the expert if this was correct. The expert assured him that was the amount the company had agreed upon.

"Did the girls react favorably to the pay increase?" asked the expert.

"They seemed to be satisfied. They didn't say much of anything."

Over the next six weeks, the production of the four girls decreased until it was practically the same as it had been before the simplified method was installed. The decline was fairly uniform for each of the four employees. The expert checked the operators several times and observed that the employees were still using the new method. He spoke to them individually, but none had any complaints, nor did any have an explanation for the current level of production.

## Problems:

1. Discuss the important ramifications of this problem.
2. Evaluate the work of the expert. Explain.
3. What action do you now recommend for the company? Why?

CHAPTER  17

# PLANNING
# OFFICE METHODS

Method facilitates every kind of business, and
by making it easy, makes it agreeable, and
also successful.
—*Charles Simmons*

AFTER we are sure that the procedure is the best possible, we seek to make
each element making up that procedure as effective as we can. This is the
purpose of planning office methods and it is basic in office management.
All physical work is accomplished by the execution of motions. For
example, task performance in the office usually involve movements by the
eyes, or the hand and arm, or the fingers and wrist.

## OFFICE METHOD STUDY

Planning efforts concentrated on a method, or the manner of work
performance of an employee performing a given type of work, is
commonly referred to as "motion study." In fact, historically the initial
attention for planning work performance was directed toward individual
tasks. Frank B. and Lillian M. Gilbreth, pioneers in this area of
management, define motion study as follows: "Motion study consists of
dividing work into the most fundamental elements possible; studying
these elements separately and in relation to one another; and from these
studied elements, when timed, building methods of least waste."[1] In other
words, it is the effort of studying an employee's motions with the view to
determine the best way of doing the task.

The superior method contains only motions to fulfill the task and these
are arranged to accomplish the work with a minimum of time and effort.

---

[1] Frank B. and Lillian M. Gilbreth, *Applied Motion Study* (New York: Macmillan
Co., 1919), p. 43.

This results in high output per employee and in a reduction of fatigue and waste. The gains possible from adopting the best methods are tremendous, for, as the Gilbreths wrote:

> The greatest waste in the world comes from needless, ill-directed, and ineffective motions. These motions are unnecessary and preventable. Their existence in the past was excusable, because there was no knowledge of how to dispense with them. That excuse no longer obtains. The methods and devices of waste elimination are known and are being constantly used. But the knowledge of how to make these great world-wide economies is being disseminated at an astonishingly slow pace.[2]

Motion study is not speedup. Motion study does not imply speeding up the movements of the employee; rather, it implies an increase in the rate of work production. There is a significant difference between these two concepts, and this difference should be clearly understood. Speeding up the employee means to hurry *all* the steps, *both the necessary and the unnecessary ones.* In contrast, increasing the rate of production through motion study means *performing only the necessary steps in a normal manner.*

### APPROACH TO PLANNING OFFICE METHODS

Planning of office methods is conducted by following the same fundamental approach already discussed in the preceding chapter. Facts are obtained, charts are used to visualize the work, every detail of the task is questioned to uncover clues for improvement, employee participation is encouraged, and greater productivity and accuracy are sought. While it follows this same general pattern, we shall concentrate in this chapter on pointing out considerations and information especially helpful in the planning of office methods. This will be material which has not yet been presented in this book. To facilitate the discussion we will stress planning efforts undertaken to improve existent methods.

### WHICH METHOD TO IMPROVE?

Repetitive tasks lend themselves most readily to planning, since they occur in volume and extend over a period of time. Furthermore, they offer large savings possibilities. The savings on each task performance might be small, but doing the task over and over again results in cumulative savings of a sizable amount. In the experience of one company, the annual savings amount to $340 per office task improved. This may appear relatively small; but on the average, over 150 such improvements are developed each year, making a yearly savings of over $50,000—a truly worthwhile goal.

Selecting repetitive tasks for improvement does not mean that special

---

[2] *Ibid.,* p. 57.

tasks do not warrant study. *Any task can be improved with sufficient planning effort.* In many instances, worthwhile savings on regular tasks have been made from analysis of special tasks. Actually, the job selected and the extent and thoroughness of the study depend upon a number of things, such as the continuity of the work, the amount of processing required, the total cost or number of people engaged in the work, the value connected with the paper handled, and the interest of the operative employee, supervisor, or analyst.

## GETTING ALL THE FACTS

As in the case of systems or procedures planning, it is necessary to have all the facts about the method in order to plan effectively. Information is obtained from a number of sources. Here again, charts are used to reveal better the detailed makeup of the method. Each of these method charts pertains to the individual employee performing a specific task. These charts differ in content and makeup, but not in purpose, from the charts used for procedure improvement. A detailed discussion of these charts, along with examples, is included at the end of this chapter.

## THERBLIGS

To assist in getting the facts, the Gilbreths developed the idea that all motions are made up of elements called "therbligs" (coined from the spelling of the name Gilbreth backwards, except for the *th*).[3] Most manual work consists of a relatively few basic motions repeated again and again. Gilbreth designated 17 therbligs; other motion analysts have arrived at a slightly different number. Figure 17–1 shows 16 commonly used fundamental motions as classified by Professor Ralph M. Barnes.

The use of therbligs is helpful in detailed studies and refinements. However, motion analysts frequently do not use the therbligs as such, but they do employ them as fundamental to their thinking. For example, it is generally recognized that economy in motion is realized when both the right and the left hands start their therbligs at the same time. The motion economist will strive to attain this condition, but he might not make a therblig analysis.

## USING THE QUESTIONING APPROACH

The questioning approach is advantageous in seeking simplification of office methods. It is actually an attitude and can be developed by anyone

---

[3] There is a difference of opinion as to the correct definition of a therblig. Some writers call it an elementary motion, while others feel that it is fundamental but of a compounded, not an elemental, nature and concerns work accomplishment.

| Name of Fundamental Motion | Symbol | Description |
|---|---|---|
| Select | St | Select refers to the choice of one object from among several. |
| Grasp | G | Grasp refers to taking hold of an object. |
| Transport loaded | TL | Transport loaded refers to moving an object from one place to another. |
| Position | P | Position consists of turning or locating an object in such a way that it will be properly oriented to fit into the location for which it is intended. |
| Assemble | A | Assemble consists of placing one object into or on another object with which it becomes an integral part. |
| Use | U | Use always consists of manipulating a tool, device, or piece of apparatus for the purpose for which it was intended. |
| Disassemble | DA | Disassemble consists of separating one object from another object of which it is an integral part. |
| Inspect | I | Inspect consists of testing a piece to determine whether or not it complies with standard size, shape, color, or other qualities previously determined. |
| Pre-position | PP | Pre-position refers to positioning an object in a predetermined place in such a way that it may be grasped in the position in which it is to be held when it is needed. |
| Release load | RL | Release load refers to that part of the cycle during which the hand is letting go of the object grasped, allowing it to slip out of the hand. |
| Transport empty | TE | Transport empty consists of moving the empty hand in reaching for an object. |
| Rest for overcoming fatigue | R | Rest for overcoming fatigue is a fatigue or delay allowance provided to permit the worker to recover from the fatigue incurred by his work. |
| Unavoidable delay | UD | Unavoidable delay refers to a delay beyond the control of the operator. |
| Avoidable delay | AD | Avoidable delay refers to any delay of the operator for which he is responsible and over which he has control. |
| Plan | Pn | Plan refers to a mental reaction which precedes the physical movement, that is, deciding how to proceed with the work. |
| Hold | H | Hold denotes the retention of the object after it has been grasped, no movement of the object taking place. |

Source: Ralph M. Barnes, "Work Methods Manual" (New York: John Wiley & Sons, Inc., 1944), p. 68

FIG. 17–1. Names, symbols, and descriptions of commonly used fundamental motions. The motion "select" is sometimes segregated into three separate motions: "search," "find," and "select."

who approaches the job with the firm belief that the manner of doing the work can be improved. Each detail of the work manner is questioned for its essentiality, possible change, combination with other motions, or simplification. The questions "What and Why?" "Where and Why?" and so forth, are utilized, as discussed in the previous chapter.

Additional questions of a method-improving nature and with purposeful intent should be developed and used. They should lead to betterment, not just a conglomeration of queries. Generally speaking, good questions are required in order to get good answers. The following list includes a number of selected questions which are worded to provide practicality and to furnish answers that are useful in bringing out possibilities for improvement.[4]

1. Questions regarding setup or workplace layout:
   *a*) Is the recipient of the form provided with a proper place to keep it?
   *b*) Are pens, pencils, erasers, and forms properly pre-positioned?
   *c*) Are desk tops and drawers kept in an orderly condition so that time spent looking for lost articles is reduced to a minimum?
   *d*) Is a desk necessary, or could the work be done as well on a flat-top table?
   *e*) Should a specially designed table be provided to facilitate the use of office machines?
2. Questions regarding tools and equipment:
   *a*) Can gathering or sorting aids be used?
   *b*) Should a machine replace hand methods?
   *c*) Are office machines properly maintained by qualified maintenance men?
   *d*) Can any foot-operated devices, such as a foot-operated stapler, be used?
   *e*) Is the type of typewriter suitable for the use to which it is put?
3. Questions regarding working conditions:
   *a*) Are unnecessary noises and disturbances eliminated?
   *b*) Is privacy assured for telephone conversations of a confidential nature?
   *c*) What precautions are taken to prevent the spread of colds and other infectious diseases throughout the office?
   *d*) Are suitable facilities provided for personal belongings?
   *e*) Could certain clerical operations, such as payroll work, be handled to better advantage on a three-shift basis?

## DEVELOPING THE IMPROVED METHOD

This can be viewed as consisting basically of two closely interrelated functions: (1) improving the employee's motions and (2) providing a suitable workplace area. In the former, the step-by-step examination to eliminate, combine, change, or simplify the motions is followed. To assist in these efforts, the questioning attitude and the principles of work

---

[4] Adapted from H. B. Maynard and G. J. Stegemerten, *Guide to Methods Improvement* (New York: McGraw-Hill Book Co., Inc., 1944), pp. 51, 56, 60–61.

simplification, already shown in Figure 16–6 are employed. In addition, certain basic guides generally helpful in improving office methods can be utilized. These are shown in Figure 17–2.

---

1. Do the work by machine, not manually, if possible. Develop the best motion for the operator with the machine being utilized.

2. Use both hands for doing work, avoiding the use of either hand as a holding device. Both hands should begin and complete their motions at the same time, moving simultaneously in opposite and symmetrical directions.

3. Analyze and eliminate, if possible, all hesitations and searches in the method to be followed.

4. Employ a minimum of motions to complete the task. Use hand motions only or, if necessary, hands and eye motions only. Arm, leg, and body motions should be infrequently required.

5. Count therbligs required by the method; the minimum number usually identifies the best method.

6. Build an agreeable sequence of motions, so that a desirable rhythm is followed in performing the task.

7. Include continuous, curved motions in preference to motions having sharp changes in direction, because the former are both less demanding and less tiring.

8. Strive to have high-priced office help do high-priced office work only. Minimize, for example, the private secretary doing strictly typist work.

9. Avoid writing the same information twice.

10. Have source document and end result in the same format, if possible.

11. Use precomputed tables or graphic indicators.

12. Make only the number of copies that are needed and used.

---

FIG. 17–2. Guides for improving office methods.

## PROVIDING A SUITABLE WORKPLACE

The best method is not possible unless the proper workplace is provided. In this connection, there are usually many possibilities for improvement. Among the most helpful are the following:

1. *Place only what is needed for the task on the desk or table top.* Do not clutter up the work area with such things as paper clips, pads, miscellaneous folders, magazines, and books which are not required in performing the task. Supplies and tools not needed should not be in the employee's way. When they are allowed to remain, inefficient motions as well as unsightly work areas are evident.

2. *Keep the employee's supplies and tools not needed for the particular task in desk drawers or in cabinets.* Supplies and tools should be stored neatly and systematically; the arrangement used depends upon the individual circumstances. Materials placed in cabinets should be indexed according to some simple plan that facilitates finding.

3. *Pre-position papers, cards, and working tools so that they are handy and ready for use as required.* This includes such things as supplying devices to hold penciled notes while typing; locating frequently used supplies such as paper clips, stapler, and rubber stamps on a rotor where easy access is possible; and putting reference materials, including books, catalogs, and lists, on convenient racks within easy reach or vision of the operator.

The arrangement of unitizing can also be followed. Under this plan, each operating unit is considered a separate entity and is supplied individually with all the tools and supplies necessary for its work. The required papers, books, supplies, and the like are located on a wall rack or in a floor cabinet near the operator's desk. For the most part, this arrangement brings best results whan a large portion of the office consists of widely dispersed and fairly independent units, although it is not limited to this particular type of setup.

4. *Utilize the normal and the maximum working areas.* The *normal* working area for the right hand on a desk top, for example, is the area determined by swinging the extended right hand and forearm only across the desk. The pivoting is at the elbow, with the upper arm being relaxed at the side of the body. The arm tends to swing out a little at the outer end of the arc. In a similar manner, the normal working area for the left hand is determined. These two normal areas overlap in front of the employee, and this overlapping area represents the location in which work requiring both hands can be performed most readily.

The *maximum* working areas are the areas determined by swinging the extended hand and entire arm, pivoting at the shoulder. Figure 17–3 shows

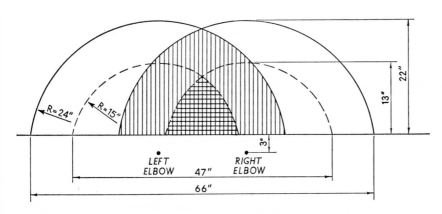

⊞ DENOTES NORMAL WORKING AREA COMMON TO BOTH HANDS

▥ DENOTES MAXIMUM WORKING AREA COMMON TO BOTH HANDS

FIG. 17–3.   Illustration of normal and of maximum working areas.

graphically the normal and maximum working areas with dimensions for an average employee.

Paper being worked on should be located within the arcs of the normal working areas common to both hands. Supplies should also be conveniently located, i.e., within the normal and never outside the maximum working areas. It should be noted that the periphery of this area is arc-shaped and not rectangular. The arrangement of the supplies and tools should also follow a pattern determined by motion principles.[5]

5. *Provide employees with pleasant physical surroundings and comfortable, correct workplaces.* Almost every day, additional evidence is found demonstrating that pleasant physical working conditions add materially to employees' satisfaction and productivity. Waste is decreased. Adequate light, for example, is an important factor in keeping errors in office work at a minimum.

An employee should be comfortable. This means that his chair, desk, table, or machine should be of such dimensions that the work can be accomplished with ease, that is, without excessive physical exertion or strain. When possible, it is usually desirable to have the employee sit part of the time and stand part of the time. Some change is apparently necessary for maximum comfort.

The height of the workplace should be such that comfortable support is given the underside of the forearm at a point slightly below the elbows. In cases where the hands are self-supported and a desk or table is used, the workplace should be of such height that the hands work at a level slightly higher than that of the elbows. In typing, for example, the forearms should be parallel to the slope of the keyboard, with the wrists slightly lower than the knuckles. The typist should sit in a position that will cause her upper arms to slope slightly forward. Sitting erect in the chair directly in front of the machine with feet flat on the floor makes it possible to type comfortably and easily.

## APPLICATION OF THE IMPROVED METHOD

After an improved method has been worked out, it is a relatively simple matter to apply it, provided the employee has participated in the planning and has a thorough understanding of why and how the new method is to be used. To accomplish method changes, there is no adequate substitute for gaining and maintaining wholesome understanding between the management and nonmanagement members. The purpose of methods improvement should be clearly set forth, and the reasons for its importance in the enterprise made crystal clear to every employee. Along this

---

[5] There are also normal and maximum working areas for the vertical work plane of an employee. The above discussion refers to the horizontal plane only because it is the common one for the office employee.

line, it helps to show examples of what has been accomplished from methods planning in other offices, and to indicate that it is a key in achieving the combination of high wages and short hours.

Everyone must realize the importance of motions in performing office work and see possibilities for improvement. This includes all department heads, division heads, supervisors, and operative employees. To achieve this goal, training can be provided; meetings with department heads and supervisors are common. They can be conducted separately for each group or combined into one group, depending upon the individual circumstances. In certain instances, supervisors may not partake freely in the discussions if management heads are also present. When this condition exists, separate groups can be formed, but management heads should never be excluded from the program; otherwise, they may lose touch with the progress and fail to see the supervisors' viewpoint.

## THE LEFT- AND RIGHT-HAND CHART

Three basic method charts will now be discussed. These are (1) the left- and right-hand chart, (2) the production study chart, and (3) the operator-machine chart.

First, the left- and right-hand chart shows the detailed motions of each hand. For this chart, six symbols are generally used:

1. Large circle — Means operation—such as something created, changed, or added to.

2. Large double circles — Means handling—such as select and pickup.

3. Double triangles, points down — Means idle.

4. Large circle with triangle inside, point down — Means hold.

5. Small circle with letter $L$ inside — Means transportation loaded.

6. Small circle with letter $E$ inside — Means transportation empty.

Here again, there is no universal agreement on the type and number of symbols to be used in this charting work. The important concepts, however, are to make certain that all the facts about the method are collected and to visualize the method being used. The symbols are merely to assist in these endeavors.

Some believe it is best to observe the actions of both hands and to indicate these data on the chart as the work progresses. Others prefer to prepare the chart by following the actions on the right hand only, the actions of the left hand only, and then combining the two charts in order to show the relationships existing according to time of execution. Attention must be given to details. A few seconds saved on an action or the elimination of a short movement, perhaps 3 or 4 inches, may seem small; but when the task is repeated over and over again, the cumulative savings in fatigue and time become highly significant.

Figure 17–4 illustrates a left- and right-hand operation chart for typing, in duplicate, original sales data sent in by field representatives. The workplace layout is sketched at the top of the chart. A number or code system can be used to identify the various materials and equipment used. Also, provisions for the inclusion of other pertinent data are made at the top of the sheet. Of special interest is the summary information, which shows the total actions by type, along with the distance the hands travel and the time taken to perform the task.

In this case, the task begins with the operator reaching with the right hand to the pile of copy blanks positioned to the right and forward of the typewriter. This action is "transportation empty," since the hand is empty, and is indicated on line No. 1 by a small circle with an $E$ inside under the symbol column for the right hand. The description "to No. 2" is written in the description column on the right. In making this transportation, the hand travels 20 inches; and this is recorded in the distance column, right hand, on line No. 1. While this is going on, the left hand is idle, so a double triangle is inserted under the symbol column of the left hand and the word "idle" written in the description column on the left.

Next, the right hand grasps a copy blank. This is a handling action and is shown by large double circles on line No. 2 under the right hand. "Grasp No. 2" is written on the same line in the description column. During this particular operation, the left hand was idle. Since this is the same as the previous entry for the left hand, no new symbol is necessary on the chart.

In a similar manner, each step of the operation is observed and noted on the form. It is important that all details be included and that extreme care be exercised to insure accuracy in this work.

A study of Figure 17–4 shows that the method can be improved. In this figure, it should be observed that the right hand moves first to No. 2, the copy blank pile. The analyst will question the necessity and purpose of this action. He will ask questions such as "Is this necessary?" "What is its purpose?" and others which will help to achieve improvement. Also, he

Subject_____ Project No._____
Operator_____ Date_____
Location_____

| 1 = ORIGINAL BLANK |
| 2 = COPY BLANK |
| 3 = ORIGINAL DATA |
| 4 = PAPER CLIPS |
| F = FINISHED WORK |
| C = CARBON |
| T = TYPEWRITER |

Diagram: F  1 / 4  2 / 3  T  C

| CHARTED BY | SHEET 1 OF 1 | METHOD BEFORE X AFTER____ | OPERATION 6 | HANDLING 23 | IDLE 4 | HOLD 3 | TRANSPORTATION LOADED (10) 131" EMPTY (12) 136" | TIME 1.25 (X) |

(X) NO TYPING

| # | LEFT HAND | SYMBOL | IN. | MIN. | MIN. | IN. | SYMBOL | RIGHT HAND | # |
|---|-----------|--------|-----|------|------|-----|--------|------------|---|
| 1 | idle | ▽ | | | 0.05 | 20 | E | to #2 | 1 |
| 2 | | | | | 0.02 | | O | grasp #2 | 2 |
| 3 | | | | | 0.05 | 16 | L | to top of T | 3 |
| 4 | | | | | 0.01 | | O | release #2 | 4 |
| 5 | | | | | 0.04 | 9 | E | to C, carbon paper | 5 |
| 6 | | | | | 0.02 | | O | grasp C. | 6 |
| 7 | | | | | 0.04 | 13 | L | to top of T | 7 |
| 8 | | | | | 0.01 | | O | release C | 8 |
| 9 | | | | | 0.06 | 25 | E | to #1 | 9 |
| 10 | | | | | 0.02 | | O | grasp #1 | 10 |
| 11 | | | | | 0.06 | 25 | L | to top of T | 11 |
| 12 | | | | | 0.02 | | O | release #1 | 12 |
| 13 | grasp #1-C-#2 | O | | 0.01 | 0.01 | | O | grasp #1-C-#2 | 13 |
| 14 | to platen of T | L | 3 | 0.03 | 0.03 | 3 | L | to platen of T | 14 |
| 15 | hold | ▽ | | | 0.02 | | O | release #1-C-#2 | 15 |
| 16 | | | | | 0.02 | 4 | E | to platen knob | 16 |
| 17 | | | | | 0.07 | | | twist platen knob | 17 |
| 18 | release #1-C-#2 | O | | 0.02 | 0.02 | | O | release platen knob | 18 |
| 19 | to keyboard | E | 6 | 0.03 | 0.03 | 5 | E | to keyboard | 19 |
| 20 | type | O | | — | — | | | type | 20 |
| 21 | to #1-C-#2 | E | 6 | 0.03 | 0.03 | 5 | E | to T platen knob | 21 |
| 22 | grasp #1-C-#2 | O | | 0.02 | 0.02 | | O | grasp platen knob | 22 |
| 23 | remove #1-C-#2 | O | | 0.05 | 0.05 | | | twist platen knob | 23 |
| 24 | to top of T | L | 3 | 0.03 | 0.02 | | O | release platen knob | 24 |
| 25 | hold | ▽ | | | 0.03 | 3 | E | to top of T | 25 |
| 26 | | | | | 0.03 | | O | grasp C | 26 |
| 27 | | | | | 0.05 | 13 | L | to "C" on desk | 27 |
| 28 | release #1-C-#2 | O | | 0.02 | 0.02 | | O | release C | 28 |
| 29 | to paper clips, #4 | E | 15 | 0.06 | 0.05 | 13 | E | to top of T | 29 |
| 30 | grasp paper clip | O | | 0.02 | | | ▽ | idle | 30 |
| 31 | to #3, original data | L | 10 | 0.04 | | | | | 31 |
| 32 | grasp #3, original data | O | | 0.03 | | | | | 32 |
| 33 | to top of T | L | 20 | 0.05 | | | | | 33 |
| 34 | release original data card on #1-#2 | O | | 0.02 | 0.02 | | O | grasp #1-#2 | 34 |
| 35 | attach clip | O | | 0.04 | | | ▽ | hold #1-#2 | 35 |
| 36 | to "F" on desk | L | 25 | 0.06 | | | O | release | 36 |
| 37 | release | O | | 0.02 | | | ▽ | idle | 37 |
| 38 | to T | E | 25 | 0.06 | | | ▽ | | 38 |

FIG. 17–4.

will observe that the right hand successively makes six transportations—three empty and three loaded—all to the same general area. Are these necessary? Can they be eliminated, combined, or simplified? Can they be made productive? Further, it will be observed that, in the beginning, the

| | LEFT HAND | SYMBOL | IN. | MIN. | MIN. | IN. | SYMBOL | RIGHT HAND | |
|---|---|---|---|---|---|---|---|---|---|
| 1 | grasp #1 | ◎ | | 0.04 | 0.04 | | ◎ | grasp C and #2 | 1 |
| 2 | to top of T | ⟁ | 19 | 0.02 | 0.02 | 16 | ⟁ | to top of T | 2 |
| 3 | grasp C and #2 | ◎ | | 0.01 | 0.01 | | ◎ | grasp #1 | 3 |
| 4 | to platen of T | ⟁ | 3 | 0.03 | 0.03 | 3 | ⟁ | to platen of T | 4 |
| 5 | hold | ▽ | | | 0.02 | | ◎ | release #1-C-#2 | 5 |
| 6 | | | | | 0.02 | 4 | ⟁ | to platen knob | 6 |
| 7 | | | | | 0.07 | | ◯ | twist platen knob | 7 |
| 8 | release #1-C-#2 | ◎ | | 0.02 | 0.02 | | ◎ | release platen knob | 8 |
| 9 | to keyboard | ⟁ | 6 | 0.03 | 0.03 | 5 | ⟁ | to keyboard | 9 |
| 10 | type | ◯ | | — | — | | ◯ | type | 10 |
| 11 | to #4, paper clips | ⟁ | 10 | 0.04 | 0.02 | 6 | ⟁ | to #1-C-#2 | 11 |
| 12 | grasp paper clip | ◎ | | 0.02 | 0.01 | | ◎ | grasp #1-C-#2 | 12 |
| 13 | to #3, original data | ⟁ | 8 | 0.03 | 0.02 | | ◯ | pull #1-C-#2 from T | 13 |
| 14 | grasp #3, original data | ◎ | | 0.03 | 0.02 | 2 | ⟁ | to top of T | 14 |
| 15 | to top of T | ⟁ | 18 | 0.04 | 0.01 | | ◎ | release #1-C-#2 | 15 |
| 16 | release on top #1-C-#2 | ◎ | | 0.02 | 0.03 | | ◎ | grasp C | 16 |
| 17 | grasp #3 and #1-C-#2 | ◎ | | 0.04 | 0.05 | 12 | ⟁ | to "2" on desk | 17 |
| 18 | hold | ▽ | | 0.02 | 0.02 | | ◎ | release | 18 |
| 19 | | | | | 0.03 | 16 | ⟁ | to left hand | 19 |
| 20 | | | | | 0.02 | | ◎ | grasp clip | 20 |
| 21 | | | | | 0.04 | | ◯ | attach to #3, #1-#2 | 21 |
| 22 | to "F" on desk | ⟁ | 25 | 0.06 | 0.02 | | ◎ | release | 22 |
| 23 | to #1 on desk | ⟁ | 10 | 0.04 | 0.03 | 16 | ⟁ | to "2" on desk | 23 |

FIG. 17–5.

right hand is occupied, while the left hand is idle. As already pointed out, motion economy results from both hands moving simultaneously in opposite directions. Therefore, arrangements should be made to have both hands moving at the same time, and in opposite directions if possible. By following this minute and careful consideration of each action, the analyst is able to simplify the work, make it easier to do, and eliminate waste.

Figure 17–5 on page 392 shows improvements for accomplishing the same work. The new work layout is sketched at the top of the sheet. Idle time has been eliminated, and simultaneous hand motions have been made a part of the method. The two transportations—empty and loaded—to the copy blanks and the two transportations to the carbon paper have been combined. A comparison study between the two charts will reveal other work simplification accomplishments. The tabular comparison shows:

|                        | Present Method |            | Proposed Method |            |
|------------------------|----------------|------------|-----------------|------------|
| Operations.............. | 6 |              | 5 |              |
| Handling................ | 23 |             | 17 |             |
| Idle.................... | 4 |              | 0 |              |
| Hold.................... | 3 |              | 2 |              |
| Transportation loaded...... | 10 | (131 inches) | 9 | (106 inches) |
| Transportation empty......... | 12 | (136 inches) | 8 | (73 inches) |
| Time.................... | 1.25 minutes | |  0.71 minutes | |

Worthwhile savings have been accomplished.

## PRODUCTION STUDY CHART

The production study chart shows how an employee spends his working time and the major functions performed. Either the employee can record his activities, or the supervisor or the planner can obtain the data by means of observation. In any event, the employee should be informed of the study and its purpose, and told why and how the recordings are made. For meaningful results, the job content should be fairly consistent from day to day, and the observed employee should neither hasten nor retard his normal efforts. The data should be collected for several consecutive days, preferably a week, in order to arrive at what would seem to be a normal pattern.

There are several ways in which the information of a production study chart can be recorded. One method consists of using graph paper with sections representing time units throughout the working day. These sections are filled in with colored pencil according to a color-identification key for the various functions performed. Another method consists of simply marking down in tabular form the various types of work done and the time each job is started and finished. The latter is illustrated by Figure 17–6. The usual identification data—employee name, date, and the like—are shown at the top. A series of vertical columns are used for the various functions, with the extreme left column utilized for time and the extreme right for comments. Since the study begins at 9:00 A.M. Monday, the insertion "Mon. 9.00" is written on the first line under the Time column. The employee is observed cleaning her typewriter, so a check mark(✔) is

PRODUCTION STUDY CHART

Sheet _1_ of _5_ Sheets

Date __3/21__  Employee's Name _Nancy Taussig_

Study By _ERH_  Division or Unit _Transcription - 32_

Computations By _ERH_  Job Title _Transcriber_

| TIME | TRAN-SCRIBING | Com-PUTING | FILING | SUPER-VISION Rcvd. | SUPER-VISION GIVEN | TELE-PHONE | HAND-LING MAIL | PERSON-AL TIME | MISC. | COMMENTS |
|---|---|---|---|---|---|---|---|---|---|---|
| MON. 9:00 9:20 | | | | | | | | | ✓20 | Cleaning typewriter |
| 9:50 | ✓30 | | | | | | | | | |
| 10:05 | | | | | | ✓15 | | | | Business Call |
| 10:18 | ✓13 | | | | | | | | | |
| 10:25 | | | | ✓7 | | | | | | |
| 10:50 | | | | | | | | | ✓25 | Rest period & Idle |
| 10:59 | | | ✓9 | | | | | | | |
| 11:08 | | | | | | ✓9 | | | | Business Call |
| 11:10 | | | ✓2 | | | | | | | |
| 11:22 | | | | | | ✓12 | | | | Personal Call |
| 11:30 | | | | | | | | ✓8 | | |
| 11:35 | | | | ✓5 | | | | | | |
| 11:50 | | | | | | | | | ✓15 | Idle |
| 12:00 | | | | | | | ✓10 | | | |
| LUNCH 1:00 1:07 | | | | | | | | | ✓7 | Tardy |
| 1:10 | | | | ✓3 | | | | | | |
| 1:40 | ✓30 | | | | | | | | | |
| 1:55 | | | | | | | | ✓15 | | |
| 3:05 | ✓70 | | | | | | | | | |
| 3:42 | | | | | | | | | ✓37 | Rest period & Idle |
| 4:05 | | | | | | | ✓23 | | | |
| 4:15 | | | | | | | ✓10 | | | |
| 4:25 | | | | | | ✓10 | | | | Business Call |
| 4:45 | | | ✓20 | | | | | | | |
| 4:58 | | | | | | | | | ✓13 | Idle |
| 5:00 | | | | | | | | | ✓2 | Cleaning up Desk |
| | | | | | | | | | | |
| | | | | | | | | | | |
| | | | | | | | | | | |
| TOTALS | 143 | — | 31 | 15 | — | 46 | 23 | 43 | 119 | 420 |
| PER CENT | 34.1 | — | 7.4 | 3.6 | — | 11.0 | 5.4 | 10.1 | 28.4 | 100.0% |

FIG. 17–6. Chart showing how an employee spends her working time. Data are secured by observing the employee.

made on the first line under Miscellaneous and "cleaning typewriter" is written under Comments. She finishes this task at 9:20 A.M. and begins transcribing. Hence, "9.20" is written on the first line under Time, and a check mark is made under Transcribing on line 2. She stops transcribing at 10:05 A.M. to telephone. Hence, on line 3, a check mark is made under Telephone, and the entry "10.05" is made in the Time column. In a similar manner, entries are made throughout the entire day.

The calculations for figuring the elapsed time per function can be made as the study progresses or at the completion of all observations. In the illustration, the ordinary 60-minute watch has been used. For the first line, the elapsed time between 9.00 and 9.20 is 20 minutes, which is recorded in the same square as the check mark under Miscellaneous. For the second line, the elapsed time is 9.50 minus 9.20, or 30 minutes. The itemized totals are shown at the bottom of the form along with the percentage figures. For example, the total time spent on transcribing is 143 minutes. This constitutes 34.1 percent of the total day's working time, calculated by dividing the transcribing time, 143 minutes, by the total day's working time, 420 minutes.

These types of data are helpful because they tell what the status of the jobs is at present and give, per employee, a picture of the overall work pattern which might form the basis for methods improvement, better supervision, and equalization of the work load. They can also be used to supply basic information for the construction of a work distribution chart.[6]

For example, a production study chart may reveal that a typist, with a typing speed of 50 words per minute, spends only 50 percent of her time typing. The remaining 50 percent is spent on other activities, most of which are nonessential, including positioning papers in typewriter, checking work, removing papers from typewriter, separating copies, cleaning typewriter, answering telephone, filing papers, and getting information from the supervisor. In this case, the effective typing production is at a rate of only 25 (50 percent of 50) words per minute. In too many offices, the sole emphasis is upon the speed of the operator. True, this is important; but when the methods improvement efforts reveal only 50 percent of the employee's particular skill being utilized, it is a challenge to the manager to eliminate such waste. The production study chart reveals such situations and assists in correcting them.

## OPERATOR-MACHINE ACTIVITY CHART

As the name implies, this chart shows the relation between the operator and the machine. Its use is somewhat limited in office methods, owing to the general nature of most office activities. It is chiefly employed to determine idle machine time and the number of machines which one operator can reasonably handle, thus in effect determining the superior method.

Figure 17–7 shows an operator-machine activity chart. Pertinent data and a sketch of the workplace layout are included at the top. Time is represented by vertical distance on the scale shown in the center column of the sheet. For example, two scale units represent two minutes, four scale units four minutes, etc. The activities of the operator are listed in the left column, those of the machine on the right.

The vertical height of each spacing in these respective columns is

---

[6] See Chapter 27 for discussion of work distribution chart.

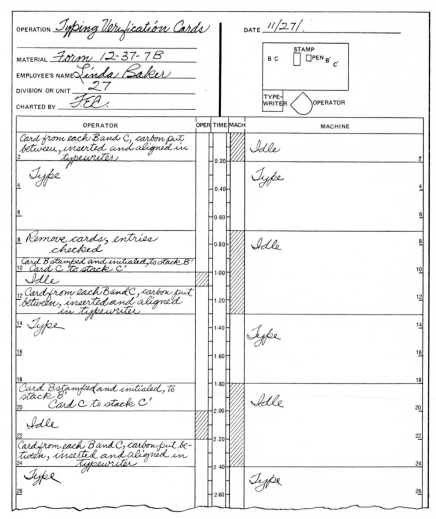

FIG. 17–7.   An operator-machine activity chart.

determined by the time devoted to the particular activity. For example, in the illustration, the first action by the operator was to "take a card from each *B* and *C*, put a carbon between, insert and align in typewriter." This required two-tenths (0.2) of a minute, so a horizontal line was drawn two units down from the beginning horizontal line. During this time, the typewriter was idle; hence, a horizontal line was drawn across the right column under Machine, two units from the same beginning line, and "idle" written in the space so formed.

Next, the operator typed. This action continued five-tenths (0.5) of a minute, so a horizontal line was drawn across the Operator column five units below the last horizontal line, or in this case opposite the 7 mark on the time scale. The space so formed was marked "type." Since the typewriter action stopped at the same time, a horizontal line was also drawn across the Machine column opposite 7 on the time scale, and the space above was marked "type." In a similar manner, the entire chart was constructed.

This method can be improved very easily. The use of multicopy stub sets with interleaved carbon offers one possibility. This would reduce the labor time per unit and increase the operating time of the machine—both contributing to greater efficiency. However, a more significant improvement would be the use of continuous-strip office forms with carbon interleaved, thus permitting the operator to type continuously until a quantity of work is finished. The checking and separating of the forms could subsequently be handled on this quantity. This method would provide a smooth and rhythmic flow of work, permit specialization upon the immediate task, and eliminate unnecessary reaching, as well as excessive finger and arm motions. Elimination of much waste would be achieved.

## QUESTIONS

1. "Any task can be improved with sufficient planning effort." Do you agree with this statement? Justify your viewpoint.

2. Discuss eight guides in achieving motion economy, using illustrations to demonstrate your answers.

3. Enumerate some actions that can be taken to provide an effective workplace to assist in the best work methods being followed.

4. Comment fully on the following: "For a given quantity of work, it is entirely possible for methods improvements to reduce employee fatigue in performing that quantity. But methods improvements usually result in increasing the amount of work performed; and as a result, the employee spends the same amount of energy or more than before the improvement. Hence, the employee is quite likely to be just as fatigued under the improved method as before the improvement."

5. For each of the following pairs, carefully point out the difference between the two identities:
   a) Therblig and the "What and Why" question.
   b) Normal working area and maximum working area.
   c) Speedup and motion study.
   d) A "handling" and a "transportation loaded."

6. As an office manager, would you agree to the suggestion that the employees fill out the data on their respective production study charts and turn these data in to you for analysis and interpretation? What would be the advantages under such an arrangement? The disadvantages?

7. List the therbligs performed for each of the following:

   *a*) An executive receiving a letter and signing it.
   *b*) A file clerk opening a file drawer, locating the proper folder, inserting a paper into the folder, and closing the file drawer.
   *c*) A stenographer folding a letter, inserting it in an envelope, sealing and placing the envelope in the outgoing mail basket on her desk.
   *d*) A typist inserting a card in a typewriter, preparatory to typing.

8. From question No. 7, above, select one of the activities listed and chart it, using a left- and right-hand chart. Point out the motions depicted on the chart which in your opinion can be eliminated, changed, combined, or simplified in performing this work.

9. Discuss the subject of "Application of the Improved Method" in the field of office management.

10. In your opinion will office methods improvement become more or less important in the future? What effect will the increasing use of office automation have upon office methods improvements? Give reasons for your answers.

11. Analyze your motions in typing a letter, or taking notes from a reference book, or sorting and then filing cards in a file. What do you conclude from your study? Discuss.

12. Draw up a tabular listing by including vertically the left- and right-hand chart, the production study chart, and the operator-machine chart. Across the top, list column headings (1) what data are shown, (2) best means to obtain these data, and (3) use or purpose of chart. Fill in the information for each column as it applies to each chart. What conclusions do you draw from your completed tabular listing?

## CASE PROBLEMS

### Case 17–1.   Beemark Company

Office manager Gary Kanel visited an exhibit of office machines in connection with an office management seminar. He was deeply impressed by the demonstration of the various operations of a particular accounting machine. Witnessing work, similar to that in his own office, being performed accurately and in a fraction of the time it required his office, Mr. Kanel decided to purchase the machine and eliminate several time-consuming operations in several departments. In time, the machine was delivered and installed. As a result, most of employee Arline Growoski's job was eliminated and she was offered a job in another department, "CC," at the same pay.

Miss Growoski protested, claiming that her job was not entirely eliminated and that those tasks remaining were given to other employees in her department. She stated that she did not like the employees in "CC" department as well as those in the department where she had now worked nearly six years. She requested that she be allowed to continue those of her tasks which the machine did not eliminate and that other work be given her to occupy her full time. She liked working at Beemark, wanted to continue to work for the company, but the decision to transfer her violated good human relations practices.

"A new work method seldom eliminates all previous duties," replied Mr. Kanel.

"We cannot do what you ask, Miss Growoski, for such a policy would prevent us from making any improvement. There isn't other work in the department for you to do. The criteria is whether the new method and our decision increase efficiency and lower costs. I am positive that they do so I must ask you again to accept the transfer."

## Problems:

1. Do you agree with Mr. Kanel? Why?
2. Could Mr. Kanel have handled this entire situation better? Discuss.
3. As Arline Growoski, what would you do? Substantiate your answer.

### Case 17–2.  Agnes Dennison

Agnes Dennison is a general clerk and is being observed for the purpose of making a production study chart. She has been informed of the study and has agreed to follow her normal work manner. The data recorded include the following: Starting at 8:30 A.M., the official office starting time, Miss Dennison cleans her desk top, checks typewriter, and arranges work on desk; at 8:41, types; at 9:03, answers a business telephone call; at 9:10, sorts requisitions; at 9:56, idle; at 10:00, files material; at 10:15, rest period, reads paperback edition of *Roses for Cindy;* at 10:30, talks with supervisor; at 10:40, runs errand for supervisor; at 10:57, types; at 11:01, answers a business telephone call; at 11:07, files material; at 11:40, makes personal telephone call; at 11:45, lunch; at 12:45, idle; at 12:55, types; at 1:25, handles supplies; at 1:40, makes personal telephone call; at 1:50, sorts requisitions; at 2:13, runs errand for supervisor; at 2:32, idle; at 2:45, rest period; at 3:00, makes personal telephone call; at 3:07 types; at 3:40, answers a business telephone call; at 3:48, idle; at 3:52, types; at 4:17, puts away work, cleans desk top; at 4:26, idle; at 4:30, official quitting time, leaves her desk.

## Problems:

1. Draw the production study chart.
2. Calculate the itemized totals of the activities of Agnes Dennison.
3. What interpretations do you make from these data? Discuss.
4. What action do you recommend as a result of the factual data assembled? Why?

### Case 17–3.  Owens Direct Mail Sales, Inc.

For purposes of sales analysis and taxes, customer orders are sorted by state. A seventh copy of the invoice prepared by the company is used. The volume fluctuates from week to week, but an average weekly volume is 15,000 orders. To do the sorting job, a rack, laid out in a straight line with eight sections horizontally and five sections vertically, is being used. The rack, which is 10 feet long and 4 feet high, sits on a long table. The 40-way sort is used because several of the states are grouped.

The operator, a tall girl, holds a batch of orders in her left hand, reads the state on the order at the top of the batch, picks the order up with her right hand, and inserts it into the bin of the rack for the particular state. The operator walks back and forth to cover the distance of the rack. She is expected to accomplish a rate of 20 orders sorted a minute, and succeeds in doing so.

Because of the volume, all the orders cannot be sorted by the operator using the rack. The overflow is sorted by another girl, who spreads the work out in little piles over several tabletops. Although the second girl works all day at this job of sorting orders, she does not accomplish as much as the girl working with the rack. From this, the office manager concludes that the rack idea is better than sorting on the tabletops. He is about to order another rack for use by the second girl; but before doing this, he has requested you to study the work method and see if any improvements for this order sorting can be developed.

## Problems:

1. What are some tentative methods you feel should be investigated to find a possible improvement?

2. What is your recommendation to the office manager?

CHAPTER **18**

# OFFICE EQUIPMENT
# AND MACHINES PLANNING

He that will not reason is a bigot;
he that cannot reason is a fool;
he that dares not reason is a slave.
—*William Drummond*

OFFICE planning includes the selection of equipment and machines to implement the proposed manner, sequence, and skill required to accomplish the work. The modern office manager cannot reasonably expect maximum output unless the best physical means are provided. Analysis and study of the various types of office equipment and machines are usually in order. In many respects, this is one of the most interesting aspects of office management. Suitable facilities have contributed tremendously to the advance and status of office management. The growth of office automation, for example, has had significant influences upon office management, as pointed out in the chapters of Part III, The Office and Automation. The use of office equipment and machines is destined to become increasingly important. They are popular and powerful forces in accomplishing office work.

## SELECTION OF OFFICE EQUIPMENT AND MACHINES

The expanding use of office equipment and machines places an increased burden and responsibility upon the office manager. He must marshal all available facts about possible facilities and help decide the best units in keeping with the particular requirements set forth by his systems, procedures, and methods planning. To illustrate, he needs to know the types of equipment available, the characteristics of each, the cost per unit of output, the initial outlay, and the maintenance cost.

More fundamental, however, is to decide whether the equipment or machine is really needed. It may be possible to simplify the work sufficiently to eliminate the necessity for mechanization. In view of the volume, type, and occurrence of the work, a nonmechanical means may be entirely satisfactory. Or it may be advantageous to farm out the work to a service bureau specializing in the work involved.[1]

If mechanization appears to be justified, the problem is one of selection. Usually careful evaluation of several aspects are required to select wisely. The decision should never be made hastily or impulsively.

The sales representatives of most office equipment manufacturers are excellent sources of helpful information about their particular products. They are very willing to be of service and will cheerfully give or try to find out the information requested. The office manager will do well to work with them, for they can keep him informed of latest developments and advise him of any special applications in other offices. This may prove an important source of ideas for improvements. Furthermore, these representatives can help in working out special applications and uses. The representative should be considered as one who is trying to help. His aggressiveness adds to his merit, as this characteristic is desirable in sales representatives.

On the other hand, the office manager, or whoever selects office equipment or machines, has definite obligations to fulfill. Good management dictates that these objectives cannot be ignored, passed over lightly, or left entirely to the sales representative.

## EQUIPMENT AND MACHINE SELECTION FACTORS

The following 12 factors should be carefully considered:

1. *The work and the manner of accomplishing it.* The purpose of the work should be clearly defined and critically examined, to assure that it is absolutely essential. Knowledge of what is probably the best way of doing the work, along with alternative effective ways, should be determined. Sometimes, work of a similar nature currently performed in the office can be used as a guide. The work and its manner of performance may strongly suggest a table rather than a desk be supplied, or a particular model of a machine be selected for it best answers the specific work requirements.

2. *The individual requirements.* The decision to utilize a particular piece of office equipment or machine should be based upon the *individual* requirements of the particular office. Use by others is not sufficient grounds for adoption. This is especially important in regard to office machines. The efficient office manager does not mechanize an office

---

[1] Service bureaus are discussed fully in Chapter 22, p. 506.

operation whenever it is possible to do so. Instead, he considers the available machines in the light of the way each one will assist in getting the work accomplished in his particular office. Basing his decision upon these factual data, he decides what, if any, machine to utilize.

However, as implied in the chapters on office automation, there is emerging a universality of data processing and distributing adaptable for all enterprises. Consideration of these universal concepts of what is necessary and what is not, from the viewpoint of effective information handling via automation, may prove them quite adequate for the individual enterprise's requirements. It could well be that in certain cases, individual requirements are stressed too much, necessitating special and high-cost operations being added.

3. *Amount and value of total time saved.* A new office machine might foster greater speeds of accomplishment, but the important consideration is not comparison of speeds but savings in total time, both in amount and value. The amount will depend a great deal upon the volume of work. Economies are usually not realized unless the unit is operating a good portion of the time. In addition, the utilization of time saved must be evaluated. To be advantageous, time saved should be used for other productive office work. If the time saved is simply dissipated and spread over other tasks, there are no economic benefits.

4. *Flexibility of use.* The extent to which the units can be used for various types of work in the office governs the economies gained. Generally speaking, if a unit being considered can be used effectively for many types of office work, its adoption usually can be justified. Likewise, the feature of expansion and contraction in order to accommodate varying amounts of paper work is normally advantageous.

5. *Price and investment.* Price is always an important managerial consideration, but it should be considered along with the services made available by the unit. That is, consideration must be given to what is received as well as what is paid out. In many instances, purchases of equipment are made on the basis that expected savings will recoup the initial investment within about one-fourth the life of the unit.

However, the factors which determine how quickly an office unit should pay for itself vary somewhat with the policies of the individual purchaser and with the importance attached to each factor. Usually, the decision is based on an evaluation of such things as (*a*) the current complete price, including installation and delivery; (*b*) if a replacement, the make, model, type, and condition of the replaced unit and its probable current market value; (*c*) the percentage of working time the unit will be used; and (*d*) the investment percentage return to the company (the effect of income taxes and overhead expenses in reducing the gross earnings should be included in this calculation).[2]

---

[2] Depreciation and the influence of trade-ins are discussed later in this chapter.

Figure 18–1 shows a quick rule-of-thumb approach to decide whether to purchase a particular piece of office equipment or machine. It is based on timesaving by personnel, as illustrated by a ratio of personnel to equipment or machine. For example, the salary cost per minute for an employee receiving $5,000 a year is approximately 5 cents. The number of thousands of dollars per year is approximately the equivalent number of cents per minute. For a $10,000 accounting machine, the cost per working day is $4. Hence, $4 divided by 5 cents per minute gives 80 minutes as the time required to be saved by a $5,000 employee to pay for the accounting machine.

| Salary per Year (1) | Approximate Salary per Minute (2) | Cost per Day for $10,000 Accounting Machine (3) | Personnel Time Required to Save (in Minutes) (4) |
|---|---|---|---|
| $ 5,000 . . . . . . . . . . . . . . . | 5.0¢ | $4.00 | 80.0 |
| 7,500 . . . . . . . . . . . . . . . | 7.5 | 4.00 | 53.4 |
| 10,000 . . . . . . . . . . . . . . . | 10.0 | 4.00 | 40.0 |
| 12,500 . . . . . . . . . . . . . . . | 12.5 | 4.00 | 32.0 |
| 15,000 . . . . . . . . . . . . . . . | 15.0 | 4.00 | 26.6 |

Column 2 is based on 250 working days a year, eight-hour day, and 83 percent efficiency.
Column 3 is based on 250 working days a year, ten-year life span.
Column 4 is Column 3 divided by Column 2.

FIG. 18–1. A quick and convenient means of determining whether an office machine will pay for itself within a reasonable period. The approach is based on determining the time required to be saved by the employee who will use the machine.

6. *Capacity of unit.* It is imperative that the unit be of sufficient size to permit efficient operations. Nothing is gained by getting a smaller desk or accounting machine than the reasonable expectancy of work volume indicates is necessary. In the case of many machines, the expected output can be judged from experience of actual users of the machine, data from the manufacturer, and actual test runs in the office. When feasible, this latter source is recommended; in fact, it is always advisable to obtain a demonstration of an office machine. Free trials, however, should be carefully qualified as to purpose, use, and extent of time; for unless this is done, a machine originally brought in for trial tends to remain, and eventual purchase may be required, regardless of selection efforts.

7. *Aesthetic values.* The appearance of the office—a desire to impress by having the latest or the finest in office equipment and machines—is an important, although sometimes subdued or concealed, consideration. Aesthetic values are highly subjective; justification for certain selections is based on personal likes. Such values have a place, for office equipment

and machines are not only a *physical* means of assisting employees to accomplish their work but also serve as a *mental* stimuli. Supplying the proper unit makes for a positive and cooperative attitude and helps place the employee in the right frame of mind to work efficiently.

8. *Employee preference.* This consideration is of great significance because the human element is vital in determining whether the equipment is properly utilized or operated. A strong bias against a particular unit prevents maximum benefits from being realized, regardless of the suitability of the unit to the work. The highly successful office manager will not force the use of a particular unit against a prejudice which the employee may have concerning that unit. Most office employees will turn out consistently the maximum work of acceptable quality when they are supplied with the equipment and machines *they feel* are the best available.

9. *Effect upon personnel requirements.* In many cases, the installation of office equipment or machines changes the requirements regarding both the number of employees and the level of their skill; and the problems of transferring, reducing, and training the work force must be considered. For example, in the case of machines, trained operators or the availability of those who are trainable as operators are foremost considerations. Furthermore, when machines are adopted to perform monotonous work, the effect upon personnel is also important, because usually a happier and more satisfied work force is the result.

10. *Forecast of work load.* As in all planning, not only must the current volume and type of work be considered, but also the probable future requirements and the adequacy of the unit to fulfill these future needs. Future requirements should be estimated for about five years, and such forecasts are sometimes quite difficult. Good management requires, however, that the unit neither become inadequate to handle the work volume several months after its installation nor stand idle a large portion of the time because of a decline in work volume which could have been predetermined.

11. *Quality of paper work.* The effect of the unit upon the accuracy and appearance of the papers should also be considered. When a machine is to replace a manual operation, increased accuracy usually will result, for machines tend to make fewer errors than human beings. Also, forms executed by machine generally have a better appearance; they are neater, more legible, and more uniform than papers which are handwritten.

12. *Need for copies and statistical data.* This consideration applies mainly to office machines selection. A contemplated machine may provide more copies of a record, and it may furnish a great deal of data of a sort and in a form not currently available. However, the important consideration is whether these available copies and data are necessary and whether they serve useful purposes which significantly aid management efforts.

## DEPRECIATION AND TRADE-IN

There is no one set of answers to the questions of how to figure depreciation and when it is economically sound to purchase a machine or to make a trade-in. The planner must refer to the accounting practices followed. Most companies consider office equipment and machines as assets; and over a period, they write them off because of depreciation. The period will depend upon the kind of product. For example, the following are common:

| | |
|---|---|
| Desks | 20 years |
| Files | 15 " |
| Accounting machines | 10 " |
| Rugs and carpets | 10 " |
| Typewriters | 5 " |

The rate used over the period can be calculated by various methods. Straight line and sum-of-digits are common, but the new "guideline form," permitted by present tax laws and designed to encourage new purchases, is gaining favor. Some companies follow the practice of charging to expense any equipment purchase of less than a stated amount, for example, $100; and any equipment purchase over this amount is put into an assets account. Other practices are also followed, but they must be reasonable and within the meaning and intent of income tax laws.

Some general overall guiding policy for trade-ins should be followed, tempered with certain adjustments based upon the individual circumstances. Several main factors influence a trade-in. First is the availability of the cash and capital resources of the enterprise. This is always present in any trade-in discussion. Second are the expected cash savings to be derived from the new unit's use. If these savings will pay for the net outlay within 24 months, a trade-in is usually in order. Third is the difference between the accrued net depreciation and the expense necessary to keep the unit operating. If the net (present book value minus trade-in) is less than the cost of repair, a trade-in is probably best.

## BUY OR LEASE

At one time, only certain types of office equipment and machines could be obtained on a leasing basis. Now, the practice of leasing has spread to practically every type of office facility. Details of leasing agreements vary widely. For example, some grant a right to purchase, after leasing for a period of time, commonly three to five years, by crediting a portion of the lease payments toward the purchase price.

Advocates of the leasing basis claim better maintenance is provided and the leasee is free from the expense and worry of keeping all units in top operating condition. In addition, leasing permits capital to be utilized in other more productive facilities. A large portion of the leasee's funds are not tied up in long-term equipment and machine needs. Furthermore, leasing permits the payments to be considered as expenses from the tax viewpoint, not as assets, as is the case with purchase. To some companies, this can be a distinct advantage. Also, leasing supplies units to meet temporary or fill-in needs. Flexibility is provided. Then too, leasing makes feasible trial usage of units. It is helpful to find out how the unit will work out before purchasing it. In contrast, many managers always buy equipment and machines if it is possible to do so. They state that in the long run, purchasing is less costly than leasing, they are free to move the facility as they like, and they can arrive independently at decisions affecting equipment or machines. Also, it should be noted that if funds are available, investment in equipment and machines in one's own business can be attractive.

## MAINTENANCE

All office equipment and machines require attention periodically in order to keep them in satisfactory condition. Ordinary use results in wear and tear, making cleaning, oiling, adjusting, and installing new parts the rule rather than the exception. Preventive maintenance, rather than remedial maintenance, should be stressed. The former seeks to catch trouble before it happens; this is accomplished by scheduling inspections at carefully determined intervals. The latter, or remedial maintenance, deals with trouble after it occurs. Preventive maintenance provides greater employee satisfaction and efficient product performance. Uninterrupted service at the lowest cost should be the chief objective. Maintenance can be handled in any of four ways: maintenance contracts, individual service calls, company-operated service, and combined leasing-maintenance contracts.

Many manufacturers, or their sales distributors, prefer to service their products in order to insure complete satisfaction; and to this end, they offer maintenance contracts which call for regular inspection, cleaning, adjusting, and oiling. Charges are made on a predetermined basis, and the rates and conditions for special service calls are usually stated. Advocates of this type of maintenance service claim that the regularity of service, the use of genuine parts, the employment of skilled, factory-trained mechanics, and the overall, long-range low cost warrant its use. This means is probably the most popular for offices of all sizes.

Individual service calls are a "when required" type of service. This is sometimes called "no service contract" maintenance. It is of a remedial nature. The age and number of units are the chief factors which influence the choice of this policy. If most of the units are new, it is reasonable to expect that they will not require repair service; likewise, when a large number are in use, it is logical that not all will require maintenance service. However, a service call on an individual basis usually costs more than one under a maintenance contract. Also, the regular cleaning and oiling of most equipment and machines are usually advisable, and these must be provided on an individual service basis when this plan of maintenance is used.

A company-operated service is followed primarily because of considerations of cost, control, or availability of service. Maintenance costs may be lower under this plan, provided there is a sufficient volume to warrant full-time maintenance employees. With a company-operated service, it is possible to exercise close control over the progress of the work, the expenses, and the regularity of inspections. In some instances, available outside services are inconvenient, owing to the remoteness of the office, and in such cases the company-operated plan may be desirable.

When a facility is leased, the leasor usually provides for the maintenance. Terms for such service are included in the lease. Both periodic and on-call maintenance are provided. Also, as a part of the agreement any design improvements in the unit or its attachments are usually supplied as quickly as available.

### OFFICE CHAIRS

Knowledge of available office equipment and machines is essential in office planning. Information on facilities commonly associated with office services (Part II) and those used with office automation (Part III) have been discussed. In the following pages, material on additional and important units is given. The first is office chairs.

The office chair is probably the most important physical facility in an office. It is personal to the employee and vitally affects the ease and comfort with which the work is done. Most office work is of a sedentary nature, a fact which further stresses the importance of the office chair. among the many types of office chairs are the familiar straight-back chair, the swivel chair, chairs that tilt, the posture chair, plain or upholstered chairs, wood or metal chairs, and chairs with or without armrests. Certain features about chairs require careful consideration by the office manager. Upholstering generally adds to appearance and comfort; but it requires periodic cleaning and, in the case of leather, "dressing" in order to preserve the material. Caster wheels made from relatively hard material are usually best for use on carpeting, while casters of softer material should be used on composition tile and wood flooring.

In the office, posture chairs are very important. The chair has three adjustments, thereby making it possible to "tailor-fit" the chair to the occupant. These adjustments include:

*1. The seat height*—so that the feet are comfortably placed on the floor and no undue pressure is present on the underside of the leg just above the knee.

*2. The backrest height*—so that support is provided the small or lumbar region of the back. The swivel joint of the backrest should be approximately one inch higher than the top of the hip bone.

*3. The backrest horizontal position*—so that the muscles covering the two pelvic bones, i.e., the glutei muscles, overhang slightly the rear edge of the seat, thus placing the body weight forward on the underside of the leg muscles.

Chair Too High
Seat pressures nerves and stops circulation just above the knee.

Chair Too Low
Steady pressure on spine causes great fatigue.

Chair Back Too High
No needed support to spine, causing slumping and a strain on back and shoulder muscles.

Chair Tilts Back Too Far
Occupant easily gets off balance, with excessive back strain.

FIG. 18–2.  Examples of common incorrect seating.

Even though available, these adjustments are frequently not used, thus incorrect seating exists as illustrated by Figure 18–2.

The major consideration about a posture chair is that it be used properly. Simply supplying a posture chair seldom assures that the benefits of good posture seating are being enjoyed. The occupant must know how to sit in the chair and must sit that way. The proper use of posture chairs improves the appearance of office employees, reduces fatigue, improves morale, and aids in the functioning of important body actions, including breathing, circulation, and elimination.

## OFFICE DESKS

An office desk provides a work surface, a temporary storage for materials being processed, and a convenient area for selected tools and machines required in accomplishing the work. The trend in desk appearance is toward smooth, streamlined surfaces. Supports touching the floor are recessed in order to conceal them from view, to permit ample toe room when standing near the desk, and to facilitate cleaning the floor. Steel desks are equipped with linoleum or plastic; lighter colors and finishes seem to be preferred. Many wood desks are finished with light stain and bleached colors. Hardware and exposed metal parts are of dull finish to avoid annoying highlights.

Further comments about desks will be centered around desk efficiency, design, and dimensions.

1. *Desk efficiency.* A desk is actually a basic working tool, and this should be kept in mind when planning. Viewing a desk as a working tool emphasizes the meaning of desk efficiency, which is influenced by (1) the design features of the desk and (2) the person using the desk. The former stresses the old adage: "A place for everything, and everything in its place." The desk and its interior are planned to give maximum service to the user. Tailor-made desk-drawer arrangements are available to aid work production. As new requirements arise, the drawers can be interchanged and rearranged as desired. Figure 18–3 suggests efficient arrangement of materials in desk drawers to meet specific requirements.

The second factor—the person using the desk—emphasizes the influence of the desk user's work habits and attitudes upon desk efficiency. The personnel element is vital and necessitates adequate instructions, training, and supervising. To assist in achieving desk efficiency, the following guides are listed:

1. Work on one task at a time and finish it before starting another. Abstain from trying to do several tasks at the same time.

2. Keep the desk free from excess papers and supplies. Have only those items on the desk that are needed. The desk top is a work surface and should facilitate immediate action.

3. Shelve material that is not urgent. For example, insert slips in magazines to articles to be read and then put them to one side for reading in off moments.

4. Strive to keep the work moving over the desk. Take action on each paper coming to the desk as quickly as possible.

5. Act on important paper work first. Have a daily schedule, and make use of a desk calendar to guide the sequence of work.

6. Dispose of all mail before going home. Do not permit a stack of mixed-up papers to remain overnight and cause a poor start the next day.

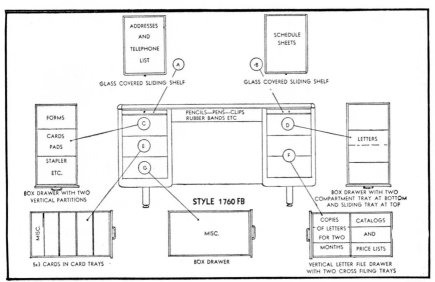

*Courtesy: Art Metal Construction Co., Jamestown, N.Y.*

FIG. 18–3.  Suggested desk-drawer layout to meet individual requirements for order department manager.

*2. Desk design.*  Desks are designed to serve particular needs. Among the most popular are those for executives, junior executives, stenographers, typists, adding and calculating machine operators, and billing clerks. Desks are available in single- and double-pedestal styles. The pedestal is the support or foundation of the desk, and it contains the drawers or a foldaway platform which houses a typewriter or some special machine. The single-pedestal desk is used in cases where a single tier of desk drawers and a smaller-size top are sufficient. Figure 18–4 illustrates several different types of desks designed to serve particular requirements.

Especially where an electric typewriter is used, a great many companies have adopted the machine platform arrangement in conjunction with the ordinary desk. Figure 18–5 shows such an arrangement. The platform can be attached to either side of the desk. Economy and efficiency are gained.

*Courtesy: Art Metal Construction Co., Jamestown, N.Y.*

FIG. 18–4.    This office features desks designed to meet specific work requirements. Observe in the foreground the fixed-bed typewriter desk; in the left background, the general-purpose desk; and in the right background, the desk with an overhang top.

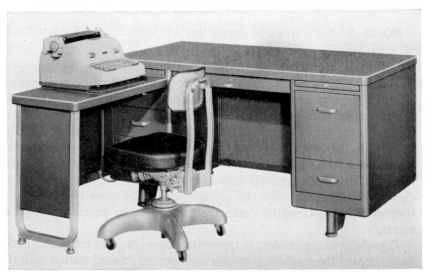

*Courtesy: Art Metal Construction Co., Jamestown, N.Y.*

FIG. 18–5.    A machine platform attached to a steel office desk.

Provided is a firmer base than the disappearing platform, more knee space, and desk drawers for supplies.

The "conference desk" has an oversized top that overhangs the pedestals at one or both ends and at the back. At meetings, it is possible for five or six people to sit comfortably around a conference desk, since ample work space and leg room are provided. The conference desk has become quite popular; it adds prestige to an executive's office. An attractive functional desk featuring modern design is shown in Figure 18–6.

*Courtesy: Herman Miller, Inc., Zeeland, Mich.*

FIG. 18–6.  A functional desk featuring modern design.

3. *Desk dimensions.* Dimensions of desks vary with the type of desk, the material used, and the manufacturer. Executive desks are usually the largest, sizes ranging from 76 x 36 inches to 60 x 32 inches being the most common. For general office work, sizes from 60 x 34 inches to 42 x 30 inches are popular. The trend is toward smaller desks. For example, most new general office desks are 50 to 55 inches wide instead of the former 60 inches, and 30 inches deep instead of 34 inches. In some companies, however, certain sizes are specified for certain uses. For example, in one company, the following applies:

| *Employee* | *Desk-Top Size* |
|---|---|
| Department head............... | 78 x 38 inches, triple overhang |
| Supervisor.................... | 60 x 36 inches, front overhang |
| Staff........................ | 60 x 30 inches or special-purpose desk |
| Clerical..................... | 60 x 30 inches |

Desks are made of various heights. Currently the preferred height is 28½ or 29 inches. It is claimed that for the average employee this height is better since it helps to maximize the employee's comfort.

## MODULAR OFFICE FURNITURE

This type of furniture consists of easily and quickly assembled modular components which, when assembled, comprise an effective functional and modern arrangement. Basic units include such "building blocks" as desk tops, desk pedestals, auxiliary tops, end supports, and filing and shelving

*Courtesy: Invincible Metal Furniture Co., Manitowoc, Wis.*

FIG. 18–7.   Modular office components assembled to provide an efficient U-shaped unit.

units. In a number of installations, modular components have been put together to form a U-shaped desk and platform arrangement as illustrated by Figure 18–7. Partition panels for privacy can be added to meet individual requirements. Components are standard and interchangeable, thus supplying flexibility and many various combinations.

## POSTING-TRAY UNIT

This equipment is commonly used in connection with machine installations and is designed to provide convenient reference to sheets or cards. Rapid removal and return of the material, quick access to accounts, locking in sheets to prevent unauthorized removal, clear vision, and a clean, orderly arrangement of records are among the features of this posting unit. Illustrations are shown in Figure 18–8.

*Courtesy: LeFebure Corp., Cedar Rapids, Iowa*

FIG. 18–8.   (*Left*) Posting-tray equipment adjustable in height from 31¼ inches for standing position to 22 inches for seated position. (*Right*) The specially designed tray expedites the posting.

## PUNCHED-CARD MACHINES

Among the most important and versatile of all office machines are punched-card machines which put information in such a form that it can be easily handled for any of a number of subsequent operations. The "punched card" is the key physical unit about which the whole process revolves. The common language supplied by this card provides the real significance to these machines.[3] They provide flexibility, accuracy, and

---

[3] Punched cards as a medium for data processing are discussed in Chapters 11 and 12.

rapidity to data processing and are employed for many different uses, including the analyzing and summarizing of statistical data, the writing of invoices, payrolls, inventory control, labor distribution, market research, sales reports, and accounts payable. They are also used to obtain correlated data. In market research studies, for example, the number of respondents who answered "Yes" to a given question, broken down according to age, income, and occupation, can be quickly obtained. Likewise, sales analyses by units, dollars, territories, and months, or manufacturing costs by various types of labor operations, can be easily determined.

## ARRANGEMENT OF DATA ON CARD

Holes are coded to represent either alphabetical or numerical information. For example, vertical columns of the card are allocated to different items. Information on months is given two columns so that a 1 in the first column and a 0 in the second is punched to indicate 10, or the month of October. The IBM card has 80 columns, the RR card has 90 columns, hence a maximum of 80 or 90 letters or numbers per card is permitted. Figure 18–9 shows the allocation of space on a punched card covering accounts receivable. In this illustration, the number 1 punched out in each of the first two columns indicates the eleventh month, or November. The code followed for punched holes was given in Chapter 12.

Laying out the punched card or deciding what information to punch in the card warrants careful thought. This emphasizes the planning function. Only information which is valuable to management, which will reveal pertinent major relationships, and which will provide the basis for meaningful subanalyses should be included.

## BASIC PUNCHED-CARD MACHINES

There are three basic punched-card machines, including a punching machine, a sorter, and a tabulator. A punching machine punches small holes in the card, representing the numerical and alphabetical information desired. The machines have many automatic features, depending upon the model and the manufacture. Figure 18–10 shows a card-punching machine.

The sorter arranges the cards according to any desired classification and in alphabetical or numerical sequence. The sorting is really a box sort. Cards are passed through the machine; and the punched hole causes a mechanism to operate, resulting in the card being directed into a specific box or pocket of the machine. Sorting at any one time is done according to one vertical column, i.e., a unit number or a letter. For example, consider the numbers in the left column of Figure 18–11 as the data to be placed in

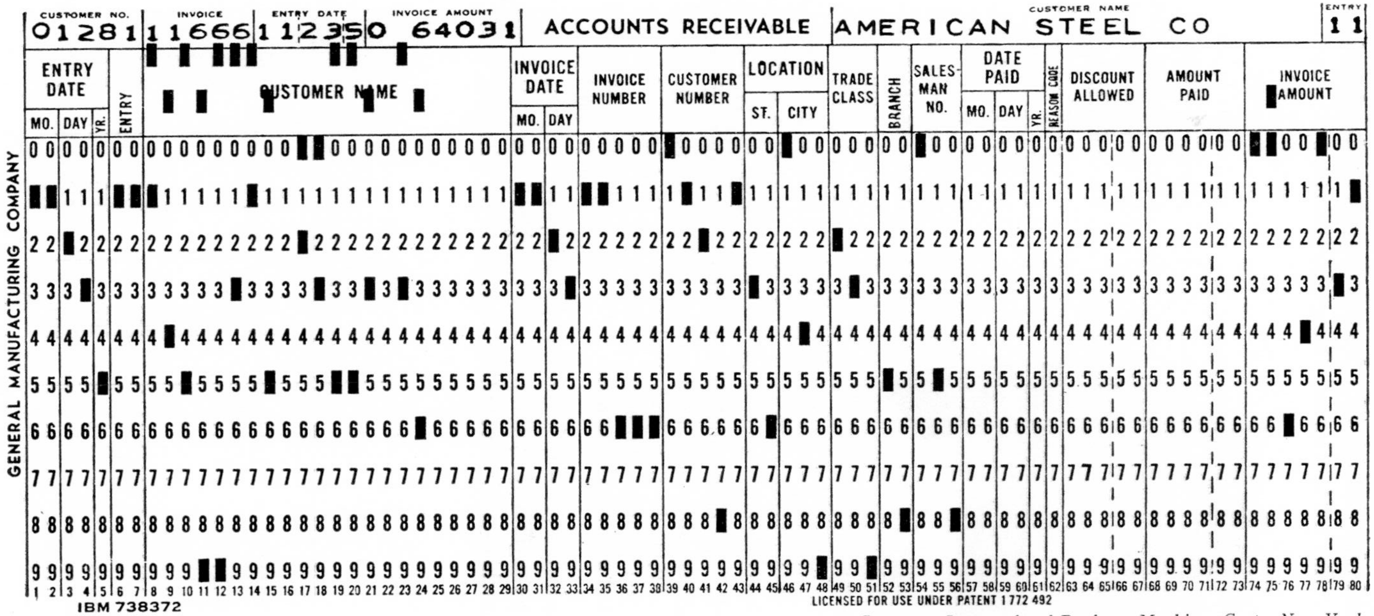

Courtesy: *International Business Machines Corp., New York*

FIG. 18–9. The space on the punched card is allocated according to the needs of the particular study.

proper numerical sequence. The first sort arranges the data in sequence according to the unit column. Then, the second sort rearranges this sequence according to the 10's column. In like manner, the third sort rearranges the 100's column, thus placing the cards in proper numerical sequence. Sorting machines are capable of handling 1,000 cards per minute, or 60,000 per hour.

*Courtesy: International Business Machines Corp., New York*

FIG. 18–10. A card-punching machine which features an automatic card control of skipping and duplicating, a fast method of duplication when desired, and a design which permits efficient and rapid operation.

The tabulator prepares printed reports from the data contained on the punched and sorted cards. These machines can print individually or in summary; a great variety of reports is possible. The number of reports that can be printed is almost limitless but depends mainly upon the information to be "read" by the machine, the forms on which the reports are prepared, and the arrangement and rearrangement of the cards. A tabulator—or as it is sometimes called, a punched-card accounting machine—is illustrated in Figure 18–12.

| Unsorted Data | Arrangement after First Sort | Arrangement after Second Sort | Arrangement after Third Sort |
|---|---|---|---|
| | ↓ | ↓ | ↓ |
| 828 | 750 | 904 | 107 |
| 107 | 460 | 107 | 191 |
| 542 | 191 | 212 | 212 |
| 904 | 542 | 828 | 375 |
| 212 | 212 | 542 | 388 |
| 375 | 904 | 750 | 460 |
| 191 | 375 | 460 | 542 |
| 750 | 107 | 375 | 750 |
| 388 | 828 | 388 | 828 |
| 460 | 388 | 191 | 904 |

FIG. 18–11.

*Courtesy: International Business Machines Corp., New York*

FIG. 18–12.  A punched-card accounting machine that provides an economic and rapid method of printing from punched cards.

## SPECIAL PUNCHED-CARD MACHINES

Special machines for specific operations are also available. A complete listing of these is beyond the scope of this discussion, but the more common ones will be included. A machine called an "interpreter" prints at the top of the card the data represented by the punched holes. This information is sometimes desired for quick identification and reference. However, many experienced and skilled operators can read the punched cards as easily as the average person reads normal print. A "verifier" can be used to check the accuracy of the holes punched in the cards. Another machine, called a reproducer or "gang punch," is designed to punch standardized information on cards. For example, data such as date and location of customer, which are repetitive for a batch of cards, can be punched at one time and not performed individually for each card. There is also a calculator, or "multiplying punch," which senses, for example, two factors prepunched in the card, computes the product, punches it into the card, and records the factors and the product on a paper.

Variable information such as meter readings, job data, and stores requisitions can be pencil-marked in appropriate spaces on a punched-card area. Then, by means of a machine called an "optical scanning punch," the variable information is read and automatically punched into the card, thus making it ready for processing.

With the developments in office automation and especially source data automation, many punched cards are now produced simultaneously with the typing of the information on a typewriter equipped with special attachments or units "connected with" the typewriter. Such machines were discussed in Chapter 11.

## USAGE OF PUNCHED-CARD MACHINES

The most common uses for punched-card machines are (1) correlating, analyzing, and summarizing data, such as sales by customer, and net

### SALES AND GROSS PROFIT BY CUSTOMER

| CUSTOMER | | | COMMODITY | | QUANTITY | UNIT | COST OF GOODS SOLD | SALES AMOUNT |
|---|---|---|---|---|---|---|---|---|
| BR. | NO. | CODE | DESCRIPTION | | | | | |
| 1 3 | 6 7 | | ACE DRUG CO | | | | | |
| 1 3 | 6 7 | 0 3 0 1 | BEAUTY SOAP REGULAR | | 1 2 | D Z | 1 9 8 0 | 2 4 0 0 |
| 1 3 | 6 7 | 0 3 0 2 | BEAUTY SOAP GUEST | | 1 2 | D Z | 2 0 4 0 | 2 5 2 0 |
| 1 3 | 6 7 | 0 3 0 3 | BEAUTY SOAP BATH | | 1 2 | D Z | 2 1 6 0 | 2 7 0 0 |
| 1 3 | 6 7 | 1 3 1 4 | SHAVE SOAP LARGE | | 2 4 | D Z | 4 8 0 0 | 6 9 6 0 |
| 1 3 | 6 7 | 1 3 5 2 | BRUSHLESS CREAM LRG | | 2 4 | D Z | 3 1 2 0 | 4 3 2 0 |
| | | | [ FOR THE PURPOSE OF THIS EXHIBIT, ONLY] [ A FEW COMMODITIES ARE ILLUSTRATED] | | | | | |
| | | | | | | | 2 7 5 0 0 ☆ | 3 7 5 0 0 |
| 1 3 | 1 0 5 | | ADAMS DRYGOODS CO | | | | | |
| 1 3 | 1 0 5 | 0 3 0 1 | BEAUTY SOAP REGULAR | | 2 4 | D Z | 3 9 6 0 | 4 9 0 0 |

### NET REVENUE ANALYSIS BY SALESMAN

| BRANCH | SALESMAN | | GROSS SALES | RETURNS AND ALLOWANCES | NET SALES | COST SALES | TRAVEL AND EXPENSE | COM |
|---|---|---|---|---|---|---|---|---|
| | NO. | NAME | | | | | | |
| 1 3 | 2 9 | A ANDREWS | 5 4 0 3 0 0 | 3 7 5 0 0 | 5 0 2 8 0 0 | 2 9 6 0 0 0 | 2 5 7 0 | |
| 1 3 | 3 2 | G DRISCOLL | 6 1 1 9 0 0 | 4 3 5 0 0 | 5 6 8 4 0 0 | 3 8 2 5 0 0 | 2 6 4 0 | |
| 1 3 | 4 5 | R M EDWARDS | 3 9 0 5 0 0 | 3 4 0 0 0 | 3 5 6 5 0 0 | 2 2 4 0 0 0 | 2 9 0 0 | |
| 1 3 | 4 7 | A H FRANKLIN | 7 5 1 3 0 0 | 4 5 0 0 0 | 7 0 6 3 0 0 | 5 1 3 5 0 0 | 2 8 0 0 | |
| 1 3 | 5 1 | J A HOLLAND | 6 2 5 7 0 0 | 4 4 1 0 0 | 5 8 1 6 0 0 | 3 8 5 5 0 0 | 2 6 2 5 | |
| 1 3 | 5 5 | L B LAWSON | 6 1 2 0 0 0 | 4 2 9 0 0 | 5 6 9 1 0 0 | 3 8 5 0 0 0 | 2 5 7 5 | |

*Courtesy: International Business Machines Corp., New York*

FIG. 18–13.   Samples of the work prepared by a tabulator of punched cards.

revenue by salesman, as illustrated by Figure 18–13; (2) preparing bills or invoices—the data on cards can be easily grouped and totaled; (3) handling accounts payable—each payment to a creditor is processed via a punched card; (4) keeping inventory records—purchases and usages by items are simple operations with punched cards; (5) preparing payrolls and distributing labor costs—checks are prepared from information on the card for each employee, and tabular lists can be quickly run as well as labor cost allocated to predetermined groups; and (6) production control—for each production operation, pertinent data and its relationship to other operations are put on separate punched cards, from which production routing and dispatching information are easily prepared.

Key considerations in the usage of punched cards include the cost and time of getting the raw data punched into the cards, the extent to which correlated or listed information will be helpful, and the value of additional facts gained from being able to interpret the data in a more feasible form. The use of punched cards is not necessarily confined to large companies. In most instances, punched cards are feasible when the data (1) are fairly repetitious, permitting prepunching for much of the data, and (2) require analysis to show pertinent relationships.

## MARGINAL NOTCHED-CARD MACHINES

These machines are used to notch precoded holes *along the edge* of a card so that sorting of the data by key classifications can be accomplished quickly and accurately. After sorting, data referring to a similar attribute, such as sales, inventories, or indirect labor costs, can be totaled and used in management reports. The process is versatile; it is applicable to many transactions, including sales orders, stock requisitions, purchase and expense vouchers, payroll records, and production control data.

The cards are available in varying sizes; for example, there are 2 x 3½-inch and 7½ x 8½-inch cards. Pertinent information is written in the center position of the card. Holes along the margins are assigned definite values depending upon their location. Identification with a particular classification is made by notching away the portion of the card between the hole and the edge. For example, in Figure 18–14, the operation number 24 can be identified by the notches in the upper left margin of the card where the 2 under the 10's and the 4 under the units have been notched. Likewise, the date, May 22, is coded in the left margin, indicating that the month is 5 and the day is 22. Observe that for any one segment, the holes of values 7, 4, 2, and 1 make possible any value from 1 through 9. Zero is indicated by no notches.

To sort cards, either a special machine or a manual means can be used. The former is recommended for large volumes of cards. The latter utilizes a single or a multiprong fork which is positioned so that it slides through a designated hole or holes in a stack of cards. By shaking the pack, the operator causes the cards with notched holes at the prong location to fall clear of the other cards. In this way a fast, accurate sort is provided.

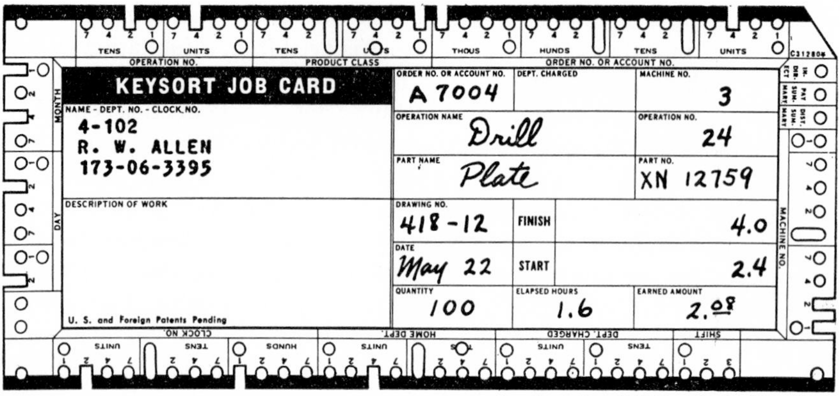

FIG. 18–14. Card punched with holes and notches to indicate definite information.

## ACCOUNTING MACHINES

In this category we include billing machines, posting machines, and bookkeeping machines. These machines are basically mechanical aids which simplify and expedite paper work. Many are equipped with "bars," or accumulating registers, which make it possible to summarize and to distribute accounts, a valuable feature particularly with records dealing with cost, sales, and payroll. These machines are not wholly automatic. Usually the proper keys must be depressed and the motor bar pushed to start each cycle of machine operation. Some are equipped with a calculating mechanism for multiplying and adding from which the operator reads the calculated amount and types it in the appropriate column. Many feature checking or proofing devices the designs of which differ with different manufacturers. In some, they consist of showing a number which is compared with an original, such as "old balance," or with an entry number, for proof of accuracy. For each horizontal line of figures, the proof-line figure must be equal to that of the old balance; otherwise, an error is in that horizontal line. In some cases, the machine locks and will not print if old entries have been picked up incorrectly. Accounting machines can be classified in a number of ways. Figure 18–15 shows some common bases for classifying machines, along with comments on each type of machine.

## DESCRIPTIVE ACCOUNTING MACHINE

To illustrate further the types of accounting machines and the kind of work done with them, several brief descriptions will be included. The first

| Basis of Classification | Types |
|---|---|
| Keyboard.... | *Descriptive Machine.* Equipped with both typewriter and numerical keyboards.     *Nondescriptive Machine.* Has numerical keyboard only. |
| Bed.......... | *Flat Bed Machine.* The printing surface and the papers are placed horizontally onto this flat bed. Advocates claim it simplifies insertion of papers.     *Platen or Carriage Machine.* The papers are inserted in the carriage, and platen is turned similar to that of a typewriter. |
| Print........ | *Single-Print Machine.* Prints two or more copies simultaneously. Papers are inserted into machine as a pack with carbon interleaved.     *Multiprint Machine.* Papers are placed side by side into the machine, which prints one paper and then moves over and prints the same data or portions of them on the other paper. |
| Style........ | *Window Machine.* Papers are placed in an opening or window; machine entries are printed while papers are held in this position. Easily handles entries in booklets, as in a bank, and expedites visual checking by operator and customers.     *Nonwindow Machine.* Papers are placed in the carriage or on the flat bed—there is no window opening of the machine. |

FIG. 18–15.   Common classifications of accounting machines.

is the descriptive accounting machine, for which the work of accounts payable can be used. For illustrative purposes, the work of a purchase journal, remittance advice, and distribution expense ledger are used. These are shown by Figure 18–16. These data are printed simultaneously by the descriptive accounting machine. The machine's typewriter is used to write in the descriptive material of the vendors' names on the purchase journal. For example, referring to Figure 18–16, the purchases from Smith Supply Company are posted January 9, for $16 and $8.50, making the balance due $170. For inventory or expense purposes, the items are distributed directly to the proper column, shown in the upper right of the figure. The item for $16 is charged to Miscellaneous account 84; and likewise, the second item of $8.50 is charged to Miscellaneous account 92. These data are printed on the respective distribution ledgers, as shown by the illustration. Distribution totals are accumulated automatically. The same machine can be used if a voucher check is used instead of a remittance advice. When due, the remittance advice is paid, less any discount allowed. Illustration of this work is not included here; but for this payment work, a check and a check register are prepared simultaneously by the same machine. A carbon copy of the check is made on the office copy of the remittance notice. Partial payments are handled by posting to suppliers' accounts during the check-

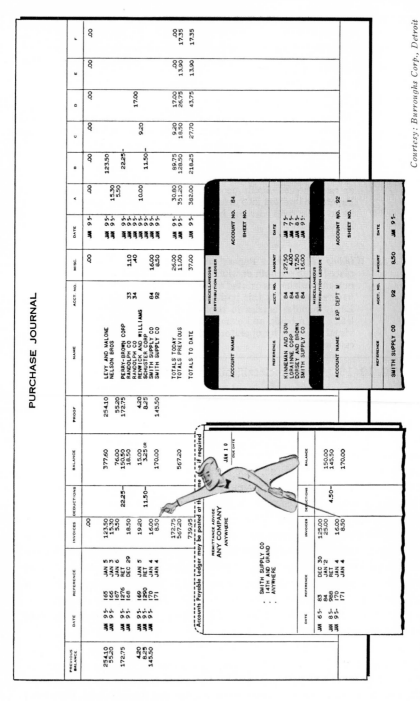

*Courtesy: Burroughs Corp., Detroit*

FIG. 18–16. Remittance advice, purchase journal with distribution, and distribution ledger prepared simultaneously with a descriptive accounting machine.

writing operation. Checks written that do not affect accounts payable, such as those to replenish the petty cash fund or for transportation charges, are written and distributed directly to the columns affected.

Different features are stressed by different descriptive accounting machines. Most are adaptable for many different types of work and are useful for any one or all types, including general ledger, accounts payable, accounts receivable, and payroll. Figure 18–17 shows a popular model. This machine features a single keyboard, program keys on the typewriter, and an electronic processing unit housed in the pedestal of the desklike

*Courtesy: Friden, Inc., San Leandro, Calif.*

FIG. 18–17. The 5010 COMPUTYPER Electronic Billing/Accounting Machine produces completed invoices at electronic speeds. Data are stored, calculations performed in milliseconds, and removal program panels are featured for unlimited machine applications.

unit. For the work of billing, the operator has only to enter figures and descriptions, and the machine automatically does the rest, including extensions, additions, deductions, percentages, discounts, subtractions, and totals. The machine automatically handles calculations in quantities of dozens and pieces, decimals, fractions, and for use in the lumber industry converts board feet into square feet and accumulates the number of pieces of lumber and the linear feet.

## NONDESCRIPTIVE ACCOUNTING MACHINE

Figure 18–18 shows a nondescriptive accounting machine. In discussing the work of this type of accounting machine, sometimes referred to as a numerical keyboard accounting machine, consider accounts receivable work in which the ledger, statement, and proof-tape journal are prepared. Figure 18–19 shows these records. To illustrate, for the last entry, the operator inserted the forms into the machine; entered the old balance, the reference numbers, and the charge by depressing the proper keys; then actuated the machine by the motor bar. The machine automatically prints all the needed information, including date, reference number, charges, and the new balance, on the three forms. To reset the machine for other accounting forms, such as accounts payable, a quick adjustment is

*Courtesy: Burroughs Corp., Detroit*

FIG. 18–18.   A modern nondescriptive accounting machine.

provided by turning a knob at either side of the machine. The letter material at the top of the ledger and the statement can be written by means of a typewriter or an addressing machine. The ledger copy is permanent and retained; a statement is mailed monthly to the customer.

## ADDRESSING AND LISTING MACHINES

Affixing addresses or other information in applications where the same information is used periodically typifies one of the popular uses for addressing and listing machines. Their widest application is probably in addressing envelopes or advertising literature. The use of these machines is beneficial wherever a small quantity of identical information must be

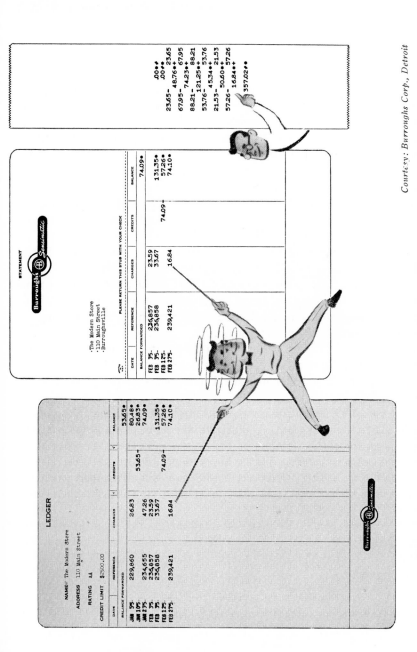

*Courtesy: Burroughs Corp., Detroit*

FIG. 18–19.  Accounts receivable work consisting of original ledger, statement, and proof-tape journal. The entries are made by the machine shown in Figure 18–18.

written repeatedly. In addition to mailing lists, the following are typical applications: names of employees along with standardized payroll information, i.e., check number and social security number; addresses on shipping labels and tags; headings on invoices and ledger cards; listing of customers; items ordered; items of storekeeping; lists of tools; tax roll; names and addresses of stockholders; and the list of dividend recipients.

There are two types of addressing and listing machines: those using metal-embossed plates and those using fiber or tissue stencils. Metal plates are made in a machine especially designed for that purpose. The plate is stamped, thus forcing the required impressions in the metal. Metal plates give very long service; they practically never wear out. The fiber stencils can be prepared on a typewriter equipped with a special platen, last a long time, but should be handled carefully. It is also possible to type or cut a punched tape which, when fed through an automatic machine for making plates, will produce them at a high rate of speed.

Most machines using metal plates permit attachments which add considerably to their value for specific operations. Included are:

1. *A cutoff device.* This permits only part of the plate to print at one time. It is useful where a portion of the information on the plate is printed in the first column of a spread sheet, another part in the second column, a third part in a third column, and so on.

2. *A selector.* By its use certain plates pass through the machine without writing. This feature is desirable, for example, when certain plates are wanted for a particular mailing. The sequence of the plates remains unchanged.

3. *A repeater.* Duplicate impressions are made from each plate before advancing to the next plate. To illustrate, the name and address might be required on the check stub and on the check, or on the statement and on the envelope. Settings for triplicate impressions are also available.

4. *A dating device.* This enters the date simultaneously with the printing of other data. It is used in connection with statements and letters.

5. *Tabbing sockets.* By inserting small metal projections into selected tabs of the plate, selective sorting of the plates is accomplished. The sockets are located along the top edge of the plate and tabs are inserted according to a code.

## MISCELLANEOUS EQUIPMENT AND MACHINES

Numbering devices are used to place numbers chronologically on incoming orders, memorandums, and other papers in order to process the papers more effectively. They are offered in a variety of sizes, capacities, and prices. Well designed, they give satisfactory service for many years.

Check protectors are employed to make out checks in perforated print so that the chances for altering the words or figures are eliminated. Different styles and types of print are available. Most check protectors are manually operated. Also offered are units that sign checks, thus eliminating much laborious and repetitious work for some executives.

Copyholders, especially helpful for stenographers doing copy work, hold papers in place at a convenient reading level. A horizontal bar guides the eye to the proper line. Since the material is held in a proper reading position, posture is aided and eyestrain, head twisting, and fatiguing refocusing of the eyes are eliminated.

A time punch prepares cards by punching the start and stop times directly into the card. The punched cards can be processed immediately and no manual computation of elapsed time or verification are required. The machine is used for labor cost analysis, production control, and machine loading. Figure 18–20 shows this machine.

Counters provide quick measurement of units and the speed of certain office work. Bank checks, cards, and labels, for example, can be quickly counted by use of these machines. Some are operated manually, while others are attached to common office machines to indicate such information as the number of strokes of typing on a typewriter or the revolutions of the cylindrical drum of a duplicating machine.

*Courtesy: Universal Time Punch, Inc., Cleveland*

FIG. 18–20.  A time-punch machine that records time records by punching directly a tab or time card.

Labeling machines prepare addressed labels in long, continuous-length strips. The back of the labels is mucilaged. The strips are cut automatically and individually for each label just prior to its being affixed to an envelope, package, or periodical. The labels are available in a variety of sizes. The speed of the machine is relatively high.

Electric staplers, used for attaching sheets of paper together, are employed for large volumes of this work. The stapling of booklets or reports, for example, is illustrative. Savings of much effort and time are gained by using an electric stapler.

## QUESTIONS

1. For what specific office machines do you believe the employees' preference would be a very important factor in machine selection? For what office machines would it be unimportant? Discuss your answers.

2. Discuss the advantages of renting office equipment and machines rather than buying them. Do you favor renting or buying? Why?

3. Carefully distinguish between each in the following pairs:
   a) Desk design and modular office furniture.
   b) Trade-in of office machine and leasing of office machine.
   c) Marginal notched cards and punched cards.
   d) Copyholder and check protector.

4. Does the supplying of a posture chair insure that the office employee who occupies it will have good posture while seated? Why?

5. What arrangement do you favor to provide for the proper maintenance of a new accounting machine in a small office employing nine people? Justify your answer.

6. Rank the following factors—flexibility of use, aesthetic values, amount of time saved—used in the selection of office equipment and machines in the order of their importance as you see it. Justify your answer.

7. Assume an office manager is considering the purchase of a calculating machine costing $750 for use by an employee receiving $4,800 a year. Explain how Figure 18–1 might assist the office manager to reach a decision regarding the purchase of the calculating machine.

8. Comment on the following quotation: "Trying out the office equipment or machine under actual conditions can go a long way toward determining its adequacy and desirability in a particular office. However, a trial has a tendency to obligate the user and may result in a purchase when such is not in order."

9. You are contemplating the purchase of seven electric typewriters for a centralized stenographic department. Three different manufacturers' makes are being considered. Basing your decision on the following data, which make of machine would you purchase?

| | ELECTRIC TYPEWRITER | | |
| --- | --- | --- | --- |
| | A | B | C |
| Unit cost................................ | $565.00 | $490.00 | $520.00 |
| Done business with manufacturer in past.... | Yes | No | No |
| Employees' preference.................. | Third | Second | First |
| Quality of work done by machine......... | Satisfactory | Satisfactory | Satisfactory |
| Aggressiveness and competency of sales representative........................... | Average | Average | Very Satisfactory |

Justify your decision.

10. Distinguish carefully between the concepts in each of the following pairs:
    a) Nondescriptive and nonwindow accounting machines.
    b) Gang punch and "optical scanning" punch.
    c) Fiber stencil and posting machine.
    d) Electric stapler and time-punch machine.

11. Discuss the use of the descriptive accounting machine in the office.

12. Name the common punched card machines, briefly relating what basic work each machine performs. In general, the usage of punched card machines can be classified into six different groups. Name four of these groups.

## CASE PROBLEMS

### Case 18–1.  Linn Company

Purchase of an office machine is being considered for work now performed manually. Either machine "A" or machine "B" will process the work satisfactorily, but the cost of the former is $3,800 installed while that of the latter is $4,500 installed. Labor cost to operate machine "A" will be $2.75 an hour, supplies, $100 a year, power, $5 a month. In contrast, for machine "B," the labor cost will be $2.60 an hour, supplies, $125 a year, and power, $5 a month. Currently, the labor cost is $2.35 an hour for the one employee required. She devotes full time to the work, which can be considered 2,000 hours a year (50 weeks x 40 hours a week). Supplies now cost $192 a year.

It is estimated that to accomplish the work machine "A" will be used about 68 percent of a normal work year (2,000 hours) or machine "B" about 55 percent. Practices followed by the company are to charge 6 percent interest on money invested in an office machine, use 10 percent annual allowance for depreciation, and 12 percent annually for taxes and machine maintenance.

### Problems:

1. Calculate the total annual costs for the first year using (1) manual, (2) machine "A," or (3) machine "B."
2. How long will it take for machine "A" to pay for itself out of savings? Machine "B"?
3. What is your recommendation for this company? Justify your viewpoint.

### Case 18–2.  The Underhill Company

A current problem in the office of the Underhill Company is keeping notes receivable accounts up to date. The majority of these notes are monthly, although some are weekly. Currently, a general ledger and a supplementary ledger in the form of a visible card index are used. When a payment is received, a receipt, in duplicate, is made out; the original is sent to the customer, and the copy is retained by the company for its records. From this copy, payments are posted to the customer or account card, all of which make up the visible card file. When posting, the balances due, discounts earned, and total paid to date are calculated and entered upon the card. Because of the volume and urgency of other work, the posting to the cards is performed about every sixth day and to the general ledger about every three weeks.

Under the present arrangement, it is difficult to be aware of all delinquent accounts immediately. Also, from time to time, serious errors have occurred in the posting of the information to the cards and to the general ledger. Finding such mistakes is a problem in itself, but more serious is rectifying the error with the customer. In addition, during the past three years, there has been a constant growth in the number of accounts, and there is good reason to believe that this growth will continue.

The office manager is considering several actions that might be taken. He is of the opinion that an office machine should be used for this work.

## Problems:

1. What are the major actions that the office manager should take?

2. Assuming that you agree with the office manager that a machine should be used, what type of office machine would you recommend? Why?

3. Describe in necessary detail how the work would be handled, utilizing the machine recommended in the answer to question No. 2, above.

### Case 18–3.    Security Insurance of Saint Louis

For the past several months, discussions dealing with modernization of office facilities have been held by executives of Security Insurance of Saint Louis. At the last meeting, approval to proceed was passed, and a committee was authorized to formulate a complete plan and submit it to the president of the company within 60 days. Approval of the committee's recommendations would be a routine matter. The prime purpose of the committee was to determine what office equipment to purchase and to keep expenditures within the authorized limits. The committee consisted of the office manager, the controller, and the personnel manager.

Since the prescribed expenditures were somewhat limited, the committee decided to purchase what was probably most important—desks and chairs. It was believed this would be a good start in the company's office modernization program. Suppliers of this type of equipment were called in and requested to submit bids. It soon became apparent that the company's tentative appropriation for this purpose was insufficient to purchase as many desks and chairs as the committee had in mind.

The controller suggested that a survey of the present equipment be made and purchases be limited to what was most in need of replacement. Several suppliers agreed to make this survey free of charge and to take the used equipment as partial payment on the new equipment. The personnel manager, however, objected to this plan, explaining that for an office employee with a new desk and chair to work alongside an employee with an old desk and chair might cause difficulty and some misunderstanding among employees.

The idea was also advanced that either new desks only or new chairs only be purchased. But disagreement over which should be purchased existed among the committee members. One committee member strongly advocated new desks, since these provide the working areas, are in full view, and contribute a great deal toward improving the general appearance of an office. In contrast, it was pointed out that a new comfortable chair probably would mean more to an employee and would result in more favorable comments by the employees.

The office manager rejected the idea that the project be held in abeyance pending the availability of more money to purchase both desks and chairs and perhaps other modernization work. He believes a beginning must be made now and eventually the entire office probably will be improved. In his opinion, to delay will bury the office modernization program indefinitely.

Problems:

1. Evaluate the viewpoints of the controller; of the office manager.
2. What alternatives are available to the company?
3. What action should be taken? Why?

CHAPTER 19

# OFFICE
# SPACE PLANNING

One of the best ways to persuade others is with
your ears—by listening to them.
                                    —Dean Rusk

ANOTHER important area of office management planning is office space planning which is *the arrangement of all physical components within the available floor space to provide maximum effectiveness and the coordination of these components into an efficient and attractive unity.* By means of space planning we seek to facilitate a good flow of office work, use office space effectively, locate equipment and machines conveniently, assist supervision, add to employees' comfort, impress favorably customers and visitors, and provide for future expansion or contraction, as the case may be. All of these are essential to proper office management and all are provided by adequate office space planning.

At the outset it is wise to recognize that space planning is not all factual or technical. We can use dimensions, lengths of work flows, percentages of effective space, and the like, but in addition to these data we must take into account the managerial climate, principal likes, and attitudes. For example, answers to basic questions such as these are needed: What image or impression should the space convey? Which is most important—cost, prestige, or appearance? Are functions performed or organization status or some other consideration to dictate the location and design of private offices? Recognizing these nontechnical factors makes the planning program realistic and lends assurance that the layout as developed will be adopted. Endless modifications are avoided. This does not mean that a passive approach should be followed. Incorporating improvements and progress is vital in planning, but practical experience

434

shows that in most cases important nontechnical considerations should be identified and utilized in space planning efforts.

## BASIC CONSIDERATIONS

Everyone seems to have ideas about office layout. Some of these ideas are excellent, while others are so impractical or incomplete that they are useless. In most instances, the help of an office layout specialist is recommended, for this assures that efficient office layout work will be done. This approach, however, does not prohibit the office manager or any executive from talking with the layout specialist and contributing to the task of evolving the best office space plans. Some companies have found that a planning committee works out very well to encourage participation in office layout work.

In order of their increasing difficulty, office layouts are for either new, remodeled, or currently used areas. New areas normally permit the most effective space utilization; completely coordinated space planning is possible. The next group—remodeled areas—sometimes poses difficult-to-solve problems, in that the building facilities are inadequate or the space modernization is incomplete. Finally, the planning of existing areas for space improvement can be both fascinating and frustrating, in that considerable improvement in space utilization can usually be brought about, but certain rigidities prevent a desired level of space efficiency being attained.

Space planning is usually a continuous type of activity. It arises when (1) a new or modified system or procedure is adopted, (2) an increase or decrease in either work or personnel is made, (3) a change in organization is made—either adding or taking away from a unit, and (4) complaints from employees are heard about their work areas suggesting elimination of the poor areas that infest the office layout.

Ineffective use of office space is a continuous liability. It contributes to office inefficiency daily, and continues to do so until an improved layout is planned and put into effect. The individual daily loss may be small; but when consideration is given the cumulative amount—for a month or a year, for example—the importance of proper layout is brought into bolder relief. Office space represents a definite cost. While it does not represent the largest portion of office expenditures, it usually does represent a sizable outlay, and it should be kept within reasonable limits.

From the viewpoint of space planning, most large offices are made up of four separate types of areas, including (1) private offices, (2) general office area, (3) service areas, and (4) storage areas. It helps to keep these in mind when preparing office layouts so that the overall viewpoint is maintained and the essentials for each type of area are included.

## SPACE PLANNING AND OFFICE SYSTEMS AND PROCEDURES

From the rational and technical viewpoint, space planning is governed and coordinated by the systems and procedures followed in performing the office work. The systems and procedures' contribution of what papers, people, equipment, and machines are used and what is done at each stage of work dictates what space planning should provide. Systems and procedures planning should be performed prior to the space planning and the latter is never divorced from the former.

Considering the office as a work area for handling information, it follows that every resource in the area is a tool to help do the work. As such each has a purpose as a coordinated unit and the space arrangement should help in integrating these various contributions. Some refer to this as "integrated space planning." It means that the acquiring of harmonious efforts toward common office goals is promoted by the office layout, or in other words, that office systems and procedures guide and are helped by the office space plans.

Emphasis should also be given to certain functions which condition the layout. These include office practices, personnel practices, records retention practices, and office services. In addition, the facilities of the building merit close attention including the number of elevators, location of the electrical distribution system—high voltage and low voltage, water, stairways, receiving and shipping areas, and special plumbing.[1] Especially important is the difference between the usable and the gross square feet area of the building. In some buildings this amounts to 30 percent of the building area, which is taken up by service cores, offset walls, columns, and primary corridors. The low efficiency of many buildings is not basically recognized, but if comparisons of office layouts in different locations are used, we must recognize that basic inefficiencies created in the construction of a building cannot be eliminated subsequently by the best of layouts.

## SPACE PLANNING AND FUNCTIONAL ANALYSIS

Many agree that space planning should be functional. It should serve to get the specific work accomplished. But to what should space planning be functional? The answer: to (1) organization, (2) function, activity, and duty, (3) office equipment and machines, and (4) communication. This leads to four types of functional analysis in office space planning.[2]

---

[1] See also Chapter 20, p. 473.

[2] These four types are from a statement by a prominent authority in office space planning, Mr. William I. Sohl, Ass't to the President and Executive Vice President, Art Metal, Inc. and Knoll Associates, Inc., New York, N.Y., December 28, 1965.

1. *The organization analysis.*  A study of organization charts is made to determine all personnel to be housed in the facility, the level of each, and formal lines of communication. Projections by organization unit for five years and for ten years are recommended.

2. *The function, activity, and duty analysis.*  The personnel activity is observed and recorded, and from this information the present work flow is revealed. The work at the present level and conditions required to execute it adequately are evaluated. Also, probable needs for five and ten years are forecast. A review of operations at each level with corresponding management member is now made and if any special studies seem appropriate, they are referred to the space planning head or committee.

3. *The office equipment and machine analysis.*  Along with the information obtained under part No. 2, data are secured on the equipment and machine requirements to perform each function, activity, and duty. This also encompasses observation of office practices followed, work station arrangements, reports prepared and used, common office policies followed, and control of traffic. We need an inventory of currently used equipment and machines, where they are located, and whether they appear suitable for continued use under either the present or a proposed layout. The need for special equipment warrants careful investigation. All these types of information are gathered during this third part.

4. *The communication analysis.*  This includes a survey of present facilities and an evaluation of their adequacy both for the present and for the contemplated facility. Not only are the number, type, and location of units important; also important are the communication aids of the physical facility itself, including size and location of ducting, floor conduits, and power lines which are required to employ the communication units advantageously.

The data from all these analyses are recorded on specially designed sheets to facilitate study. Some include questions to ask, others diagrams to fill in, and still others call for listing specific information under designated columns. This latter means is used for recording the inventory of equipment and machines. Figure 19–1 shows a portion of work sheets developed from the communication analysis. If such data are not compiled and used, it may subsequently be found that telephones have to be changed, outlets are incorrectly located, and unsightly conduits must be attached to the floors and ceilings.

It is extremely helpful to determine by organization units the approximate space needed. This is derived from data of the above analyses. Space requirements result not only from the people on the payroll but also, and more important, from the equipment and machine requirements of each member. We need therefore to keep the following data for each employee: name, functional title, units of equipment and size of each, machines and size of each, and other or miscellaneous area requirements. These can be

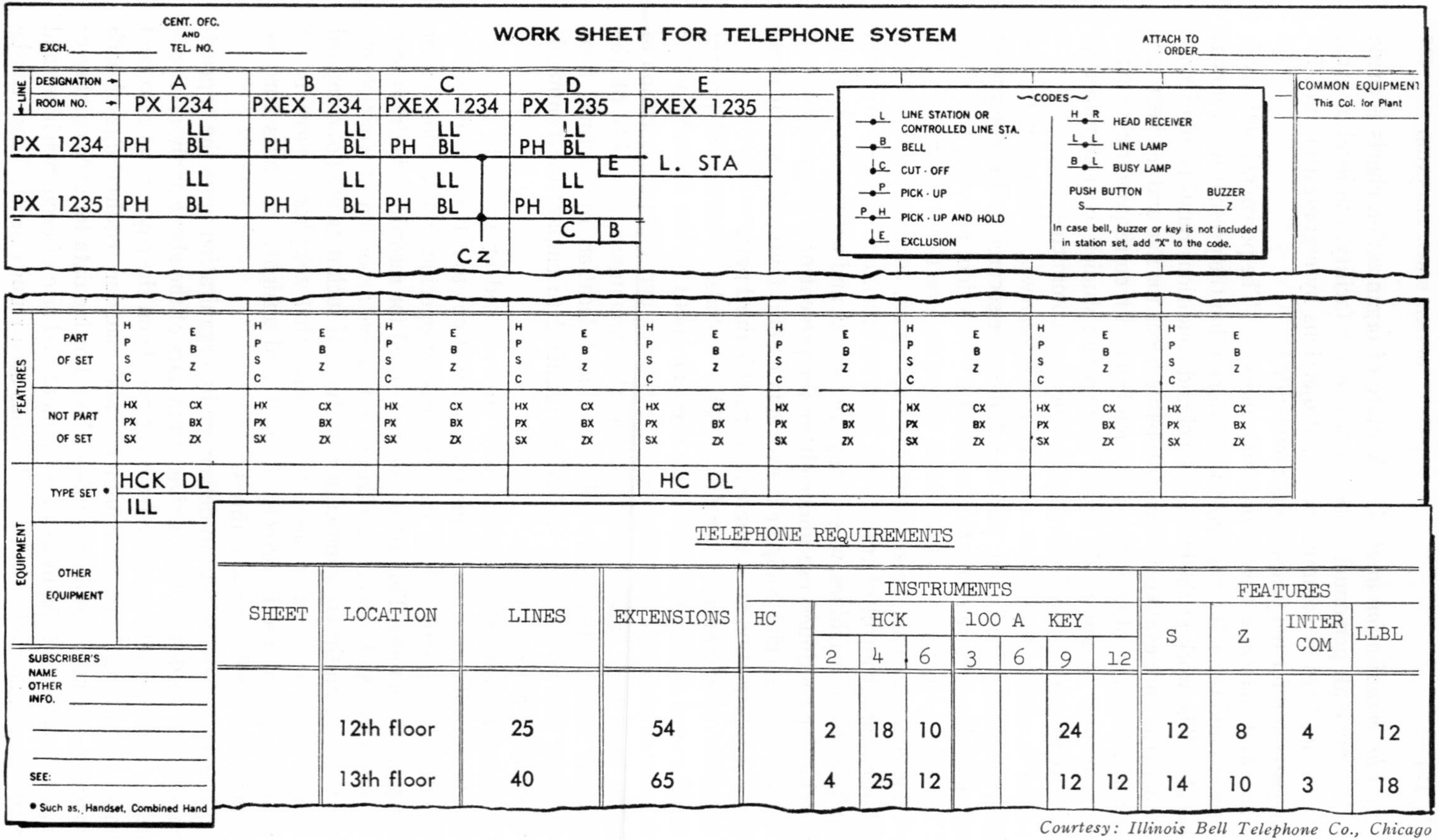

# WORK SHEET FOR TELEPHONE SYSTEM

EXCH. _____  CENT. OFC. AND TEL. NO. _____  ATTACH TO ORDER _____

| LINE DESIGNATION → | A | B | C | D | E | COMMON EQUIPMENT (This Col. for Plant) |
|---|---|---|---|---|---|---|
| ROOM NO. → | PX 1234 | PXEX 1234 | PXEX 1234 | PX 1235 | PXEX 1235 | |
| PX 1234 | PH LL BL | PH LL BL | PH LL BL | PH LL BL | | |
| PX 1235 | PH LL BL | PH LL BL | PH LL BL | PH LL BL | L. STA | |

CODES ~

- L  LINE STATION OR CONTROLLED LINE STA.
- B  BELL
- C  CUT-OFF
- P  PICK-UP
- P H  PICK-UP AND HOLD
- E  EXCLUSION
- H R  HEAD RECEIVER
- L L  LINE LAMP
- B L  BUSY LAMP
- S  PUSH BUTTON
- Z  BUZZER

In case bell, buzzer or key is not included in station set, add "X" to the code.

## FEATURES

| PART OF SET | H P S C | E B Z | HX PX SX | CX BX ZX |
| NOT PART OF SET | H P S C | E B Z | HX PX SX | CX BX ZX |
| TYPE SET • | HCK DL | | | |

## EQUIPMENT

OTHER EQUIPMENT

SUBSCRIBER'S NAME _____ OTHER _____ INFO. _____

SEE: _____

• Such as, Handset, Combined Hand

## TELEPHONE REQUIREMENTS

| SHEET | LOCATION | LINES | EXTENSIONS | HC | HCK | 100 A | KEY | S | Z | INTER COM | LLBL |
|---|---|---|---|---|---|---|---|---|---|---|---|
| | | | | | | | | | | | |
| | 12th floor | 25 | 54 | 2 | 18 | 10 | 24 | 12 | 8 | 4 | 12 |
| | 13th floor | 40 | 65 | 4 | 25 | 12 | 12 | 14 | 12 | 3 | 18 |

INSTRUMENTS — FEATURES

FIG. 19–1.  Telephone work sheets used in space planning.

the heads of columns for our spread sheet. Projections for future periods can be included in the extreme right columns, if desired. Incidentally, such data will show the specific makeup of personnel accounting for the anticipated greater space requirements. From these sheets detailed space needs are easily obtained.

A quick and helpful comparison should now be made. One should calculate the square feet of usable space and compare it with the square feet of space needed. This will reveal whether there is too little, too much, or enough space. If there is too little, some rigorous adjustments must be made at once. If there is too much, the surplus should be either utilized for additional purposes, screened off in readiness for future expansion, or rented. Leaving it open and idle may well result in adjacent units spilling into these areas, and after this happens, space control is lessened and an orderly expansion program is ignored.

## WHO GOES WHERE?

The next task is to determine the general location of the various units within the total usable space. For this purpose, functional flow studies are used. They show who works with whom and what goes where. Flow is either (1) by papers or (2) by people. We try to minimize the latter, but both must be used. Usually there are key papers about which work of certain units revolve. Tracing the movement of such papers supplies clues as to what units should be related and in what sequence. Data from the communication analysis are also beneficial in this respect. Probably the most reliable data come from an analysis of the systems and procedures. Even though time-consuming and somewhat complex to carry out, it is normally well worth the work.

Our efforts result in showing the relationship of components and can be illustrated graphically by a block diagram as given in Figure 19–2. Each block identifies the department or unit to be included in the layout. The width of the line joining two blocks indicates the quantity of work flow and the physical requirements for communication between these two units. Keeping in mind these relationships of components, the overall work flow, and the nontechnical factors fostered by top managers, the space planner strives to fit the requirements into the usable space so that the work can be accomplished efficiently and under pleasing physical conditions. In this evolving of the layout, knotty problems arise. Trial and error, patience, and experience assist, but also helpful are utilizing certain layout guides and space standards, and following certain layout steps. However, before presenting these latter aids, a brief comment about the use of CRAFT should be made.

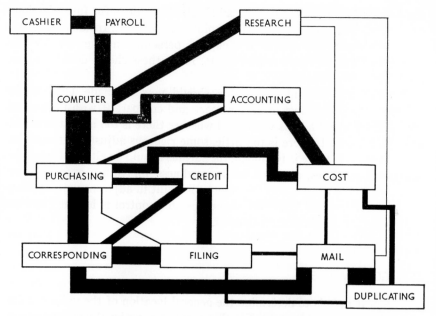

FIG. 19–2.    Block diagram showing relationship of components.

## CRAFT

One of the newer and more interesting means for determining the best relationship of components is CRAFT (Computerized Relative Allocation of Facilities Technique).[3] This technique gives an answer which is difficult to improve upon. A diagram is drawn showing how the units are related to each other. Adjustments are then made to find the arrangement of units having the best relationship contributing to the effectiveness of the totality, as measured by cost or time (some measurable unit) for the various work flows and communication efforts. Input data to the computer start with the total cost of work flow and communication for a given pattern. Then, the change in the total cost brought about by two units exchanging positions is calculated. Subsequently calculations by the computer proceed through all combinations of exchanges among the units. For 20 units or departments, and using paired exchanges, some 190 calculations are required. If any unit is to be considered not a candidate for exchanging positions, it can be so programmed. Hence, by means of a computer, the relationship among components to provide the total minimum cost of work flow and communication can be precisely determined.

---

[3] E. S. Buffa, G. C. Armour, and T. E. Vollmann, "Allocating Facilities With Craft," *Harvard Business Review,* March–April, 1964.

The printed output shows the physical locations. Each printed column and each line represent a given measurement like 10 feet, so that 5 columns by 20 lines represents 10,000 square feet. Within this area the letter F, for example, in 2 adjacent columns and of 3 adjacent lines deep represents an area 20 feet by 30 feet, or 600 square feet for filing. Its position is the best for filing, considering the total layout, and is shown relative to that of all other units or departments. Armed with such information, we know what units to locate adjacent to what other units and have the structural framework for the most effective layout.

## BASIC LAYOUT GUIDES

There have been developed a number of layout guides which when followed help to provide an effective office arrangement. Not all of these can be followed in any one layout; but in general, the more that are included, the better the layout. The list includes:

1. Utilize one large area in preference to an equivalent area of small parcels. The single large area permits better lighting, ventilating, supervising, and communicating.

2. Use uniform-size desks in any one area. This gives better appearance and promotes the feeling of equality among employees.

3. Keep filing cabinets and other cabinets at uniform height in any one area to improve general appearance.

4. Use straight symmetry in layout. Avoid offsets, jogs, and angle arrangements.

5. Give major preference to the dominant flows of work and communication needs. Provide for straight-line work flows and avoid backtracking, crisscrossing, and unnecessary movement of papers.

6. Place related departments adjacent, and keep jobs of a similar nature in close relationship.

7. Locate departments which normally have many visitors from the outside near the entrance; or if this is not feasible, make provisions so that this traffic will not disturb other departments.

8. Locate vending machines, fountains, and bulletin boards where they will cause least distraction and congestion.

9. Provide for maximum work loads.

10. Have the work come to the employee, not the employee go to the work. Keep employee flow to a minimum.

11. Locate supervisors at the rear of their work groups, so that they can easily observe what goes on in the work area.

12. Place all employees so that they face in the same direction. Do not have employees facing one another.

13. Arrange desks so that ample natural light comes from a little back and over the left shoulder.

14. Avoid private office locations which cut off natural light to the adjacent general office area.

15. Do not have the employee facing a window, too near heat sources, or in line of drafts.

16. Use movable partitions for walls, as they are easy to install and can be quickly rearranged at will. Part-way partitions with plain or opaque glass permit good light and ventilation.

17. Provide sufficient floor electrical outlets for office equipment and machines.

18. Place units requiring noisy equipment and machines in an area with soundproofing to avoid disturbance to others.

19. Put files and frequently used equipment near the employees who use them. Abstain from putting all files at dead wall space.

20. Place filing cabinets back to back.

21. If a corner is required, consider the possibility of providing it with filing cabinets.

22. If possible, provide lounging areas where employees can relax during rest periods, talk informally, and eat lunch.

23. Provide convenient and adequate rest-room facilities.

24. Anticipate and provide for future changes. Keep the layout flexible.

## SPACE STANDARDS

The amount of space to be allocated for any given work station or department is subject to a great many considerations. The type of office work, the physical units, the shape of the area, the general effect desired, and the location of service facilities are examples of factors to be taken into account. Of prime importance are the individual circumstances of each case. Judgment and experience must be used in determining the correct allocation of space.

The following are helpful:

1. *Desk space standards.* Fairly uniform space standards have been evolved for common office units, such as desks and chairs. For example, when 60 x 34-inch desks are arranged as single units with aisles adjacent, or when they are arranged in pairs, end for end, with aisles adjacent to each desk, the minimum space standard from back to back of desks is about 72 inches. See Figure 19–3 (top illustration). These arrangements provide about a 3-foot strip for the chair and for getting to and from the desk. The bottom illustration of the figure shows space standards for three desks placed end for end. Of the three plans shown in this figure, plan No. 2 requires the smallest area per clerk; in contrast, plan No. 1 requires the most.

2. *Office corridor standards.* Main corridors should be from 5 to 8 feet wide, depending upon the amount of traffic to be handled. A 5-foot aisle

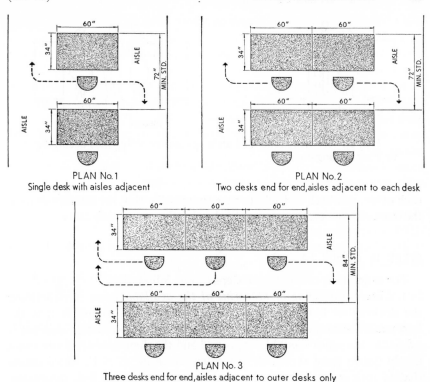

PLAN No.1
Single desk with aisles adjacent

PLAN No.2
Two desks end for end, aisles adjacent to each desk

PLAN No.3
Three desks end for end, aisles adjacent to outer desks only

FIG. 19–3. Minimum standards for back-to-back arrangement of desks under different floor plan layouts.

can normally accommodate around 850 people in five minutes. Main aisles in an office area should be from 4 to 5 feet wide, and the range of secondary aisles should be from 3 to 4 feet wide. Cross aisles should be provided about every 50 feet.

3. *Filing cabinet space standards.* The spacing of ordinary filing equipment depends upon frequency of use and functions of the material filed. Pertinent data include:

| Material | Type of Cabinet | Position of Filing Cabinets | Aisle Space |
|---|---|---|---|
| Active | Ordinary | Facing same direction | Drawer depth plus 24 inches |
| " | " | Facing each other | Two drawer depths plus 36 inches |
| Inactive | " | Facing same direction | Drawer depth |
| " | " | Facing each other | " " |
| Active | Side or lateral | Facing same direction | 24 inches |
| " | " | Facing each other | 30 inches |

The first two arrangements are illustrated by Figure 19–4. When a quantity of ordinary filing cabinets are used, always arrange them facing

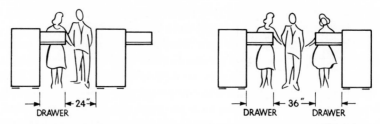

FIG. 19–4.  Recommended aisle spaces for active files according to their arrangement.

each other, i.e., back to back, to save space. Likewise, for lateral cabinets, the most economical arrangement is having them face each other.

## STEPS IN OFFICE LAYOUT

For general expediency these steps can be followed:

1. *Secure a drawing or blueprint of the available area.*  In obtaining the drawing or blueprint, care should be exercised to insure that the information shown is accurate and complete. In the event that no print is available, the space should be measured and the dimensions indicated on a neatly drawn hand sketch. A convenient scale is $\frac{1}{4}'' = 1'$, which means that $\frac{1}{4}$ inch on the drawing is equal to 1 foot of actual floor dimension. The exact location and size of radiators, windows, building offsets, and door swings, and the location of columns, pipes, electric light outlets and wiring, ducts for telephone wiring, running water facilities, and entrances and exits are important. Frequently, the ability to adapt a suggested layout depends upon the completeness and accuracy of these data. A building offset incorrectly spotted, or the omission of a radiator, can necessitate changes and alterations in a proposed layout and cause an otherwise acceptable layout to be rejected.

2. *Determine the areas of main traffic movement.*  These areas will depend upon such things as the size and shape of the space available and the general type of office. The location of building facilities such as entrances and exits, stairways, elevators, rest rooms, and the like will suggest areas of greatest travel. From this information, the location of the main corridors, storage rooms, reception rooms, and wardrobe rooms in the layout will be suggested. These represent space required for other than personnel occupancy.

3. *Formulate tentative answers regarding the use of reception room, conference rooms, and private offices.*  A complete discussion on the use of these areas is made later in this chapter. For purposes of illustration, assume that, for the time being, the tentative answer is to use a reception room, two conference rooms, and six private offices in the top management

group and one in each of the five departmental groups. These data are then added to the listing of physical units that must be provided.

4. *Study and coordinate the data found from the organization, activity, equipment and machine, and communication analyses.* Developing this overall picture is not easy, yet it is not especially difficult. We can identify the number of employees and the equipment and machines required for each organization unit. We also have the total size of the area needed for each organization unit, and we know, as stated above, the relationship among the units in terms of flow and communication—as shown in the block diagram. Matching the major segments of the space requirements against usable space available sounds like a herculean task and the work does resemble working a jigsaw puzzle. But bit by bit, an adjustment here and there, key areas begin to shape up and the entire layout begins to unfold satisfactorily. Consultation with the leaders of those to occupy the tentative spaces can be used. Valuable suggestions are received and conflicts, such as several groups wanting the identical space, can be resolved.

5. *Make templates to scale of all physical units (or use models), and identify clearly.* A template is a scaled pattern, made of cardboard or paper, which is used to represent the floor area occupied by a physical unit. The scale of the templates must be the same as that of the drawing showing the available area; as already pointed out, a scale of $\frac{1}{4}'' = 1'$ is convenient. Frequently, the shape of the templates is confined to that of a square or a rectangle; and in most cases, this is satisfactory; but there are instances where the details of cutoff corners, rounded corners, and the like should be included in the templates, as the final arrangement may hinge upon these considerations.

A separate template should be made for each physical unit considered in the layout. For purposes of identification, the name of the unit and of the basic group by which the unit is to be used should be stamped or printed on each template. It is also possible to use different colors representing different physical units to help visualize the work. Where a conference room and private offices are considered, templates covering the overall floor dimensions should be made and clearly identified.

Instead of templates, small-scale, three-dimensional models of the physical units can be used. These office models are dimensionally accurate and show at a glance the arrangement of the office. Many people can visualize the layout more clearly from scale models than from a technical drawing with which they may be unfamiliar. Complete kits, consisting of several hundred pieces including desks, chairs, files, machines, coat racks, and building columns, are available.

Also available are magnetic templates and magnetic models that can be used along with a steel-covered piece of plywood serving as a base. The magnetic templates or models hold fast to the steel-plywood base, yet they can be moved to show different layouts. The base can be attached to a wall, thus providing convenient viewing adequate for a group of people.

6. *Arrange templates or models for each basic group within its respective tentative area.* The suggested layout is determined by moving and shifting the templates or models to various positions so as to arrive at an effective arrangement. This phase of layout is a tentative trial-and-error process. It requires considerable time and cannot be rushed. If magnetic templates or models are used, they can be moved about as desired; yet, when released, they hold a fixed position. When the contemplated layout is completed, a picture of it can be taken and white paper copies made so that convenient reference sheets are provided.

7. *Check entire tentative layout, and make minor adjustments as required.* After the units in each group have been arranged in the best manner, the next step is to review the entire layout in order to see that it is a well-knit arrangement which will meet the particular needs. Pay particular attention to the contribution of every major unit making up the total layout. Check for the work flow through the entire office and continually review the general appearance of the entire layout. Usually, minor adjustments are made to achieve the overall effect desired.

8. *Indicate by appropriate markings the major flows of work and the telephone and electric wiring; also, include the name of the employee to be located at each unit.* This information is necessary in order to gain a complete understanding of the layout. The location of electric wiring outlets is especially important where groups of electrically driven machines are used. In many cases, some wiring arrangements must be provided for getting current to each desk.[4] The name of the employee at each work unit is helpful to the office executive in visualizing the arrangement.

9. *Recheck related layout with each respective basic group and, after securing respective sanctions, submit the overall plan to the top managers for final approval.* The first basic group to consult, of course, is the top managers. Point out where the executives will be located, what facilities are provided, and the chief considerations determining the recommended layout. Generally, minor changes will be suggested, and they can usually be incorporated. The same approach is followed with each group head. If consultation was practiced as suggested in step No. 4 above, the suggested plans are usually viewed favorably. However, if there are doubts and questions, an explanation of the recommended layout should be made, with the reasons carefully pointed out in a simple, logical way. After all groups have OK'd their respective layouts, the entire plan is submitted to the top managers with the statement that this layout has the approval of each group head. Acceptance by the top managers is then usually little more than a formality.

---

[4] See pages 473–75 of Chapter 20.

## OVERALL SPACE ESTIMATES

Studies show that a value of 60 square feet of usable space for each *ordinary clerical employee* is a desirable standard; and when an office layout calls for this amount, the space utilization is considered by some to be highly satisfactory. The value of 60 square feet per ordinary clerical employee is arrived at in this manner:

> 54-inch desk and chair, 54″ x 72″ = 27.00 sq. ft.
> Aisle per desk, 18″ x 72″ =  9.00 sq. ft.
> Miscellaneous (files, aisles, etc.) = 24.00 sq. ft.
> Total = 60.00 sq. ft.

But space requirements vary with the equipment and machines needed, and hence, so-called allowances of square feet per employee are unrealistic and fluctuating. They are at best foggy guides. Some surveys show 75–80 square feet per clerical employee as typical in a fairly large clerical area. Estimates for other personnel include:

> Top executive...................400–450 sq. ft.
> Intermediate executive..............275–300 sq. ft.
> Supervisory executive...............110–125 sq. ft.

These data are more valid primarily because there is more uniformity in what equipment and machines an executive or a supervisor is provided. They are helpful as broad estimates.

However, to repeat, there is no fast rule for the standard number of square feet per office employee. The amount of space to allow is influenced by the nature of the work, the available total area, the extent of service areas, the need for privacy, the number and type of equipment and machines, and the shape, exposure, and obstructions within the total space itself. One office with a value of 77 square feet per clerical employee may have an excellent layout, while employees of another office with 77 square feet per clerical employee struggle under cramped office conditions.

## THE PRIVATE OFFICE

Decisions regarding the use of a private office should be made only after ample consideration has been given to the individual circumstances. A private office should be employed when its use is dictated by facts and unbiased judgment. It should never be provided simply because it has always been provided for a particular job or because requests and sometimes pressure have been brought to bear. Figure 19–5 shows two effective private office layouts.

Those in favor of a private office will usually seek to justify their views upon three considerations: (1) prestige, (2) suitable space for work requiring high concentration, and (3) proper accommodations for confidential work. Most top management members are supplied with private offices. This helps add weight, influence, and respect to this group in the eyes of other employees and of visitors to the office. In addition to top managers, there are other members of the office who, for reasons of prestige, probably merit separate private offices. They include department heads and professional people. In many cases, however, the department head can perform the most effective supervision when located in the general area of his unit with additional individual space.

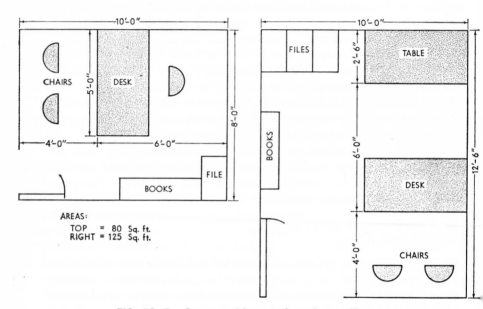

FIG. 19–5.  Suggested layouts for private offices.

The second major consideration, to provide suitable space for work requiring high concentration, can usually be determined objectively. Creative work, such as writing advertising copy and preparing difficult reports, usually justifies a private office. Likewise, employees doing intricate analysis, original planning, close mental work, and work requiring exclusive attention with a minimum of distraction merit a private office.

The third important reason, proper accommodations for confidential work, is significant in work involving research, planning, control, and consolidating recapitulations of important statistics. Likewise, the conversations during personnel selection interviews are of a confidential sort, and it is best to conduct them in a private office. However, the importance of confidential work can be overemphasized, and extreme care should be exercised in determining whether this consideration actually warrants a private office.

On the other hand, their relatively high cost is a paramount objection to private offices because, with them, space utilization is about 35–50 percent that of the open-area arrangement. The value of square feet per employee in a private office will usually exceed 105–110. Also, the buying, erecting, maintaining, and, in case of alteration, moving of partitions entail expenditures which cumulatively amount to quite sizable figures.

The use of private offices may interfere with supervisor effectiveness. The closeness of the supervisor to the employees, his familiarity with problems as they arise, and his being at the heart of all happenings in his unit are the types of things that are usually lost when the supervisor is segregated by a private office. In order to see that an order is carried out properly, it is frequently best to be close at hand to give instructions, check performance, and provide encouragement.[5]

Furthermore, private offices complicate the heating, ventilating, and lighting of these areas as well as of adjoining areas. Individual segments of space, set off from the large area, require special arrangements to supply these services, all of which mean additional materials and labor.

Moreover, private offices prevent other arrangements which work out equally well or better. Such arrangements include the use of movable partitions, railings, and modular furniture with partitions. These are discussed in the following paragraphs.

## MOVABLE PARTITIONS

For segregating the private offices needed and dividing the office space as the approved layout requires, the use of movable partitions is winning increasing favor. Movable partitions are made from metal or wood and are easily erected, dismantled, and relocated. They are prefabricated and factory-finished. Wiring and outlets are laid in the baseboards and joints. A variety of styles, colors, and finishes are offered. Panels with recesses for bookcases, alcoves for drinking fountains, provisions for door openings, and with or without glass (crystal or obscure) in the top areas are among the many available kinds offered to fit requirements for every type of working space. Various heights, ranging from the railing to the ceiling, are available. Door units can be selected from either single or double models; they may be hinged, double-acting, or sliding. The partitions are soundproof, with insulating material in the center or core.

Partitions from about 36 inches to 84 inches in height are very popular. They afford privacy, yet do not interfere with ventilating and lighting as

---

[5] In the main office of the Martin Company, Baltimore, Md., there are no interior walls or room dividers. The only sign of top executive status is placement in corner areas furnished no differently from the nonexecutive areas.

much as partitions extending from the floor to the ceiling. In many cases, a 36-inch partition is used to surround the work area of one person, thus affording many advantages of a private office at much less expense and trouble. However, movable partitions creating the effect of private offices have, in some instances in their initial usage, resulted in employees behind the partitions becoming loud and boisterous. In such cases, an educational job on how to use "partitioned offices" has corrected the situation.

For partitions higher than 36 inches, the use of clear glass for the upper portion of the partition is highly satisfactory. This design permits the occupant to look out and see what is going on—an important considera-

*Courtesy: General Fireproofing Co., Youngstown, Ohio*

FIG. 19–6.    Effective use of movable office partitions.

tion for a supervisor's office; it also minimizes the obstruction to light, and the cost is reasonable. Sometimes, a frosted or obscure glass is preferred. Figure 19–6 shows an installation of movable office partitions.

Movable partitions afford great flexibility in office layout; they make it economically possible to fit the available space to new layouts whenever the need occurs. The panels can be used over and over again. Not only space flexibility but also space control and high material salvage are thus realized. Changes in layout can be made overnight or during a weekend. In many instances, the cost of erecting movable partitions is only 15 per-cent of that of immovable tile and plaster walls. Furthermore, the use of movable partitions eliminates objectionable inconveniences such as noise, commotion, debris, dirt, waiting for plaster and paint to dry, and, after partition installation, the cleaning of rugs, draperies, and furniture.

Railings are used, especially in banks, with outstanding success. The old layout idea of having executives in private offices concealed in the rear of the bank has given way to the modern plan, whereby executives are in the front, open portion of the bank area, with offices, if divided, separated by low railings. This arrangement is of relatively low cost, minimizes the need for special lighting and heating facilities, makes a pleasing appearance, and is convenient for both the officers and the customers.

## MODULAR EQUIPMENT

Modular equipment and its availability with partition panels was pointed out in Chapter 18.[6] Such units give a private office effect and satisfactorily meet many privacy and prestige requirements. Popular arrangements can be assembled from interlocking, interchangeable component units.

Modular-type arrangements save floor space and increase efficiency. Figure 19–7 illustrates a comparison between conventional desk units and modular units, with a saving of 22.4 percent of floor area resulting from the use of the modular units. At the same time, the smaller space is more convenient and provides an adequate work area.

## RECEPTION ROOM

The reception room creates the initial impression of the enterprise upon the visitor, and it is true that initial impressions are often lasting ones. The reception room should have an attractive, inviting appearance. Displays of the company's products or services are very effective and assist in building good will. Keeping the room clean is basic. Chairs should be kept in a straight line, with newspapers and magazines arranged neatly on a table, and ash trays should be kept clean. It is also well to include some sort of cloakroom facilities to the reception room.

Whenever possible, the reception room should not handle ordinary and necessary traffic between different areas in the office. Employees walking across the reception room create a disturbing influence and distract from the dignity of the entire office. To prevent this condition, it is best to provide a passage for regular office traffic which bypasses or goes around the reception room.

## CONFERENCE ROOM

For meetings in privacy, a conference room is highly recommended. Most private offices are not suited for the handling of meetings. With a conference room, the participants can be arranged more satisfactorily, a

---

[6] See Chapter 18, page 414.

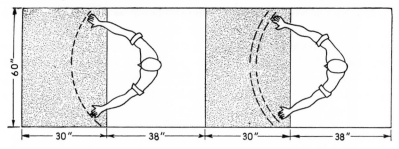

DESK AREAS = 3,600 SQ. IN.    TOTAL AREA OCCUPIED = 8,160 SQ.IN.

## CONVENTIONAL DESK UNITS

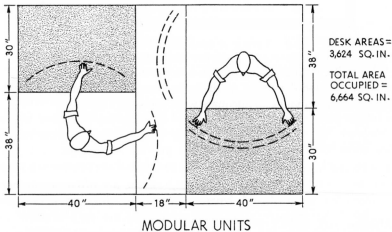

DESK AREAS =
3,624 SQ. IN.

TOTAL AREA
OCCUPIED =
6,664 SQ. IN.

## MODULAR UNITS

*Courtesy: Globe-Wernicke Co., Cincinnati*

FIG. 19–7.   A comparison of conventional desk units with modular units shows that, for the same number of employees and approximately the same desk areas, the modular units save nearly 23 percent of floor space (8,160 square inches compared with 6,664 square inches).

greater number can usually be accommodated, and each one can have a convenient place to write or to take notes. Furthermore, the meeting is placed on a businesslike basis, with a minimum of interference and distractions. The conference room should be located conveniently where traffic in and out of the room will be least disturbing to the other office employees. Figure 19–8 shows dimensions of a well-planned conference room layout.

### WARDROBE FACILITIES

Wardrobe facilities can be provided either by having separate rooms—locker or cloakrooms—or by placing wardrobe racks in the office areas. If

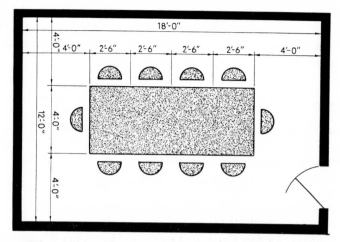

FIG. 19–8.  Layout of conference room for ten people. The table is 4 x 10 feet. For each two additional people to be accommodated, add 2 feet 6 inches to table length and to room length.

the former plan is used, provision should include separate rooms for men and women. When racks are used, they can be located throughout the office areas. Units are available which provide storage for coats, hats, overshoes, umbrellas, and the like for as many as three persons per square foot of floor area.

## PLANNING THE OFFICE MOVE

Office layout changes necessitate moves—sometimes small, sometimes large. It is best that these be well planned. A detailed office layout should be developed. The approach should be along the lines outlined in this chapter. This means that employees will know of the move, and they should. When the layout is determined, inform them of decisions they will want to know about, such as the general decor to be used, where they will be located in the new layout, the approximate time of the move, and outstanding features of the new arrangements. When the layout is finalized, number each item in it. Then tag and number all equipment and machines to designate their exact location in the new layout. For large moves a code of different colors and letter prefixes is effective, i.e., red (second floor), C (cost department), yellow (third floor), L (library), etc.

Schedule the move over a weekend or vacation period. Allow a maximum of 60 continuous hours (Friday 6:00 P.M.—Monday 6:00 A.M.) and arrange for an adequate number of trucks and crews. Items to be placed in remote and farthest areas should be moved first, after which should come those located adjacent to the entranceways. By assigning key employees to serve as deputies of specific areas the moving work is greatly expedited. These deputies help coordinate the move, direct traffic, check to see that correct items are placed in the correct locations in their areas, and answer questions.

## QUESTIONS

1. Discuss the subject, Space Planning and Functional Analysis.
2. Identify each of the following:
   a) CRAFT as used in office space planning.
   b) Integrated space planning.
   c) Office space planning.
   d) Templates.
   e) Movable office partitions.
3. What information does Figure 19–2 convey and how is this information used in office space planning?
4. Comment on the following statement: "Money spent in redecorating and re-furnishing a reception room can better be spent in fixing up the office proper. The reception room has little, if any, relationship to the efficiency with which the paper work of an office is accomplished."
5. In your opinion, should an office supervisor be located at the front, rear, or center of his or her work group? Should he be facing in the same direction as, or in an opposite direction from, the work group? Give reasons for your answers.
6. What are some office space standards that you would use in making an office layout?
7. Name 12 office layout guides that you feel are of major importance.
8. Approximately how much office space would you allot to each of the following:
   a) Two desks end for end (60 x 34-inch desk), aisle adjacent, chair for each desk.
   b) Private office for top executive.
   c) General office space for eight clerks.
   d) A conference room for ten persons.
9. Describe the layout of an office with which you are familiar, and point out several ways in which you feel it might be improved. Give reasons for your suggested changes.
10. What are your ideas concerning the use of private offices in a modern office layout? Substantiate your viewpoint.
11. Do you agree with this statement: "While a standard number of square feet to allot for each office employee is admittedly convenient and impressive, it simply is neither practical nor realistic. You can't design effective office layouts by relying on a set of selective and somewhat arbitrary space data."
12. Give some realistic suggestions for an office manager to utilize when planning the office move.

## CASE PROBLEMS

### Case 19–1.  Iola Products, Inc.

Tom Hance (*sales representative*):  Absolutely. Side filing is efficient. Mr. Conrad, you can file twice as much material per square foot of floor space with side filing as you can with the conventional four-drawer file.

Bernard Conrad (*office manager*):  That's difficult to believe. What are the dimensions of a side filing unit?

Hance:  The dimensions are 13 inches by 36 inches. The unit is 36 inches long.

Conrad:  And the regular four-drawer file is about 15 inches by 28 inches?

Hance:  Yes, that's right.

Conrad:  What's the capacity in filing inches of a side file?

Hance (*referring to manual*):  In filing inches, let's see. Here you are. Filing inches for a 13-inch by 36-inch side filing unit are 204. For a 15-inch by 28-inch four-drawer filing cabinet, it is . . . ah . . . 102 filing inches.

Conrad:  202?

Hance:  No. It is 102.

Conrad:  All right, 102. Now, our available space is 9 feet 6 inches by 21 feet 2 inches. There is a 30-inch door in the center of one 21-foot-2-inch side. How many side file units can I get in there?

Hance:  I'll figure it out. Will you wait a couple of minutes?

Conrad:  Surely. Go ahead.

### Problems:

1. Is this statement correct? "You can file twice as much material per square foot of floor space with side filing as you can with the conventional four-drawer file." Substantiate your answer, showing calculations.

2. What is the answer for Mr. Hance in reply to Mr. Conrad's inquiry regarding the number of side filing units in the given area? (Hint: Consider first the units arranged mainly lengthwise—along the 21-foot-2-inch dimension, and second, along the 9-foot-6-inch dimension.)

3. Aside from space requirements, briefly discuss other factors Mr. Conrad should take into account.

### Case 19–2.  United Utilities, Inc.

Telephone inquiries from customers are answered by employees of the customer service department of United Utilities, Inc. The office area in which this department is located is 20 feet by 24 feet. This space formerly was used as a conference room, has all inside walls excepting along one 20-foot dimension which is open adjoining a general office area. The space is equipped with one large table, 8 feet by 12 feet, and a number of chairs. When the customer service department was assigned here, the supervisor and seven employees occupied spaces around the table with the supervisor at one end. Business grew as new services were offered by the company. About six months ago, there were one supervisor and 12 employees seated around the table. The arrangement was: the supervisor and one employee at one end, three employees at the opposite end, and four employees on each side of the 12-foot dimension. Space had to be provided for two more employees and it was decided to bring in an available 3-by-5-foot table, place it to one side of the larger table with the 5-foot side parallel to the 12-foot dimension of the large table, and seat an employee on each of the two 5-foot sides.

Although this arrangement provides a space for each employee, it is not wholly satisfactory. The office manager realizes that this type of work requires patience, concentration, and skill in using the telephone. He has decided to rearrange the work area in order to minimize confusion and distraction. Also, he believes an assistant supervisor should be appointed and the 14 employees divided into two groups of seven employees each, with a supervisor directing one group and the newly appointed assistant directing the second. He has asked you to plan the improved office layout.

## Problems:

1. Draw several alternative layouts that will meet the general suggestions of the office manager.

2. Which alternative do you recommend? Why?

## Case 19–3.  Hanover Company

To provide needed warehouse space and locate the production control department near the center of its major operations, it has been decided to make certain layout changes. Production control has a manager, an assistant manager, and eight clerks. Currently, they share an office area with the traffic department, which employs 32 persons, including four managers. The present arrangement is illustrated by the drawing on page 457.

Production control is located in the area shown by the upper part of the drawing. Two of the available private offices are vacant. All production control will be moved to another floor of the building. The traffic department, now located within the lower three-fourths of the illustrated area, will be moved and consolidated within the upper portion of the illustrated area, specifically the top 80 feet, making an overall area of 50 feet wide and 80 feet long. The traffic department is growing; and if possible, adequate space for four managers and 40 clerks should be provided. The remaining or lower space, namely, 50 feet wide by 30 feet long, will be taken over for needed warehousing purposes.

## Problems:

1. Prepare your recommended office layout for the traffic department. A scale of one-quarter inch equals one foot is very satisfactory.

2. Point out the desirable features of your proposed layout.

3. Do you believe that your proposed layout will be better for the traffic department than that which they are now using? Substantiate your answer.

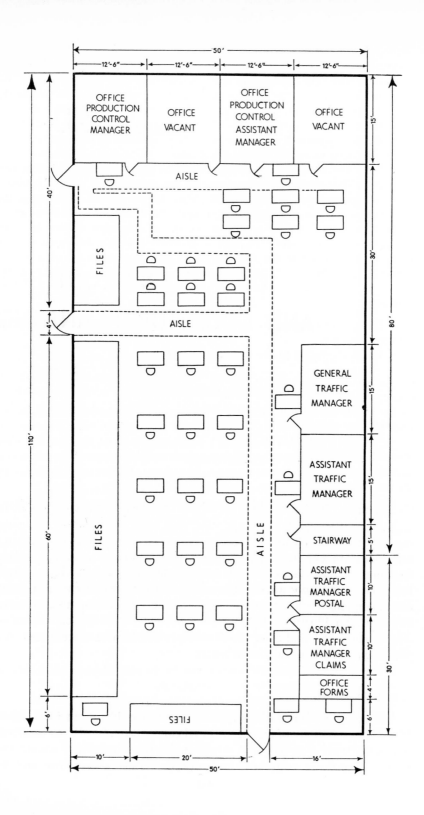

CHAPTER **20**

# OFFICE ENVIRONMENT AND LOCATION PLANNING

It is common to overlook what is near by
keeping the eye fixed on something remote. In
the same manner present opportunities are
neglected, and attainable good is slighted by
minds busied in extensive ranges and intent
upon future advantages.

*—Samuel Johnson*

THE GENERAL physical working conditions under which office work is done
and the location of the office are additional areas where proper planning
can be of genuine help. Among the major factors of physical working
conditions are (1) light, (2) color, (3) music, (4) air, and (5) sound.
Planning for these factors should not be handled separately. They are all
interrelated, not only among themselves, but also with location, layout,
equipment and machines, and all the other major planning areas already
discussed. To illustrate, lighting is dependent somewhat on the color
scheme employed, and color conditioning is tied in with office layout. All
planning must be carefully coordinated.

## OFFICE LIGHTING

Adequate light is one of the most important considerations in an office.
Many office tasks are of an exacting and close nature. Small print, carbon
copies of typed material, and poorly handwritten notes are among the
regular hard-to-see materials that must be handled. The office and its

458

surroundings should assist employees to see rapidly, easily, and comfortably. The advantages of such conditions are illustrated in Figure 20–1.

Without light, there can be no sight; and for light itself to be seen, it must be *associated with surfaces*. Light and surfaces are closely linked. This means that the entire working environment must be taken into account when considering lighting questions because the surfaces affect the light which, in turn, regulates the ability to see. For an object to be seen, it must stand out from all other things around it. That is, contrast is necessary.

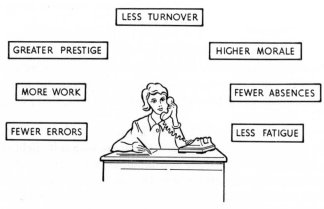

FIG. 20–1.   A well-balanced program of lighting in the office provides many advantages.

We need to remember three characteristics of light: (1) quantity, (2) brightness, and (3) diffusion. These are crucial to whether we have adequate lighting.

1. *Quantity of light.* A common measurement of light is a footcandle which is *the amount of direct light one foot distant from a standard candle.* A rule of thumb for rough estimating is that, for small rooms, one watt per square foot of area provides 15 footcandles. Thus, a 100-watt bulb in a room 10 feet x 10 feet will provide approximately 15 footcandles of light. The amount of light also depends upon the distribution of the light sources; for example, that provided by a single 100-watt bulb will differ from that supplied by four 25-watt bulbs, because of the difference in the light diffusion. Recommended values of illumination are shown in Figure 20–2.

2. *Brightness of light.* Brightness is determined by the amount of light reflected from an object. The effective light for seeing is the reflected light, not the light from the source. If the object to be seen reflects very little of the light cast upon it, the object is relatively difficult to see and in this case possesses a low reflectance value. The ratio of the light a surface

RECOMMENDED VALUES OF ILLUMINATION FOR OFFICE WORK

| Type of office or work | Footcandles recommended on working area |
|---|---|
| Difficult seeing tasks | 150 |

such as auditing and accounting, business machine operation, transcribing and tabulating, and bookkeeping

Ordinary seeing tasks................................................100

such as private office work, general correspondence, and work in conference rooms, active file rooms, and mail rooms

Casual seeing tasks................................................ 30

such as in inactive file rooms, reception rooms, stairways, washrooms and other service areas

*Source: Illuminating Engineering Society, New York*

FIG. 20–2.

reflects, divided by the amount of light it receives, is the reflectance value of that surface. For example, a smooth finish in white has a reflectance value of about 0.90, or 90 percent; in medium yellow, 0.65; and in dark green, 0.07.

Brightness is also important because it controls contrast, which affects seeing. The human eye sees best when the areas within its field of vision, such as a desk and its immediate surroundings, are approximately of the same brightness. An undesirable situation is that in which the light is concentrated on the desk area, and the surroundings are dark. Under these conditions, the pupils of the eyes are continually expanding or contracting in their adjustment to the bright and dark areas. This makes for eye fatigue and difficulty in concentrating on the work. For the visual area, which is generally described as about 30 degrees in all directions from the eye, the ratio of the brightness of the light source to its background should not exceed 3 to 1. Lighting fixtures and their arrangements influence this ratio. From the practical viewpoint, too great a brightness contrast can cause glare, which comes either from the source of light or from smooth, highly polished surfaces. (See Figure 20–3.)

Greatest visibility is usually reached when there is a maximum color contrast between writing and its background. It is difficult to read when there is little contrast between the paper and the printing, for example, white on white, white on cream, or black on black. On the other hand, white chalk marks on a blackboard or black print on white paper affords a high contrast and helps the seeing process.

3. *Diffusion of light.* In order for an object in any spatial position to be seen clearly and easily, diffusion of light is required. Light should not be absolutely uniform. Some shade and shadow provide variety and their effect is normal to the eye; but harsh, strong, contrasting shadows are annoying and should be avoided. Well-diffused light is sometimes referred to as a "soft" light. Proper diffusion of light is obtained by having light in

FIG. 20–3.    Glare prevents office employees from working effectively.

different amounts come from an adequate number of sources and directions.

## SOURCES OF LIGHT

Sources of office lighting include natural, fluorescent, and filament bulbs. Natural light varies throughout the day and from day to day and usually, other sources of light must be used to maintain the required amount of light. Natural light has beneficial psychological effects. An employee usually feels better and has a sense of less confinement when he can look out occasionally and see daylight, observe the weather, and the like. It would seem advisable to have natural light visible even in cases where it is a very minor light source, but a number of modern offices have solid outside walls and rely on artificial light exclusively.

Fluorescent light enjoys wide acceptance in offices. Practically all new offices and most of those remodeled are using this type of light source. Fluorescent light is closer than any other artificial light to the color of natural light, and it provides large amounts of illumination at relatively low operating costs. To illustrate, the light output of a 40-watt fluorescent tube is nearly twice that of a 40-watt filament bulb. Also, the surface area of a 48-inch-long fluorescent tube is roughly ten times that of the filament type; this characteristic helps to distribute the light more uniformly.

Filament-bulb light is still an important source of artificial lighting. Improvements in filament-bulb shape, type of glass, and length of life have been achieved. However, the filament bulb has certain objectionable characteristics, including the yellowish color of its light that looks different from the color of natural light, the large number of bulbs that are necessary to supply a sufficient amount of light under today's office-lighting requirements, and the heat generated from these masses of bulbs.

Sources of light can also be classified as either (1) general lighting or (2) supplementary lighting. In the former, the entire area is lighted to a prescribed level of illumination. The source is usually a number of fixtures in or suspended from the ceiling. The second, or supplementary lighting, consists of illuminating a relatively small area, like a desk top or a portion of an office machine. Supplementary lighting is used advantageously not only in providing the desired decor in private offices, reception rooms, and hallways but also for increasing the illumination of a fixed office work position or where the area involved is relatively small.

## BASIC DESIGNS OF LIGHTING SYSTEMS

The four basic designs of lighting systems are: (1) direct, (2) semidirect, (3) indirect, and (4) semi-indirect. Under direct lighting, light from the luminaire is permitted to travel directly to the working surface. This gives a "hard" type of light, and diffusion is not too good. Glare may be high, shadows are sharp, and the ceiling is usually dark. Generally, it is the least preferred type.

The design of semidirect lighting allows some of the light from the luminaire to travel upward to the ceiling, whence it is reflected downward to the working area. Most of the light, however, travels downward directly to the working area. A semidirect system illuminates the ceiling and lessens the effect of deep shadows.

In the case of indirect lighting, the light travels upward to the ceiling, where it is reflected downward to the working area. This provides a light which is "soft" and relatively free of sharp shadows. Actually, the ceiling is the source of light to the work area; therefore, it should have a high reflection value. But since the employee cannot completely ignore the ceiling, the possibilities of glare and too intense ceiling brightness must be taken into account.

With semi-indirect lighting, most of the light travels upward to the ceiling and then down to the work area, but some of the light is allowed to travel directly downward. As with indirect lighting, the ceiling is, in effect, the main source of light. The direct light helps increase the amount of light on the work area, but consideration must be given to its possible contribution of objectionable shadows and glare.

## ARRANGEMENT OF FIXTURES

Generally speaking, with fluorescent lighting, it is more comfortable to view the fixtures *crosswise*, not lengthwise. Especially is this true in a large office. In a small office, this consideration is relatively unimportant. However, there is one important exception—the use of luminous-sided fixtures with glass or plastic sides. These units should be viewed lengthwise for greatest comfort, regardless of the area size.

Some uniformity or symmetry of the lighting fixtures is usually desirable for better general appearance. The arrangement should bring out the architectural and decorative features that assist in producing a cheerful working environment. Long rows of fixtures may be interrupted or designed with an occasional break, but the foremost considerations are

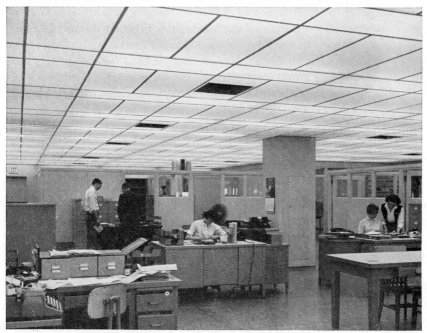

*Courtesy: Illuminating Engineering Society, New York*

FIG. 20–4. An office with ceiling completely luminous can supply excellent light.

proper lighting without serious glare and a coordinated lighting system. Fixtures can be suspended from the ceiling or recessed into it. The design of having the ceiling completely luminous is also popular. For this purpose, "floating-panel luminaires" can be used. They are economical, easy to install, and create a pleasant atmosphere. Figure 20–4 shows an installation of this design.

## OFFICE LIGHTING AS AN INVESTMENT

Expenditures for proper office lighting represent a sound investment. A well coordinated lighting system represents about 2 percent of total operating costs of a large office, compared with 0.5 percent normally spent for obsolete, inadequate lighting. This increase of 1½ percent is minute when related to all the comfort, greater accuracy, and psychological advantages of proper office lighting. And it is even more so when compared with office productivity where many studies show 10–15 percent gain obtained from providing proper lighting.

Maintenance has a significant bearing on any lighting investment. The practice of replacing bulbs on a regularly scheduled basis is gaining favor. This simplifies maintenance and maintains proper lighting levels. Also needed are periodic cleaning of the luminaires, proper wattage of bulbs, and correct voltage. In one study involving eight locations, the footcandle output was raised from an average of 11.8 to 46.2 footcandles, or an increase of over 350 percent, by cleaning the dirty fixtures, using color of high reflecting value for the walls and keeping them clean, replacing aging bulbs, and supplying the correct voltage.

## COLOR CONDITIONING IN THE OFFICE

Color not only beautifies an office but also improves conditions under which office work is performed. The gains from color properly used are not only aesthetic and psychological but economic as well. Color cannot be used indiscriminately in the office. Its use requires an understanding and an appreciation of color harmony and compensation.

It is now well established that color affects the human emotions, senses, and thought processes. For example, color usually has an important influence upon one's blood pressure and disposition to relax. A certain color will impress the minds of some individuals with a particularly favorable feeling or thought; another color will have the opposite effect. Some colors give a lift; others impart a depressed feeling. Some tend to hasten mental action, others to retard it.

Colors in the range of yellow, orange, and red are regarded as "warm" colors; they usually have the psychological effect of encouraging warmth and cheer. In contrast, cool colors, including blue, violet, and dark green, generally produce a subduing effect of restraint and calmness. Tints such as buff, beige, and ivory are moderately stimulating, while pale violets and blues are depressing.

For example, during August, the walls of a New England office were painted blue. The following winter, the employees complained of the office being cold, even though the normal temperature of 70 degrees was maintained. Then, the temperature was raised to 75 degrees, but complaints still continued. The blue walls were then redecorated to warm yellow and green. The temperature continued at 75 degrees. Now, the employees protested that the office was too warm. A return to the temperature of 70 degrees resulted in the ceasing of the complaints.

## SELECTION OF COLORS

The general color scheme of an office can follow one of many arrangements, depending upon individual preferences. A proper color balance, however, is needed and this means the use of a few colors correctly, not a variety haphazardly. The current trend is toward the monochromatic, which describes the use of various shades of one color for floors, walls, and draperies, together with one bright accent color. As a beginning point, the desk is selected in a particular color. With this basic color determined, the floor covering is selected to harmonize correctly with the desk. Then, lighter shades of the floor covering can be used for walls and draperies. The accent color can be in the chair or accessories such as pictures, desk pieces, and lamps. Figure 20–5 shows a suggested color guide to obtain a coordinated color pattern in an office.

| When Desk Is— | Use Carpet of— | Use Walls of— | Use Draperies of— | Use Chair, also Pictures, Desk Accessories, and Lamps of— |
|---|---|---|---|---|
| Gray | Gray | White | Gray | Red |
| Gray | Rust brown | Light gray | Rust | Yellow |
| Walnut or mahogany | Green | Beige | Chartreuse | Dark yellow |
| Walnut or mahogany | Beige | Light blue | Light blue | Dark yellow |
| Bleached or blond finish | Light brown | Beige | Beige | Orange |
| Bleached or blond finish | Charcoal | Gray | Yellow | Coral |

FIG. 20–5. Suggested color guide for a coordinated color pattern.

Additional specific color suggestions include:

1. *For the general office.* Ceiling in white, walls faced by employees in soft, cool colors; one or more of the walls may be in a warm color such as light yellow. Wall colors should harmonize.

2. *For the conference room.* Light and neutral colors are preferable, but some carefully utilized strong colors are usually necessary to stimulate occupants.

3. *Reception room.* Neutral colors are usually best. Avoid sharp contrasts. Limited and careful use of vivid colors is in order.

4. *Corridors.* Light colors are usually needed because of lack of daylight.

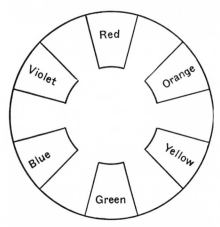

FIG. 20–6. Sketch of color wheel, showing relationship of primary colors —red, yellow, and blue. Secondary colors are made by mixing adjacent colors named on the wheel. A combination of all the colors shown produces a neutral gray.

The use of a color wheel also aids in proper color selection. A sketch of this wheel is shown by Figure 20–6. The primary colors are red, yellow, and blue; they are located on the wheel at equally spaced distances. Secondary colors are obtained by mixing adjacent colors on the wheel. For example, red and yellow give orange. Colors directly opposite each other on the wheel are complementary colors. Green, for example, is the complement of red; blue, of orange. Toward the center of the wheel are the grayer shades which color experts use to minimize the possibility of color violence. The main ways to secure pleasant and harmonious color effects are:

| *Use* | *Such As*<br>(*Refer to Color Wheel, Fig. 20–6.*) |
|---|---|
| 1. Complementary colors | Red and green, the colors directly opposite each other. |
| 2. Split complementary colors—actually a triad, two colors adjacent to the direct complement of the third color | Green-blue and green-yellow, the two colors adjacent to green, the direct complement of red. |
| 3. Triads—three colors equidistant from each other | Red, yellow, and blue. |

## COLOR AND LIGHTING

Color has a significant influence upon the lighting of an office. Light colors increase the utilization of light; dark colors decrease the lighting intensity. This is because light colors reflect the light rays, whereas dark colors absorb the light rays. For these reasons, any normally dark area will lighten up when lighter colors are used for the ceiling, walls, and floors.

Natural lighting varies slightly in color. Light predominantly from one particular direction usually has a characteristic tinge; to compensate for this condition, the use of complementary colors is usually recommended. This is illustrated as follows:

| When Predominant Natural Light Source Is— | Light Is Slightly Colored by— | Recommend Use of— |
|---|---|---|
| Northern light | Bluish tinge | Warm color |
| Eastern light | Neutral | Neutral color |
| Southern light | Yellowish tinge | Cool color |
| Western light | Reddish tinge | Cool color |

Furthermore, the use of color influences the apparent proportions of an area. This is due to the reflecting and the contracting light effect brought about by the different colors. Dark colors seem to advance an area, light colors to retreat it. Hence, the dimensional effect of a long narrow room can tend to be equalized by the use of a dark color on the end walls and a lighter shade of the same color, or of a harmonizing hue, on the other walls. Similarly, the proportions of a square area can be made to appear elongated.

## MUSIC CONDITIONING

Music serves as an environmental work aid because the physiological and psychological power of sound in musical form may be used to produce an improved behavior pattern. "Music while you work" programs are designed to improve working conditions, relieve mental and visual fatigue, reduce nervous tension, and make the employees feel better in general. Such programs are popular and they are effective.

In a survey of over 35,000 employees, 90 percent stated they liked music while they worked; an equal number credited music with making their work more enjoyable; and nearly 85 percent said it helped to break the monotony of their work.[1] The types of office work showing the maximum benefits include filing, mail room, typing, reception, keypunching, and verifying. In a large public utility, the productivity of cards punched increased 18 percent when music was added. Common gains in other offices include a decrease in absenteeism and in nonessential employee conversations.

The music is functionally controlled, which means that it is specifically arranged, orchestrated, and recorded to accomplish a specific goal. Distracting and attention-getting music, such as heavy brass effects and solos, is excluded. The music is stimulating and designed to fit the specific office work as well as the temperament of the employees. Music during the first part of the morning consists of a bright opener followed by

---

[1] *An Answer to Worker Tension* (a booklet published by the Muzak Corporation, New York, 1960).

moderately bright music, such as several waltzes. Music of maximum stimulus is played during late morning and afternoon. Light classics and slower swing tunes are usually predominant in programs for office employees. The music is played for specific intervals only because best results are usually obtained from this type of pattern. It is either "piped" from a central sending studio, or a self-contained unit providing the music is installed in the office. The expense is nominal, approximating $1 per day for a small office and 10 cents per month per employee for a large office. The inexpensive addition of a microphone to the subscriber's equipment automatically converts the installation to a public-address system.

## AIR CONDITIONING

Air conditioning regulates atmospheric conditions by controlling the four basic elements—temperature, circulation, moisture content, and cleanliness. It is possible to control only three, or two, or, in fact, just one of these elements; but such control is more correctly termed partial rather than complete air conditioning. Either a central or individual units can be used. Varying sizes and capacities are available. Individual units for a small group of offices or for part of a floor area have grown in popularity. Some are designed for a single room and are portable. The cost of air conditioning is reasonable. Not only does it aid health and comfort, but it also offers economic advantages. Higher productivity and decreases in cleaning and decorating costs are prominent.

## TEMPERATURE, HUMIDITY, AND VENTILATION

The temperature in many offices is too high. This leads to discomfort and drowsiness. Regulators should be installed on the heating apparatus so that excessive temperatures are not reached. It is well to become "thermometer-conscious" and to keep the office temperature within reasonable limits, that is, 70–74 degrees Fahrenheit.[2]

Humidity, or the amount of moisture in the air, definitely affects the comfort and efficiency of a human being. At the same temperature, moist air feels hot and dry air feels cool. Excessive dampness may cause physical discomfort of a respiratory nature and induce a heavy, languid feeling. Likewise, excessive dryness or very low humidity frequently induces a feeling of parchedness and nervous irritability. "Relative humidity" is the term used to describe the intensity of moisture saturation in the air. A recommended relative humidity for an office is from 40 to 60 percent.

---

[2] If air conditioning is used, the recommended temperature range is from 68 to 82 degrees Fahrenheit, depending upon the outside temperature. Too great a differential between outside and air-conditioned areas is undesirable.

When the relative humidity is 20 percent, the office air is too dry; when the humidity is 70 percent, the air is too moist.

Lack of proper ventilation can make a person feel sleepy and unduly tired. At 70 degrees Fahrenheit, an adult human body at rest gives off a small amount of heat, which must be carried off by the surrounding air; otherwise, the body becomes unduly heated. The normal ventilation requirement is about 2,000 cubic feet of air per person per hour. Drafts should be avoided. Usually, the best practice is to have the air circulating from a number of outlets so that it is distributed evenly over the entire area. For nonair-conditioned areas, fans help considerably in providing adequate ventilation. Also, window ventilators permit incoming fresh air without causing direct drafts to blow on any one person. The practice of opening windows and airing the office for short, stated periods during midmorning, noon, and midafternoon does much toward expelling stale air and freshening up the office.

## SOUND CONDITIONING

A noisy office is seldom an efficient office. Noise is unpleasant, distracting, and costly. It makes for difficulty in concentrating, in using the telephone, and in turning out accurate office work. According to physicians, noise causes transient changes in blood and brain pressure, a quickening pulse rate, and indigestion. So-called "getting used to noise" is misleading. One may temporarily be unaware of its effects; but over a period of time, one becomes excessively fatigued and irritable as a result of noise.

Noise has no definite pitch and quality, whereas in a musical tone, these properties are fairly well defined. Sound can be defined technically as "vibrational energy." The oscillation of these waves of energy, or sound waves, traveling through the air stimulates the auditory nerves; and this, in turn, results in a perception of the sensation and a consciousness of sound. Among the chief characteristics of sound are (1) pitch—frequency of the vibrations, (2) intensity—the energy of the vibrations, (3) quality —the mode or type of vibration, (4) reverberation—the sustaining qualities after the sound has stopped at its source, and (5) the expectancy and acceptance of the individual. Of greatest concern is loudness, which is primarily determined by both intensity and pitch, with emphasis on intensity. Actually, the phenomenon of increasing loudness follows a rather complex physical law. To have a relative measurement of the range of sound intensities, a unit of measurement called a "decibel" is used. One decibel is about the smallest change in sound that the human ear can detect. The decibel scale shows the relative values from the lowest to the highest human audible sound intensity. For convenience, the scale is measured logarithmically. The lowest value is zero, the beginning of human audibility, to approximately 110, which represents the sound of thunder. Figure 20–7 shows a table of sound identification and the corresponding decibel ratings.

VALUE OF NOISE LEVELS EXPRESSED IN DECIBELS

| | |
|---|---|
| Threshold of hearing | 0 |
| Noise in average home | 32 |
| Quiet office | 37 |
| Quiet radio in home | 40 |
| Noise in city (residential district) | 45 |
| Restaurant clatter | 50 |
| Noisy office | 57 |
| Stenographic room (large office) | 70 |
| Noisy factory | 85 |
| Boiler factory | 97 |

*Source: Americana Corporation, "Encyclopedia Americana,"*
*Vol. I (New York, 1955), p. 107.*

FIG. 20–7.

The means for controlling noise in the office include:

1. *Reduce and, if possible, eliminate the source of noise.* Place felt pads under typewriters and adding machines, and rubber cushions under various types of office equipment. Soundproofing cabinets such as illustrated in Figure 20–8 are effective. Proper lubrication of file drawers,

*Courtesy: Gates Acoustinet, Inc., Menlo Park, Calif.*

FIG. 20–8.  The cabinet over the machine is an effective noise reducer.

doors, desks, and chairs contribute further to noise reduction. Appeals to employees can be made, stressing consideration for others and the importance of eliminating unnecessary conversations.

2. *Locate office in a quiet space.* The top floors of a building are usually less noisy, since they are further removed from street traffic.

Relocation within the building to avoid direct exposure to noise sources or to highly congested areas can also be made.

3. *Segregate noise sources from the rest of the office.* Locate all noisy equipment and machines in a separate room off to one side. If this is not feasible, concentrate the chief noise sources in one area; this is better than having them scattered all over the office.

4. *Use sound-absorbing materials for office floors, ceilings, and walls.* Sound travels in waves and is reflected from glazed or nonporous surfaces in the same way that light is reflected. Under these conditions, sound continues to travel in all directions and bounces back and forth until its energy is absorbed; then the sound dies out of its own accord. This condition usually makes for a noisy office.

When acoustic treatment or sound-absorbing material is used, the sound dies out faster. The same sounds exist as before, but they are not permitted to reflect repeatedly until dissipated naturally. Carpet eliminates virtually all floor noise. Also, drapes and curtains made of soft fabrics help to absorb sound. Acoustic material for covering ceilings and walls is available in several forms. One common type is a fibrous mineral tile, about 12 x 12 inches in size and perforated. It is available in thicknesses ranging from ½ inch to 1¼ inch, and can be attached either by a special cement or by means of nails or screws. Another common variety is a mastic type material which is spread on the surface and dries, leaving a porous surface. In some instances, a loose, fibrous material is used, along with a separate hard facing material that has numerous perforations.

## LOCATING THE OFFICE

The remainder of this chapter will deal with location planning. Most offices are located in one of the following places: (1) in the factory building, (2) in a separate building adjacent to or near the factory building, or (3) in an office building far removed from any factory building. In the first two cases, the office location depends upon the factory location, which is usually determined with reference to factory needs only. However, in the third case, the office location can be determined in line with the particular needs of the individual office. For any of these three cases, the office space within the prescribed or selected building must also be determined.

A number of factors usually are considered. The problem is how to evaluate all the factors and give the proper weight to each. For this purpose, a chart like that shown in Figure 20–9 can be used. The selected factors are listed on the left, and beneath each factor are statements designed to help identify the intended meaning of the factor. Opposite each factor is a series of numbers indicating the range of points or values which have been assigned to that factor. Also, the points assigned reveal the relative importance of each factor. Those shown are suggestive only. In an actual case, the factors selected and the weights given each one are determined by the evaluator. However, to make comparisons among different possible locations valid, the same chart is used for evaluating the several sites under consideration.

|  | Excellent | Good | Fair | Poor |
|---|---|---|---|---|
| 1. Adaptability of space: <br> Is the space adaptable to the needs of the office? Is there room for expansion? | 60 | 45 | 30 | 15 |
| 2. Building facilities: <br> Are entranceways, wiring arrangements, outlets, ducts, fire protection, and other *fixed* facilities adequate? | 60 | 45 | 30 | 15 |
| 3. The proximity of office building to business factors: <br> Is the building near to customers; to transportation facilities; to shopping centers, restaurants, and hotels; and to mail facilities? | 44 | 33 | 22 | 11 |
| 4. The cost involved: <br> Is the rate reasonable and in keeping with competitive prices? | 40 | 30 | 20 | 10 |
| 5. Natural lighting and ventilating provided: <br> Is the exposure on the north, east, south, or west? Does it have large glass areas? Do windows face the street or open lots? Are ceilings high? | 28 | 21 | 14 | 7 |
| 6. Characteristics of the building: <br> Does the building have a favorable appearance, good name and address that are easy to pronounce and remember, and adequate floor load and ceiling height? | 24 | 18 | 12 | 6 |
| 7. Freedom from dirt and noise: <br> Is the general area free from dirt and noise? Is the area itself clean and quiet? | 24 | 18 | 12 | 6 |
| 8. Stability of tenants: <br> Do tenants of the building tend to stay put (are moving and transferring the exception)? | 20 | 15 | 10 | 5 |
| Maximum total..................... | 300 | 225 | 150 | 75 |

FIG. 20–9.   Chart used to determine office location selection.

## ADAPTABILITY OF THE SPACE

Top priority is accorded adaptability of the space, for that which is selected should permit suitable arrangement of the various office organization units; it should be of adequate size and shape. For the most part, rectangular shapes are best; and where requirements permit, occupancy of an entire floor is usually preferred. Individual circumstances alter cases;

but normally, it is more economical to travel 10 feet vertically, i.e., between floors, than 150 feet horizontally, i.e., on the same floor.

Preferably the space selected should permit future alteration and office expansion. Future requirements mean more than just securing space greater than that needed for current requirements. Consideration must be given to where and how future changes will alter present space provisions. Usually, future considerations are taken care of either by leasing entire floors and subleasing what is not now required or by securing options on adjoining areas. Some office executives feel it is desirable to provide space arrangements to accommodate at least five years of future expectations.

The difference between a site's "rental space" and "usable space" should be noted. Usually, one pays for rental space, which is the area measured between the inside surfaces of the outer boundaries. It includes areas for columns, projections, pilasters, and window arrangements necessary to the building. The usable space is the effective area which can be used for the office. Frequently, 10 percent of the rental space cannot be used, and commonly the figure is higher.

## THE BUILDING FACILITIES

Building facilities were mentioned in Chapter 19, but more needs to be stated about them because they are important in location planning. A building facility includes any device or feature incorporated in or attached to the building which assists in using the space with convenience and efficiency. In brief, a building facility must be fastened to the building, or installation is required to finish the building. As stated in the previous chapter, building facilities include a long list of items, among which are entranceways, elevators, stairways, wiring arrangements, air conditioning, hallways, columnar spacing, janitor closets, water accessibility, noise control features, means of fire protection, and other fixed facilities.

Adequate wiring facilities are one of the big considerations in building facilities today. Separate runways are used for (1) low voltage, including telephone and communication systems, and (2) high voltage for normal electrical current as well as that of higher voltages. For electrical current, many older office buildings are wired for about 2 watts per square foot of floor area, whereas the current recommendation, due to the number of electrical machines, is about 6 watts per square foot. Wiring capacity is limited by the cross-sectional area of the conduit, and to increase wiring capacity requires either larger conduits or new-type conductors. The former is expensive, since most conduits are buried in concrete. One alternative is to attach a new, larger conduit on the surface. A better solution is use of a new type of wire with very thin but effective insulation. Its use permits greater copper capacity in the conduit; hence, in some instances, the old wiring can be replaced with this new type and the present conduits employed.

The modern need for quantities of electrical wires has given rise to the use of cellular steel floors. At the top left portion of Figure 20–10 is shown a series of galvanized steel cells spaced close together, providing continuous in-floor passageways throughout the entire floor area. Various cross-sectional areas and spacings of the cells are available. These steel cells

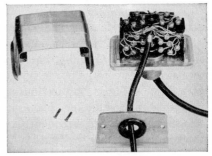

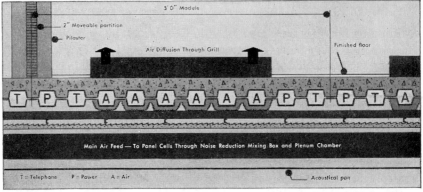

Courtesy: Inland Steel Co., Chicago

FIG. 20–10. *Top left:* Close-up of cellular floor construction. *Top right:* Components of telephone outlet fitting. *Bottom:* Suggested arrangement for use of cellular floor for telephone, power, and air needs.

serve as a subfloor over which the concrete is poured. However, before pouring concrete, steel header ducts are fastened directly on top of the steel cellular flooring and at right angles to the cells. In turn, the header ducts are connected to the desired distribution lines in the cells, from whence the proper distribution line is connected to an outlet. In the illustration, two outlet fittings are shown. Easily installed anywhere along the cell length, they are available in many designs to meet various functional requirements. For example, in the top right illustration of Figure 20–10 are shown the components of a compact aluminum outlet fitting for telephone service; it features three connecting blocks with a capacity of 15 pairs of telephone wires or 30 separate wires. Additional flexibility is made available by cellular steel floors in that, via conduits beneath the cells, additional wire connections between designated points can be utilized. The cellular steel floors also provide unobstructed underfloor ducts for heating and air conditioning, as well as for other uses. The bottom illustration of Figure 20–10 suggests a combination of air, electrical, and telephone cells.

It should be noted that construction and remodeling work is subject to building code requirements, which specify the design and the type of construction that is permitted. Use of certain materials may be forbidden, or stated design principles must be followed for certain structural parts. Requiring all buildings to have at least two entranceways may be included in a building code, the purpose being to reduce the fire hazard. Usually, some flexibility is provided, certain alternatives and choices being designated. Portions of some building codes have remained the same for a number of years, while others have been modified from time to time. Code requirements are enacted and enforced usually by local government.

## PROXIMITY OF OFFICE BUILDING TO BUSINESS FACTORS

When the location covers an office building, the following factors should be given careful consideration:

1. *Customers and others in same business.*  The proximity of the building to those who are in almost daily contact with the office is a very important consideration. In the first place, closeness to customers is generally considered advantageous. This is true when personal interviews and associations are frequent, but relatively minor when activities with customers are by telephone or by correspondence. Secondly, closeness to others in the same line is viewed with favor. This closeness encourages discussions of common problems among occupants, helps simplify the problems of the building manager, and adds to the convenience of customers and clients dealing with occupants of the building. There is, for example, a tendency for offices of financial houses, law firms, real estate firms, insurance agencies, and public utilities to locate in buildings in the financial district. Also, in many cities, specialized buildings to accommodate particular types of business offices are available; for instance, motion-picture offices may be located in the film exchange building and stockbrokers' offices in the stocks and bonds building.

2. *Transportation facilities.*  Convenient and low-cost means of getting to and from the building must be available not only to employees but also to outside representatives, visitors, and delivery and messenger men. Out-of-the-way places, necessitating transferring and long waits for buses, trains, or taxicabs, are a distinct disadvantage.

3. *Retail stores, restaurants, and hotels.* Convenience to retail stores might well contribute to the growth of the business. For example, domestic financing enterprises have found it helpful to locate in or near retail stores; medical doctors likewise find that areas near retail stores are good locations. The availability of restaurants is another consideration. Employees like to have a selection of handy eating places for noon lunch, or for evening meals when overtime work is necessary. A lack of eating places might necessitate providing a company cafeteria or dining room. Also, nearness to hotels is, in many cases, a distinct advantage in the location of an office.

4. *Mail facilities.* Good mail facilities should always be secured and given consideration in the selection of an office location. Frequent pickups and deliveries, with convenient accessibility to a post office, can contribute very materially to operating efficiency.

## THE COST INVOLVED

The cost of office space is of cardinal importance; however, it should always be considered along with the other location factors discussed. The cost of office space is expressed in dollars per square foot per year. To illustrate, assume an office measures 30 x 40 feet and the rental is $5 per square foot. The cost per year is 30 x 40 x $5, which equals $6,000, or, on a monthly basis, $6,000 divided by 12 equals $500.

The cost per square foot varies with many factors, such as the size of the city and general business conditions; but in order to gain some idea of the range in rates, a high of around $9 to a low of around 25 cents per square foot can be used. The top figure represents space in the better locations and buildings of the larger cities, while the latter may be converted factory space in a relatively poor location. Included in the square foot cost are services such as air conditioning, running water, wall maintenance, and elevator service. In many respects, the price is subject to negotiation with regard to what is included.[3]

## NATURAL LIGHTING AND VENTILATING PROVIDED

Since lighting is very important in an office, the availability of daylight and the building facilities for providing artificial light should receive prime consideration. Any area that provides much daylight is normally favorable. Exposures facing the north are generally preferred, as northern light is of a steady and soft type. Eastern exposures are next in preference, followed in order by southern and western exposures. Normally, the outside wall areas should utilize a maximum of glass area and be not less than one-fifth of the floor area. Windows extending almost to the ceiling

---

[3] See also page 479 for discussion of "Provisions of Lease."

permit a maximum amount of natural light to reach the inner areas of the floor space. Artificial light, however, will also be required and for this purpose adequate fixtures, electrical outlets, and lighting provisions must either be available or be provided. Agreement on the amount of artificial light to be utilized and the cost of installing and maintaining the necessary fixtures is a further important consideration.

It is imperative that an office be well ventilated. Careful observation should be made of the prospective space area to determine if adequate ventilation is possible. Spaces with few windows, a small number of openings to air ducts, low ceilings, and window openings on inside courts normally do not provide sufficient ventilation. However, with air conditioning, many of these shortcomings can be overcome.

## CHARACTERISTICS OF THE BUILDING

The general appearance of the building, its size, reputation, age, available services, and technical factors should be taken into account. In considering these things, decisions are made based on such factors as whether the building is modern or old, whether the building name is in good repute, whether the name and address are easy to pronounce and remember, and whether the building is well advertised. Also considered are the building services, including the elevator service, janitor service, and night protection.

An important technical factor is the allowable floor live load. At least 75 pounds per square foot are needed and a value of 100 pounds is desirable for complete versatility of layout. The floor-to-ceiling heights should be a minimum of 8 feet; however, for large areas, 10–12 feet is more appropriate. Low ceilings create a feeling of congestion and make the office difficult to ventilate; high ceilings make lighting, noise-reducing, and heating efforts difficult. Furthermore, columnar spacing must be considered, for it affects office layout, especially the location of main partitions that are joined to columns. A spacing of 20 x 20 feet or more is acceptable; spans less than 18 feet are normally unsatisfactory for efficient office utilization. Along the outside walls, a constant dimension of approximately 5 feet, center to center of window sections, or alternating windows and piers, expedites locating partitions and accommodating new units of equipment and machines.

## FREEDOM FROM DIRT AND NOISE

Certain elements are extremely disturbing to office workers and should be avoided whenever possible. Dirt, smoke, and soot are objectionable, and their presence in an office location and area should be avoided. Street noises are bothersome and interfere with efforts of mental concentration. In addition, the surrounding tenants' types of businesses, with special reference to the amount of traffic and the operations performed, might also be important from the viewpoint of noise.

## STABILITY OF THE TENANTS

Generally it is considered advantageous to locate an office in a building where the tenants are stable. Frequent moves by tenants in and out, and alterations, are undesirable from the viewpoint of solid, substantial enterprises. Various studies seem to indicate that real estate companies, law firms, and financial houses are among the most stable. Their office needs remain fairly constant, and they seem disposed to remain in one location for relatively long periods. In some cases, their tenure in the same location extends for 25 years and longer. In contrast, manufacturers' agents and advertising agencies tend to move more frequently. However, many of these remain in the same location for 10 or 15 years; and while this is relatively less, it still reflects a strong element of stability.

## OWN OR RENT

In most discussions regarding the office location, the question arises: "Is it better to own or to rent?" This question involves policy and can be answered only by the top managers. Certain considerations should be made, however, and these are as follows.

The advantages in owning include:

1. The building can be tailor-made for, or remodeled within technical limits to meet, the particular needs of the enterprise. However, needs change; sometimes the building becomes obsolete or at least not as convenient as first planned.

2. There is an element of prestige for an enterprise in owning its own office building. The name of the enterprise can be used for the building, and the publicity value can be quite high.

3. There is a possibility of income from renting out a portion of the building. This procedure allows also for flexibility in future expansion.

4. Permanency of location is obtained. This might lend stability to the enterprise and, in addition, permit continuity of a desired name and street address.

5. A relatively safe investment is afforded. An office building represents an equity in which the capital invested is fairly secure.

In contrast, the main advantages of renting are:

1. Freedom of top managers from care and worry in connection with ownership. The problems of building maintenance and repairs are avoided.

2. Finances of the enterprise are more flexible. Large amounts of capital are not tied up in one relatively long-time investment. The renter is free to invest any surplus in the most productive channels.

3. Changes in office location can usually be made more freely. The enterprise is not wedded to one location.

4. A satisfactory arrangement is provided for the small enterprise whose office requirements are not elaborate.

The "sale and lease back" arrangement, being heard of more and more, describes a transaction in which an investor buys a building from a seller and in the same transaction gives the seller a long-term lease on the building. The seller continues to occupy the building, pays rent, and is free of the responsibility of building upkeep and operation. For the seller, the deciding issue to enter into a "sale and lease back" arrangement is his financial position, especially that of taxes and his desire for liquidity of his capital.

## PROVISIONS OF LEASE

The legal right of a tenant to occupy a given office space is consummated by means of a lease. Actually, *a lease is a form of contract by which one party conveys real estate to another party for a period of time at a specified compensation.*

A lease is in effect for a stated period of time. Office leases usually run for one, three, five, ten, or twenty years, and in some instances longer. Payments are usually made monthly, with the first payment due at the time the lease is executed; this first payment customarily applies as rent for the first month or stated period. Sometimes, an advance of three months' rent is made at the beginning of the lease period, and this is held by the lessor as evidence of good faith and intentions on the part of the lessee.

The different agreements or clauses contained in a lease depend upon the type and value of the real estate involved and the number of subjects upon which the lessor and the lessee believe a definite written agreement is advisable. A lease can be specially written, or it can be a standard form. Normally, the lessor provides janitor service, heat, running water, elevator service, window shades, and fire-protection apparatus. He usually has the right to change the name and street address of the building; designate all sources for sign painting, ice, towel service, and the like; have passkeys to the premises; and enter the premises at all reasonable hours for inspection, repairs, and alterations. On the other hand, the lessee usually provides floor coverings, partitions, Venetian blinds, awnings, ventilators and fans, and intercommunication units.

## QUESTIONS

1. Of the five major factors of physical working conditions in an office, which one do you believe is most important? Justify your answer.

2. Discuss the importance of light quantity, brightness, and diffusion upon the attainment of adequate lighting in an office.

3. An office manager heard many favorable comments concerning the adoption of of "music while you work" in various offices. Believing this might be desirable in his office, he arranged, through the office supervisors, to ask his entire office

force if they would like to work to music. The response was overwhelmingly in favor of having music. Accordingly, the office manager purchased a wide selection of "long-play" records and two record-playing machines—one machine for each of the two main office areas. What benefits or difficulties do you feel might result from the office manager's action. Explain your answer.

4. Discuss the psychological effect of color upon office employees.

5. What is the meaning of each of the following terms:
   a) Semi-indirect design of a lighting system.
   b) Decibel.
   c) Footcandle.
   d) Relative humidity.

6. At an office management meeting, Mr. Alexander Messinger, an office manager, tells you that his general office is quite noisy. What suggestions can you give Mr. Messinger to combat the office noise?

7. In your own words explain how the chart shown in Figure 20–9 is used.

8. As an office manager, would you favor the "sale and lease back" arrangement in connection with acquiring suitable office space? Why?

9. Of the various major factors given consideration in locating an office, which two factors do you believe are most important? Justify your viewpoint.

10. Select two office buildings in the community in which you now live, and make a survey to determine their suitability with respect to (a) the characteristics of the building, (b) the cost involved, (c) the adaptability of the space, and (d) freedom from dirt and noise for each of the following prospective tenants:
    a) A sales representative requiring desk space and a room for small samples.
    b) An insurance office requiring a total of about 1,800 square feet, including a reception room, a room about 15 x 25 feet for salesmen, and general office space.
    c) A medical doctor who needs a reception room, an examining room, and, if possible, a small room to one side for his records and library.
    Write your results in a suitable form, using a sentence outline type of presentation.

11. Define each of the following:
    a) Rental space.
    b) Allowable floor live load.
    c) Building facility.
    d) Lease.

12. Discuss the subject of building facilities as applied to office location and building.

## CASE PROBLEMS

### Case 20–1.   Consolidated Truck Terminal, Inc.

The general offices of Consolidated Truck Terminal, Inc., occupy the top floor, 100 feet by 200 feet, of a three-story building which is about 60 years old and located in the older industrial section of a midwestern city. The building faces north along a 100-foot length; windows make up almost the entire wall on the west, south, and east sides.

Private offices are located along the entire south side and form an L-shape extending 100 feet from the southern face along the west wall, and 20 feet from the southern face along the east wall. A general office area across the space, that is from west to east, 50 by 100 feet, is occupied by rows of desks facing south. There are four rows (west-east) and five rows deep (north-south) on the west side of the 50-by-100-foot area, and a like or symmetrical arrangement of desks on the east side. The desks of the outer row are flush against the wall; distance between desks along west-east direction is 4 feet. The four rows take up about 32 feet along the west-east distance from the wall. The center portion of 26 feet [100 − (2 x 32)] is used for a main aisle, stockroom, duplicating room, and rest rooms.

Until a new building was constructed on the lot immediately east of the building, natural light was usually sufficient for the two rows of desks by the windows on the east building side. Now, the occupants of the east two outer row desks must use artificial lighting at all times, as is true for the occupants of the four inside rows of desks. Indirect filament-bulb lighting is used and, in the opinion of many of the office employees, does not give enough light for eye comfort. The occupants of the two western outer rows of desks do not have ideal lighting conditions and complain of the glaring direct sunlight coming in through the windows.

The desks and chairs in the office are as old as the building itself. The desks are wooden and have been subjected to long, rough usage. Many of the female employees have complained of getting snagged hosiery from the inside desk legs. The chairs, swivel type without armrests, have rollers and as an employee works at her desk, the chair tends to roll away unless the wooden caster wheels are flat on one side.

For ventilation, the windows are opened from the top and bottom with a board resting on the sill at an angle to deflect the direct breeze upward. This is usually all right for the occupants of the outer two rows of desks; but the four inner rows get all the breeze, which is fairly strong with a normal wind. Hot-water radiators are located along the walls at the base of the windows. In the winter, the men employees complain that the office is too warm and open the windows; then, the women complain that the office is too cold. Since the office is on the top floor, the heat from the roof in the summer is quite noticeable.

The general manager agrees that the physical working conditions in the office are not ideal, but states that the corporation does not have the money "to fix up the office." However, repeated employee complaints about the working conditions led him to believe that perhaps he should do something so he decided to air-condition the office. He reasoned this would aid every office employee alike so it should contribute to employee harmony.

The first day of the air-conditioning operation was a hot day in August. Some of the employees praised the new installation as a real contribution and progress in providing a decent place in which to work. Quite a few employees, mainly female, complained about the office being too cold and of drafts from the air ducts. They said they could not stand the blasts of cold air.

## Problems:

1. Evaluate the actions taken by the general manager.

2. Would you have made the same decision as the general manager? Justify your answer.

3. How would you handle the present complaints about the air conditioning?

## Case 20–2.   Nikko-Sanwon Chemical Company

This company, an integrated manufacturer of vinyl plastics, produces and sells three major categories of such plastics, including (1) vinyl chloride polymer resins, (2) "PUC" compounds, and (3) calendared vinyl sheeting and polyethylene film. These products are used in a variety of applications such as insulation for wire, flooring, toy components, luggage, and bookbinding.

The sales office of the company is located in the Merchandise Mart, near the Loop in Chicago. In this office, 12 salesmen and 26 clerical personnel are employed. The office is convenient for buyers and is a prestige location where a representative can bring customers and impress them favorably. In addition, "the Mart" is very accessible for employees, who can live in any part of the greater Chicago area and reach the office without trouble.

One of four manufacturing plants of the company is located in the southwest area of the city, some nine miles from the Loop area. Adjacent to this plant is a large warehouse which was constructed two years ago. There is ample space available in the warehouse to house the sales offices, now in the Merchandise Mart. In the opinion of Mr. Tashio Umeda, president of the company, the sales office should be removed to the warehouse. This would reduce overhead and consolidate Chicago operations in one location. However, through Mr. Leonard Griffin, the vice-president of sales, Mr. Umeda discovers that many of the salesmen and office personnel do not favor such a move. Some of them have stated that they will quit if the move takes place.

Mr. Umeda strongly feels that the move would be best for the company from the long-range viewpoint. However, he wishes to retain all his present employees if this is possible and suggests that the company (1) reduce the working hours to $7\frac{1}{2}$ hours daily from the present 8 hours, but keep the pay the same; (2) establish a free service to assist employees to find satisfactory housing quarters in the southwest area of the greater Chicago area; and (3) organize car pools, with the company compensating the employees whose cars are used.

### Problems:

1. What additional information do you feel appropriate for Mr. Umeda to consider before reaching a decision on whether to move the sales office?

2. Outline the program of action that you recommend Mr. Umeda take. Substantiate your recommendations.

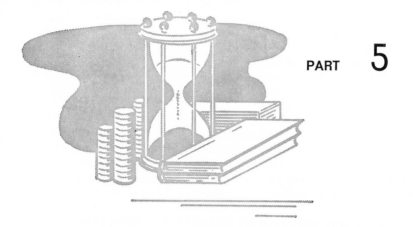

# PART 5

# OFFICE MANAGEMENT—

# CONTROLLING

*Controlling, a fundamental function of office management, consists of determining what is being accomplished, evaluating it, and, if necessary, applying corrective measures. Basically, controlling is performed to see to it that what is planned is being accomplished.*

*Controlling is extensive; there is no single type of managerial control that is all-inclusive. Some types have to do with the amount of work to accomplish, while others concern the accuracy to be achieved, the practices to follow, the use to make of time, or the dollars to expend. Five chapters comprise Part 5 of this book; they cover completely the essentials of managerial controlling as applied to office work.*

# CHAPTER 21

# CONTROLLING:

# FORMS, SUPPLIES, STANDARDS

Have a purpose in life, and having it, throw
into your work such strength of mind and
muscle as God has given you.
—*Thomas Carlyle*

CONTROLLING is performed by the office manager to insure that the provisions of his planning will take place. It can be viewed as the familiar management follow-up either to confirm operations taking place as desired, that is, according to plans, or to reveal deviations that necessitate corrective action so that the office goals will be achieved. Normally, verbal and written reports are made to supply information as to what is being accomplished. These reveal whether the prescribed process is being followed, the proper number of people employed for each type of work, the quality of work attained, the amount of expenditures, and if the work is being completed on time and when wanted.

Controlling is a fundamental function of office management and consists of (1) *determining what is being accomplished,* (2) *evaluating it, and* (3) *if necessary, applying corrective measures.* The most effective controlling can be applied to complete and well-thought-out plans. When the goals and planned means for attaining them are not clearly set forth, the controlling must of necessity follow an indefinite, indecisive pattern.

## CONTROLLING OF OFFICE FORMS

Let us start our discussion of controlling by considering an area which is common to all offices, one in which controlling is important, and one

485

about which we are familiar. This is the area of office forms. In nearly all enterprises, forms have a tendency to continue indefinitely regardless of need. The root of much office inefficiency stems from this situation. In addition, new forms are started whether the information desired is now contained in existent forms or can be secured by a slight modification in these forms. These facts are recognized by many executives who believe operations in their respective enterprises would be greatly improved if proper control over office forms were exercised. In addition, many studies show that the *functional* considerations of forms—time spent in using the forms and their aid in getting information recorded, transmitted, and processed—represent by far the greater cost of forms as well as the greater opportunities for improvement. *Physical* considerations—size and weight of paper, and printing cost—are important and must be taken into account, but they are relatively minor. For each dollar spent to purchase forms, somewhere between $15 and $25 are spent to process the forms. Taking the average of $20, this means that a multiple-copy form costing $60 per thousand involves a processing cost of $1,200. By eliminating unneeded forms, much time, effort, and money can be saved.

Well, what can be done about it? The answer: Exercise effective forms controlling. Start with the first step, common to all controlling, stated above. It is: Determine what is being accomplished.

## DETERMINE WHAT IS BEING ACCOMPLISHED

For this purpose, current information on the various forms now being used, what respective purposes they serve, and specific data on their contents and identification are required. To these ends, the following steps are recommended.

1. Announce to all employees the existence of the forms control unit, and explain its function and its authority. Be specific as to who is the head of it. In many cases, the head may be the office manager. Other members of the unit should include key personnel who are qualified and can give support to the office forms control efforts from different departments of the enterprise.

2. Freeze all forms activity at its *status quo*. Announce that any additions or changes must be taken up and cleared through the forms control unit.

3. Obtain at least two copies of every office form used in the enterprise. Use one copy for a centralized forms control file, the other for purposes of analysis, as described below.

4. Make out a tabulating card for each form indicating its (1) function, (2) numerical designation, and (3) construction features. File these by numerical designation and use as cross-reference with the centralized file. Office forms are employed to assist in any of the following

functions: report, request, record, instruct, follow up, authorize, cancel, order, apply, acknowledge, estimate, route, schedule, and claim. Segregating the forms by their major function assists analysis.

5. File each form in the centralized file according to function. This will bring together every form that is similar in nature regardless of its design, its name, or where it is used.

6. Secure a listing of all the office systems and procedures used in the enterprise.

7. Mark all forms in the centralized file according to the system or procedure in which they are used.

With the big growth in SDA (source data automation) and computer usage, the trend in forms procurement has been to consider all forms of one system or procedure at the same time. This approach recognizes the interrelatedness of the forms. Suggestions are made and bids are received for the complete form requirements per system or procedure. This way, better prices and services are obtained.


## EVALUATION OF PRESENT FORMS

The second step is to evaluate what is being accomplished. That is, in our controlling sequence we now seek to determine how well the present office forms are serving the enterprise. For this purpose, several different but related activities can be undertaken. Questionnaires sent to those using the forms frequently prove effective. It is helpful for the person in charge of forms control to meet separately with each department head and discuss improvements. These meetings can be followed by group meetings for all department heads in order to decide what improvements can be made in forms that affect more than one department.

In evaluating the present office forms, it is not uncommon to analyze the existent forms to determine if any can be (1) eliminated, (2) combined with others, or (3) improved. The emphasis is upon functional considerations. The form's adequacy to meet the work requirements consistent with efficient office management is of foremost importance. Results achieved are sometimes amazing. In the case of one prominent Chicago company, the total number of office forms was reduced from 1,182 to 368.

Figures 21–1 and 21–2 show how forms can be combined to improve office efficiency. Originally, four separate forms—shipping label, invoice, shipping memorandum, and packing slip—were typed separately. Subsequently, the four forms were combined and now require only one typing. In Figure 21–2, a copy has been raised to show the shipping label in the upper left corner, the receiving memorandum in the upper right, and the packing slip below. These are separated by tearing apart at the perforations.

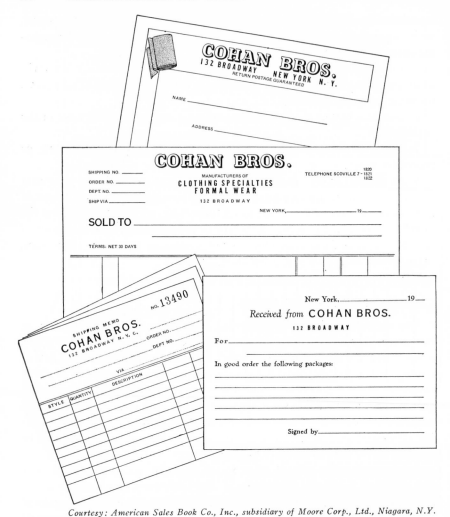

Courtesy: American Sales Book Co., Inc., subsidiary of Moore Corp., Ltd., Niagara, N.Y.

FIG. 21–1. Forms used by a clothing manufacturer. *Top to bottom:* Shipping label, invoice, shipping memorandum, and packing slip.

In addition, physical considerations are taken into account—the size of the forms, correctness for filing, cut without waste, and easy folding for enclosure in an envelope. Also, the weight of paper for the original and each carbon, the use of different colors of paper, and their essentiality in the particular form are carefully reviewed. Specifications are checked—the type of ink, punches, and perforations are investigated. The ordering quantities and rates of consumption are compared.

These indicated efforts actually point up two major activities: (1) the disclosure of possible improvements in the current work accomplishment and (2) the establishment of standards. The former can be justified as a

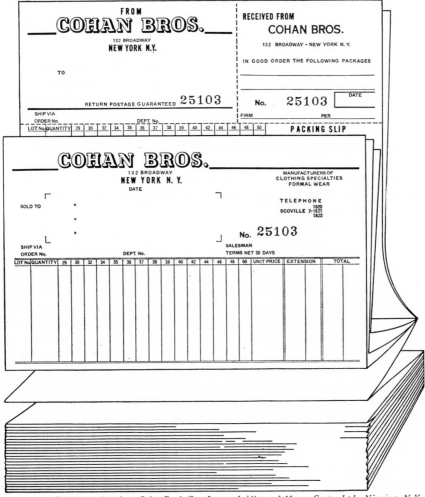

*Courtesy: American Sales Book Co., Inc., subsidiary of Moore Corp., Ltd., Niagara, N.Y.*

FIG. 21–2. A combination of the four forms shown in Figure 21–1. Now, the same amount of work is accomplished in one typing operation instead of in four.

planning activity, but the activity is triggered by controlling and the closeness of these two fundamental activities is demonstrated by this illustration. Often the controlling simply poses questions as to what might be done, but the actual doing of it and working out the details is delegated to the planner. Also, it must be added that the evaluating does not always include attempts to improve. In many cases it is simply a counting or a measuring task. For example, consider control of quality. Usually the evaluation is to grade the quality being achieved. Is it satisfactory or not? There may be no suggestions or direct attempts to improve the quality being attained. The assignment is either to accept or to reject what is made. Of course, this is a limited and narrow viewpoint; it fails to maximize its possible participative contribution from its advantageous position.

The second major activity mentioned above is the establishment of standards. Standards are discussed later in this chapter, but for now they are identified as *base lines of reference*. That is, to evaluate what is being accomplished, we compare it to its standard. In the case of office forms, for example, we would develop standards we believe suited for the company's needs. Such standards for forms would give stability, uniformity, and continuity to our controlling efforts. This does not mean that the work of forms control becomes static. Quite the contrary; it is dynamic. As the needs of the company change, the standards and the forms used will also change.

## APPLYING CORRECTIVE MEASURES

The third step in controlling is to *apply corrective measures, if necessary*. This includes redirecting the efforts in a manner to insure that the recommended modified work means are followed. In the case of office forms, controlling includes bringing about the establishment and use of office forms deemed proper and effective. Also, the forms controller or organization unit would have the authority to purchase forms and to review and pass on any and all forms if it were concluded that this was the best way to acquire the forms the company should have. The personnel involved in this phase of controlling should have sufficient status so that others will take them seriously. They must work well with others in the company. Suggestions by others should be encouraged and their cooperation won.

## GAINS FROM CONTROLLING FORMS

What is gained by having effective controlling of office forms? In a numerical arrangement, the answer is (1) retention of only necessary forms, copies, and items on forms, (2) prevention of issuing unnecessary forms, (3) improvement of forms to allow for ease of data entry, filing, and reference, (4) distribution of forms for those having justifiable reasons for receiving them, (5) production of required forms by the most appropriate process, (6) reduction of limited-use forms and expansion of general-purpose forms, and (7) review periodically of all forms in use in order to keep them in line with current needs of the enterprise.

## CONTROLLING OFFICE SUPPLIES

Let us now turn our attention to another common area, that of office supplies, and consider controlling in this area. Office employees need proper supplies if maximum productivity is to be attained. The lack of a typewriter ribbon, an order pad, envelopes, or letterheads might cause serious delay in getting out important office work. In addition, supplies represent an investment of capital. An office of 100 employees might easily have $10,000 worth of stationery and supplies on hand. Lack of reasonable controls over office supplies results in extravagance, needed items being out of stock, excessive prices being paid for certain items, and obsolete material remaining in the stockroom.

Fundamental to satisfactory controlling of supplies is adequate planning, which includes these essentials:

1. Locate the stockroom in a convenient space that is not desirable for clerical work. Be sure it is clean and dry. Enclose the area, and keep it under lock and key. Provide adjustable shelving, arranged for easy accessibility to supplies and most effective use of space.

2. Eliminate marginal stock items such as infrequently used and slow-moving items. Most office stockrooms are burdened with such supplies, which interfere with the smooth operation of the stockroom.

3. Arrange the stock according to some orderly plan. Index all items by number or code, and have a handy reference available to locate any item quickly; arrange forms by their numbers. Place heavy items on the lower shelves and light items on the upper shelves.

4. Establish realistic maximum and minimum quantities for each item, as well as the ordering point. These can be based on judgment guided by past experience. The analysis of the requirements for each item will help attain a balanced inventory of supplies. As a normal practice, it is usually best to buy small quantities at frequent intervals. For each item, the amount purchased should be in line with the rate of consumption, the time required to receive a replenishment from the supplier, the quantity considered minimal for the functioning of effective management, and the savings in cost, if any, which are achieved through larger quantity purchases of the item.

5. Limit the quantity of supplies issued at any one time to about a two-weeks' supply. Large quantities of supplies encourage waste; too-small quantities involve excessive requisitions and trips to the stockroom. Also, in many cases, it has been found that the practice of packaging supplies in small units helps to economize their use. Furthermore, all issuance of supplies might be confined to one day out of the week or to certain dates during the month. This tends to promote planning the need for office supplies and to concentrate the work of control over supplies. In the event that supplies are needed in the interim, a special requisition and approval from the office manager can be required. This practice tends to discourage requests for supplies at irregular times.

With this as a foundation, our major controlling efforts will follow the same sequence already mentioned of (1) determining what is being accomplished, (2) evaluating it, and (3) if necessary, applying corrective measures. For this purpose, the following list of activities can be applied:

1. Place one person in charge of the stockroom, and delegate complete authority and responsibility to him.

2. Issue supplies only upon authorized written requisitions, which should be made out, in most cases, by the department head or by the supervisor of the unit receiving the supplies. File these requisitions in case they are needed for future reference. Maintain a journal or record by departments of what is issued, when, and to whom. Make a periodic inspection of this record to ascertain if consumption of supplies appears to be normal in the light of past requirements and volume of work handled.

3. Inform supervisors, by means of monthly statements, of the costs of office supplies issued to their respective units. This will help to keep the supervisor conscious of the importance of office supplies; and the supervisor, in turn, will reflect this attitude to the individual employees.

4. Hold campaigns periodically to encourage reduction of waste of supplies by employees. The creating of an intense desire by office employees to stay within prescribed limits of usage and to conserve supplies ranks among the most effective measures to develop.

5. Determine if less costly items could be substituted for certain present supplies. Usually, an arrangement providing for pretesting different products, or at least a willingness to try them out, is in order. Using a limited variety of some items can assist controlling efforts and reduce costs.

6. Exercise periodic follow-up to help insure that the supplies are needed and meet requirements. An effective practice is to select at random a requisition for supplies and investigate it thoroughly. Find out how the item is used, who uses it, whether it is the best for the specific use, and whether the price paid for it is reasonable and in line competitively. Answers to these questions either will confirm that a satisfactory job of acquiring supplies in being done or will uncover areas which require remedial action.

## CONTROLLING AND STANDARDS

It was mentioned earlier in this chapter that standards are commonly used to evaluate what is being accomplished. Standards are so important in controlling that the remainder of this chapter will be devoted to them. First, one should clearly understand what is meant by "standard." *A standard is something established by either custom or authority in order to gauge such things as quality, performance, and service of any factor used in management.* It may be thought of as a basis of reckoning, i.e., a basis of comparison. Most standards represent the best current knowledge of an item or practice formulated and accepted to meet the needs of present conditions.

Specifically, standards do not imply or reflect perfection. A material standard for paper designated by the manager of an office means that paper of these particular specifications is the type desired by the manager and is satisfactory for the specific purpose in mind, taking into account such things as the type of printing press, the price range, and the desired finished product. The standard provides him with a reference line to evaluate the paper.

Standards not only facilitate controlling, but they are also important to the other fundamental functions of management, including planning, organizing, and actuating. For example, in planning, standards are the essential media for determining what components are required for establishing the sequence of successive operations. In other words, standards provide the common language for carrying out managerial work in areas such as expressing what is to be done, discussing, allocating, and instructing.

## EXTENT OF STANDARDS

Standards apply to all factors of an enterprise. For example, there exist, in management, standards for each of the six M's—i.e., Men, Materials, Machines, Methods, Money, and Markets. This means that modern managers have established recognized bases of reference for each of the six factors. For example, concepts such as "standard" material and "standard" machine are common in the office, but less commonly identified standards are "standard" man and "standard" money. The concept of a standard man is frequently used in personnel work when considering what qualifications a man must possess to fill a particular job, while standards in money or the financial part of an enterprise are very well illustrated by expressions of standard costs.

In many offices, the basic types of standards, along with the type of area covered by each, are shown by the following:

| Basic Standard | Area |
|---|---|
| Work: | Measurements of the quantity and the quality of accomplishment |
| Tools: | Desk, file, machine |
| Conditions: | Amount of space, equipment layout, lighting, floor covering |
| Process: | Filing methods, mail distribution, handling of accounts receivable, duplicating process |

Under tools, for example, a standard for a machine might designate the specific type, capacity, speed, and possibly the name of the manufacturer.

Furthermore, this designated machine would probably be expected to be used for certain work. In this case, the machine standard serves for purposes of controlling.

## ADVANTAGES OF STANDARDS

The use of standards in management provides tremendous advantages, including:

1. *Aid managing.* The performance of the management process is expedited by the use of standards. Identification and measurement of quality, performance, and capacity of the factors used by a manager constitute the supports upon which the managerial functions can be predicated.

2. *Provide a common basis for understanding.* Standards provide a common terminology, or a common language, between the employee and supervisor or between the buyer and seller. Through the use of standards, it is possible to determine exactly what is being discussed or investigated.

3. *Aid in securing coordination.* Standards serve as focal points around which revolve most problems of management. The synchronization of the various factors used by a manager depend, in the final analysis, upon the synchronization or interplay of the various standards which are brought together.

4. *Reduce waste.* Standards help to determine definite requirements. Losses resulting from obsolete equipment, inefficient methods, and excess materials are kept at a minimum when good standards are employed and strictly enforced.

5. *Promote better utilization of employees.* Standards help to achieve the goal of utilizing personnel within carefully defined and known limits. Executives are encouraged to do executive work—not routine work. Likewise, supervisors are expected to carry out the job of supervising—not that of an operative employee with only the title of supervisor.

6. *Encourage simplicity.* Standards tend to eliminate unusual and complicated practices. The very nature of standards and their interrelatedness tend to encourage the use of simple descriptions and easily understood terms. Also, wide usage encourages understanding of the standard.

7. *Act as stimuli to research.* Standards help to localize areas in which improvements might be made. They serve to help state the problem and to assist the researcher in concentrating on a problem of relatively limited scope.

8. *Provide effective connecting links between the findings of research and the application of research results.* Standards serve as the contact points for the application of research findings. New discoveries and improvements are introduced via the standards; and in this manner, the

beneficial contributions of research are utilized with a minimum of time and effort.

9. *Provide interchangeability of part and machine.* Each component may be so specified and accurately determined by the use of standards that it is entirely feasible to use any one of a group of similar components. By means of standards, it is possible to insure that all units of part $X$ will be identical within the limits set up by the standards.

10. *Make mass production possible.* Standards permit the handling of each component separately; thus, specialization may be practiced and the gains thereof realized. Difficult and complex jobs requiring long and strenuous training periods are reduced by the use of standards to relatively simple tasks, yet at no sacrifice in the total amount of work accomplished.

## MEANS OF EXPRESSING STANDARDS

Various means of expressing standards can be used, including the following:

1. *Written specifications.* Simply a detailed statement of the requirements that must be followed or that must be met by the factor under consideration.

2. *Model.* A typical sample, a miniature representation, or an exact representation of a specimen of the factor considered standard.

3. *Accepted rule or regulation.* An established course or guide prescribed by a person in authority.

4. *Unwritten customary procedure.* The habitual usage or generally recognized practice as shown by past experience.

5. *Verbal communication.* The conveyance of thoughts and opinions concerning the standard by means of spoken words.

Convenience has tended to associate or group certain of these means with certain factors employed by managers. For example, a standard method is usually expressed by one of three means—a written specification, an unwritten customary procedure, or a verbal communication. In contrast, a standard material might be expressed by any of these means plus a model. Figure 21–3 shows the means most commonly used to

| Factor | Written Specification | Model | Accepted Rule or Regulation | Unwritten Customary Procedure | Verbal Communication |
|---|---|---|---|---|---|
| Men | X | ... | X | X | X |
| Materials | X | X | ... | X | X |
| Machines | X | X | ... | ... | ... |
| Methods | X | ... | ... | X | X |
| Money | X | ... | X | X | ... |

FIG. 21–3. The means most commonly used to express standards according to the factors of management.

express standards according to factors. To illustrate, for machines, the standard is usually expressed by a written specification or by a model. Figure 21–4 shows a methods standard expressed by means of a written specification. In this case, the method is precisely stated; it tells exactly what to do and minimizes the possibility of misunderstanding.

## CHANGE AND STANDARDS

Standards are changed primarily for two reasons: (1) to gain improvement and (2) to recognize the interdependence of standards within an

---

Every error which is made in posting a passbook or ledger card must be corrected by an adjusting entry on the savings machine, as described in the following paragraphs. No erasures are permitted.

If the wrong old balance is posted in the machine, the correction should be made as follows:

1. If the old balance is picked up incorrectly and detected immediately, the Clear and Sub-Total lever is merely brought to the "Clear Balance" position and the balance cleared.

2. If the error is found after posting the old balance and the deposit or withdrawal, but before extending the new balance, the incorrect old balance is to be set up and the Overdraft key depressed (with the book and card out of the machine), and the correct old balance is to be set up on the Old Balance key. The book and card are then to be inserted and the correct new balance extended.

3. If the error is not detected before the new balance is posted, the correct old balance is to be picked on the Old Balance key (with the book and card out of the machine). If the entry was a deposit, the amount is to be recorded under the Overdraft key. The card and book are then to be inserted and set to the line immediately below that on which the incorrect balance appears and the correct new balance extended. The word "Balance" is to be written beside it and an ink line drawn through the incorrect balance.

4. If the error is not detected until the cards are proved at the end of the day, the procedure in (3) above is to be followed, except that the card only can be corrected. A Caution signal should be placed on the card so that the book will be corrected when next presented. The customer should be advised of the error and asked to present his passbook for verification as soon as possible.

*Source: First National Bank of Boston, "Manual for Savings Tellers" (Boston, 1943), pp. M1 and M2*

FIG. 21–4. A methods standard in the form of a written specification.

---

enterprise. Experience shows that after a standard has been set, it is common to try to improve it. This is as it should be, for progress in management is dependent in large measure upon improvements in standards. In addition, the setting of a standard seems to place a level below which future standards will not be set.

The interdependence of standards can be comprehended best by considering an illustration. For a given task in an office, assume standards have been set up for the material, machine, and method. These three standards are interdependent and may be called "associated standards." The employee, in order to accomplish the task, must use the standard material in the standard machine and follow the standard method. Figure 21–5 in the second column, illustrates the present standards for the material, machine, and method. The employee is to use 12-pound, 8½ x 11-inch paper in an 11¼-inch-roll typewriter, and he is to make five copies, using ½-inch spacing between vertical columns.

| Factor | Present Standards | Standards after Changes | Reasons for Changes in Standards |
|---|---|---|---|
| Material.... | 12# white bond paper, size 8½″ x 11″ | 16# white bond paper, size 17″ x 22″ | New sheet size requested by top management members. Larger sheets necessitate heavier paper. |
| Machine.... | 11¼″-roll typewriter | 19¼″-roll typewriter | Larger roll needed to accommodate new paper size. |
| Method..... | Insert paper in machine, make five copies, leave ½″ spacing between vertical columns. | Insert paper in machine, make four copies, leave 2″ spacing between vertical columns. | Number of copies reduced from five to four because of heavier paper used. Increased spacin ; improves appearance of sheet. |

FIG. 21–5. Illustrating the interdependence of associated standards. The standard for material was changed upon request of top management members. This change in the standard for material necessitated a change in the standard for machine and also in the standard for method.

Now, suppose that a change is made in the standard of the material from 12-pound, 8½ x 11-inch paper to 16-pound, 17 x 22-inch paper. In order to handle this new weight and size of paper, it is necessary to change the machine standard from an 11¼-inch to a 19¼-inch-roll typewriter and to change the methods standard from making five copies to four copies and from allowing ½-inch spacing to a 2-inch spacing between vertical columns. These changes in standards and the reasons for making them are shown in concise form in Figure 21–5.

*In general, a manager should review all standards when any one standard is revised.* This is especially important for associated standards, but it also applies for standards of a similar group. All methods standards, for example, should be reviewed whenever a change is made in any one methods standard, because in this way possible sources of improvement and the bettering of all methods standards can be discovered and adopted. To repeat, *standards are not independent, they are interdependent.*

## AMERICAN STANDARDS ASSOCIATION, INC.

For some years the American Standards Association, Inc., and the Administrative Management Society (prior to 1963 known as the National Office Management Association) have worked together in efforts to establish office standards which it is hoped will prove useful to many managers. The American Standards Association does not set standards; it provides the machinery whereby every group concerned in any project has a right to participate in the setting of the standards. The program includes the establishment of office standards for each of the following major groups: office equipment and furniture, paper for office use, office supplies, business machines, personnel, physical and physiological factors, and office forms, records, and procedures. Figure 21–6 shows an office standard for basic sheet sizes and standard stock sizes for bond papers and index Bristols. By its use, a reference level for managerial controlling is provided.

## OFFICE STANDARDIZATION—MEANING AND IMPLICATION

The wide adoption of a limited number of standards in a particular area can lead to standardization. For example, when a company adopts certain stated standards regarding the type and size of desks it will use, the practice is known as standardization. A degree of uniformity is implied in all standardization. In many instances, standardization deals with an industry, not with just one enterprise. Both the needs and the benefits of standardization are in proportion to the complexity of managing the particular enterprise or industry.

Typically, a number of considerations must be included in standardizing an office item. For desks, the considerations might include size, appearance, utility, comfort, interchangeability, construction, maintenance, depreciation, and initial cost. How much weight to give to each of these factors is primarily a question of judgment, although weights in proportion to the relative costs of the factors might be developed. Standardization can be applied to any number of office areas, such as chairs, files, machines, lighting, forms, procedures, employment qualifications, and training programs.

From an *economic* viewpoint, there is little doubt that office standardization is beneficial. Such economic factors as simplified control, greater quantities of work achieved, advancement of office production techniques, and assistance in managerial decision making are among the virtues generally pointed out.

| | Division 2 |
| NOMA | Paper |
| OFFICE STANDARD | NOMA |
| | N2.1 - 1955 |
| | ● |
| | ASA |
| | *Reg. U. S. Pat. Off.* |
| | X2.2.1 - 1955 |
| | *UDC 676.3.001.3:389.172 |
| | ● |

### Basic Sheet Sizes and Standard Stock Sizes for Bond Papers and Index Bristols

(An American Standard)

#### 1. Scope

1.1 The scope and purpose of this standard is to list the basic sheet sizes and standard stock sizes of bond papers and index bristols in order to encourage the use of normally available sizes.

#### 2. Definitions

2.1 For purposes of this standard, the terms listed below are defined as follows:

2.1.1 **Basic Sheet Size,** as defined in the Dictionary of Paper* is a certain sheet size recognized by buyers and sellers as the one upon which its basic weight is figured. Usually, it is also the one which prints, folds, and trims most effectively.

2.1.2 **Standard Stock Sheet Sizes** are the sizes of paper normally stocked by most paper merchants and most paper mills and from which the sizes commonly used in the office are cut with a minimum of waste.

2.1.3 **Bond Paper*** is a grade of writing or printing paper originally used where strength, durability, and permanence are essential requirements, as in government bonds and legal documents. Its use has extended into other fields, such as business letterheads and forms, where strength and permanence, though important properties, are not so essential; this accounts for the wide range of quality in this type of paper. These qualities are obtained through the use of rag pulp, bleached chemical wood pulps, and mixtures of these fibers in the manufacturing process. Although bond paper is a typical writing paper, almost all of it is subjected to some form of printing before use. Therefore, it must have good printing qualities which, however, are not as important as writing and erasing qualities, clean-

liness, formation, finish, color and freedom from fuzz. It is usually made in basis weights from 13 to 24 pounds (17 in. x 22 in. per 500 sheets).

2.1.4 **Index Bristols*** are bristols used principally for index records, business and commercial cards. They are a group of cardboards made on the Fourdrinier or cylinder machine at different basis weights. They are made of homogeneous stock (such as rag, sulphite, or bleached sulphate pulp) or by pasting together two or more plies of the same kind of paper, and finished and sized for pen and ink work. The usual basis weights are 180, 220, 280, 340, and 440 pounds (25.5 in. x 30.5 in. per 1000 sheets).

*The Dictionary of Paper, published under the auspices and direction of the American Paper and Pulp Association, 122 East 42nd Street, New York, N. Y. (Copyright Second Edition 1951.)

#### 3. Standard Stock Sheet Sizes†

(All Dimensions in Inches)

| Bond Papers (Rag Content or Chemical Wood Pulp) | Index Bristols (Rag Content or Chemical Wood Pulp) |
| --- | --- |
| 17 x 22‡ | 20½ x 24¾ |
| 17 x 28 | 22½ x 28½ |
| 19 x 24 | 22½ x 35 |
| 22 x 34 | 25½ x 30½‡ |
| 24 x 38 | |
| 28 x 34 | |
| 34 x 44 | |

† The Standard Stock Sheet Sizes listed in this standard, except for the 22½ x 35 size Index Bristol, are identical with those listed in Simplified Practice Recommendation R22-40 for Paper of the U. S. Department of Commerce.

‡ Basic Size.

NOTE: When the direction of the grain is important, it should be specified.

● **Approved as American Standard by the American Standards Association, Inc.—Aug. 16, 1955**
● **Sponsor: National Office Management Association.**  *Universal Decimal Classification

**NATIONAL  OFFICE  MANAGEMENT  ASSOCIATION**
**WILLOW GROVE, PA.**

*Courtesy: American Standards Association, Inc., New York; and National Office Management Association (now the Administrative Management Society), Willow Grove, Pa.*

FIG. 21–6.  A written office standard.

However, from the *social* viewpoint, there has been much discussion, and differences of opinion exist. Proponents claim that due to standardization the level of both the skilled and the semiskilled employee has been raised; a measurement of performance is provided; the uniformity among similar jobs has widened the market for employee's services; and the employee can develop proficiency in a definite, prescribed area of endeavor. In contrast, those opposed to office standardization claim the employee is deprived of his dignity as an employee—valuable skill and enthusiasm for his job are lost; the range within which the employee may exercise his skill is narrowed; the employee is without the overall picture, of which his efforts are a small part; and the dull and drab work life, with work interest and outlook impeded, can make the employee an undesirable citizen in his community.

## QUESTIONS

1. Enumerate and discuss the steps essential to determine what is being accomplished as the initial work in connection with controlling office forms.
2. Discuss the evaluation of present office forms as a definite step in the controlling of office forms.
3. State three benefits derived from the controlling of office forms. Discuss one of these benefits in some detail.
4. Can controlling exist without planning? Planning without controlling? Management without controlling? Explain your answer.
5. In your opinion, what are the three most important advantages of standards in office management? Point out and discuss your major reasons for selecting these three advantages.
6. Give a brief explanation for each of the following:
    *a*) Model for expressing a standard.
    *b*) Interdependence of standards.
    *c*) Base line of reference.
    *d*) Associated standards.
7. In efforts to improve existent office forms used in an office, should emphasis be given to functional or to physical considerations? Substantiate your answer.
8. Discuss the extent and importance of standards in the field of office management.
9. As an office manager, what actions would you take to provide adequate management over office supplies?
10. Do you favor office standardization? Cite reasons to support your viewpoint.
11. Can controlling take place without the use of a standard? Elaborate on your answer.
12. What are your reactions to this statement: "Satisfactory standards being recognized, base or reference points remain constant, thus supplying the characteristics of solidarity and firmness required to build and expand controlling efforts."

## CASE PROBLEMS

### Case 21–1.  Clenndenning Company

Ted Woodruff filled out a form for one pad of paper, a box of paper clips, and six large manila envelopes. He deposited this form in the office supplies control basket on the table near the door to the office supplies room. Ted was following the "help yourself" supplies arrangement which has been followed by the company for some time. The filled out forms were collected and reviewed weekly by Craig Mc-Kelvey, the assistant office manager, who used the information for reordering supplies reaching a low inventory. Actually, the current system did not work too well. Shortages of items were frequent and Craig McKelvey believed that some employees failed to fill out the required form correctly or, in some cases, not at all. He therefore spent some of his time watching the action around the storeroom to see if he could discover the cause or causes of discrepancies in the supplies. He observed Ted entering the storeroom and emerging ten minutes later with a large wrapped bundle under his arm. Going to his desk, Ted placed the bundle in a desk drawer and resumed his work.

Later, at quitting time Craig observed that Ted removed the bundle from his desk drawer and started down the aisle with other employees leaving for home. Just before passing the doorway leading to the reception room and then to the outside, Ted was stopped by Craig who inquired if the package he had was his own. Ted said that it was. Craig's questions and disclosures resolved that the bundle contained expensive company supplies. After further questioning Ted admitted he was taking the supplies home for use by himself and his family. He added that he frequently did company work at night in his home. Relieved of the bundle, Ted was permitted to go home, but was requested to report to Edward Lasser, the office manager, first thing in the morning.

Next morning Mr. Lasser told Ted his action was strictly against company policy and he was discharged. Ted asked for another chance, pointing out that he had been with the company four years, and other employees took supplies all the time from the storeroom without filling out any form whatever and many of these supplies were taken by the employees to their homes.

## Problems:

1. What major conditions have contributed to this situation taking place?
2. Evaluate Ted's behavior. Craig's behavior.
3. Did Mr. Lasser handle the situation correctly? Why?

### Case 21–2.  Benton-Donohue Company

For the past several months, Mr. Richard E. Schubert, the office manager, has been giving serious consideration to the establishing of standards for posture chairs which his company purchases. Mr. Schubert believes that standards are necessary for three chair classifications—executive, supervisory, and clerical. For each of these groups, a particular model, design, upholstery, and color would be determined and used throughout the entire office.

To substantiate his viewpoint, Mr. Schubert points out that the use of such standards would greatly improve the appearance of the office and save much time in purchasing. Also, chair purchases could be made at better prices for the company. But probably of even greater importance would be the elimination of comparison of chairs by employees of the same general organizational level. For example, one supervisor would not compare his chair to that of another supervisor and feel that he had a better or an inferior chair by comparison. Chair equality would be attained.

The controller suggests that the employees of each office division should be permitted to select the chairs they want. In other words, chair standards should extend within an office division only. Any other standards arrangement would conflict with personnel interests and possibly with the type of work performed. Furthermore, he believes that the company should give its chair business to several suppliers. Competition should be encouraged; otherwise, the company might find itself at the mercy of one supplier.

The president of the company does not see anything wrong with employees of the same organizational level using different chairs, and he asks two questions of the office manager: (1) "How are you going to determine the standards for chairs in our office?" and (2) "What are the tangible savings from adopting the use of chair standards?" As the president sees it, the answer to question No. 1 is so involved that the company should not undertake the project. In addition, many employees would question the results and their use regardless of what would be determined. In answer to the second question, it appears that additional expenditures, not savings, would be incurred. Not one, but groups of chairs would probably have to be purchased if chair standards were adopted. Also, the possibility of taking advantage of lower prices on the chair market would be minimized, and further improvements in chair design and manufacture would be discouraged.

## Problems:

1. Do you agree with the viewpoint of the controller? Discuss. Of the president? Discuss.

2. What action do you recommend that the office manager take? Why?

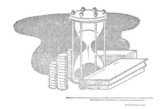

# CHAPTER 22

# CONTROLLING OFFICE
# QUANTITY AND QUALITY

Our greatest obligation to our children is to
prepare them to understand and to deal
effectively with the world in which they will live
and not with the world we have known or the
world we would prefer to have.
*—Grayson Kirk*

CONTROLLING quantity is prominent and important in office management.
In most offices, the volume of work is likely to be quite large during some
periods and, conversely, quite small during other periods. This fluctuation
appears to be in the general nature of office work. A study of the demands
upon an office over a comparatively long period of time will usually reveal
a rhythmic pattern in office activities. For example, it may be found that
peak loads are generally experienced on the first day of each week, every
Friday, or the last few days of each month.

These conditions require controlling effort to minimize the fluctuation
and make the work more manageable. When the peak periods are known
fairly well in advance, quite adequate means for handling them can be
determined. However, in other cases, the demands upon an office are
continually changing, and where this condition exists, the work of
controlling is difficult.

## THE PROBLEMS OF QUANTITY VARIATION

Perhaps the most important problem incurred because of variation in
the quantity of office work is that of getting the work finished when it is
needed. Adequate control can assist tremendously in this respect. Also,
work fluctuation creates a "feast or famine" situation in the factors
utilized in performing the work. For any given period, how many people to

503

hire, what machines to employ, and which methods to adopt are typical questions. On the one hand, the reduction of idle machine and personnel time are paramount; while on the other hand, lack of sufficient capacity in machine or manpower is of foremost consideration. Another disturbing problem is the designating and the handling of rush or special work. In most instances, this designation means little in determining work priority, because the terms are applied to practically all the work. Furthermore, the supplying of accurate information concerning the stage of completion for certain office work is complicated by work fluctuation. Information on the progress being made, the number of units completed, and the probable finishing time is not readily supplied when the work volume is characterized by steep peaks and deep troughs.

## QUANTITY CONTROLLING EFFORTS

Several fundamentals should be kept in mind when performing quantity controlling. First, it is mandatory that adequate knowledge and information about the things being controlled and which affect quantity of work are available and supplied. Data on personnel, systems and procedures, machines, cost, and due dates must be known. In this respect, standards are helpful, as discussed in Chapter 21. Second, the control efforts should be coordinated, viewing the totality of the work. Quantity control cannot be left to the individual employee. Unbalanced and sporadic work loads are eliminated in part by taking into account the complete and inclusive work requirements for definite periods. Also, the best practice is to have the controlling under the direction of one individual or an organization division designated to handle this function. Third, quantity controlling should be constructive in its ultimate effect. It is an energizing, positive action, not a depressant. The controlling should make it possible for the manager to give more attention to getting the work out, planning efforts, making decisions, improving methods, and reducing costs.

For quantity controlling, the step of determining what is being accomplished is considerably clarified by expressing the office work in measurable units. Such expressions are necessary for accurate quantity controlling. We are dealing with amounts of work and specific measurements of it are basic for the control efforts to have meaning and purpose. "A lot of office work" is subject to an infinite number of interpretations. We also need accurate and fast means of communication between the one doing the controlling and the employee doing the actual physical office work. In the smaller office, or where the supervisor initiates his own means of control, no particular difficulty is encountered with this requirement. However, when centralized controlling is used, fast intercommunication service is necessary between the line operators and the controlling unit.

Evaluating what is being done, an essential step in all controlling, takes on special meaning in controlling quantity. The planned sequence of operations for each type of work should be utilized, otherwise the controlling is usually diminished. In many instances, the office system or procedure will supply this information, but details covering a specific job are sometimes also necessary. This is especially true in the case of "bottleneck" areas. Along with the prescribed sequence, we need reasonable time expectancies for completion of the work, i.e., time standards should be available. Knowing when, how much, and for how long the controlling efforts are applied are decisions which should be guided by the utilization of office time standards.[1] In addition, the evaluation should emphasize and be tied in with getting the specific work accomplished. In controlling office quantity it is easy to digress and find the efforts really perpetuating a control mechanism or program as such. Care must be taken to direct and keep the evaluating of quantity "on the beam."

Applying corrective measures, if necessary, consists in part of seeing that the initial control plans are enforced faithfully or revising the control actions in view of the unfavorable results being obtained and experience in controlling work. The corrective actions take many different forms and are strongly influenced by the personal preferences of the controller and the circumstances of the particular office.

## MEANS OF CONTROLLING OFFICE WORK FLUCTUATION

The question now arises: "What specifically can the office manager do in order to meet the problems inherent in the fluctuation of the office work volume?" The answer lies in employing either initially, or subsequently as suggested by events as they unfold, one or several major means. Eight possibilities are offered here:

1. *Employment of part-time help.* This possible solution is self-evident and will not be discussed in detail. In certain cases, the use of part-time help is entirely satisfactory; but experience seems to indicate, in general, that part-time help may not be as reliable, efficient, and cooperative as regular employees. Also, the cost of recruiting, hiring, and training part-time employees might be excessive. Flexibility of the work force, however, is gained by the use of part-time people.

It should also be noted that some service bureaus specialize in supplying skilled office help in the client's office for a specified short-term period.[2] Help obtained in this manner is usually competent and can be recruited upon short notice, but the cost is higher than that of regular employees doing the same work.

---

[1] Measuring and timing office work is the subject of Chapter 23.

[2] Service bureaus are discussed several paragraphs below.

*2. Overtime work.* Although commonly resorted to, this solution to the problem of work fluctuation is not entirely satisfactory. For occasional overloads, it may represent the simplest solution. However, when the amount of work during regular hours is light and frequent peak loads are common, the working of overtime is open to serious question as the best way of handling the problem. For one thing, overtime increases unit labor cost considerably. Consider a common case in which an employee works eight hours overtime. These eight hours are paid for at the rate of time and one half. In effect, these overtime hours increase the unit labor cost by 8.33 percent, calculated by dividing 52, the hours paid for, by 48, the hours worked, or 1.0833, an increase of 8.33 percent.

There is also the question of employee fatigue. Over an extended period, there is reasonable question whether the rate of output during the overtime hours will be the same as that during the regular work hours. The rate of production during overtime tends to fall below the normal production rate. Most office managers will concur in the statement that an office employee working an extra two or three hours after a normal eight-hour working day will not produce an extra two-eighths or three-eighths of a normal day's work. The amount will be less—in some instances, considerably less.

Furthermore, legal restrictions must be taken into account. Federal and state laws regulate the type of work and the hours which an employee can work in certain occupations. Where female employees are involved, the regulatory statutes may be of special importance.

*3. Forming mobile units.* In some offices, it is possible to form "flying squadron" units which are moved from area to area to help handle excessive work loads. Normally, the office must be fairly large to utilize this method. However, the same idea is used informally in most small offices by shifting the employees around when and as the work requires. Utilizing mobile units necessitates employees with comprehensive training in a number of different types of office work. Hiring and maintaining such employees present some difficulties, but can be managed satisfactorily.

*4. Calling service bureaus to do the work.* Office overloads or work which is of a special nature can be handled by outside enterprises which specialize in this type of work. Most of these so-called service bureaus are independently owned business firms, but some are units of office machine manufacturers. Service bureaus are located in all major cities throughout the United States; several are nationwide in scope. Some are specialists operating, for example, computer or punched-card installations only; but many offer complete services in typing, calculating, tabulating, filing, transcribing, duplicating, and direct mailing. Service bureaus offer vast experience and competent, specialized personnel to handle complex jobs. The service is fast. For example, one service bureau completed, for a client, inventory calculations involving 3,500 hours of work within three working days. In view of the service provided, the cost of service bureaus is usually reasonable.

It should be observed that these outside service bureaus are useful to the office manager for more than meeting peak loads or emergency problems. They are also helpful when purchase of particular office machines cannot be justified by the office because of its size or the amount or character of the work. Also, a service bureau can be engaged to serve as a laboratory to test the value of a new means of handling office work before the necessary equipment is purchased.

5. *Stress centralization in organization.* One of the strongest justifications for centralization in office organizing is the more effective handling of peak loads.[3] When the excess work is (1) mainly basic activities such as typing, computing, copying, sorting, and filing and (2) concentrated in different departments at different times, the centralized organizational approach has real merit.

6. *Use of cycling.* Cycling is an arrangement whereby papers are processed throughout a period according to an orderly plan rather than as a group—for example, at the beginning or end of each period. In other words, by means of cycling, the work is spread out evenly throughout the period. The practice of cycling has been used in connection with the mailing of statements and is commonly referred to as cycle billing. The same practice, however, can be applied to other types of office work.

Cycling has been used for a long time by public utility companies in sending out their bills for service. Meters are read, for example, in a certain section of the city, bills mailed, and payments specified by a certain date. Several days later, other meters in another section of the city are read, bills mailed, and payments requested by a date which is a few days after that of the previous group.

Many department stores operate on a cycle-billing basis under which each account is posted once a month, but statements are mailed for a different section of accounts on different days throughout the month. The accounts can be divided into 20 or fewer groups, depending upon such things as the volume of postings, the number of accounts, and the number of trays required to house the accounts.

Figure 22–1 shows a chart which gives the divisions for 20 cycles. Going from the outer to the inner circle of this chart, the data represented are, respectively, the accounts, the cycle numbers and closing dates, and the cycle mailing dates. For example, to the right of and slightly above the center of the chart, accounts "Cle to Coon" have cycle number 6.01. The 6 of this number indicates that the closing date is the sixth of the month.

---

[3] See Chapter 26.

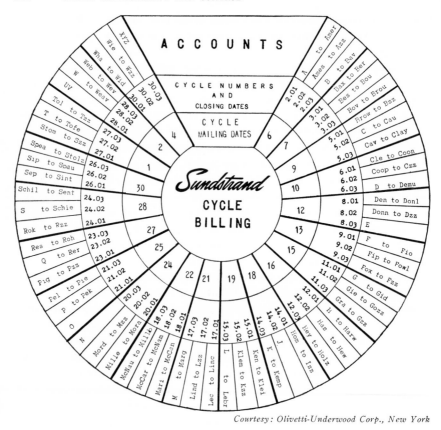

*Courtesy: Olivetti-Underwood Corp., New York*

FIG. 22–1. Chart used to establish cycles in a cycle-billing system.

The cycle mailing date is 10, i.e., the tenth of the month, which allows four days after closing accounts to prepare the statements for mailing to customers.

7. *Maintain work backlog.* This means utilizes a reservoir of work, so to speak, in order to level out the peaks and valleys of the office work flow. When certain work can be postponed or moved up, this approach works out quite satisfactorily. The attempt is to make each day an average day.

An alternate approach is to mix urgent with nonurgent office work. Certain tasks of the office, such as bringing records up to date, replenishing supplies, and putting headings on certain papers, can usually be performed during slack periods. When work having high priority is received, it is processed immediately, the nonurgent work being laid aside for the time being.

8. *Orderly work flow through routing, scheduling, and dispatching.* This approach consists of establishing specific channels by which the

office work is to be accomplished, placing time values on each successive step so arranged, receiving information on progress of work, and issuing authorization for work to proceed from step to step. It emphasizes the controlling of the work quantity and the use of time in work performance. Each of the major components of this approach—routing, scheduling, and dispatching—will be discussed.

## ROUTING

*Routing is the determining of the route or channel through which the work travels and the sequence of operations required for the completion of the work.* For most offices, routing is determined by the system and procedure used. In some instances, the choice of a particular machine or of a certain area may be fixed by the routing process, but this is the exception rather than the rule with most office work. Commonly, a route sheet, showing the sequence of operations, is prepared. In addition, for each operation, the allocated time and the department in which the work is to be performed are indicated.

A practice sometimes followed is to place the office work in a heavy manila envelope with the route sheet attached on the outside. A copy of the sheet is retained by the person or department doing the central control work. In some instances, the form of the route sheet is printed on the envelope to prevent possible loss of the route sheet in the office.

## SCHEDULING

*Scheduling is the assigning of time values to the work sequence—the determination of when each operation starts and when it should be completed.* The extent to which office work can be scheduled depends upon the individual circumstances; but usually, a great deal can be scheduled, including billing, key punching, tape perforating, tabulating, transcribing, check writing, order writing, and inventory taking.

The common practice in scheduling is to work backward from the time specified for completion. An allowance is made for each operation required by the work; and in this manner a starting time is determined. For example, if the time set for completion of a job is 4:00 P.M., Thursday, June 12, and the work requires 18 hours' time, this means that the work should start 18 hours before that time and date, or 2:00 P.M., Tuesday, June 10.[4]

The three common means of scheduling include use of:

1. *Folders.* In certain instances, this simple and quite effective informal means of scheduling office work can be used advantageously.

---

[4] This is based on working hours from 8:00 to 12:00 noon and from 1:00 to 5:00 P.M., five days a week.

Under it, a given number of units of work are placed in each of a number of folders. These are distributed by the supervisor, who notes to whom each folder is given, the starting time, the machine or workplace used, and the completion time the batch of work in the folder should take. The employee is told the amount of time the work should require. Upon return of the completed work, the time taken is noted, and the process is repeated. The supervisor is the key controlling person under this arrangement. He has knowledge of the work on hand, the amount completed, the amount in process, and when it should be finished.

Best results are obtained when the amount of work in each folder is a reasonable amount—probably that requiring an hour or less for completion. Some prefer to call this *short-interval scheduling* and are enthusiastic about the excellent results it brings. It features assigned amounts of work that an employee easily comprehends, frequent and certain follow-up, good time utilization, and adoption of the basic tenet that telling an employee when you expect him to complete a specific job before he starts it usually helps in meeting the schedule.

2. *Visible index cards.* Data required for formal and complete scheduling can be handled on cards. For this purpose visible index cards providing signals for control purposes works out very well.[5] A separate card is made out for each machine, desk, or workplace. The signals featured by this type of equipment are moved to specific positions along the margin of the card to designate specific scheduled times. Scanning the cards quickly reveals what equipment is available for work and what jobs are currently being worked on.

3. *Charts.* Another effective means of recording scheduling data is by the use of charts. One of the original types, called the Gantt chart, was devised by Henry L. Gantt. The basic principle used is that work planned and work accomplished are shown on the same chart in relation to each other and also in their relation to time. The items are listed in a column, with corresponding capacities or data on maximum scheduling loads shown in an adjacent column. Other columns are used for time units, such as hours, days, weeks, or months.

Figure 22–2 shows a Gantt chart representing the scheduling of work for department 13, in which six posting machines are used. In this figure, a main time column represents one week, as shown by the date filled in at the right and top of each time column. To illustrate, the column headed "Dec. 3" means the week ending December 3. In this case, there are five divisions under each main time column; the divisions represent the five working days in the week. The data for each machine are shown in the identified horizontal sections of the chart, i.e., machine No. 1-N by the top horizontal section, machine No. 2-B by the second horizontal section, etc.

---

[5] See Chapter 6 for discussion on visible equipment for filing.

For each machine, the work, scheduled by weeks, is indicated by the light line and the total cumulative work scheduled by the heavy line. Thus, for posting machine No. 4-B, work time scheduled for the week ended December 17 is three days, which represents 960 postings (3 x 320); and the total amount of time scheduled for this machine for the six weeks' work is twelve days. The **V** mark on the top of the chart shows that the chart represents the status as of that date, which, in the illustration, is December 14. This type of Gantt chart is termed a load chart, since it graphically represents the load assigned to each machine and likewise reveals the idle or available time. Successive additions can be made on the chart by extending the proper lines; a redrawing is not necessary.

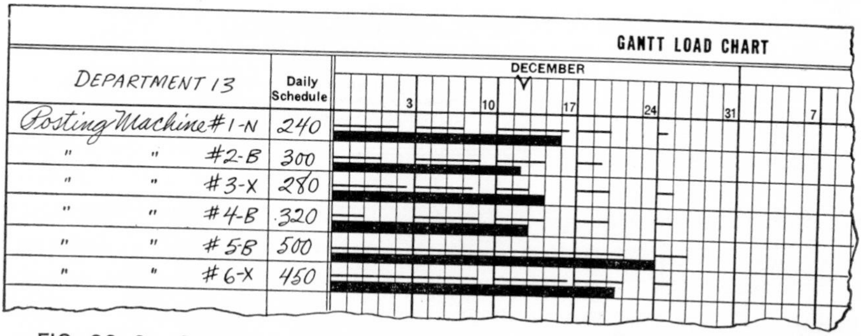

FIG. 22–2. Gantt load chart, showing graphically the degree of utilization of machines, idle time, and time available for scheduling.

Another type of scheduling chart combines the principles of the visible card and the Gantt chart. It has the general appearance of a large, visible card file with the overlapping card pockets hanging vertically. (See Figure 22–3.) Scheduled items, such as operations, machines, or work stations, are shown in the extreme left column of the chart; time is indicated along the horizontal axis. A separate pocket is used for each scheduled item. At the extreme left of each pocket is placed a card which gives frequently used information about the scheduled item, with the identifying data appearing in the visible margin. The remaining portion to the right in each pocket is used to show graphically the scheduled operations and times allotted for the particular item. To do this, two types of cards are used: (1) operation cards and (2) time insert cards. The former are printed card forms used to indicate data about the operation and the scheduled time. Operational information is written on the card with the scheduled time information shown in the bottom margin of the card. The latter are printed strips of paper placed in the visible margin to show the time scale along the horizontal axis. The strips are folded lengthwise, with the turned-up stub showing the printed scale.

When the operation card is tucked in the visible margin and behind the insert card, only the colored strip of the operation card is visible; and the length of this strip indicates the amount of time required to do the work. The exact placement of the card is determined by the scale of the insert card in the visible margin. Since a colored strip indicates scheduled time, it follows that white space indicates free or unscheduled time.

*Courtesy: Remington Office Systems Div., Sperry-Rand Corp., New York*

FIG. 22–3. *Top:* Close-up of scheduling chart. *Bottom:* Installation in office of a large manufacturer.

## DISPATCHING

Dispatching is putting into action and adequately following up the routing and scheduling plans; it represents true controlling and is made up of a signaling to go ahead and a checking to see that action is taking place when and where it is wanted. For office work, dispatching is usually quite simple. It is frequently done informally by the supervisor, however, when the volume and different kinds of office work warrant it, employees doing only dispatching work can probably be employed advantageously. Quite often, it is desirable to use a central control board which graphically visualizes the dispatching of the many different jobs which are started, moved through the office, and completed.

Many different types of control boards exist, including the three-hook, spring-clip, peg-string, and grooved-strip types. The last two are most adaptable to office work. Figure 22–4 shows a peg-string board, which has the controlled items on the left side and such things as time, operations, and departments in separate sections across the top. The board has a series of small holes into which pegs are inserted. For each item in the left column, there are two horizontal rows of holes. The top row is used to indicate the scheduled operations, the bottom for the actual progress. Thus, comparison between the two is easily made.

To show the scheduled operations, a peg with a string attached is inserted in the proper hole corresponding to the operation and time value. The string, which extends from the left of the board to the peg, is always taut, thus giving the impression of a horizontal line. Pegs inserted in the bottom row of holes show the actual progress. For quick reference, an assortment of different pegs, having contrasting colors, shapes, and markings on the top, is employed. A quick glance at the board shows the times for dispatching, what work is behind schedule, and what work is ahead of schedule. A vertical cord representing a specific time and date, frequently a "today line," is used to assist in visualizing these conditions. Each day, for example, the cord is moved to the right a distance equal to one day on the time scale. All data are kept up to date on the board by moving the pegs to the proper positions representing the current condition.

The first line, pocket No. 1, of Figure 22–4 covers order No. 101. The large round peg shows that this order is in department No. 6. To the right and under July, the small round peg indicates that the order was received July 11. The peg with the string attached to it is shown under July 25, which is the scheduled completion date of the current operation. The "today line" is at July 21. Hence, this order is to be completed in four days. In contrast, order No. 103, in the third pocket, was scheduled for completion on July 16 and is five days behind schedule. This order is in department No. 6, which should be consulted to determine what can be done to get the order moving. The square pegs to the extreme right of the board indicate the scheduled dates for finishing the orders. Order No. 101, for example, is to be completed August 12.

In contrast, the grooved-strip board has horizontal cardholder strips for insertion of tickets representing work lots. The extreme left column is used for work-lot numbers, and the remaining columns are headed by department names. Cards are made out for each work lot. As the work progresses, the cards are moved on the board to correspond with the

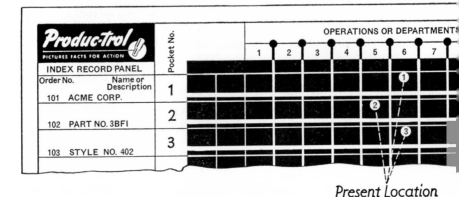

Present Location
of Order

FIG. 22–4.   A closeup view of the peg-string board.

correct department location of the work. In some instances, the time is shown horizontally. When this is done, separate tickets can be made for each operation on each work lot, as well as for the scheduled starting and finishing times indicated on each card. In this manner, the helpfulness of the board is increased by showing the scheduling function.

## OFFICE QUALITY CONTROL

Another important area of office controlling is that applied to the quality of work. Poor quality impedes the essential services of an office. A poorly typed letter, an incorrectly executed office form, an error in extending the cost data, or a misspelled name on a customers' list diminishes the effectiveness of information handling. Some of the work must be done over, some can be "fixed up" by additional expenditure of time and energy, and some is used "as is"—with errors or misstatements undetected, and promising the possibility of subsequent waste. Generally speaking, lack of adequate control over quality can result in three types of losses. First, paper work errors can cause a wrong decision to be made. Failure to process an inquiry properly might result in the loss of the prospective sale from a very important customer. Second, poor quality can result in loss of good will. A customer's payment improperly posted, or mailing out an incorrect billing, are examples. Third, loss in time and money is incurred in detecting and correcting office errors. Frequently, this loss is unnoticed; nevertheless, it is present.

## OFFICE QUALITY CONTROL APPROACHES

The same basic three-step pattern of control already emphasized for forms control and quantity control is followed for quality control.

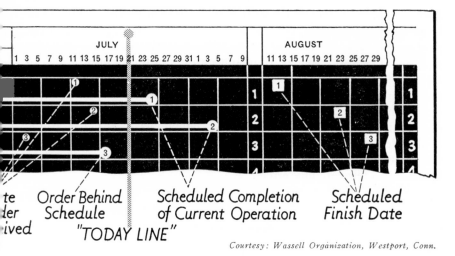

te    Order Behind    Scheduled Completion    Scheduled
der    Schedule    of Current Operation    Finish Date
ived    "TODAY LINE"

*Courtesy: Wassell Organization, Westport, Conn.*

However, the more effective approaches used for this area are sufficiently different from other controls to warrant discussion here. The specific approach adopted will depend upon the particular type of office work, the personnel, the cost of maintaining quality, and the possible effect of an error in the work. First, a practice of checking every segment of all work can be followed. This constitutes 100 percent inspection—i.e., each letter or each column of figures is gone over to verify the correctness of the work. Second, a policy of either spot or sample checking can be followed. In the case of spot checking, every third or perhaps fifth document or segment of work is checked. For sample checking, a group which is representative of the total is determined statistically and is subsequently checked to determine the quality level of the total work being performed. Third, the office work can be inspected by means of statistical quality control (SQC), an approach based on statistical methods and the laws of probability. It is more than a "look-see" after the work is completed. SQC provides signals and information that work is satisfactory or not as it is being processed. Thus, if errors are occurring beyond the acceptable limits, the processing can be stopped, corrected, and then resumed.

## STATISTICAL QUALITY CONTROL

Natural phenomena and their relationships are statistical in character. Repeated productive operations of the same thing will provide a distribution of values. This can be evidenced either by measurement on each of a quantity of similar items or by repeated measurements of the same thing on the same item. This follows because of the inherent characteristics of the measuring method.

The distribution of values can be shown graphically by means of a curve, with the values represented on the horizontal scale and the frequency of the values on the vertical scale. For our purposes here, it can be stated that when the phenomena are natural, sufficiently large, and of random selection, most of the values will cluster in the center around a representative average value, while other values in the group will tend to taper off to the left and to the right of this average. The result is what the statistician calls a normal, or bell-shaped, curve, as shown by the curve *MMM* in Figure 22–5. To illustrate, if the errors of inventory recorders are counted, it will be found that most commit, let us say, five errors, while a few commit three, and still fewer commit one error. Likewise, to the right (or greater than five errors), there will be some with seven errors, and a few with nine errors.

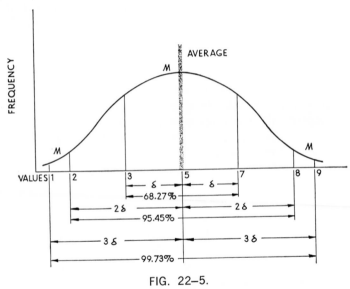

FIG. 22–5.

Based on statistical mathematics and the laws of probability, the statistician can determine the normal dispersion or spread of these data. Commonly, a value known as a standard deviation is calculated. Within a standard deviation to the left and to the right of the average are contained 68.27 percent of the values of the series. Within two standard deviations to the left and to the right are 95.45 percent, and within three standard deviations, 99.73 percent of the values. These concepts are shown in Figure 22–5.

## CHANCE AND ASSIGNABLE CAUSES

These statistical relationships are utilized in developing effective means to control the quality of work. For a series of data, it is known statistically what variations from the average can be expected on account of the inherent characteristics of the phenomena. Variation within a definable area is inevitable and is *the result of chance*. However, variation outside the definable area can be discovered and subsequently corrected. In other words, statistical quality control reveals when a variation is due to *other than chance*, i.e., when *an assignable cause* is present. But it does not tell what the cause is. Investigation and analysis are required to find and remove the assignable cause.

## CONTROL CHART

A graphic device known as a control chart is constructed and used for plotting data and showing variations from the acceptable goal or standard. The values of the limits placed on the chart are determined statistically. In this work, the statistical concepts of the normal curve, the average or normal quality value, and the limits of variations that are due to chance are determined.

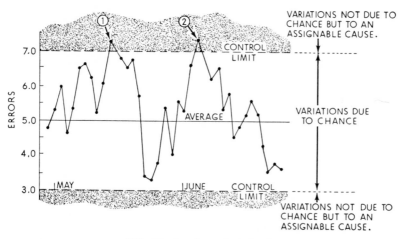

FIG. 22–6.    A control chart.

Figure 22–6 illustrates a control chart. This can be thought of as developed from a normal, or bell-shaped, curve placed on its side, so that the area in which variations due to chance occur is represented by a horizontal band. In the illustration, this band is from 3.0 to 7.0 errors. The average or normal expectancy due to the inherent nature of the work is 5.0 errors; however, the quality of the work will vary from 3.0 to 7.0 errors because of chance. It is inevitable and is not assignable to a cause. When the quality measurement goes outside this pattern of variations—for example, as indicated by points 1 and 2—the cause is not chance but an assignable influence which should be discovered and eliminated. It might, for example, be a defective tabulating key mechanism on the typewriter, paper slipping in the machine, or a space bar that is not working properly.

In a control chart, the frequency of plotting the data depends upon the quality and value of the product controlled. Usually, the values are obtained from a sample of the work—that is, a representative number of the total are selected and checked. This may be once every 15 minutes, or perhaps once a day. The value of these selected units is representative statistically of the total being processed.

A different control chart is usually established for each control station. This is done because the work being quality controlled at one station may differ considerably from that at another station.

To reiterate, SQC stresses preventive rather than remedial action. When more than 7.0 errors are found in a batch of work, indicated by point 1 in Figure 22–6, the work is stopped, and the reason for this assignable amount of errors is discovered and corrected before the work is permitted to continue. Thus, processing a large quantity of work and subsequently finding much of it defective is avoided. Usually, the trend of the readings is indicative. For example, the increasing readings climaxing to point 2 in Figure 22–6 point to the occurrence of such a reading as 2 outside the control limits. Many feel that trends leading to readings near the control limits can be used as signals to look for an assignable cause without waiting for the actual reading to exceed the control limits.

## IMPLEMENTING SQC IN AN OFFICE

To initiate statistical quality control, it is first necessary to find out the current quality level of the operation. A fact-finding survey of from two to four weeks is recommended, the exact time depending upon the variety and complexity of the work being done. A description of the error, its probable cause, and an estimate of the time required to correct it provide additional helpful information.

The quality levels and the control limits should then be determined. It is usually best to concentrate on the key areas or locations. This tends to give control over the entire work of the office. Some errors can be eliminated entirely by the use of such techniques as process improvement, machine operation, and simplified office forms. When the error can be eliminated—i.e., all the factors causing it, the need to control such errors is likewise eliminated.

The next step is to establish the sampling plans so that economical and statistically sound representations of the total values will be used. This resolves itself into a problem of statistics, but a practical understanding of the included problem is necessary.

Installation of the program is usually a simple task, but close supervision and expert assistance, if needed, should be supplied. Like all new programs, that of statistical quality control gives rise to questions and to situations demanding on-the-job decisions.

The program should be reviewed periodically to check on results and make minor adjustments deemed advisable. Of course, if the nature of the work changes, the quality control efforts should be reviewed to determine if any modifications are needed.

## QUESTIONS

1. As an office manager, would you favor forming mobile units to meet fluctuating work requirements? Justify your stand.

2. Point out the relationship, if any, in each of the following pairs:
   a) Time insert cards and overtime work.
   b) Quality control and dispatching.
   c) Scheduling and routing.
   d) Routing and office layout.

3. Indicate what means probably would be used to handle the peak office work load caused by each of the following:
   a) Granting discounts on all bills paid by the tenth of the month following the month in which purchase was made.
   b) Finishing a payroll by Friday morning of each week.
   c) Completing an inventory over a weekend for a large manufacturing company.
   d) Issuing licenses to car owners of a state during the first two months of the year.

4. Explain the meaning of "scheduling by folders" and indicate where its application is probably most desirable.

5. Discuss the meaning, objectives, and means of dispatching in the controlling of office work.

6. Talk with an office manager and inquire if maintaining quality of work is a problem in his office. If so, evaluate practices followed to minimize it. If not, how do you account for its absence? Make a brief report of what you discover.

7. Discuss the subject, quantity controlling factors, pointing out the fundamentals of which to be mindful.

8. What different approaches can an office manager follow with regard to quality control? Discuss.

9. Identify each of the following:
   a) Unassignable cause in statistical quality control.
   b) Cycle billing.
   c) Service bureaus.
   d) Gantt chart.

10. Does statistical quality control stress remedial or preventive action? Use Figure 22–6 in explaining your answer.

11. Errors in the work of filing at the central files have reached the level where reasonable work flow is impeded. During the past three months, the office manager has made several minor changes in the handling of the filing work with the intent of making it easier to perform and making an error less likely. During

this period, data compiled show the following: (1) quantity of work up 2.3 percent, (2) number of filing employees at beginning of period, five, number at end of period, five, (3) filing supervisor's rating, average. What action do you now recommend the office manager take? Why?

12. Many feel that office work must be 100 percent accurate and free from mistakes. In the light of statistical quality control, is this belief reasonable? Should an office manager expect this degree of quality? Discuss.

## CASE PROBLEMS

### Case 22–1.  Oakson Company

Shortly before quitting time at 4:45 P.M., supervisor Joseph Ayer noticed four employees of his department, the factory office, getting ready to go home. He called them over to his desk.

MR. AYER:  You are working overtime tonight—till 8 o'clock at least. (*The employees stared for a moment, then one of them,* WALTER BROWN, *spoke.*)

MR. BROWN:  Is there something wrong? How come we must work? I don't get it.

MR. AYER:  There is nothing wrong. We simply have to get caught up in our work. I told you day before yesterday we were working overtime tonight.

MR. BROWN:  Well, I can't work tonight. And I don't recall getting any notice about working overtime.

MR. AYER:  I told you while you were standing right where you are right now. And that's all you need.

MR. ROBIN (*another employee*):  Mr. Ayer, I did not get any memo about overtime tonight.

MR. AYER:  You don't need a detailed written message delivered to you personally. I told you and that's sufficient.

The men worked past quitting time. About 5:30 P.M. Mr. Ayer told them that he was going down the street for a sandwich and cup of coffee and asked if they wanted to join him. All replied in the negative. When Mr. Ayer returned to the factory office at 6:05 P.M., he found that his four employees had gone for the day.

Problems:

1. Assume you are Mr. Robin and first thing the following morning Mr. Ayer talks with you privately. What explanation or defense for your action would you give? Why?

2. What action do you recommend Mr. Ayer take? Why?

### Case 22–2.  Ferguson Company

Numerous complaints were being received dealing with the slowness of processing customer orders. The central office handles all order processing and sends documents to the company's 11 warehouses for shipment of merchandise. It is the general manager's desire to process all orders and send them to the mail room within 24 hours of receipt of order. He suspected this time requirement was not being met. To investigate the situation he conferred with the manager of systems and procedures, Mr. Herman Ottoman, and it was agreed that Mr. David Cosand, a systems analyst with the company, would talk with the general manager, study, and suggest measures to effect improvements. Subsequently, while interviewing the general manager, Mr. Cosand suggested that a study be undertaken to determine how long it was taking to process an order. However, the general manager believed a simple control record based on a sampling of orders should be tried. As the general manager saw it, from a portion of the completed work, the amount of elapsed time from receipt to completeness could be determined, but more important, the elapsed time up to each department or major work station could be found for any given department or station. Hence, a pattern of orders, such as orders station 1 from the first day after initial receipt, orders station 1 from the second day of receipt, and so forth, could be revealed.

Mr. Cosand agreed that this was entirely possible and practical. He expressed the belief that this would give some factual measurement of the problem, but would not solve the difficulty, namely, completing customer orders more quickly. He also pointed out that to him the proper control to attain was (1) knowing exactly what kind of service is being supplied and (2) comparing this against the service goals established by management. The former would be gained by following the general manager's suggestion. To this the general manager heartily agreed, but added that remedial measures would be needed to upgrade the service to the level desired and this, in turn, would require knowledge of how the orders are now processed.

Accordingly, Mr. Cosand studied the practices now being followed in processing the orders. He found that (1) orders are sent to the sales department, where they are reviewed; (2) when review is completed, usually around noon, orders are sent to credit department for checking; (3) thence they go to the order department, where orders are extended in dollar amounts and merchandise availability is checked; most of this work is not completed by 5:00 P.M. and it frequently extends until noon the following day; (4) orders passing credit and merchandise availability requirements are sent to invoicing; all orders being invoiced have been in possession of the company at least a day; (5) completed and checked invoices are sent to the mail room at 4:00 P.M. daily for mailing to warehouses.

## Problems:

1. Give your understanding of the general manager's concept of a control record to indicate the service being rendered, i.e., data showing the elapsed time for completion and likewise the elapsed time up to each department, and explain how these data could be used advantageously. Illustrate your answer with a chart, if you desire.

2. What additional types of information do you feel it advisable for Mr. Cosand to obtain? Why?

3. What recommendation do you believe Mr. Cosand should make? Why?

## Case 22-3.   Dallas Dandy Petroleum Products, Inc.

Distribution of "Dallas Dandy" petroleum products is made by sales to independent dealers and by direct sales to certain customers by the corporation's bulk plants and commission agents. These bulk stations number about 200 and are widely dispersed geographically. Products sold directly by bulk plants are recorded by means of customer delivery tickets which are listed on a sales report by an office employee at the bulk station. On any given sales report, there might be listed 15 to 500 tickets. The bulk plant reports from one to five times a week, depending upon its volume of business.

For customer billings, sales reports, and tax reports, the company follows the practice of processing a particular month's business for all bulk plants within the first three working days of the following month. Hence, all bulk plants are requested to have their sales reports in the office by the second working day of the following month. This creates a large volume of work at the first of each month.

Various plans to meet the peak work requirements were used, but none proved entirely satisfactory. The office manager was resigned to the fact that it was just "one of those things" and they would have to do the best they could. Later, he got the idea to establish a group of "special clerks." These were chosen from various departments and were selected because of their experience and flexibility. Their regular assignments were normally work of little priority value; they could be done at any time during the month. When the month-end volume of work arrived, these special clerks, as many as were needed, were added to the first department which received the work. As the work moved along to subsequent departments, so did the special clerks. When the rush period was over, they returned to their regular assignments.

The arrangement devised by the office manager worked satisfactorily for several months; then, complaints grew from customers regarding errors in papers sent them. For the month just ended, 378 complaints were received. Normally, about 50–60 complaints had been received each month, none of them too serious. Since there were about 20,000 active customer accounts, the office manager had accepted 50–60 as probably a normal state of affairs. But when the complaints jumped to 378, he became very concerned. He discussed the problem with the various supervisors, who assured him they would make special efforts to insure better quality work. The following month, the mistakes reported by customers reached 443. The office manager was certain that corrective action must be taken at once. How many papers erred in favor of the customer, about which the company heard nothing, also worried him. He was certain his superior would find out about the situation and demand a solution to the problem. He reasoned that he had better have the right answer and a plan in operation before he was "called on the carpet."

## Problems:

1. What are some of the major alternatives open to the office manager?

2. Do you believe the present "special clerks" arrangement can be made to operate satisfactorily? Substantiate your answer.

3. What program of action do you recommend for the office manager? Why?

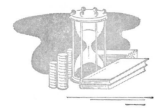

CHAPTER **23**

# CONTROLLING
# OFFICE TIME-USE

Time is cried out upon as a great thief; it is
people's own fault. Use him well, and you will
get from his hand more than he will ever take
from yours.
　　　　　　　　　　*—Elizabeth Wetherell*

A MAJOR AREA of controlling is that of time-use which deals with the
accomplishing of work *within specific time limits*. It is very well to get
the office work completed, but how long should it take to do it in keeping with fair, reasonable, and adequate time controls? Here again we
follow the familiar controlling steps of (1) determining what is being
accomplished, (2) evaluating it, and (3) if necessary, applying corrective measures. But to follow these steps in reference to office time-use,
we encounter the problem of office work measurement to which time values can be prescribed.

## OFFICE WORK MEASUREMENT

For time-use controlling to be effective, we must first know the amount
of work to which the time controls are being applied. To state that the
work should be completed within 5.5 minutes implies a given quantity
of work completed within this period. This means that measurement of
office work is required.

To measure means to determine quantity. For control of time-use, we
measure work, we measure time, and relate the two together. To illustrate, it is common to speak of so many orders processed within a given
time. The number of orders becomes meaningful when tied with the
quantity of time.

Measurement of work concerns accomplishment or productivity. It has to do with results; it does not deal with the amount of energy expended, although in many cases this may be in direct proportion to the work output. Work measurement can be considered a tool in that it helps a manager (1) to distribute work loads fairly, (2) to define job success in tangible units, (3) to analyze employee performance, and (4) to highlight where remedial help is needed.

Much of the work in an office can be measured fairly accurately and inexpensively. The extent in any given case will depend upon the particular type of office tasks performed; but usually from two-thirds to three-fourths of all work in an office can be measured. It is true that difficulty in measurement is encountered, for example, when the office work is nonrepetitive and irregular, or when it is primarily mental rather than manual. These are impediments; but with study and analysis, the ultimate objectives of measuring the office work can be achieved and surprisingly useful and reliable results obtained. It is erroneous to accept the belief that work measurement cannot be set for office work.

## MEASURING UNIT

To measure requires a recognizable unit. There are many different units that can be used, the selection depending mainly upon the type of office work. For example, typewritten work can be measured by typing area or sheets, and purchase orders by the number written. Sometimes, the quantity can be determined very easily by means of counting devices on machines; and frequently, the relationship of the weight of paper to the amount of work can be employed. Other examples of work-measuring units in the office are the number of invoices written, the amount of postage (dollar value) used on outgoing mail, the weight of incoming mail handled, the reams of paper used in duplicating work, the number of paychecks prepared, the inches of card stacks filed, and the number of credit investigations made.

The unit used should be easy to identify, count, and understand. For each related application, it should possess uniformity of scope and definition. Generally speaking, the unit preferred is that which comes into existence as the result of an essential, clear-cut office operation. This characteristic aids identifying and counting.

In some instances, the selection of a satisfactory unit is extremely difficult; while in other cases, there are several available and acceptable units. In the latter case, for example, typewritten work can be measured in units of (1) pages, (2) standard-length lines, (3) key strokes, (4) square inches of typed material, or (5) cylinders or disks from which material is transcribed. The choice is guided by the individual characteristics of the work under consideration. No one unit is best under all conditions. For example, the number of pages is satisfactory provided the pages are approximately uniform in the amount of typed material and in difficulty.

Accurate measurement is desirable and should be sought; but in the case of office work, this can be carried to uneconomical extremes. Too precise or too detailed measurements can result in bulky and sometimes cumbersome data which are ineffective in practical application.

## MODIFIED WORK MEASUREMENT UNITS

A modified unit to measure office work is frequently used. To illustrate, the unit of a purchase order of a company may not be satisfactory because all purchase orders are not identical. Some require five lines of typing, others eight lines, and for exceptional orders, the filling out of special forms is necessary.

To combat these hurdles, modified work measurement units can be employed. One common example of this is to use a "block of orders" instead of a single order as the basic measurement unit. A quantity of 200 orders may make up a block of orders. The content of the individual order may vary considerably, but the content of 200 orders will normally be quite like that of another 200 orders. Thus, a work measurement unit possessing reasonable comparability is provided.

Also, the work measurement can be considered over a period of time, i.e., for 10 or 15 days. During such a period, the average makeup of the modified unit will be fairly constant, that is, comparing one 15-day period with another 15-day period.

Another approach is to employ what can be termed "the core operation." Under this modified work measurement unit, the office work of an entire system or procedure, or any part of it, is expressed by a single unit, considered the core or the most important operation and the one around which most of the other work of the system or procedure, or the totality being measured, depends. To illustrate, the incoming order might be considered the core. All processing in connection with this order, such as credit investigation, correspondence, billing, and the like, is tied up with the handling of the incoming order. These activities increase as the incoming orders increase, and vice versa. By measuring the core, it is feasible to get a reasonably accurate measurement of all the work. Common core operations include number of policies handled, applications processed, orders received, items on order, units shipped, sheets duplicated, bills sent out, requisitions made, or checks written.

## TIMING OFFICE WORK

Common practice associates time measurement, or the aspect of duration, with the work measurement. Time is an all-important factor. To punch a given number of cards or to file a definite quantity of orders is an accomplishment, but the important question is: Within what time limits can this be done? How long should it take? How much time should elapse from the start to the finish? Time is the element which is basic and common to all work. It is a vital basis of effective controlling.

For any given case, it is customary to identify the measurement of work and also that of time as "time study." Formally defined, *time study is the determination of a satisfactory work output and of the time required to complete a given number of work units regularly.* The unit may be an entire task or any part thereof. Time is usually expressed in minutes per piece or 100 pieces, or at a rate of so many pieces per hour.

The values from time study are called "time standards" and are used by managers as bases of reference for controlling. More specifically, time standards help the manager of office work, in that:

1. *A basis for work distribution is provided.* Time standards give the office manager the means for determining the volume of work and the number of employees required to get the work out. They afford the establishment of a "fair day's work," and they make it possible to plan the office operations.

2. *The office work can be scheduled.* Knowledge of the time to be allocated to different tasks expedites the arrangement of the order of work according to a predetermined timetable. By this means, full utilization of all production factors can be more nearly attained. And better control over scheduling and individual work assignment are possible. Information on the starting and completing dates for the various tasks can be determined and the office can supply excellent service.

3. *Effectiveness of department, division, or individual can be determined.* An indication of what the working force should accomplish is provided. The question is not "Is the employee always busy?" but "What does the employee accomplish?" The actual productivity compared with standard productivity is known. It is therefore possible to distinguish the efficient from the inefficient employee or group. Remedial action to improve the work of the inefficient personnel can be taken.

4. *Control over labor costs can be exercised.* Time standards make it possible to compare standard against actual labor costs. Control can thus be applied and corrective action taken if costs are out of line. Also, the tendency is to reduce labor cost where good time standards are used.

5. *Morale and labor relations are improved.* With time studies, the employee knows what is expected of him, and this makes office work more interesting. Having an objective—an end in view—lends encouragement so that office work does not seem like an endless mass of detail. Generally, the employee will be happier and do better work when he knows what and how much he is supposed to do, and upon what basis his efforts will be judged. Time standards remove favoritism; they provide factual information and treat all employees alike. In addition, by

means of standards, basic data are obtained which provide help in measuring supervisory effectiveness and formulating employee promotions and training programs.

## PRELIMINARIES OF OFFICE TIME STANDARDS

Before attempting to set any office time standard, it is well to observe several key considerations. First, tell the office employees that time standards are going to be determined. This is by far the best course to follow. Time standards affect employees and they will want to know about them. Enlightened managers take the initiative and share information concerning the purpose, means, and personnel doing the work of establishing standards. Furthermore, managers should answer all questions directly about the time standards program because the ultimate success of the program depends greatly upon the employees' cooperation.

Identify carefully the beginning and the end of the task for which the time standard is being established. This may sound elementary, but a precise definition is helpful. Generally, it is best to have the end of the task cycle followed immediately by a repetition of the task cycle. Exclusion of work, or time between cycles, should be avoided, if possible.

Select the means of determining standards that appears best considering the particular circumstances involved. As will be pointed out in the following discussion, different means of establishing time standards exist, and they vary in respect to various criteria. To highlight this information, Figure 23-1 has been included. For example, the cost of determining the time standard varies from low to high, among the six means included. These data are relative and serve as a guide only. Individual considerations determine which means to utilize in a specific case.

## SUBJECTIVE JUDGMENT

Time standards set through subjective judgment are sometimes referred to as rule-of-thumb standards. They are based only on the experience and guess of the management member. It is strongly recommended that the manager refrain from the use of such time standards. Even when an accurate guess in establishing the standard has been made, it is extremely difficult to explain and justify the estimate. Frequently, disagreement over the guess arises and may cause problems.

## PAST PERFORMANCE RECORDS

This means consists of recording what is happening. To illustrate, assume billings written as the work unit. The recordings will show accomplishments day by day or week by week as follows: the number of

| Criteria | Subjective Judgment | Past Performance Records | Work Sampling | Standard Time Data | Stopwatch Study | Standard Data from Stopwatch Study |
|---|---|---|---|---|---|---|
| 1. Cost of determining | Low | Medium | Medium | High | High | High |
| 2. Time to measure and establish standards | Fast | Fast | Average | Slow | Average | Slow |
| 3. Training and skill required | Low | Low | Low | High | Average | High |
| 4. Relative preciseness | Low | Medium | Medium | High | High | High |
| 5. Group or individual work application | G or I | G or I | G or I | I | I | I |
| 6. Assistance in methods improvement | Low | Low | Low | High | Average | High |
| 7. Satisfactory for work variation by volume | Yes | Yes | Yes | No | No | No |
| 8. Satisfactory for work variation by type of work | Yes | Yes | Yes | No | No | No |
| 9. Acceptance by employee | High | High | Medium | Medium | Low | Medium |
| 10. Interruptions to work operations | Low | Low | Medium | Low | Medium | Low |

FIG. 23–1. Comparison of office time measurement techniques.

units on hand at the beginning of the period, the number received during the period, the number completed, and the number at the end of the period. These are basic data. The actual performance time standard is derived by dividing the number of total man-hours worked by the number of billings processed. Trends, variations, maximum work loads, and the like can be evolved and subsequently utilized in controlling the work.

Data can be gathered either by the supervisor recording the amounts of work completed along with the corresponding times taken for each of his employees, or by having each employee record his work completed and the time taken to do it. Simple forms can be used, and cooperation of the employee is essential. To secure this, it is well to explain carefully and in some detail the purpose, operation, and need of the plan.

Standards arrived at from this approach have management value.[1] In many respects, they are particularly helpful for groups of office employees doing fairly similar work. It should be observed, however, that standards obtained from past performance records are really *records of "what is," rather than "what should be."*

## WORK SAMPLING

Work sampling is a means employing random observations whereby the ratio of delays and of elements of work to the total process time is determined. It is based on the law of probability. If a comparatively large number of observations are taken at random intervals, the ratio between the observed frequency of a particular activity to the total number of observations taken will approximate the correct percentage of that activity. The technique consists of intermittent but frequent spot checking of the activity of one or more office employees and the recording of the activity at the moment it is observed. From the work sample obtained, the time spent on each type of operation in relation to the total time available is determined.

Figure 23–2 clarifies the manner of establishing office time standards from work sampling. Column 1 shows the different types of work observed and column 2 the observations of each type, making up a total of 1,810 observations. Column 4 reveals that the total work time period over which these observations were made was 22,485 minutes. From official records and counts, we obtain the data of column 5 on work volume for the total work time period. With these basic data, we calculate the remaining data as shown in Figure 23–2. To illustrate, referring to line 1 the calculations for the value under column 3, 540 divided by 1,810, or 29.8 percent; for column 4, 29.8 percent of the total units,

---

[1] For example, they are usable in federal offices where watch time study is prohibited by clauses in appropriation bills.

22,485, or 6,700 minutes; for column 6, 6,700 minutes divided by 5,135 units, or 1.31 minutes per unit. The time standards by type of office work are shown in column 6. We have assumed that the total of 22,485 minutes was spent in the same proportion as the observations made.

By work sampling, it is possible to determine effective utilization of time, causes and extent of interference with effective accomplishment, flow of work through an office, and the amount of time devoted to various activities by an employee. The office manager of a large insurance company found, by means of work sampling, that a low utilization of personnel and machines existed in the company's data-processing center. Using these facts as a springboard, the manager, within eight months,

| Type of Work (1) | No. of Observations (2) | Percent (3) | Minutes (4) | Work Volume (5) | Unit Time Standard [(4) ÷ (5)] (6) |
|---|---|---|---|---|---|
| 1. Type | 540 | 29.8 | 6,700 | 5,135 | 1.31 min. |
| 2. Calculate | 217 | 12.0 | 2,698 | 5,135 | 0.53 " |
| 3. Check | 154 | 8.5 | 1,911 | 5,135 | 0.37 " |
| 4. File | 142 | 7.9 | 1,777 | 7,460 | 0.24 " |
| 5. Sort | 80 | 4.4 | 989 | 7,460 | 0.13 " |
| 6. Telephone | 133 | 7.4 | 1,664 | 514 | 3.24 " |
| 7. Misc. | 120 | 6.6 | 1,484 | — | — |
| 8. Idle | 105 | 5.8 | 1,304 | — | — |
| 9. Personal (includes lunch) | 319 | 17.6 | 3,958 | — | — |
| Total | 1,810 | 100.0 | 22,485 | | |

FIG. 23–2. Determining time standards from work sampling observations.

by means of control programs, increased machine utilization 17 percent, released 12 rental machines, and won enthusiastic support of supervisors and employees for work sampling as a technique for making jobs less complicated and more productive. Many believe work sampling is one of the most practical and economical means for appraising the time required to perform office work.

Work sampling data can be secured by means of observations by the supervisor. The degree of reliability obtained is increased by increasing the number of observations. The method is economical and measures cyclic effect, a very important concept in most office work. However, it is not practical to take a sampling of too many breakdowns of a job. Work sampling is better suited to broad operations. It is recommended for standards for purposes of cost control, group effectiveness, planning personnel needs, and for taking corrective action. Care must be taken to avoid purposeful behavior by the employee being observed. For example, when the observation starts, the employee may not continue to work at his normal pattern but strive to appear busier and begin moving papers, straightening up his desk, and engaging in similar activities. Such actions decrease the accuracy of the data. To combat this, use the supervisor or a stationary observer throughout the study so that the employee does not know when to exercise purposeful behavior. However, the stationary observer eliminates cost advantages of work sampling and reverts to the all-day study with its relatively high costs. Probably the best ways to eliminate purposeful behavior are (1) to use and train the supervisor as the observer and (2) to explain thoroughly the need and manner of performing the study in order to win the employee's complete cooperation.

## STANDARD TIME DATA

The data for this means of determining time standards are based upon fundamental motions or muscular movements for which basic time standards have been developed. The time values vary with the nature of the motion and the conditions under which it is made. For example, movement of an arm 4 inches is given a certain time value, turning the wrist has another value, etc. Most standard time data are expressed as tables of values. To utilize this material, the standard time data man analyzes each manual operation into the basic motions which are necessary in performing the task. The time for each required basic motion is taken from the table of values and added to determine the time standard for the entire task.

Figure 23–3 shows the standard time values for the elemental motions required to obtain and put an original sheet of paper into a typewriter. On line 4, for example, right hand, the elemental time of 0.0016 of a minute is the time allotted for a motion, *F1,* meaning fingers open 1 inch; and the elemental description is *GR,* meaning grasp. Similarly, on line 5, the standard time value of 0.0080 of a minute is given *A20D,* arm extended 20 inches to *M,* or move, sheet to typewriter.

Standard time data are predetermined time values for definite basic motions. By their use, time standards can be set before the work is actually performed—especially useful in planning a new or a changed system or procedure. Standard time data are best suited for high-volume, repetitive tasks where manual motions predominate. Even though applicable for reading and mental computations, it is often difficult to convince employees of the data's validity for such work. The better known standard time data systems are Work Factor, Methods-Time Measurement, and Office Manning Controls.

## STOPWATCH STUDY

The time standard developed from this source applies to specific work done under specific conditions, including the workplace, method, and

**OPERATION NAME** Obtain and put an original sheet of paper into typewriter    **DEPT.** Sales Analysis    **SHEET** 1 **OF** 2

| NO. | ELEMENTAL DESCRIPTION | MOTION ANALYSIS | ELEM. TIME | CUMULATIVE TIME | ELEM. TIME | MOTION ANALYSIS | ELEMENTAL DESCRIPTION | NO. |
|---|---|---|---|---|---|---|---|---|
| 1 | | | | .0080 | .0080 | A20 D | R to sheet | 1 |
| 2 | | | | .0080 | - | Ct Gr | 1st Gr | 2 |
| 3 | | | | .0103 | .0023 | F1P | Separate | 3 |
| 4 | | Wait | .0119 | .0119 | .0016 | F1 | Gr | 4 |
| 5 | R to sheet | A20D | .0080 | .0199 | .0080 | A20D | M sheet to typewriter | 5 |
| 6 | Gr sheet | 1/2 F1 | .0008 | .0207 | .0008 | Hold | | 6 |
| 7 | Approach typewriter roller | A1SD | .0034 | .0241 | .0034 | A1SD | Approach typewriter roller | 7 |
| 8 | A1 (OTS-TD .074") | 1-1/2A1SD | .0051 | .0292 | .0008 | 1/2 F1 | R1 sheet | 8 |
| 9 | GD 5" | 1-1/2A1SD | 0%.0015 | .0307 | .0054 | A8D | R to roller knob | 9 |
| 10 | IND | A1SD | .0034 | .0341 | .0008 | 1/2 F1 | Gr roller knob | 10 |
| 11 | INS | A1D | .0026 | .0367 | .0056 | Wait | | 11 |
| 12 | R1 paper | 1/2 F1 | .0008 | .0375 | .0031 | FS180° | Turn roller knob | 12 |
| 13 | R to carriage release | A80 | .0054 | .0429 | .0008 | 1/2 F1 | R1 roller knob | 13 |
| 14 | Gr carriage release | 1/2 F1 | .0008 | .0437 | .0031 | FS180° | R to roller knob | 14 |
| 15 | | | | .0445 | .0008 | 1/2 F1 | Gr roller knob | 15 |
| 16 | | | | .0601 | .0156 | .0078x2 | Repeat elements Nos.12-15 | 16 |
| 17 | | Wait | .0192 | .0629 | .0028 | FS45°SD | Turn to final line | 17 |
| 18 | Depress carriage release | F1 | .0016 | .0645 | .0016 | Hold | | 18 |
| 19 | Push carriage to 1st position | VA4SD | .0048 | .0693 | .0048 | VA4SD | Pull carriage to 1st position | 19 |
| 20 | A1 (OTS-TD .100") | 1-1/4A1SD | .0043 | .0736 | .0043 | 1-1/4A1SD | A1 (OTS-TD .100") | 20 |

TOTAL SELECT TIME _____ x _____ CONVERSION = _____ HPC    STANDARD PRODUCTION PER HOUR (100 + HPC) _____ EHO

REMARKS:

*Courtesy: Wofac Corp., Haddonsfield, N.J.*

FIG. 23–3.   Data from a standard time study.

material. It is not a universal time standard. The work selected for study should be repetitive and of sufficient volume to warrant careful analysis. The proper workplace should be resolved and the work motions economized. There is no point in establishing carefully set time values for work that is performed ineffectively and is soon to be improved. The variable job elements which are affected by changing conditions should be under control. The stopwatch should be one which reads directly in one-hundredths (0.01) of a minute. Keeping all values in these units simplifies calculations. The watch should also provide means for snapping back the hands to zero after each reading if the "snap-back" method is desired.

The employee selected for observation should be an above-average type, not because he accomplishes more work, but because he will probably have the best motions and rhythm in his work. This does not mean that the time standards to be determined will require an above-average worker. Discussion of this point is given several paragraphs below. Complete cooperation of the employee must be secured. This means, among other things, explaining what is being done, and why, plus answering any questions the employee may have. When ready, take a position a little to one side of and behind the employee. To become familiar with the task, watch the completion of it several times.

The job is divided into components or small motions that can be observed and timed. An illustration of such components for the work of posting material requisition notices on card files is shown by Figure 23–4. The eight components heading up a like number of columns are hand-printed across the top of the form.

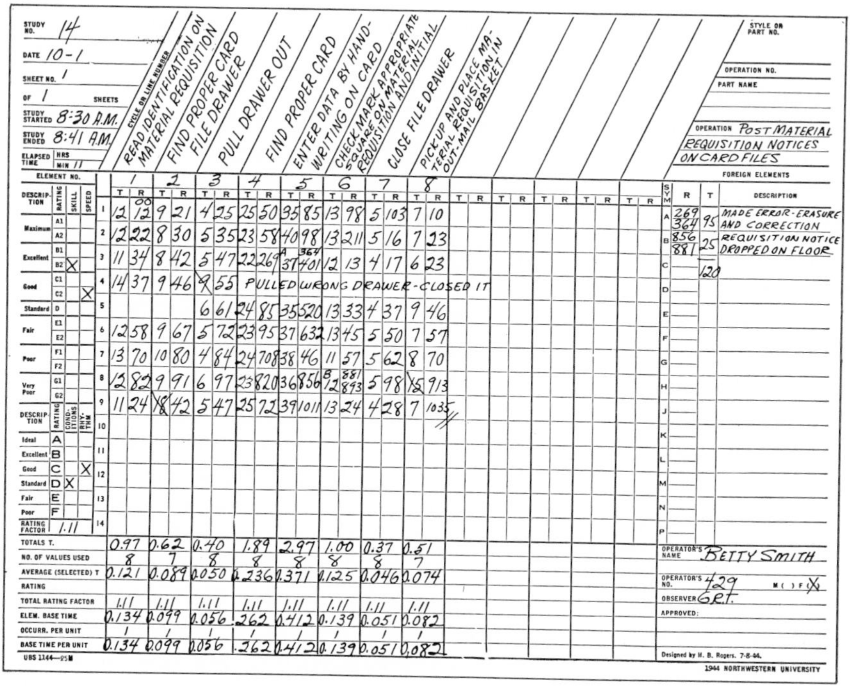

FIG. 23–4. Time-study data sheet for an office task.

Next, the time observations are recorded. The starting time is written in the space provided (upper left of Figure 23–4). Make certain the stopwatch hands are set at zero. Start the stopwatch at the beginning of the first element; and at the completion of this element, note and record the watch reading on the first line in the first column under the letter $R$, which stands for Reading. At the completion of the second element, note the watch reading and record it on the first line of the second column under the letter $R$. In Figure 23–4, the reading at the completion of element 1 is 12; at the end of element 2, 21; at the end of element 3, 25; at the end of element 4, 50; and so on. In this illustration, the "continuous reading" method is being followed, not the "snap-back" method.

At the end of the last element, let the watch continue to run; and in like manner, repeat the task-cycle-recording readings on the second line. Continue this procedure until a sufficient number of cycles have been timed to indicate some commonness in the elapsed time per element. Usually, about eight or ten cycles should be recorded, but some analysts claim readings should be taken for at least 15–20 minutes. It is also possible to determine mathematically how many cycles represent a reliable sample so that a true representation of the work is obtained.

Variations from the proper sequence are recorded as "repeats" on the immediate line below, or, in the case of interruptions, by footnoting and explaining in the space located on the extreme right of the form. To illustrate, referring to Figure 23–4 again, on the third line under element 5, an interruption occurred and is footnoted by the letter $A$. At the right of the form, a description is given that the employee made an error, erased, and corrected. This "foreign element" took place between watch readings of 269 and 364, or a total of 95, which is actually $^{95}\!/_{100}$ of a minute. Another interruption is shown by footnote $B$ on the eighth line under element 6.

We want the time standard not for the above-average employee observed, but for the average or normal employee. The adjustment to normal is known as "leveling"; to do this, observations of the observed employee's skill, effort, working conditions, and consistency are made during the study. Recordings for these factors are written on the left side of the form in Figure 23–4. As a guide, a leveling chart, such as that shown in Figure 23–5, is usually used. The algebraic values of the ratings are obtained from this chart; and in the case illustrated, the following will apply: skill B2, or +0.08; speed C2, or +0.02; conditions D, or 0.00; rhythm C, or +0.01; adding, we get +0.11 (0.08 + 0.02 + 0.00 + 0.01). This total added algebraically to unity gives 1.11, which is the leveling or rating factor and is indicated on the form near the bottom of the left-hand column in Figure 23–4.

The time elapsed for each element is calculated by subtracting the preceding from the immediately following cumulative reading and recording under the appropriate column headed $T$, which stands for Time. To illustrate, in Figure 23–4, on the first line, the value 9 under $T$ in element 2 is obtained by subtracting 12 from 21; the value 4 under element 3 is obtained by subtracting 21 from 25. Other values of time elapsed for each element are obtained in like manner.

Now, the time standard can be calculated by:

1. *Finding the representative, observed, elemental time.* To do this, study the time taken by elements shown by each vertical column under $T$, strike out the abnormal times, and find the average—usually the arithmetic average of the remaining times. In the illustration given in Figure 23–4, the abnormal time of 18 for element 2 on line 9 has been

| SKILL | | | SPEED | | |
|---|---|---|---|---|---|
| +0.15 | A1 | Superskill | +0.13 | A1 | Killing |
| +0.13 | A2 | | +0.12 | A2 | |
| +0.11 | B1 | Excellent | +0.10 | B1 | Excellent |
| +0.08 | B2 | | +0.08 | B2 | |
| +0.06 | C1 | Good | +0.05 | C1 | Good |
| +0.03 | C2 | | +0.02 | C2 | |
| 0.00 | D | Average | 0.00 | D | Average |
| −0.05 | E1 | Fair | −0.04 | E1 | Fair |
| −0.10 | E2 | | −0.08 | E2 | |
| −0.16 | F1 | Poor | −0.12 | F1 | Poor |
| −0.22 | F2 | | −0.17 | F2 | |
| CONDITIONS | | | RHYTHM | | |
| +0.06 | A | Ideal | +0.04 | A | Perfect |
| +0.04 | B | Excellent | +0.03 | B | Excellent |
| +0.02 | C | Good | +0.01 | C | Good |
| 0.00 | D | Average | 0.00 | D | Average |
| −0.03 | E | Fair | −0.02 | E | Fair |
| −0.07 | F | Poor | −0.04 | F | Poor |

*Courtesy: Stewart M. Lowry, Harold B. Maynard, and G. J. Stegemerten, "Time and Motion Study" (New York: McGraw-Hill Book Co., Inc., 1940), p. 233*

FIG. 23–5.  Performance-rating chart.

discarded. The average of the selected $T$ values is 0.089, as shown near the bottom of the column. This was calculated by dividing 0.62 by 7.

2. *Apply the leveling factor.* To do this, multiply the average $T$ value by the leveling factor. In the case illustrated, this is 0.089 times 1.11, which gives 0.099, the elemental base time. Since the $T$ value occurs once per unit, the base time per unit is the same, namely, 0.099, which is written on the bottom line of the column.

3. *Total base times and add allowances for personal needs, fatigue, unavoidable delays, and the like.* The sum of the base time per unit is 1.235 (0.134 + 0.099 + 0.056 + 0.262 + 0.412 + 0.139 + 0.051 + 0.082). An allowance of 20 percent as a lump sum is added, making the adjusted value of 1.482 (1.235 + 20 percent of 1.235). This is, of course, in minutes. Expressed as units per hour, the value is 40.5. Calculation of the adjusted value along with information regarding the working conditions, the material and equipment used, and a sketch of the workplace are included

for identification and future reference on the reverse side of the time-study sheet shown in Figure 23–4.

## STANDARD DATA FROM STOPWATCH STUDY

This means utilizes predetermined or standard data values derived from the data of many actual stopwatch studies from which it is possible to determine the basic allowable times for elements which are common to many tasks.[2] To do this, relationships between time and some meaningful variable, such as distance, size, or weight, are determined. For example, consider the element "pulling file drawer out." From many actual stopwatch studies, the time values for this element are obtained. Some of these values will be for pulling file drawers out a distance of 6 inches, others 10 inches, still others 14 inches, etc. By mathematical analysis of these data, the relationship between time and distance traveled for the element "pulling file drawer out" can be determined. From this relationship, the amount of time for this element can be predetermined, based on the distance the drawer travels. In similar manner, relationships can be determined for the size of the drawer and the weight of the material in it. The relationships so developed can be expressed as tables of values, as equations, or as graphs.

## EXAMPLES OF OFFICE TIME STANDARDS

The following office time standards have value in connection with various types of office work. They are included here to be helpful in a comparative way only. They were determined for specific conditions prevailing in a particular office and should be used as guides, not goals.

|  | *Units*<br>*per Hour* |
|---|---|
| 1. Typing: | |
| Type name and account number on card | 180 |
| Type labels from typewritten copy | 135 |
| Type ledger cards | 105 |
| Type report, double space on 8½ x 11-inch paper, one original and one carbon copy | 10 |
| Type address on envelope | 85 |
| 2. Calculating and checking: | |
| Compute products of 3-digit number by 3-digit number, using machine | 500 |
| Add 20 numbers in a column (each number is 3 digits) by machine | 2 |
| Compare columns of figures on tape or report, with columns of figures in like order (number of digits per figure compared equals 5) | 4,800 |
| Count items on a tape, or lines on a sheet | 9,400 |

---

[2] "Elemental motions," as used here, means the smallest motions that can be observed and read for time. It does not mean elementary motions or therbligs, which are discussed in Chapter 17. Therbligs usually are of too short a duration to be measured by a stopwatch.

3. Accounting:

Pull from source, post account to ledger sheet by machine, and replace sheet. . .   130
Make entries in ledger (manual). . . . . . . . . . . . . . . . . . . . . . . . . . . . . . . . . . . . .    40

4. Filing and sorting:

Sort correspondence papers for filing. . . . . . . . . . . . . . . . . . . . . . . . . . . . . . .   480
File correspondence papers in alphabetical file. . . . . . . . . . . . . . . . . . . . . . .   180
Sort 5 x 3-inch cards alphabetically. . . . . . . . . . . . . . . . . . . . . . . . . . . . . . . .   300
Locate and pull addressing plates from alphabetical file. . . . . . . . . . . . . . .   420

5. Miscellaneous:

Hand-fold 8½ x 11-inch sheet with one fold. . . . . . . . . . . . . . . . . . . . . . . .1,200
Seal ordinary envelope (manual). . . . . . . . . . . . . . . . . . . . . . . . . . . . . . . . . .   450
Assemble three sheets of paper, 8½ x 11 inches, and insert in large 9 x 12-inch
    envelope. . . . . . . . . . . . . . . . . . . . . . . . . . . . . . . . . . . . . . . . . . . . . . . . . . . . .   575

## PERT

Before closing this chapter a few words about PERT (Program Evaluation Review Technique) are in order. PERT deals with time controlling from the large, overall viewpoint of several related systems and procedures making up what can be termed a project or a network activity. Multistage industrial operations as the development of certain government defense projects or the construction of several buildings simultaneously by the same contractor may constitute the project. A chart is prepared to show the composite necessary operations for the total project. From the beginning to the end of this network activity, there are typically several paths of work sequence that can be followed. Using the chart as a guide, the time required for the longest sequence of operations is computed; this is known as the "critical path," because it time controls the completion of the entire network. A delay in any task along this path would necessarily delay completion of the entire network. In contrast, delay in any other jobs of the project not included in the critical path could, within limits, be delayed without retarding the whole project. Usually some 85 percent of the individual jobs are found in this category; thus, 15 percent of the jobs are critical in content and sequence to the completion of the entire project within a stated period. In other words, PERT highlights the key or critical jobs or work. The office is included in that these efforts require additional or revised information on short notice, or new information as necessitated by changes in plans and schedules.

## QUESTIONS

1. Why is it necessary to measure office work? Why not just time the work and determine the time standard from these data? Discuss.

2. Indicate what measuring unit you would recommend, and your reasons why, for each of the following:

*a*) Duplicating a monthly report.

*b*) Verifying the accuracy of bank checks written.

*c*) Answering correspondence dealing with sales.

*d*) Receiving office visitors.

3. In your opinion, is purposeful behavior by the employee being observed a challenge in most of the common means for determining office time standards? Discuss.

4. Explain Figure 23–2 in your own words.

5. Give an example of a modified work measurement unit in connection with office work and explain how it is used.

6. Explain the following: "Past performance records are actually 'what is,' rather than 'what should be.' "

7. Why should a stopwatch time study be made only after the proper workplace has been provided and the motions economized? Are there any exceptions? Explain.

8. Distinguish carefully between the concepts in each of the following pairs:

*a*) Time study and stopwatch study.

*b*) Elemental time and "critical path."

*c*) Work sampling and "snap-back" watch readings.

*d*) Leveling factor and allowance for personal needs.

9. Name and discuss four major advantages in having time standards. Are these advantages to managers exclusively, to nonmanagers exclusively, or to both managers and nonmanagers? Explain.

10. Comment on the following: "The adjustment of observed data to give proper consideration for what is an average employee appears vital in a stopwatch time study. In contrast, the concept of an average employee is ignored when the means of work sampling is followed. This is inconsistent and demonstrates that neither means provides accurate time standards."

11. What is PERT and for what purposes is it used? Use an illustration in the office management area to explain your answer.

12. For what types of office work and under what conditions would you recommend time standards established by standard time data? Discuss.

## CASE PROBLEM

### Case 23–1.  Lorne Company

A contact-type duplicating machine is located in the corresponding section of an office where it is convenient to make a duplicate of a letter with handwritten answer on the bottom of the sheet. Use of the machine, however, is for company business by anyone in the office. Both the manager of the credit section of the office and the assistant sales manager of the sales department office, immediately adjacent to the main office, have requested the general manager of Lorne Company to buy each of them a contact duplicating machine. The credit manager states that he uses the duplicating machine very little now because the one in corresponding is being used when he wants to use it. Many times a number of copies were being made and this means too long a wait for him to use the machine. The assistant sales manager points out that the present machine is being cleaned or temporarily out of order too much. He believes it would save his employees much time to have their own duplicating machine.

The general manager asks Michael Miller, the office manager, to look into the situation and give him recommendations as to what to do. Accordingly, Mr. Miller decides to conduct a work sampling study. After some observations and talking with the supervisor of corresponding, he reasons that there are logically eight categories for observation, including (1) machine nonavailable—being used by other than corresponding, (2) machine in use by corresponding for either 1, 2, 3, 4, or 5 or more copies, (3) machine not in use but ready for immediate use, and (4) machine being cleaned or temporarily out of order for any reason. He believes 450–500 observations over a three-week period will provide adequate data. Proceeding with the study, the following data are obtained:

|  | *Observations made in* | | |
|---|---|---|---|
|  | *Week No. 1* | *Week No. 2* | *Week No. 3* |
| Unavailable | 22 | 19 | 18 |
| Being used for |  |  |  |
|   1 copy | 24 | 30 | 41 |
|   2 copies | 22 | 26 | 17 |
|   3 copies | 3 | 1 | 6 |
|   4 copies | 6 | 11 | 6 |
|   5 copies or more | 5 | 7 | 4 |
| Not in use | 46 | 55 | 57 |
| Being cleaned or temporarily |  |  |  |
|   out of order | 13 | 13 | 10 |

## Problems:

1. Complete the table of data by calculating the number of observations (*a*) in each category, (*b*) in each week, and (*c*) in total for the study.

2. Determine the percentage of observations accounted for by each category and the corresponding minutes per workday (480 minutes) for each category.

3. Are the work sampling data complete and conclusive enough to provide the general manager with satisfactory answers? Explain.

4. What recommendation should Mr. Miller make? Why?

## Case 23–2.  Kingman Company

The time data on page 540 are for typing 3 x 5 reference cards. For this work, an allowance of 15 percent is given for personal needs and delays. Office hours are from 8:00–11:30 A.M. and 12:30–4:30 P.M., with a 15-minute "break" in mid-morning and again in midafternoon.

The operator is seated at a desk with typewriter in middle, new cards are at her upper left, finished typed cards at her upper right. Information to be typed is on a list placed on the desk at one side of the typewriter. The first work element is picking up a card, inserting into typewriter, and positioning. The succeeding elements

| DATE 11-10-6- STUDY No. 59 SHEET No. 1 OF 1 SHEETS | ELEMENTS: PICK UP CARDS / TYPE & WRITER / TYPE 3 LINES / REPRODUCE TYPE & CHECK / STAMP CARD / WRITE IN CODE NUMBER / PUT IN BOX TO RIGHT | FOREIGN ELEMENTS | | |
|---|---|---|---|---|

| NUMBER | | 1 | 2 | 3 | 4 | 5 | 6 | FOREIGN ELEMENTS | | |
|---|---|---|---|---|---|---|---|---|---|---|
| NOTES | LINE | R | R | R | R | R | R | SYM / R / T / DESCRIPTION | | |
| | 1 | 00/.11 | .24 | .31 | .39 | .53 | .56 | A .32/.42 | BREAK, ERASE AND OVERTYPE |
| | 2 | .66 | .82 | .98 | .96 | 1.11 | 1.13 | B .07/.15 | DROPPED CARD ON FLOOR, PICKED IT UP |
| | 3 | 1.22 | 1.36 | 1.42 | 1.51 | 1.66 | 1.69 | C | |
| | 4 | 1.79 | 1.93 | 1.98 | 2.06 | 2.72 | 2.24 | D | |
| | 5 | 2.32/2.42/2.55 | 2.62 | 2.69 | 2.94 | 2.86 | | E | |
| | 6 | 2.96 | 3.07/3.15/3.22 | 3.30 | 3.46 | 3.49 | | F | |
| | 7 | 3.60 | 3.72 | 3.80 | 3.88 | 4.03 | 4.06 | G | |
| | 8 | 4.17 | 4.30 | 4.36 | 4.45 | 4.60 | 4.63 | H | |
| | 9 | 4.73 | 4.86 | 4.91 | 5.00 | 5.15 | 5.18 | I | |
| | 10 | 5.27 | 5.39 | 5.45 | 5.53 | 5.67 | 5.71 | J | |
| | 11 | 5.81 | 5.94 | 6.00 | 6.08 | 6.22 | 6.25 | K | |
| | 12 | 6.35 | 6.49 | 6.54 | 6.61 | 6.76 | 6.79 | L | |
| | 13 | | | | | | | M | |
| | 14 | | | | | | | N | |
| | 15 | | | | | | | O | |

SKILL / EFFORT
A1 A2 SUPER — A1 A2 EXCESSIVE
B1 B2 EXCELLENT — B1 B2 EXCELLENT
C1 C2 GOOD — C1 C2 GOOD
D AVERAGE — D AVERAGE
E1 E2 FAIR — E1 E2 FAIR
F1 F2 POOR — F1 F2 POOR

CONDITIONS / CONSISTENCY
A IDEAL — A PERFECT
B EXCELLENT — B EXCELLENT
C GOOD — C GOOD
D AVERAGE — D AVERAGE
E FAIR — E FAIR
F POOR — F POOR

GENERAL RATING FOR STUDY: SKILL EFFORT COND. CONST

STUDY STARTED 10:00 / STUDY FINISHED 10:15 / OVERALL TIME

TOTALS "T" / NO. OBSERVATIONS / AVERAGE "T" / MINIMUM "T" / MAXIMUM "T" / RATING (S.E.C.ACT.) / LEVELING FACTOR / L.F. x AVE. "T" / % ALLOWANCE / TIME ALLOWED

are indicated on the time-study sheet. Any errors in typing are caught and corrected by the operator. The number of rejects due to typing errors is nil.

## Problems:

1. Compute the time standard for the indicated work in cards typed per hour.

2. How many typed cards would you expect during a regular working day? Explain.

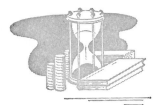

<br />

CHAPTER **24**

# OFFICE
# COST CONTROLLING
# AND BUDGETING

The greatest difficulty of the intellectual is
distinguishing the important from the
unimportant.
                    —*John P. Grier*

IMPLIED in every office accomplishment is that the work be completed
satisfactorily and within a certain cost. Managerial success in many
cases lies in understanding and utilizing cost information. Answers to
what things cost, how these costs are figured, and the meaning of the
final results in terms of cost are fundamental to the work of the effective
office manager. More important, questions of cost must be answered if
the enterprise is to continue, at least from the long-range point of view.
The area of cost controlling in office management is therefore of utmost
significance.

Cost, as we will use it here, means the *dollar amount expended for the
ownership, use, or service of every component making up and employed in
the execution of the work*. Cost is a matter of money outlay for manual or
mental work planned, accomplished, or in process of being achieved.

### COST AND THE OFFICE MANAGER

Many managers consider cost the common controlling medium, since
other types, such as those for quantity, quality, and time-use, can be
expressed in terms of cost. But other media of controlling should be
used when they are believed to be superior under the particular cir-

<br />

<br />

<br />

<br />

<br />

<br />

<br />

<br />

541

cumstances. Cost is not an objective in itself, but simply a means, and an important one, used by a manager. It helps the manager, especially in the act of controlling, to direct the various activities so that within stated limits the goals will be realized.

Decision making is usually greatly influenced by the consideration of cost information. Whether to install a new procedure, to purchase a new office machine, to perform a new service, or to revise a form design are decided with the aid of cost information. Sometimes, the question is an-

## COST SAVINGS ESTIMATE

DEPARTMENT NO. __78__

DATE _9/7/_

DESCRIPTION _Adopt work layout and method described by M-240_

NOTE: ALL COSTS FOR ONE YEAR

| COSTS | PRESENT | PROPOSED | SAVINGS |
|---|---|---|---|
| LABOR | $2875 | $2130 | +$745 |
| MATERIAL | 925 | 800 | + 125 |
| MACHINE TIME | 750 | 1035 | - 285 |
| OTHER (WRITE IN) | | | |
| TOTAL | $4550 | $3965 | $585 |

ACTION ____ _Recommended and approved on Oct. 3, 1958 by executive_ ____

_committee, R. C. McGinnis, Chairman._

APPROVED AND PUT INTO EFFECT BY __ _CRM._ __

FIG. 24–1.   A cost savings estimate.

swered almost entirely on the basis of cost. In addition, cost also helps justify a managerial action. Recommendations for a change usually include the cost before and the cost (estimated) after the change is effected. Likewise, if an alteration has been made, the wisdom of this move is frequently confirmed by a "before and after" cost picture. Figure 24–1 illustrates one type of form that can be used.

An office manager keeps informed of many office practices by means of cost information. Many of the items in reports dealing with accomplishments, and also in ordinary financial statements, are expressed in cost. The number of employees; supplies used; inventory on hand, in process, or finished; charge for floor space occupied; charge for office machine usage; and the like are expressed in dollar values, estimated from cost data.

Cost also serves as an effective medium for coordinating managerial activities. For example, it is helpful in determining the program of action that will achieve the required results, yet maintain the proper balance. The selection and extent of managerial efforts, their timing, and direction can be executed in an orderly manner. Actions predicated on guesses or on hit-and-miss bases are minimized.

Cost information provides the office manager with clues to places where waste can be reduced or eliminated. While curbing waste is a desired result of all controlling, it is especially so in the case of cost. The very nature of cost information focuses attention on what was paid out and what was received. This leads to waste reduction. To illustrate, a study of duplicating costs might uncover uneconomical runs and the use of improper paper for the specific purpose. In addition, cost information reveals fluctuations in cost which can be followed up by investigations to determine the reasons and subsequently apply remedial measures. In this case, cost data supplied the tip-off to quantity controlling.

The effective use of cost information leads logically to the maintaining of satisfactory cost levels and, beyond this, to the lowering of these cost levels. Progressive reductions in cost appear to be a normal state of affairs in a progressive economy. The eternal challenge is to achieve better office work at less cost.

## APPROACHES TO COST REDUCTION

To gain significant office cost reduction, three approaches appear essential: (1) Concentrate on the items offering greatest cost reduction opportunities, (2) develop a cost-consciousness among all employees, and (3) establish an effective cost control program. This three-pronged attack, when efficiently applied, is practically certain to reduce costs.

## ITEMS OFFERING GREATEST COST REDUCTION OPPORTUNITIES

Certain items normally offer greater cost reduction possibilities than others. Those representing the big items, the ones on which the most money is now being spent, and those of a cumulative and repetitive nature usually offer the best opportunities for lowering costs. Some research and probing may be required to find this type of information for a particular office.

In most offices, however, the major expense is wages and salaries— employees are the key cost. A breakdown of total office expenses under typical conditions is usually of a pattern similar to the following:

| Item | Percentage of Total Costs |
|------|---------------------------|
| Office wages and salaries | 70% |
| Supplies, postage, telephone | 15 |
| Purchase and maintenance of office equipment and machines, rent, light, and heat | 15 |
| Total Costs | 100% |

In other words, nearly three out of every four office dollar costs are for people. Interestingly this pattern has remained about the same during the past several decades, even though office automation is now used extensively. To increase efficiency, this suggests the use of less employees, or the more efficient use of those presently employed. Stressing people as the core of office cost reduction, Fred E. Shelton, Jr., suggests careful examination of four areas: (1) office supervision, (2) habit patterns, (3) servile attitudes, and (4) methods of administration.[1]

## COST-CONSCIOUSNESS AMONG EMPLOYEES

Cutting cost is not a job restricted to managers. It is a job in which every employee can and should participate. Interest in costs is fundamental because it is a means contributing to employee security. To reduce costs is a way of keeping an enterprise fit so it can continue to operate successfully and meet its responsibilities.

Cost information can be used to develop a cost-consciousness among employees. A feeling of the importance of cost and its use throughout the entire enterprise must be achieved for cost to have greatest value. Every member on the payroll, from the top executive to the lowest employee, should be made aware of and encouraged to think in terms of cost. When the employees are cost-minded, a basic and broad beginning toward improving operations has been accomplished. Thinking in terms of cost is necessary for greatest efficiency.

To accomplish this aim, suggestions pointing out possibilities for lowering office expenses are helpful. Figure 24–2 shows this in graphic form and brings out the fact that cost permeates all office activities. Every employee has the opportunity to be cost-minded and to reduce costs. In addition, accurate cost information should be disseminated to all supervisors and employees who are charged with those costs and for which they are responsible. By this means, cost is given important and meaningful status. Employees are quick to recognize this and will seek to use cost as a guide in their everyday tasks.

## ESTABLISH EFFECTIVE COST CONTROL PROGRAM

As pointed out throughout these chapters on controlling, three steps make up controlling and consist of determining what is being accomplished, evaluating it, and applying corrective action if necessary. These same steps hold true for cost controlling. A complete discussion of each step will be supplied, highlighting considerations pertinent to cost controlling.

---

[1] Fred E. Shelton, Jr., "Wanted: Cost Reduction," *Office Executive* (June, 1956), pp. 9–11. This is an excellent article. Mr. Shelton is an executive of the Standard Register Company, Dayton, O.

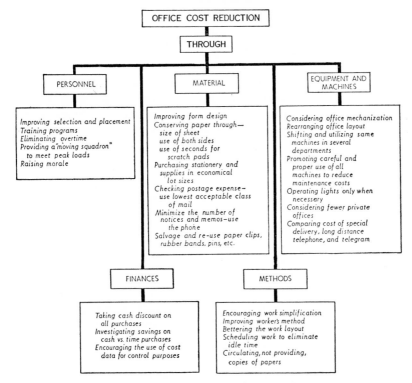

FIG. 24–2. Possibilities for the reduction of office costs.

## DETERMINING WHAT IS BEING ACCOMPLISHED COSTWISE

Obtaining the facts on cost, classifying them by type, and arranging them to expedite quick reference are fundamental in determining what is being accomplished costwise. Sources of cost information include ledgers, cost journals, payroll records, purchases, and records of service charges. Better results are usually secured by concentrating efforts in several selected areas. It is well to take into account these considerations:

1. *The data should be accurate and timely.* In the modern office, frequent changes may be made to improve the operations. These changes are sometimes of a major sort and necessitate a new collection of cost data in order to reflect an accurate measurement of current expenditures. Even in the case of minor adjustments, the resultant effect may be sufficiently large to invalidate a considerable portion of previous cost information. Cost data should be closely affiliated and apply to the current situation; otherwise, their value is questionable.

2. *The data should apply to well-defined components.* Usually, in studying cost data, the most important figures are not the totals but the

individual cost figures, covering each component of those which collectively make up the total cost. Sufficient details must be included in all cost information to maximize its managerial value. No single factor tells the whole cost story.

In addition, the "cost per unit" should be used. The unit cost is the important concept. Comparison of a $300 actual cost with a $200 expected cost is not valid. If the work accomplished is 150 units and the expected output was 100 units, the true values become:

$$\text{Actual} = \frac{\$300}{150 \text{ units}} = \$2 \text{ per unit,}$$

$$\text{Expected} = \frac{\$200}{100 \text{ units}} = \$2 \text{ per unit,}$$

which demonstrates that the actual unit cost did not exceed but is equal to the expected cost.

3. *The data should be completely identified as to (a) general type and (b) individual specifications.* A means of classifying cost is essential to effective cost controlling. In fact, the term "cost" in and of itself is practically meaningless. The varieties of cost are almost endless, the different types depending upon the degree and kind of work covered. To facilitate understanding, information concerning "cost of what to whom" is needed.

Several general type identification arrangements will be given. The first, based on the elements of material, labor, and overhead, includes the following:

| *Element* | *Segregation and Meaning* |
|---|---|
| Material cost: | Direct material cost—expenditures for materials which are or become a part of the product (office forms and letterheads, envelopes, and postage). |
| | Indirect material cost—expenditures for materials which are not a part of the product but are necessary in the carrying out of the work (typewriter ribbons, erasers). |
| Labor cost: | Direct labor cost—expenditures for labor attributable to and having a bearing upon the product or service (billing-machine operator, typist). |
| | Indirect labor cost—expenditures for labor not attributable to or in an unbroken connection with the product or service (methods man, janitor). |
| Overhead cost: | Expenditures which do not belong exclusively to any part of the material or labor (rent, light, heat, managerial expense, telephone). |

The second arrangement utilizing a functional basis consists of total costs made up of:

I. Production costs, under which are:
   A. Production overhead costs
   B. Production direct costs
   C. Office cost consisting of:
      1. Office overhead cost
      2. Prime office costs
         a) Direct office material cost
         b) Direct office labor cost
II. Sales costs, under which are:
   A. Sales overhead cost
   B. Promotion, travel, and advertising cost
   C. Salesmen's compensation cost
      1. Wage payment cost
      2. Commission and bonus cost

These arrangements are illustrative only and are not complete.

Many managers find that apportioning office costs for a specific period to the main office systems and procedures brings very satisfactory results. Specific estimated and actual costs for informational outputs or units of office production can be determined wherever appropriate. Many types of cost analyses are thus possible, such as determination of cost trends and expected office cost incident to various managerial decisions.

Identification as to individual specification is also necessary. This includes information of the particular office operation covered, such as date, location of operation, and operation number. A tabular arrangement of these data is usually satisfactory. In some instances, the data are written in a coded form to preserve their confidential nature. Either cards, letter-size papers, or large spread sheets can be used.

### EVALUATING THE COST EXPENDITURE

To evaluate the cost we need to (1) know what cost is satisfactory and (2) compare this actual cost with the cost deemed satisfactory. For the former, the amount can be determined in several different ways. One is to arrive at the amount from past experience, giving ample consideration to general economic changes and conditions. Another is a judgment or estimate of what is received for a given expenditure. This is in the nature of an educated guess. In addition, standard costs can be employed. These are predetermined costs calculated to represent the amount of expenditure for material, labor, and overhead considered normal for the performance of the work. Theoretically, when the work is done by a standard employee with standard material and under standard conditions, the total dollar expenditure should be the standard cost. Generally speaking, the evaluating of cost expenditures by standard costs is superior because they reflect an analytical, studied, and reasonably accurate cost expectancy. Where standard costs have been established some time ago, they must be adjusted to reflect current conditions. These adjustments are called variances and may be either positive, i.e., added to the standard, or negative, i.e., subtracted from the standard.

The use of standard costs gives rise to several outstanding advantages. Basic references are provided to orientate managerial efforts, strict accountability for deviations from the established standard cost can be placed on those responsible for the deviations, and cost analysis is simplified. In contrast, standard cost usage has its shortcomings. For example, the units of expression are dollars and hence are subject to fluctuating value; personnel must be especially trained for standard cost work so that proper interpretation and use of the standard data are made; and in cases of special work, standard cost data cannot be used unless serious adjustments are made. While all these objections are valid, they are not particularly serious. Dollar values tend to remain *relatively* the same even though they do fluctuate in absolute value. It is probably true that some guide to acceptability, although it be found wanting in many respects, is better than none at all. Also, most efforts to guide the performance of work must, of practical necessity, be tempered with judgment.

After we have a fairly firm idea of what cost is satisfactory, we can compare the actual cost to this expectancy and thus determine whether the actual expenditure is greater, the same as, or less than the acceptable level. From this comparison, the performance efficiency is revealed. If the expenditure is less than the amount considered satisfactory, an investigation is made to determine if the work performed was of acceptable quality and quantity and if the satisfactory cost level is proper. On the other hand, where the actual cost exceeds the established satisfactory level, an investigation might be made to check the satisfactory level or, more likely, to analyze the actual cost to see in what way it can be brought into line.

The comparison work is expedited by cost reports giving detailed information on expenditures and compiled at the end of each day, week, or month. For maximum assistance, the report should show the plus or minus deviations from the expectancy for each item and, what is very important, should include sufficient data to establish trends. In many instances, the comparison of actual with expected cost is included under budgetary control, which is discussed later in this chapter.

## APPLYING CORRECTIVE ACTION IF NECESSARY

For the most part, this step includes efforts to reduce expenditures in those cases where actual costs are exceeding the satisfactory cost level. In many cases, the data apply to what has already happened, so that the corrective action is for some future date. However, it is vital to evaluate costs and to seek the reasons for present values. To illustrate, investigation of an increasing trend in office personnel costs may reveal poor selection techniques and high turnover. The remedial action might include a testing program, retraining of interviewers, and specific employee training efforts.

Although costs are detailed in terms of specific office functions, it is necessary to retain the overall viewpoint in deciding the corrective action. A reduction in one expense might increase another, making a total net gain in expenses. For example, centralized office costs may be reduced, but the work has been shifted to branch offices where the costs increase. Other illustrations are reducing the amount of light, resulting in an increase of time required to do the work; and eliminating interoffice telephone service, with the resultant increase in time spent by employees in delivering messages personally.

Another consideration is how to utilize all time and space gain or savings derived from the corrective action. The controlling is ineffective if it permits the former overage to dissipate among other work. For example, consider a six-hour task requiring eight hours to be completed. Through effective cost controlling the eight hours is reduced to the proper six-hour level. But actually the correction is effective only if these two hours saved as a result of the controlling are used to perform other work. Likewise, an additional office machine may save the time of one person out of three; but unless the third person is transferred and put to other work, the net result costwise is not a saving but only a machine added.

What we are saying is that for cost controlling to be effective, it is necessary (1) to check and see that the corrective steps are followed and (2) to know, as a consequence of these revisions, what the new results will be. The first point is achieved through personal means—observation and working with supervisors. For the latter point, some simple type of reporting can be instituted. For these reports to have greatest value, they should be made on a weekly and, in some instances, on a daily basis. It is important to know immediately if costs are getting back into line both for individual and for total costs. Receiving reports at relatively long intervals of time might mean needless continuation of costly practices or receipt of information when it is too late to do anything about it.

Cost controlling is a job that never ends. It varies in intensity with the particular needs of the office and the enterprise, the skill of the personnel assigned to and interested in it, and the beliefs of the top management members. It takes time and is laborious work, but it is well worth the effort. Best results are usually obtained from continuous, not sporadic, efforts.

## OFFICE BUDGETS

An important device for implementing controlling, usually associated with cost, is a budget. When a manager speaks of using a budget, he actually has two concepts in mind: the budget and budgetary control. Each of these can be defined formally in the following manner: *A budget is a device consisting of an orderly arrangement of data determined by computed guesses and covering all phases of the enterprise for a definite future period of time.* On the other hand, *budgetary control is the process of using the budget by comparing actual results with the computed guesses in order to correct either the estimates or the causes of the differences.*

The budget and budgetary control are interrelated and must always be considered jointly. A budget without budgetary control is useless from the managerial viewpoint ; and budgetary control without a budget is meaningless.

## WHY USE A BUDGET?

Preparation of a budget requires planning, and practicing budgetary control necessitates orderly controlling. Thus, the use of a budget assists a manager in performing these two fundamental functions of management and in closely relating them for practical purposes. Specifically a budget helps the office manager by encouraging a desired balance among the various office activities. The overall viewpoint is promoted. The use of a budget also helps to reveal weaknesses in the office organizational structure. Those units in which expenditures are excessively high can be marked for managerial attention. Furthermore, the decision making of a management member is facilitated by the factual information of goals and respective accomplishments shown by the budget.

It should be noted, however, that a budget is a managerial tool—a means of assistance to a manager, not management itself. Budgets are not automatic in their operation. Care in their compilation and wise, meaningful interpretation of the data are required. In addition, the use of budgets requires time. Current ills are not cured overnight by budgets. The discovery, correction, or elimination of undesirable conditions cannot be hurried. Also, budgets are limited by the accuracy of the forecasts. Reviews about every month or three months should be scheduled so that new developments or changes of conditions are reflected in the budget. We will say more about budget reviews later in this chapter.

## KINDS OF BUDGETS

It is possible to draw up a budget for almost any department or division of an enterprise. Frequently, separate budgets are made for sales, production, purchasing, finance, labor, and general expense. These are then combined into one budget, which is sometimes termed the "master budget" or simply the "budget."

As stated above, most budgets are cost-controlling devices and therefore are prepared in dollars, but physical units, or any other term which is useful and convenient, can be used. Quite often, where physical units are employed, the dollar values are also shown. When this practice is followed, it should be noted that not only units but also unit cost, i.e., price, must be forecast, and this can prove quite difficult.

It is sometimes desirable to show in a budget not only the allowances at a certain level of activity but also the allowances at various other levels. Such a budget is referred to as a *step budget,* and its value lies in predetermining and thinking through the action to be taken should variations from the estimated goal arise. Actually, the work of preparing a step budget is not as difficult as it may at first appear. Deviations are estimated from the allowances for the established goal. Some items will vary directly with the volume; others will tend to rise or fall with the operating level, but not in direct proportion to it; others will remain the same regardless of the operating level.

## ALL BUDGETS CONCERN THE OFFICE MANAGER

The office manager should use all the budgets employed in an enterprise to find out the plan or projected trends in operations which will affect the amount of office work. Included in the various budgets of an enterprise are those for sales expense, production, purchasing, and general expense, as will be mentioned in the following pages. From these various budgets, knowledge of changes such as an increase in advertising literature to be mailed, a change in the number of bills payable, the development of new sales markets, a new policy regarding billing practices, and a reduction in the number of purchasing orders can be ascertained and this information utilized to have the office provide its necessary functions.

Ordinarily, the office manager is active in the preparation of (1) the cash budget and (2) the office expense budget. In the case of the cash budget, the extent of office activities affects the cash requirements of the enterprise. The purchase and trade-in of office machines and equipment, the expansion or contraction of any office function in order to keep it in balance with changes elsewhere in the enterprise, or simply action to cut down office expenditures are illustrations of the office's influence on the cash budget.

The office expense budget is the individual budget covering office activities and is one in which the office manager is vitally interested. Typical items include supervision, clerical payroll, stationery, supplies, postage, telephone and telegraph service, reception and messenger service, purchase and maintenance of office machines and equipment, rent, and light. As already indicated, comparisons are made with the estimated amounts.

Figure 24–3 shows a portion of an office expense budget. In this case, entries of actual expenditures have been made for the months of January and February. Expenses for February are nearly $400 in excess of the

OFFICE EXPENSE BUDGET FOR THE YEAR 196–

| ITEM | JANUARY | | FEBRUARY | | MARCH | |
|---|---|---|---|---|---|---|
| | Estimate | Actual | Estimate | Actual | Estimate | Actual |
| 1. Stationery and envelopes.. | $  75 | . . . . . | . . . . . | $  83 | $  50 | |
| 2. Supplies............... | 50 | $  68 | $  35 | 21 | 35 | |
| 3. Postage................ | 35 | 35 | 35 | 35 | 35 | |
| 4. Telephone and telegraph... | 185 | 173 | 185 | 186 | 185 | |
| 5. Reception and messenger service.............. | 450 | 440 | 450 | 440 | 500 | |
| 6. Magazine and book subscription.............. | 18 | 18 | . . . . . | . . . . . | . . . . . | |
| 7. Maintenance of machines and equipment*........ | 40 | 53 | 40 | 62 | 40 | |
| 8. Purchase of machines and equipment*........... | 440 | 291 | . . . . . | 165 | 200 | |
| 9. Rent.................... | 80 | 80 | 80 | 80 | 80 | |
| 10. Light................... | 22 | 21 | 20 | 21 | 20 | |
| 11. Traveling expenses*....... | 80 | 135 | 80 | 40 | 80 | |
| 12. Employees' welfare....... | 50 | 60 | 50 | 47 | 50 | |
| 13. Clerical payroll*......... | 3,750 | 3,870 | 3,750 | 3,920 | 4,000 | |
| 14. Supervision payroll*...... | 1,140 | 1,140 | 1,140 | 1,170 | 1,300 | |
| 15. Miscellaneous (list)....... | 25 | . . . . . | 25 | . . . . . | 25 | |
| Install new electric outlet | . . . . | 3 | . . . . . | . . . . . | . . . . . | |
| Fix door at north exit.... | . . . . | . . . . . | . . . . . | 18 | . . . . . | |
| Total............. | $6,440 | $6,387 | $5,890 | $6,288 | $6,600 | |

* These items must be justified by details on supplementary sheets.

FIG. 24–3.   An office expense budget. Supplementary sheets are used to show the details of certain items which are selected on the basis of judgment and experience.

estimate. A study of the itemized data for this month shows that clerical payroll, machine and equipment purchases, and supervision payroll are the items chiefly responsible for the increase. Further investigation of these expenses should be made.

## PREPARATION OF THE BUDGET

An interesting graphic representation of the sequence of budget preparation is shown in Figure 24–4. The total estimated income is determined from expected sales and other sources of income. From this

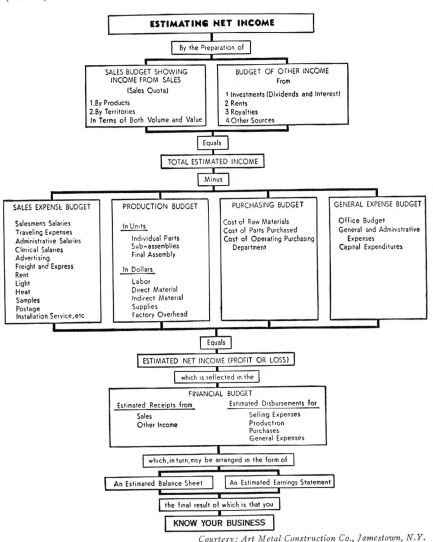

Courtesy: Art Metal Construction Co., Jamestown, N.Y.

FIG. 24–4. A normal sequence of budget preparation. The chart shows the coordination of the various individual budgets and the type of information found in each one.

total estimated income are subtracted the expenses of sales, production, purchasing, and general expenses. This gives the estimated net income or loss, which can be reflected in the financial budget, an estimated balance sheet, and an estimated earnings statement. The chart shows some of the details included under each individual budget.

Usually, the sales budget is developed first, since in many cases all other activities are predicated on what the sales expectancy picture is. Using the predicted sales as a basis, the plan for production, purchasing, and the like can be drawn up.

However, in some cases, this approach is reversed. The beginning is made by estimating the approximate income needed to provide a fair return on capital invested in the enterprise; then, one works back to determine the sales required, the production, and so on. There are variations of these two approaches, as well as other methods.

Most procedures for budget making consist of a series of steps somewhat like the following:

1. A conference of top management members is held to discuss trends and general outlook and to formulate broad policies regarding activities throughout the coming year.

2. The basis for the entire program, including sales and net income, or some other entity, is first drawn up by the executive in charge of the particular activity. It is then submitted for discussion and approval to the remaining top management members.

3. Each department head then prepares a budget for his own separate activity, guided by the data in the basic budget.

4. These budgets covering separate departments are submitted to the officer in charge of the budget. Generally, this is the controller or the budget officer.

5. A conference between the designated officer and each department head is then held for the purpose of thoroughly discussing and, when necessary, revising the respective individual department budget. Sometimes, a budget committee is used, in which case the budget officer transmits the estimates to the committee along with his recommendations.

6. After a tentative agreement on each individual budget has been reached, the master budget meeting is called. At this time, each individual budget is submitted and discussed. If necessary, adjustments are made, and final approval is obtained. This approval is generally contingent upon a final OK by the general manager or the president.

7. When finally determined, the budget is written up in its approved form, and copies are sent to all persons charged with carrying out a major portion of the plan. In like manner, copies covering specific parts of the master budget are distributed to lesser executives who are responsible for the execution of a particular portion of the plan.

## THE BUDGET PERIOD

The data of a budget apply to a definite period of time. The length of this period varies, however, because of several important considerations, one of which is the ability to make reasonable forecasts covering conditions affecting the work. All comparisons are made with the forecast data. It therefore follows that for valid comparison, the budget should cover only a reasonable future period, usually one year or less.

Other considerations include the normal cycle for completion of the work, the fiscal period utilized, and the intended use of the budget. That is to say, the budget period selected should be long enough to include any seasonal or characteristic variations of "up and down" changes brought about by sales and production cycles. When fiscal income and expenditure are key considerations, the budget period should coincide with or fit into the time pattern already existing for other financial controls. And if the budget is to serve as a quarterly check, the time period should include a three-month period. If the purpose is a semiannual check, a six-month period will be used.

The most common period covered is one year, with breakdowns for quarterly and monthly periods. The year usually coincides with the calendar year, although if operations are on a fiscal basis, the fiscal year is used. Customarily, the forecasts are subjected to revision and addition, either monthly or quarterly, as new conditions become known.

## REVISION OF BUDGET

Generally, the forecast will be made during November and December for the following year. Then, the revising and adjusting can follow any of a number of plans, but the following three are the most frequent:

1. *Periodic budgeting.* This plan provides for major revisions three times a year—in March, June, and September—for the remaining months of the year. For example, in March, a reforecast for the period April through December is made. If needed, revisions can be made at other times of the year as well.

2. *Progressive budgeting.* This arrangement furnishes definite times for major revisions throughout the year, such revisions covering definite periods following the revision date. For example, assume that revision times are bimonthly or at the end of February, April, June, August, October, and December, and that the period covered is six months. At the end of February, revisions would be made for the following six-month period, March through August; at the end of April, revisions are made for the period May through October; and so on. Revisions made at times other than the definite dates usually apply to the current budget only.

3. *Moving budgeting.* Under this plan, a forecast for 12 months is maintained by adding a month as each month is completed. To illustrate, at the completion of October, 1968, a forecast for October, 1969, is added; therefore, the 12-month forecast would cover November, 1968, through October, 1969. Revisions in the forecasts covering the intervening months are made when necessary.

## MAKING BUDGETING MORE EFFECTIVE

Several salient points merit mention before closing this chapter. The effectiveness of budgeting is enhanced by:

1. *Formulating the broad boundaries of the initial budget from the top down and subsequently filling in needed data from the bottom up.* The best budget is everybody's budget. If the budget resembles the form of an edict from top managers, it becomes a punitive club instead of an effective tool of management. The general goals and necessary broad constraints are set forth by top managers, who are in a position to visualize these needs. To supply the practical means for reaching these goals, middle and supervisory management members should be given the opportunity to participate in the formulation of the budgets that affect them. Suggestions from nonmanagement members should also be encouraged. In this way, interest, enthusiasm, and acceptance of the budget by all personnel are developed.

2. *Setting specific targets.* Budgeting exists to help accomplish specific goals within specific expenditures. Budgets are not simply official means to approve or disapprove specific expenditures only. It is erroneous for a manager simply to accept $x$ dollars to run his department, for such a viewpoint fails to include a specification of the assignment to be accomplished for these $x$ dollars. How much informational accomplishment is to be expected, i.e., how many checks processed, letters written, or inquiries handled?

3. *Providing for emergencies.* To help in meeting day-to-day problems easily, budgeting should include plans for what to do, if. . . . Actions commonly change from those anticipated. The work force is increased or decreased, training is altered, layouts rearranged, promotions reduced. Flexibility is vital in budgeting. The successful meeting of objectives usually requires application of reason and intuition at all levels. Unless adequate provision for emergencies is made, budgeting can be feared as an inviolable instrument that instills unsurmountable rigidities into the operations.

4. *Including realistic goals.* The best budgets reflect neither undue optimism nor pessimism. They do not call for better results than sound judgment indicates will be achieved. Likewise, they don't view the future as unduly difficult, with things getting worse and resulting in the inevitable need to cut costs regardless.

5. *Looking at favorable as well as unfavorable variances.* The natural tendency is to be most interested in unfavorable variances and to take proper action to correct them. However, it is frequently beneficial to review the favorable variances too. Some may cover activities that can be improved by application of technical advances, while others may be

combined with other activities or even eliminated in view of current requirements.

## QUESTIONS

1. Name the major approaches to office cost reduction, and discuss briefly the one you feel is most important.
2. State concisely the meaning and give an example of each of the following:
   *a*) Cost as medium for coordinating managerial activities.
   *b*) Indirect material cost.
   *c*) Cost-consciousness by employees.
   *d*) Cost control.
3. What are the advantages in an office manager using standard costs? The disadvantages?
4. Would you say that costs are important in the making of most major decisions by an office manager? Why?
5. In determining the facts regarding cost, discuss the need for the cost data to apply to well-defined components. Give illustrations to clarify your answer.
6. Explain Figure 24–2 in your own words.
7. Which of the following can serve as objectives of an office manager?
   *a*) Costs.
   *b*) Reduction of costs.
   *c*) Budgets.
   *d*) Standard cost.
   Explain your answers.
8. In your opinion, can an office be managed effectively without a budget? Defend your answer.
9. As an office manager, what basic arrangement for revising the budget would you follow? Why?
10. Discuss the consideration of providing for emergencies in efforts to make budgeting more effective.
11. Miss A believes that if an item is in the budget, it is sufficient justification for spending that amount in order to utilize funds advantageously and keep them in balance. In contrast, Miss B claims that, whenever possible, savings on every budget item should be made in order to keep costs at a minimum. With whom do you agree? Give your reasons.
12. Do you agree with the statement: "All budgets concern the office manager"? Explain your answer.

## CASE PROBLEMS

### Case 24–1.  Kenneth Allbright

The office of which Kenneth Allbright is office manager is to be subjected to cost analysis and control. To date, office costs have been considered under the single classification of overhead expenses and it is the belief of the top managers that efforts should be directed toward getting office costs known and reducing them if possible. In their opinion, there is much waste in the office. Time is not effectively used, office supplies are wasted, copies of reports are excessive, expense accounts seem to be padded, and some supervisors appear to do very little work. Accordingly, Kenneth Allbright was asked to join Mr. Herman Kushbaum, the controller, and several of his staff to formulate a plan for launching the office cost program.

Mr. Kushbaum is delighted to take part in this project because he feels the opportunities for "making a good showing" are tremendous. He recommends that cost information on key office work be established as the initial effort. "This will tell us where we are, then we can concentrate our efforts on those costs that are excessive," he comments. Data on the cost per invoice written, and the cost per payroll check written will serve as excellent starting points in his opinion. In contrast, Kenneth Allbright feels this is the wrong approach to cost analysis and reduction. He believes it is going to be very difficult and expensive to establish meaningful costs for many of their office operations. In his opinion the use of any cost formula is subject to so many interpretations that the whole effort is meaningless. Mr. Allbright strongly advocates efforts to foster an awareness of cost by each office supervisor and employee. This is the only way, he maintains, to launch the program and it is without doubt the most effective means of bringing the office costs down.

### Problems:

1. With whom do you agree, Mr. Allbright or Mr. Kushbaum? Why?

2. To what extent will the development of standard office costs aid the company?

3. What are your recommendations to the top managers of this company? Discuss.

### Case 24–2.   Office Automation Institute

Having successfully offered one-, three-, and five-day seminars for office work, the managers of the Office Automation Institute, OAI, now contemplate a two-week or ten-day session program. They would like a minimum of 50 paid registrants and are mailing 3,000 announcements at a cost of 11¢ each for the mailing and $375 for preparing and printing these announcements. Each registrant will receive seminar materials estimated to cost the institute $36.50 per enrollee. Meetings will be held at the conveniently located Hotel Davis, which charges $25 a day for a conference room having a capacity of 92. The group will be served lunch each conference day in a special catering room of the hotel, for which a charge of $3 per person, including tips, is made. Also, hot beverages will be supplied at midmorning and again at midafternoon in the rear of the conference room. For this service, a charge of 75 cents per day per enrollee will be made. A total of 14 instructors will be used to cover the various subjects; but only two different instructors for any one day will be scheduled, each handling the group for half a day. Compensation for an instructor for half a day is $75 plus his lunch regardless of whether he instructs in the morning or in the afternoon. Special equipment, including a slide and a motion-picture projector, will be needed for five days; it is estimated that this will cost $30 per day.

As a policy, the institute requires a minimum margin of approximately 30 percent of the total income from a seminar. That is, if the total income is $1,000, the institute strives to keep expenses at no more than $700. Registrations from mailings for other seminars have ranged from 1.9 percent to 5.1 percent of the total number of mailings sent out. However, the managers of the institute are at a loss to know whether these response ranges are valid for a seminar such as they are now planning.

## Problems:

1. Discuss the major problem facing the institute.

2. Calculate the approximate registration fee that the institute should charge for the office automation seminar.

3. What plan of action do you feel the institute should follow? Why?

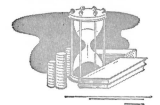

CHAPTER 25

# OFFICE MANUALS

We have too many people who live without
working, and we have altogether too many who
work without living.
                              *—Charles R. Brown*

OBTAINING desired control over the efforts of employees is assisted by the
use of complete and up-to-date office manuals. Authorized information
dealing with the policies and practices of the enterprise; recommended
systems, procedures, methods, and standards to be followed; and the
regulations regarding employment can be given in a simple, direct, and
uniform manner by means of manuals. *An office manual is a written
record of information and instructions which concern and can be used to
guide the employee's efforts in an enterprise.* Actually, it is a guidebook—
a source for data believed essential for the highest performance of the
job.

## EVALUATION OF MANUALS

Essentially, an office manual is a device to assist in the orientation of
employees. It can help to make instructions definite, to provide quick
settlements of misunderstandings, to show each employee how his job fits
into the total organization, and to point out how he can contribute to the
achievements of office objectives as well as to maintain good relationships
with other employees. On the other hand, manuals aid management
members significantly. Manuals relieve management members of having
to repeat similar information, explanations, or instructions. They not only
force decisions on policies and procedures—thoughts about them must be
put into writing—but they also provide constancy to them. Employees
come and go, but the manual stays. The training of newcomers is
enhanced. Both the delegation of authority and management by exception

are promoted by the use of manuals.[1] Furthermore, manuals assist in reducing gaps, obsolete activities, and needless office work duplication.

In contrast, there are some managers who do not advocate the use of manuals for any of a number of reasons. Among the more common criticisms are that manuals "cost too much," "are too much work," "stifle initiative," or "won't work in our case." In some cases, these objections are no doubt justifiable; but for many enterprises, the use of manuals appears to be beneficial. The great majority of nonusers of manuals are small companies where informal communication and mode of operations are considered sufficient.

---

1. Center authority and responsibility for the manual program.
2. Write to the level of the employee who will use the manual.
3. Maintain a distribution list—distribute only those manuals that are needed in each case.
4. Use color to emphasize identity of binder or printing matter.
5. Keep manual simple in arrangement of material and in language used.
6. Adopt adequate indexing and cross-referencing.
7. Use numerous visual aids—charts and illustrations.
8. Keep manuals up to date.
9. Highlight changes and revisions.
10. Audit the material periodically.

---

FIG. 25–1.    Basic requirements for success of office manuals.

Figure 25–1 lists the basic requirements for success of office manuals. More will be included about these requirements throughout the pages of this chapter.

## TYPES OF OFFICE MANUALS

Different offices have need for different manuals. The type is determined by answering the question: "What is the purpose to be served?" In some instances, a single purpose only is served; while in others, several purposes are to be fulfilled. The number and the kind of purposes are determined by the individual circumstances.

Manuals can be written to cover a variety of subjects, including policies, organizational structure of the enterprise, employment, indoctrination, supervision, job instruction, standard work practices, computer data processing, history of the enterprise, and specialized or departmental practices such as in the accounting, corresponding, filing, engineering, purchasing, or sales department. However, for convenience, the major

---

[1] Delegation of authority is discussed in Chapter 28, p. 616; management by exception in Chapter 9, p. 203.

types of manuals, along with their respective purposes, can be set forth as follows:

| *Type of Manual* | *Purpose* |
|---|---|
| Manual of policies | To state the policies of the enterprise or office. |
| Manual of operations, or standard practices manual, or job instruction manual | To inform employees of established methods, procedures, and standards. |
| Manual of office rules and regulations, or handbook on employment | To give concise information on benefits, operating rules, and employment regulations. |
| Historical Manual | To provide historical information about the enterprise. |
| Multiple-purpose manual | To supply selected items from any area or subject deemed desirable and helpful in the work performance. |

## MANUAL OF POLICIES

As set forth in Chapter 15, a policy is a basic guide to action. It prescribes the overall boundaries within which activities are to take place and hence reveals broad managerial intentions or forecasts broad courses of managerial action likely to take place under certain conditions. To illustrate, promoting employees solely on the basis of merit is a policy. It states the guide for promoting, but it does not tell who will be promoted. Likewise, the payment of salaries above the prevailing amounts in the community for similar work, consistent with the economic well-being of the enterprise, is another example of a policy. Knowing the policies of an enterprise provides the main framework around which all actions are based. Policies furnish the background for an understanding of why things are done as they are.

A manual of policies puts into writing the policies of an enterprise. It has been said that a policy does not really exist unless it is in writing. To decide each case on its individual merits and to convey this decision verbally is not in keeping with modern management thinking. Proponents of a manual of policies cite these advantages: (1) Written policies require managers to think through their courses of action and to predetermine what actions will be taken under various circumstances; (2) a general program of action for many matters is provided, and only the unusual or exceptional matter requires the attention of the top managers; (3) a framework is provided within which the manager can operate freely; and (4) written policies help to insure equitable treatment to all employees.

On the other hand, there are those who object to having a manual of policies. Among the important points they mention are the following: (1) Policies are extremely difficult to write accurately and completely—the interpretation of words and phrases sometimes leads to serious misunderstandings; (2) written policies make it difficult to keep policies flexible, as is frequently required by changing conditions; and (3) knowledge of policies should be confined to those persons charged with their execution— the top executive, department heads, or supervisors, as the case might be.

## MANUAL OF OPERATIONS

A manual can serve as a convenient source for information on how the work is to be done. The authorized steps can be listed; and supplementary information, in the form of diagrams, sketches, and charts, can be included in order to clarify the data. The standards and guides to be followed are usually included.

The contents of this type of manual can be pointed toward any one or all of the following:

1. *Individual tasks and jobs.* Illustrative is the manual which explains how to operate and use an adding machine. The importance of keeping accurate records can be emphasized and information included describing the parts and operations of an adding machine, practice lessons, and an explanation of the practices of the company. A glossary of terms is sometimes included to clarify the work.

2. *Departmental practices.* Manuals of this type contain a statement of the duties of the department. Its divisions are defined, the supervisors listed, and their responsibilities indicated, along with outlines and procedures for operating. The work of departments, such as sales, purchasing, accounting, and research, is often set up and described in departmental manuals.

3. *General practices in a special field.* This type of manual is becoming more popular, for it furnishes valuable general information which is usable in special lines of work. Its adoption is mainly in large offices, although in certain instances the small office can benefit from manuals of this type. Systems and procedures manuals and those for computer data processing are illustrative. Each of these vary considerably in makeup. However, a somewhat typical page from a systems and procedures manual will give the number, title, and subtitle of the system or procedure, the organization units affected, a general statement of the system or procedure in one paragraph, an outline of the material classified by major headings, with important actions numbered and listed under each heading. Concluding are original issue date, revision date, and signature of authorizing manager.

## MANUAL OF OFFICE RULES AND REGULATIONS

Manuals are an excellent medium in which to explain employee benefit plans, including such things as group insurance, hospitalization, and savings facilities. Questions regarding the use of the company library, cafeteria, and recreation club can also be answered. In addition, the prescribed guides for conduct are included and cover such items as sick allowances, the use of rest periods, conduct regarding smoking, solicitation for money in the office, the sale of tickets, hours of employment, holidays, vacations, office etiquette, rest periods, telephone usage, and recreational provisions. As already stated, a manual of this type is identified either as a

---

### GENERAL OFFICE ROUTINES

DESKS—Keep your desk clean. It's a workbench, not a catchall. Never allow a lot of old-fashioned relics to accumulate on it. File everything away in its natural place, and dispose of obsolete matter. (The job of filing is an important one and is not to be neglected or allowed to pile up.)

Avoid having decorations on the desk that might tip and spill, such as flower containers, ink bottles, sponge cups, etc. Keep such things in safer places.

Clear all desks and tables before leaving the building. Any papers or letters of a confidential nature must be put away, never left on the desk top. All lights are to be turned off, fans and ventilators disconnected, and blinds raised. Typewriters should be covered when not being used.

DUSTING—Each office is to be thoroughly dusted each morning—during the day too if necessary. No one need resent dusting—it's part of the job.

Pens should be filled, pencils sharpened and water bottles filled first thing in the morning. See to it that ash trays are kept clean throughout the day. If blotters are used, make sure soiled ones are replaced.

Typewriters should be dusted morning and night, type cleaner applied weekly.

SUPPLIES—If you are responsible for handling supplies for the office, check them regularly and make sure that you are not running low. Keep a list at your desk of supplies that will soon need to be requisitioned (use form 527 for ordering). All requisitions must be authorized by the department head.

HOURS—Arrange hours if possible so the office will not be unattended at any time. If it is impossible for someone to be present during lunch hour, do not leave without making arrangements with someone else to take any important calls.

CALLERS—It is much better to have an understanding with your superior regarding his wishes in the matter of announcing callers, the persons he wishes to see and those he does not, rather than to guess at the proper procedure in each instance.

Keep an accurate, up to date list or notebook of telephone numbers and addresses, business as well as personal. Such a list should be readily accessible. Add to it regularly so it will be of value both to you and your superior.

---

*Source: Butler Brothers, "Secretaries' and Stenographers' Handbook" (Chicago, 1946), p. 20*
*Reproduced here by special permission.*

FIG. 25–2. Page of a manual used by a large national distributor of general merchandise.

manual of office rules and regulations or as a handbook on employment. However, for psychological reasons, the manual may be given a title like "You and the XYZ Company" or "Getting Along at XYZ." Such a manual helps to orientate and to inform the employee by giving him specific answers to all the elements of his work surroundings, thus promoting understanding and harmonious relationships. Figure 25–2 shows a sample of the type of information included in this kind of manual.

## HISTORICAL MANUAL

Many employers feel that it is important to give employees information regarding the history of the company—its beginning, growth, accomplishments, present management, and current status. This gives the employee an insight into the tradition and thinking behind the enterprise with which he is associated. It probably makes for better understanding, increases morale, and helps the employee to feel that he "belongs"—that he is a part of the company. Giving an employee a picture of the whole helps him to fit himself into the total picture. Manuals, of course, are excellent means for conveying this type of information to employees. The story of the enterprise usually can be told on several pages; and quite frequently, it can be a part of a message written by a major officer. Historical information is commonly included as the introductory portion to a manual of office rules and regulations.

## MULTIPLE-PURPOSE MANUAL

This type of manual represents a combination of any two or all of the types discussed above. The company's needs, the size of the enterprise, and the philosophy of the top managers usually determine the makeup. The outline of a multiple-purpose manual might include the following:

1. Title.
2. Foreword.
3. Table of Contents.
4. Company History.
5. General Policies of Company.
6. Organization.
7. Company Departments—Functions, Authorities, and Responsibilities.
8. Office Regulations.
9. Office Supplies and Maintenance.
10. Personnel Points—Hiring, Promoting, Terminating, Sick Leave, Employee Benefits, and Social Activities.

11. Miscellaneous.

12. Index.

## SOURCES FOR MANUAL MATERIAL

Probably one of the best sources of material for a manual is manuals used by other enterprises. Looking over what has been included in manuals of another company suggests what topics might be covered. However, the manual should be personalized to meet the particular needs of an enterprise.

Additional data can be secured from a number of other sources. Such data might include (1) minutes of board of directors' meetings, (2) reports of executive conferences, (3) speeches and published articles of executives, (4) bulletins and company circulars, (5) agreements with employees and contracts with unions, (6) grievance records, (7) company magazines or similar publications, and (8) interviews with executives, especially the personnel manager, training director, and supervisors.

Experience shows that, with time, it will be desirable to eliminate certain material and to add other material. The additional material might be secured from the above sources or, because of the unique nature of the information, may be secured from a special source. For example, instructions in the correct use of a new office machine would probably be secured from the manufacturer or seller.

## PREPARATION OF MANUALS

Some orderly process must be followed in the preparation of manuals if they are to be inclusive and to be completed within a reasonable period of time. The process followed depends a great deal upon the individual in charge of this work. In general, however, it will be helpful to follow a procedure along these lines:

1. *Announce to all members of the enterprise that a manual is to be prepared.* Solicit their suggestions and ideas as to what should be included. Appointing a committee of employees often encourages their participation in the preparation of the manual. As a result, better understanding and greater acceptance and use are usually gained. Special attention should be directed to supervisors, for they are usually rich sources of excellent material.

2. *Draw up a list of all the subjects to be covered by the manual.* The purpose of the manual, the cost, and managerial judgment will determine, for the most part, what items are included. Proper subheadings should be made under each main topic, and the list should be arranged according to the contemplated main divisions or sections of the manual. A big time-saver in this respect is to use a separate card for each topic and file behind

guides. By this means, material can be classified quickly and the list or outline changed with a minimum of effort.

A logical arrangement of the material is most commonly used, but this sequence is not necessarily the most effective in all cases. Consideration should be given to placing the vital information or that which is most interesting in the beginning, using the last portion of the list for data of less importance.

3. *Write the information under each subject.* It is advisable to use headings—major and minor—so that the material is well organized and the reader can follow it easily. Check the source data to help insure accuracy in all writing. Source material can be numbered and indexed, and this means of identification tied in with the writing by means of marginal notes. Keep the prospective reader in mind—write so he will want to read the manual and understand what it is intended to mean. A simple, friendly, and sincere style is best. Short words and sentences should be employed. Narrative style is common, but the playscript format is very effective.[2] Include charts, cartoons, diagrams, and examples of proper forms, letters, and reports in order to gain greater clarity. These illustrations should be in an inexpensive, rough form until it is decided, as described below, whether they will be included in the final manual. All material should be presented in the "normal flow of work" sequence. The amount of detail depends upon the importance of the subject.

4. *Prepare a limited number of copies for key executives, supervisors, employee or union representatives, and several key employees.* Have them read the manual and submit criticisms and suggestions. Quite often, better ways of expression are found in this way. Sometimes, subjects can be combined, major items previously overlooked can be added, minor points strengthened, and the entire manual improved.

5. *Revise the manual and give it to top management members for approval.* Corrections and suggestions from the previous step are incorporated. It is well to include a separate statement to the effect that the entire contents are in agreement with the philosophy of top management members and are acceptable to the employees.

6. *Send the approved manuscript to the printer or the party doing the actual mechanical production work.* The manual can be published by any of several different methods, including xerography, mimeograph, offset printing, or letterpress.[3] The quantity, appearance, and cost will probably determine the process used. Details regarding size, paper, and type of binding must also be decided. Generally, it is well to seek competent advice in these matters.

The size $6\frac{1}{4}$ x $4\frac{1}{2}$ inches is excellent for a booklet intended for

---

[2] Playscript is discussed in Chapter 3, p. 50.

[3] See Chapter 5 for discussion of duplicating processes.

carrying in the pocket. If the manual is to be used as a reference book on a desk, an 11 x 8½-inch size is very satisfactory. Other popular sizes include 9⅛ x 6 inches, 8½ x 5½ inches, and 5⅛ x 3¾ inches. Pages of these sizes can be cut, with minimum waste, from sheet sizes usually carried by the printer.[4]

The number and size of the pages in the booklet generally determine the weight of paper used. When the number of pages does not exceed about 24, a thick paper can be used; but where a greater number of pages is involved, a thinner stock is used, to eliminate unnecessary bulk. For page sizes under about 8½ x 5½ inches, a paper of about 60 pounds is used. When the size is greater, paper of about 70 pounds is employed.

---

PAGE SIZE—

If printed, the 6 x 9-inch page size is effective. This is the typical book size. If typed, the 8½ x 11-inch page size will be preferred by most employees.

ARRANGEMENT OF MATERIAL—

Place sections most frequently used at front of manual.
Related sections should be placed close together and interrelated by cross-references.
Set sections apart by stiff divider page of different-colored paper.
Either tab sections for ready reference, or use a divider of page size to facilitate a margin index.

REMEMBER TO—

Make the cover attractive by using a clear, brief title and well-selected artwork.
Include a table of contents and an index so that the reader can quickly find what he is looking for.

---

FIG. 25–3.   Helpful suggestions for preparation of manuals.

Make the headings stand out on the page by the use of white space around them, or color may be employed. Color increases the cost; but in many cases, the effect brought about by such things as a colored border, headline, or illustration justifies the additional expense. For additional suggestions see Figure 25–3.

The type of binding may be either side or saddle wire stitching, screw post, prong fasteners, ring binder, and wire or plastic edge binding. The

---

[4] In the case of loose-leaf and many bound manuals, it is customary to give the dimension of the binding side first. Thus, an 11 x 8-inch size means the binding is on an 11-inch side. The dimensions used in this discussion follow this practice. In contrast, and at times somewhat confusingly, in specifying dimensions of index cards, the horizontal dimension is named first, followed by the vertical dimension. For example, an 8 x 5 card means 8 inches horizontally and 5 inches vertically.

choice will depend primarily upon usage, amount of material, appearance, and cost.[5]

## DISTRIBUTION OF MANUALS

It is paramount in the distribution of the manuals to provide a copy to everyone concerned with and in need of the information the manual contains. The extent of distribution depends upon the size of the enterprise; in most cases, one copy of the manual should be available for ready reference in at least each department or division. In cases where manuals pertain to specific jobs, copies should be readily available to every employee on such jobs.

To increase the readership of the manual, it is sometimes given to the employee only during an interview. His attention is directed to specific pages, and he is encouraged to read the entire booklet. In some cases, depending upon the type of manual, it is mailed to the employee's home with an accompanying letter. Forewarning that the manual is to be used as the subject for a forthcoming meeting or group discussion is a very effective means of encouraging readership. In addition, sometimes the employee is requested to sign and to return an enclosed card in the manual as evidence of reading the complete booklet; and in other instances, questions are asked on the card to measure the employee's understanding of the manual contents.

## MANUAL MAINTENANCE

The problem of keeping the manual up to date is ever present. In most enterprises, changes are taking place constantly, owing to new work being added or improvements in current work being made. Revisions of and additions to manuals are constantly in process. New pages must replace the old and be distributed to all holders of the manuals. These changes may be covered either by single sheets or by entire supplements. Frequently, amendments are written on colored paper to attract attention to the change. Also, notations made in red ink in the manual will point out those parts which have been changed, omitted, or amended. When many changes cause the manual to be difficult to read and use, it should be rewritten.

All changes in manuals should be cleared through a central control unit so that proper authorization and conformity in results are obtained. If this is not done, needless confusion and misunderstanding will result. The revised sheets should follow the established form of the manual. New material will probably be added every three to six months, together with

---

[5] See Chapter 5, page 105, for detailed discussion of this subject.

certain modifications in the old material. Limited research shows that nearly 90 percent of all managers prefer a three-ring binder, which facilitates the insertion of revised sheets.

An old saying is that the three R's of manuals are easy reading, reference, and revision. Much emphasis is placed upon the last R— revision. To aid manual maintenance an excellent practice is to find out what users of the manual think of it. For example, do they believe it is:

1. *Readable*—effective writing style, good format, and easy-to-read print?

2. *Illustrated*—where needed, and in sufficient detail?

3. *Practical*—titled properly, directions clearly given, adequate coverage of material and effectively indexed?

4. *Modern*—attractive appearance, and up-to-date in content?

## QUESTIONS

1. What are some common purposes for which an office manual can be used?

2. Justify the viewpoint of an office manager who does not favor having a manual of policies. Do you agree with this viewpoint? Why?

3. List and briefly comment on six basic requirements for success of office manuals.

4. Are you of the opinion that for most offices a manual is beneficial? Substantiate your answer.

5. For each of the following, indicate in what type of office manual you would expect to find the information:

   *a*) Practices to be followed in computer data processing.

   *b*) Conditions under which books from the company library can be borrowed and taken home.

   *c*) The philosophy and working principles followed by Jonathan Rosewell Heinmann, founder of Heinmann and Hertz, Inc.

   *d*) General office routines to be followed by all office employees.

6. Is an office manual of greater importance in a large or in a small office? Justify your answer.

7. Name and evaluate the important sources of material for manuals.

8. Discuss the subject of manual maintenance.

9. Distinguish carefully between the elements in each of the following pairs:

   *a*) Manuals and standards.

   *b*) Historical manual and manual of office rules and regulations.

   *c*) An 11 x 8½-inch manual and an 8½ x 11-inch manual.

   *d*) Managerial controlling and manuals.

10. Enumerate and discuss briefly the major steps in the preparation of a manual.

11. Discuss the subject, distribution of manuals.

12. It has been suggested that a manual be written that would be adaptable for use by all offices. Spaces for individualized "fill-ins" would be provided. Do you believe such a manual is feasible? Explain.

## CASE PROBLEMS

### Case 25–1.  Van Debur Corporation

After three days on her new job with Van Debur Corporation, Marilyn Veit, a private secretary for the treasurer of the corporation, had an interview with her superior. She expressed the opinion that the morale of the office employees seemed low, especially of those in the correspondence section. She believed it would help to prepare a manual for them which, among other things, would give information about the corporation's history and the importance of its products as well as definite aids in typing letters and sundry tasks of employees in the section. The treasurer listened attentively to the suggestions, congratulated Marilyn, and authorized her to get together her ideas and some samples of what the proposed manual would be like. He informed the office manager of his decision. The office manager reports to the treasurer.

Marilyn talked with the supervisor of the correspondence section, who offered to assist in every way possible. However, she told Marilyn that a manual would not improve morale. What the employees want is more money, but the corporation will not give it to them. She explained the work to Marilyn and gave her samples of work requested. When Marilyn suggested talking to one or two selected employees of the department, the supervisor countered that this was not advisable, so Marilyn dropped the request. Later, in talking with the treasurer, Marilyn learned that none of the office departments had a manual, that any conversation with office employees should be cleared with their supervisors, and that the corporation very infrequently changed systems in use, the tendency being to stay with established conditions and practices of conducting the work.

### Problems:

1. Enumerate the types of information you suggest be included in the proposed manual.

2. Do you believe the proposed manual is appropriate and will be helpful? Discuss.

3. What action do you suggest Marilyn Veit take? Why?

### Case 25–2.  Sovereign Products Company

During a conversation with a business friend at the Meadowdale Country Club, Mr. Gregory E. Brady became very interested in office manuals and their use in the management of an office. His country club friends told him a public relations firm, Richards and Associates, had gotten together a very attractive and informative office manual for them. Mr. Brady is vice-president of finance for Sovereign Products Company. Several days later, he called his office manager, Mr. Rodney Custer, to his office, and the following conversation took place.

BRADY: I've asked you to come in, Rod, to discuss the use of an office manual in our office. What do you think of our having a manual?

CUSTER: Well, Mr. Brady, you will recall—or no, I guess that was before you came here, that—well, we had an office manual some eight years ago. But its usage declined; and during the past year or so, I guess you could say we have no manual at all.

BRADY: That was my understanding—we do not have an office manual. How come we got away from having a manual? Why don't we use it, Rod?

CUSTER: I don't know, sir. It doesn't seem to be missed.

BRADY: Others use one. Maybe we are missing out on something. I think we should have one. Seems to me in an office our size, with 72 employees, we. . . .

CUSTER (interrupting): It's 82, sir.

BRADY: Are we up to 82? The more we could use a manual, I would judge. It would help reduce office costs and lighten the burden on our office supervisors. Don't you think so?

CUSTER: Well, it could, I suppose.

BRADY: Yes. Custer, I'd like you to see what you can do toward bringing out a new, up-to-date manual for our office.

CUSTER: Yes, sir. I am very busy right now, sir, and I really don't have anybody who can write well enough to do this.

BRADY: Well, see what you can do, and let me know.

Mr. Brady held the matter in abeyance for four weeks. He then called a representative of Richards and Associates to his office and discussed the possibility of this firm writing a manual for the Sovereign Products Company's office. He gave the representative a copy of the old manual used by the office at one time, and offered several suggestions about what the contents of a new manual should include. Immediately after this conversation, he telephoned Mr. Custer, told him what he (Brady) had done, and requested that Mr. Custer submit any ideas about the new manual and its contents to him.

Five weeks passed, and there was no word from Mr. Custer. Richards and Associates were called in again by Mr. Brady, who authorized them to proceed and make up a sample or dummy copy of a proposed new office manual. A month later, the sample was submitted and approved by Mr. Brady and also by Mr. Custer, whom Mr. Brady asked "to look it over." Subsequently, the manual was printed and distributed to key personnel.

Now, six months later, Mr. Brady has information based on sources he considers thoroughly reliable that the office manual is not being used.

### Problems:

1. Is there a problem faced by the company? Substantiate your answer.

2. Discuss the actions taken by Mr. Brady, emphasizing what you consider the good and the bad points.

3. What do you recommend Mr. Brady do now? Why?

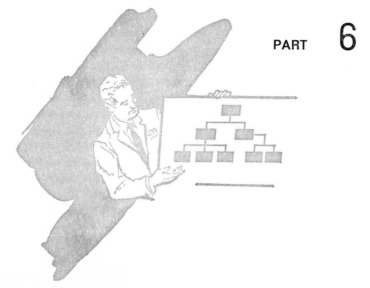

# OFFICE MANAGEMENT—ORGANIZING

*Organizing is the next fundamental function of office management to be discussed. This includes apportioning the office work to be done, assigning the various parcels of work to specific members of the work group, and establishing the proper work relationships among them. Office organizing must be kept up to date so that vigorous teamwork is maintained. Effective organizing is essential in managing an office. The five chapters that follow deal with office organizing.*

# CHAPTER 26

# THE OFFICE ORGANIZATION

Concentration is the secret of strength in politics, in war, in trade, in short, in all management of human affairs.
—*Ralph Waldo Emerson*

ORGANIZING is a fundamental function of management and it becomes a necessity when two or more people work together. Decisions must be made regarding who does what work, who reports to whom, what members are in a certain work group, and who decides what types of issues. Organizing deals with these basic questions.

Answers to these questions provide an organizational framework within which talented individuals can contribute to the common goal of both their enterprise and themselves. The framework or structure utilized should assist and promote the collective efforts, but in the final analysis it is people, and only people, who determine the success or failure of organizing efforts.

## MANAGEMENT AND ORGANIZING

Organizing makes possible the effective operation of a group. It is the basis for necessary teamwork among the various members of a common enterprise and helps blend together their efforts. Organizing guides the work by the various members not only to serve as a single coordinated force toward a common goal but also to utilize the particular individual specialty of each member toward achieving the major goal. In essence, the value of the individual's contribution is enhanced and, at the same time, the accomplishments of the group are increased. Every member, management and nonmanagement, knows how he and his work fit into the total picture, what he is to do, when and where he is to do it, and who, if anyone, helps him.

Organizing enables a manager to enlarge his scope of operation, that is, it makes it possible for a manager to accomplish much more than he could as an individual. It provides the means for using effectively the work of other people, and it sets the groundwork for the development of people. In fact, success in management requires effective organizing; failure to organize properly limits any manager's ability to manage.

Organizing provides a satisfactory climate for achieving an informed and satisfied work force. It avoids needless duplication of effort. It gets individuals to work effectively as members of a team, not separately as single individuals. It avoids confusion and misunderstanding as to who is to do what work. It prevents "buck-passing," an excessive number of managers and nonmanagers, and misinformed members of the group.

## OBJECTIVE AND ORGANIZING

Organizing, like the other fundamental functions of management, is influenced and guided by the objective being sought. Organizing is, or should be, performed to achieve a definite objective, and this goal determines the organizational type and structural makeup needed.

To evaluate competently an office organization requires relating it to the particular objective for which the organization is designed. The question "For what objective is the group organized?" is a cardinal consideration in organizational efforts. The paper work required in one enterprise may differ from that in another enterprise. The centers for paper-work processing are not identical in all organizations. Top managers' ideas of what paper work should be performed by what departments differ among enterprises. Some companies are local, others national, and still others international in scope. Also, some have only one line of related products, while others have multiple lines of products. These considerations help shape the objective and, in turn, are utilized to mold the organization.

## MEANING OF ORGANIZING

*Organizing is the allocating of the total work to be done among the work group, establishing the relative authority and responsibility of each individual who is placed in charge of each work component, and supplying the proper work environment.* In organizing, a manager is concerned with (1) work—how to distribute it, (2) people—who is going to do what work, (3) relationships—what is the relative authority and responsibility among the "organization units" formed by the work distribution and the respective people doing it, and (4) work environment—what tools and workplaces will best contribute toward maximum work accomplishments. From the managerial viewpoint, organizing logically associates the numerous functions of an enterprise and the people performing these functions. In addition, it establishes definite relationships among the people who are performing these functions.

Office organizing, like all organizing, is a dynamic, not a static, process. As a result, changes take place in an office organization; this is the common occurrence rather than the exception. Changes in an office organization take place for many reasons, such as changes in the objectives of the enterprise, changes in personnel, and changes in the conditions outside the office or of the entire enterprise. The student of office management must fully realize that organizing is an active, living entity—it is not a passive, rigid concept. The effective office manager normally changes his organization from time to time in order best to meet the current requirements. This subject of organizational dynamics is so important that an entire chapter in this book, Chapter 29, is devoted to it.

## RELATION OF OFFICE TO ORGANIZATION OF ENTERPRISE

Since office work and its management are performed to supply a needed service to other major activities of an enterprise, it is advisable first to consider office organization in relation to the organization of the entire enterprise of which the office is an important part. It is common to think that in the typical organization, the major activities to be performed are production, sales, and finance. Each must be done satisfactorily if the enterprise is to survive. The creating of a utility for others is basic for most enterprises. This, in turn, necessitates selling efforts, so that the product or service is made available to buyers. The producing and selling efforts necessitate financing activities, in that ample capital must be obtained and maintained.

In addition to these three major activities, there are frequently personnel and the office, which are included to assist the main functions. Many feel that both personnel and the office are major activities, and that each should be accorded organization position and status on a par with production, sales, and finance. Sound arguments can be advanced to justify this viewpoint. In the case of the office, for example, the trend toward more and more automation, the use of computers, and the general recognition of the vital contributions of the office give increasing weight to this viewpoint. In keeping with this approach, and as pointed out in Chapter 2, many prefer the term "administrative management" to "office management," the belief being that the former more accurately describes the content and importance of supplying information by processing papers and the contributions of such efforts to an enterprise.

Any attempt to justify one major activity as the most important in an enterprise is purely academic. Actually, all the major activities are needed. For example, production requires sales, financing gives rise to paper work, personnel assists production, and paper work expedites sales efforts. Our interest here is organization in the management of the office; and the vital concept for our purpose is to remember that office work is done to help fulfill other major functions—it is not performed apart from them. Production activities such as cutting, sewing, machining, assembling, painting, drying, and packing are assisted by the work of the office. Likewise, typical sales activities such as merchandising, analysis of markets, and selling efforts are helped by the office. And the same is true of finance and personnel, for many records and papers are needed in each.

## ORGANIZATIONAL CONTENT AND PLACEMENT OF THE OFFICE

The questions can now be asked: "What activities should be included in the office?" and "Where should the office organizational unit be placed in the organization of the entire enterprise?" The answers must be known so that organizational relationships can be identified both within the office itself and between the office and major organizational units of the enterprise. These relationships can be termed (1) intradepartmental— among the activities making up the office, and (2) interdepartmental— among the office and other major organizational units of the enterprise. The interdepartmental viewpoint is especially helpful because it emphasizes the facilitating and service aspects of office work.

Actually, to designate an organizational unit as "the office" can be confusing, for it is likely neither to be in one location nor to include all office activities. To reiterate, office work is not an activity in and of itself; it is a part of and employed in almost every function. Office work contributes information needed in performing the major functions of production, sales, finance, personnel, and other functions, such as engineering, research, and purchasing, which are necessary in a particular organization.

Logically, from the organizing point of view, the required office work should be located where it can be performed at lowest cost, assist best in achieving the stated objectives, and supply the highest service to those using it. This is determined by giving consideration to a number of factors, of which the following are important:

1. *Type and nature of the enterprise.* The content and the placement of the office function are affected greatly by the dominance of the production, sales, finance, or personnel activities. If the enterprise is primarily one for production—a large manufacturer, for example, selling its entire output to several large buyers—the office unit probably will be of relatively small importance. However, in a predominantly financial

enterprise, the work will be of relatively great importance. To illustrate, in a bank or insurance company, office work is usually of much greater importance than it is in a manufacturing company. Likewise, in a governmental enterprise, the office unit normally occupies a position relatively high in the organizational structure.

2. *Importance attached to office work.* If top managers of an enterprise recognize the work of the office as of relatively high significance, the tendency will probably be to bring it together into one organizational unit and place this unit high in the organizational structure. But if office work is considered minor, although necessary, it probably will be performed by the department needing it and coordinated as completely as possible with the primary activities of the respective department.

3. *Degree of office mechanization used.* Up to a certain level, the adoption of office machines has small effect upon the organization structure. But when machines capable of processing huge quantities of work or of performing work historically handled by several departments are adopted, the result organizationwise is to consolidate the work, shrink the department, combine departments, and change the organizational framework. This can readily be seen in the case of computers and their impact upon office organizing. Significant changes take place likewise when source data automation (SDA) is adopted, and also to some degree when high-speed accounting machines, punched-card machines, automatic typewriters, and duplicating machines are installed.

4. *Extent of centralization of office functions.* Since office work occurs throughout the entire enterprise, from the president's office to the lowest-paid clerk, it is possible to have it performed in dispersed locations, under the jurisdiction of the unit in which it arises. When this practice is followed, the office function is dispersed and either combined with, or made subordinate to, other organizational units. In its fullest application, this dispersion extends to the smallest and lowest organizational unit of the enterprise. In contrast, a directly opposite arrangement might be used. In this case, the office work is fully concentrated and is placed in the hands of a single executive who is completely responsible for all office activities in the organization.

These two conditions, however, are extreme. From a practical viewpoint, seldom is either used. An intermediate or modified arrangement between these two extremes is commonly followed:

1. Office work is located and performed by major departments, and each department head is fully responsible for the office activities in his own department.

2. Office work is distributed among all departments, but one person is placed in charge of this office work in order to achieve reasonable coordination.

3. Certain office work is centralized in one unit and placed under one

manager. The remaining office work is performed in the unit in which it arises and is supervised by the regular department head of that unit. This arrangement is quite popular. It is interpreted in different arrangements, and the more common of these are discussed in the following paragraphs.

## THE OFFICE SERVICES ARRANGEMENT

As pointed out and discussed in Part 2, so-called office services, including corresponding, report writing, mail and office communicating services, duplicating, calculating, filing, and records retention, are frequently included in the office organizational unit and placed under the "office services manager" or in some cases the "office manager." However, all these services are not always centralized, the notable exceptions being corresponding, report writing, calculating, and filing. Furthermore, even when all these services are referred to as being centralized, they are only partially so—some of certain services being located in various units throughout the entire organization structure.

The adoption of an "office services" unit arrangement means that the manager in charge of office work has a dual managerial task. First, he should manage the services unit; and second, since office work is being performed in various other units in which it arises, he should counsel with the executives of these various units and help them accomplish their office work in the best manner. This second task is of paramount importance and in many respects establishes the true status of the office manager in any organization structure. Actually, it is identifying what office work is and demonstrating to other managers in the organization how best to accomplish this type of work, in essence providing the office work viewpoint to all managers of the enterprise. All use office work; hence, help in how to use it effectively constitutes a real service. Figure 26–1, top left illustration, shows graphically the office services arrangement.

## THE SYSTEMS AND PROCEDURES ARRANGEMENT

As recognition that the "systems approach" can increase office efficiency, many companies have established an organization unit to facilitate this particular viewpoint and effort.[1] The exact format, content, location, and authority of this organizational unit varies considerably from company to company. For our purposes here, it is identified as the "systems and procedures department"; but other common titles are systems department, procedures department, methods department, or business services department. Probably none of these titles identifies

---

[1] The systems approach is discussed in Chapter 9, pp. 197–205.

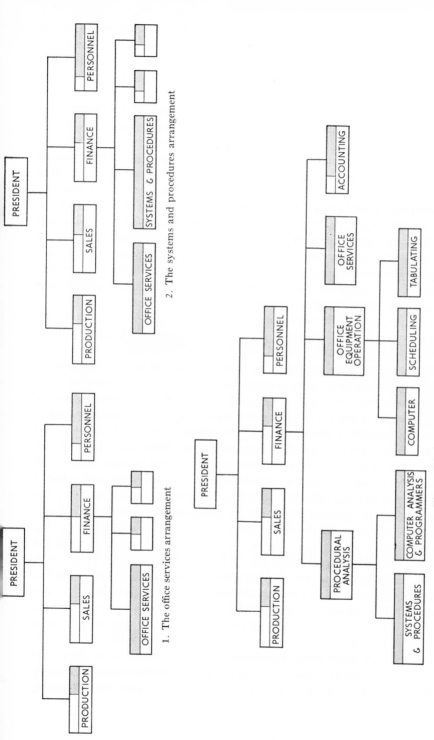

1. The office services arrangement

2. The systems and procedures arrangement

3. The modified systems and procedures arrangement

FIG. 26-1. Various organizing arrangements of office work with reference to the entire enterprise. The shaded areas approximate the relative amount of office work.

completely and clearly the work performed. For discussion purposes, we have assumed that this unit is subordinate to the major unit of finance. It is also common to subordinate it to the controller's office. Any or all of the following activities may be included in the systems and procedures unit: (1) office systems, procedures, and methods design and implementation—to determine and use the proper office operations, their best sequence, and the manner of performance to get the office work accomplished efficiently; (2) computer analysis and programming to operate the computer; (3) analysis of other office machines and equipment in order to advise what type of machine or equipment should be used for a specific type of office work under the prescribed conditions; (4) office layout and working conditions—to recommend the most effective arrangement of office facilities and the physical surroundings to supply; (5) office standards—to relate useful levels of performance or frames of reference in order to evaluate achievement; and (6) office work simplification—to point out ways to eliminate waste of all kinds and get the office work out more effectively. The systems and procedures arrangement is illustrated by the top right illustration of Figure 26–1.

## THE MODIFIED SYSTEMS AND PROCEDURES ARRANGEMENT

As computer usage has increased, some companies have adopted what might be termed a modified systems and procedures arrangement. Here the procedural analysis for systems and computer facilitation is separated from the implementation of the machines. Experience has shown that above certain levels or volumes of activity, the work of computer and other office machine scheduling and usage are best segregated from the design and analysis functions for these machines. The bottom illustration of Figure 26–1 shows this arrangement. Note that the procedural analysis section includes (1) *all* systems and procedures work throughout the company in one unit and (2) the work dealing with computer analysis and programming in another unit. The head of the procedural analysis section coordinates the activities of systems and procedures men and that of the computer analytical personnel. Also, observe that the computer analysts and programmers make up *one* unit in order to maintain close organizational ties between these related activities.[2]

## THE ADMINISTRATIVE SERVICES ORGANIZATIONAL ARRANGEMENT

Primarily because office automation has increased and especially as the strong trend toward computers has taken place, the organization of those supplying information has been modified to better meet current needs.

---

[2] See Chapter 9, p. 206.

The concept of an "administrative services" organizational unit on par with other major units of an enterprise has developed and is winning favor. This arrangement places most of the office work under a single administrator. The top illustration of Figure 26–2 shows the administrative services arrangement. For illustrative purposes only, the units under administrative services are shown as systems and procedures, machine operation, and office services. Observe that the efforts of designing how the work will be accomplished (systems and procedures) is segregated from that of implementation (machine operation). Also, that analyzing and programming essential for computer usage is concentrated in a separate unit from that of the efforts designing the means to be used for the paper work in general. Modern electronic machines make it feasible to handle a large part of the paper work of an enterprise in one organizational unit. However, even under the administrative services arrangement, some office work is performed in other major units, simply because it is easier, more convenient, and of greater service to perform some of the office work in these other units.

Having an administrative services unit is a departure from the initial and still widely used arrangement of having the office unit include the computer group and the entire unit under the finance or the controller major unit. The main reason for favoring the finance vice-president or the controller was that he could move with freedom across organizational lines, was already associated with office machines and procedures, and the work to be done by the computer—notably payroll, accounts payable, and accounts receivable—was already his responsibility. But as experience was gained and applications broadened, the automatic assignment of computer stewardship to the finance executive or controller was questioned. It was reasoned, and quite correctly, that the office organization should take into account:

1. *The objectives of the computer usage.* Is reduction of office cost or improvement of managerial information primary? Can a computer assist and take an increasing role in the overall management process of the enterprise?

2. *The scope of the applications.* The broader the range of applications, the stronger the reasons for a separate administrative services unit. For example, if the usage is broadened in scope from processing of routine data to sophisticated management decision making, the chances are that a separate unit will be the more effective organizational vehicle.

3. *The organizational strength of the finance executive or the controller.* It is readily apparent that the man in charge of an activity determines its contribution and importance. The manager should comprehend the tremendous contribution of better information, creating effective systems and procedures, and harnessing the huge potential of the computer. In addition, competence in working effectively with, and

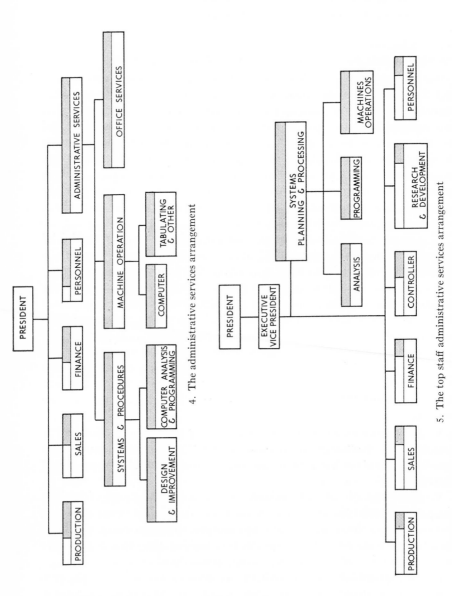

4. The administrative services arrangement

5. The top staff administrative services arrangement

FIG. 26–2. Two administrative services organizational arrangements each of which provide top recognition and status to office work efforts. The shaded areas approximate the relative amount of office work

securing action from, major executives and having the support and confidence of top management are essential. In many instances, the finance executive or the controller meets these requirements fully while in other instances there appears to be an inadequacy.

## THE TOP STAFF ADMINISTRATIVE SERVICES ARRANGEMENT

The bottom illustration of Figure 26–2 represents a simplified form of a large enterprise with an extensive informational services unit and large-scale electronic data processing. Responsibility for all this work is fixed in a department executive reporting directly to the executive vice-president. This department serves as a service group to all other departments including the vice-president of finance or the controller. Also, the department head has charge of small paper work staffs maintained by some of the major departments such as sales and research and development. These small staffs are not shown in the figure.

This arrangement permits company-wide coordination of all paper-work systems. It identifies informational activities with the top management and enhances the enlistment and support of department heads. The informational needs can be determined objectively without predisposition to a particular means or solution. Either manual, semimechanical, or complete computer application can be evolved and installed after all alternatives have been carefully evaluated. An avowed goal of this arrangement is to improve the quality of information made available to management members.

## CENTRALIZATION AND OFFICE ORGANIZING

"Centralization of office activities" means the physical concentration of such activities into a single group, with the management over them vested in one person. For example, in centralized filing, all filing work for an entire office is done by a filing section and managed by a filing chief. Centralization is concentration.

Actually, the concept of centralization can be considered from the viewpoint of (1) physical location or (2) management. This, in turn, permits four possibilities, namely, (1) physical location centralized and management centralized, (2) physical location not centralized and management centralized, (3) physical location not centralized and management not centralized, and (4) physical location centralized and management not centralized. Illustrations of these four possibilities, along with comments for each, are shown in Figure 26–3.

A key consideration in office organizing is the degree of office work centralization from the management viewpoint which is adopted. As already indicated, the degree of centralization of "office services" varies

POSSIBILITY 1

PHYSICAL LOCATION : CENTRALIZED
MANAGEMENT :          CENTRALIZED

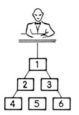

COMMENT : COMMON CONCEPT
OF CENTRALIZATION

POSSIBILITY 2

PHYSICAL LOCATION : NOT CENTRALIZED
MANAGEMENT :              CENTRALIZED

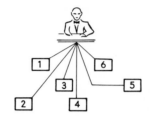

COMMENT : COMMON BUT SOMETIMES
NOT FULLY COMPREHENDED
AS A TYPE OF CENTRALIZATION

POSSIBILITY 3

PHYSICAL LOCATION : NOT CENTRALIZED
MANAGEMENT :          NOT CENTRALIZED

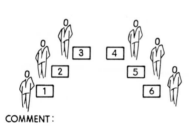

COMMENT :
SERIES OF INDIVIDUAL UNITS.
ACTUALLY NO CENTRALIZATION
CONCEPT EXISTS

POSSIBILITY 4

PHYSICAL LOCATION : CENTRALIZED
MANAGEMENT : NOT CENTRALIZED

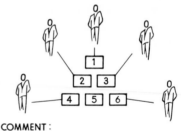

COMMENT :
RELATIVELY RARE CONCEPT OF
CENTRALIZATION - LITTLE USED

FIG. 26–3.   The four possibilities of centralization.

among different enterprises; by no means do all enterprises have a department akin to the systems and procedures department, and relatively few have some form of an administrative services department. Equipment analysis, for example, may be handled by the executive handling the particular function for which the equipment will be used; likewise, the executive of the operating department may have charge of standards applying to paper work in his unit. A computer may be located solely within one department such as research and development and this arrangement is satisfactory providing the single department has sufficient work to require the full time of the computer. The particular organizational pattern followed depends upon many factors, but the degree of centralization is vital and merits further comment.

## EVALUATION OF OFFICE CENTRALIZATION

The current trend appears to be toward centralization. Office automation, use of computers, consolidating fragmented clerical functions, and taking organizational measures to stop the spiraling of overhead costs are among the major reasons for this trend. A suggested approach to determine the feasibility of centralization of office work is discussed in Chapter 29.[3] Specifically, the advantages of office centralization include:

1. Flexibility is given the organization. Work peak loads can be readily handled, office machinery utilized fully, and the effects of labor shortages reduced to a minimum.

2. Equitable wage schedules are fostered. The measurement of office output is encouraged, and comparisons of wages for similar work are possible.

3. Training of office employees is expedited. New employees can be added to centralized groups without seriously affecting the operations of the group. The retraining of old employees for new jobs is also well adapted to a centralized type of organization.

4. Methods of office operation can be applied uniformly and quickly. Standards common to several organizational units can be established.

5. Cost of performing office work is decreased. Supervisory costs are lowered, the costs of investment and maintenance of machines are lowered, and the amount of floor space is frequently reduced.

6. Labor specialization is practiced. Employees become highly efficient and are continuously employed on work necessitating their highest individual skill and ability.

On the other hand, there are many who feel that better results are obtained from a noncentralized, or decentralized, organizational arrangement of the office work. To substantiate their view they point out that:

1. Much office work is confidential and should be handled by the unit in which this confidential trust is placed.

2. The work is performed by those who may not be familiar with the detailed requirements. Minor changes and corrections cannot be made on the spot.

3. Effective planning and controlling are difficult to exercise since the executives most familiar with the use and purpose of the paper work are not near at hand.

4. Work is done without regard for urgency or importance to the individual office unit. Delays may take place. The efficiency of each unit may be hampered.

---

[3] See pp. 637–38.

5. Costs may increase due to nonproductive transporting and handling time required.

6. Employees of a "generalist" nature are not developed. Some versatile persons with overall viewpoints are essential in all enterprises.

It should also be added that for a noncentralized office arrangement to provide satisfactory results, certain organizational requirements should be met. These include (1) a clear understanding and agreement among all management personnel of the office goals and the basic policies to be followed, (2) written statements covering office work decision making to be performed by nonoffice management members, (3) an effective reporting to the office manager of what decisions concerning paper work are being made by nonoffice management members, and (4) a follow-up and post-decision audit should be maintained. When such practices exist, sound decentralized decisions can be made and an effective organization maintained.

## THE OFFICE ACTIVITIES

For instructional purposes, it is helpful to enumerate the various office activities that can exist in an enterprise in order to afford a panorama of office work. As indicated above, the location and arrangement of office activities assume a variety of patterns and relations. The following is not intended to represent any particular office or serve as a specific recommendation.

The many and various office activities, segregated by six major divisions, include:

1. Office automation (deals with utilization of computer and of SDA, source data automation).
   1.1 Computer analysis and programming.
   1.2 Operation of computer.
   1.3 Determination and application of SDA.
   1.4 Filing and storage of media—punched cards, punched tape, magnetic tape, and so forth.
2. Office services (includes activities commonly thought of in reference to office work).
   2.1 Correspondence and office reports.
       2.11 Stenographic and typing work.
       2.12 Billing.
   2.2 Communicating services.
       2.21 Mail and messenger services.
       2.22 Telephone and telegraph.
   2.3 Calculating.
       2.31 Data for reports.

    2.32 Statistical data.

  2.4 Filing.

  2.5 Records retention.

3. Office planning (encompasses activities dealing with what office work will be performed, when, where, and how).

  3.1 Determination of objectives, policies, systems, procedures, and methods.

    3.11 Routines and flow of office work.

    3.12 Design and use of office forms.

  3.2 Use of office machines and equipment.

  3.3 Research.

4. Physical facilities of the office (consist of activities pertaining to the securing, using, and maintaining of physical factors needed for performing office work).

  4.1 Location and arrangements.

    4.11 Office layouts.

    4.12 Office lighting, ventilating, and noise control.

  4.2 Purchasing.

    4.21 Office machines.

    4.22 Office furniture and equipment.

      4.221 Desks, chairs, and filing cabinets.

    4.23 Office forms and supplies.

      4.231 Storage and issuance of same.

5. Office controlling (consists of activities of work measurement and comparison to see that office work is performed as planned).

  5.1 Operational analysis.

    5.11 Office standards.

      5.111 Office systems, procedures, and methods.

      5.112 Office forms.

      5.113 Office machines, furniture, and equipment.

    5.12 Office work simplification.

    5.13 Office work measurement.

    5.14 Office manuals.

  5.2 Work and cost control.

    5.21 Routing and scheduling.

    5.22 Peak work load handling.

    5.23 Cost analysis and office budgets.

6. Office personnel (includes employee motivation and relationships with fellow employees, with the job, and with the public of the enterprise).

  6.1 Office employment.

    6.11 Recruitment, selection, and placement.

      6.111 Interviews, tests, and references.

    6.12 Transfers, promotions, and terminations.

6.2 Salary administration.
>    6.21 Job description and evaluation.
>    6.22 Job performance rating.
6.3 Office training.
6.4 Welfare.
>    6.41 Grievances.
>    6.42 Suggestion system.
>    6.43 Office safety.
>    6.44 Office employee benefits—pensions and hospital insurance.

## QUESTIONS

1. Explain why organizing enables a manager to enlarge his scope of operations.
2. If specialization helps in getting work accomplished, should not all office work in an enterprise be performed in a centralized location and under the management of one head? Justify your answer.
3. Identify each of the following:
   a) Work division as an essential of organizing.
   b) Organizing.
   c) Organization unit.
   d) The administrative services arrangement of office organization.
4. What relationship, if any, exists between managerial objectives and organizing? Discuss the significance of your answers in the study of office management.
5. Do you agree with the statement, "Organizing is the work of setting up a hierachy of managers and determining who supervises whom and what unit does what thing or things"? Explain your answer.
6. Discuss Figure 26–2 in your own words, pointing out what you consider the chief points of interest from the viewpoint of organizing.
7. Elaborate on the statement, "No organizational unit should be designated as 'the office.' Such a statement is both incorrect and confusing."
8. Discuss the relation of the office to the organization of a large company. Is this relationship important in office organizing? Why?
9. Briefly discuss what in your opinion are the four most important advantages of centralization. Of decentralization.
10. Relate where you believe the computer should be located organization-wise in a medium-sized manufacturing company. Justify your answer.
11. Justify your answer to each of the following:
    a) Does centralization give flexibility to an organization structure?
    b) Do organizing and organization structure have essentially the same meaning?
    c) Does the concept of centralization in organizing always mean from the viewpoint of management?
    d) Is coordination the main purpose of organizing?
12. Discuss the meaning of the term "centralization" as used in managerial organizing.

## CASE PROBLEMS

### Case 26–1.   Harper and Reeves, Inc.

The corporation maintains three offices, one for each of its three separate manufacturing plants in Chicago, Boston, and Oklahoma City. All consolidated reports of the corporation's activities are prepared in the Chicago office, which is considered the main office. Six months ago, new machines were installed in the Chicago office and just ten days ago it was announced that most accounting as well as all statistical tabulating work used primarily for forecasting and sales purposes now performed in Boston and Oklahoma City were to be moved to the Chicago office. The move would start in 30 days and require approximately 40 days to be consummated.

This change gives rise to organizational problems. In the Chicago statistical tabulating unit, for example, there were initially six employees, and the supervisor Paul Isham directed the group informally and kept a close personal touch with all the employees and their work. With rapid increase in sales and a demand for more precise data, Mr. Isham's unit has grown to ten employees during the last 120 days. Now with the centralization of statistical tabulating services in Chicago, Mr. Isham's unit is expected to acquire an additional 12 employees, one of whom is the former supervisor of the Oklahoma City statistical tabulating unit. The office manager is concerned about providing adequate supervision so that the new tab summaries and reports are correctly and promptly prepared and that the old established work is continued satisfactorily in the future as it has been in the past.

### Problems:

1. What are some major alternatives open to the corporation?

2. What organizational arrangement do you recommend for the Chicago statistical tabulating unit?

3. Evaluate this recommended organization unit, discussing important advantages as well as disadvantages.

### Case 26–2.   Wrightwood Manufacturing Company

Eugene Beesley, aged 36 years, an industrial engineer, came to the Wrightwood Manufacturing Company about two years ago. He was assigned to the industrial engineering department of the manufacturing division. His work record showed him to be a highly competent and qualified man, and the company felt very fortunate in acquiring his services. During the first few months with the company, he handled several projects admirably well; and when the office requested an engineer to assist in some office work measurement, Beesley was given the assignment. Soon he became extremely interested in office work and the possibilities it offered for improvement. To his way of thinking, "the paper mill" offered tremendous opportunities. He worked diligently and established many standards.

Nearly a year ago, the office manager quit to move south on account of his wife's health. Beesley's dynamic qualities and eagerness, together with his competency, suggested to the company's vice-president of general services that he was the man for the office manager's job. Discussing the proposition with several of his colleagues and finding no opposition, the vice-president offered the office manager's job to Beesley, who accepted.

He was elated at the prospect. Within his first two months on the new job, he submitted a new coordinated plan for office operations which would save the company a considerable sum. His office supervisors believed the plan excellent and supported him. Beesley held many conferences with several top executives, including the vice-president of general services, the vice-president of sales, and the vice-president of finance. He also talked with various groups in each of several units. Beesley believed he should talk to these various personnel of the company because many of his proposed changes in paper work would affect them.

After six months of trying to make headway with the office improvement program, Mr. Beesley began to feel that he was not getting anywhere. His superior, the vice-president of general services, kept giving him special work to do, which work Beesley classified as strictly "busy" work and of no real importance. One job was an investigation of the reception service; another, of the trend in the number of items included on a typical order received by the company. Also, at the suggestion of the president of the company, Beesley visited several large offices using computers and also spent several days each with two different computer manufacturers. Reporting back to the president on the results of these visits, Beesley's impression was that the president had little interest in the visits and would rather not hear about them.

Another three months passed, and things continued about the same. Beesley kept busy on special assignments which he believed were whims of the company's top executives. He felt that he was achieving nothing that could not be accomplished by reports from company people in the various units affected. He arranged an interview with his superior and challenged the situation. He received a vague response. Thinking over the situation for several days, Beesley decided to quit and tendered his resignation.

## Problems:

1. Should the company accept Beesley's resignation? Why?
2. What do you think the real problem is in this case? Explain.
3. What action should be taken, and by whom? Discuss.

# CHAPTER 27

# OFFICE ORGANIZING—
# WORK DIVISION AND PEOPLE

*The talent of success is nothing more than
doing what you can do well; and doing well
whatever you do, without a thought of fame.*
*—Henry Wadsworth Longfellow*

IT IS implied in the previous chapter that for organizing to take place,
work is divided, forming clusters of tasks, and people are assigned to
these tasks. The resulting "work division–people assigned" segments
provide the nuclei of organization units. How to divide the work and the
important considerations in assigning people to vitalize the organization
are discussed in this chapter. We start with work division because, in the
great majority of cases, this is the superior approach. A manager must
coordinate what is done, not who is doing it. Also, the work is relatively
permanent, it changes less frequently than the interests and abilities of
personnel. Furthermore, to formulate organization units primarily on the
basis of personnel often results in unusual combinations of duties that are
difficult to manage and for which the securing of replacements is arduous.
However, the "people–work" division approach is used and in some
instances with outstanding success.

## WORK DIVISION

There are many different means for dividing the work in office
organizing, including (1) by function, (2) by process, (3) by customer,
(4) by product, (5) by territory, and (6) by project. An organizer can use

any means he desires, and commonly several means are employed in the same organization structure. What best helps to achieve the objective should be used. In a bank, for example, for the top levels, functions may be used; whereas the loan department may be divided by customer—loans to manufacturers of plastics, chemicals, and paper; loans to manufacturers of food processors and package machines; or by product—commercial loans or personal loans. Office work division by territory is common for offices designed to serve sales organizations. The territory divisions constitute the main segments of the sales organizational structure, and the offices serving such organizations are likewise segregated and located throughout the country. Work division by project in office organization has been used very little as of now. It utilizes the idea of work division being a project or a major and complete program. Assigned to a project is a complete team which is permitted to work on the project assigned until either successful completion or an authorized termination is ordered, at which time the team is disbanded and new projects are activated with newly formed teams believed appropriate for the new work involved. Large research development agencies of government are using project organization with great success. In the future it may become an important segment of office organizing.

The most common means of departmentation is by function, which can be defined as *the normal or characteristic operation of an activity*. Filing, for example, is a function in that it is an activity which always has characteristic identities, and these identities are usually considered the proper action of filing. In management, it is common to speak of "functions," such as the function of producing, the function of selling, and the function of financing. For example, the function of producing means the normal or characteristic operation of producing goods or services. In turn, any function covering a broad scope of action such as producing can be broken up into component functions of a relatively limited scope. For producing, these component functions may include the function of designing, the function of plant layout, the function of fabricating, the function of assembling, the function of inspection, the function of production control, and the function of purchasing.

The same function may be performed by two or more people and likewise, the same person may perform two or more functions. Illustrative of the former is a group of clerks all doing the same work, for example, checking billings in a department. The latter case is illustrated by the receptionist who greets and directs visitors, opens and sorts the mail, and types letters.

## EXISTENT DIVISION OF WORK

For an existent organization, data on the current work divisions as well as who performs the different tasks can be surveyed and recorded on a work distribution chart. Basically this is a spread sheet which shows, for a given time period—usually a week—the type of work and the time spent on each job by each employee in the office organization unit under review. The basic information can be obtained from the supervisor or the employees. Probably more objective data are obtained by observing each employee and recording information on his activities. However, this approach is relatively expensive.

Figure 27–1 shows a work distribution chart. A vertical column is used for each employee, along with one to indicate the time spent on each activity. The functions performed are listed in the first column on the left. This chart gives a graphic, overall picture of the work done and the work divisions in effect. In addition, it reveals the relative amounts of time put

| OFFICE FUNCTIONS | TOTAL MAN HOURS | LOIS MILLER Unit Supervisor | MAN HOURS | BETTY HEIDT Stenographer | MAN HOURS | RUTH TORFF Order Clerk | MAN HOURS | EDITH WRIGHT File Clerk | MAN HOURS | SYLVIA GAZEL Telephone Switchboard Operator | MAN HOURS |
|---|---|---|---|---|---|---|---|---|---|---|---|
| Correspondence | 54 | Read and route Dictation | 9 / 10 | Takes dictation Transcribes | 10 / 20 | Types labels and materials for files | 5 | | | | |
| Computing | 32 | Figures prices | 3 | Figures prices | 2 | Figures prices | 15 | Figures prices | 12 | | |
| Filing | 21 | | | | | Files correspondence Finds letters in file | 2 / 5 | Files correspondence Finds letters in file Classifies correspondence | 4 / 6 / 4 | | |
| Handling mail | 26 | Opens mail Time stamps mail | 2 / 5 | Stamps mail | 2 | Opens mail | 5 | Stamps mail | 4 | Opens mail Stamps mail | 3 / 5 |
| Miscellaneous | 67 | Answers questions Answers telephone inquiries Supervises | 8 / 2 / 1 | Cleans typewriter Gets supplies Arranges advertising stuffing material | 1 / 2 / 3 | Answers telephone inquiries | 2 | Errands for postage stamps and supplies Maintains tickler file for follow-ups | 8 / 8 | Operate switchboard | 2 / 32 |
| | 200 | | 40 | | 40 | | 40 | | 40 | | 40 |

FIG. 27–1. Work distribution chart.

on each office function and the extent of work division. From the "people assigned" viewpoint, the chart shows what skills are required, whether special skills are being wasted, whether too many employees are performing the same function, and whether an employee is doing too many unrelated tasks.

## INDIVIDUAL JOB CONTENT

From the organizing viewpoint, individual job content is the contribution to the objective made by the individual performing the particular job. The activities assigned or the individual job content can be viewed as what the employee is required to perform because of the organizational position and relationship occupied in the organization structure.

Effective organizing requires that each employee have definite tasks that he understands, can perform, and that encourage his personal development. When these requirements are met and the necessary physical facilities and adequate supervision are provided, the individual is in an ideal work situation where real accomplishments are possible.

The division of work to be done must be carried out to the individual job level. That is, the department functions must be divided ultimately into jobs for each individual. Unless this is done, the managerial work of organizing is incomplete, and the group of people connected with the enterprise cannot perform as a whole or contribute with a unity of action.

## JOB SPECIALIZATION

All organizing requires some specialization. Most managers agree that no one person can do everything equally well. The need for allocating total work and capitalizing upon what a person can perform best have resulted in job specialization. Complex work is divided into relatively simple components, each accomplished effectively by employees specializing in that single operation or in a group of similar operations. The question is not whether to have job specialization but to what extent job specialization should be carried. In organizing, the office manager must decide this question as exemplified by determining the work makeup of each organizational unit and what is done by each member of that unit. Too many and too varied tasks for one employee are generally avoided. On the other hand, a job of very limited scope is not used, presumably to minimize the problem of monotony and lack of employee interest in his work.

In some enterprises, where the office organizing has utilized job specialization to a great degree, provisions such as job rotation, "music while you work," rest periods, and keeping the employee informed of all major enterprise operations have been adopted to maintain high morale and to make the organizational structure effective. For the most part, the degree of specialization has not been questioned. However, in some companies, an attempt to broaden the job scope has been advanced. This is commonly referred to as *job enlargement*. These efforts have given surprising results, such as reduced office costs, improved quality of work, better teamwork, and lower absenteeism. These results, which must be interpreted carefully, indicate that there are both economic and social limits to job specialization. The degree and form of job specialization to follow presumably depend upon the type of office work and the individual doing it. More specific information is needed to derive definite recommendations, but it appears that the prevalent ideas concerning job specialization should be modified.

## WORK DIVISION ARRANGEMENTS

Generally speaking, work divisions for the top level of an organizational structure are made on the basis of functions. Divisions for the intermediate levels usually are either by type of product, by customer, or by territory. Common at the lower office organizational levels are work divisions by any of these three arrangements: (1) serial, (2) parallel, and (3) unit assembly. Work division by product, customer, or territory is self-explanatory; but further discussion of the serial, parallel, and unit assembly is warranted.

In the serial arrangement, the work division is extended to a series of small tasks, each task being performed by a specialist in that particular type of work. Moving progressively from task to task, the work advances until completed. The serial arrangement is the same basic plan as the familiar factory assembly line, commonly found in production plants. In some quarters, the term "production line basis" is used to describe the serial arrangement in the office. "Consecutive handling" adequately describes this arrangement.

The parallel arrangement permits a series of needed and separate tasks to be performed by one individual or a work team. The employee or employees, as the case might be, do not specialize in performing one task but gain proficiency in accomplishing several tasks. Frequently, the tasks are related, but this is not necessary. To implement the parallel arrangement, the total work is divided into two or more major parts, and each part is assigned to an employee or group of employees. The basis for dividing the work into parts can be any of many factors, for example, by letter of the alphabet, number, territory, type of merchandise, or major subject. From the individual's viewpoint, the scope of the work is relatively large under the parallel arrangement. The term "concurrent handling" can be used to identify this arrangement.

The unit assembly arrangement provides for different employees to perform different work steps upon the same work items at the same time. It can be termed "simultaneous handling." Each step is done by a specialist in his particular type of work. Coordination of the various tasks is a prime requirement under this arrangement, for the separate tasks usually do not require identical times to perform. The unit assembly arrangement can be thought of as a cross-blending between the serial and the parallel arrangement.

Figure 27–2 shows these three basic arrangements in graphic form. The work considered pertains to the handling of customers' orders and consists of three separate operations, including (1) credit approval, (2) inventory check, and (3) pricing. Assume a work force of three employees, Nancy Brown, Sharon Hewitt, and Virginia Walker. The serial arrangement is shown at the top of the figure. For simplicity, each separate operation has been considered a separate task, and one employee has been assigned to each task. In contrast, the parallel arrangement is shown at the center of Figure 27–2. In this illustration, the total customer order-handling work has been divided into three parts that parallel each other. Each part consists of all three separate tasks of the work, that is, credit approval,

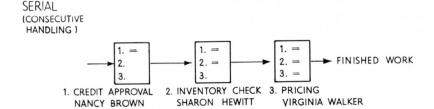

SERIAL
(CONSECUTIVE
HANDLING )

1. CREDIT APPROVAL    2. INVENTORY CHECK    3. PRICING
NANCY BROWN            SHARON HEWITT          VIRGINIA WALKER

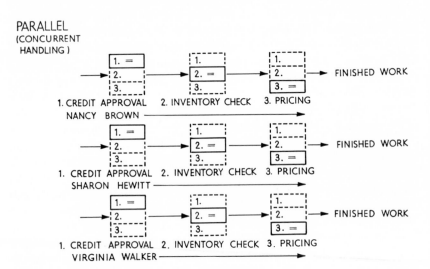

PARALLEL
(CONCURRENT
HANDLING )

1. CREDIT APPROVAL    2. INVENTORY CHECK    3. PRICING
NANCY BROWN

1. CREDIT APPROVAL    2. INVENTORY CHECK    3. PRICING
SHARON HEWITT

1. CREDIT APPROVAL    2. INVENTORY CHECK    3. PRICING
VIRGINIA WALKER

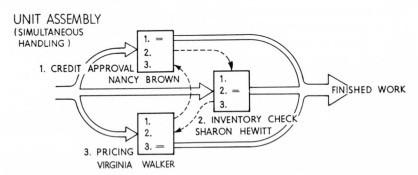

UNIT ASSEMBLY
(SIMULTANEOUS
HANDLING )

1. CREDIT APPROVAL
NANCY BROWN

2. INVENTORY CHECK
SHARON HEWITT

3. PRICING
VIRGINIA WALKER

FIG. 27–2.  Illustrating the serial, parallel, and unit assembly arrangements of work division.

inventory check, and pricing. As illustrated, employee Nancy Brown performs all three tasks or operations, and so do each of the other two employees, Sharon Hewitt and Virginia Walker. The bottom illustration of Figure 27–2 shows the unit assembly arrangement. Here, specialization is practiced by each employee, but the work sequence is not identical for each item. Nancy Brown performs credit approval; while at the same time, Sharon Hewitt performs inventory check, and Virginia Walker does pricing.

## WHAT ARRANGEMENT TO USE

Like many other practices, the question of whether to use the serial, parallel, or unit assembly arrangement cannot be fully answered by a "Yes" or "No." Normally, for any given office, the tendency is toward the prevalence of one, but seldom will it be used exclusively. Individual circumstances govern, with consideration given to cost, employees' interest in their jobs, quality of work, preferences of managers and employees, and the overall objectives.

More specifically, the serial arrangement of work division requires a sufficient work quantity of a particular type to keep an employee fully occupied in its performance. Quantity and specialization are close "buddies." Also, mechanization tends toward a serial arrangement. Most office machines handle a large volume of work, and their cost usually requires a high percentage of utilization throughout the workday. In some instances, the job content is so complex and the tasks so heterogeneous that some breakdown in the work is necessary to acquire and maintain employees for the work. When this is the case, the serial arrangement is usually followed. In addition, some office work, if performed by one employee, would incur a sizable loss of time in shifting from one operator to another. For example, a job consisting of typing, then calculating, followed by checking and resumption of typing, may show low efficiency. Selecting the serial plan frequently follows when the skill needed is of a special type, due to scarcity or the amount of training that can economically be provided. It is usually not feasible to dilute the efforts of the employee possessing a needed skill in a specialty. An expert in operating punched-card equipment should not type and file letters as a part of her regular job duties. Another condition normally suggesting the adoption of the serial arrangement is when great uniformity in handling certain portions of the office work is required. The signing of checks and bank drafts can be cited as an illustration.

In contrast, the parallel arrangement is usually followed when better work performance appears to be associated with a complete understanding and handling of the particular subject matter. An overcharge in a billing to a complaining customer might best be handled in its entirety by one employee. Furthermore, when the "start to finish" period for the work performance must be reduced, the parallel arrangement may be superior. Under this pattern, delay in work processing, or loss in time by papers traveling from operation to operation, is avoided. Less handling and idle time generally result when the papers are processed by employees working under a parallel arrangement. In some cases, by keeping the division of work too small, an employee is deprived of helpful overall checks in the work. When this situation exists, the parallel arrangement automatically provides the solution. It should also be observed that with parallel groups performing similar cycles of work, it is possible to hold contests, compare work accomplishments of each group, and inject other competitive devices in managing the work. Such measures help stimulate high productivity. In addition, the parallel arrangement helps to eliminate duplication of efforts such as reading and checking if such is present when high specialization is followed. Under the parallel pattern, one employee familiarizes herself with the contents of the paper by a single reading and a single checking. Finally, the parallel arrangement is suggested where the circumstances indicate that greater interest and enthusiasm by employees probably will be gained from having a greater variety of work in the job makeup.

The unit assembly arrangement permits work to start at an operation other than the first in the sequence of tasks. This makes it possible to start processing the work simultaneously at different operational stages. In other words, the performance of work operation No. 3 need not wait until No. 1 and No. 2 are completed. In certain situations, this is a definite advantage. Furthermore, flexibility in machine utilization and in work scheduling are provided. Usually, completed work is obtained more rapidly under the unit assembly arrangement; for this reason, it is employed for special rush and emergency work. Specialization is practiced to a great degree under this arrangement; but as stated above, sometimes the coordination of the individual work processing poses a difficult problem.

## JOB ANALYSIS

Job analysis is a formal means of determining the job content. It can be defined as follows: *Job analysis is the process of critically examining the components of a job, both separately and in relation to the whole, in order to determine all the operations and duties.* In short, job analysis deals with facts about jobs and what is required for competent performance. Typical of data included are the forms and materials handled, the equipment and machines used, the methods utilized, the frequency of the operations, the amounts and kinds of skill required, and the degree of concentration needed. Such information is extremely useful in management because (1) the scope of the job becomes definite, (2) the identity becomes fixed, and (3) definite association between job title and content is established.

Job analysis is customarily and quite correctly thought of as an activity logically a part of personnel activities because it is basic in the performance of many personnel department functions. For example, job analysis is the basis for determining the relative worth, compensation-wise, of jobs; it facilitates hiring and placing, can be used for formulating training needs, and serves to identify promotions and transfers. These are truly personnel functions in character and are discussed in Part 7 of this book. However, inasmuch as job analysis does identify the job and its content, it is included in this discussion dealing with organizing. As already pointed out, really effective and complete organizing work requires specific work divisions at the individual level. Job analysis helps supply this requirement.

## OBTAINING JOB ANALYSIS DATA

In the case of new work or a new organizational unit, the manager doing the organizing must decide the characteristics of the newly created job or jobs. In a going office, however, three methods of securing job analysis data are possible: (1) interview and observation, (2) conferences, and (3) questionnaires. For the first method, the analyst goes to the employee, asks questions about the job, and observes what the content of the job is. While this method is satisfactory for office jobs, it is probably most popular for factory jobs. In the second method, the employee is called into conference and verbally describes his job to the analyst, who records the information. This method usually requires more time than the others, takes the employee from his job, and may interfere with the work routine. In the third method, a questionnaire is sent to the employee, who fills in the information. This method is used in cases where the employees can intelligently handle clerical details and are more or less accustomed to paper work. It is commonly used for most office work. The federal government has employed this procedure successfully for over 50 years. Frequently the questionnaires are supplemented with short observations and interviews, especially for the more important jobs.

Whatever method is adopted, it is advisable to secure within practical limits as much information as possible about each job. It is usually better to have too much than too little data. Commonly the data are recorded on a prepared form, called a job analysis report. This form serves as a reminder to answer definite questions and thereby secure all the needed facts, so that no part of the job is overlooked. It also expedites recording the data in a standardized manner, thus making it easier to handle and interpret the information. Figure 27–3 shows a portion of a job analysis form.

## JOB DESCRIPTION

The information on the job analysis form actually describes the job. However, when this information is written in a more descriptive style, the

JOB ANALYSIS

Present title of job ———————— Department ————————
1. What is the general purpose of this job?
2. What duties are performed in the *usual* course of the work? (Tell from where work is received, what is done with it, and where it is sent.)
3. What duties are performed only at stated intervals? (Give answers by daily, weekly, monthly, etc.)
4. In what organizational unit is this job presently located?
5. Does the job entail supervising other employees? (Explain.)
6. If there are any special training courses essential in order to perform the duties of this job satisfactorily, name them.
7. What past experience is *necessary* for a new employee to have in order to perform the duties of this job?
8. What are the *most* difficult parts of this job?
9. What are the *least* difficult parts of this job?
10. About what proportions of this job require sitting, ———%; standing, ———%; moving about, ———%?
11. What machines or other equipment are operated?
    Regularly:
    Occasionally:

FIG. 27–3.  Portion of questionnaire used for job analysis.

term "job description" is frequently used. While the format used for writing these descriptions varies, they usually contain a summary of the job, the work performed, and the qualifications generally considered essential. (See Figure 27–4.)

Job descriptions are useful in the work of organizing. The duties and the lines of authority, if any, are clearly set forth. Job descriptions also help bring about better understanding within an enterprise because they point out the qualifications required of an employee on the particular job, help in selecting persons best fitted for the requirements of the job, and assist in acquainting the new employee with his job.

Current practice tends to use the terms "job description," "job statement," and "job title" to identify progressively contracting descriptions of the job. A job statement is used to furnish a quick picture of the job. To illustrate, in Figure 27–5, the job content of "programming manager" is condensed to a single paragraph. A job title is simply a common name for a job. However, job titles are commonly inadequate to identify a job satisfactorily. For example, the title "secretary" is used to identify jobs of different makeup, as illustrated by the two job statements in Figure 27–6. *The title plus the job content are necessary for accurate identification.* This is important in office organizing where work division and organizational unit creation must be decided.

# JOB DESCRIPTION

DATE_____

JOB TITLE__ _JUNIOR ACCOUNTANT_____ _GRADE_VI____CODE_____

SUMMARY:                Under general direction of Comptroller and immediate
                        supervision of Accountant, performs general accounting
                        duties and prepares special reports as assigned.

WORK PERFORMED:   Maintains records of cash receipts and/or disbursements,
                        posts related subsidiary records. Posts various journal
                        entries and adjustments, maintains record of Supply
                        Department receipts and prepares minor financial statements.

                        Handles correspondence, verifies tabulations and reconciles
                        bank statement. Assists in distributing work to temporary
                        help, prepares monthly reports and special statements.
                        Performs related work, such as figuring per capita and
                        expense ratios. Operates office machines as required.

                        May supervise work of accounting clerks, typists for
                        temporary periods, etc. and performs similar duties as
                        assigned.

QUALIFICATIONS:   Normally requires three to five years' training and
                        experience, including two years' general accounting train-
                        ing plus three years' company accounting experience as
                        an Accounting Clerk.

*Courtesy: J. D. Moore Organization, Park Ridge, Ill.*

FIG. 27–4.  A job description written in an effective form.

## IMPORTANCE OF PEOPLE IN ORGANIZING

As stated in the beginning of this chapter, organizing can logically start with work division, and the divisions created serve as focal areas for organizational units. In turn, the work within each organizational unit must be accomplished, directly or indirectly, by people. Up to this point, attention has been directed to the work aspect of organizing; but equally important, and in the opinion of many of greater importance, is the "people aspect" of organizing. In fact, it would be difficult to overemphasize the importance of people in organizing.

Successful organizing helps provide the means for getting effective results through people's efforts. It provides for the adequate development and placement of people. While work division and assignment are

*Programming Manager:* Reports to director of procedural analysis. Supervises administrative assistant programmer. Is responsible for planning and organizing all programming activities for the computer; maintaining essential records of the programming department; directing, motivating, and evaluating personnel; and participating in the planning of computer usage.

FIG. 27–5.   Job statement of programming manager.

important, they are not the end objective in organizing. The main goal is to make it possible for a group of people, called employees, to work cooperatively and efficiently. The total work is segregated by functions so that each individual of the work group can perform a portion of the total work in the best possible manner. The expression "Organization is people" is trite; nevertheless, it stresses the importance of people in the work of organizing. It brings out the basic idea that people constitute the center about which revolve the organizational concepts of the work to be done, the authority, and the work environment.

In the final analysis, the organization structure is a tool—it provides the grouping of specific activities and of people for the purpose of applying management. Work is accomplished by people or machines operated by people. Organizing does not accomplish any work objective; it must be implemented with people. Hence, one of the biggest jobs of a manager is to form or maintain an organization structure which permits the proper placement and the development of employees. Some claim that almost any organization structure will prove satisfactory as long as the right people are operating it. Others lay great stress on the proper division of work and relationships. No doubt, both are important. However, the point here is that people are vital in organizing; they can make or break any organization structure.

*Secretary:* Takes dictation, using shorthand, and transcribes the dictated material into a neat typed format; makes appointments for executive and reminds him of them; answers and makes telephone calls; handles personal and important mail; writes routine correspondence on own initiative; maintains executive's files.

*Secretary:* Takes dictation, using either shorthand or a machine; transcribes dictation from either shorthand notes or a machine; interviews people coming into the office, directing to other employees those who do not warrant seeing the executive; answers and makes telephone calls.

FIG. 27–6.   Job titles may be identical, but the respective job statements may differ.

It follows, therefore, that a sound organization structure is necessary for effective employee performance. This is true because organizing deals with and sets forth such basic issues as what is to be done and by whom, and who decides what. This view of organizing has been compared to that of writing the story for a motion-picture film. It sets the stage and predetermines what is to take place. How well it takes place, i.e., the quality of the motion picture, depends in great measure upon the actors—the personnel element.

Personnel has a decidedly marked effect upon the structure of an organization. When, for example, the ratio of skilled to unskilled employees is high, the pattern of the organizational structure might be far different from that for one where the ratio is low. The reason for this, in part, is the relative importance of supervision and the placement of different functions at different levels in the two structures.

Organizing affects and is affected by the human side of group activities. The sought-for coordination among different activities is more correctly stated as the coordination among *the employees* performing the different activities. After all, the work is divided so that it can be accomplished by the group. How effectively the various members of the group work together as a team toward achieving the objective is the paramount consideration.

## MANAGER'S ATTITUDE AND ORGANIZING

Organizing reflects a manager's attitude and thinking in that it reveals the understanding of a manager for the essentiality of the human element and how this resource is to be regarded. Just allocating the work, assigning employees to neatly conceived endeavors, and granting carefully defined authority to selected persons is insufficient. The people assigned to certain tasks and the creation of certain working relation among themselves must be handled with great care. There is genuine skill in having logical work divisions tie in respectively with an adequate consideration for who is to do each respective component of work.

An office manager implements regard for the human element in his organizing work by recognizing and appreciating the value, as well as the limitations, of his employees. This is not a one-shot proposition but a continuing, ever searching effort to keep up to date on how the employees available to him can best be brought together to work toward a common goal. The supervisor in charge of the mail room, for example, reflects from the human-element viewpoint the office manager's thinking, organization-wise, of the supervisor's value, including his strong and weak points for his particular supervisory job. The job content, a result of work division, is presumably what the office manager thinks it ought to be; likewise, the authority granted is what the office manager thinks it ought to be—all or at least a big portion of it is with reference to the office manager's human-element evaluation of the supervisor. In this sense, it is sometimes said that an organization structure reflects the shadow of its manager. However, it appears more appropriate to state that an organization structure *reflects the light or understanding* of its manager.

Concentration on men's strengths pays organizational dividends. A manager holding firm convictions about an employee's abilities to perform the work competently tends to instill confidence in the employee and develops his will to do successful work. At the same time, the manager must realize that not all men can do all things. To assume otherwise can lead to disaster in his organizing. Yet, by proper managerial motivation, leadership, and lifting a man's vision to higher planes, the common man can be stimulated to achieve uncommon things.

However, the office manager who experiences the greatest success in organizing is a realist and accepts people available to him for what they really are. He recognizes that most organizational structures, and particularly the area of which he is a part, are the result of many decisions which took into account various considerations, some of which were controversial and contained imponderables. He also realizes that organizing is a "give and take" proposition between what is to be done and who is assigned to do it. Essentially, it has a compromise characteristic. The chief criterion, however, is to get the work accomplished adequately and maintain a continuity of satisfactory work achievement.

## ORGANIZING AND SOCIAL IMPLICATIONS

There is a strong "rational" feature about formal organizing. It is designed, the components are purposely related, and jobs within it are carefully defined. The justification for such activities is that to do otherwise would be wasteful and haphazard. On the other hand, there is the question whether this "rational" characteristic restricts individual creativity and initiative. Does it fully meet social as well as economic needs?

Superior organizing releases potentials, creates opportunities, and stimulates the growth of its members. Most superiors want neither weak subordinates nor those clearly more capable than they. The demand is for obedient conformists who "follow the rules," do their jobs well, and handle the emergencies satisfactorily. Too rigid or too rational an organization structure may encourage passive short-time prospective employees who value only their immediate abilities. They may obtain little psychological satisfaction from their work, and to satisfy most of their human needs they may go outside the organization. In such a situation the employee may even develop an attitude that he is paid for the dissatisfactions he experiences.

What is the answer? How can both economic and social needs be met? You cannot have all employees totally independent and actively pursuing what goals their respective social needs suggest. This would make for a very difficult situation—something like "all fleas and no dog." But it is reasonable to relate organization goals with those of the individual employee. To the degree that these goals are compatible, the employee attains personal satisfaction in achieving the organization's goal. Also, social needs vary among individuals and, fortunately, the organization requires different kinds of jobs and relationships so that it appears feasible to attain satisfactory combinations of individual needs and jobs. In addition, many managers feel that the answer lies in decreasing the dependency and submissiveness of the employee by providing him with greater responsibility and a larger scope of job. The need is for "bigger" jobs and less specialized and narrow small jobs. Finally, required is greater recognition of the fact that organizing provides a facility through which employees join together to support efforts of truly competent leaders and for more productive efforts benefiting others as well as themselves. So called "loners" such as writers, artists, and composers can be viewed as achieving significant accomplishments mainly by working alone, but their works are known and perpetuated through organizations. Were it not for these organizations, the loners and their creations would sink into obscurity.

## CHALLENGE OF ORGANIZATION AND PEOPLE TO MANAGERS

A major challenge of organization and people is to integrate fully the work being done by the people of the various units into a cooperative and coordinated whole. This sounds fairly simple, but acquiring it in actual practice is a different story. People are not entirely unpredictable, yet they certainly cannot be considered the same as machines. Based on available knowledge, the intricacies of the human mind are far more difficult to understand than the chemical reaction of several compounds. Consider, for example, an individual working as a member of a group. He is an individual but, at the same time, is affected by the group. If he were removed from the group and analyzed, the investigative results would have to be greatly qualified because he is not the same person he was when integrated into his organizational unit.

Another and perhaps eternal challenge is to develop a favorable organizational climate in which people are stimulated and permitted to grow. Environment is among the strongest influences to which an employee is exposed. Every organization provides environmental stimuli that affect its members, and likewise the members affect the organization. Favorable surroundings conducive to the development of a way of life, operating under the arrangement devised by organizing, must be provided. The competency of an employee may be curbed due to improper organizational relationships, or his full contribution may never be realized if he is placed in the wrong organizational unit or is not supplied the proper work environment. In the best of organizing work, there is spirit, an attitude of mind, a belief in people and what they can accomplish. A solid organization structure is not built on form or body alone.

Finally, in the work of organizing, there is the challenge of utilizing all available resources, especially people, to their utmost. The tendency is to create new authorities, new units, and to go out and get "new faces." Adequate regard should be paid the tried and true. It is not always wise to discard the traditional for something new, mainly because it is new. Good organizing requires concentration on fundamentals. From a practical viewpoint, a manager must use in the best possible manner what is available to him. At the same time, changes and newness cannot and should not be avoided, for progress demands and is a part of something different.

## QUESTIONS

1. Relate the more common bases of departmentation at the various levels of the organization of an enterprise.
2. Discuss the means for obtaining office job analysis data. Which means do you prefer? Why?
3. What are the significant differences between the concepts in each of the following pairs?
    a) Job statement and project organization.
    b) Office function and work divisions.
    c) Serial work division arrangement and job analysis.
    d) Job enlargement and job specialization.
4. Do you agree with this statement, "People constitute the essential makeup of an organization. Hence, it is logical as well as advantageous to begin organizing efforts by finding out what people are available and what each of them can do best." Justify your answer.
5. Under what general conditions would you recommend the parallel arrangement of work division? Justify your answer.
6. You have been asked to give a short talk on the subject, "The Effect of An Office Manager's Attitude Upon His Organizing Work." Outline the main topics of your proposed speech.
7. Explain Figure 27–1, highlighting the main concepts that this illustration shows.
8. Relate in specific ways the application of human relations to the work of organizing.
9. Many writers and composers have achieved greatness working alone—without an organization at all. Does this demonstrate, in part, that perhaps in management there is a tendency to overemphasize the importance and contribution of organization? Why?

10. Relate why organizing is a challenge to the alert manager.

11. Discuss the social implications inherent in organizing.

12. Do you agree with the following? "Organization structure is a tool; in and of itself it does not accomplish any work objective." Explain your answer.

## CASE PROBLEMS

### Case 27–1.  Sondak Company

The supervisor of the filing department did not work Thursday afternoon in order to attend to some personal business. About 4:00 P.M. the office manager decided to look around the office and observed four file clerks seated around a table in their department engaging in casual conversation. Three other file clerks were busy filing papers and the two clerks in the adjacent purchasing department appeared to be busy filing cards in the purchasing files maintained by the purchasing personnel. The office manager watched for about three minutes then walked over to the filing table. Addressing one of the seated file clerks he asked, "Are you finished with your work?" The employee answered, "Yes, sir. I've completed my afternoon quota of 900 papers. The standard is 225 an hour, you know. I am OK now." Smiling broadly she added, "You know the old adage, a clean desk or table indicates executive ability."

The following morning the office manager called the filing department supervisor to his office and related the incident to her.

OFFICE MANAGER: I should think that they would at least help finish the filing work of their department. They could also have given the purchasing girls a hand as it was obvious they were swamped with work late yesterday afternoon.

FILING SUPERVISOR: I have told them to keep working, but they have the attitude that after accomplishing their day's standard work requirement, they can stop working and waste time. They insist that they have the right to set their work pace.

OFFICE MANAGER: I just don't understand it. Emphatically, they do not have a right to stop work and loaf because their quotas are fulfilled. Who told them they did? You never did, did you?

FILING SUPERVISOR: Absolutely not. But I can see why they would not go over to purchasing and help there.

OFFICE MANAGER: Yes? Why?

FILING SUPERVISOR: They're adhering strictly to department lines. Our instructions and the office manual are quite specific on this point. . . . In other words, purchasing personnel are to do purchasing work, and filing personnel the filing department work.

OFFICE MANAGER (*nodding his head*): Yes.

## Problems:

1. What is the problem?
2. Justify the filing department employees' viewpoint.
3. Specifically, what contribution can organizing make?
4. What action should the office manager take? The filing supervisor? Why?

## CASE 27–2.   King-Mullin Corporation

Manufacturers of devices to control, confine, and utilize the flow of liquids under pressure, this corporation has grown tremendously during the past five years. Its fluid system components are being used in the aircraft field, missiles, lift trucks, hydraulic accumulators, air control valves, and similar applications. Currently, there are a total of 20 persons in the headquarters or Los Angeles office, including the general manager, who is the chief executive of the corporation and runs the business for the small number of owners. There are also 2 salesmen who are on the road all of the time, 9 engineers in a research and development unit reporting to the factory and production manager, and 156 persons in manufacturing. The 20 people in the office and the work done by each follow. The number in parentheses following each title indicates the number of employees with that job.

1. *Assistant to the purchasing agent.* (1) Types the letters of this department and handles the files of this unit. Reports to the purchasing agent and personnel director.

2. *Assistant sales manager.* (1) Handles advertising; works with the advertising agency; plans catalogs and brochures, displays, and sales portfolios; corresponds with distributors and customers. Reports to sales manager.

3. *Billing clerk.* (1) Types the invoices, maintains her own files of the customers billed. Reports to the controller.

4. *Bookkeeper.* (1) Keeps the books, types bills, and also does some filing work. Reports to the controller.

5. *Controller.* (1) Directs the work of the accounting department; makes up various financial reports, cost analysis, and office employees' payroll; and hires new employees for the office. Immediate superior is the general manager.

6. *Correspondent.* (2) Dictates letters on machine and sometimes to a file clerk or typist, makes up shipping schedules and cost estimates. Reports directly to the sales manager.

7. *Cost accountant.* (1) Makes up factory payroll, assists the controller with cost analysis work and other reports, and does some typing and filing. Reports to the controller.

8. *File clerk and typist.* (2) Alternates between filing and typing, takes shorthand, and is responsible for office supplies. Is under the direct supervision of the sales manager.

9. *General manager.* (1) Actually the president of the corporation, he coordinates the entire operations of the corporation, makes major decisions, and interprets broad policies.

10. *Order clerk.* (1) Enters incoming orders and is secretary to and reports directly to the sales manager.

11. *Purchasing agent and personnel director.* (1) Handles all purchasing and is personnel director for factory workers only. Immediate superior is the general manager.

12. *Sales manager.* (1) Handles contacts with customers, either personal or by mail; travels about 50 percent of the time; and manages the work of the sales department. Reports to the general manager.

13. *Salesman.* (4) Calls on prospects and customers, secures orders, takes care

of customer inquiries by telephone. The sales manager is the immediate superior of all salesmen.

14. *Secretary to the general manager.* (1) Performs secretarial work for the general manager, which work requires about 35 percent of her time; during the remainder of her time, she helps the other departments. Reports directly to the general manager.

15. *Switchboard operator.* (1) Operates the telephone switchboard and does some typing. Reports to the general manager.

Within the next four months, a small computer will be delivered and installed at the company. This addition is mainly the result of the efforts of the general manager, who is confident that it will prove very valuable for problems in the company's research and development work, analyzing sales, and improving office work. For this latter application, he has received little or no encouragement from the controller, who, to date, has shown little interest in the forthcoming computer or its application to the regular paper work of the corporation and prefers not to disturb the present means of processing papers.

## Problems:

1. Draw an organization chart of the office.

2. Evaluate the present office organization, pointing out what may be its strong and weak points.

3. Where do you suggest the forthcoming computer unit be placed from the standpoint of organization? Why?

# CHAPTER 28

# AUTHORITY AND ORGANIZATIONAL RELATIONSHIPS

The work an unknown good man has done is
like a vein of water flowing hidden underground,
secretly making the ground green.

*Thomas Carlyle*

THE VARIOUS organizational units made up of work divisions and people assigned to them must be related, or formally tied together, so that they provide a unified group which can operate effectively toward obtaining common objectives. Relating these units leads to the subject of authority.

*Authority is the right to act or to exact action by others, within a prescribed area.* With the concept of authority is associated the power to make decisions and to see that they are carried out. The compliance aspect of authority is not confined to coercion or force; more commonly, it is gained by means of persuasion and requests.

## CHARACTERISTICS OF AUTHORITY

Authority has definite limitations. First of all, it must, from the management point of view, be used in conformity with the efforts to achieve the accepted goals of the organizational unit. It is not used by an office manager as his whims or wishes might suggest. Also, the use of authority is influenced by the people with whom it is being employed. The exacting of certain actions by others must be within their capacity to perform. To illustrate, trying to enforce a decision impelling an inexperienced file clerk to operate a modern bookkeeping machine would be a ridiculous misuse of authority.

The relative position in the organization structure normally indicates the degree of authority from the formal viewpoint. But the amount of decision-making power and ultimate enforcement may be modified by the popularity or acceptance of the one in authority by the person being influenced by that authority. Managerial competence to gain enthusiastic cooperation, to acquire respect, and to inspire may be lacking despite the formal authority established by position in the organization structure. This also means that a person with little or no formal authority established by reason of his position in the structure might actually possess extensive authority due to his integrity, knowledge, and skill. In punched-card accounting, for example, others may seek suggestions from a certain individual and do what he recommends. Although the person may not be formally in charge, he actually possesses significant authority. Situations of this type may be of a temporal nature or may exist for long, continuous periods.

In many office organizational units, situations of an unusual or emergency nature arise from time to time. They may not be provided for in the regular organizational arrangement. In such circumstances, the person assuming the authority has derived it from what is called the "authority of the situation." This usually is temporary and exists until the person normally in charge assumes authority over the unusual event.

The relationship established by authority is either of two major types, (1) vertical and (2) horizontal. Vertical authority relationships are those between different organization levels and concern the superior-subordinate association. Horizontal authority relationships deal with organizational units within an organizational level and concern the manager-to-manager association within the same organization level.

Lastly, authority is dynamic. Within prescribed limits, its makeup is changed according to the specific conditions and requirements of the group or the individual. It is not always applied to the same degree or intensity. This characteristic emphasizes the manager's skill or application of his authority.

## SPAN OF AUTHORITY

In writing of relationships among organizational units and the subject of authority, the question arises: How many immediate subordinates can a manager manage effectively? The number is commonly referred to as "span of control" or "span of management." For our purposes here, it is believed the term "span of authority" is appropriate and helpful.

In a given case, there is probably an optimum number of employees who should be immediately subordinate to an executive in order that most satisfactory managerial results are obtained. The number should be large enough to utilize the executive's full time and ability, yet not so large that his efforts are diluted over too wide a span. The proper span of authority depends upon many considerations.

The organizational level at which the managerial work is performed appears to be important. At the higher levels, few might report to their immediate superior; while at the lower or operative levels, many might report to one superior. Also, the type of work is important. To illustrate, a supervisor of draftsmen might adequately direct the work of 15 draftsmen, depending upon the particular type of drafting work performed. Generally speaking, a relatively broad span of authority can be used. In addition, adequate consideration must be given to whether all the immediate sub-units are of equal size and importance, whether they must be given equal attention by the supervisor, and whether the caliber of personnel requires a large or a small amount of supervision. Where the makeup of the work is fairly stable and little communication between units is required, a broad span of authority usually proves satisfactory. Furthermore, the geographical distance between activities affects the span utilized.

Some managers prefer a span numbering from four to eight. Originally, this quantity came from the military, where rapid change in plans and operations may be necessary because of enemy action. However, in business organization, the span should be determined by keeping in mind the considerations mentioned above. The number used may well be four to eight, but it need not necessarily be this amount. The span of authority appears to be increasing in many business enterprises. In some instances, successful operations are reported with spans of 10 to 12 persons at the top levels and with 20 to 25 persons at the lower levels. In the final analysis, the number of subordinates reporting to a manager should be limited to what he can effectively manage.

It is appropriate to point out that span of authority deals with the number of persons reporting to a manager, not the number of persons having access to a manager. The two can be greatly different. Also, span of authority is confined to *formal* authority relationships. Actually, in most enterprises, there are usually many informal authority relationships. These result from the existence of social interests and relationships among employees and are frequently different from the economic formal relationships established.

## ORGANIZATIONAL RELATIONSHIPS AND SPAN OF AUTHORITY

It is interesting to note how the number of relationships increases as the number of persons supervised increases. First, consider a manager, M, with two supervisors, A and B. In this case, there are six relationships:

M with A, M with B, and A with B, plus the reverse of each, assuming the initiative is taken by the second-named party; i.e., the additional three are A with M, B with M, and B with A. Now, assume that M increases his number of supervisors from two to three, or an increase of 50 percent. What happens to the number of relationships with which M may now be concerned? They increase from six to 18, or an increase of 200 percent. The third supervisor, C, makes for these additional 12 relationships: M with C, B with C, A with C, M with AB, M with BC, and M with AC, plus the reverse of these six relationships. This is summarized in Figure 28–1.

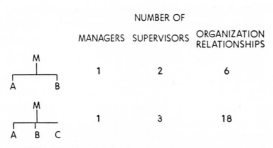

FIG. 28–1.  Data showing the rapid increase in organizational relationships as the number of persons increases.

Wide spans of authority make for a high number of organizational relationships, while short spans make for a low number of relationships. Not all the relationships are of equal importance, but they should be taken into account when determining the span of authority.


## RESPONSIBILITY

When a management member is given or assumes authority to perform specific work, an obligation to perform the work is created. The acceptance of this obligation is known as responsibility which can be defined as follows. *Responsibility is the obligation for the carrying out of a duty and what one is accountable for in the execution of an assigned task.* That is, responsibility can be viewed as having two parts: (1) the obligation to secure results and (2) the accountability to the one from whom the authority is received. Commonly responsibility takes the form of a list of duties. These are general statements—they do not spell out every detail of what is to be performed.

Being obligated to secure results and being accountable automatically puts a person under pressure and develops his sensitivity to gain satisfactory results. Typically, in a business enterprise the board of directors appoints a president who is expected to manage the business.

His obligation to secure results and his accountability are well known. In turn, by means of organizing, he shares his authority and responsibility with individuals. In fact, this is one of the main purposes of organizing.

Efforts to develop responsibility in management members takes many different forms, but an effective practice is to provide the holder of authority and responsibility with a list of questions to improve the exercise of his authority and to stimulate his enthusiastic acceptance of his responsibility. Figure 28–2 illustrates the type of questions that can be asked.

---

1. Do you make a continuing review of excess office processing capacity?
2. What five office work areas require most of your time? Should they?
3. Have you investigated to find out if your instructions are understood?
4. Are you keeping up with the latest developments in office machines that might be used in your organizational unit?
5. Are written procedures brought up to date?
6. Do you receive any useless reports or documents?
7. Do you take an individual interest in each of your subordinates?

---

FIG. 28–2.  Questions to develop management responsibility.

## DELEGATION OF AUTHORITY

A very important concept in organizing is delegation of authority. This is the granting or conferring of authority by one executive to another. Usually it is thought of as being from a higher to a lower level, as is commonly the case within business enterprises. However, in some organizations of government and some religious groups, delegation of authority is from a lower to a higher level and from one level to another on the same plane. Hence delegation can be downward, upward, or outward.

By means of delegation, an executive spreads his area of managerial influence and makes an organization structure meaningful. Without delegation, an executive restricts his managerial actions to those that he himself can perform. In fact, organizing does not become fully effective until delegation of authority is practiced.

Figure 28–3 illustrates the importance of delegation of authority in an organization. At the top of the illustration, office executive A has three assistants, 1, 2, and 3. In turn, assistant 1 has chiefs 11 and 12 reporting to him; likewise, chief 11 has subordinates 21 and 22; and chief 12, subordinates 23 and 24. The employees reporting to executives 2 and 3 are shown by the illustration. President A delegates proper authority to his executives 1, 2, and 3. The former two, 1 and 2, delegate authority to their subordinates; and in turn, these subordinates delegate authority to their subordinates. In contrast, executive 3 is trying to do all the managerial work of his organizational unit himself. He does not delegate authority to either 15 or 16, who likewise do not delegate to 29, 30, 31, or 32. This failure to delegate authority actually paralyzes this portion of the organizational structure under executive 3. To a great extent, the employees reporting to executive 3 may just as well not be management members of the organization. There is in reality no formal authority structure below executive 3.

In delegation, the delegator always retains his overall authority for the delegated duties. He does not surrender or permanently release his authority. He does grant the right for others to act officially within the specific areas. Only the authority needed to carry out successfully the

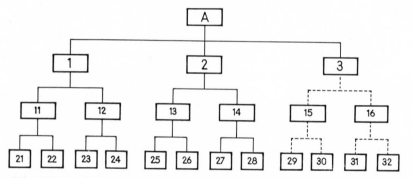

FIG. 28–3.  Failure to delegate authority by office executive 3 tends to paralyze the organization established under him.

assigned functions is or should be delegated. This makes for the tapering concept of authority and simply means that in most organization structures the authority becomes successively smaller or tapered as successively lower horizontal levels of the structure are considered.

Since an authority delegator retains in the ultimate all his authority, he likewise retains in the ultimate all his responsibility. He cannot evade a failure of a subordinate by saying it was the fault of the subordinate. The superior retains the ultimate responsibility and is accountable for what is or is not achieved by his organizational unit.

From the practical viewpoint, delegation of authority is either specially granted or inherently implied in the job. In the former case, it is given to an individual in order that he may act to perform the management which is essential in achieving the objective. In the latter case, the authority is inherently tied up with the job, so that whoever holds the job or performs the delegation function in the organization structure automatically possesses the authority which goes with that position. In any enterprise, therefore, authority is contingent upon such things as the delegation of those already in authority, the traditional structure of the organization, and the character and mental characteristics of the individual.

## PROBLEM OF DELEGATION

One of the big problems in organizing is to get managers to delegate authority. Ideally, the proper delegation should exist at each delegator-to-delegatee level throughout the entire structure, and the delegation should extend as close to the level or point of action as possible. This makes for effective organizational action and encourages initiative by employees at each organization level. But in practice, some managers are reluctant to delegate. They fear that if authority is delegated, the right decision may not be made, and the work will not be handled correctly. Their belief is that they must keep in close touch with activities and decide most issues. In some instances, they may not fully realize the amount of authority needed by a subordinate to get the work done properly. In other instances, the manager states that he has delegated authority but at the same time criticizes his subordinates when they make and enforce decisions without his advice.

Delegation of authority is not easily acquired. The natural tendency is to do work yourself if you are the one charged with doing it. And if the work is important, there is all the more reason for doing it yourself to make certain that it is done right. These habits develop quite commonly because most persons acquire managerial status after doing nonmanagerial work. The latter type emphasizes doing the work yourself and doing it well; the reward can be promotion to managerial work. But success in managerial work requires getting work achieved by and through others. Failure to realize this fact plus difficulty in making the needed change in thinking, i.e., acquiring the managerial viewpoint, not the direct operative viewpoint, contribute to the lack of delegation by a manager.

It is common for the amount and extent of delegation of authority to be arrived at informally by trial and error. The subordinate makes a decision or tries out a certain practice; and if no reprimand results, he assumes the management work performed is within his province. In many cases, the status of delegation of authority is the result of an infiltration process over a long period of time. Slowly but surely, authority for certain matters has been turned over to the delegatee. Commonly, verbal statements establish the amount of delegation of authority; and in a relatively few instances, the superior gives specific delegation of authority in writing.

## DEVELOPING DELEGATION OF AUTHORITY

The first requirement for developing delegation of authority is to realize the need for it. A manager must recognize that as long as he is limited to doing what he can accomplish himself, he will always be short of time and limited in his achievements. The alternative is to acquire aides, train them, and permit them to do the job, even if their manner of doing it differs from how the manager might have done it. Competent aides are mandatory for group efforts to reach greatest heights. A manager's need is to multiply himself. It is nonsense to try to lead the band and play all the instruments, too.

Furthermore, for delegation to work effectively, certain criteria can assist materially. Important is the establishment of definite goals and clear policies, for these give guidance to the subordinate and keep him from going too far astray in the fulfillment of the tasks. Work which is routine and which is covered by definite policies should offer little delegation difficulty. Clear and timely communication, complete instructions and orders, and definite job identifications are also helpful. And the use of broad controls expedites delegation, for they can supply the desired checks to determine whether the work is being accomplished satisfactorily.

Lastly, belief in delegation is necessary. An office manager must want to make delegation successful; he must strive to help it succeed. Among other things, he will not interpret delegation as distributing the work to others, sitting back, and observing if they make good or not. Rather, he will select the delegatee carefully and offer counsel readily to him, being careful not to give him answers, but to help him find the answers himself. The office manager must be willing to see his subordinates make mistakes and charge the cost to management training and the strengthening of his organization. Effective delegating does not just happen. From the very beginning, it takes much effort, time, and persistence to develop the art of authority delegation and to keep it alive.

## LINE AUTHORITY AND STAFF AUTHORITY

Full comprehension of organizing also requires knowledge of the types of authority, their respective characteristics, and when to use what type for which purpose. The two main classifications of authority are (1) line and (2) staff. A manager can have either or both. When a manager has line authority, he is called a "line manager" and normally exercises direct command over the work of all members in his unit, but there are certain exceptions, as discussed below. Characteristically, the authority relationship is of a superior-subordinate type, forming "a line" from the top to the bottom of the structure. It is the authority used to accomplish directly the major goals of an enterprise and exists at all levels of the organization structure.

Staff authority, the second major classification, is made up of several different types including (1) advisory staff, (2) functional staff, (3) service staff, and (4) control staff. All of these are commonly termed "staff authority," yet they are dissimilar in important respects, and the common identification of staff is unfortunate. A manager with staff authority is a staff manager. A clear understanding of these various types of staff authority helps clarify vital relationships in organizing. All are in use and are believed necessary. Their specific application depends upon the individual organization.

## ADVISORY STAFF AUTHORITY

The word "staff," according to Webster, means "a pole carried in the hand for support." Therefore, staff authority pertains to assistance or support, and this concept was the initial identification and use given staff authority. Much of this assistance and support takes the form of being advisory and is appropriately called advisory staff authority. Specifically, a manager with advisory staff authority normally counsels or advises, in

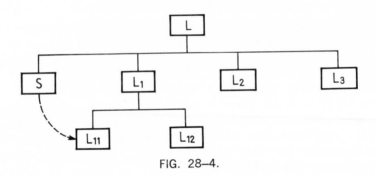

FIG. 28–4.

his specialty, the manager having line authority. Advisory staff is a manager-to-manager relationship and can exist within any organizational level.

In Figure 28–4, line manager L has four subordinates, S, $L_1$, $L_2$, and $L_3$. The latter three are line executives, while S is an advisory staff executive. His job essentially is to counsel and advise L in his (S's) specialty so that L can do a better job. The counsel and advice of S can be accepted in whole or part and utilized by L in managing the organizational group; or L can reject the advice of S, since L is in direct command of the unit. In some companies, the practice of "compulsory staff service" is followed. This requires a line executive to listen to his staff executives, but the final decision and enforcement rests with the line executive. When the managers are competent, this practice aids them in their respective tasks. Also, in some enterprises, the "completed staff work" doctrine is followed. This emphasizes the presentation of complete solutions by the advisory staff to the line executives. Piecemeal recommendations are avoided; and stress is placed on supplying assistance, not placing the line man in a predicament with questions regarding what he wants investigated or what data should be included in a report. Of course, the line man and the staff man should talk things over, but in a constructive way, with each making contributions.

## FUNCTIONAL STAFF AUTHORITY

In office management, the use of functional staff authority is especially common. It concerns specific functions only and is delegated from one manager to another manager who is not related to the former by formally established authority channels. It can be conferred by a line to a staff manager, or vice versa. To illustrate, in Figure 28–4, line manager L may delegate to his subordinate staff executive, S, the authority for S to issue orders concerning a specific work activity directly to $L_{11}$, who is a line manager. In this case, the authority possessed by S is functional staff. Actually, L is delegating a qualified amount of line authority for a specific activity to S. The delegated authority is limited to a particular activity and applies only to the authority relationship in this activity between S and $L_{11}$. Good management practices would include L's informing $L_1$, $L_{11}$, and $L_{12}$ that this functional staff authority exists. Functional staff authority expedites efficiency and is convenient. Its use, however, must necessarily be limited; otherwise, established authority relationships are neutralized. Some specialized activities of the office from time to time require a competent office executive to explain and enforce office procedures to nonoffice personnel in order to insure proper handling and good administration. Such situations are solved by the use of functional authority.

## SERVICE STAFF AUTHORITY

When speaking of office organizing, the term "service unit" commonly arises. Its justification is primarily economy and improved work performed or service offered by the unit. Purchasing, general office services (mail, telephone, and reception service), and legal counsel are examples of service organizational units. Generally, the head of such a unit possesses service staff authority which actually includes some line authority, as persons are expected to request the service organization unit to perform for them a service included in the service unit's makeup and, furthermore, to be bound by the decisions made by the service unit in its specialty. To illustrate, the manager of billing may not purchase supplies and equipment. This is done for him by the purchasing unit, and the billing manager abides by the decisions and actions of the purchasing unit.

Service staff authority applies both within and outside of the service unit as it pertains to this specialized service work. In addition, some service organizational units utilize functional authority when delegated, that is, they have jurisdiction over specific work performed by others not normally or formally under the authority of the service unit. In some instances, the service unit's authority is limited to the strictly advisory. The unit recommends and counsels in work regarding its specialty, but the decision as to what to do and its enforcement are not within the province of the service unit.

## CONTROL STAFF AUTHORITY

In many organizations, there are units that perform essential work for achieving the major goals of the enterprise; yet, their work is of a specialty nature and is not supplied on a strictly advisory basis. The contribution is indirect insofar as the chief objectives are concerned; but when necessary enforcement of decisions is present, considerable line authority over the particular function in the enterprise may be present. For example, these conditions frequently exist for an auditing unit, or a procedural analysis organization unit, or one dealing with office standards. Requests by such a unit to line managers to supply certain financial information, to use financial standards supplied, and to abide by pre-scribed auditing practices are not on a "take it or leave it" basis by the line managers. The requests are essential for required managerial control and when they can be enforced by the auditing unit, such a unit has control staff authority. In a very real sense, it includes aspects of ultimate line authority. Enforcement is usually voluntary because the line managers realize that the specialty offered is important and that, if necessary, compliance with requests can and will be forthcoming.

## ORGANIZATION CHARTS

*An organization chart is a graphic representation of an organization structure.* It can be thought of as a picture of the organization structure; it shows the organizational units, the relationships, and the existing lines of authority.

To draw an organization chart, use the outline approach. First, list the main functions; next, place those functions which are subordinate to the main functions under the proper main function in the outline list; then, place under each subordinate function the minor functions which properly belong under the respective subordinate function. In this way, a list is developed which shows the main functions, the subordinates under each main function, and the minor functions under each subordinate. This outline form is then transformed into the graphic form which makes up the organization chart.

The chart may also be prepared by starting with the person of highest authority in the organization structure and working down by determining who reports to this top person and what activities each person handles. This procedure provides the information for the first level of management below the chief executive and may be followed for each consecutive layer. From the information so gathered, the organization chart can be constructed.

An organization chart simply helps in visualizing the organization structure; it insures neither good organization nor good management. However, it does compel the organizer to put down in black and white what the structural relationships are. This crystallizes his thinking and clarifies fuzzy, but important, details which might otherwise be overlooked. Specifically, the main advantages of an organization chart can be listed as follows: (1) a clear, overall concept of the organization is obtained; (2) the main lines of authority and responsibility are brought out in full relief; (3) promotional possibilities are provided; and (4) the assignment of titles is simplified.

## THE LINE ORGANIZATION

The line, or scalar, type of organization, which was used extensively in our early industrial development, is one of the oldest organization forms. It uses line authority exclusively. This type of organization is still quite popular and is frequently employed by proprietors of small businesses and for other enterprises where the number of employees is small.

The line organization is characterized by direct lines of authority from the top executive to the various assistants, and direct from them to the employees at the operative level. Each member is fully responsible for the carrying out or the actual performance of the job to be done. Throughout the entire structure, each member is in complete charge of all activities within his particular organization segment. Authority and responsibility are greatest at the top, and reduce or taper as successively lower levels of management are considered.

The line type of organization is illustrated in Figure 28–5. Line authority exists between the president at the top and the employees at the bottom. The line authority may be thought of as a scalar type, in that it reduces by scales or steps. To illustrate, the connection is from the president to the vice-president of finance, to the manager in charge of office work, to the supervisor of the mail, telephone, and reception services section, and to the clerks of this section. The vice-president of finance is in complete charge of finance, including the work of the manager in charge of office work and the manager in charge of credits, disbursements, and equities of the company; the manager in charge of office work is, in turn, in complete charge of that particular segment of the organization

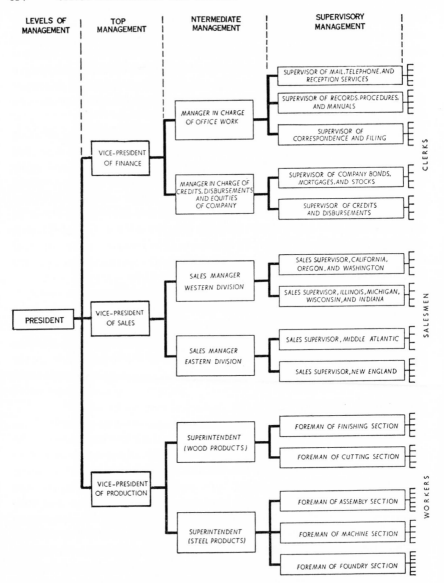

FIG. 28–5.  A line organization.

and specifically over the supervisors of correspondence and filing; records, procedures, and manuals; and mail, telephone, and reception services.

The advantages of the line organization include the following: Authority and responsibility are definitely fixed, and the person who has that authority and responsibility is known to all; the structure is very simple and hence readily understood by all personnel; discipline is easily maintained, since each worker and each boss knows what is expected of him and in which areas he is to operate; decisions can be quickly reached; the fact that a single boss who is in complete charge makes for a minimum of delay in decision reaching; and lastly, the line organization offers splendid training opportunities for the development of executive talent. The line officer is charged with getting things executed; he must be a doer; he must get the work accomplished.

In contrast, the line organization also has its disadvantages. Perhaps most outstanding is that, relatively, specialization of work is not practiced. Particularly is this true at the intermediate and supervisory management levels. Another disadvantage is the difficulty of securing coordination. Each lord is master of his own house or his unit of the organization, and the coordination between any two line units of the same organizational level is obtained solely by the strong leadership of the man at the top in charge of the several line units. The tendency is for the head of each unit to develop a rather independent unit and to think only of his own unit's activities, without much regard for other necessary functions of the enterprise. In fact, some believe that the line organization probably places too much emphasis on the managers. Another disadvantage is the difficulty of forming organizational units; this is particularly true in cases where the unit is not suggested by the process. Frequently, insufficient opportunity is afforded to modify and to change existing units from the viewpoint of the total organization structure.

## THE LINE AND STAFF ORGANIZATION

When staff authority relationships are added to a line organization, the resultant organization is called a line and staff organization which is extensively used. In this type, line managers have line authority to carry out the activities, but their efforts are qualified by staff managers who have authority to carry out their particular work. Both line and staff managers are considered essential, and all are believed needed to accomplish the work effectively. More precisely this means that the line and the staff managers comprise a winning team of managers with varying degrees and types of authority. In the team effort, all are required. None should be thought of as inferior; for if in fact they are, then either they should be replaced or their area of operation should be eliminated.

The chart of a line and staff organization is shown in Figure 28–6. The line part of this organization, basically the same as that shown in Figure 28–5, is represented by the diagram *outside* the areas of the dotted circles, and the areas *inside* the six circles represent staff organizational functions. On the left, under production, for example, the jobs of plant manager, chief inspector, and methods and standards manager constitute staff activities. Likewise, under the vice-president in charge of sales, the jobs of

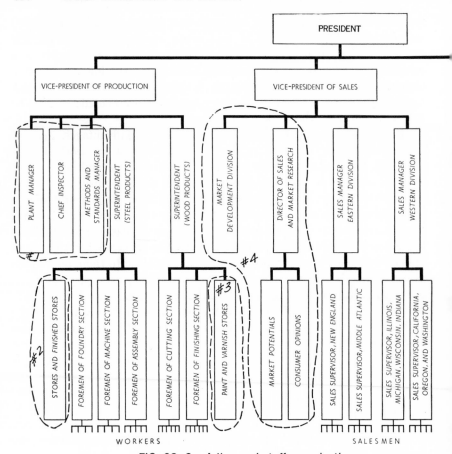

FIG. 28–6.  A line and staff organization.

market development and sales and market research constitute staff functions. The entire portion of the chart to the right, under personnel, is circled, since personnel is a staff function to the entire organization. Areas enclosed by circles 2 and 3 represent staff functions at lower levels of management. Staff functions can exist at all levels. Note in particular that even though a function is staff, the organization for carrying out that function may be of a line organization type. To illustrate, under the vice-president of sales, the directorship of the sales and market research division is a staff activity to the organization structure as a whole; but the sales and market research division itself is organized as a line organization, with the work of market potentials and consumer opinions under it.

The advantages of the line and staff organization are many. First, the lines of authority are fairly well fixed, good discipline can be attained,

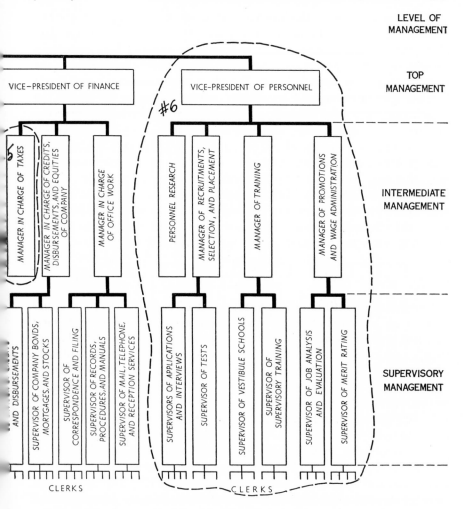

decisions can be reached after desirable deliberation, and the principle of specialization can be utilized to the extent of practical limits. Second, coordination can be improved because the line officers are supplied with factual data concerning activities both within and outside their own units. Third, flexibility is provided for the organization structure to expand or contract, as conditions warrant. New activities can be added and old ones discarded without seriously affecting the organization structure. Fourth, proper balance among all the activities, line as well as staff, can be maintained. Fifth, more opportunities are afforded to match the desires, capacities, and interests of personnel with the job, since a greater variety of jobs involving different duties, responsibilities, training, and background is required.

The disadvantages of the line and staff organization center around the relationships existing between the line and staff managers. In the first place, the line manager may tend to ignore the advisory staff manager's counsel, so that the expert information provided is never used. Second, the staff manager may tend to ignore the ideas of the line manager simply because specialization and expertness are supposed to be under the jurisdiction of the staff manager. Third, the staff manager may overstep his prescribed staff authority and even attempt to take over line authority which is out of his realm of activity. Fourth, a considerable number of staff managers are not good salesmen, and many staff contributions are not fully used partly because other managers are not convinced of the merits of the staff's work. Fifth, line orders, staff advice, and staff orders may be confused by members of the organization structure, with the result that the *what, when, where,* and *how* of activities are not clearly known to either the managers or the nonmanagement members.

## USE OF COMMITTEES

Committees constitute an important part of most organization structures. They can exist at any organizational level, be of short or of long life, and deal with various subjects. Many are delegated line authority, that is, they not only discuss and decide issues but also secure compliance of others with the decision. Such a committee is sometimes called a "plural executive." However, probably most committees have advisory staff authority. Their purpose is to discuss and recommend. In some cases, they simply receive information, classify it, and make it available for others to use.

The committee may be viewed as an important modification or addition to the main type of organization. Just as staff modifies the line to form a line and staff organization, so the committee may also be added to form a line, staff, and committee organization. In this case, the committee element adds an excellent medium to the organizational structure for discussion and educational group meetings. Also, the committee acting in an advisory capacity serves as an excellent addition.

A committee offers several outstanding advantages. First, it permits organization members to take an active part; thus, better cooperation is obtained. Second, it helps to secure coordination. Men and women from different departments have the chance to see the organization's needs as a whole; they have a chance to discuss these problems with their fellow supervisors and employees. Third, the committee is an excellent source of collective advice, ideas, and opinions for top managers. Fourth, the committee offers an excellent medium for educational and training purposes.

In contrast, a disadvantage of the use of a committee is that it divides responsibility. There is no single individual fully responsible. Second, the committee is weak in carrying out activities. It commonly lacks decisive action and follow-up. Third, most of a committee's decisions are the result of compromise—a "straddle the fence" variety. Usually, the majority rules; and this might tend to bring prejudice, secret agreements, and bargaining, rather than facts only, into the committee's decisions. Fourth, committee meetings usually require a great deal of the members' time. There appears to be little doubt that a sizable amount of this time is wasted and might better be spent by members on their individual tasks.

## QUESTIONS

1. Discuss some common and general characteristics of authority.
2. Point out the difference between the terms in each of the following pairs:
    a) Span of authority and horizontal authority relationships.
    b) Service staff authority and a line organization.
    c) Responsibility and "authority of the situation."
    d) Compulsory staff advice and plural executive.
3. Outline the identity, implication, and importance of span of authority in organizing.
4. How can management responsibility be developed in delegatees? Use an example to illustrate your answer.
5. Is it possible for an enterprise to have a member without (a) authority, (b) responsibility, or (c) authority and responsibility? Explain.
6. Enumerate the major reasons why managers do not delegate authority. What inferences do you draw from this state of affairs?
7. Describe an organizational arrangement illustrating the use of service staff authority. Of control staff authority.
8. Relate the advantages and disadvantages in the use of committees in office organization structures.
9. Mr. A is a line executive of department X. Also in this department is Mr. B, an advisory staff executive reporting to Mr. A. Clearly state the organizational relationship between Mr. A and Mr. B.
10. Discuss several ways in which the delegation of authority by an office manager can be developed.
11. Briefly discuss the advantages in a manager using a line and staff organization.
12. Describe a situation illustrating difficulties encountered due to a lack of utilizing the completed staff work doctrine.

## CASE PROBLEMS

### Case 28–1.  Mathews Company

It is true that Mr. Paynter is a very busy man. The work load is heavy, but based on much organizational study and carefully established work standards, there are ample work divisions and employees in each division. Mr. Paynter reports directly to the vice-president of finance, and reporting to Mr. Paynter are six supervisors, including, respectively, the heads of (1) corresponding, (2) order billing and invoicing, (3) office procedures and methods, (4) mailing, (5) filing and records retention, and (6) office services. Mr. Paynter is known to run a "tight ship." He permits his supervisors to make routine decisions only and frequently there are differences of opinion as to what is a routine decision. He sees to it that he is in on every decision affecting (1) any hiring, promoting, or terminating of an office employee, (2) any office employee's pay adjustment, (3) any change in currently followed procedures or methods, (4) any purchase of office equipment, machines, or supplies, and (5) any contemplated change in office policies. In addition, Mr. Paynter personally directs the office suggestion system, edits and approves changes and modifications in the office manual, and supervises the receptionist, two telephone switchboard operators, and the four members of the office janitorial staff working day and night hours.

The president of the company has expressed his dissatisfaction with the office to his immediate subordinates, the vice-presidents of sales, production, and finance, respectively. He states that he waits an unduly long time for office information, there are many delays in preparing reports, processing customers' orders seems to take longer than it should, and "it takes a month and three summers to get a new idea adopted in the office." He has observed idle office machines during his walks through the office. He personally likes Frederick Paynter. Paynter is a hard worker, always willing to help, is extremely agreeable, dresses well, and is conscientious about his work. If anything, he appears overly cooperative. With all the office employees, now 83 in number, the president feels the office should be far more effective than it is.

### Problems:

1. As you see it, what is the major problem?
2. What action do you recommend the president of Mathews Company take? Why?

### Case 28–2.   Paul Lawrence Chadwick

Paul Lawrence Chadwick is the head of a staff unit, the office work simplification unit; he reports to the office manager. In turn, the office manager reports to the president of the company. Chadwick works hard, has a multitude of ideas, and at times becomes discouraged because of the delay and inactivity on many suggestions for improvement made by his organization unit.

What he believed to be an excellent suggestion, from the viewpoint of both less effort required to do the work and lower cost, was submitted to the office manager in a report some six weeks ago. Since that time, Chadwick has asked the office manager several times what he thinks about the suggestion and receives the answer: "We are looking into it." Chadwick feels, however, that the office manager is just "stalling."

A few days after the last time Chadwick spoke to the office manager, the latter suffered an injury in an automobile accident. It was announced that he would be unable to come to work for at least four weeks; while he was absent, his duties would be taken over by the assistant office manager. Chadwick has little respect for the assistant office manager's abilities. Likewise, the assistant office manager feels that Chadwick is too precise and spends company money on a lot of impractical ideas. The two do not get along too well.

Chadwick believed the suggestion embodied in the last report to the office manager to be so important that, in the company's best interests, delay in its adoption should not be tolerated. Based on past experience, he was convinced the assistant office manager, now in charge, would take no action on it. Accordingly, he explained the new procedure to the supervisor whose department, direct mail, is affected and to a small number of line employees in that department. At Chadwick's insistence the new means was tried out. For the next several weeks, careful records of time expenditures were made by Chadwick, and these were compared with expenditures under the previous arrangement. Savings of $23 a day, or approximately $6,000 a year, were indicated through the use of the new means. Chadwick wrote the report concerning the installation and the results obtained and submitted it to the president of the company, with a copy of the report being sent to the "office of the office manager."

Two days later, the office manager returned to his job; and during the course of "welcome back" conversations, the president referred to the report and asked a few questions about it, which the office manager could not answer, explaining he was not familiar with it. Returning to his office, the office manager called in his assistant and inquired about the new process being used in the direct-mail department. The assistant knew nothing about it. The office manager's secretary, overhearing the conversation, located the copy of Chadwick's report to the president and gave it to the office manager.

## Problems:

1. What action do you feel is proper for the office manager to take? Why?

2. Do you approve of Mr. Chadwick's action? Justify your answer.

3. What general impression do you gain concerning the organization of this company?

# CHAPTER 29

# DYNAMIC
# OFFICE ORGANIZING

The greatest mistake you can make in life is to
be continually fearing you will make one.
—*Elbert G. Hubbard*

ORGANIZING is a vibrant, living activity. Change takes place whether or
not it is planned because organizing is what it is. Work demands change,
relationships and interactions of employees change, and the views of top
managers change. The astute management member not only recognizes
this, but he strives to utilize the inevitable changes to update his
organization and thus employ the best possible work groupings, personnel, and relationships in keeping with current demands.

Too often, an existent organization expands or contracts without any
genuine direction or guidance by the managers. New functions and new
personnel are added and the organization just grows, or in contrast,
functions are combined, peculiar organization relationships established,
and personnel placed on jobs requiring but a small portion of their
capacities. Or a needed organizational adjustment may be postponed
indefinitely—the outmoded organization being permitted to give rise to
difficult managerial problems. More precisely, this failure to recognize
organization dynamics and utilize them constructively leads to these
undesirable conditions:

1. The functions become disproportionate in their relationship to each
other when judged by the relative importance of each function to the
objectives of the enterprise.

2. Important functions are neglected, or they are subordinated to other
functions; either condition makes it difficult to carry out the requisite
activities.

3. New functions of a planning nature which might greatly strengthen the organization are ignored.

4. Capable men are confined to mediocre jobs.

5. Authority relationships become blurred; differences arise over who is supposed to decide what.

6. The necessary coordination among the major functions is decreased, since the personnel for each major function tend to stress their individual activity exclusively.

## RESPONSIBILITY FOR ORGANIZATION CHANGES

All things considered, the organization used is the result of managers' thinking and implementing in this area of management. Especially is this true of top managers, for their attitudes and thoughts tend to mold the organization structure adopted. They cast the die and decide, sometimes arbitrarily, what the organization pattern will be and when and where changes in it will be made. To some degree, top managers are influenced by their subordinates regarding what changes in the existent structure should be made. But in most cases, organizational suggestions initiated by subordinates are conditioned by them in order to insure approval by the top managers. The location, timing, and extent of any organizational modification is regulated ultimately by the top managers.

Fortunately, the growing practice among enterprises of updating and improving the organization structure at regular intervals is being recognized as advantageous. For example, in some companies, this task is assigned to one individual within the organization. He works closely with the various management members, discussing possible organizational improvements with the managers who would be affected by such changes, and encouraging them to offer their ideas and participate in developing needed organizational improvements. Having an individual to head up the activity of possible organizational changes is an effective way to insure that attention will be given this important work. A number of large, well-known companies have established a special organization unit for the sole purpose of studying and recommending organization changes and improvements. They report excellent results for these "organization evaluation" units.

## ORGANIZATION CONTINUITY

The continuity of an organization is conditioned chiefly by (1) the work—both its flow and its type—and (2) the time element. A relatively stable and continuing organization usually results when the flow of work is steady. Modifications in organization structure are likely to be minor and infrequent. The line as well as the staff functions are usually well defined and known. On the other hand, when demand for the products or services is irregular, the predominant idea is usually to meet current requirements; and generally, the organization is of a line type, with relatively few staff functions. It tends to be a "nothing or all" existence.

Under the consideration of type of work, assume that office A handles the same work day in and day out and that office B handles a certain type of work X for a part of a month, work Y for another part of a month, and work Z for still another part of a month. The structural organization of office A will probably differ from that of office B, and the personnel must be attuned to changes periodically as a normal state of affairs. Office A probably will emphasize staff elements. Office B, on the other hand, will tend toward a line type of organization in which most employees can perform several activities with equal skill.

Organizational continuity is also affected by the time element. A structure set up temporarily to accomplish an emergency task might be far different from one set up to exist over a long period of time. Organization structures having little continuity are usually very simple. An office group to handle registrations for a one-day convention might well be organized quite differently than a group organized to handle tax registrations. Or consider the example of a crowd of people organized to put out a fire in the neighborhood. They probably will be organized far differently from the firemen of the local fire department. The crowd of people will probably organize so that every member does something physical to put out the fire. It is unlikely that there would be any staff advisory members. Speed of action would be paramount and at the conclusion of the fire, the group would be dissolved. In contrast, the local fire department probably utilizes not only direct fire fighters but also a trained staff of experts in carrying out the task of fire fighting. Through time, the fire department has developed an efficient, highly coordinated organizational structure. And it is permanent—it is not dismantled after each fire-fighting experience.

## NEED FOR ORGANIZATIONAL BALANCE

Organizing, to be effective, must represent a balance among the various activities in relation to their real worth and contribution. An office is not all billing, all tabulating, all procedures analyzing, all filing, or all anything else. It is a proper balance and blending among the many activities believed essential. The effective organizer thinks in these terms, yet he recognizes that organization dynamics has a significant effect upon the maintenance of this balance.

Normal changes within an organization take place in different areas and to different degrees. This results from current popular interest, research and development, and personal managerial intent. To illustrate, the records retention unit spurts in size due to a strong swing in managerial thinking on its importance; or systems and procedures develops into a central activity of those concerned with paper-work processing, and organizational units within which this type of work is performed are expanded and given greater authority.

The result of these localized changes may tend to make the entire organization unbalanced. In some instances, the strengthened unit needed just that to place it in proper balance with the other organizational units. But frequently, the strengthening does not stop at the point of balance; it continues until a state of imbalance among the units is again present.

The meaning of organizational balance is subject to a great many interpretations. Good organizing maintains the relative importance of the various functions. Too frequently, however, managers continue to improve what is already relatively effective. Bettering the weak areas would be more helpful from the viewpoint of the entire organization. An important part of the problem is not to place all strong managers of the enterprise in one or a few organizational units. Success begets success. Commonly, the strong manager tends to attract trainees with the greatest managerial potential, and the more proficient manager tends to develop good managers under him.

In analyzing an office organization, it may be found that certain activities such as corresponding and billing appear grossly overemphasized relative to their importance in view of all the other office activities. Further study may reveal that the past experience and work of the office manager was in the area now seemingly too large or being given too much emphasis. Why is this? Because there is a human tendency by managers to emphasize and manage well those activities in which they are most interested and experienced. If the office manager "knows" corresponding, this work will tend to be organized and managed well. On the other hand, if he knows very little about office personnel research, this activity may be somewhat neglected and not developed to its required relative importance.

## MAJOR INFLUENCES BRINGING ORGANIZATION CHANGE

From what has already been stated, it is evident that there are many factors which bring about change in an organization. To exhaust a list of causes is beyond our purpose here. But four major influences will be discussed in detail because they represent important considerations in organization dynamics. These four influences are (1) the process and machines used, (2) the relationships followed, (3) the degree of centralization practiced, and (4) the personnel employed.

## PROCESS AND MACHINES USED

As indicated in Chapter 27, the process quite often determines the main components of the organization structure. In the handling of a purchase order, for example, receiving, costing, billing, and mailing may contribute the main components. However, research and concentrated efforts for improvement may evolve a different process for the handling of purchase orders. Information in a different form or time sequence may be adopted to reduce costs. It is also possible that some computer means or duplicating improvement might revolutionize the old process into one that is different and brand new. This, in turn, would mean organizational changes.

Closely allied with process changes are the machines used. Mechanization may use the identical process, but it may perform the work in such a manner and at such speed that changes in the organizational pattern are necessary. Certainly, when the office work is being accomplished largely by manual means and is changed to one of mechanical processing, organizational modifications are in order. Mechanization may eliminate certain functions and change others, resulting in the need for different people, at least in the sense of the displaced people being retrained for the new work, and new organizational relationships being established.

## THE RELATIONSHIPS FOLLOWED

There is an old saying that "authority clusters around the person willing to accept it." The employee of managerial competence, ambition, and desire for authority tends to acquire additional wanted authority. Hence, over a period, authority tends to be increased by such individuals; and as a result, organization relationships change, at first in practice, and ultimately formally, in keeping with conditions as they have developed.

In Chapter 28, it was pointed out that for a small organization many functions are usually grouped into each organization unit, the total number of such units is small, a line type organization is used, and the number of relationships is relatively low. In contrast, when few functions are in each organization unit, the number of units is large, a line and staff type of organization is used, and the relationships are relatively high in number. In either of these cases when the relationships are altered, there is a necessity of change in the organization structure. There can, in fact, be an organization change caused by a modification in relationships only; a change in functions or in their grouping or in personnel is not necessary.

## THE DEGREE OF CENTRALIZATION PRACTICED

A key contributor to organization change is the movement either to or from centralization. As already stated the current trend is toward more and more centralization of office work. In and of itself this makes for organization changes. But the degree of centralization should not be determined by following blindly what others may be doing. The soundest approach is to make an objective study within the given enterprise. For this purpose, a four-step program can be followed:

1. *Determine the major centers of office work activity.* Essentially this is an inventory showing, by centers, the name, location, number of employees, major work performed, quantities of work, and equipment utilized. From these data, it is possible to identify the areas offering the greatest potential for improvement. The use of a simple form such as that shown in Figure 29–1 is helpful in this recording work.

CLERICAL FUNCTIONS INVENTORY

| COMPANY: | | INFORMATION BY: | | DATE: | |
|---|---|---|---|---|---|
| WORK GROUP | LOCATION AND DEPARTMENT | NUMBER OF EMPLOYEES | | MAJOR WORK PERFORMED | OFFICE MACHINES AND EQUIPMENT USED |
| | | SUPERVISORY | NON-SUPERV'Y | | |
| | | | | | |
| | | | | | |
| | | | | | |
| | | | | | |
| | | | | | |
| | | | | | |

FIG. 29–1.   Recording form to simplify inventory of clerical functions.

2. *Ascertain the productive efficiency of these centers.* Find out if any relationship exists between the volume of work processed by a group and the work output per person in that group. In general, a high volume of available work per person is related to high individual productivity. This results partly from the fact that there must be a sufficient work volume to keep an employee busy throughout the work period. Figure 29–2 shows that for a given enterprise, the greater the number of billings processed, the higher the employee productivity or billings processed per employee. Each dot in the figure represents a district office of the company. In the case of two district offices, the number of billings processed is about 420, and the corresponding productivity per employee is 73 and 77, respectively. When the volume of work is higher, at 700 or 750, as in other

district offices, the productivity jumps to 97. This suggests gains to be derived by centralizing all billing work ; but before this conclusion can be reached, the analyst should conduct similar investigations for other clerical work performed in the district offices, such as credit and collections, and accounts receivable, to determine if a similar pattern emerges. From this range of information, the feasibility of consolidation can be demonstrated.

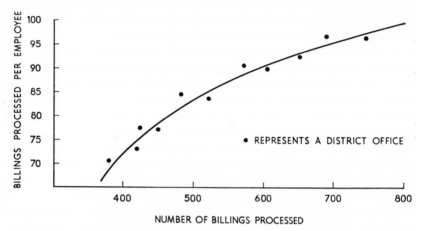

NUMBER OF BILLINGS PROCESSED

FIG. 29–2.   Relationship between average productivity per employee performing billing processing and number of billings processed for each of 11 district offices.

*3. Establish an optimum number of major office work centers.*   We are trying to answer the questions : To what degree should the centralization be pursued ? Do you collapse office work done in 11 district sales offices to six or three regional office service centers, or some number in between ? In some cases, the optimum size can be determined for the data utilized in step No. 2 by noting the volume point at which definite plateauing takes place, that is, employee productivity remains constant regardless of the work volume. Using this optimum work volume as a base, the number of district offices can be determined. But this mathematical answer usually must be qualified by nonmeasurable factors, such as the potential office mechanization, the need of communication between the organizational units, the cost of conversion, employee training required, and the vulnerability and risk involved should the centralized units become incapacitated due to equipment breakdown, strikes, or disaster.

*4. Decide on the location of the major office work centers.*   Top managers normally make this decision, keeping in mind certain criteria among which are the present organization structure, the personnel involved, the availability and cost of labor, and the likely direction of the company's future growth and paper-work requirements.

## THE PERSONNEL EMPLOYED

Of all the influences contributing to organization change that of personnel employed is the greatest and most significant. It merits full discussion which will now be given. Change due to personnel comes about in three different ways: (1) the manager believes a different organizational arrangement will prove advantageous; (2) the manager recognizes that some personnel have changed and desires to utilize better their possible contributions; or (3) the manager is confronted with the problem of labor turnover—some employees leave, and replacements must be found for them, or the employee requirements of the office change.

Certain types of people tend to work together effectively as a group, while others never seem to reach the level of expected cooperation. The reasons are many; but presumably most important are differences in personalities, capacities, and relationships among the group's members. Various predetermined personnel measurements and devices can be employed to place employees better, but trial-and-error, probationary, or temporary placement approaches are widely used. Nothing, it seems, completely takes the place of actually trying the employee out and observing what is achieved from this trial. This shuffling of personnel makes for organizational changes and is done in the interests not only of employee social satisfaction but also for production efficiency.

Most managers recognize the fundamental truth that with time, their employees change. They acquire new knowledge, new skills, new interests, and new attitudes. This is inevitable; in fact, it is promoted by managers in management development programs and many efforts of motivation. But it is perhaps more important that people change because it is a natural evolutionary process which takes place as a person increases in age, participates in more experiences, and reflects on life and its meaning. An office job satisfactory to a young woman of 20 probably will not satisfy her when she reaches 26. She will seek a change, and the alert manager will recognize this and do something about it. Later, at age 35, it could well be that no job in industry will satisfy her, as her interests and desires are now centered on work in connection with her own family. The point here is that no person remains static. Some change more rapidly than others, but change they do. Managers, in their organizing work, should take these personnel changes into account; and this means the organization structure will be dynamic.

Sooner or later, all offices have the problem of employee replacement due to the normal state of affairs of some employees leaving the office or the employee requirements of the office changing as the office work either expands or contracts. A basic need of every office is to supply and to maintain a satisfactory working force. To do this, likely candidates must be located and those best qualified selected and hired. This brings up the important subject areas of recruiting and selecting office employees, and the next several pages will be devoted to a discussion of them.

## RECRUITING

The recruitment of employees is a permanent activity. Increased emphasis is placed upon this work during peak business periods, but the problem of securing the right employees confronts most offices most of the time. There are always separations because of marriage, illness, voluntary leaves, terminations, and death.

Recruiting has four major aspects: (1) the determining of future needs, (2) the evaluating of the recruiting process for different types of office jobs, (3) the establishing of contacts helpful for referrals of candidates, and (4) the preparing and distributing of appropriate material used to promote recruiting efforts. Knowing the quantity and quality of candidates to seek and when to seek them constitutes the first requirement of effective recruiting. People of the skill, attitude, and interest that the office requires should set the background for recruiting efforts. Following this, attention should be directed to the sources utilized and the contacts established. Many office managers have found that appropriate recruiting literature is definitely helpful in aiding recruiting efforts.

Limited data reveal that the number of applicants hired to the number rejected is in the ratio of 1 to 7, and that over $200 is spent for each office employee hired. These data suggest that recruiting can be improved. What can be done? Probably foremost is the use of more accurate and complete job specifications. When the job requirements are vague, the likelihood of finding a satisfactory candidate is considerably lessened. No available source can supply its maximum recruiting assistance when the information supplied is insufficient and not clearly stated. Another improvement possibility is the avoidance of delay in hiring the likely candidate. In too many cases, a qualified candidate is lost because of a lack of promptness in dealing with the applicant from the time of application to the time the decision to hire or not to hire is rendered. A third area is developing the reputation of the particular office as being a good place to work. The office possessing this valuable public good will commonly has a satisfactory group from which outstanding candidates can be selected.

## SOURCES OF OFFICE HELP

Generally speaking, a variety of labor sources is desirable and needed to meet recruitment goals. The "best" source usually must be qualified regarding the type of office job, the geographical location, the prominence of the company, and the skill with which the recruiter uses a particular source. The proper personnel viewpoint is to work with a number of different sources of office help. Better people usually can be selected if there is a group from which to choose.

Among the more common sources are:

1. *Persons recommended by present employees.* This is usually a very good source, but caution must be exercised to avoid favoritism. Some companies post notices on bulletin boards encouraging employees to recommend friends who might be seeking employment.

2. *Former employees.* This group constitutes an excellent source. However, careful screening and selection techniques are required to avoid a "come and go" atmosphere. Frequently, satisfactory part-time employees can be obtained from this source.

3. *New employees.* The person just hired usually knows somebody else who is looking for a job. Satisfactory results are usually obtained if candidates are put through the regular selection channels.

4. *Employment agencies.* It is well to utilize this source. Some agencies are public, others are private. The former charge no fee; the latter do, and the charge commonly is made to the employer. Agencies have broad contacts and experience; they try to supply likely candidates for vacancies.

5. *Schools—including vocational advisory boards.* This is one of the better and larger sources of office employees. Some companies keep in close touch with high schools, business colleges, and universities, and send representatives to talk with students about to graduate. Many schools have placement offices and will cooperate fully with prospective employers. It is well to develop schools as a source of office help. The candidates usually have formal training but limited business experience.

6. *Institutions for the rehabilitation of handicapped persons.* Frequently, very capable people can be secured from this source.

7. *Voluntary applicants.* It is a good practice always to see people who come in looking for a job. Frequently, this source offers excellent personnel, but it cannot be relied upon as the sole source of help.

8. *Advertising.* Newspaper, radio, and television advertising are effective media for securing a number of candidates. Good coverage is usually obtained; but all respondents will not be fully qualified, and the normal weeding-out process must be used.

## SELECTION OF OFFICE HELP

Choice of a candidate is normally based on a comparison between (1) what the job requires for successful execution and (2) what the applicant has to offer. For the most part, the better the balance between these two factors, the better the selection work, and the more likely is the attainment of a satisfactory working force. Under job requirements are such attributes as the amount of formal education, knowledge, experience, and physical considerations. Under what the applicant offers are his fund of knowledge, experience, intelligence, physical attributes, and personality. This matching effort, however, must not be thought of as an exacting operation. On the contrary, it is quite flexible. Job requirements should be used as a guide. Frequently, a satisfactory person does not have the *exact* qualifications desired; but with time and experience, he may well prove satisfactory on the job.

The use of vocational requirements facilitates the selection. For example, the suggested minimum vocational requirements for the job of beginning stenographer might be established at ability to type at a rate of 55 words per minute on straight copy material for a ten-minute period, with five errors or less; to perform shorthand writing at 100 words per minute; to transcribe notes of unfamiliar material at the rate of 35 words per minute for a ten-minute period, and to produce work of mailable quality; to transcribe from a machine, at the rate of 10–12 letters per hour each letter consisting of two to three paragraphs. Progress is being made by various associations in getting office managers to request employees who meet definite vocational standards and in getting schools to train students toward these standards.

## TOOLS OF PERSONNEL SELECTION

There are a number of selection tools that assist in deciding which candidate should be placed in what job of an office organization structure. Discussion here includes the tools of (1) application form, (2) interview, (3) references, (4) physical examination, and (5) tests.

1. *Application form. The application form is a written record providing a means of securing and maintaining the more obvious personnel information, such as identification, education, work history, and activities of the applicant.* It is particularly helpful for selection purposes. Sufficient information should be obtained, but superfluous information should be avoided. All questions asked should serve a definite purpose in evaluating the candidate's possible value to the office.

For the higher-level jobs, it is often quite helpful to ask several questions designed to gain some insight into the candidate's general attitude toward life and his ability to write and to organize material. To illustrate, questions such as the following might be asked: "In narrative form, give us a résumé of your major accomplishments, hopes, and ambition." "Will you tell us about your special qualifications not covered elsewhere in this application?" "What unusual business situations have you encountered, and what did you do about them?"

2. *Interviews.* One of the basic tools in the selection process is the interview. It provides the opportunity for meeting the applicant and observing his verbal ability, appearance, general personality, and attitude, as well as the chance to "get together and talk it over." The face-to-face meeting with the applicant offers possibilities of information afforded by no other means.

The objectives of the employment interview are to exchange information and to make a favorable impression upon the applicant. Unless these conditions are accomplished, the interview is not wholly satisfactory. The exchange of information is essential to intelligent selection. Creating a favorable impression reflects the interviewer's ability to gain public goodwill by securing a favorable attitude of the applicant toward the office, whether he is hired or not.

To assist interviewing, it is a good practice for the interviewer to have a list of items he wishes to cover. The accuracy and quality standards on previous jobs held by the candidate, the supervisory practices liked, and the grades received in school are illustrative of areas to cover that will make for effective interviewing. Second, rating charts can be used. By this means, a written record of the relative intensities of the important factors is made by the interviewer. A third interviewing aid is oral trade questions. An idea of the candidate's competency is obtained through the use of these questions, which are concerned with names of office machines, office operations, general knowledge of office jobs, and the like. Fourth, an interviewer's guide, designed to help secure essential information, can be used. The interviewer asks the questions on the guide and records the answers given by the applicant as favorable or unfavorable. Fifth, interviewing practices shown by experience to be effective should be followed. These include:

*a*) Putting the applicant and yourself at ease.

*b*) Explaining clearly what the job is—the duties, responsibilities, chances for promotion, working conditions, and so forth. If possible, read or let the candidate read the job description.

*c*) Using language appropriate to the educational and experience background of the applicant—language that does not reveal your own attitude.

*d*) Encouraging the applicant to talk by asking questions that begin with *why, when,* and *how.* Avoid questions that can be answered by a "Yes" or "No."

*e*) Interrupting the applicant only when what is being said is irrelevant. Start speaking after the applicant has paused for at least ten seconds.

*f*) Letting the applicant ask questions.

*g*) Granting sufficient time for the interview, but not prolonging it to the point of boredom or useless repetition.

*h*) Keeping your interviews fresh. Periodically change the questions and the sequence in which they are asked.

3. *References.*   Managers usually like to obtain information on the applicant from previous employers and responsible persons currently acquainted with him. Reference checking is a helpful means in appraising not only the candidate's cooperation and dependability but also the candidate's probable skill, interests, and abilities. On the other hand, there are many who believe references are frequently unreliable. Members of this school claim inaccurate evaluations are provided; either excessive praise or excessive criticism is supplied.

The value of references depends upon the knowledge and character of the person supplying the reference information. Qualifications include being fully familiar with the demands of the job, knowing the candidate extremely well, supplying information with absolute honesty, and exercising sound evaluating judgment. These qualifications appear to be filled best by professional people and by former employers.

In a great majority of cases, agreement on these points exists:

*a*) References from former employers are more reliable than those supplied by personal friends of the candidate. Former employers can verify dates of employment, salaries, type and quality of work performed, and attendance record.

*b*) Telephone reference inquiries produce better results than mail. By telephone, a depth of detail can be acquired, and people given as references are usually more willing to speak frankly than to put the same comments in writing.

*c*) Reference information should be obtained *before* a full interview. Data can be checked, and selected areas for discussion or further probing can be chosen for the interview.

4. *Physical examination.*   The main purpose of the physical examination is to determine the type of work the applicant is physically best suited to perform. It shows one of several situations: (*a*) that the candidate is physically able to do certain types of work; (*b*) that he is fit for limited service only in specific jobs; (*c*) that with certain adjustments and treatments, he will be suited for jobs of a particular sort; or (*d*) that he is physically unfit, and proper corrective action cannot be taken. Physical examinations help to raise the standard of physical fitness, to increase work output, to lower accident rates, to decrease turnover, and to lessen the amount of absenteeism caused by sickness.

5. *Tests.*   This is the last personnel selection tool to be discussed. *Tests are measurements of personnel aspects secured by scientific methods of observing and recording in certain standard situations.* The measurements are normally qualitative and are believed to be related to success in performing the work. But tests determine what a candidate can

do, not what he will do. A test score is an indication of the probability of the candidate's success or failure as determined by his possession of the attributes measured and the importance of these attributes in the work accomplishment.

Several terms in connection with tests should be familiar to the office manager. These include:

a) Validity of test. This refers to the relationship between the test score and accepted or known facts about the attribute measured by the test. To illustrate, the most desirable employees among the present employees should make a high score; the average employees, a lower score; and the least desirable employees, the lowest score.

b) Reliability of test. This deals with the consistency of the test in yielding similar results when given on different occasions. In other words, the same approximate results should always be obtained with the same group and the same test.

c) Standardization of test. When a test has been found, through a process of experimentation, to have both validity and reliability, it is commonly referred to as a standardized test.

d) Norms of test. A series of numbers indicating performance scores of large numbers of persons who have taken the test are called "norms." They serve as guides for comparison of scores.

There are on the market today a great number of tests designed to measure the many different attributes considered significant in personnel work. The National Business Entrance Tests, sponsored jointly by the Administrative Management Society and the United Business Education Association, offer a battery of tests covering machine calculation, stenography, typing, bookkeeping, filing, and business fundamentals. Those who pass these tests are given a card or certificate of proficiency which is evidence of having successfully passed certain standardized clerical tests.

A 12-hour examination program is utilized for Certified Professional Secretary candidates. The examination, prepared annually, consists of personal adjustments and human relations, economics and business organization, business law, secretarial accounting, stenography, and secretarial procedures. Successful candidates are given a CPS identifying card and are permitted to wear a CPS pin.[1]

Among the many types of single-trait tests, the following are probably of greatest importance in office management: (1) the intelligence test, (2) the clerical test, (3) the personality test, and (4) the interest test. Figure

---

[1] For further information on the National Business Entrance Tests, write the Administrative Management Society, Willow Grove, Pa.; for information on the Certified Professional Secretary tests, write National Secretaries Association, 222 West Eleventh Street, Kansas City, Mo.

| Name | Contribution | General Content of Test | Basic Implications | Examples of Standard Tests | Main Purpose of Test |
|---|---|---|---|---|---|
| Intelligence and Mental Alertness Tests | Indicates one's adequacy in a number of types of work. | Problems on information and of judgment and reasoning. Questions dealing with contrast or comparison. Memory tasks. | What a person has absorbed is a fair indication of what he will or can absorb. Differences in background are not taken into consideration. Little indication of how the indicated ability may be applied. | Army Alpha (Original and Several Revisions) Benge Test of General Knowledge The Henmon-Nelson Test of Mental Ability The O'Rourke General Classification Test Otis Self-Administering Test of Mental Ability The Pressey Senior Classification and Verification Psychological Corporation Scott Company Mental Alertness Test | To make preliminary selection. To gain an insight to the applicant's ability to understand and to manage ideas. |
| Trade and Clerical Tests | Helps to show the degree of achievement possessed by a candidate for this specific type of work. | Questions appraising vocabulary level. Ability to notice details. Problems in simple calculations and arithmetic reasoning. Competency in performing clerical work. | Candidate having achievement of certain level and above will probably execute the job requirements most effectively. | Benge's Clerical Test Blackstone Stenographic Proficiency Tests Minnesota Vocational Test for Clerical Workers National Business Entrance Tests O'Rourke's Clerical Aptitude Test Psychological Corporation Shellow's Intelligence Test for Stenographers Thurstone Examination in Clerical Work, Form A | To determine applicant's knowledge of a specific trade or profession. To select candidates having at least a certain minimum of relative ability to perform work in a particular field. |
| Personality Tests | Indicates the presence or absence of traits, or group of traits. | Single item questions which are answered with "Yes" or "No." Single words suggested—applicant names words which he associates with this single word. | Applicant will answer questions honestly. The make-up of the personality is related to the situational demands of a job. | Beckman Revision of Allport A-S Test California Test of Personality Heidbreder's Personal Traits Rating Scale, Form 2 Humm-Wadsworth Temperament Scale Laird's Personal Inventory C-2 | To appraise those qualities which are pivotal in a situation and probably will determine the degree of future success of candidate on the job. |
| Interest Tests | Aims to determine the extent of the candidate's genuine interest in a particular type of work. | Questions to indicate the correct use or identity of machines and devices. | One's latent or developed interest in a certain type of work is closely related to the energy, persistence, and contribution which he gives to that work. | Brainard-Steward Specific Interest Inventory Strong's Vocational Interest Blank, Form A Thurstone Vocational Interest Schedule | To determine the degree of interest which a candidate has for different types of work. |

FIG. 29–3.  Comparison of various tests on significant factors.

29–3 shows a comparison of these four types of tests, revealing for each one the contribution, general content, basic implication, names, and main purpose.

Testing is a specialized field, and best results are usually obtained when the work is performed by qualified testing experts. Trained personnel, either on a part- or full-time basis, can be engaged.

## FORMAT FOR REORGANIZING

Work of reorganizing should follow a definite pattern. The following format is effective:

1. *Make an inventory of the present organization.* It is absolutely essential to know the precise identity of the organization structure being reorganized. Assumptions and guesses in this respect lead to unnecessary trouble and work. The correct name of each organizational unit, the exact work performed, the employees performing what work in each unit, the line and the staff authority relationships existing among all the units should be carefully ascertained and set down in writing.

2. *Write a description for each job.* Although it requires much time and detailed effort, preparing a written description of each job is usually extremely helpful. In no other way will the reorganizer fully realize the exact content of the various work segments and how they are related. Preparing written descriptions also greatly assists in securing clues as to what work might better be placed other than where it is in the present organization.

3. *Analyze current organization, and evaluate proposed changes.* This step is guided mainly by the objectives of the entire organization and the part that each component is expected to contribute to the goal accomplishment. Knowledge of the people available to perform the various tasks is also essential. This can be gained by researching the personnel records and talking with the supervisors or with the employees themselves. Some means of recording information in a logical order should be followed. Data common to all employees should be obtained so that reasonable comparisons can be made.

From all this information, the proposed organization is gradually evolved. Several different ideas, encompassing different work divisions, people, and relationships, are tentatively drawn up. Subsequently, each arrangement is evaluated, noting what appear to be its strong and its weak points, the probable hurdles involved in putting it into force, the effect upon the personnel to be changed, the possibility of acquiring needed new personnel, the training which will be required, and similar considerations. Tentative arrangements should be discussed with various management members and affected personnel to gain their appraisals and exchange reactions regarding the advantages and disadvantages to be incurred and the consensus regarding what should be done. Based on the results of this overall investigation, the decision is made as to the makeup of the reorganization to be used.

4. *Determine the phases or steps to be taken from the present to the proposed organization.* It may be deemed wise to institute the reorganization at once. In situations where an extremely inefficient or costly organizational structure exists, it may be best to implement the change without delay. However, in many cases, the gradual shifting from the present to the ultimate organization takes place in several phases or steps. Normally, this makes for greater acceptance by the employees, who will go along with a small change but will balk if the modification is too large or believed radical from their viewpoint. Individual situations may govern the timing of the change. For example, the retirement or resignation of a key executive may signal the most opportune time to adopt change. However, regardless of the reason, in each instance the plan of what is to be done and by whom should be worked out in advance. To reorganize without adequate predetermination and study usually leads to poor results.

Figure 29–4 illustrates the phases of reorganization that might be followed by a company whose present office organization is like that shown by the top diagram. Note that seven managerial chiefs report to the office manager. It is desired to reduce the number of chiefs reporting directly to the office manager, to install and use a computer, and to consolidate relative functions in order to get a more tightly knit and effective organization structure.

The first phase in this reorganization is shown by the middle illustration of Figure 29–4. Procedures and research has been given the subfunctions of work simplification and the newly created standards section. Under the new unit of physical office facilities is placed office layout and office purchasing. The correspondence and reports unit now includes filing along with reception, mail, and communicative services consolidated into one subunit. The computer unit is added and initially will process data in connection will billing and payroll. Accounts payable remains a separate unit, as does duplicating; the head of each reports directly to the office manager.

The second and final phase consists of adding systems to the procedures and research unit and transferring this enlarged unit to the computer section. Work simplification with standards and a manuals unit under it report directly to the office manager. Duplicating is transferred and becomes a subunit under correspondence and reports, while accounts payable is placed under the computer organizational unit.

5. *Take necessary reorganization action.* The last step is to put the reorganization into action. Once it is decided what changes to make and a time schedule established, definite action should be taken. To hesitate or

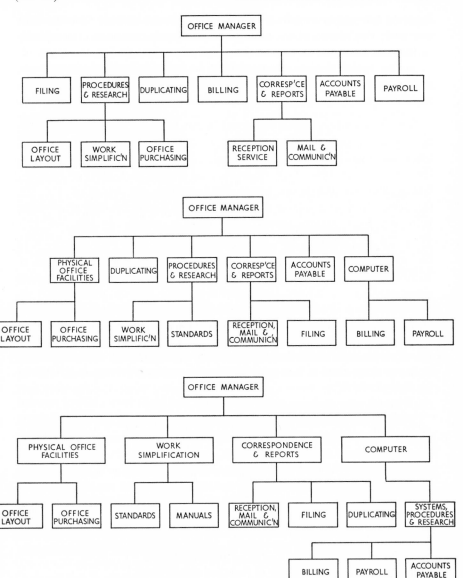

FIG. 29–4. Phase charts are commonly used in reorganizing. The present organization is illustrated by the top chart. The first phase of changes to be made is shown by the middle chart. Subsequently, the organization of the middle chart is changed to that shown by the bottom phase chart.

display indecisiveness can hamper the entire reorganization. A positive viewpoint, fairness, and pointing out the "reasons why" generally assist in getting good results.

It is important to give the reorganization time to prove itself. Time is required for people to adjust to new assignments, become familiar with new authority relationships, and utilize new formal channels of communication. All managers should be thoroughly indoctrinated in the reorganization, be able to answer questions concerning it, publicize its advantages, and counsel any employee in need of such help. Successful reorganization plans always include these important follow-up features.

Specific attention should be called to the fact that the above list does not include copying the organization of another enterprise in a similar business. Organizing is highly personalized and should be tailor-made for the specific objectives, type of work, and people of a given enterprise. Needs and circumstances vary. Basic guides are available for the construction of an effective organization and should be used in keeping with the basic requirements. The work is similar to the architect designing a building. The best architect does not copy an existing building. He employs basic guides of building and engineering and creates a structure that meets the specific and personal needs of his client.

## QUESTIONS

1. Comment fully on this statement: "The old adage of keeping an organization in balance is so much academic nonsense. Activities are never in balance; some are always more important than others. Hence, it is perfectly natural and nothing to worry about to have organizations that are not in balance. It is a natural state of affairs."

2. What are some of the undesirable conditions that result from a lack of any real planning for organizational change?

3. Carefully identify each of the following:
   a) "Validity of test."
   b) Phasing in reorganization.
   c) Certified Professional Secretary.
   d) Application form.

4. Explain how establishing an optimum number of major office work centers tends to result in organization centralization.

5. Regarding tests for selection purposes, answer each of the following:
   a) What is the main contribution of personality tests?
   b) What is the main purpose of trade and clerical tests?
   c) What are the basic implications of intelligence and mental alertness tests?

6. Do you agree with this statement? "For a given enterprise, personnel changes over a period, but the organization remains fundamentally the same. If more managers kept this basic truth in mind, there would be less organizational problems." Why?

7. In what ways do you believe the recruiting of office employees can be improved? Are you of the opinion that these improvement means are practical and can be accomplished? Explain.

8. Explain the meaning of Figure 29–4 in your own words.

9. Relate several examples of the time element affecting organizational continuity.

10. A friend of a present employee has been interviewed, tested, and her references checked. She is recommended to the supervisor of department K-5, who hires her. At the end of a four-week period, it appears she cannot perform the work satisfactorily. Is the personnel selection, supervision, company, or employee at fault? Explain your answer.

11. Are organizational changes brought about by changes in the process and machines used? Elaborate on your answer.

12. Stage an interview with an applicant for the job of correspondent. Bring out the important factors that make an interview successful. Summarize your techniques.

## CASE PROBLEMS

### Case 29–1.   Foster-Myers Company

Experience with personal interviews and background checking for personnel selection and placing was proving unsatisfactory for Jack Echols, office manager of Foster-Myers Company, a regional chain of variety stores. To correct the situation, Mr. Echols decided to enlist the help of testing. He realized that tests were not a perfect selection media yet he was impressed by the statement of a competitor who claimed that with interviews alone only 28 percent of all new employees hired turned out to be really above average employees, whereas when an interview plus tests were followed, the percentage of above average employees jumped to 46 percent.

Accordingly, tests were used by Mr. Echols in selecting private secretaries for executives of the company. These tests were designed to measure learning, memory, alertness, adaptability, creativity and flexibility in thinking. The results obtained proved extremely satisfactory, so much so that in talking with the president of the company about this program, Mr. Echols was urged to use these tests throughout the office organization. Currently, the company needed a typist in the purchasing department and a typist in the sales analysis department. Of seven applicants, Mr. Echols, by interviewing, selected five to be tested and from the results of testing selected the two best girls. They were placed in the jobs and were well received. The supervisor of purchasing congratulated Mr. Echols on his providing such an excellent new employee. However, at the end of the eighth week the girl placed in the sales analysis department quit and three weeks later, the girl in purchasing was absent and telephoned her supervisor that she had decided to leave the company. Upon hearing this news, Jack Echols stated, "I'm through with tests. It's like I've been saying, the best approach is to hire any likely candidates and just try them out. Maybe they stay a few days, a few weeks, a few months, perhaps a few years. But you never know. Scientific personnel selection and placement? That's a schoolroom term."

### Problems:

1. Evaluate the actions and beliefs of Mr. Echols.

2. What action regarding selecting and placing of employees should the company follow? Why?

## Case 29–2.    Express Cartage Company

Some 20 years ago, this company started with one truck and one driver, who is now president of a thriving cartage business. Initially, Mr. Tom Flanagan, nicknamed "Gabby" by all his close friends, had his wife, Angela, prepare all the paper work in connection with the business. As the business grew, he hired Phideas Plummer, then aged 43 years, as a bookkeeper, and soon, there were a junior bookkeeper reporting to Phideas and a sales manager with two salesmen reporting to Mr. Flanagan. A little later, August Wagner served as an assistant to Mr. Flanagan in the operations department, which had grown to a fleet totaling six trucks and drivers.

About five years ago, it became apparent that something would have to be done about Phideas Plummer, who, although quite proficient at keeping books, was indeed a poor manager. At this time, Phideas had the title "office manager," with two bookkeepers and a file clerk reporting to him. He seemed to have become very irritable, was curt with the employees, and seldom was able to supply Mr. Flanagan with information requested. Since he had been with the company for 15 years and knew the business, there was reluctance to let him go. Accordingly, one of the bookkeepers, Mrs. Myrtle Ashenbrenner, aged 48 years, was made the office manager and given two girls, one who would take care of billings and the other to do the filing. Mr. Plummer continued to handle bookkeeping, including accounts receivable, and had one helper.

About six months ago, further changes appeared imperative. Phideas Plummer was getting more cantankerous and just did not seem to know the meaning of co-operation with the other employees. However, his three people, an accounts receivable accountant and two general accountants, voiced no difficulty with him. Myrtle Ashenbrenner, now with the company 11 years, failed to show any aggressiveness in managing the office. She seemed content to run only her unit, consisting of herself, handling credit matters, a billing clerk, and a filing clerk. It was quite obvious that she and Phideas Plummer did not get along, even though there was no evidence of discord between them. The company now had a very competent sales manager, Peter Ferreti, who had a secretary, a file clerk, and three salesmen reporting to him. "Gabby" Flanagan was very well pleased with the work of Mr. Ferreti; and in talking over the problem of having a better office manager, they agreed that Miss Eileen Fogarty, currently private secretary to Mr. Flanagan, should be given this job. Miss Fogarty is a very reliable employee; all of her six years with the company have been as Mr. Flanagan's private secretary. Her present age is 29 years. When offered the new job, Miss Fogarty was not too enthusiastic but stated if it was what Mr. Flanagan wanted, she would accept it.

At that time, the office unit consisted of a telephone switchboard operator, two stenographers who also did filing work, a watchman, and a purchasing clerk who bought items up to $300; over this amount, the purchasing was done by Mr. Flanagan. The operations unit, still headed by August Wagner, had a file clerk and 16 drivers and trucks.

Mr. Flanagan is today still dissatisfied with the operation of the office. He does not know what to do about it although he has given some thought to it. He has asked you for assistance.

## Problems:

1. What are your reactions to the changes made in the organization of this company?

2. Draw a chart of the current organization.

3. In your opinion, what are the major problems requiring managerial attention?

4. What recommendations would you give Mr. Flanagan? Substantiate your suggestions.

# CHAPTER 30

# PRINCIPLES OF

# OFFICE ORGANIZING

Personal soundness is not an absence of
problems but a way of reacting to them.
—*Donald W. MacKinnon*

EFFECTIVE organizing is a challenge to every manager. It cannot be achieved by any mechanistic discipline or technological process. The best approach appears to include knowledge of basic organizing truths plus skill in their application, taking completely into account the individual considerations. Ever changing economic and social developments add to the challenge and necessitate much time and effort by the manager in maintaining a sound and effective organization.

## BENEFITS OF GOOD ORGANIZATION

A good organization is well worth the time and effort required to design, evaluate, and modify it as changing conditions demand. There are numerous benefits derived from good organization, among which the following are vital:

1. *Enables a manager to multiply himself.* One man can accomplish a limited amount of work; but by means of organizing, he can spread his influence and achieve much more work. A man through good organizing attains greater work accomplishments than is humanly possible working alone.

2. *Prevents needless duplication of work.* The entire work to be done is analyzed and divided with the resultant necessary work components determined. No more and no less work than that made up by these components need be done.

3. *Encourages labor specialization.* The dividing of the work, neces-

sary for organizing, is compatible with the use of labor specialization. Special skills and work efficiencies are harnessed by good organization.

4. *Provides a basis for evaluating performance and capabilities of employees.* Good organization helps define specific work to be done, outlines in what areas decisions are to be made, and indicates who is accountable for what work.

5. *Reveals logical personnel advancement possibilities.* The sequence of promotion, which jobs are related, and the relative importance of each are stressed by good organization.

6. *Assists salary and wage administration.* The relative importance and difficulties of different jobs revealed by organization can assist in developing an equitable salary and wage administration. In some cases, jobs of the same organizational level have similar wage ranges.

7. *Expedites formal communication.* Definite channels of relationships among all organizational units are established by organization, and these channels serve as official means for communication among the organizational members.

8. *Resolves differences among managers concerning identity and coverage of their respective managerial authority.* Organization spells out the relative authority for each management member. The areas in which decisions and their enforcement are authorized are clearly established; they are not left to chance.

9. *Minimizes bypassing established authority relationships.* Who is to report to whom is clearly established in good organization, and every manager knows who is to help him accomplish a definite task.

10. *Increases cooperation and coordination of the group's efforts.* Good organization places emphasis upon cooperation with others; and the formal division of work, together with specified authority relationships, fosters coordination.

11. *Places activities into manageable units.* The work of each unit can be planned effectively, expanded or contracted as required, and adequately controlled. In addition, the group can be of a size and composition which permit high morale, commonness of purpose, and effective leadership.

12. *Permits an orderly approach to reorganizing.* A known structure exists within which employees can work together effectively. Mistakes in this structure can be brought to light quickly; they need not be perpetuated. Necessary changes can be planned, considering all important aspects of the change; correction by expediency is unnecessary.

## ORGANIZING PRINCIPLES

The above list is quite formidable and certainly worth striving for. However, from the practical viewpoint, at any given time, different degrees in attaining these benefits exist. There are several reasons why this is true. In the first place, the personal influence of top executives upon the structure of the organization is exceedingly important. Men differ in their beliefs, and not all top executives view an organization structure with identical opinions and convictions. Also, the enterprise may lack the funds required to set up the ideal structure. Certain functions, recognized as important, are not a part of the organization structure simply because top managers cannot see their way clear to finance these activities. In addition, there is a tendency to stay with the old and established form of organization structure rather than to change to a new and untried form. Enterprises tend to build up customary practices, and these traditions tend to maintain an organizational *status quo*. Finally, there usually exist agreements, bargains, and favors among members of an enterprise. Contracts with certain individuals to perform certain functions, and understandings among members of an immediate family or relationship, may be cited as examples.

However, the maximum of benefits should be sought. How are these obtained? By applying definite organizing principles developed over a long period of organizing study and experience. These principles are general truths, not laws. They should be viewed as common guides to action. Universal and valid for an organization structure set up to achieve any major objective, their application to office organizing is particularly helpful to the progressive office manager.

Thinking in terms of principles instead of isolated instances makes for trust and confidence; at the same time, skill in applying knowledge is enhanced. Success in the specific application of any organization principle depends upon the individual circumstances. In certain instances, these principles are merely some of the factors which should be taken into account, along with other factors considered important in the individual case. A total of 16 principles will now be discussed. Important points of the previous chapters on organizing will be reiterated in this discussion.

## CONSIDERATION OF THE OBJECTIVE OF THE ENTERPRISE

The very first principle to be considered is the objective of the enterprise. Answers to the question "What is the aim of the enterprise?" or "What is the enterprise trying to accomplish?" are fundamental considerations in any organizing effort. The objective permeates all activities within an enterprise and influences their number and the extent to which they are carried out.

It is extremely difficult to judge the effectiveness of an organization structure without an adequate knowledge of the objective of the enterprise. What would be considered efficient for one objective might well be considered very inefficient for another objective. For example, the objective of cleaning the streets in a small town after a heavy snowstorm might require an organization structure which is entirely different from the structure needed when the objective is to distribute samples of products in ten cities throughout the United States. Or consider the organizational differences between two offices, one for a large insurance company using a computer, the other for a small manufacturer of necessity using basically manual office methods. Because the objectives are different, the type, number of functions, and personnel of the one structure would be entirely different from those of the other.

## UTILIZATION OF FUNCTIONS AS ESSENTIAL COMPONENTS

The essential functions of the enterprise should constitute the main elements of the organization structure. The nature of the enterprise determines the main functions; and these, in turn, determine the essential components upon which the organization structure should be built. Furthermore, the functional approach promotes the objective viewpoint in organizational structures and minimizes the subjective influences of the individual.

The grouping together of similar functions helps to form strong major groups; the tendency to split activities is minimized. Not only does grouping of like functions with like functions afford great strength to an organizational structure, but it also provides great flexibility; functions may be modified, new functions added, and old functions eliminated easily and simply without disturbing the essential structure of the organization.

In addition, the utilization of functions as the essential organization components helps to define clearly the various functions and to prevent uneconomical overlapping and duplicating. Working directly with functions helps to concentrate attention on them, and clear concepts of activities tend to be developed.

## ESTABLISH REASONABLE ORGANIZATIONAL UNITS

The functional approach assists in dividing the total work along a logical basis. To form practical organizational units, the various work divisions must be assembled into effective units from the standpoint of organizing. In establishing these organizational units, consideration must be given to many physical factors such as the size of the unit, the quantity and scope of work, the way it is done, the need for verifying the work of one unit by another, the extent of continuous flow, and the permanent nature of the work. The advantages of specialization are sought, but employee job interest must also be won. In addition, and possibly of greater importance, is consideration for the management member who will take charge of this unit. What are his special attributes, his shortcomings, ambitions, accomplishments, and training? If no manager is available, what qualifications will be sought; and is there a reasonable possibility that such a manager can be hired? Furthermore, adequate thought must be given to evaluating the proposed nonmanagement members of the unit, the capacity and skills required, personnel relationships to be integrated, and the wishes of the contemplated prevailing management member.

In addition, the reasonableness of the organizational unit is affected by the influence of the span of authority. If organizational units of relatively small work scopes are established, there normally is a tendency to use wider spans of authority than if the reverse—units with large work scopes —is adopted. The span should always take into account the preference and managerial ability of the supervisory executive.

## DEFINITION OF EACH JOB

To define each job of an organizational structure makes for better organizing. The activities to be performed should be prescribed in complete yet simple language. The duties and the responsibilities should be noted as well as the authority relationship between the job being defined to that of other jobs in the structure. Such work helps the organizer to utilize constructive and creative thought in his efforts and to see more clearly the division of work and the relative organizational position of the person assigned each component work segment.

Organization charts and job descriptions are helpful media in this work, but special attention should be given organization manuals. The format can follow any one of many different patterns; but specific information regarding the title, the organizational unit, responsibility, and authority are usually included. Getting this information down in black and white helps to clarify overlapping operations, eliminate duplications, and assign duties to specific areas. However, when the material for an organization manual is collected and written by each manager in charge of each respective unit, interest is stimulated in better organizing work, and general understanding among executives throughout the structure is gained. Organization manuals are also helpful in training the executive incumbent as well as his successor, and they provide official answers to organization questions for the given enterprise.

## ORGANIZATIONAL MEASUREMENT OF PRODUCTIVITY

Organizing can assist in efforts to measure productivity and this fact should be recognized in performing organizing work. Too frequently productivity measurement is thought of as being a separate activity entirely divorced from organizing. But for improving management it is helpful to assign work into organization units in such a manner that measurement of its accomplishment is expedited. An organization unit itself can represent an effective cluster of work which can be quickly delineated from that of the total enterprise, related to specific man-hours expended, and evaluated quickly.

In many respects, organization units can provide the segments or basis for measuring productivity similar to cost centers being used in cost controlling efforts. Actually, good organizing expedites controlling—some of our most practical controlling measures are obtained via organizing, for it is organizing that deals with work assignments for whom and with what relationships to associated activities of the enterprise. Organizing can be used to raise efficiency and progressive management requires that this fundamental need be recognized and used.

## CONSIDERATION OF THE HUMAN ELEMENT

The motivating power behind any organizational structure is the personnel of that structure. For a function to be performed, a responsibility to be assumed, and an authority to be exercised, the presence of human beings is required. Therefore, adequate consideration for the human element of any organizational structure is of prime importance.

Psychologically, the fact of individual differences is well established. What one person seeks, another abhors. The aims of one may differ widely from those of another. The capacity for creative work of "A" might be unusual, while that of "B" is such that he can think of a new idea only after extended and considerable effort. Likewise, the intellectual curiosity of one person might be concentrated upon mathematics, while that of another is very broad, covering many major subjects.

The various functions to be performed differ in any organizational structure so that there are many functions to be performed by many different types of persons. This condition is not paradoxical, as might first be expected. Rather, it is extremely fortunate, for it makes it possible to match a person of certain likes, capacities, and curiosities with the particular function which requires those particular characteristics.

Placing the right person in the right job supplies an enormous motivating power. The assigned job should meet his current capacities and interests. Proper placement makes for overall harmony within the organization and helps determine whether the person fits into the aims and purposes of the organization and methods of operation. Secondly, it provides for high efficiency among the organization members. A person does his best when he is engaged in a function which fits fully his individual characteristics. Thirdly, there is the advantage of a better social order. The employee feels that he is doing the things which he believes are worthwhile and that he is contributing to society according to his individual ability. In addition, he is engaged in work which places him in an environment which gives him social satisfaction.

In some cases, the entire organizational structure is built around the available personnel, giving minor consideration to the functions. A big advantage in this approach is that all the unique characteristics of all the available personnel are utilized to the very utmost. Good results can be obtained. However, the big disadvantage in such a practice is that the necessary replacements are extremely difficult to make, because it is frequently almost impossible to find a person with the exact characteristics of the person being replaced.

## PROVISION OF EFFECTIVE LEADERSHIP

Leadership is always outstanding in the success of any enterprise. The structural relationships of an organization may be very poor; yet, wonders may be accomplished through effective leadership. On the other hand, the relationships may be excellent; yet, little can be achieved if its leadership is poor.

Leadership implies the ability to show others the way to attainment of wanted goals. Managers have excellent opportunities to do this by means of their organizing efforts. For example, the manager can, through his organizing, assist the subordinate in concentrating his efforts on work which not only is in keeping with the enterprise's demands, but also supplies satisfaction and status to the subordinate. Also, by lending him needed encouragement and help by means of leadership and example, the manager can accomplish more with less effort and time, and the strength of the organization is increased.

Organization units can serve as focal points around which employee enthusiasm and accomplishment revolve, provided adequate leadership in an effective organization is utilized. In fact, leadership conditions all management development and it provides the real spirit of an organized group and stimulates the group members to peak performance far above what they actually thought could be attained.

## UNITY OF EFFORT ATTAINMENT

One of the main purposes of organizing is to secure unity of effort by the group. The different segments of the organization should be put together into a neat mosaic that permits and encourages the total as well as each part to contribute its maximum toward the work to be done.

No one should report to more than one superior, and there should be one superior for every organization member. An attempt to operate under any other set of conditions results in conflicting orders, confusion by the employee, and dissatisfaction by the manager. In addition, the manager faces the problem of proper allocation of his time, giving loyalty to divided interests, and spreading his efforts too thinly.

Yet it must be remembered that unity of effort should be carried to a reasonable degree only. Employees in this day and age deserve some leeway and freedom of action regarding performance of their particular work. The broader outlines of work are provided, but the employee has the liberty to make some decisions regarding his particular efforts and thus accomplishes both the work aim provided and satisfies his own personal goals.

## DETERMINATION OF CLEARLY DEFINED CHANNELS OF AUTHORITY AND RESPONSIBILITY

In every structure, there is some personnel directive which is manifested through the instructions, orders, systems and procedures that are transmitted through organization channels. This personnel directive is one of the most important means of obtaining effective group effort, and it can operate efficiently only when clearly defined channels of authority and responsibility are provided within the organizational structure.

Each member of an enterprise not only must know what to do, but must know that his work is looked over to determine if it is being done correctly. Definite channels eliminate the so-called "horizontal gaps" in organization structures, i.e., areas at any given organizational level which are not covered by a channel of authority and responsibility. When horizontal gaps exist, the functions and activities of the personnel in such areas are not adequately synchronized with those of the other parts of the structure, and inefficient overlapping of personnel control activities is usually present.

## ESTABLISHMENT OF DEFINITE AUTHORITY AND RESPONSIBILITY

Not only must the channels through which authority and responsibility flow be clearly defined, but also the authority and responsibility themselves must be definite and known to all concerned. Defining the authority assists in gaining the needed coordination among the various component efforts, and it enables vertical coordination between superior and subordinates throughout the entire organization to be effective.

Defining authority does not mean spelling out every detail of what a manager can and cannot do. It prescribes in what broad areas the manager shall make decisions; and by means of objective identifications, policies, and communication, the manager directs his efforts to specific work. Thus, the manager's initiative, creativity, and enthusiasm are stimulated, not thwarted, by the careful defining of his authority. This makes for effective management.

Responsibility implies an individual trust, a dependence upon an individual to perform an assigned task promptly and efficiently. When one is vested with responsibility, it is up to him and to him alone to see that the job is carried out satisfactorily. Defining responsibility tends to develop the individual and to increase his reliability. When an individual knows exactly the task and the activity for which he is being held fully responsible, he tends to overcome common obstacles and to perform his tasks promptly and thoroughly. Human beings like to measure up to the requirements made of them. In addition, defining responsibility aids in getting work accomplished. When responsibilities are defined, it is known who is responsible for each particular activity; and with this knowledge available, the proper person for a specific function can be seen quickly and directly, without waste of time.

Responsibility should be fixed at a level as low in the organization structure as is consistent with the capability of the personnel at that level to assume responsibility. The lower the level, the greater the benefit to the total organization personnel. Furthermore, benefits of developing future managers of the enterprise, increasing the individual's feeling of worth, and minimizing disciplinary problems can be cited.

## ESTABLISHMENT OF CLIMATE FOR DELEGATION OF AUTHORITY

Delegation of authority by a manager is vital because it makes organization meaningful. Failure to delegate means failure to reap the benefits of organizing. Many managers are reluctant to delegate; and frequently, delegation is practiced to a limited degree only. To request a manager to delegate seldom brings about the desired practice. Other steps must be taken.

Establishing a work climate that is free from frustration and fear is probably a cardinal guide to follow in encouraging delegation. Managers must be made to feel that turning over carefully selected assignments to their subordinates is the proper thing to do and that their superiors approve of such action, even when the subordinate does not perform the assignment in the same manner that the manager would and the results are short of the expected accomplishment. The deficiency is charged to the development of managerial skill.

The climate should be one of managers believing in their subordinates, recognizing their competence or lack of it, and willing to take a calculated risk to gain ultimately a better work force. The underlying theme followed is that a manager grows most when he builds subordinates the most.

## PROVISION FOR COEQUALITY OF AUTHORITY AND RESPONSIBILITY

Another important principle of organizing is that the authority of any manager should be coequal with his responsibility and, vice versa, his responsibility coequal with his authority. The association between authority and responsibility is intimate and arises from accomplishing the same work. As pointed out in Chapter 28, making decisions and enforcing them regarding specific work (authority) also entails the obligation to perform this work (responsibility) by accepting and using the delegated authority.

Authority and responsibility are therefore akin to an object and its image in a mirror. If one exists, the other exists also in a coequal status. Authority commensurate with responsibility is needed before responsibility becomes meaningful; and likewise, responsibility without commensurate authority has dubious managerial value. Effective managers keep this principle of organizing in mind and see to it that for any manager, coequality of authority and responsibility is present.

## HOLD THE ORGANIZATIONAL LEVELS TO A MINIMUM

In the interests of having an organization that is closely knit, adaptable to necessary changes, and high in productivity, it is normally advisable to hold the organizational levels to a minimum. What the precise number of levels should be depends mainly on the size of the enterprise and the type of work performed. For most business enterprises, seldom should there be more than five levels beneath the chief executive. To have more encourages "run-arounds."

The number of organizational levels is closely associated with the span of authority followed. Wide spans usually make for few levels, whereas narrow spans normally necessitate a larger number of levels. In the former case, the organizational structure is referred to as a "flat organization"; in the latter, as a "tall organization." Coordination vertically is relatively easily obtained in the flat organization; and in contrast, it is more difficult in the tall organization because of the depth created by the organizational levels. On the other hand, and because of the same reasons, coordination horizontally is relatively easy within the tall organization, but relatively difficult within the flat organization.

Communication is more effective and direct when few levels of organization are used. This follows because organizational levels tend to distort and to serve as insulators to communication. When communication must penetrate many levels of organization, both the content and the speed of the communication may be altered with each succeeding level pierced. The difficulties exist in communication not only from the top down, but also from the bottom up.

## ATTENTION TO COORDINATION OF THE ACTIVITIES

Coordinating implies the smooth working together of the various activities which make up the total effort expended in achieving the prescribed work. Coordination can be thought of as aiming toward a perfect meshing or a harmonious adjustment. By means of coordination, a manager obtains a smooth synchronization of all necessary activities, each performed at the desired place and time. An illustration of a situation in which coordination is paramount is that of a symphony orchestra, where various musical sounds of many instruments, consisting of different tone qualities, pitches, timbres, and quantities, are all coordinated or blended together in such a manner that the end result is smooth, melodious music.

Organizing is intended to provide a vital means for coordinating the activities of a group. This integration of efforts, in the opinion of many, is the ultimate deciding factor in organizing. Without order and arrangement, there are quite likely to be disjointed efforts and a hodgepodge of mental and physical toil incompatible with the objectives of the enterprise.

Each member of a group should know not only his own immediate goal but also the common goal of his fellow workers, so that recognition can be made of a common interest and the obligation of mutual service. To reach the peak of coordination, each member must accept the basic purpose of the enterprise, understand why this achievement is essential, know his part in these efforts, and be informed of the progress as it is achieved. This implies a self-imposed type of discipline by each member upon himself in order to win status as a true "mutual server."

## PROVIDE FLEXIBILITY IN ORGANIZATION

In all organizing work, it is fundamental to remember that no organization remains the same for long. Recognition of this dynamic quality should be taken into account in all organizing, and this necessitates providing flexibility in the organization. Within a given period, products and services are added, others are discontinued, while many others are modified. Likewise, processes change, with resultant change in makeup and relationships of organizational units.

It is in personnel that the most prominent changes will take place. As pointed out in Chapter 29, in the normal course of events, some people will leave the enterprise, and others will join it. Some will request transfers; others, because of new skills or experience acquired, will seek better jobs both within and outside the enterprise. Also, changes in process, mentioned above, contribute to the need for personnel changes. The astute manager realizes that these changes are inevitable and provides some flexibility in his organization to cope with them. Organizations change, some increase, some decrease. None remain completely constant.

## APPLICATION OF SIMPLICITY

Simplicity has been defined as "that delightful perfection between too much and too little," and the best all-around organization structures are those which encompass simplicity in their makeup. A complex structure is almost certain to make difficulties for a manager. Likewise, an organization structure that excludes necessary functions is a serious handicap to the success of the enterprise. A good organization structure includes only the necessary functions, no more and no less, and establishes the relationship among the necessary functions in the simplest possible manner.

The known rules of nature are comparatively simple; the natural way to perform a task, to relate one's work to that of another, or to accomplish a common goal, is to do it the simple way; it is against normal business instincts to do anything in a complex and involved manner. The true concept of a particular function—what is to be done, when, and how—is best understood by people when they are informed in simple language and in a direct manner.

Efforts to make an organization structure seem profound by adding unnecessary functions, giving old functions new names, and developing complex relationships between the functions make for confusion. Efficient managers work with things that are simple; they understand them better; and they know that simplicity brings the best results.

It is appropriate to quote from a statement attributed to Sir Henry Deterding of the Shell Oil Company, who said:

> There is a master key to success with which no man can fail. Its name is simplicity, simplicity I mean in the sense of reducing to the simplest possible terms every problem that besets us. Almost every man can succeed if only he will simplify everything in his life. That has been my working theory for forty years. As a very young man I stumbled upon this fundamental truth that everything that is complicated is wrong. Simplicity rules everything worth while. Whenever I have met a problem which after taking thought I could not reduce to simplicity, I have left it alone.

If more managers would follow this suggestion, our managerial efforts would certainly improve.

## QUESTIONS

1. Discuss how a good organization helps to (1) increase cooperation and coordination of the group's efforts and (2) supply an orderly approach to reorganizing.

2. What is an organization principle, and how can an office manager use it?

3. When a manager delegates authority to make his organizing effective, is he not increasing the organizational levels which should be held to a minimum? How do you resolve these seeming differences in organization principles?

4. A great deal of importance is attached to the objective in evaluating an organization structure. Why is this?

5. What basic guide or guides in organization have been violated in each of the following?
   a) Failing to recognize and include certain functions in the organization structure.
   b) Assigning the responsibility for a single function to three people.
   c) Organizing an office exactly like that of another highly successful office.
   d) Excessive "buck-passing" when emergency work fails to be completed on time.

6. Is there such a thing as an "ideal" organization? Explain your answer.

7. As you see it, could we say that granted sufficient competent leadership we would not need organizing? Why?

8. Discuss the organizational principle, "Provide for Organizational Measurement Of Productivity."

9. What is the meaning of each of the following managerial terms or concepts?
   a) Coequality of authority and responsibility.
   b) "Horizontal gaps" in an organization structure.
   c) "Tall organization."
   d) Formal communication.

10. What is your understanding of unity of effort in organizing work? How far should it be carried to attain the best organization? Why?

11. As business operations become more complex and the paper work arising from them becomes more voluminous, do you feel it practical to feature simplicity in an office organization structure? Explain.

12. Discuss your reactions to this statement: "Responsibility is a personal possession and loses its significance when thought of in reference to groups as commonly found in the usual discussions of organization."

## CASE PROBLEMS

### Case 30–1.  Toole-Heedsman Corporation

The operations of the Toole-Heedsman Corporation are worldwide, with plants and offices located in the United States, South America, Europe, Asia, and northern Africa. Mr. Robert M. Fitzgerald, director of systems, procedures, and office machines, has two assistants, one for systems and procedures, and one for office machines. Mr. Fitzgerald finds that he must spend much of his time away from the corporation's main office in New York and quite often it happens that one of his assistants is out of town the same time Mr. Fitzgerald is absent. Under the circumstances, Mr. Fitzgerald has followed the general practice of delegating much work of a semiexecutive nature to his private secretary, Mrs. Irene Best, who has been with the company for 17 years, the last five with Mr. Fitzgerald and before that, eight years with Mr. Fitzgerald's predecessor.

Officially Mrs. Best has no recognized line authority and issues orders only in the name of Mr. Fitzgerald. It is the opinion of the personnel manager that Mrs. Best is not fitted by training or personality for promotion to any other job in the office. Actually, she has become a fixture in the office, becoming well-nigh indispensable to her superior, Mr. Fitzgerald. She has knowledge of the policies, traditions, and routines of the various departments of the company.

Long experience has made Mrs. Best expert in keeping "in the clear" and in avoiding responsibility, and thus in many instances she is heartily disliked by junior executives, who resent her arbitrary assumption of authority but who, nevertheless, are reluctant to register a complaint with their superior or Mr. Fitzgerald because of the recognized dependence of the latter upon Mrs. Best to assume the burden of routine administration.

As a result, Mrs. Best has come to occupy a position of authority out of all proportion to her direct responsibility, and to some exerts an irritating influence detrimental to the morale of many office employees.

### Problems:

1. What are the chief weaknesses of the organization situation described above? What advantages?

2. What suggestion would you make to improve the situation?

3. How would you go about getting top managers to accept your suggestions?

### Case 30–2.   The Ryan and Harrison Company

A total of 52 employees are classified as office workers in this company. The office manager is in charge of one telephone operator, two mail clerks, four timekeepers, two billing clerks, two duplicating machine operators, and a receptionist. The controller is in charge of ten accounting clerks, three bookkeepers, a purchasing agent, and three purchasing clerks. The sales manager has a regular force including ten stenographers and three file clerks. The remaining office workers are dispersed throughout the company and report to the chiefs of their immediate and respective units.

The office manager believes his unit should include the correspondence work, but the president of the company has done nothing about the suggestion. He is not sure that the office manager could handle the work properly, and he does not want to interfere with getting sales correspondence out promptly nor to offend the sales manager. The controller is a very forceful and conscientious man who keeps in close touch with every operation performed in his unit. He insists that all decisions concerning work of his unit be cleared through him. He justifies this practice as an effective means of keeping costs in line. His work load is very heavy, but he has repeatedly turned down the suggestion to appoint an assistant, explaining it would increase office costs too much. It is common for the controller to work until 7:00 o'clock several evenings a week and to come down to the office for a part of Saturday morning. Some of his associates chide him by telling him: "You can win a promotion in an easier way" or "You should work steady during regular working hours." The controller resents these comments, but says nothing in reply. The sales manager, being a very busy man, has only limited time to supervise the stenographers; so he has the secretary to the president, an elderly woman, take charge of the stenographers and file clerks.

There is very much independence between units with little cooperation between them. The stenographers usually will not type any letters unless they pertain to sales. Occasionally, the controller comes into the office manager's department and directs people what to do. The purchasing agent does not cooperate with the office manager, giving as the reason that the office manager has no authority over purchasing. The general atmosphere around the office spells independence. Some of the clerks feel that they are being "picked on" because more work is piled on them, while others just sit around and look busy.

## Problems:

1. In your opinion, what are some plausible reasons leading to the present condition of this company's office, that is, what might lead to the formation and existence of this office?

2. From the viewpoint of organizing, evaluate the present office of this company.

3. What action do you feel should be taken to improve the company's office organization?

# PART 7

# OFFICE MANAGEMENT—ACTUATING

*Many practitioners feel that actuating is of foremost importance in office management. To attain greatest managerial efficiency, office employees must be inspired to use their highest attainable skills and capacities in work they are genuinely interested in doing.*

*Actuating includes the creating and the continuing of the desire by each employee to achieve work goals willingly and enthusiastically. It can be thought of as the ability to get others to do the work you want done because they want to do it.*

*The following five chapters are devoted to office managerial actuating.*

# CHAPTER 31

# MOTIVATING

# OFFICE PERSONNEL

You will never stub your toe standing still. The
faster you go, the more chance there is of
stubbing your toe, but the more chance you
have of getting somewhere.
            —*Charles F. Kettering*

In the ultimate, all management must be accomplished by and through people. It is people who make or break the management of any office. Experts in office management recognize this. Materials, equipment, and machines can all be readily replaced; they can even be insured against loss. But capable and loyal human beings cannot be replaced, nor can their loss be adequately insured. Efforts to develop and maintain competent and cooperative human beings must be made and this means that human motives must be understood and actions taken according to that understanding.

Most employees want and will respond favorably to help. They want to develop, to perform greater service, to acquire status, and to contribute importantly. This means that in many respects a manager is really a helper of employees. His task is to help his followers do their best. His challenge is to get employees to do more for him than they will for others. This means that knowledge of people's behavior and skill in influencing them are extremely important attributes of the manager. We are not concerned directly with the achievement of one big happy family of employees as such, but toward the achievement of a contented group as an essential in accomplishing the task to be performed. We manage to get work accomplished effectively, but we can do this and at the same time make the employee's work life happier and his work more meaningful and satisfying.

## HISTORICAL DEVELOPMENTS OF VIEWPOINTS TOWARD EMPLOYEES

Our viewpoint toward employees was not always as it exists today. Actually, we have progressed through several stages. At one time, an employee was considered in the same light as a commodity—something to be bought on the open market, and of a fairly uniform quality. Later, the so-called machinery conception of labor became prominent; the employee was considered a producing unit and his value measured in terms of the goods produced. After years of struggle and unhappiness, a new concept of employer-employee relationships gradually evolved. It was that an employee is a human being and that his welfare is important; hence, the employer should encourage and supply various welfare services deemed desirable. A paternal attitude toward the employee developed. This represented an improvement over the employee's previous status, but it was not the answer to satisfactory employer-employee relations. Many employees were suspicious of these welfare efforts and resented being the children of a paternalistic policy. Since the period of around 1915–20, the concept that an employee is a human entity and must be treated as such has gained headway. This means that consideration for an employee's psychological makeup and recognition and utilization of his desires, attitudes, interests, and motives are as important as attention to his physical efforts, perhaps even more so.

As thinking along this human-entity line progressed, the basis for a great many current practices developed, including the idea that individuals vary in their personal aptitudes and interests, that no two people respond identically to the same opportunity, that different jobs require different abilities, that the emotional makeup of the employee is important, and that the prevailing spirit or feeling of the work force affects its productivity. A "mutuality of interests" between employer and employee is being recognized. This means that both have an interest in the well-being of the enterprise and that the relationship between employer and employee should be a harmonious working together toward their common objectives, which are compatible over the long-run period of time.

## MOTIVATING EMPLOYEES

The question can be asked: "How do you motivate employees?" A logical approach is to find out the wants of the employees and either satisfy these wants in managerial activities or supply reasonable explanations why they cannot be fulfilled. Many studies have been conducted to discover the important wants of employees. The survival or biological needs, sometimes referred to as economic, include the desire for adequate food, clothing, and shelter. What constitutes adequacy in these areas will differ among people, and likewise the degree of motivations to acquire satisfaction of these needs will vary. However, in normal economic times, these survival needs are met; and when they are taken care of, much of the employee's concern is then turned to the satisfaction of emotional and social needs. For example, he wants to know that what he is doing is worthwhile and has merit, that he is accepted and approved by his fellow men. For most employees, their daily work is expected, at least in part, to supply these needs by providing an opportunity to demonstrate their talent, acquire prestige, and gain recognition.

Studies along this line reveal listings of the psychological and social wants of employees. The wants vary somewhat depending upon the study, but most include the following: job security, opportunity for expression, chance to develop and grow, information about changes that will affect them, equitable pay, personal help when requested, recognition for accomplishments, treatment as human beings, and effective supervision.

Knowing these wants, the next step is to set operations in action in order to satisfy them. Here is where the real skill of motivating enters. Employees' wants are not identical for each group or for each member of a group. Furthermore, the wants do not remain constant; they vary from day to day. And the reaction to the same stimuli may differ widely among employees.

Most people want to do their share—and more. It is the task of the manager to provide a working climate in which this basic desire of an employee is completely fulfilled. From time to time, a person is encountered who wants to "get by" without doing any work, dislikes most fellow employees, has little ethics in his dealings with others, and is against most proposals by people with whom he is associated. Such a person is sick emotionally and mentally. Study shows that in many instances, this is not the way he would like to be; but he got this way owing to his past experiences, his beliefs, or the conditions to which he was exposed. Quite frequently, it is found that this type of person actually wants help. Proper understanding and motivating can straighten him out, but it may take much time and patience.

## MOTIVATION BASIS

The most successful motivation is self-direction by the employee. The urge or desire should come from within the individual, not from someone else in the form of an outside force. Hence, successful motivation usually means providing a work climate that permits the employee to act in a manner that satisfies his own needs. Our knowledge of motivating is increasing daily, but there still remain many unknowns in this fascinating subject area. Agreement is usually voiced with the statement that every employee has a motivation response and this response can be fostered and utilized by managers creating opportunities, removing obstacles, providing guidance, and encouraging growth. The implementation or taking of actions, however, rests with the employee.

Figure 31–1 lists some basic concepts to remember in dealing with people. These concepts can be utilized in motivating employees, the application depending upon the particular circumstances in the individual case.

---

1. People like to help others. Ask for their opinions.
2. People like to feel important and needed. Acknowledge their contribution and recognize their help occasionally in front of others.
3. People like to be encouraged. Help them see the successful accomplishment of their aims and ambitions.
4. People like good listeners. Let people talk about their accomplishments and disappointments. Give the other fellow a real hearing.
5. People like to be brought into the picture when talking about yourself. Give your conversation a "you" angle. "You will find this of special interest because. . . ."
6. People like a word of praise whenever merited.
7. People like a choice, if possible. Let a person decide for himself; help him reach conclusions, but do not make decisions for him.
8. People like to avoid embarrassment and being "boxed in a corner." Give a person an "out" and a chance to save face.
9. People like people who keep well groomed. Keep your body clean, clothes neat. This is a subtle way of saying to others, "I care about your opinion of me."
10. People like their image to be accepted. Strive to sense what this image is and let them know that you understand their picture of themselves.

---

FIG. 31–1. In dealing with people, remember these concepts.

## LEADERSHIP

Vital in supplying a motivating environment is leadership. People prefer to be with a successful leader. Being a part of victorious accomplishments, following a man who has demonstrated an ability to get things done, and having firsthand experience in observing successful management in action are in and of themselves highly motivating to an employee. Members of a group receive strong stimuli from effective leadership; and in turn, a strong leader acquires his position, in part, because of his ability to motivate members of his group.

What is leadership? It has been defined in a number of different ways; but for our purposes here, we can consider that leadership implies a threefold meaning:

1. *Skill to direct—to show the way.* A leader possesses the ability to guide people—to point out the proper means for attainment. This leadership characteristic usually means that the leader is out in front

leading, not in back pushing. While not directly applicable, the concept can be illustrated by considering a piece of ordinary wrapping twine. When the front end of the twine is directed and guided along desired paths, the rest of the piece of twine will follow. In contrast, when the twine is pushed, it follows no predetermined path and flounders in an aimless direction.

2. *Ability to win cooperation and loyalty.* A leader is able to get people to act jointly and to work toward a common goal. All efforts of the group are knit together and concentrated into one large force toward the attainment of the objective. This unity of operation is accomplished by strong and enthusiastic feelings, so that each member has a deep sense of obligation to the leader.

3. *Courage to carry on until the assigned task is accomplished.* A leader is dauntless and ever confident that the task to be done will be completely accomplished. He has implicit faith in the success of his actions and gives a feeling of confidence and positiveness to all associated with him.

People like to be led by a dynamic leader. They like to be led by a person who clearly envisages the goal, who knows how to achieve that goal, and who goes out after it. Once the decision is made as to what the goals are and what people must do to achieve them, leadership at all levels of the organization plays a dominant role in seeing that they are accomplished.

## COMMUNICATION

High on the list of what to do to gain effective motivation is communication. Employees want to know what is going on and especially to be informed about achievements, problems, or changes that affect them. The normal tendency is to underrate the importance of communication. An aggressive and sincere communicative effort will do wonders toward achieving a cooperative, confident, and enthusiastic working force. An informed employee is usually a good employee. Employees like to be told firsthand about new policies and why they are being adopted, and they feel that they have a right to know about changes to be made in existing conditions.

Most difficulties of communication can be classified under the headings of either telling too little or assuming complete understanding of communication. Both of these habits tend to detract from our communication effectiveness. Managers should take the initiative and supply full information to employees. Dependence upon "word of mouth," or believing that "everybody knows that—it's common information," leads to incomplete and frequently incorrect information. The employee is eager to know any news in which he is involved. He wants to be informed, not coddled. Any information that will help him do a better job ranks high in his preference.

Tell an employee something you want him to understand, and the chances are 12 to 1 he will not fully understand you. Why is this? Because many believe that the act of writing or telling another certain information completely fulfills their job of communicating. However, to communicate effectively requires definite skills and knowledge. Included among these criteria are the following:

1. *Communication is two way.* One tells, informs, or requests; the other listens, asks, or interprets. Without listenership, the communication just does not exist. As Thoreau put it: "It takes two to speak the truth—one to speak, the other to hear it." Listening is an art and requires effort. For best results, involve the listener as soon as possible. Asking leading questions such as the following are effective: "How do you feel about . . . ?" "Well, what do you think—will it work?" "Now, what other information can I give you?"

2. *Think before you write or talk.* Some people are so intent on communicating that they start to write or talk before evaluating the situation and organizing their thoughts. As a result, they confuse the reader or listener. Before communicating, it is a good idea to decide: (1) Why do you want to say anything? (2) What do you want to say? (3) What is the objective in saying this? and (4) What do you know about the receiver or listener?

3. *Use effective words—focus words and mutually known words.* Focus words help to spot the key points in a communication. The listener or reader is assisted by phrases such as: "Our goal is to. . . ." or "To summarize, . . . ." These expressions aid in drawing inferences and value judgments. The use of mutually known words is essential. To describe the wage structure as "lucrative" reduces real communication if the receiver does not know the meaning of the word.

4. *Practice empathy.* Communication is assisted by the sender placing himself in the position of the receiver and judging the message from the receiver's point of view. This guide helps win acceptance by the receiver and emphasizes his interests, goals, and fears by giving the receiver what he wants to hear or read.

5. *Create a follow-up.* The recipient should be given the feeling that he can return with questions or ask clarification on any part he fails to understand. Offering assistance and closing with expressions such as: "Call me if any questions arise," or "Let's get together again next Monday noon and . . . ," are usually effective in this respect.

## COMMUNICATION MEDIA

Normally, the formal lines of communication should be employed. These are the same connecting links as "lines of authority," discussed in

Chapter 28. Organization shows relationships, and these relationships are made meaningful by exercise of both authority and communication. In fact, authority to put decisions into action necessitates communication. The traditional office grapevine is effective as a dispenser of information. It can never be completely eliminated, people and communication being what they are. The wise manager recognizes this and uses the grapevine as an auxiliary, but is exceedingly careful that accurate, complete, and timely messages are conveyed through the normal channels so that half-truths and incomplete information are not spread by the grapevine.

Many communication media are available. The selection depends

| Medium | Features | Organizational Level for Which Effective |
|---|---|---|
| Conversation | Man-to-man, forthright personal relationship | All organizational levels |
| Letters | Excellent for statistical data and where permanent record is desired | Top managerial and supervisory levels |
| Pamphlets and booklets | Suitable for large volume of material | All organizational levels |
| House organs | Adequate coverage satisfactory for reminders and announcements | All organizational levels |
| Motion pictures, radio, and television | Dramatize presentation; helpful in training, relating company history, and special achievements | All organizational levels |
| Speeches | Impressive for special events and celebrations | Top managerial and supervisory levels |

FIG. 31–2.  Media available for communication purposes.

chiefly upon the type of information and the type of employees to be reached. Figure 31–2 suggests the features and the organizational level for six selected media.

## SUGGESTION SYSTEMS

A suggestion system is a means by which employees can submit their ideas to a manager and, if these ideas are adopted, receive an award, usually consisting of an amount of cash. Generally, the suggestions concern ways to save time, to reduce waste, to improve quality, or to simplify practices and procedures. A suggestion system can be a strong employee motivator because the employees are given the opportunity to say something, to feel that the company is "their company," to think of constructive ideas, and to contribute to the progress and betterment of the enterprise.

In addition, the economic gains can be quite large. Financial gains are made by the company as well as by the successful suggester. But these gains should not be stressed to the exclusion of the others mentioned. A suggestion system is far more than a mechanism for the buying of useful ideas.

Each and every suggestion should be answered promptly with reasons for decisions reached. Replies can be by individual letters or personal interviews; it is not a good practice to post lists on the bulletin board. Replies to turndowns, i.e., those suggestions receiving no award, must contain the reasons why such action is taken. This practice is recommended because it (1) lets the employee know that his suggestion was evaluated; (2) reveals whether the judging committee understood his idea; (3) helps him to become better informed, inasmuch as he is told why his idea was not worthy of an award; and (4) prompts him to continue to try and stimulates further thinking. The amount of the reward must be worthwhile and must offer some inducement to the employee. Many companies have found that $10 is a minimum figure to use and that maximum awards based on 10 percent of the savings for the first year are satisfactory.

Suggestion systems have a tendency to become dormant; for this reason, they must be continually promoted. Showmanship, publicity stunts, and promotions can be used to keep the program alive. Devices which have proved successful include the following: attractive suggestion forms; appealing and well-located suggestion boxes bearing the sign "Have you deposited your suggestion here today?"; attention-getting posters; reminders in payroll envelopes; and notices in company papers.

The suggester's identity is unknown to the investigator in some systems. This anonymity is obtained by means of a numbering and coupon arrangement on the suggestion form. The suggester retains a numbered coupon which corresponds to the number of the suggestion. Under this arrangement, impartiality on the part of the investigators is promoted. In contrast, other systems require the suggester's signature, a practice which affords close contact with the suggester.

Suggestion stimulators can be directed to all employees in order to encourage their participation in the suggestion systems. Letters and announcements can be used; or more direct and definite means may be utilized, such as the manager asking: "What can you suggest to save time in the filing department?" Employees then start thinking of ways to improve that department. This practice appears to bring usable results, but it involves a serious disadvantage. It directs attention to fields foreign to the employee. A suggestion system is supposed to enable the employee to take advantage of the things he already knows but which have not as yet been used to full advantage. Directing his attention to new fields, therefore, might mean a loss of excellent ideas stemming from his intimate on-the-job knowledge.

## MERIT RATING

Employees must be clear as to what is expected of them and how they are to be judged. This is a keystone of effective motivating. In addition, the typical employee wants the answer to the question: "How am I doing?" If highly successful, he would like to know it; if mediocre or even unsuccessful, he would like to know it, and why. Furthermore, it is motivating to him to know that his employer has an interest in him, is willing to give praise when deserved and to point out his shortcomings when existent, so that he can improve himself and satisfy his superior.

Merit rating, also commonly termed performance rating, should not be compared to the inspecting of a product on an assembly line. It is not an X ray of the employee. It is a two-way understanding between the employee and his supervisor involving the setting of objectives for the employee to develop himself and the means for achieving these objectives. Merit rating can be viewed as an inventory of the most valuable asset of the enterprise—its employees. Such efforts are essential to effective management; they constitute an important tool of managerial actuating and provide information helpful in many ways. Among the important uses of merit rating are:

1. To assist in developing the supervisor's critical evaluation of the employee's worth.

2. To provide a record of the progress of new employees or those in training.

3. To indicate areas where training is needed.

4. To let the employee know what management members think of his performance.

5. To uncover employees of unusual abilities along specific lines.

6. To guide personnel work in promoting, demoting, or transferring an employee.

7. To justify increases in wages within the established job range.

## MERIT-RATING PLANS

Merit rating is accomplished by rating the employee on a number of predetermined factors. These factors are considered to be directly associated with, as well as indicative of, the employee's performance on the job. They should be carefully selected and include only those factors necessary to give adequate data. Usually, six to eight factors are sufficient, as the use of too many might lead to carelessness in rating, and too few might distort the ratings. Information which is available elsewhere, such as attendance, punctuality, and length-of-service data, should not be included in the merit-rating form. In each case, however, the factors selected are considered to be applicable to the employee, not to the job requirements.

There are four basic types of merit-rating plans: (1) employee comparison, (2) man-to-man basis, (3) check lists, and (4) charts. The first is an elementary form of ranking in which a comparison of the relative performance of employees is determined. Normally, the employees under a given supervisor or in one department are ranked, from the most satisfactory at the top of the list to the least satisfactory at the bottom of the list. The ranking can be by separate traits or on an overall basis.

In the man-to-man type, the employee is rated by comparing him to another employee believed to exemplify the highest rating of the particular factor being considered. Sometimes, a rating scale, established by the highest, middle, and lowest exemplary employees, respectively, is used. Thus, on the quality of dependability, for example, employee A is compared with each of the three employees included in the rating scale and is then given a rating it is believed he deserves. The man-to-man basis is not widely used in offices because it is rather complex and time-consuming. Difficulty is encountered in selecting the employees to use in the rating scale, and wide variations in the characteristics of those selected appear common.

Check lists consist of a series of statements or questions dealing with the employee's performance. Frequently, the statements have different values or weights which are unknown to the respondent. Questions which can be answered either "Yes" or "No," or by "It applies to this employee" or "It does not apply to this employee," are used. The following illustrates a portion of a check list:

| Item | Scale Value* |
|------|------|
| 1. He works at a slow but steady pace. | 5 |
| 2. He is usually ahead of his work schedule. | 3 |
| 3. He gets along with fellow employees. | 8 |
| 4. He makes few mistakes in his work. | 10 |
| 5. He asks for considerable time off. | 7 |
| 6. He usually thinks of the company first. | 4 |

* Not included in form supplied to rater.

Charts are probably the most common type of merit rating used in an office. This is because they are easy to use, readily understood, and accepted by both the raters and the ratees. The chart type consists of a list of selected traits, each accompanied by a scale indicating different degrees of the trait. The rater indicates on each scale the extent to which the employee displays that respective trait in his work. For guidance to the rater, short descriptions for various degrees are usually provided. Figure 31–3 shows a performance-rating chart.

**BLUE CROSS - BLUE SHIELD PLANS**
**CHICAGO**

**PERFORMANCE RATING**

NAME:_____    DATE of RATING:_____

DEPARTMENT:_____    JOB CLASSIFICATION:_____

| JOB KNOWLEDGE | How Well Does This Employee Understand The Requirements Of Job To Which Assigned: | | | | | |
|---|---|---|---|---|---|---|
| | Thoroughly understands all aspects of job. | More than adequate knowledge of job. | Has sufficient knowledge to do job. | Insufficient knowledge of some phases. | Continually needs instruction. | |
| QUALITY OF WORK | How Accurate, Neat And Complete Is The Work: | | | | | |
| | Consistently neat, accurate and thorough. | Careful worker seldom needs correction. | Work is acceptable. | Occasionally Careless —needs checking. | Inaccurate and careless. | |
| CO-OPERATION | Does This Employee Work Harmoniously And Effectively With Co-Workers And Supervision: | | | | | |
| | Exceptionally willing and successful as a team worker. | Usually tactful and offers to assist others | Gets along well enough, no problem | Cooperation must be solicited, seldom volunteers. | Tends to be a troublemaker. | |
| RESPON-SIBILITY | How Does This Employee Accept All The Responsibilities Of The Job: | | | | | |
| | Accepts all responsibilities fully and meets Emergencies. | Conscientiously tries to fulfill job responsibilities. | Accepts but does not seek responsibility. | Does some assigned tasks reluctantly | Indifferent—avoids responsibilities. | |
| INITIA-TIVE | How Well Does This Employee Begin An Assignment Without Direction And Recognize The Best Way Of Doing It: | | | | | |
| | Self starter: makes practical suggestions. | Proceeds on assigned work voluntarily and readily accepts suggestions. | Does regular work without prompting. | Relies on others: needs help getting started | Must usually be told exactly what to do. | |
| QUANTITY OF WORK | How Much Satisfactory Work Is Consistently Turned Out By This Employee: | | | | | |
| | Maintains unusually high out-put. | Usually does more than expected. | Does sufficient amount of work. | Inclined to be slow. | Inadequate turn-out of work | |
| DEPEND-ABILITY | How Faithful Is This Employee In Reporting To Work And Staying On The Job: | | | | | |
| | Places company interests ahead of personal conveniences. | Punctual and does not waste company time. | Generally on the job as needed. | Some abuses — occasionally needs to be admonished. | Chronic abuses of working schedules. | |

COMMENTS:_____

_____

_____

Rated By:_____    Discussed With Employee: By_._____

Is any action being taken to help this employee improve his performance?  ☐ No  ☐ Yes—Specify_____

_____

_____    Dept. Manager_____

RB—9-7-59    (See Reverse Side For Instructions in Rating)

*Courtesy: Blue Cross—Blue Shield Plans, Chicago*

FIG. 31–3.  An effective performance-rating chart.

## ADMINISTRATION OF MERIT RATING

Merit ratings are formally made about twice a year. The supervisor normally is charged with the responsibility of rating employees. Sometimes, assistance is given by his superior or by a member of the personnel department; and in some instances, several superiors who are in intimate contact with the employee rate him, in order that more than one judgment of his performance will be available. In most cases, the supervisor knows or should know most about the performance of the employee in his division or unit. Actually, no competent supervisor depends upon a rating form or waits for a given time of the year to appraise his employee. It is a continuous job. Formal and periodic merit rating helps codify results and insures that some orderly appraisal is taking place.

An interview between the employee and the management representative affords an opportunity for a forthright discussion on the employee's performance. Each factor of the merit rating can be discussed in a constructive and factual manner. Recognition of the employee as an individual can be increased and employee good will be enhanced. The interview can be highly objective, because preplanning and concentration upon specific topics are feasible.

Employee self-appraisal is another helpful technique. When office employees are fully informed in advance of the purpose, operation, and application of merit rating, they make remarkably accurate self-appraisals. There is some tendency, however, for the better employees to underrate themselves, and the problem employees may overrate themselves. Employee self-appraisal helps to give the *how* and *why* of merit rating to the employee. He knows what is expected of him and uncovers areas in which improvements can be made. Self-analysis encourages self-development. Self-appraisals can be recorded on special forms provided for this purpose. They supplement the regular ratings determined by management-designated raters.

Since judgment and subjective factors are so important in merit rating, it is advisable to supply a training program for raters in order to help secure intelligent and well-considered ratings. Training helps to implement the plan properly and constructively. The rater must understand the purpose of the form and what method to follow. Competent rating work is a key area of satisfactory merit rating. Also, it is important to provide retraining periodically, so that new developments in employee-rating work and future plans can be brought to the attention of the raters. A retraining program also aids in reviewing the principles of good rating with each rater before each rating period.

Review by a management panel is highly successful in many companies. Funneling all ratings within an enterprise through one body makes for better control and greater uniformity of ratings. Employees who are qualified for promotions, transfers, training, and salary increases are readily identified. Likewise, those requiring remedial action are identified, and proper measures can be taken.

In administering merit rating the following considerations warrant attention:

1. Top management backing for merit rating is essential to its success.

2. Merit rating should serve primarily to motivate employees, to inventory personnel, and to improve the working force.

3. The rating form should include only those traits that cannot be measured objectively by standard personnel records.

4. Only those traits of greatest importance to an employee's progress should be utilized; usually, eight to ten traits are adequate.

5. To expedite comparisons and the rating work, rate all employees on one trait, then all on the second trait, and so forth.

6. Normally, and in keeping with statistical probability, of the ratings for many on a single trait, a few will be low, a few will be high, and the greatest number, perhaps 60 percent, will be average.

7. Each trait should be a single one, not compound; should be defined objectively, not subjectively; and should be in terms of work performed on the job.

8. Ratings should be based on observations of definite and concrete actions.

9. Ratings of an employee should be discussed with him in private by the rater.

10. Periodic training and retraining of raters are essential for success of a merit-rating program.

## PROMOTIONS, ABSENTEEISM, AND TARDINESS

Promotions are motivating in that they afford satisfaction to the average individual in his desire to develop, to advance, and to improve his status. Most companies have the policy of promoting from among their present employees whenever possible. This requires keeping a sharp eye open for the discovery of promotable personnel—those people who demonstrate a desire to advance by qualifying for a better and more responsible job. Qute a few managers, however, feel that some of the vacancies for better jobs should be filled by candidates from outside the enterprise. By this means, it is contended, new ideas, new attitudes, and different methods of operation are brought in which tend to foster an active, healthy condition.

The initiative for promotion work belongs with the manager. Without prodding, the manger should see that worthy people are promoted. The knowledge of whom to advance is gained through records covering each employee's merit, competence, and length of service. Actually, promotion implies two-way action. It calls for action by the managers—to open up avenues along which employees can advance; and it calls for action by employees—to qualify themselves for advancement.

The failure of an employee to report on the job when scheduled to work is one of the difficult personnel problems with which the average office manager must cope. Absenteeism disrupts the smooth flow of work; either the work stops completely, or extra work is forced upon another employee. There is no single cure for absenteeism. It is an individual problem and the correction must suit the particular case. Records revealing who is absent, how long, how often, and why give information on where to concentrate corrective efforts.

Among the various motivating means used to reduce absenteeism are pointing out to employees the importance of being on the job, talking with each absentee upon return and thoroughly discussing the cause and explanation offered, checking to see if the right person is on the right job, maintaining a continued health program, allowing a definite number of days off per year, requiring absentees to make up time, and showing some outward thanks and appreciation to those employees who are always on the job.

Bad timekeeping on the part of employees indicates a disrespect for others and a lack of dependability. Tardiness is contagious. When one or two continue to come into the office late, the idea gets in the minds of other employees that such behavior has managerial approval. Being early is as much a habit as being late. The hour at which work starts has little influence on the problem. The tendency to procrastinate must be corrected and the importance of keeping time obligations stressed.

An effective motivating means consists of creating a strong employee interest in promptness. Supervisors should set good examples and always be on time themselves. They should also keep reminding the employees about the importance of being on time. In many instances, the employee simply fails to allow himself sufficient time to get ready for work. Dependence upon hairline transportation connections and failure to allow extra time for travel under bad weather conditions are common causes. The means of correction here are self-evident.

In many offices, a tardy employee is required to report first to the office manager or to the timekeeper, where an explanation is given verbally for the tardiness and a form filled out indicating the reason why. The idea of going through a "lot of red tape" helps discourage tardiness. The imposition of a penalty, such as making up time lost or doing the least desirable work, proves effective. However, before using such a plan, it should meet the approval of the employees, who should agree to "go along with it." One company uses a unique plan which brings surprisingly good results. An employee's name is selected at random from the payroll list;

and promptly at starting time, the employee is called on the telephone. If he answers, indicating presence and promptness on the job, he receives a reward of $20.

## EMPLOYEE ECONOMIC SECURITY

Various arrangements are now available to help provide a measure of economic security to employees. These arrangements have a motivating influence and are beneficial in that they assist in supplying economic aid in case of sickness or old age. Also, at the time of death some help is given dependents of the deceased employee. These economic security measures have been brought about through the efforts of companies and employees and the influence of state and federal laws, among which are unemployment insurance regulations, workmen's compensation laws, and social security regulations. The form, purpose, and content of these various plans vary considerably and require special study for complete understanding.

The discussion here will be confined to three arrangements, including:

1. *Hospitalization plans.* These plans are a form of insurance which pays a portion of hospital expenses resulting from all nonoccupational illnesses or accidents suffered by the employee. Premiums are usually paid by the employee, although in some instances the company contributes toward the plan. Under a typical plan, costs might be $10 per month for an unmarried employee for semiprivate accommodations. The amount of cost varies with such factors as the number of employees in the plan, their sex and age, and the benefits provided.

2. *Pension plans.* These provide regular payments to an employee retired from service. The great majority of large enterprises now have such plans. They make it possible not only to give needed relief and to grant rewards for long service but also to retire older employees, thus permitting the employment of younger persons as replacements. This helps keep the work force alive and vibrant, and the existence of a retirement pension plan makes for high morale and attracts better employees.

The cost of a pension plan can be paid by either the company or the employees, or both. The amount of retirement pay generally provided is about 50 percent of the average rate for the five-year period preceding retirement. The trend is toward a reduction in the waiting period for eligibility and the elimination of high age requirements of participants for pensions. Programs under which the employee contributes are also becoming more common. The plan should be based on a sound actuarial basis. It is usually advisable to employ the services of specialists in this field.

3. *Group insurance plans.* Protection for individual employees as

members of a group is provided by group insurance plans. Usually, employees are eligible only after a stipulated period of service and in an amount relative to their earnings. The company or the employees may pay the full cost of the plan, or the cost may be assumed jointly. Employees are usually able to secure protection at a cost below that of individually purchased insurance of the same protection. The exact nature of the policy varies with different plans; the basis of all is straight life insurance coverage, but this frequently is supplemented with other benefits.

## EMPLOYEES' RECREATIONAL ACTIVITIES

Recreational activities have motivating influence, but they also help provide a balance between work and play. A well-rounded program of recreational activities is an important part of personnel activities because it improves employer-employee relations, increases efficiency, and makes for healthy, satisfied employees. Such activities may include the following: archery, baseball, softball, basketball, tennis, horseback riding, golf, bowling, horseshoe pitching, swimming, hiking, band, glee club, photography club, and amateur shows.

The participation of management members in recreational activities should consist of a readiness to furnish advice, to offer suggestions, and to lend assistance *upon request.* Managers should not attempt to force inclusion of certain activities or to run the program. Any semblance of paternalism should be avoided.

In guiding the development of the program, the following approach is usually helpful:

1. Measure the adequacy of the activity to find out the total number of employees who can participate.

2. Examine each existing activity to see if it is attracting a capacity number of employees.

3. Investigate public and private recreational facilities to determine how and when they can be used.

4. Find out what is included in programs of other companies.

5. Publicize the existence of the activities so that all employees who can and want to participate may do so.

## SUGGESTIONS FOR EFFECTIVE MOTIVATING

Certain general guides which, in many offices, have proved successful in motivating employees will now be given. To some extent, these are a review of what has already been stated; but in the following form, they can prove helpful and convenient.

1. *Believe in yourself and in other people.* Effective motivating starts

with a genuine belief both in yourself as a management member and in the people under your direction. A manager must sincerely believe that he can motivate and must want to motivate his employees. Belief in employees means thinking and promoting the idea that they can plan better, exercise authority better, and do their work better, and giving them the opportunity to do so.

2. *Set a good example.* The management member should demonstrate by his actions the kind of effort he would like his employees to exert. Performance on the part of the leader, his attitude, and his work habits tend to set a pattern which employees copy. Important in this consideration is to keep busy—everyone, including the supervisor, should have enough meaningful work to do. Failure to provide ample work results sooner or later in employee dissatisfaction and a lack of justification for the money spent in their employment.

3. *Place employees in proper jobs.* Employees normally will give their best efforts in work they like and feel competent to perform. They need to have assignments they are capable of performing. Finding the field of endeavor best suited for each individual employee's capacity and interest, as well as following up to insure that each member is on the best job for which he is currently adapted, will assist in stimulating the employee's best efforts.

4. *Stress participation.* Rare indeed is the person motivated to unusual achievement without some participation in the planning, discussion, and decision making of the activity in which he is going to take a part. Actually, this is a basis for practicing delegation of authority.[1] An employee wants to say something about conditions that affect him. Employees want to be asked their opinions about factors involving their work. They appreciate an audience. By such means, the employee gains the feeling that his employer has an interest in, and cares about, those working for him. Likewise, the desire "to get ahead"—to advance, to win status and prestige—tends to be satisfied when participation is stressed. In some companies, weekly meetings among members of a department are held in order to bring the employees into the task of operating the department by seeking their counsel.

5. *Keep employees informed.* It is a natural human tendency to want to know what is going on, why this or that operation is important, and what changes are being considered—in short, to be kept informed. This adds to an employee's sense of belonging and of being an integral part of the organizational structure. Employees want to feel they are valued members of the team. Communicating effectively with people is essential in motivating them.

6. *Give adequate incentive and reward.* This can and does take many

---

[1] See Chapter 28.

different forms including the amount of wages, the granting of special privileges, the conferring of titles, and the instilling of competition between departments or among employees. To illustrate, the amount of compensation, as well as a proper differential between jobs, is important. Employees want comparable pay for comparable jobs, and salaries that are "in line" with those of other enterprises in the area. They may be less interested in the amount of their own pay than in the relationship of their pay to that of other employees. Individual recognition, awarding of honors, and seniority can be cited as common means of granting special privileges, but these rewards are conferred within the limits of well-publicized policies. Employees can be greatly motivated when the reward offered has significant value to them.

7. *Recognize achievements of employees.* Most employees want to feel useful; they want their efforts to be appreciated. In short, they want recognition. Credit where credit is due and a sincere expression of satisfaction from the employer for a job well done are effective motivating means. The practice of holding periodic talks in private with each employee is also highly recommended. In this way, the employee is individualized, he is afforded recognition, he can voice his feelings about aspects of his job, and a better employer-employee understanding can be established.

8. *Develop group spirit.* Motivation is assisted by making employees feel they are a part of the group and are needed on the team. In this respect, various employee recreational activities can be used to good advantage. The group spirit among an interested and participating number of employees is also fostered by giving them certain facts and an objective, then letting them, as a team, come up with a recommended course of action. In one company, the employees are given a profit and loss statement based on the work they performed and are requested to tie this in with the major objectives of the company.

9. *Give information about the job itself.* To be motivated effectively, each employee must believe his work is wholesome and important. The relationship of his assignment to the entire office and to the aims of the company should be clearly brought out. It is helpful to point out why the particular equipment and machines are supplied so that an attitude of pride in performing work well and in being a part of the enterprise is developed.

10. *Provide an opportunity for job security.* Almost every employee is concerned about having steady work—not being laid off or losing his job. Security is the main reason for demanding restrictions on the type of work that an employee can perform. Also, adequate financial support for old age or to take care of illness or accidents is an important security want of the employee. Providing this wanted security can have a stimulat-

ing effect upon the employee. However, it is necessary to keep him aware of it and to point out that work accomplishments effectively attained are the best means of achieving and maintaining job security.

11. *Employ fear judiciously.*    Fear is a negative force; but when properly used, it can serve as a very strong motivator. The apprehension of not wanting certain happenings to take place can cause a person to exert unusually strong efforts in the direction away from the unwanted event.

12. *Exercise strong leadership.*    All normal persons are motivated by competent leaders. The typical employee wants a leader who knows what he is doing, can speak authoritatively, never makes promises he cannot keep, builds confidence, and takes prompt disciplinary action whenever necessary.

## RESEARCH IN ACTUATING OFFICE EMPLOYEES

Why is the successful actuating of office employees one of the most helpful of all managerial skills? The answer, in part, is because typically the office employee calls upon only a fraction of his full potentiality in performing his job. Managers commonly do not tap the ultimate of what an employee is capable of doing. The main reason is because available motivating tools and their application are inadequate. Much more needs to be known about motivating and how to apply it.

It is hoped that research will supply the answer. Research is a lucrative source of new techniques, new methods, and new information. It seeks to appraise by objective means. It strives to answer such questions as "How well is the job now being done?" "Can it be improved?" and "What will create more interest in performing their work?"

Good research starts with basic factual knowledge about each employee. Included are records of what motivating techniques were used and the results obtained from each. Evaluation of results in order to codify relationships between application and accomplishments is essential. In addition, adequate and complete personnel records are necessary. Success in providing such records depends chiefly upon the content and number of records used, the accuracy of the recorded data, and the analysis and interpretation given them. Available standardized personnel forms will be found helpful, but these should be reviewed in terms of what is essential for the particular program. Among the more common records are: personnel history of the employee; employee's application form; physical examination findings; results of selection tests; identification record; data on training; merit ratings; seniority ratings; safety record; first-aid record; record of attendance, warnings, and demerits; salary and earnings; and termination.

In addition, a personnel record folder on each employee is very helpful. This folder consists of a collection of all personnel records pertaining to the employee; it gives the complete story on that employee and makes this information available for instant reference. Normally, it contains the records listed above; but in some cases, either more or less records may be retained.

## QUESTIONS

1. Do you agree with this statement? "Managers are really helpers of employees. If this fact were more universally accepted, we would improve our management tremendously." Justify your viewpoint.

2. To demonstrate a concept of dealing with people, refer to Figure 31–1, and give an example of bringing the other person into the picture when talking about yourself.

3. How important do you feel the actuating of office employees really is? Elaborate on your answer.

4. Draft a merit-rating chart that to you seems satisfactory for a "programmer—computer section." Justify your recommended chart.

5. Indicate what medium of communication you would recommend for each of the following, along with your reasons for its use:
   a) Announcing that the company has just received a large order for a newly developed product that seems destined to reach sales of $1 million within the next 12 months.
   b) Giving employees the data on the company's contribution to the employees' pension fund for the year just ending.
   c) Advising the discontinuance of operations at Plant C in Big Ridge, Michigan.

6. Name eight merit-rating practices that normally should be kept in mind for most satisfactory results from the viewpoint of both employee and employer.

7. What is meant by each of the following?
   a) Merit-rating factors.
   b) Paternalistic attitude toward employees.
   c) Two-way communication.
   d) Employees' recreational activities.

8. Justify the viewpoint that leadership is a strong motivating force in management.

9. Six months ago, company "XYZ" established a suggestion system, which unfortunately has proved to be very ineffective. You are asked to investigate the system and make recommendations for improvements. Describe your approach to a procedure in this assignment.

10. Of the 12 means of motivating employees given in this chapter, which 5, in your opinion, are probably the most effective for most cases? Why?

11. Do you favor the use of periodic self-appraisals by employees? Why?

12. What area of motivating employees do you feel warrants considerable research over the next five years? What types of additional information would you like discovered?

## CASE PROBLEMS

### Case 31-1.  Howe Products Company

The supervisor of the card-punching and tabulating department, Edward Pierce, went to his superior, office manager Byron Duffel, and inquired if there was danger in letting a company romance continue. He explained that one of the women employees in his department was apparently quite interested in a Mr. Daniel Schloesser, an executive in the systems and procedures department. It probably had been going on for six to eight months and everyone in card punching and tabulating seemed to know about it.

DUFFEL:  Who is the girl?

PIERCE:  Agnes Cushman.

DUFFEL:  She's a very good worker, if it is the one I'm thinking about. She has long black hair, short, rather stocky, big brown eyes?

PIERCE:  Yes, that's Agnes.

DUFFEL:  Well, this Schloesser man must be 40–45 years old. I would guess Agnes at about 25 years.

PIERCE:  I believe the records show she is 28 years of age.

DUFFEL:  I don't know too much about Schloesser—whether he's married or has been married.

PIERCE:  I've heard very little about him. Nothing about a wife or family of his. Do you think I ought to do anything?

DUFFEL:  I guess it's their own private affair.

PIERCE:  Yes, I guess it is. Yet, on the other hand, he's coming over and talking to her quite a bit. And she gets far more telephone calls now, but I don't know if they are from Schloesser or not. Some of the other girls are making kidding remarks to Agnes and she doesn't seem to be taking them too well.

### Problems:

1. What should Mr. Duffel say to Mr. Pierce? Why?
2. What action, if any, should Mr. Pierce take? Mr. Duffel?
3. In general, what do you feel should be done about company romances? Why?

### Case 31-2.  Asbury Company

Due to a heavy snowfall, Asbury Company had little opportunity to contact its employees personally to tell them the company would be closed for the day. It was believed that the streets and roads could be cleared sufficiently for operations to resume the following day. The decision not to open was made about 6:30 A.M. About ten minutes later a company official telephoned a release to two ratio stations to announce that the company would be closed for the day.

Although the radio stations carried the announcement of "no work" once every 15 minutes, beginning at 6:45 A.M. and ending at 9:00 A.M., six office employees and eleven shop employees showed up for work and were sent home. Working hours are 8:30 A.M. till noon and from 1:00 P.M. till 5:00 P.M.

Two days later, a letter, signed by 14 of the 17 employees showing for work, was received by the company paymaster. In this letter, the employees claimed four hours pay because, as they put it, "We were not adequately notified in advance not to come to work." The general manager of the company contends that they were and points out that radio is an acceptable communication medium in emergencies. The spokesman for the 14 employees counters that the company is not being fair about the matter.

## Problems:

1. Evaluate the position taken by the 14 employees.
2. What alternatives are possible for handling this situation?
3. How would you have handled this as the general manager? Why?

## Case 31-3.   Kubera Company

Edmund DuBarry is a cost clerk, has been with the company two years, and performs satisfactory work. Several months ago he purchased for his home a stereo set and a quantity of long-play records. Soon after that he developed the habit of humming and whistling at his work. His sounds were somewhat lacking in artfulness, but Edmund apparently derived much satisfaction from his efforts for he continued with them off and on throughout the entire day. Fellow cost clerks working near Edmund made no complaints, but to his supervisor, Harvey Olsen, "the sounds" were very disturbing. At first, he had hoped that Edmund would "stop the music" after a week or so of such goings on. But the practice persisted.

Finally, Mr. Olsen spoke privately to Edmund and requested that he stop his humming and whistling during working hours as they were distracting, in bad taste, and not in keeping with a well-run office. Edmund complied and was quiet for several days. Then he again started humming and whistling while on the job. After a couple hours of this, Mr. Olsen walked to Edmund's desk and in front of the entire department shouted to Edmund, "Stop it." Edmund did. Then after several seconds, Edmund stated softly, "None of the boys here in the department have complained. All of us are doing our work. The trouble is supervisors don't want to adjust to individual employee differences, but employees are expected to adjust to individual manager differences." Mr. Olsen told Edmund to keep quiet and get to work. Edmund said nothing.

## Problems:

1. Is there a problem here? Discuss.
2. What do you believe would have happened had Mr. Olsen said nothing to Edmund DuBarry?
3. What should Edmund do now? Mr. Olsen? Justify your views.

CHAPTER **32**

# OFFICE SALARY
# ADMINISTRATION

That man is truly free who desires what he is
able to perform, and does what he desires.
—*Rousseau*

COMPENSATION is motivating to an employee. Man does not work for
money alone but for what he can do with the money he receives.
Fundamental are his needs for food, clothing, and shelter and the
challenge to satisfy these needs is motivating; but after providing
adequately for them, man seeks to fulfill other wants and takes on tasks
and seeks compensation sufficient to satisfy these other wants. Hence, the
monetary reward for performing work is a fundamental consideration in
actuating and helps get.work accomplished that otherwise might not be
accomplished.

## ADMINISTRATION OF COMPENSATION

There are a myriad of influences affecting office salary administration.
At any given time some factors are tending to push salaries up while
others are having the directly opposite effect. And these respective forces
are of varying degrees. The subject of compensating can become quite
complicated. To simplify our discussion, we will identify three considerations which are normally of major significance in the office area. These
include (1) salary surveys, (2) salary differentials, and (3) salary
patterns.

Salary surveys are conducted to find out what enterprises are paying so
that you can keep your salaries competitive and in line. Great care must
be taken to make certain that valid comparisons are being made. As
pointed out previously, one of the greatest sources of error involves

identical job titles, with wide differences in job content. Likewise, what is actually being produced may differ. For example, in company "A" an accounting machine operator may be paid $95 a week and perform 20 transactions an hour whereas in company "B" an accounting machine operator is paid $95 a week and performs 16 transactions an hour. Is a comparison between the two $95-a-week salaries truly meaningful? Salary surveys are helpful but not conclusive. Frequently they are performed by a trade association, a professional society, an organization of manufacturers, or similar enterprises. Each participating company receives a copy of the results, which are coded to mask the sources.

Salary differentials exist and are justifiable because job requirements differ. Work that requires higher knowledge and skill normally commands a higher salary than work requiring lower knowledge and skill. That salary differentials should exist is generally accepted; the real question is, "What differential is fair and just?" In addition, wage differentials exist between different geographical areas. Office salaries in San Francisco, for example, are higher than those in Memphis. Furthermore, office salaries for the same type of office work can vary within San Francisco. A typist for an import-export firm may receive less salary than a typist in a San Francisco bank.

Salary patterns tend to be formulated by the leading enterprise or enterprises in an area and in many instances these patterns are adopted by other enterprises in the area. This follow-the-leader practice can be extremely rigid or somewhat flexible, in which case the leader enterprise can have an influence, but its policies and practices may not be adopted in totality. Leader or pilot enterprises, however, usually in some degree affect salary administration actions and constitute an influence with which to reckon.

Job evaluation, or some adaptation of it, is used by most office managers to keep office salaries paid in line with what others are paying for similar work, to provide proper wage differentials, and to be competitive salarywise. In addition to job evaluation, the core of most office salary administration programs includes consideration of how well the incumbent is doing the particular job, regard for the amount paid for "fringe benefits," and recognition of certain social and economic influences. Each of these will be discussed. We will start with job evaluation.

## JOB EVALUATION

The concept of the job and its relative worth are considered in job evaluating, which can be formally defined as follows: *Job evaluation is the determination of the relative value of each individual job in an enterprise and is arrived at by means of a systematic procedure using jobs or selected job factors for comparison or measurement.* There are four main methods of carrying out job evaluation work, including (1) ranking, (2) classification, (3) factor comparison, and (4) point.

1. *Ranking Method.* The jobs within an enterprise can be arranged according to their relative difficulty. A ranking of the jobs is thus obtained; and in this manner, the relative importance of each one is established. The job at the top of the list has the highest value, and the job at the bottom of the list has the lowest value. The usual procedure is (1) to rank the jobs in an individual department and (2) to combine all departmental rankings into one composite ranking.

Figure 32–1 illustrates the results which might be obtained from this

### ARRAY OF JOBS ACCORDING TO RANKING METHOD

| Rank No. | Name of Job | Earnings per Week* |
|---|---|---|
| 1 | Accounting clerk I | $120 |
| 2 | Purchasing clerk | 116 |
| 3 | Traffic clerk I | 112 |
| 4 | Cashier | 108 |
| 5 | Accounting clerk II | 104 |
| 6 | Traffic clerk II | 100 |
| 7 | Cost clerk | 96 |
| 8 | Tabulating-machine operator | 92 |
| 9 | General bookkeeper | 88 |
| 10 | Correspondent | 84 |
| 11 | Stenographer | 80 |
| 12 | Switchboard operator | 76 |
| 13 | Typist I | 72 |
| 14 | File clerk | 68 |
| 15 | Typist II | 64 |
| 16 | Office boy | 60 |

* In uniform variation from top to bottom.

FIG. 32–1.

method. For example, the job of "accounting clerk I" was considered of greater value than the job of "purchasing clerk," while the job of "office boy" was ranked lowest in the office. If the weekly salary of the top job is set at $120 and that of the lowest job at $60, then the rank order of the intermediate jobs, assuming a straight-line or uniform variation, is shown in the last column in the illustration.

2. *Classification Method.* Under this method, a predetermined number of job classes or groups are established, and the jobs are assigned to these classifications. For example, the job classes, from highest to lowest, might include:

Class A.  Executive
    Office manager
    Office departmental supervisor

Class B.  Skilled
  Purchasing clerk
  Traffic clerk
  Cashier
Class C.  Limited skilled
  Tabulating-machine operator
  Stenographer
  Switchboard operator
Class D.  Unskilled
  File clerk
  Office boy

In this method, the jobs within each grade frequently must be graded further to show more adequately the existing relationships. To do this, the ranking method, previously described, can be employed.

3. *Factor Comparison Method.*  Jobs can also be evaluated according to predetermined factors which have been established as a measure of ranking. Customarily, a key-job comparison scale is established and used for this purpose. Job factors are listed across the top and the dollars per week or salary-rating schedule in the left column. The scale provides the means for applying *salary rates* to job relatives as needed.

Assume four job factors: education, experience, responsibility, and working conditions. On each of these factors, each key job is ranked. Generally, eight to ten jobs are considered key jobs, selected on the basis of the jobs requiring widely different amounts of the job factors being utilized. To illustrate, for the "accounting clerk I" job, the rating values given for each of the job factors might be:

| | |
|---|---:|
| Education | $ 36.00 |
| Experience | 28.00 |
| Responsibility | 44.00 |
| Working conditions | 12.00 |
| Total | $120.00 |

In other words, from the key-job comparison scale, it is possible to determine what portion of the present salary of a job is being paid for each factor.

This scale is the measuring device for evaluating all other jobs in the company. Other jobs are fitted into this scale, with the key-job evaluations being used as guides. To illustrate, consider the job of "tabulating-machine operator." The evaluator would first read the job analysis sheet for this job. Then, concentrating his attention on the factor of education, he judges where under the education column the job of tabulating-machine operator seems to fit. He might decide that this job requires a little more education than a certain key job but less than another key job. Hence, he would evaluate "tabulating-machine operator" between the two considered key jobs. In similar manner, the job is evaluated according to the other job factors, and the other jobs in the company are evaluated in a similar manner.

4. *Point Method.* In this method, job factors are selected, and each is assigned a maximum number of points or credits. The selection of job factors is qualified by the following: that each job factor (1) exists in all the jobs to be evaluated, (2) varies in amount in the different jobs to be evaluated, and (3) is mutually exclusive of other job factors. The maximum point value assigned to each factor is determined by its relative importance. This is governed primarily by the judgment and experience of the analyst. Normally, from eight to fourteen factors are used. Those most common include skill, experience, education, responsibilities, working conditions, effort, and supervisory requirements.

Each selected job factor is defined in clear and simple language. The degree or intensity of each selected factor is broken down, and points are assigned for each level of the factor. Figure 32–2 shows these data for the factor "responsibility for loss," which has been given five levels, *A* through *E,* ranging in value from a low of 3 to a maximum of 50 points. Figure 32–3 illustrates 11 job factors selected for use in the evaluation of clerical and supervisory jobs. In this case, the data showing the level and the points of rating, along with pertinent comments for the job of "junior accountant," are indicated for each factor. Note that under factor No. 4, "responsibility for loss," the rating level of *B* is valued at 15 points, which was arrived at by referring to the guide shown by Figure 32–2.

## PRICING THE JOB

The ultimate aim of job evaluation is to determine the job price or rate of pay. Jobs of high evaluation should command high rates of pay; in general, the higher the evaluation, the higher the pay. The immediate problem is to determine what the rate of pay should be when the evaluation is a known amount. The job prices to be established must be consistent (1) externally (rates within the enterprise are in line with the rates paid outside the enterprise) and (2) internally (rates within the enterprise are directly associated within the evaluations).

External consistency is accomplished by securing the current wage rates in the area from salary surveys conducted by enterprises specializing in this type of work or from local governmental offices. Sometimes, to supplement available information, a thorough salary survey must be made. It is also well to remember that accurate job descriptions and productivity data add greatly to the usefulness of salary survey results.

Internal consistency is determined by comparing the job evaluations with the rates paid. In some cases, this can be done by a simple comparison of columnar data. Very often, however, a graphic representation helps to visualize this comparison, especially when the point

4. Responsibility for Loss

| Level | LEVEL DEFINITION | Points |
|-------|------------------|--------|
| A | Nature of work involves negligible opportunity for loss. Normal or reasonable care required and all work is verified or proved by repeating entire operation. | 3 |
| B | Nature of work is such that more than normal or reasonable care is required to prevent loss. However, work is checked by proving against totals or some standard rather than by repetition of operation. | 15 |
| C | Nature of work involves moderate but constant opportunity for error, limited only by daily or subsequent spot check or examination. Great care should be exercised to prevent loss. Potential serious loss from errors in transcription or computation. | 27 |
| D | Good judgment must be exercised regularly to prevent loss. Work is of such nature that complete and correct performance is hard to control, reliance being placed on the individual. Work subject to general supervision and occasional review. | 38 |
| E | Work of such a nature that commitments are made which may involve the entire bank. Work is frequently released without any check being made or is checked only by individual doing the work. A high degree of financial responsibility is involved. | 50 |

*Courtesy: J. D. Moore Organization, Park Ridge, Ill.*

FIG. 32–2. Illustrating the different levels of "responsibility for loss" and the number of points assigned to each level.

system of evaluation has been used. Commonly employed is a chart or scatter diagram in which existent wage rates are plotted on the vertical axis and evaluations on the horizontal axis. A curve showing consistent relationships between rates and evaluations can then be drawn on the chart. The deviations of actual rates from this curve can readily be spotted, and jobs overpaid or underpaid with respect to their evaluation can be quickly observed.

Figure 32–4 is a scatter diagram showing the relationship between wage rates and evaluations. The plotted points are indicated by the small

| | | | | | | |
|---|---|---|---|---|---|---|

**CODE** ............................................................. **SALARY GRADE** ........ VI .................................................................

**JOB TITLE** ........ JUNIOR ACCOUNTANT .................................................................................................................

### CLERICAL AND SUPERVISORY EVALUATION

| | NO. | FACTOR | RATING LEVEL | RATING PTS. | JOB REQUIREMENT |
|---|---|---|---|---|---|
| **SKILL** | 1 | Essential Knowledge | D | 84 | Requires a knowledge of advanced accounting methods and procedures and a working knowledge of company financial policies. |
| | 2 | Experience and Training | G | 73 | Normally requires 3 to 5 years' training and experience, including 2 years' accounting training plus 3 years' company experience as an Accounting Clerk. |
| | 3 | Analytical Requirements | C | 27 | Requires analysis of figures and data which vary in content but follow general patterns of application |
| **RESPONSIBILITY** | 4 | Responsibility For Loss | B | 15 | Requires more than normal care to prevent loss due to miscalculations. However, work is usually checked against totals. |
| | 5 | Confidential Information | B | 6 | Involves preparation and use of limited confidential matters in the Accounting Department. |
| | 6 | Contacts Public and Internal | B | 28 | Involves routine contacts with persons where detailed subject matter must be presented satisfactorily. |
| | 7 | Individual Initiative | B | 12 | Involves initiative in planning details of own work. |
| **EFFORT** | 8 | Mental Effort | C | 15 | Requires moderate mental effort to solve problems of accounting. |
| | 9 | Physical Effort | A | 6 | Involves light physical effort with intermittent standing and sitting at comfortable intervals. |
| | 10 | Work Conditions | A | 0 | Working conditions are excellent. |
| | 11 | Supervisory Requirements | FX | 18 | Involves immediate leadership over Accounting Clerks and Typists. |
| | | TOTAL POINTS | | 284 | |

*Courtesy: J. D. Moore Organization, Park Ridge, Ill.*

FIG. 32–3. Job factors, ratings, and comments for the job of "junior accountant."

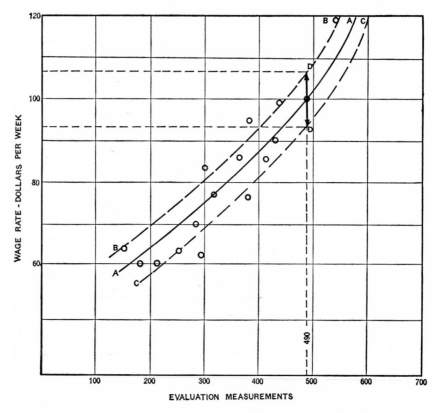

FIG. 32–4.  Scatter diagram showing relationship between wage rates and evaluation measurements.

circles. Curve *AA* has been drawn in and represents what is considered to be a consistent relationship between rates and evaluations. Curves *BB* and *CC* have been drawn in for reasons discussed in the paragraphs that follow.

### JOB PRICE RANGE

From a practical viewpoint, the office manager is interested in more than a job price for each job. What he really wants is (1) *a price range for each job,* not a single price for each job; and (2) *a price range to cover a group of jobs,* not just one job. A price range provides flexibility and makes for a better salary plan. Furthermore, when a group of jobs are within one price range, the entire task of wage determination is simplified.

Referring again to Figure 32–4, a wage range has been indicated by the two curves *BB* and *CC* drawn on the chart.[1] The job of "traffic clerk II," for example, evaluated at 490 points, has a range from $93 to $107 per week, indicated by ordinate *DD* on the chart.

To provide a group of jobs within one price range, it is customary to group jobs into classes so that all jobs in the same class have the same price range. In other words, jobs of the same worth are put into the same class. The number of job classes depends primarily upon the total number of jobs, and the spread between the highest and the lowest job. Usually, a total of six to ten job classes is sufficient in most offices.

As already discussed, the classification method of job evaluation automatically puts the jobs into various classes. On the other hand, when any of the other methods of job evaluation are used, the alignment of jobs is arbitrarily divided into different numbers and levels or classes.

## ADVANTAGES OF JOB EVALUATION

A solid foundation for an office salary administration is supplied by job evaluation because it (1) shows the relative value of office jobs within a company, (2) assists in the evaluating of new office jobs, (3) helps obtain a satisfactory wage level for all office jobs within the company, (4) helps to eliminate salary inequalities by putting office jobs having similar requirements in the same salary range, and (5) affords factual data for the settling of salary disputes. It is imperative, however, that the work of determining job content, grades, and price ranges be kept up to date by regular, periodic checkups. The content of many jobs changes in the normal course of events; and this, in turn, frequently changes the relative values of the jobs. Likewise, changes in the general wage levels appear to be the usual rather than the exceptional happenings.

## HOW WELL THE INCUMBENT IS DOING HIS JOB

Up to this point we have confined our discussion to what the job is worth. Let us now consider an equally important concept in office salary administration, namely, how well the incumbent is doing his job. For this purpose, merit rating, discussed in the previous chapter, is commonly used. In some programs, merit rating tempered with seniority is followed. The justification for this approach is that the employee who has been on the job for a long period tends to perform the work better or at least knows more about how it should be performed. This viewpoint, however, is open to question, but in offices where it is followed, it is usually popular and brings quite satisfactory results.

---

[1] Frequently, a constant percentage change from the center line is used to establish the outside range lines. For example, for $50 median, the range is $45–$55; for $90 median, the range is $81–$99.

Bonus arrangements are employed by some companies to demonstrate approval of satisfactory office work accomplishments. Usually the payments of bonuses commemorate special occasions, such as Christmas, a birthday, or an employment anniversary. These payments commonly amount to sizable sums—perhaps an extra month's pay or, in some cases, as much as 20 percent of a year's salary. They are given to share the results of profitable operations, to recognize outstanding service, to continue a traditional custom, or to improve employee morale.

Financial incentive plans are another means of recognizing how well the incumbent is doing. These plans provide for total compensation based to some extent on the amount of work accomplished instead of strictly on the basis of time spent at work. Generally speaking, financial incentive plans are not common in offices, but their use is growing. The more common incentive office work includes transcribing, card punching, order processing, and billing.

## FUNDAMENTALS OF OFFICE INCENTIVE PLANS

There are two fundamental concepts in practically all office incentive plans: (1) a base or standard amount of work output and (2) the amount of wage payment which will be given for production below standard, at standard, or above standard. The first concept, the base amount of work output, can be determined by past performance records, by time studies, or by guess. Customarily, this standard amount of work is expressed as 100 percent. The amount of work which is established as standard is extremely important, for it is commonly, but not always, the point at which the incentive pay begins. The second concept, or pattern of the amount of wage payment, varies with the incentive plan. Some plans guarantee base rates up to standard; others do not. Some divide the excess above standard equally between employee and employer, while others share the overflow according to various percentages.

The same general type of plan can be used for a group as for a single employee. The group can be used when the nature of the work is such that its segregation among individual employees is very difficult or costly. The group incentive pay is figured first, than divided among the members according to either the individual base wage rates, the number of hours worked by each member, the individual gross base pay, or on some other agreed basis.

Incentive wage plans should be tailor-made to suit the particular office and to achieve the particular objectives desired from the plan. The following guides are helpful:

1. Incentive plans should have the backing of the top managers.

2. The best incentive plan is usually the simple plan. It should be thoroughly understood by all concerned.

3. There should be a close relationship between reward (incentive pay) and results (contribution).

4. An incentive based on the individual employee is generally better than one based on a group.

5. The work output should increase as well as the amount of salaries.

6. The base or standard production amounts should be carefully determined—preferably by measured time studies.

7. The number of temporary standards should be held to a minimum. When standards are temporary, this fact should be known to all concerned.

8. The incentive wage should be neither guaranteed nor limited. In most instances, the base wage should be guaranteed.

9. The standards should be reviewed for possible revision whenever any change is made in the material, machine, or method used.

10. If indirect production employees, such as messenger boys, receptionists, and telephone operators, are included in the plan, they should be affiliated on some measurable basis, such as the maintenance of an acceptable ratio between the total indirect man-hours to the total direct man-hours, or the total indirect man-hours to total work output. This tends to keep the indirect man-hours under control.

## FRINGE BENEFITS

Another major area of modern office salary administration is fringe benefits. These include (1) legally required benefits—social security, unemployment, workmen's compensation requirements, (2) pay *away* from the job—paid leaves, vacations, and holidays, (3) pay *on* the job for time off—employee meetings, overtime pay, and shift premium pay, and (4) special benefits—service awards, meal allowances, relocation expenses, and tuition aid. Various estimates point to an average of about 28 percent of total base payroll costs constituting expense for fringe benefits. The trend in the amount of fringe benefits has been steadily upward during the last decade. Wage experts predict fringe benefits will represent 40 percent of payroll costs by 1980.

Many office employees give considerable weight to the fringe benefits included in a job. The dollar "take home" pay is adjusted in view of the fringe benefits received; and it is common to find an office employee preferring to work for a particular concern where the dollar salaries are average or even low, but the numerous fringe benefits provided make for an attractive total remuneration.

A big need in the fringe benefits area is for employers to explain and publicize their benefit programs. Too frequently complicated mathematical formulas and legal phraseology are communicated in response to simple employee questions. As a rule, employees want simple answers, not problems. They want to know their benefit position. What is available to an employee and his dependents if and when an emergency arises is what he wants to know. The wise office manager tells him in language that he can understand.

## SOCIAL AND ECONOMIC INFLUENCES

Last of the major areas of office salary administration discussed here is social and economic influences. A number of factors could be discussed under this heading, but the discussion here will be limited to (1) career influence and (2) the supply of and demand for office jobs. Career influence is made up of what an employee is looking forward to when he accepts a job and the influence of this ambition on his work. The pay for a job may be too low, in terms of what the job requires; but because of career influence, the employee willingly forgoes the higher and appropriate pay in order to get ultimately to a job he wants. The case of a young law graduate in a law office illustrates this point. On the other hand, the career influence may cause a job to be rated too highly by the employee, based on the actual job requirements. The job might be of the dead-end type and offer no usable training or advancement beyond a well-known level. In this case, sufficient salary must be paid to secure and hold the proper type of employee.

For the most part, salary rates are affected by the condition of supply and demand. These economic factors are dynamic; they change with time and exert a "push and pull" effect on salary rates. As a matter of practical consideration, recognition must be given to significant changes in the supply and demand for employees of specific skills. *Temporarily,* minor adjustments might have to be made in order to alleviate serious labor shortage difficulties. For example, current conditions may make it necessary to start a new employee at a figure higher than the usual starting wage but still within the range of the job. Or in unusual cases, the rate may be outside the job range; but such a condition usually does not last and might be viewed as an emergency case. If it does persist, however, it is well to revalue the job and change the classification, thus giving reality to the salary administration plan.

This does not mean that the salary ranges established primarily through job evaluation should be ignored whenever the labor market is either generally tight or loose. It does mean some deviation for some jobs —generally very few—which have become out of line because of the effect of current economic forces. As a matter of fact, the job-evaluating factors, such as education, experience, and responsibility, are themselves functions of time and of the economic forces of supply and demand. It is therefore reasonable to expect some minor adjustments in salary rates as a result of the influence of supply and demand for employees of specific office skills.

## QUESTIONS

1. Justify the viewpoint that compensation has a motivating influence upon an employee.
2. Define each of the following:
   a) Salary patterns.
   b) Job evaluation.
   c) Financial incentive plan.
   d) Price range for a group of jobs.
3. Discuss the use of salary surveys in office salary administration.
4. Would you say that job evaluation is scientific in its determination of the value of a job? Why?
5. For an office employing 750 employees, can the wage rates be externally, but not internally, consistent? Internally, but not externally, consistent? Elaborate upon your answers.
6. As an office manager, would you favor a financial incentive plan as a part of your salary administration program? Justify your viewpoint.
7. In your opinion, are bonus payments to employees effective actuating efforts? Why?
8. Which method of job evaluation do you consider the simplest? The most accurate? The easiest for employees to understand? Substantiate your answers.
9. As you see it, point out the importance and the contribution of fringe benefits in office salary administration.
10. Explain Figure 32–3 in your own words.
11. What basic employees' desires does a financial incentive provide? Are these of major or minor importance in office management?
12. What steps do you feel might be taken to make an office employee more aware of the fringe benefits he is receiving?

## CASE PROBLEMS

### Case 32–1.  Forsythe Company

Arthur Kadell was being paid $625 a month. He joined the company three and one-half years ago, was promoted to his present job on which he has received two pay increases. Due to the installation of a computer and changes in work content, Arthur Kadell's job will no longer be necessary. His supervisor told him not to worry, that he would be transferred to another job. Meanwhile, he will continue on his present job for approximately the next two months while the changeover is being made.

Some seven weeks later, Mr. Kadell is informed that he will be transferred to another department and job which will pay him $540 a month, and he will retain his full seniority and company benefits. Mr. Kadell protests, claiming he should continue to receive his present rate of pay. He reasons that the company offer gives him a cut in pay through no fault of his own; he has a good work record with the company, and prior to now, nothing has been said about his having to take less pay. He adds, "Had I known this, I would have started looking outside for something else the minute I found out my job was to be eliminated."

## Problems:

1. What further action do you feel Arthur Kadell should take? Why?
2. What should the company do? Why?

### Case 32–2.  Prychinski Manufacturing Company

Much of the office work was paid for on an incentive basis. Cleo Reitsma and Stella Mikalski, employees in the mailing room, were given time standards for direct mail work including folding brochures, stuffing into envelopes, sealing, and stamping. Any savings in time based on these standards earned incentive pay in addition to a guaranteed hourly base wage. Times were reported daily on "employee cards" which also served as time cards from which the company's direct labor costs were figured. In checking over the cards for one day's work the supervisor, Tony Perfeth, suspected that Cleo and Stella had not reported their production on work that he was certain they had completed. When all employees had gone home for the night he checked the direct mail work area and found the suspected batch of work completed and neatly piled up in a secluded part of the area. He said nothing to anyone about his discovery.

Several days later in checking the employee cards, Tony noticed the suspected batch of work was reported in yesterday's work by Cleo and Stella. He reasoned that they had withheld their production to report it a later day so that they would receive more incentive pay for the later day. For the day when production was withheld, they received guaranteed base pay only even though they did not reach standard. The net effect was more money for Cleo and Stella. Tony called them to his office and accused them of falsifying work records. At first, they stated they did not understand what Tony was talking about. Then Stella readily admitted they had juggled their production figures. But, they insisted, this is a fairly common practice and Tony has never told them not to do this, that he must know of the practice, and that he has never warned the employees of this practice. As they see it, they simply were tardy in reporting.

## Problems:

1. Use arbitrary figures to show how withholding production by Cleo and Stella would result in greater net earnings to them.
2. What action should Tony Perfeth take? Why?

### Case 32–3.  Sawyer-Chesky, Inc.

The office manager, Ron Seydell, is of the opinion that fringe benefits for the office employees have become excessive. Some years ago, the company started the practice of giving all office employees coffee and doughnuts free of charge during the morning and afternoon "breaks." Mr. Seydell favors cutting this out. Also, a parking space was leased by the company several years ago, and office employees were permitted to park free on this lot. With the increase in business and office employees, the lot has become inadequate. There is a second parking lot available; but rather than keep adding to company costs, Mr. Seydell feels that the whole idea of the company supplying free parking space should be abandoned.

In talking over the situation with his associates and the personnel director, Mr. Seydell has met opposition to his proposal. The personnel director, in particular, feels very strongly that the employees will resent, even though they may not openly say so, any action by the company to take away the parking service and convenience. True, this costs the company an average of about 36.7 cents per week per employee, points out the personnel director, but he contends that it is money well spent. The free coffee and doughnuts involve 16.2 cents per day per employee.

The office manager agrees that the grumbling should be held at a minimum when the company stops picking up the "tab" for these extras. He contends that office costs must be reduced. Something has to be done about these fringes, which are excessive, in his opinion. What started as little extras and niceties are getting out of hand. The parking question will get the company involved more and more as time goes on. And in his opinion, the advantages, if any, of the company supplying free coffee and doughnuts are quite intangible; and to think of this as being a favor to the employees is simply ridiculous. To quote Seydell's own words: "The company is paying the employees a good wage. Let them buy their coffee and doughnuts if they want them. It's not the company's responsibility."

## Problems:

1. What do you think of Mr. Seydell's recommendations? Why?
2. Can you see any merit in the company retaining these benefits? Discuss.
3. What plan of action do you feel the company should take? Why?

# CHAPTER 33

# DEVELOPING
# OFFICE EMPLOYEES

Only the individual can make himself a better
manager. The company and the boss can help.
But in the long run all personal development is
just that—personal.
                    —*Richard S. Reynolds, Jr.*

THE PLANNED development of employees is the goal of formal employee
training efforts. It is vital in managerial actuating and has grown
tremendously during recent years. Employee training is an everyday
activity in most enterprises. Employees acquire their training either by
means of planned and well-administered programs or by a hit-or-miss
method which includes learning by mistakes, by trial and error, and by
absorption. Since training is vital and goes on continually, progressive
managers have set up definite training programs so that proper direction
and control can be given to make the employee's work contribution more
useful to the enterprise.

## FUNDAMENTALS OF DEVELOPING

Most employees are developing most of the time through the acquisition of additional knowledge and skill. This is a perfectly natural process.
The sources include personal performance, behavior of other employees,
hearing, observing, and imitating. These means are commonly referred to
as "experience." Development from these sources places a strong emphasis
on what is practical and is conditioned extensively by experiment and
accident. As such, it is neither an efficient means nor necessarily
applicable to the employee's job.

Intentional efforts to teach someone can be far more effective, provided

708

the efforts are properly managed. Beginning with what the trainee now knows and can perform, it is possible to determine what the trainee must know and be able to do in order to perform successfully particular work assignments. The differential between what is now known and what is needed constitutes the gap which training seeks to fill. This gap is reduced gradually, because learning is a gradual process. An employee learns bit by bit, not all at once. Knowing the gap to be filled and considering the gradual doses which can be absorbed by the trainee and in what sequence, the formal training operation can be set in motion. Usually, tie-ins or association of new concepts with knowledge or skills already possessed by the trainee proves effective in training work.

There exist today many different schools of thought about the means of training. However, the objective should be foremost in determining the form of training to provide. Fundamentally, all instruction should (1) proceed from the known to the unknown, (2) go from the simple to the complex, and (3) follow the order of "prepare, present, and apply."

There exist today many different schools of thought about the means of training. However, the objective should be foremost in determining the form of training to provide. Fundamentally, all instruction should (1) proceed from the known to the unknown, (2) go from the simple to the complex, and (3) follow the order of "prepare, present, and apply."

Basic considerations in the activity of acquiring knowledge and skill warrant emphasis in our discussion at this time. Of prime importance is the trainee's personal interest in learning. Economic or social gains may motivate him, but a stimulus must be present. Necessarily, people start from where they are in any training effort, and they are most likely to want to learn when they see what is taught is helpful to them. In addition, the trainee must be in a receptive mood, emotionally settled, and free from worries, personal troubles, and anxieties. Lastly, it must be recognized that the trainee must learn for himself; he must subject himself to the learning process. The instructor's role is primarily one of guidance and stimulation.

Figure 33–1 lists some key points in learning. Keeping these simple truths in mind will assist anyone who is helping others to develop.

---

1. A person learns best what he likes best.
2. A person learns by doing; watching or listening is insufficient.
3. A person remembers longer if he understands the *why* of the knowledge.
4. A person tries harder for rewards than he does to avoid punishments.
5. A person learns fastest when the teaching makes it easier for the learner to learn.

---

FIG. 33–1. Some key points in learning.

## OBJECTIVES OF SUPERVISORY TRAINING

Three basic requirements are common to most successful supervisors: (1) technical proficiency, (2) facility in visualization, and (3) ability in human relations. Under technical skill are included such things as effective application of one's knowledge of specific techniques in handling and processing information, office practices, office layout, and the like. Essentially, technical skill deals with tangible operations and is the most common type of skill possessed.

Facility in visualization means the capacity to picture mentally the managerial operations, to envision their relations, to exercise creativeness, and to evolve means for accomplishing definite goals. It involves intangibles, it includes perception of the management process, and it implies possession of an all-inclusive conceptual viewpoint and understanding about all the elements through which the major tasks will be accomplished. It is especially important for the office supervisor.

Ability in human relations is essential to supervisory ability and growth. Much of the discussion in this section of the book deals with this topic; but for emphasis, it can be repeated that knowledge and skill in human relations deals with manager-nonmanager relationships, the general attitude toward people, the evaluating of human motivations, and the winning of loyalty, support, and willing cooperation.

## OBJECTIVES OF EMPLOYEE TRAINING

Comparing respective job requirements to the qualifications of the employee performing the jobs will reveal certain areas in which employee training might prove helpful. Future plans of the office, anticipated increases in personnel, and changes in methods are direct and basic sources for determining the objectives of an employee training program.

Each employee should have complete knowledge of what constitutes his job and what its relationship is to other jobs in the organization. This should not be left to chance. Planned efforts in the form of a training program should be utilized to get job content information to each employee. Improved relations are a certainty when the employee understands completely what his job is, the relationship of his work to other work in the department, and, in time, that of his department to the entire organization structure.

Up-to-date knowledge of operating policies and procedures is another important and common objective in office training. Information on personnel practices should be made known to all. Likewise, the general scope of desired public relations and the quality of paper work required are among the types of information which should be a part of every employee's knowledge.

Each employee should have knowledge of the best known methods of doing his work. It is not sufficient for managers alone to have this knowledge; a manager must see to it that the employees also know, for only then is a satisfactory efficiency in work output possible.

Also, recognition or advancement should be extended when training is completed satisfactorily. This may take the form of improved status, public recognition, increased earnings, or promotion. It is a mistake for an enterprise to develop an employee for a better job or to improve or add to his knowledge and skill without subsequently offering him a job on which he can use the newly acquired ability, either in the present or at some future date, within or outside the enterprise.

## ADVANTAGES OF TRAINING

When the above objectives are attained definite advantages accrue. One who really manages makes use of training to help him manage. To the management member, training assists in improving his planning, controlling, organizing, and actuating. For example, creating effective plans, maintaining proper standards of quality, building a satisfactory organization structure, delegating authority, and stimulating employees are all assisted by effective training.

In addition, the responsibility of supervision is lessened. Training does not eliminate the need for good supervision but it reduces the requirement for detailed and constant supervision. A well-trained office employee is self-reliant in his work, because he knows what to do and how to do it. Under such conditions, close supervision is ordinarily not mandatory.

Also, the best available methods of performing the work can be standardized and made available to all employees. High levels of performance become the rule rather than the exception. The advantages of past knowledge and experience can be retained.

Furthermore, office employees, well trained, will usually show a greater increase in, and a higher quality of, work output than will an untrained group. Employees do a more intelligent job and make fewer mistakes when they possess the know-how, have an understanding of their jobs and of the interdependence of one job and another, and know the *why* of the company's policies and procedures. And it is important to note that morale can be boosted effectively *after* the employee knows what to do.

On the other hand, these advantages are not obtained without a price. Certain difficulties and possible losses are incurred and should be recognized in any training program. First of all, regular office work is likely to be interrupted or delayed by time spent in training. The output of the trainee might be temporarily reduced. Also, training might foster dependence upon others for solutions to challenges which the employee should think through for himself. Self-reliance and capacity for new ideas might be stifled. Furthermore, competent training leaders are difficult to obtain. When mediocre instruction is utilized, not only may the results of the training be below what is expected, but they may actually prove harmful.

## TYPES OF TRAINING

Training can be classified in many ways. One useful classification is training for present jobs and training for future jobs. Another is training for any or all of the following: job knowledge, job skills, and attitudes. Still another is training for basic information, for personal development, and for specific production in definite work application. A useful list showing the range and types of training may be outlined as follows:

1. *Preemployment Training.* This deals with the type and amount of instruction needed by inexperienced employees prior to their entering the office. This training is generally provided by educational institutions outside the enterprise, such as high schools, universities, business colleges, night schools, and correspondence courses. Preemployment training is generally broader and more fundamental than the other types of training. It is intended to provide basic skills. Likewise, it sometimes is of a theoretical nature, in contrast to the practical aspect of the other types; it seeks to provide an intellectual background and to develop the art of thinking and reasoning.

2. *Induction Training.* The objective of induction training is to provide the new employee with the information necessary for a complete knowledge and understanding of practices and procedures of the enterprise. Included in this aspect of training are welcoming the new employee to the company, explaining the office rules and regulations, acquainting him with employees' benefits, informing him of the company's policies and operations, and telling him what is expected of him as an employee. The new office employee's impression of the company is frequently formed during the first several hours at the new job. Introductions should be made to the new employee's department head, fellow employees, and those supervisors with whom he will be associated. If it is possible, an introduction to one of the officers is also helpful, as this gives the new employee a feeling of worth and helps him to visualize the extent of the company. Experience shows it is a good idea to give the employee some job which he can do without too much instruction and then leave him by himself. This gives the new employee a chance to digest some of the new surroundings. Follow this up with contacts about every hour or so throughout the rest of the day. Encourage the new employee to ask questions.

3. *On-the-Job Training.* This type of training aims to give the employee the necessary skill required for a specific job. It seeks to fill the

gap between the ability the worker can supply and the ability the job requires. The job can be either that of the present or some future assignment. In some cases, the job is of a higher grade than the employee's present one; in other words, the employee is being prepared for promotion. The makeup of on-the-job training takes many different forms, including lectures in specific subjects, practice on new machines, job rotation—including all jobs of a certain group, special assignments of a temporary nature, understudying a junior executive, special courses, reading assignments, and special workshops by professional associations.

TYPES OF TRAINING GIVEN TO VARIOUS CLASSIFICATIONS OF EMPLOYEES

| Classification of Employee | Type of Training | Training Required |
|---|---|---|
| New | Induction | To give information relative to the job and to the policies and practices of the company. |
| | On-the-job | Specific training in the important details of the employee's job. To help the employee acquire the necessary knowledge and skill. |
| Seasoned | On-the-job | To instruct in changes in procedures, routines, policies, and new equipment. Also, to prepare for jobs of higher grade (promotion). |
| Transferred | Induction | To give information relative to new duties and work environment. |
| | On-the-job | Specific training in the important details of the new job. To help the employee acquire the necessary knowledge and skill. |
| Supervisor | Supervisory | To give information relative to the theory and practical application of supervisory techniques. |

FIG. 33–2.

On-the-job training stresses just that—on the job—but some of the training may be acquired, in part, outside the enterprise. The entire program, however, should be carefully coordinated.

4. *Supervisory Training.* One of the most important types of training in any enterprise is supervisory training. Training of supervisors is vital because of their essentiality in management. Special courses in supervisory training have been designed, and many of these are generally considered effective. Discussion of supervisory training is included in the chapter on office supervision (Chapter 35).

Figure 33–2 indicates the type of training which is given to employees of different classifications or circumstances. For example, the new employee is given induction training and on-the-job training. The former provides information relative to his new job and to the policies and practices of the company; the latter includes specific training to help him acquire necessary skill.

## MAKE-UP OF TRAINING PROGRAM

In addition to ample consideration for the fundamentals of training, the objectives sought, and the types of training available, the makeup of any training program should devote sufficient thought to (1) the trainees, (2) the instructor, (3) the training period, (4) the training material, and (5) the training methods.

1. *Trainees.* Proper selection of trainees is of major importance if permanent, gainful results are to be obtained. A trainee should be trained for the kind of job he likes and is fitted to perform. In this respect, training is closely related to the selection of personnel. Evidence is quite conclusive that careful screening of candidates for training raises the effectiveness of the training work.

In the case of supervisory training, it is best to include all supervisors and those considered for promotion to such posts. Excluding some employees on the basis that they do not need the training or that they are already doing their work satisfactorily is a poor policy. Even outstanding supervisors profit from well-managed training programs, and their presence assists in many ways the less competent supervisors in attendance.

2. *Instructor.* A key figure in a good training program is the instructor, as a capable teacher contributes immeasurably to its success. Qualified instructors may be obtained from inside or outside the company; however, many office employees are not good teachers. The efficient employee does not necessarily have the ability to teach. Instructors need many qualifications besides knowing how to do the work. A good teacher has the skill to instruct and is tolerant, understanding, and patient. Also important is an appreciation for the value of the training work in relation to the enterprise and an understanding of what the employee goes through in order to acquire the skill and knowledge which the program is designed to achieve.

3. *Training Period.* The length of the training period depends upon the skill to be acquired, the trainee's learning capacity, and the training media used. For example, a simple indoctrination program for clerks may require an hour a day over a period of a week, while a course in accounting machines may be given two hours a week for 15 weeks. The use of effective visual material usually helps to reduce the training time. Some training directors claim that effective visualization reduces the teaching time by upward of 35 percent. Also, certain means of training such as programmed instruction, discussed below, which is of a visual nature, is reputed to save up to 70 percent of training time.

To maintain interest and to secure maximum accomplishment, no single session should last longer than two hours. One hour is even better. The best practice is to pay employees for training time if the course relates in any way to their work. Many states have laws or rulings affecting training time; and in addition, certain federal laws are applicable. Controversial issues are likely to appear if the employee does any productive work during the training time, if the training is outside regular working hours, of if the training work is intended to train the employee for a new or additional skill. It is advisable to check federal and prevailing state laws to help determine whether trainee or company time should be used.

4. *Training Material.* A text or some written material is usually desirable as a basis for instruction, review, and reference. For most subjects, a satisfactory book can be selected; but in instances where the course content is of a special nature, it may be well to prepare material for this specific use. A complete outline of the entire course should be made with the main topics included under each meeting or session. When a text is used, the parts to be covered must be clearly indicated; and assignments which require some preparatory time should be made for every meeting. This helps to keep the program on schedule, points the meeting toward definite subjects, and usually assists in the progress and satisfaction of the trainee.

5. *Training Methods.* There exist many different office training methods. For convenience, we will confine this discussion to the following 12 different methods, listed alphabetically: coaching and counseling, computer assisted instruction, conferences, demonstrations, guided experience, in-basket technique, job rotation, lectures, problem solving, programmed instruction, role playing, and understudy method. Choice of office training method depends upon many factors, including the objectives of the training, the number of trainees, the preferences of the instructor, the type of material to be covered, the cost, the time allotted, and the wishes of the trainees.

Coaching and counseling are normally work-centered and fact-centered individual efforts aimed to convey useful work information and to improve skill. Coaching emphasizes "setting up the plays," but permitting the employee to carry them out as best he can. Motivation and practical instruction are essential. The instructor must have the respect of the trainee, understand how he feels, and possess an ability to use analogies and demonstrations. Counseling stresses assisting an employee to recognize his strengths and weaknesses in fulfilling the requirements of his job. The counselor spends most of his time listening. His role is to help the trainee help himself, to become independent in his own right, and to build confidence in himself. The amount of direction and assistance given depends upon the individual being counseled. Both coaching and counseling emphasize a person-to-person individualized relationship. Essentially, it is an informal rather than a formal method of training.

The computer assisted instruction (CAI) is one of the newer means of instruction. The trainee takes a course by means of a computerized teaching machine. Instructions, questions, and guidance are stored in the computer and presented to the trainee by means of a typewriterlike communications terminal linked to the computer. Up to 12 trainees can hook into the course at the same time. After giving an identification number to verify trainee and course, the first question is written out by the computer on a continuous paper form of the terminal unit. In a course on statistics, for example, the first question might be, "How is the arithmetic average calculated? Type answer." If you answer, "By determining the number in the series appearing most frequently," the computer will answer immediately, "That answer is incorrect. The arithmetical average is not determined by the frequency of a number in the series but by averaging mathematically. Will you answer again?" Prompted by the hint, you now type the answer, "Add the numbers of the series and divide this sum by the quantity of numbers in the series." To this the computer will answer, "Correct," then proceed to the next question. To date, CAI appears to work best in conjunction with a human teacher who can answer questions and conduct periodic seminars. Computer trainees retain more material than conventional trainees and in a test of a statistics course needed only 13 hours to complete what requires 45 hours in an ordinary classroom.

The conference method permits trainees to express themselves orally and to exchange thoughts, and enables the instructor to judge the trainee's understanding of the subject material. The conference method is especially popular in supervisory training. Trainees are encouraged to express themselves freely. A group of about 20 participants is the ideal size for best results from the conference method. Demonstrations provide forceful presentation of how the job is done. This means stresses learning by eye rather than by ear and is especially helpful for jobs where physical skills are vital. The guided experience method utilizes evaluation of the trainee to reveal his weaknesses; then, the causes of these weaknesses are decided, and experience to remedy them is planned. Extreme care is taken to select the proper work assignments so that the trainee's shortcomings are ultimately removed. The assignments vary and include such things as writing reports, serving on committees, solving specific problems, performing research work, and working on normal day-to-day tasks. Like coaching and counseling, the guided experience method can be considered a highly personalized, informal type of training.

The in-basket technique realistically simulates actual office conditions. Actually it is in the nature of a business game. From two to about fifteen play the game which ordinarily takes two hours—one hour actual playing time and one hour of discussion among the players following conclusion of the game. Each trainee or player sits at a desk on which there is an "in" and an "out" basket, paper, and pencil. Instructions are given by the instructor indicating, for example, that you have certain helpers and you are leaving on your three-week vacation tomorrow. Identical packets of papers are then placed in the "in" baskets of all players. These papers require your office managerial attention. A typical packet may contain three letters, five memos, a telegram, two reports, and four telephone messages. Each trainee studies the materials and writes what he believes is the most appropriate action, clips the material to the original paper,

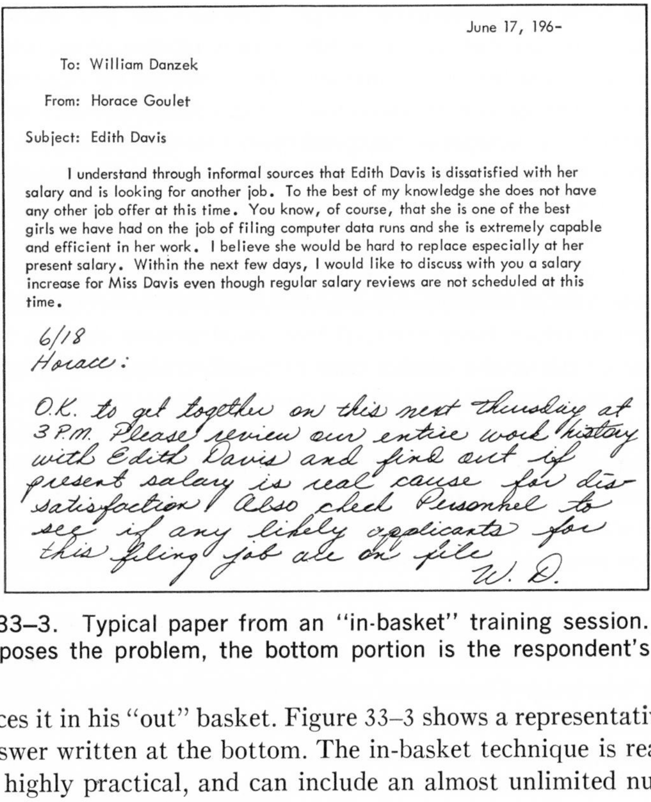

June 17, 196-

To: William Danzek

From: Horace Goulet

Subject: Edith Davis

I understand through informal sources that Edith Davis is dissatisfied with her salary and is looking for another job. To the best of my knowledge she does not have any other job offer at this time. You know, of course, that she is one of the best girls we have had on the job of filing computer data runs and she is extremely capable and efficient in her work. I believe she would be hard to replace especially at her present salary. Within the next few days, I would like to discuss with you a salary increase for Miss Davis even though regular salary reviews are not scheduled at this time.

6/18
Horace:

O.K. to get together on this next thursday at 3 P.M. Please review our entire work history with Edith Davis and find out if present salary is real cause for dis-satisfaction. Also check Personnel to see if any likely applicants for this filing job are on file

W. D.

FIG. 33–3. Typical paper from an "in-basket" training session. The top portion poses the problem, the bottom portion is the respondent's answer.

and places it in his "out" basket. Figure 33–3 shows a representative paper with answer written at the bottom. The in-basket technique is reasonable in cost, highly practical, and can include an almost unlimited number of potential problems and situations.

Job rotation, sometimes referred to as the "merry-go-round" basis, rotates trainees among different organizational units, thus providing the trainees with overall knowledge of the company's operations and the work done by each unit, and the opportunity to participate in the affairs of the various units. This method assists the individual to think in terms of universal managerial principles rather than the immediate activities at hand. Lectures are effective for initially explaining information to trainees. They should be carefully prepared, reinforced by the use of charts, sketches, and models, and presented by a qualified speaker. The means of problem solving is effective when the problems are well selected and bring out considerations pertinent to the work at hand. In short, solving the problems should meet specific development needs, such as an ability to analyze and relate given facts, to determine the problem to be solved, to read and to substantiate the recommended actions to be taken. Unless a developmental need is met, this method of training may be inadequate, time-consuming, and ineffective.

Programmed instruction is self-instruction and utilizes a systematic method of presenting information to the trainee. Presented one step or frame at a time, the material can be easily understood and absorbed. The increasing difficulty between two subsequent frames is narrow so that advancement is gradual but continuous and complex material is encountered only by the trainee prepared for it. The trainee advances at his own individual pace and learns at the speed most convenient for him. For each frame, he is required to select an answer from several alternatives and checks his answer with the approved reply. Thus immediate feedback is provided. He proceeds only after knowing the correct response to the question of the immediate frame. Programmed instruction incorporates sound instructional principles in that the trainee is actively participating in the teaching-learning process, the material is presented to lead each trainee into making the correct response, uniformity and consistency of instruction are possible, and the trainee advances gradually from the simple to the complex aspects of the material. Various research studies reveal the effectiveness of programmed instruction. To illustrate, in imparting knowledge of how to operate a modern office machine, training time required 31 percent less time with the trainees retaining 53 percent more knowledge compared to that obtained with conventional methods. Furthermore, programmed instruction permits training on a decentralized basis, is suited for individual training—a group is not needed, and the instructor can concentrate on special problems of training; he need not spend the majority of his time on routine training work.

Role playing narrows the gap between talking about what should be done and actually doing it. For training purposes, the playing out of a typical problem situation can be quite effective. It is especially helpful in situations involving employee relations. The method permits the trainees to participate, to gain an insight into their own behavior, and to look at the problem from many different viewpoints. By means of the understudy method, the trainee works as an assistant or helper to his teacher, thus acquiring familiarity with the work and practices of his teacher, who normally is an employee at the same or higher organizational level as the trainee. Experience with dynamic events and acquaintance with the atmosphere and position in which the trainee will eventually perform are acquired. On major issues, the trainee may be required to submit complete data affecting the issue along with his recommendations for action. In this way, thinking is stimulated, and the accepting of responsibility is encouraged. The understudy method is commonly used in supervisory training.

## COST OF TRAINING

Training costs money. Many analyses of its cost are unrealistic, in that comparisons are made between the expenditures of "no training"—actually a misleading term—and those of a formal training program. The fact is that training costs are tangible and intangible. Erroneously, the latter group is commonly ignored in the cost of training.

Under tangible training costs are training materials, nonproductive time of trainee, and nonproductive time of employee instructor, or fee charged, if an outsider. Under the intangible classification are such things as a longer time for the trainee to attain a reasonable level of production, loss of employees seeking better job opportunities, time of experienced employees asked to "show me how to do this" by the trainee, loss due to work spoilage and errors, practicing of poor work methods, and improper work viewpoints and attitudes being permitted to develop and spread.

Training is a necessity in modern management, and reasonable expenditures for it should be made. The amount depends upon the needs and the aims of the office. However, costs should be kept under control. Management members should have some idea of what is being accomplished for the expenditures being made. This brings up the question of training effectiveness.

## EFFECTIVENESS OF TRAINING

From the managerial viewpoint, it is an excellent idea to measure the effectiveness of training efforts. The evaluation, however, must be in terms of a particular training problem. This problem may be expressed in the form of questions, such as:

1. Has the training increased production?
2. Has there been a decrease in the number of errors?
3. Has there been a reduction in labor turnover?
4. Has there been a reduction in absenteeism, requests for transfers, and number of grievances?
5. Has the attitude, work environment, and enthusiasm of the office work force improved?

It is usually best to measure effectiveness by departments or by some homogeneous group, for the problems of measurement become quite complex when the entire office is considered. It is advisable to make comparisons between office groups as units. A good procedure is to use as a control one group which is characterized by little or no formal training, by training of a particular type, or by a different method of training. Special care should be exercised to see that the groups compared are reasonably similar with respect to such factors as age, sex, and time of week, month, or year.

Evaluating the results of training is not, however, a simple matter. Many companies make little effort to evaluate training results as such, or they are satisfied with general overall indications of the training's worth. It is difficult to determine what factors contribute to employee development.

It is possible to overdo training to the point that the efforts and costs in its behalf exceed the highest estimates of benefits within a reasonable period. Training should be carefully managed; it should not be engaged in simply because "it is the thing to do." It is a continuous, not an "off and on," activity. It can start on a small scale and subsequently increase as the benefits become known and the needs and progress of the enterprise dictate.

As a guide, these points should be kept in mind: (1) Office training is desirable and necessary and is performed regardless of whether a formal program is carried on or not; (2) office training must be tailor-made to fit the specific need of the enterprise; (3) the questions of *what* training should be conducted, and *when, where,* and *how,* require answering; (4) office training should be based on the needs of the office as shown by job analysis, prevalence of errors, low work output, employees' attitudes, and supervisory effectiveness; (5) office training should be preceded by careful selection of trainees; and (6) the training of office supervisors is vital.

## QUESTIONS

1. Justify the viewpoint that training is a vital actuating force in management.
2. Point out and briefly discuss the significant differences between the objectives of supervisory training and those of employee training.
3. What interpretations do you give to the following statement: "One who really manages makes use of training to help him manage"?
4. Discuss programmed instruction as a means of office training, indicating whether you favor its use, along with your reasons why.
5. Do you agree with this statement: "All known training means have an element of artificiality in them. Of necessity they must operate under an assumed arrangement. This leads to the fundamental principle that actual practice—learning by doing—is the superior teaching process. There is no satisfactory substitute for experience which emphasizes application of the employee's knowledge to the task that confronts him at the particular time"? Justify the position you take.
6. Do you believe an employee training program is a good investment? Why?

7. While office training may be highly desirable, it also has some disadvantages. Briefly relate several of these disadvantages.

8. A new employee has just completed a two-week indoctrination training program given by a bank. The training director of the bank has rated the new employee as unsatisfactory, basing his opinion on the training results. Should the new employee be placed on the job, asked to repeat the training, or dropped from the payroll? Explain your answer.

9. Carefully identify each of the following:
   *a*) In-basket technique of office training.
   *b*) Computer assisted instruction.
   *c*) Induction training.
   *d*) Intangible costs of training.

10. Using Figure 33–1 as a guide, relate a learning experience that bears out the validity of several key points listed.

11. Give an example illustrating an occasion when you would recommend the use of demonstration as the means of office training. The use of role playing. The use of understudy method.

12. Discuss the subject of the training period utilized as a key consideration in the makeup of an office training program.

## CASE PROBLEMS
### Case 33–1.  Mitchell Company

Martha Cole is an excellent typist and has been with Mitchell Company for three years. The office employees total 12 people and work in an informal, pleasant, and friendly environment. The bookkeeper announces her resignation effective in six weeks. She is getting married and will move from the city. Martha is asked whether she would like to do the bookkeeping work which would give her more pay. She replies that she would, but has very little knowledge of bookkeeping. The sales manager, who manages the office, then explains that the company will enroll her in a school, pay her tuition, and she can learn bookkeeping. The class meets evenings twice a week and starts in two weeks. Martha is elated at the opportunity.

Martha enrolls at the school and is also shown key points of the bookkeeping work by the bookkeeper before she leaves. After a month of being on the bookkeeping job, it appears to those around Martha that she is having some difficulty mastering the new work. But Martha does not complain and does not ask any co-workers for assistance. On Wednesday morning of the following week, Martha is absent. In a telephone call by her at about 10:00 A.M. she explains that she has quit her job. When asked why, she replies, "To accept another position." A telephone call to the school reveals that she has been absent from classes for the past two weeks.

Problems:

1. Discuss some plausible explanations for Martha's behavior.

2. What might the company do to avoid reoccurrence of situations such as indicated by this case?

3. What action do you recommend the company take? Why?

## Case 33–2.   Gulf Grocery Wholesale Company

Total management personnel from the supervisory level up is 87 men and women, of whom 45 are operative supervisors. Main office organization units include credit and collections, order writing, billing, accounting, purchasing, personnel, stock, correspondence, mail handling, advertising, filing, research, company library, and watchman services. The company's executive committee wishes to initiate a formal supervisory development program. Business is expected to increase on an average of 10 percent per year for the next decade. The company operates in six states and sells grocery items to over 1,400 retail grocery outlets.

### Problems:

1. Outline the general features of your recommended program, noting the probable schedule of events.

2. Do you feel a program such as that requested by the executive committee is the best way to develop office supervisors for the company? Why?

## Case 33–3.   Schmidt Company

"Here's your desk. You can get yourself squared away, and I'll be back as soon as I can," stated supervisor Ruth Frey to new employee Harriet Walters. The desk was similar to a seeming multitude of other desks, all inhabited by employees working on their jobs. All, that is, except those wondering who the new employee was, how she got the job, and what kind of person she was. After standing a few minutes, Harriet Walters sat down at her desk, pulled each of the six desk drawers open in sequence, and scanned the miscellaneous papers thereby revealed. She came across an old newspaper and out of curiosity placed it on the top of the desk and began reading a news item. After reading for perhaps ten minutes, Harriet suddenly sensed that someone was standing at her side. Looking up, she saw a well-dressed, middle-aged man, Mr. Joseph McMurry.

McMurry:   Reading of newspapers during office working hours is not permitted, Miss . . . a . . . er. . . .
Harriet:   Walters. Harriet Walters is my name.
McMurry:   Yes. Yes, thank you, Miss Walters. So may I suggest that you put the newspaper away and be on with your work?

With this statement, Mr. McMurry walked away. Harriet thought she had better tell Mrs. Frey about the incident, so she walked over to Mrs. Frey's office and told her. Mrs. Frey listened, smiled, and then stated: "Don't worry about it. Here, take this manual back to your desk and scan the material. Some of it is outdated, but you'll find it informative and interesting. I'll be over just as soon as I can."

Harriet returned to her desk and read the manual for over an hour. Then, Mrs. Frey brought a batch of papers and requested that Harriet check the addition of a column of figures on each paper. Any errors were to be indicated by writing in the correct figure in red pencil. This work continued until a bell rang, and Harriet noticed everyone leaving his desk. Glancing at her wristwatch, she noted it was 12:00 noon. Assuming it was lunchtime, she grabbed her purse, walked to the lobby, and started to leave by the main entrance. Stopped there by a watchman who requested her "pass" to leave, Harriet returned to the office, but found no one around whom she could ask about the needed pass. After Harriet had spent several minutes wondering what to do, she saw a girl from the factory processing office walk by; after a formal greeting, and learning of Harriet's plight, she asked Harriet to join her for lunch in the company cafeteria.

Shortly after the start of the afternoon session, Ruth Frey approached Harriet at her desk, told her she (Ruth Frey) was free now, and proceeded to explain how to perform a fairly simple job of arranging cards alphabetically. In addition, Mrs. Frey brought several more batches of paper on which lists of figures were to be added and checked. After spending some 15 minutes with Harriet, Mrs. Frey left. She returned twice during the afternoon and found Harriet busy and doing the work correctly.

## Problems:

1. Is there a problem here?

2. What suggestions do you feel are in order to Harriet Walters? To Ruth Frey? Discuss.

# CHAPTER 34

# SAFETY AND

# TRADE UNIONISM IN THE OFFICE

Underlying practically all our attempts to bring
agreement is the assumption that agreement is
brought about by changing people's minds—
other people's.

—*S. I. Hayakawa*

PROVIDING a safe place in which to work and an orderly process mutually evolved for determining the general conditions under which the work will be done are major attributes in actuating employees. In this chapter we will discuss first the subject of office safety. Following this the main highlights of office trade unionism will be presented.

### OFFICE ACCIDENT OCCURRENCE

Accidents can and do happen to office employees; they enjoy no automatic exemption. These accidents come about in a number of ways. For example, some cleaning fluids used on office machines are inflammable, and cases are on record where the fumes from the cleaning fluid were ignited by a spark from the electric motor of the machine, resulting in a flash fire which caused severe burns to office employees. Severe falls and injuries result from slipping on highly polished floors and running on stairways by women in high-heeled shoes. Reclining too far back in a chair can result in the occupant's being thrown with considerable force; and serious, sometimes permanent, injuries have been suffered by office employees in this way.

724

There is a cause for every accident. It is some defect or lack of action which must be corrected in order to prevent a recurrence of the accident. Falling down a stairway is not a cause; it is a result—an accident. The causes may be loose papers on the stair treads, inadequate lighting on the stairway, or the employee's failure to watch where he is stepping. These conditions must be rectified in order to achieve better safety results.

Some writers have classified the causes of accidents under three headings: mechanical, physiological, and psychological. These terms are self-explanatory. Under mechanical causes, for example, are classified such things as improper lighting, unguarded machines, and technical defects in equipment. Physiological causes include bad eyesight and age

Courtesy: "GM Folks," General Motors Corp., Detroit

FIG. 34–1. The practices illustrated commonly result in accidents. These pictures were especially posed for accident prevention promotional work.

of employees; psychological causes cover such things as the employee's tendency to take unnecessary chances, carelessness, horseplay, and temporary emotional and mental disturbances. These causes are interrelated and must be attacked jointly in most practical activities designed to reduce accidents. Figure 34–1 illustrates practices that frequently result in accidents.

## MANAGERIAL SAFETY ACTION

Experience and records show that accidents can be reduced; in fact, most can be prevented entirely. The best course of action for preventing accidents depends upon the circumstances in each particular case. Some advocate the so-called triple E program, which consists of engineering, education, and enforcement. That is, the first step is to engineer all equipment and machines with safety guards, cutoff switches, and other devices to make them as safe as is technically possible. Next, education for all employees is provided, to instill work habits and practices for winning high safety achievements. Last, enforcement insures that safety regulations are carried out.

This means that the initiative rests with the manager, but he must win the cooperation of the employee to make office safety really effective. Aggressive managerial action is required. Merely supplying a safe working place is insufficient. The manager must also see to it that safety measures are recognized and enforced; but what is more important, he must accomplish this with enthusiastic approval and encouragement by the nonmanagement members.

## INITIAL SAFETY STEPS TO BE TAKEN

Hazards causing accidents must be identified before they can be eliminated. Available safety information reveals that the main types of office accidents have to do with slipping, tripping, handling materials, being hit by falling objects, and striking against objects. Among the more common hazards which result in office accidents are:

Defective electric cords lying across aisles, and loose connections
Paper clips and thumbtacks on the floor
Loose linoleum or carpeting
Slippery floors
Open desk drawer or file drawer
Tilting backward too far in office chair
Sharp burrs on edges of metal office equipment
Sharp pointed pencils placed in upright position in handkerchief coat pocket
Broken glass desk top
Exposed moving parts of office machines
Splinters and loose veneer on wood desks and chairs
Bottles, papers, or books stacked on top of filing cabinets
Protruding pencil sharpeners and power and telephone outlets
Reading while walking
Running in aisle, on stairways, or through doorways

Assistance in locating hazards to eliminate is provided by a check list such as that shown in Figure 34–2. In addition, an analysis of the accident reports can help in locating areas that need attention.

With factual data as a background, steps can be taken to incorporate needed safety actions into a program. Usually included are the following:

## OFFICE SAFETY INSPECTION DATA

Carefully inspect the office, and for each question, check whether a hazard exists. If "Yes," briefly note the important details.

| QUESTION | DOES HAZARD EXIST? | | COMMENTS (GIVE LOCATION AND DETAILS.) |
|---|---|---|---|
| | Yes | No | |
| 1. Are aisles obstructed? | | | |
| 2. Do pencil sharpeners project over desk or table? | | | |
| 3. Are file drawers kept closed when not in use? | | | |
| 4. Are machines properly guarded? | | | |
| 5. Are glass desk tops broken? | | | |
| 6. Are there any sharp metal projections on any equipment? | | | |
| 7. Is electrical wiring concealed? | | | |
| 8. Are office accessories insecurely placed? | | | |
| 9. Are papers and waste properly disposed of? | | | |
| 10. Are facilities for smokers adequate? | | | |
| 11. Are materials stacked on desks or cabinets? | | | |
| 12. Are extension cords used extensively? | | | |
| 13. Are floors too highly polished? | | | |
| 14. Is carpeting loose or worn? | | | |

FIG. 34–2.   Portion of a form designed to assist in determining safety hazards.

1. *Educate employees to possible dangers.*   Each employee should be made thoroughly aware of all the possible dangers of his job. All the details that make for safety should be carefully explained. These efforts can be planned and made a regular part of the job process and the training work. In this manner, the correct way of doing the job, which is also the safe way, becomes habitual. Safety is built right into the job—it is a part of the job.

2. *Provide safe work areas.*   Supplying all the necessary provisions for safe working places and equipment for employees is paramount. Office floors should be covered with nonslippery material; adequate lighting should be provided; desks and chairs should be free of sharp edges.

3. *Promote first-aid service.*   Insistence upon first-aid treatment for minor injuries means little if adequate facilities are not available. When these facilities are provided, managers show that they wish all injured employees to receive treatment promptly.

4. *Make safety clothing available.*   The use of special clothing designed to protect employees from injuries should also be included. Plastic aprons, for example, should be available to employees working around large quantities of ink, glue, and cleaning solutions. Likewise,

finger guards should be provided to employees doing work where the chances of suffering paper cuts are quite high.

5. *Maintain good housekeeping practices.* Good housekeeping in the office is essential for good safety work. The habits of orderliness and cleanliness contribute to good office safety because they help to set good examples for employees and to keep the office personnel safety-minded. Stairways should be kept clear of all loose objects; aisles should be marked for traffic lanes; an adequate number of wastepaper baskets should be furnished; and regular cleanup service should be provided.

## OFFICE SAFETY RECORDS

Effective accident prevention work requires that adequate records be kept of all accidents. It is important to know what accidents happened, where, when, the types of injuries incurred, and the conditions which caused them. By studying such data, a manager is able to take intelligent corrective action and knows where to stress safety efforts.

There are two widely used and accepted indexes in safety statistics: (1) the frequency rate and (2) the severity rate. These names are self-explanatory: The frequency rate measures the occurrence of accidents, and the severity rate measures the seriousness of accidents. The indexes are used to show the relative values and trends within any group and the comparisons among different groups.

1. *Frequency rate.* The frequency rate can be defined as the number of disabling injuries suffered per million man-hours worked. The formula is:

$$\text{Frequency rate} = \frac{\text{Number of disabling injuries} \times 1,000,000}{\text{Total number of man-hours worked}}$$

Disabling injuries are frequently referred to as "lost-time accidents arising out of and in the course of employment." The National Safety Council classifies the following types of injuries as disabling injuries:

*a*) Death.

*b*) Permanent total disability. Any injury or combination of injuries suffered in one accident which permanently and totally incapacitates an employee from following any gainful occupation. Loss of both eyes or of both hands is an example.

*c*) Permanent partial disability. Any injury suffered in one accident which results in the loss of any member or part of a member of the body but which does not result in death or permanent total disability.

*d*) Temporary total disability. Any injury suffered in one accident which results in no permanent injury but which prevents the injured person from returning to a regularly established job within 24.hours after the start of the shift during which he was injured.

The total number of man-hours is best obtained from payroll records or time cards. If these are unavailable, the number can be estimated by multiplying the average number of employees by the average number of hours worked during the period considered.

2. *Severity rate.* The severity rate is the number of days charged as a result of injuries per million man-hours worked. The formula is:

$$\text{Severity rate} = \frac{\text{Time charged (in days)} \times 1,000,000}{\text{Total number of man-hours worked}}$$

Days charged are sometimes called "days of disability." However, the time charged away from the job does not accurately measure the severity of the accident. Therefore, tables have been set up indicating an arbitrary number of days which should be used for various types of accidents. For example, an accident resulting in death or in permanent total disability is charged at the rate of 6,000 days for each case. This is approximately 20 years. A permanent partial disability resulting in the loss of a hand is charged at 3,000 days.

THREE-YEAR FREQUENCY AND SEVERITY RATES OF SELECTED INDUSTRIES

| INDUSTRY | FREQUENCY RATES | | | | | SEVERITY RATES | | | | |
|---|---|---|---|---|---|---|---|---|---|---|
| | 1958–60 | 1959–61 | 1960–62 | 1961–63 | 1962–64 | 1958–60 | 1959–61 | 1960–62 | 1961–63 | 1962–64 |
| Offices................ | 0.65 | 0.69 | 0.68 | 0.76 | 0.71 | 115 | 158 | 117 | 127 | 130 |
| Automobile........... | 2.34 | 2.13 | 1.91 | 1.73 | 1.77 | 258 | 249 | 228 | 215 | 207 |
| Chemical............. | 3.54 | 3.44 | 3.42 | 3.30 | 3.25 | 528 | 476 | 489 | 419 | 395 |
| Construction.......... | 17.97 | 18.70 | 19.07 | 19.08 | 19.08 | 2,350 | 2,247 | 2,296 | 2,376 | 2,498 |
| Lumbering............ | 23.82 | 23.64 | 20.43 | 18.40 | 17.37 | 2,375 | 2,166 | 1,760 | 1,596 | 1,642 |
| Printing and Publishing. | 6.66 | 6.92 | 7.07 | 6.81 | 7.48 | 369 | 338 | 313 | 258 | 411 |
| Steel................. | 3.29 | 3.30 | 3.25 | 3.31 | 3.34 | 794 | 796 | 739 | 713 | 695 |
| Tobacco.............. | 6.65 | 6.48 | 6.06 | 5.88 | 5.78 | 307 | 266 | 332 | 399 | 440 |

*Compiled from National Safety Council, Inc., "Accident Facts" (Chicago, 1961–65)*

FIG. 34–3.   Comparison of safety statistics.

Available safety data show that the office frequency rates and severity rates are among the lowest of any industry classification. This is shown in Figure 34–3. It is encouraging to note that with several exceptions, the rates are declining for every industry—safety is progressing.

Records on accident costs are also helpful in improving safety accomplishments inasmuch as the amount of expenditure has some relationship to the efforts directed to this area. Budgets of these costs are desirable, and actions to get the most benefits for a given expenditure should be encouraged.

It is a well-known fact that accidents are expensive. The loss might be in money, skill, time, human suffering, work output, or interruption in the flow of work. The hidden or incidental costs of accidents are much greater than the measurable direct costs. Such things as the cost of hiring and training new employees, the interference with production, and the loss of good will are sizable expenses not generally though of in connection with the costs of accidents. The ratio of hidden to direct costs of accidents may be as high as 4 to 1, which means that total accident costs are far greater than most people realize.

## OFFICE SAFETY PERSONNEL

It is important that there be a recognized head of office safety work. This person should be given complete responsibility for the direction and guidance of all office safety efforts. The person in charge might be the office manager himself, or the office manager might appoint a subordinate to the job. Generally, the safety director need not spend all of his time on safety, but it is advisable for him to devote a certain amount of time regularly to the program.

Department heads are the key personnel in accident prevention work. In many respects, the success of the entire safety program depends upon the supervisors. It is promoted by the cooperation of the department heads, and they can do more than anyone else toward keeping the employees safety-minded. Furthermore, supervisors can correct unsafe conditions, they can see that safety rules are followed, that first aid is provided in case of accident, and that proper reports are filled out.

Because participation promotes acceptance, the use of a safety committee with rotating membership is recommended. A five-member committee, with membership rotating bimonthly, usually works out very well. The system of replacements should be such that not more than two new members are added at any one time, thus insuring that the remaining three members are familiar with the work of the committee. The work of this group is advisory. It submits suggestions for the reduction of accidents within the office. Frequently, the safety committee may also:

1. Sponsor accident prevention contests.
2. Review safety suggestions made by the employees.
3. Make regular safety inspections of the office.
4. Suggest additions and changes in safety rules.
5. Post safety materials on the bulletin boards.
6. Maintain the first-aid equipment.

## PROMOTING SAFETY CONSCIOUSNESS

The mental attitude of the employee toward safety is exceedingly important in accident prevention work. There is a great deal of truth in the saying: "The best safety device in all the world is located an inch or two above the eyebrows." The employee who "thinks safety" and who has developed a safety consciousness "from the ears up" has gone a long way toward preventing accidents.

All efforts designed to keep safety on the employee's mind and to keep accident prevention a live subject in the office will help substantially in the safety program. Although it may seem strange, it is a common occurrence for people to be careless. Safety-mindedness requires alert-mindedness. Safety work is a continuous process, requiring constant reminders to the employee to work safely, to avoid taking chances, and to keep safety foremost in his thoughts. The task is not an easy one, but persistence and steadfastness of purpose will achieve good results.

It is a truism that for the most part, people attach the same degree of importance to activities as do their leaders. If the managers believe in, and are actively engaged in, accident prevention work, then this same spirit will be picked up by the employees. The safety example set by managers is important in attaining a good safety record.

In addition, safety rules should be explained, and the reasons for their rigid enforcement given to the employees. The entire safety program can be seriously handicapped if there is any letdown in either the education or the enforcement of safety rules. Quite often, having the rules in writing is helpful.

Also, employees should be informed of safety fundamentals. This can take various forms, including articles in company papers, talks at meetings, informal suggestions to employees, movies, and safety instruction cards. This latter medium provides the employee with pertinent suggestions about safety and serves as a series of timely reminders, helping to keep safety on the minds of the employees. Figure 34–4 shows several examples of safety instruction cards.

Pictures, posters, and cartoon sketches can also be used to arouse the employee's interest in safety. It is usually best to have this material specific in nature, telling the employee what to do under particular conditions. Giving the employee general safety cautions and slogans is probably of limited value. It is usually well to supplement this type of safety promotion with intensive individual follow-up. The bulletin boards used should be located in areas that are frequently seen, accessible, and in full view.

Lastly, safety contests are helpful. They stress the competitive spirit and usually rely upon the employee's desire to excel. An award in the form of a plaque, banner, special pin, or money may be given the individual, group, or department having the best safety record for a given period. A reversal of this technique can also be used, and it is generally effective. In this case, a booby prize is given the unit having the poorest safety record, with the requirement that this "award" be displayed prominently. This approach appeals to the employee's pride and to his desire to escape any designation which makes him look ridiculous. Like

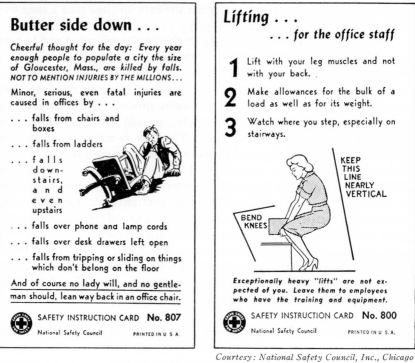

FIG. 34–4.   Safety instruction cards.

all promotional plans, safety contests must be publicized and made acceptable to the employees.

## THE OFFICE AND TRADE UNIONS

Trade unions for office employees have existed for a number of years. Among the oldest are the editorial employees of some newspapers, organized around 1890; the National Association of Letter Carriers, created in 1892; and the Brotherhood of Railway and Steamship Clerks, organized in 1899. These early unions were loosely organized, judged in terms of present-day standards.

During the following several decades, other office unions came into being, among which are the following: the National Federation of Post Office Clerks (organized in 1906), the American Federation of Teachers (1916), the National Federation of Federal Employees (1917), and the American Federation of Governmental Employees (1932). With time additional office unions were formed. Today, there are several hundred strong office unions within the United States. Estimates vary as to their total membership, but it is probably close to 10 percent of the total number of office employees. This may appear minor, but it is a composite figure of all office employees; and in certain enterprises, the extent of office unionization assumes a prominent position.

## MANAGEMENT–TRADE-UNION RELATIONS

When a union exists in an office, managers are required to bargain with the authorized representatives concerning "wages and other conditions of employment." In other words, a process which might be called "collective cooperation" is used, whereby employers and representatives of employees arrive at agreements covering compensation and the conditions under which employees will work. This usually means that policies concerning matters such as wages, discharge, discipline, and transfer must be discussed with the union representatives and incorporated into a mutually agreed upon labor contract. Subsequently, decisions utilizing these policies are made by management members but are frequently subject to question by and explanation to the union, via an established grievance procedure. In essence, the union wants to be consulted and to present its views in matters affecting its members during the decision-making process so that the decision reached will be in keeping with its views. The ultimate decision, however, is made by a management member; but from the practical viewpoint, the decision must be acceptable to the representatives of the employees in order to be entirely effective.

## WHY OFFICE EMPLOYEES JOIN OR DO NOT JOIN UNIONS

The growth in office unionization has been slow. Various surveys reveal that office employees do not join a union for these major reasons:

1. *Possible loss of social status and prestige.* Identification of office employees is with "those in the know." The typical office employee works in street clothes; he is around, sees, and sometimes meets the executives of the company. He believes his work is of a high type, is dignified, and has prestige. Frequently, it is looked up to.

2. *Receiving certain benefits of unionism without being members.* In many instances, the benefits negotiated by unions of nonoffice employees are passed along to the office employees of that enterprise. This practice has been termed "a free ride" for the office employees. The practice may be questioned, but it does exist.

3. *Satisfactory working conditions.* Most office employees feel that they work in an area which is cleaner and quieter than that in which many other employees work. Also, they may consider the work safer and not as physically tiring.

4. *The basic characteristics of most office employees.* They are conservative and inclined to stay with the old rather than to try out the new. In addition, about two-thirds of the office employees are women,

many of whom are interested in working in offices for only a limited period of time.

In contrast, what is the answer to "Why do office employees join unions"? Among the various reasons, these appear most prominent:

1. *Discontent with present earnings.* Especially is this true when comparisons with wages of factory employees are easily made and the differential between the two are great. Among the greatest contributors to this discontent are slower rates of wage increases for office compared to factory employees, shrinking advantage in fringe benefits enjoyed by office employees, and wage raises for lower-class office jobs without comparable wage adjustments in middle and top office job classes.

2. *Lack of security.* The wide changes taking place in the office, especially growing automation, add to the office employee's fear of losing his job.

3. *Supervisors who are not well trained or informed.* The employees want better work guidance, communication, and participation in matters that affect them.

4. *Lack of a feeling of justice.* Formalized procedures to permit handling of grievances of office employees or to represent them adequately to management representatives are not provided. The employees believe there is no adequate means for them to get their "gripes" to top managers' attention.

## CHARACTERISTICS OF CONTRACTS

The majority of current office-union contracts are tailor-made to suit the special conditions of the individual offices. There is, however, some similarity of contracts, since most of them cover the same subject topics. Most contracts contain clauses covering such matters as recognition of the union, union status, union security, salaries, hours of work, seniority, employment procedures, transfers and dismissals, grievance procedures, penalties, maternity leaves, and severance pay. A discussion of several of these subjects follows.

1. *Union recognition clause.* A "recognition of the union" clause points out that the union named in the contract is fully recognized by the employer; frequently, it also states what jobs and what employees are covered by the contract. Sometimes, a statement is included to the effect that the union will not accept into membership those employees in the excluded groups.

2. *Status of union.* Union status concerns the relationship of members of the union with the company. In general, there are three kinds of union status:

1. *Union shop.* Nonunion members may be hired; but after a certain period, they must, as a requirement of employment, become union members.

2. *"Maintenance of membership" shop.* All employees are not required to join the union, but all present union members must retain membership during the time the contract is in force.

3. *Exclusive bargaining shop.* The union is recognized as the exclusive bargaining agent for all employees, but no employee is compelled to join it or to remain a member.[1]

3. *Wage rates.* Clauses on wage rates frequently include the recognition of job classifications and wage rates for each class. Minimum rates only might be stated. Uniform adjustments, either in amount or in percentage, may be provided; and the effective date of such adjustments may be included.

The following is a typical contractual statement pertaining to wages.

SECTION 2. The wage schedules as set forth in this schedule, attached hereto as Exhibit B and made a part hereof, shall apply and be in effect as of July 1, 1967, and shall remain in effect for the life of this agreement.

SECTION 3. Overtime compensation and deductible time lost shall be computed by dividing the monthly salary by one hundred seventy-three and one third (173⅓) to arrive at an hourly rate to be used for such computations.

4. *Layoffs and seniority.* While most unions favor the governing of layoffs and rehires on seniority, they will grant a statement to the effect that seniority shall govern when the employee involved has the ability to do the work under question. Questions arising in connection with seniority are sometimes clarified by the practice of preclassifying employees either by occupation or by departments or divisions. In this way, employees making up a fairly comparable group are associated together.

To illustrate:

SECTION 3. A reduction in working forces resulting in demotions and layoffs will normally be on a departmental seniority basis except for stenographers and filing clerks, who will be on a company-wide basis.

5. *Penalty clauses.* Penalty provisions provide punishment for members who violate parts of the contract. Penalties might be in the form of reductions in pay, temporary or permanent layoffs, or less severe disciplinary measures, depending upon the nature of the violation.

## CONTRACT LIMITATIONS

It is not feasible to write a collective bargaining contract which covers every possible source of difference between the employer and the employee. A brief contract stating the points in simple terms usually is

---

[1] The Labor Management Relations Act of 1947 outlawed in interstate commerce (1) the closed shop—in which the employer agrees to hire only union members, and all employees must continue their good standing in the union during their terms of employment and (2) the preferential shop—in which preference in hiring and in layoff is given union members.

sufficient. Attempts to cover all contingencies in great detail will result in complicating the contract and in making it extremely difficult to interpret. Arguments about language technicalities lead to disputes which usually cause trouble.

There must be a spirit of cooperativeness on the part of both interested parties; they must want the contract to work. When both parties have this attitude, even the skimpy and legally poorly written contract can help to expedite harmonious relations. Without this attitude, the success of a well-written contract can be seriously curtailed.

In many respects, questions involving the legal rights are peripheral quizzes—they do not penetrate to the real core of management-union cooperation. Managerial actions and techniques conducive to production and mutual cooperation are paramount considerations, as well as the union's appreciation of the inherent characteristics and conditions under which the office must operate. Recognition must be given to the development of the various elements and changes affecting the general background in which the contract is made. These include technologic, economic, and social modifications that today's enlightened managers and nonmanagers recognize and accept.

## LABOR MANAGEMENT RELATIONS ACT OF 1947

A long list of labor laws make up the legal background upon which current management-union cooperation is administered. But for our purpose, the provisions of the Labor Management Relations Act of 1947, commonly referred to as the Taft-Hartley Act, and the Landrum-Griffin Act of 1959 can be considered as making up the current labor legislation. There are also important state labor laws. We are omitting them, however, in order to keep this discussion a reasonable length. The Landrum-Griffin Act of 1959, among other things, permitted employees to file with the government complaints about the acts of their union leaders. Most of the complaints to date have dealt with questions pertaining to voting by union members in union affairs, and the misuse of the dues by union officers.

The Labor Management Relations Act of 1947 is the important legislation that sets forth the major provisions of management-labor cooperation. By this law, a National Labor Relations Board (NLRB) was established with the power to hear testimony, render decisions, and decide the appropriate unit for purposes of collective bargaining. The board serves mainly in a judiciary capacity. A general counsel and his staff prosecute the cases brought before the board. Among the other important provisions of this law are (1) unfair labor practices, (2) strike controls, and (3) checks on unions. These provisions will now be discussed.

The Taft-Hartley Act forbids unfair labor practices either by the employer or by unions or their agents. Unfair labor practices by an employer include (1) interfering with or restraining employees from forming or joining a labor union, (2) dominating or influencing a labor organization, (3) discriminating in the hiring or in the conditions of employment of any employee because he is a member of a union, (4) terminating employment or discriminating against any employee for any charge made or testimony given under this law, and (5) refusing to bargain collectively with representatives of his employees.

Practices which constitute unfair labor practices by unions or their agents include (1) coercing or restraining employees in connection with their joining a union, (2) charging "excessive or discriminatory" union initiation fees (the meaning of "excessive or discriminatory" is determined by the labor board in cases where there is an authorized union shop contract), (3) refusing to bargain collectively with the employer, (4) participating in jurisdictional strikes, and (5) practicing "featherbedding," i.e., making the employer pay for services not performed.

Charges of unfair labor practices on the part of either employer or union are investigated, complaints issued, and prosecution carried on before the National Labor Relations Board by the general counsel, who has exclusive authority to prosecute unfair labor practices. He is appointed by the President of the United States and has general supervision over all attorneys employed by the board, except trial examiners and legal assistants to board members.

Basing its decision on the preponderance of evidence and testimony, the board decides whether any defendant named in the complaint is guilty of an unfair labor practice. If he is not guilty, the findings are stated, and an order is issued dismissing the complaint. If he is guilty, the board states its findings and causes a cease and desist order, prohibiting the continuation of the unfair practice, to be served on the guilty party. For enforcement of its orders, the board has the power to petition the Circuit Court of Appeals with jurisdiction where the unfair labor practice occurred.

Under the subject of strike controls, the Taft-Hartley Act provides that 60 days' notice must be given the other party before the normal termination of a labor contract. The Federal Mediation and Conciliation Service must be notified at least 30 days after the 60-day notice if no agreement is reached. This provision is, of course, intended to help settle the differences of opinion. Lockouts and strikes are prohibited during the notice period. There is no compulsory arbitration or court injunction right against a legitimate noncritical strike, i.e., one not threatening "national health and safety" or affecting an entire industry.

In contrast, threatening lockouts or strikes affecting "national health and safety" or an entire industry may be delayed 80 days by the

President in this manner: A board of inquiry may be appointed to determine the facts involved in the dispute. A report stating these facts, along with each party's statement of its position, is filed with the Federal Mediation and Conciliation Service, and the contents are made known to the public. In addition, the President at this time may, through the Attorney General, seek a court injunction against the lockout or strike. If the injunction is issued, there follows a period of 60 days in which to bring about a settlement. If this is not reached, the National Labor Relations Board holds, within the ensuing 15 days, a company-by-company election on each employer's last offer of settlement and certifies same within five days to the Attorney General, who then moves to dissolve the injunction. Then, the President submits a comprehensive report of the proceedings to Congress, along with any recommendation which he deems fitting and proper for appropriate action.

With reference to checks on unions, the law provides that a union may seek an election under NLRB supervision or file an unfair labor practice charge with the board. For such action, the union must previously file (1) pertinent union information and (2) noncommunist affidavits by each officer of the union.

The pertinent union information is filed annually with the Secretary of Labor. The report must include name, title, compensation, and allowances for each of the union's three principal officers and for any other officer or agent of the union if the aggregate compensation and allowances of any one of these persons exceeded $5,000 for the preceding year. The report must also include the manner of election or appointment of these officers or agents; the amount of initiation fees and regular dues; a statement showing the procedure followed for such things as qualifications for union membership, levying of assessments, authorization for bargaining demands, for strikes, for disbursement of union funds, and for the basis for expulsion of members; and a report showing receipts and expenditures for the fiscal year and total assets and liabilities at the end of the fiscal year. All union members have a right to a copy of their union's financial report.

The affidavits by union officers can be filed either contemporaneously with a union action privileged by the act or within the preceding 12-month period. The affidavit is a sworn written statement signifying that the union officer is not a member or affiliate of the Communist Party and does not believe in, belong to, or support any organization believing in or teaching the overthrow of the United States government by force or by illegal or unconstitutional methods.

There are additional important provisions of the act that merit mentioning. They include:

1. Union shop agreements must be in accordance with the prevailing state law and are void in states that forbid them.

2. An employee or a group of employees can petition that the union's authorization to enter into a union shop contract be withdrawn; such a petition must contain the signatures of 30 percent of the employees represented by the union. However, only one election on union security can be held each year.

3. In instances of authorized union shop contracts, the failure of a member to pay union dues and initiation fee is the only cause for loss of good standing with the union for which an employer can be forced to discharge an employee.

4. Union dues checkoff is allowed only with the employee's written consent.

5. If the majority of professional employees desire a union, they can be represented, if they wish, by a union other than that representing the production workers.

6. The individual employee can present grievances directly to his supervisor, provided the union representative is informed and given an opportunity to be present. Settlement of the grievance can be made if such settlement is not contrary to any terms of the existing union contract.

7. The employer can refuse to bargain with a union of foremen or supervisors. They can have their union, but the employer need not bargain with them if he does not choose to do so.

8. Unions as well as employers can sue and be sued for violations of contract under this act. Judgments against unions must be collected from them, not from the individual employees.

## HANDLING CONTROVERSIES

Ideally, the manager and the union representative should solve their differences by means of interpreting the labor contract, bargaining, or mutual agreement. In practice, however, this does not always take place. Hence, to handle controversies, several methods are available, including the following:

*By mediation.*  Both parties agree to use a third party, or mediator, in order to compromise or reach an agreement. He may relay one party's opinion to the other or act as a chairman in getting the parties together to relate their beliefs and opinions. In addition, the mediator may define the basis of the dispute and show the legal meaning of the agreement, thus indirectly demonstrating how settlement might be reached.

*By conciliation.*  Each party may ask for a conciliator who serves as an intermediate and seeks to settle the dispute. In contrast to that of the mediator, the work of the conciliator is aggressive; he may be said to take the offensive. The conciliator may induce one party to accept certain requests of the other or may give advice as to the manner of settling the dispute. To bring about agreement, conciliators depend upon such things as their ability, prestige, and knowledge of all facts in the case. They have no legal power to compel acceptance of any terms.

*By arbitration.* The parties may use voluntary arbitration to settle their differences. To do this, both parties agree to submit the case to a neutral, impartial third party or umpire. It is usually agreed that the arbitrator's findings will be accepted as final.[2]

In actual practice, the terms "mediation" and "conciliation" are used synonymously. As previously stated, the Taft-Hartley Act provides that a 30-day notice of a change in or termination of a labor contract must be filed with the Federal Mediation and Conciliation Service. This makes it possible for the service to get the differences settled before an open break has occurred.

## IMPROVING MANAGEMENT-LABOR RELATIONS

The current status of management-labor relations can be considered quite satisfactory, but improvements are possible. To meet better the challenge of bargaining, advance greater harmony, and gain greater management-union cooperation, the following recommendations are made:

1. *Utilize competent managers more intensively.* Application of the best minds is necessary to find the superior means of bettering management-union relations. Time has brought improvement, but much remains to be done. Managers need to take the offensive and acquire an enlightened view on their role in collective bargaining. They should find out the real reasons behind the union demands. Progress in the following areas would be highly beneficial: bettering the communication with and motivation of employees, smoothing out the business cycle, improving management techniques, training more efficient employees, and broadening the educational background of managers and of labor leaders.

2. *Establish mutual agreement on rights of management.* Managers desire freedom to meet their responsibilities and resent any restrictions upon functions which they believe essential for performing their job. Traditionally, managers want no restrictions on their right to hire, fire, discipline, and maintain order and efficiency. On the other hand, unions feel that one of their main functions concerns the welfare of their members. They are interested in all matters which involve the employee; conditions of employment, they reason, are of vital concern to them.

Experience shows that the initiative and firm policies taken by managers determine to a significant degree what action the union takes. It is possible to include in the contract the principal managerial rights and

---

[2] K. Braun, *The Settlement of Industrial Disputes* (Philadelphia: Blakiston Co., 1944), p. 29.

"Arbitration," as discussed here, applies to reaching a contract agreement and is not the common type of arbitration which deals with the interpretation and application of existing contracts to specific disputes.

specify these as managerial functions; but acceptance by the union is a debatable question and depends upon individual circumstances and precedents, and the character of the rights. There are some who feel that a policy of specifying managerial functions has a limiting effect, since unions might claim participation in matters not specifically stated. However, this might be handled by stating that all existing functions now carried out by managers shall remain functions of management.

3. *Recognize and reconcile the aims of managers and of unions.* Too frequently the goals of managers are unknown to unions and likewise, the goals of unions are a mystery to managers. The goals of each should be identified and analyzed. When this is done, they appear compatible and able to exist in harmony. Such a disclosure forms a solid foundation for building better relations and understanding. The goals of managers usually include (1) an equitable income for the owners, (2) a reasonable income for contingencies, expansion, and improvements, (3) a good reputation for products and services, (4) a reputation as a good place to work, and (5) a favorable attitude by the public. Among the union's chief aims are (1) security of employment, (2) wages consistent with a decent standard of living and commensurate with the quality and quantity of work output, (3) consultation and opportunity for suggestions in shaping policies, (4) employee recognition and status for work well done, and (5) good working conditions.

4. *Practice empathy by managers and by union representatives.* Each should strive to recognize fully the problems of the other. Neither party should ask for concessions which, if granted, would jeopardize the existence of the other. Both should seek for something workable, since any other approach leads to strife. It is simply recognizing the facts of office life—that managers are here to stay and also that unions are here to stay.

5. *Accept complete responsibilities by managers and by union representatives.* This is fundamental. Both managers and unions should be capable, willing to accept and to assume their respective and complete responsibilities. Agreements made in good faith should be carried out, and any subsequent adjustments found desirable should be made in accordance with the mutually agreed upon procedure.

6. *Recognize all interested parties.* It is well to note that there are actually *three, not two,* interested parties in a labor contract: (1) the employees, represented by the union; (2) the owners, represented by managerial personnel; and (3) the consumers, or general public. The negotiators are usually only the managers and the union representatives, but the agreements they reach should be consistent with the public interest. Disagreements resulting in strikes or shutdowns obviously affect public interest. Likewise, agreements which are contrary to the public interest can be very damaging; although more subtle, they can probably

have a greater effect upon certain members of society than upon the initial disputants.

7. *Develop closer association among managers, union representatives, and employees.* Managers should know the union representatives, union representatives should know the managers, and both should know the employees. They should know each other as fellow human beings working together. A spirit of cooperation and understanding should prevail; for all three are bound together, and they must strive for mutual, not separate, survival.

8. *Establish a mutually agreeable basis for conducting collective bargaining.* Most managers would like to operate on the familiar business basis. To them, the process is orderly, and contracts represent agreements satisfactory to both, which in case of violation means redresses enforceable by court action. However, evidence seems to indicate that in some instances, unions are not certain that the traditional business code is the best medium. They are driven by a passion for improvement of the employees' lot and, in many respects, believe collective bargaining and the attainment of satisfactory management-union cooperation are more in the nature of a social and political procedure than a business procedure. For collective bargaining improvement to take place it appears mandatory that these extremes be brought together in some way or a mutually agreed basis be established.

In conclusion, it can be stated that progress in the above eight areas will require time. They are essentially long-range developments and both managers and labor representatives must allow time for ideas to be absorbed. Improvements do not just happen overnight; they evolve; they take time.

## QUESTIONS

1. Explain the meaning of the statement: "The best safety device is located an inch or two above the employee's eyebrows."

2. Assume you have just been appointed safety head in an office employing 150 people. What steps would you take to initiate an effective safety program?

3. With reference to office safety, explain in your own words what is meant by a frequency rate of 8.0? A severity rate of 160.0? If the severity rate is divided by the frequency rate, such as 160.0 divided by 8.0, giving a value of 20.0, what is the meanings of the value, 20.0? Discuss.

4. Do you agree with the following statement: "Office safety is readily accepted by employees mainly because it is for their benefit. Rigid enforcement of safety regulations smacks of the dictator approach. Employees are human beings and do not have to be pushed into being safe employees."

5. Are committees effective in promoting safety among office employees? Substantiate your answer.

6. Select one of the two illustrations shown in Figure 24–1. Assume you are an office supervisor and observe the condition shown by your selected illustration. What action would you take? Be specific.

7. Relate briefly the meaning of each of the following:

   *a*) Accident costs.

   *b*) Good housekeeping practices.

   *c*) Union shop.

   *d*) Mediation.

8. What are some important union unfair labor practices forbidden by the present federal labor law?

9. In company RST, the office employees are nonunion, and the factory employees are members of a union. Recently, as a result of collective bargaining, a 4 percent increase in wages was given factory employees. At the same time, a like increase was given office employees.

   *a*) Do you feel the office employees are justified in accepting this increase?

   *b*) How can the managers of the company justify the increase to office employees?

   *c*) Should the office employees join the union?

   Give reasons for your answers.

10. Is the work of the office manager changed by the existence of a union in his office? Explain.

11. On what basis do you believe office layoffs and rehires should be handled? Justify your viewpoint.

12. In a unionized office, should an office employee take his work problems to his supervisor, the union steward, or a member of the personnel department? Justify your answer.

## CASE PROBLEMS

### Case 34–1.   Eberhart Machine Company

The supervisor of the duplicating department asked two duplicating machine operators to clean up their desks and tidy up several cabinets of paper located in the department. The operators refused, claiming such work was neither in their job classification nor in their job description. The discussion went on for 35 minutes, with no work of any kind being done. Finally, the supervisor stated: "Either the two of you do the work as I direct and file a grievance about it later if you like, or you go home." The operators went home. They stated: "Our union will back us up. We don't have to do cleanup work."

The following morning, when they reported for work, the personnel manager came to their places of work and told them each had been given a five-day suspension for refusing instructions of their supervisor. One of the operators replied: "We didn't disobey our supervisor. She gave us a choice either to do the work or to go home. We chose to go home. She did not warn us we were subject to disciplinary action if we went home. Ask her; she is standing right over there."

Said the personnel director: "The supervisor didn't have to warn you. Employees are supposed to work as directed and not go home. There is nothing in the job description that says you're not supposed to do reasonable cleanup work, and the request made of you was certainly reasonable. You chose to ignore supervisory direction and to risk discipline."

"We'll take this up with our steward and higher-ups if need be," replied one of the operators. "You can't do this to us."

## Problems:

1. What action should be taken now by the personnel director? By the supervisor?

2. What decision do you believe should be reached? Why?

### Case 34–2.    Bellows Company

Not much attention was paid to office safety by the office manager because, in his opinion, there were too many more important things demanding his time. True, there have been very few serious accidents in the office of Bellows Company during the past several years. However, three days ago, an employee in the filing department pulled out the top drawer of a five-drawer file and before she realized it, the entire file cabinet tipped and fell on her. She suffered an arm injury in trying to prevent the file from falling and a broken ankle when her foot was caught under the file. She required hospitalization and latest word is that she will be away from work for at least three weeks.

The office manager deeply regretted this accident happening in his office. He believed some safety measures probably were in order so he wrote a personal letter to each office employee, explaining that an accident had occurred, the company's strong desire to maintain a safe office, and each office employee's responsibility to exercise care to avoid possible accidents in the future. In addition, he urged each office supervisor to cooperate fully in helping to keep the office a safe place in which to work. He also posted several notices on the office bulletin board suggesting, "Be careful. Office accidents do happen. Do not take chances. Help avoid serious injury to yourself." For the most part, these efforts were well received, but some of the employees argued that the office manager was splurging and wanted to look pious in light of the accident that occurred in the filing department.

Yesterday, a fire started in the duplicating division of the company's office. Two employees suffered minor burns in extinguishing the flame, and some damage was done to a desk and to carpeting. An investigation revealed that the cause was carelessness on the part of an employee, who had placed a lighted cigarette on the edge of his desk. The lighted cigarette had fallen into a wastebasket filled with papers, and the fire had started.

## Problems:

1. What are your reactions to the handling of the situation by the office manager after the accident in the filing department? Explain.

2. What action do you recommend that the office manager now take? Why?

# CHAPTER 35

# SUPERVISING
# OFFICE EMPLOYEES

The secret of good direction does not consist in
solving problems but in identifying them.
—*L. A. Appley*

THE OFFICE supervisor is a key figure in the managerial work of actuating. Almost every plan, policy, and decision originated at the top of the organization structure must filter down through the supervisory level. Because of his strategic location both to influence and to implement the many actuating techniques, the supervisor is extremely influential in motivating employees, in developing them, in promoting safety, and in building teams which carry out specific duties.

An organization unit is what it is largely because of the supervisor's influence. Actually, many problems are reduced to simple tasks when supervisors are competent and get complete cooperation from their employees. The accomplishment of satisfactory office production and the establishment of a favorable work climate depend in large measure upon the quality of office supervision. The supervisor is charged with seeing that the work in his unit is performed within a reasonable time and at a reasonable cost. He is the ultimate regulator of what is accomplished.

## THE SUPERVISOR'S STATUS

The supervisor is at the critical focal point about which the top managers' wishes are distributed and the operative employees' desires are concentrated. He is the point of contact between management members and nonmanagement members. To many employees, the supervisor represents management.

Usually, a supervisor is thought of as being below the executive level.

745

The supervisor's work is similar to that of the executive; but the scope of the work, the matters on which decisions must be made, and the general overall executive work are not as broad in the case of the supervisor as in the case of the executive. For convenience, a "supervisor" can be defined as *a management member working at an organizational level where personal oversight of tasks assigned to small groups is assumed in order to assure satisfactory performance.*

## THE WORK OF THE SUPERVISOR

Actually the supervisor's work, in great measure, consists of getting work performed properly by others. This is the heart of supervisory success. A person who insists upon doing everything himself never makes a satisfactory supervisor. Most failures in supervision are in getting things done through people. It is not always the employee's fault, although this is the common explanation.

It is possible to classify the work of the supervisor in a variety of ways. Since the supervisor is a management member, the following outline appears logical and helpful.

Under planning, the supervisor has such activities as:

1. Participating in the formulation of establishing objectives for his unit.
2. Understanding and knowing the work to be done.
3. Knowing and interpreting company policies to the employee.
4. Keeping up with new developments.
5. Improving current methods being followed.

Controlling encompasses the following work by the supervisor:

1. Following stated practices and procedures.
2. Utilizing standards established for the work.
3. Evaluating work output in terms of cost.
4. Checking accuracy and quantity of work.
5. Minimizing peak work loads.

Organizing efforts by the supervisor include:

1. Delegating work to others.
2. Allocating the work among members of the unit.
3. Placing similar work in the same unit.
4. Establishing proper authority relationships among members of a unit.
5. Keeping employee-work relationships up to date.

The supervisor's managerial actuating efforts deal with:

1. Informing employees of changes.
2. Evaluating and disciplining employees.
3. Developing understudies.
4. Securing teamwork and harmony among employees.
5. Increasing the value of employees.

## KNOWLEDGE AND SKILL OF THE SUPERVISOR

To perform his work effectively, the supervisor must have certain knowledge and must be able to do skillfully certain activities. Knowledge requirements of the supervisor vary from one office to another, but the ability to perform certain activities skillfully is fairly constant regardless of the office and its type of work.

The basic knowledge needs are:

1. *Technical knowledge.* This includes knowledge of systems, procedures, materials, office forms, equipment, and the manner in which results are used. Much of this knowledge might be acquired while one is serving in a nonsupervisory capacity. The supervisor should know enough about the detail work that is done to provide the necessary leadership to those performing the tasks and to plan and control their work so that orderly and reasonable rates of accomplishment are realized.

2. *Knowledge of responsibilities.* This includes comprehension of the company's policies, rules, and regulations; of the extent of the supervisor's authority and responsibility; and of matters on which he can make final decisions. An acquaintance with basic information about organization, management, collective bargaining, communication, budgeting, and any area of direct or indirect concern in the particular supervisory job appears to be a minimum requirement.

Basic needs concerning what the supervisor's skills are:

1. *Skill in teaching.* Whether a supervisor gives specific instructions on a particular task or makes assignments in fairly broad terms, it is necessary that he pass along his knowledge to others and develop them. This, in turn, calls for skill in teaching and is a prime means for making supervision more effective. Generally, an employee is more satisfied, has greater interest, and will be more industrious when informed clearly what work is wanted and how it is to be performed. This means that the supervisor should have skill in instructing, so that a well-trained work force is available.

2. *Skill in methods improvement.* Better utilization of materials, machines, and manpower is the constant aim of progressive managers. Some methods of performing work are inherited, others are hastily thrown together, while still others are copied from similar operations. All can be

improved. Skill in analyzing, supplemented by ingenuity, usually results in improved ways of performing work.

3. *Skill in human relations.* This sometimes suffers as a result of the pressure and volume of day-to-day work. Working with and getting along with people are vital to the supervisor. This emphasizes the important areas of understanding the behavior and attitudes of individual employees and of recognizing and using basic human motivations.

## RELATIONSHIPS WITH OTHERS IN ORGANIZATION

The destiny of a supervisor is controlled largely by other people. Almost everything he achieves comes as a result of their approval. Good relationships with others in the organization are therefore paramount for the supervisor. It is the supervisor who provides the intended meaning to organizational relationships. He is the one who coordinates at his point of operation all the decisions made by those with staff authority to those with line authority. And he is the one who tempers the planned means of performing work to the actual realities of work performance at the point of their performance. For convenience we can view the supervisor's relationships as those dealing with organization members (1) above the supervisor and (2) below the supervisor.

With reference to the first, the supervisor is expected to implement a specific portion of a plan at the operative level. To do this, he is given instructions, receives specialized assistance from various staff members, attends indoctrination meetings, and communicates with his superiors. In these relationships, the astute supervisor discovers that certain practices assist him appreciably. He should:

1. *Have firm belief in essentiality of supervisory work.* The effective office supervisor believes that the office is a vital part of the enterprise and that his efforts to help manage the office work are fundamental to the success of the enterprise. He should reveal this belief by viewing enthusiastically his opportunity to contribute to the success of the office.

2. *Focus appeals to superior's greatest interests.* Normally these are improved service, lower costs of operation, and increased net income. The office supervisor who shows how his unit will help achieve these goals will capture the attention and support of his superiors. Actually, with some concentrated thinking, it is not difficult to do this, but some showmanship should be used in presenting the idea. For example, for a project lowering the costs of operation, the mere statement, "The savings to be realized are $12,000," is not nearly as effective as "The savings to be realized are greater than the net income realized from increasing our sales $125,000." Both statements mean the same thing, but the second one is far more effective to top-level managers.

3. *Expect some resistance to suggestions and new ideas.* Some top and middle managers favor a sort of "do not disturb things, let them be as they are" attitude. Especially is this true if there are no complaints and things are running quite smoothly. The feeling is: "Why take a chance? Let well enough alone." The possibility of this condition's existing in any particular case should be realized and taken into account by the office supervisor.

4. *Act in a manner to justify recognition as a member of management.* Too frequently, recognition of supervisors as management members is lip service only, the recognition is by decree only. Nothing tangible is done to make supervisors a part of management or to make them feel that they are. To overcome this condition, supervisors can offer, as a group, suggested measures to their superiors to give them proper recognition and justify them (the supervisors) as the best means for obtaining certain goals of top management and for the overall improvement of the total management team. Top priority should be given the adopting of written statements outlining the supervisor's authority and responsibility, adequate compensation, and direct two-way flow of management information. These activities, along with other important ones and the tools for achieving them, are shown in graphic form in Figure 35–1.

With reference to the second category of relationships—those with organization members below the supervisor—a number of considerations can be stated. Much of the success of a supervisor depends upon his ability to develop and maintain good relationships with his work group because, as a manager, he accomplishes the work by means of this group's efforts. The supervisor is expected to utilize his employees' capacities and interests effectively. He assigns employees definite work, points out certain goals, and gets them to want to perform accurately and do a satisfactory volume of work. In addition, he is called upon to review and evaluate the work performance of his employees, and to answer questions concerning the methods in action to accomplish the work. Various means can be used by the supervisor, depending mainly upon the type of employee, the work situation, and the kind of office work.

A supervisor's relationships with members of his group emphasize use of motivating and human relations practices. To avoid repetition, we will briefly outline the following five guides that a supervisor should follow:

1. *Judge members of his group by their good qualities.* Work is achieved by positive attitudes, not by stressing lack of abilities and skills.

2. *Make every personal contact helpful and constructive.* Take the viewpoint that you are trying to assist every member of your group achieve the ultimate of his potential.

3. *Get your group members to participate in your plans.* Modify plans to strengthen them and to uncover and eliminate objections; and adopt

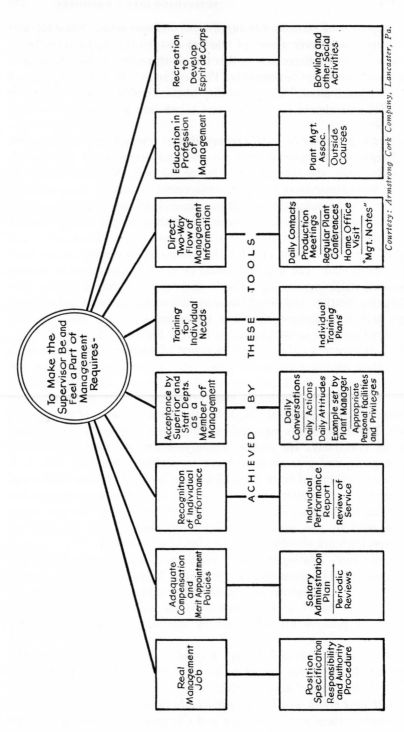

FIG. 35-1. The supervisor in management.

To Make the Supervisor Be and Feel a Part of Management Requires—

Real Management Job

Position Specification
Responsibility and Authority Procedure

Adequate Compensation and Merit Appointment Policies

Salary Administration Plan
Periodic Reviews

Recognition of Individual Performance

Individual Performance Report
Review of Service

Acceptance by Superior and Staff Depts. as a Member of Management

Daily Conversations
Daily Actions
Daily Attitudes
Example set by Plant Manager
Appropriate Personal Facilities and Privileges

Training for Individual Needs

Individual Training Plans

Direct Two-Way Flow of Management Information

Daily Contacts
Production Meetings
Regular Plant Conferences
Home Office Visit
"Mgt. Notes"

Education in Profession of Management

Plant Mgt. Assoc.
Outside Courses

Recreation to Develop Esprit de Corps

Bowling and other Social Activities

ACHIEVED BY THESE TOOLS

Courtesy: Armstrong Cork Company, Lancaster, Pa.

the plan that will achieve the predetermined goal most effectively and serve the interests and desires of the group to a maximum.

4. *Eliminate opposition of interests among your group.* Find out common motives and areas of identical purpose. These should be emphasized in supervisory work. Strive toward group unity and effective teamwork.

5. *Give instructions clearly.* Be certain the basic idea is identified and transferred to the recipient of the instruction. Do not take anything for granted. Provide sufficient details.

Figure 35–2 shows a daily check list for a supervisor to appraise himself in his relationships with his work group.

| | *Yes* | *No* |
|---|---|---|
| 1. Do I impress people as knowing my job? | | |
| 2. Do I plan my work so that each member of my group is fully occupied? | | |
| 3. Do I follow the rules that I require of my members? | | |
| 4. Do I have time to talk over with my members problems that are bothering them? | | |
| 5. Do I have control of myself before I discipline any member of my group? | | |
| 6. Do I maintain recognized quality standards? | | |
| 7. Do I insist that each member meet reasonable work outputs? | | |
| 8. Do I see that each member keeps his working place in an orderly condition? | | |
| 9. Do I make certain that satisfactory working conditions are maintained? | | |
| 10. Do I treat each member of my group as I would like to be treated? | | |

FIG. 35–2. Daily check list for supervisor's self-appraisal.

## COACHING AND COUNSELING

In Chapter 33 we indicated coaching and counseling as methods used in office training work. A discussion of coaching and counseling appears warranted at this time because the office supervisor has frequent occasion to make use of them. Coaching stresses the values of information and inspiration. The particular data needed for a given situation are supplied and the unique capacities of members of a group are both stimulated and integrated by a coach. In contrast, counseling emphasizes leading a person to self-insight and improvement by means of carefully selected questions and suggestions along with skillful listening. To get the person to see what he can do to improve his accomplishments is the goal of counseling. It can be viewed as a suggestive and supportive technique to instill self-motivation in the person being counseled.

To be able to use coaching and counseling successfully it is first necessary to make clear what you want the employee to do and to be sure that he knows it too. This supplies the needed orientation and something toward which he can measure his progress. Second, be sensitive to capabilities, behavior, and likes of the employee. Some excel in physical pursuits, others rank high in mental endeavors. Some are "detailists," others comprehend mainly broad generalities. Find out these individual differences and be guided by them in coaching and counseling. In brief, know your employee. Next, stress the immediate future. Concentrate on the present job. Reach agreement on what is to be done for the next day, next week, or next month at most. It is easy to make commitments for three or four years ahead and then gradually forget about them. Fourth, stay with specific, concrete examples. Talk about actual happenings. Discuss actual incidents and their effect upon his work and standing. Lastly, use constructive criticism. Tie in with his work and bring out ways which would make for improvement. Stress the potential gains and the feasibility of his achieving them.

## SUPERVISING FEMALE EMPLOYEES

Since the majority of office employees are female, the subject of supervising female employees is important. In many respects, what has been stated about supervision applies equally to female and to male employee. Certain additional suggestions, however, may prove beneficial. A cardinal point is to give very careful consideration to women's work assignments. They do many things extremely well, but usually are outstanding on work requiring manual dexterity, caring, and mediating functions. That is, women are more likely to do better in work where patience, interest in human beings, and human needs are considerations. But women, like men, should be encouraged to do what they can do or what they can learn to do. It is also helpful to treat each female employee as an individual. Many women feel that their problems are different— even though other women have the same problems. Let them stand as individuals, in fact, encourage this viewpoint which usually meets with favorable response.

Pay correspondingly greater attention to the workplace of women employees. Women want "a nice place to work," including a clean, attractive area with good decor. They are actively aware of their surroundings. An opportunity for socializing, conversing with others, and allowance for family obligations are also desirable. Furthermore, exercise authority, but don't be a tyrant. Women office employees expect authority to be used and they won't rebel against it. What they won't tolerate is tyranny. Finally, recognize certain facts about the psychology of women. They tend *to show* their emotions more readily than men, probably because it is more culturally acceptable in our society. Moods in women differ and change throughout the day. With ten women employees there can be ten different moods at one time. These moods vary or multiply during the day. Frequently, female supervisors are more rigid than male supervisors would be. This is because there is a tendency for women supervisors to act as they think men would act under the same situation. The answer here is to point out that the best supervisor is both firm and considerate. Fairness must be a part of all supervisory efforts. Also recognize that all supervisors must earn the respect and confidence of his or her subordinates. It is inevitable that the work group test the new supervisor.

## THE SUPERVISOR AND PLANNING

Effective supervision requires thorough planning. The successful supervisor has found that planning enables him to gain his goal with a minimum of effort. Planning helps the supervisor to maintain the proper balance in his work; major objectives are given the major portion of his time and effort. Also, planning makes for orderliness in supervision; actions are thought through. Likewise, areas of nonaction are predetermined. The supervisor knows what he is going to do and when he is going to do it.

Failure of the supervisor to plan his work results in inefficiencies and makes the job of supervision more difficult. Frequently, the lack of planning results in a failure to meet expectancies or to anticipate and to prevent supervisory problems before they occur. Other indications of lack of planning are tardiness in getting work accomplished, excessive costs, not enough time to finish the work, low morale, lack of direction to the group, waste of material, loss of employees' time, and an absence of overall coordinated effort.

Adequate planning will help disclose to the supervisor the proper time for the presentation of an idea or program to his superiors or to his subordinates. Logically, this is when they are in a receptive mood or are puzzled with a problem for which the idea or program is a solution. Timing, however, is very important; and in many cases, it is wise to draw up an entire plan, *file it away,* and let it stay filed away until the most opportune time arrives.

When this time arrives, the best technique is to submit the plan, request approval or acceptance, and give reasons why it should be followed. This approach gives the initiative to the supervisor, and the advantage commonly lies with the one having the initiative. An army with unrivaled offensive power is usually the victor; a football team with a terrific offense is extremely difficult to defeat. Games are usually not won by the team which cannot score; the best they can hope for is a tie score, or a "break" which brings them an unexpected victory.

## EFFECTIVE TIME-USE BY THE SUPERVISOR

Basic to supervisory success is the wise use of time on the job. To this end, the office supervisor can concentrate on essentials—the really important tasks. The best supervisors perform key tasks only and do not let themselves get involved in endless details. Unnecessary work is quickly identified as such and abolished. Also, for most supervisors, the completion of a task once it is started makes for efficient time utilization. Tasks not quite finished are the vexation of many supervisors. Staying with a job until it is finished and not giving in to interruptions are key habits to be followed. In addition, the budgeting of one's time is a time-saver. The time-minded supervisor decides what tasks he had to perform, estimates the time for each, and schedules these time periods through his workday. This approach helps utilize time more effectively and establishes goals that are achieved during the day, thus providing a sense of satisfaction. Furthermore, the office supervisor should acquire speed in reading and become more selective in what is read. Few adults receive reading training beyond the elementary school level. Many people read at this pace, which is a serious detriment to their efficiency in time utilization. By practice and accelerated reading courses increases up to 75 percent in reading efficiency can be attained.

With better utilization of time, a proper balance among the various facets of the supervisory work should be attained. An equitable appraisal of all the various supervisory tasks must be made and compared with established levels of satisfactory performance. For example, data on cost, quantity of work achieved, quality of work, number of grievances, number tardy, number absent, and labor turnover rates are helpful. Trends in these data are significant. Also, changes in some factors may help predict future changes in others—frequently before either the difficulty or the favorable accomplishment is revealed by standard operating reports.

## AUTHORITY AND SELECTION OF OFFICE SUPERVISORS

In a relatively small enterprise, the general manager, who in many cases is also the owner, has supervisory authority over each employee. The general manager makes the decisions that concern job requirements, keeps the employee informed about changes and the progress of the business. With growth of the company and the resultant spreading of the gap between top management and nonmanagement members, it is generally agreed that supervisors must narrow the gap and conduct many of the needed managerial relations with employees.

The size and complexity of the enterprise, as well as the viewpoint toward employees, tend to modify the supervisor's authority. Unfortunately, in many offices, it is not clear what the office supervisor is expected to do. The former concept of the supervisor "running his unit," with complete authority to hire, fire, change work sequence, make improvements, and handle operations in any way believed satisfactory, has changed considerably in many offices. This lack of a clear-cut understanding is due to the very nature of the job—the fact that the work of supervision is so varied, the scope so large, and the activities involved so numerous. However, the transition can be said to have been brought about by the use of staff members to assist and to render advice to the supervisor in carrying out his work. In some cases, it is believed that the work of office supervising has become so complex that expert help to the supervisor is an absolute necessity. In contrast, others are of the opinion that staff helpers usurp authority and take over activities which constitute the fundamental duties of the supervisor. For example, in many offices, the supervisor does not interview and select new employees, but he does have a voice in the final hiring.

Selection of office supervisors can be considered the beginning of effective supervision. From what has already been stated, it follows that a supervisor's qualifications are different from those of an operative employee. The employee having the longest service, the highest production volume, or the longest no-tardiness and no-absenteeism record is not necessarily the best selection for a supervisory job. Much of the work the supervisor is called upon to perform differs from that of the operative employee.

The first step in the selection of office supervision is to determine the background and characteristics needed for the supervisory jobs. Such information can be used to set the minimum employment qualifications and standards. Preparation of such information should take into account the realities of the specific condition.

The actual task of selection is assisted by the use of any one or all of the following: (1) appraisals of the candidates, (2) written tests, (3) interviews, and (4) evaluation of experience and training. The first, or appraisal of candidates, can take many different forms, including inquiry of the candidate's present superior, talking with those acquainted with the candidate's work performance, and discussing with friends the candidate's activities in clubs and other groups outside the office.

Written tests are increasing in usage, but they probably do not yet qualify as a common means for office supervisory selection. Tests are designed to measure work, personality, and technical factors. They provide a means to screen initially a large number of candidates, and they stress objective evidence instead of someone's opinion and judgment. However, considerable criticism has been leveled against tests in which it is pointed out that they concentrate on selected areas rather than the "entire man," that some candidates are practically certain not to reveal their true ability by written word, and that the candidates answer test questions for a prescribed situation in one way, yet for the same situation perform in a different way under actual working conditions.

As pointed out in Chapter 29, interviewing is perhaps the most common means of selection, and this statement includes supervisory selection. The face-to-face meeting, the opportunity to clarify ambiguous written statements, and the flexibility to shape the interview to the individual case make for the wide use and popularity of the interview method.

Finally, the evaluation of experience and training provides a practical element to the selection method followed. A detailed investigation of the candidate's work history is sometimes undertaken. Thus, elements which might be overlooked in the other selection approaches are brought into the program. Knowledge of the enterprise and technical competence are illustrative of these elements.

## SUPERVISORY TRAINING

Strictly speaking, any educational activity designed to prepare the candidate for supervisory work or to improve the supervisor in carrying out his duties successfully can be termed "supervisory training." The field is quite broad and deals with many, yet related, subjects. Supervisory training is not confined to learning to perform a set of movements more efficiently but includes the development of attitudes, control of emotions, and the broadening of one's views. Keeping the supervisor fully informed constitutes one of the biggest challenges in supervisory training. Conditions are constantly changing; new developments are taking place; and in most cases, the supervisor finds himself confronted with new personnel, new attitudes, and new problems.

Excellent work in supervisory training is being accomplished by the members of the Training Within Industry Foundation, a nonprofit organization which advocates gaining maximum results from employed people through better supervision. Years of intensive research and many office tryouts with groups of supervisors have helped develop highly successful training programs for supervisors. Among the more important for normal office use are:

1. *Job instruction.* The *JI* course consists of five two-hour sessions and is intended to give skill in instructing. It is especially helpful where there is work involving long break-in periods, numerous errors, or difficulty in getting the office work out on time. To illustrate the content,

the course consists of four main parts: (*a*) preparing the employee, (*b*) presenting the operation, (*c*) trying out the performance, and (*d*) following up on performance.

2. *Job relations.* Known as the *JR* course, this also consists of five two-hour sessions. It helps provide skill in leadership and is recommended where there are too many misunderstandings among employees and complaints are numerous in the human relations area.

3. *Job methods.* This *JM* program likewise is five two-hour sessions. It gives skill in improving methods through practice sessions and on-the-job coaching. This program is effective in finding better methods of accomplishing office work.

4. *Job economics training.* Known as the *JET* course, this requires five 1½-hour sessions and presents the basic principles upon which the United States economy operates.

5. *Discussion leading.* This *DL* course of four three-hour sessions is designed to give skill in getting participation in meetings and in discussing thoroughly matters of common interest.

6. *Program development.* The *PD* course is intended for the instruction of one person in a company who has responsibility for designing and conducting training programs in his company or some unit thereof. The normal time required for this course is five days, dispersed among two or three weeks, to permit specific application of program material to the trainee's company.

In addition, the following means of supervisory training are helpful and widely used:

1. *Company supervisory schools* in which organized classes in problems of supervision are studied.

2. *Individual study* of the various available materials on the theory and practice of supervisory work.

3. *Conferences and seminars* that afford discussions with supervisors of other departments, group training, and an opportunity to talk over problems of mutual interest.

4. *Dramatized meetings* in which supervisors act out their problems, this acting-out to be followed by discussions and comments to bring out possible improvements in the handling of problems.

5. *Observation of and talks with employees* to gain a better insight into their jobs and their attitudes.

6. *Interviews with top management members* to gain advice and suggestions regarding what supervisory action might be taken under various circumstances.

7. *Involvement in an actual situation,* handling the work of supervision with a "learn by doing" technique. Uusually, some background data are desirable before using this means of obtaining information.

## SECURING EFFECTIVE SUPERVISION

Much material is available concerning how to be an efficient supervisor. Some of it is quite idealistic and contains many platitudes. The subject is broad, but the following ten points are included in order to indicate, in general, the type of activity which is recommended.

1. *Treat all workers alike—show no favoritism.* The successful supervisor operates objectively; his personal likes and dislikes are not permitted to influence his work.

2. *Practice consultative supervision.* This practice includes talking things over with the employees and giving them an opportunity to suggest the best way to accomplish a task. Such a procedure makes for a cooperative work force and recognizes the fact that no one has a monopoly on good ideas.

3. *Enforce all rules and regulations promptly.* Usually, nothing is gained by delaying action in cases where violations are involved. In fact, delay might be interpreted as a lack of decisiveness and an inability to cope with the situation.

4. *Keep your instructions simple, and repeat them frequently to the new employee.* Good supervision requires mutual understanding between the supervisor and the employee. In addition, a patient, helpful attitude must be assumed, particularly in working with the employee who is not yet fully familiar with all the job requirements.

5. *Insist upon and stress the need for each employee to give a full day's work for a full day's pay.* Satisfactory work outputs are the chief responsibility of every supervisor.

6. *Watch waste—material loss and time loss.* One of the chief foes of efficiency is waste. Guarding against this enemy will add significantly to the work output.

7. *Keep fully informed on company policies and their interpretation.* The supervisor is constantly called upon to interpret company policies to the employees. Knowing the policies and keeping informed of any changes and additions is a supervisory "must."

8. *Secure employees' opinions regarding supervision.* Through some means, such at attitude surveys, spot interviews, casual conversations, and discussion groups, find out what is bothering the employees and what "gripes" are developing. Adequate and correct information at the right time and place may avoid much needless trouble.

9. *Develop capable assistants.* Good management requires that qualified replacements be available to maintain the supervisory force at a satisfactory number and caliber. Failure to develop an understudy jeopardizes the supervisor's chances for promotion.

10. *Let top and middle management members know what you are doing and why.* Because supervision is vital to the enterprise, top and

middle management members should know what supervisory action is taking place. Effective supervision requires complete backing by these members, and one of the best ways to retain this endorsement is to tell them what is going on, along with the various reasons why.

## QUESTIONS

1. What are the basic skills an office supervisor needs? Discuss briefly the one you feel is most important.

2. Justify your viewpoint toward this quotation: "With more and more specialists and expert staff people being used in the modern office organizational structure, the importance and status of the office supervisor has decreased. He is not as important as formerly. In many cases, he decides virtually nothing, his superiors telling him what to do."

3. Relate a situation showing how an office supervisor successfully used counseling in her work.

4. Identify each of the following:
   a) Supervisor.
   b) Coaching.
   c) JI course for supervisory training.
   d) Technical knowledge of office supervisor.

5. As an office manager, what practical recommendations would you make to assure more efficient supervisory services? Explain.

6. Discuss the work of an office supervisor in what might be considered a typical office.

7. Discuss several considerations to keep in mind in supervising female employees.

8. "The advantage usually lies on the side taking the initiative." Explain this statement, citing examples from your own experience.

9. Justify the statement that the supervisor provides the intended meaning to organizational relationships.

10. What means can an office supervisor use in order to make better use of her time?

11. Draw up a program for the recruitment and selection of office supervisors for a large office. Assume candidates will be recruited from both within and outside the enterprise.

12. Discuss the relationships between the supervisor and those above her in the organization.

## CASE PROBLEMS

### Case 35–1.  Moyer Manufacturing Company

After considerable thought and talking it over with other management members, office manager Maurice Stetler decided to terminate the employment of Elmer Pick who in Stetler's opinion is not the type of employee wanted by the company. Employed three years ago as a programmer in the computer group, Elmer demonstrated little initiative, was careless about his appearance, and was not thorough in his work. When hired, he was what Stetler describes as a marginal recruit. More important, however, as a reason for his dismissal was Elmer's poor job attitude. Especially during the past year, Elmer showed lack of interest in his work and repeatedly gave silly reasons why certain programs could not be constructed when all the time they are being designed and implemented.

Elmer Pick was given his discharge notice. He went to his supervisor to protest, but was surprised to find that his supervisor, Jerome Carroll, was also given his dismissal notice. Jerome curtly told Elmer that he (Jerome) didn't want to hear any gripes. Said Jerome, "I've put up with you too long, Elmer, and now it has cost me my job." Jerome requested and received an interview with Maurice Stetler. Jerome pleaded for another chance, stating that no warnings of company dissatisfaction had been given him. He had erred in trying to run his unit with incompetent people but this was all the personnel department sent him. He would change this, however, if given another opportunity. Maurice Stetler stated he would reconsider the entire matter, but frankly as of now, he believed the termination should be carried out.

Later the same day, Elmer Pick called at Mr. Stetler's office and requested reinstatement of his job. "I need the work badly," he explained. "I've been here for a spell and certainly seniority means something around here." Mr. Stetler answered, "All facts have been considered. Primarily, it is your poor job attitude. But your personal record will read "resigned voluntarily." Elmer thanked him and added, "Let me ask you something. What is poor job attitude? I'm a member, or I was, of a poorly run department. The fact that you are letting Mr. Carroll go is proof of that. If a guy is in an atmosphere of poor supervision, how do you expect him to be a 'Willing Willie' especially to all the half-baked and wild ideas they bring you. Now that you are getting rid of Mr. Carroll, things should be better. Your charges against me are vague, Mr. Stetler. You have no records or witnesses to prove I didn't do the work or had any wrong view toward it. And, as I say, I want to keep my job. I need it."

## Problems:

1. Discuss what are probably the major factors leading to the situation as presented in this case?

2. What further action do you recommend be taken by Jerome Carroll? By Elmer Pick?

3. As Maurice Stetler, what would you do? Why?

## Case 35–2.  Kirkland Company

The supervisor of the accounting department has resigned due to ill health. His assistant, Harold Steward, age 62, has been offered the job, but has declined, explaining he prefers to continue in his present job and feels the supervisor's job should be given to someone else. He suggests Rebecca Clarke, age 57, who has been with the company over 35 years. She started as a clerk, is pleasant, accurate, and dependable. "She knows our accounting work from A to Z," states Mr. Steward, continuing, "I know the company has never had a woman supervisor, but an exception should be made in Miss Clarke's case."

There has been some thought that an outsider should be brought in to inject some new supervisory thinking into the company. Preliminary investigation shows that qualified candidates are scarce and will probably require paying a higher salary than the present supervisor is receiving. Also, attention has been directed to promoting the assistant supervisor of the billings department to the accounting supervisory job. While crossing of departments is not new with the company, accounting has always been considered a special area requiring definite knowledge and background. Accounting supervisors have always come from the accounting department. Yet, the assistant supervisor of billings is a highly competent man with some accounting knowledge, well liked, and possessing a flair for motivating employees.

Henry Briggs, age 34, has 12 years of accounting service with the company. He is the company's oldest male accounting employee, attends university evening classes, and expects to receive his degree, with a major in accounting, a year from next June. He is very ambitious, somewhat impatient, wants things done in a hurry, and tends to stay by himself preferring to read or study. His work is entirely satisfactory. It is known he has a great interest in office automation and many of the newer ways of processing accounting data. The second oldest accounting employee from the employment view is Gertrude Bryant who has been with the company for 21 years. She started at age 28, after her husband was killed in an auto accident. With three children to support, she has worked steadily since that time. Her children are all grown up now, but she continues to work because she enjoys it and as she says, "I can use the money." She accomplishes much work, is reserved yet very friendly and is a good conversationalist.

### Problems:

1. What is the major problem in this case? What are the minor problems?

2. Discuss your recommended action to resolve the company's major problem, as you see it.

3. What person or persons (title or titles) should probably carry out your recommended action? Explain.

### Case 35–3.  Peerless Products, Inc.

In the accounting department are 14 employees who—Edgar Crawford, the supervisor, believes—make a very effective team. One employee, Bernard Oakton, aged 30 years, married, with three children, started a tax service company last year. He assisted a number of people to prepare their income tax returns and made several hundred dollars extra. As a result of this work, he secured the part-time job of keeping the books for two small businesses. By working several evenings and weekends, he was able to do this work. Although it was confining, he did not mind, as he could use the extra money; and he thought that with some luck, the business might develop into an independent accounting firm of his own.

Oakton has never said anything about this outside work to Edgar Crawford, who nevertheless knows about it through friends and the grapevine. There is no company policy pertaining to such matters, and Crawford has said nothing to Oakton about the outside work. But he has observed that Oakton looks tired, even the first thing in the morning, and for the past six weeks has been absent quite often from his regular job. About two weeks ago, he heard that Oakton had hired a part-time helper to assist him on these outside assignments.

Last week, Oakton was absent for a day and a half. When he reported for work at noon, Edgar Crawford requested that he come to his office and fired him.

BERNARD OAKTON: This is the rawest deal I ever heard of. I wasn't here because my wife is ill. I wanted to explain this to Marcey (*the telephone switchboard operator*); but while holding the line, I was cut off.

EDGAR CRAWFORD: Yes? Well I'll tell you something. I do not believe you.

OAKTON: Well, now I. . . .

CRAWFORD: You're trying to misrepresent your absence, which is another reason why you deserve to be fired. And if you were cut off on the switchboard, why didn't you call back to offer your explanation? You know as well as I do that company rules require notification from anyone who is not going to report for work on a regular workday.

OAKTON: Sure, I know that. But the phone call has nothing to do with it. You're sore because of my outside business.

CRAWFORD: I did not say that.

OAKTON: It's what you're thinking, all right. I know. But let me ask you this, Mr. Crawford. You've known about my outside work and never said anything. So what gave you the right to get tough about it all of a sudden and terminate my employment?

## Problems:

1. What do you believe Bernard Oakton should do now? Why?

2. What should Edgar Crawford do? Why?

3. Could the circumstances that led to this problem have been eliminated? Explain, showing how and why.

INDEX

# INDEX

*This book was set in 10½ point Old Style #7, leaded 1½ points, and 9 point Old Style #7, leaded 2 points. Part and chapter numbers are in Folio Medium; part and chapter titles are in News Gothic Light. The size of the type page is 27 by 45½ picas.*